Communications in Computer and Information Science 1384

More information about this series at http://www.springer.com/series/7899

Arsénio Reis · João Barroso ·
J. Bernardino Lopes · Tassos Mikropoulos ·
Chih-Wen Fan (Eds.)

Technology and Innovation in Learning, Teaching and Education

Second International Conference, TECH-EDU 2020
Vila Real, Portugal, December 2–4, 2020
Proceedings

Springer

Editors
Arsénio Reis
University of Trás-os-Montes e Alto Douro
Vila Real, Portugal

João Barroso
University of Trás-os-Montes e Alto Douro
Vila Real, Portugal

J. Bernardino Lopes
University of Trás-os-Montes e Alto Douro
Vila Real, Portugal

Tassos Mikropoulos
University of Ioannina
Ioannina, Greece

Chih-Wen Fan
National Hua-Lien University of Education
Hualien City, Taiwan

ISSN 1865-0929 ISSN 1865-0937 (electronic)
Communications in Computer and Information Science
ISBN 978-3-030-73987-4 ISBN 978-3-030-73988-1 (eBook)
https://doi.org/10.1007/978-3-030-73988-1

This Springer imprint is published by the registered company Springer Nature Switzerland AG
The registered company address is: Gewerbestrasse 11, 6330 Cham, Switzerland

Preface

TECH-EDU is an international forum for academicians and researchers to present their current work regarding technology and innovation in education. The second edition of the International Conference on Technology and Innovation in Learning, Teaching and Education (TECH-EDU 2020) was held online during December 2–4, 2020, due to the COVID-19 pandemic situation.

This forum brought together two communities: the community of those who work in specific educational areas incorporating technology as a way of enhancing or extending the educational possibilities of their work, and thus offer new ways of learning; and the community of those who work in fields of technology and explore its potential in different educational contexts. The meeting of these two communities at TECH-EDU 2020 was an opportunity to present the most recent advances in research on the incorporation of technology in education and in its different contexts.

TECH-EDU 2020 received researchers' contributions from four continents (Asia, Europe, North America, and South America).

The tasks of submission, peer review, and note of acceptance or rejection, were undertaken using the T4People Conference Management System. All contributions received were submitted to a double-blind review process with two reviewers per paper, and the initial texts, if accepted, were reformulated according to the indications of the reviewers. Of the 79 papers submitted to TECH-EDU 2020, 42 were accepted for the conference.

TECH-EDU 2020 had a considerable variety of contributions. The accepted papers were presented in nine sessions distributed over the three days. The contributions have been grouped into five topics in this volume:

- Digital resources as epistemic tools to improve STEM learning. Nine papers that show how digital resources, provided by technology, can be used as tools or epistemic tools to promote Science, Technology, Engineering and Mathematics (STEM) learning in different contexts, subjects or teaching levels. Some of the papers also describe the instrumental orchestration required to convert digital resources into epistemic tools.
- Digital technologies to foster critical thinking and monitor self- and co-regulation of e-learning. Seven papers that explore digital technologies to promote high cognitive levels of complexity as critical thinking in higher education or to monitor self- and co-regulation of learning in different contexts.
- The COVID-19 pandemic: changes in the educational ecosystem and remote teaching. Eleven papers that consider the effects of the COVID-19 pandemic in the educational ecosystem, new challenges and opportunities relating to the role technology can play in education, or the vulnerabilities that have become evident and that need to be understood and addressed.
- Transforming teaching and learning through technology. Ten papers that explore the usage of data mining in various educational areas or extend the possibilities for

transforming teaching and learning settings with the technologies that enable collaborative work, in several educational contexts.

Educational proposals using technology to foster learning competences. Five papers that present work exploring new proposals of articulation between technology and education to foster learning competences using games, robots, or augmented reality.

This diversity of papers opened up the door to link the two different communities and left a lasting mark in the research field of technology and innovation in education. We would like to thank everyone involved in the organization and running of the conference, the keynote speakers, and all of the participants, for making it such a successful and enjoyable event.

February 2021

Arsénio Reis
J. Bernardino Lopes
João Barroso
Tassos Mikropoulos
Chih-Wen Fan

Organization

Conference Chair

J. Bernardino Lopes	University of Trás-os-Montes and Alto Douro, Portugal

Conference Co-chairs

Tassos A. Mikropoulos	University of Ioannina, Greece
Chih-Wen Fan	National Hua-Lien University of Education, Taiwan

Organization Chair

José Paulo Cravino	University of Trás-os-Montes and Alto Douro, Portugal

Organization Committee

António Marques	University of Trás-os-Montes and Alto Douro, Portugal
Cecília Costa	University of Trás-os-Montes and Alto Douro, Portugal
Daniela Pedrosa	University of Aveiro, Portugal
Dennis Paulino	University of Trás-os-Montes and Alto Douro, Portugal
Hugo Paredes	University of Trás-os-Montes and Alto Douro, Portugal
João Barroso	University of Trás-os-Montes and Alto Douro, Portugal
Paulo Martins	University of Trás-os-Montes and Alto Douro, Portugal
Tânia Rocha	University of Trás-os-Montes and Alto Douro, Portugal
Sofia Hadjileontiadou	Democritus University of Thrace, Greece
Sofia Balula	Universidade de Lisboa, Portugal
Arsénio Reis	University of Trás-os-Montes and Alto Douro, Portugal

Conference Scientific Committee

Alexandre Pinto	Instituto Politécnico do Porto, Portugal
Ana Balula	Escola Superior Tecnologia e Gestão de Águeda, Portugal
Ana Paula Aires	University of Trás-os-Montes and Alto Douro, Portugal
António Barbot	Instituto Politécnico do Porto, Portugal.
Antonio Coelho	Universidade do Porto, Portugal
Armando Cruz	Instituto Politécnico de Viseu, Portugal
Armando Soares	University of Trás-os-Montes and Alto Douro, Portugal
Arnaldo Santos	Universidade Aberta, Portugal
Athanassios Jimoyiannis	University of Peloponnese, Greece
Carla Morais	Universidade do Porto, Portugal
Clara Viegas	Instituto Politécnico do Porto, Portugal

Cecília Costa	University of Trás-os-Montes and Alto Douro, Portugal
Cruz Matos	University of Trás-os-Montes and Alto Douro, Portugal
Danial Hooshyar	University of Tartu, Estonia
Daniela Pedrosa	University of Aveiro, Portugal
Dennis Beck	University of Arkansas, USA
Eva Morais	University of Trás-os-Montes and Alto Douro, Portugal
Evely Boruchovitch	University Estadual de Campinas, Brazil
Fernando Martins	Instituto Politécnico de Coimbra, Portugal
Floriano Viseu	Universidade do Minho, Portugal
George Fessakis	University of the Aegean, Greece
Gonçalo Matos	University of Trás-os-Montes and Alto Douro, Portugal
Gustavo Alves	Instituto Politécnico do Porto, Portugal
J. Bernardino Lopes	University of Trás-os-Montes and Alto Douro, Portugal
Jonathan Kaplan	Université Lumière Lyon 2, France
Jose Bidarra	Universidade Aberta, Portugal
Julien Mercier	Université du Québec à Montréal, Canada
Lisbet Ronningsbakk	The Arctic University of Norway, Norway
Maria Felicidade Morais	University of Trás-os-Montes and Alto Douro, Portugal
Maria Loureiro	University of Aveiro, Portugal
Maria M. Nascimento	University of Trás-os-Montes and Alto Douro, Portugal
Melpomeni Tsitouridou	Aristotle University of Thessaloniki, Greece
Nada Dabbagh	George Mason University, USA
Paula Catarino	University of Trás-os-Montes and Alto Douro, Portugal
Paulo Martins	University of Trás-os-Montes and Alto Douro, Portugal
Pedro Fonseca	University of Aveiro, Portugal
Pedro Tadeu	Instituto Politécnico da Guarda, Portugal
Pei-Yu Cheng	National Cheng Kung University, Taiwan
Raymond LaRochelle	University of Delaware, USA
Ricardo Nunes	UNICAMP, Brazil
Ricardo Queirós	Escola Superior de Media Artes e Design, Portugal
Rodrigo Lins Rodrigues	Universidade Federal Rural de Pernambuco, Brazil
Roger Hill	University of Georgia, USA
Sandra Vasconcelos	University of Aveiro, Portugal
Sofia Dias	Universidade de Lisboa, Portugal
Sofia Hadlileontiadou	Democritus University of Thrace, Greece
Tassos Mikropoulos	University of Ioannina, Greece
Teresa Bettencourt	University of Aveiro, Portugal
Thrasyvoulos Tsiatsos	Aristotle University of Thessaloniki, Greece
Ting-Ting Wu	National Yunlin University Science and Technology, Taiwan
Vanda Santos	University of Aveiro, Portugal
Vassilis Komis	University of Patras, Greece
Vítor Rocio	Universidade Aberta, Portugal
Vítor Santos	Universidade Nova de Lisboa, Portugal
Xana Pinto	University of Aveiro, Portugal
Yannis Dimitriadis	University of Valladolid, Spain

Contents

Digital Resources as Epistemic Tools to Improve STEM Learning

Converting Digital Resources into Epistemic Tools Enhancing STEM Learning 3
J. Bernardino Lopes and Cecília Costa

The Use of Kahoot, GeoGebra and Texas Ti-Nspire Educational Software's in the Teaching of Geometry and Measurement 21
Paula Sofia Nunes, Paulo Martins, and Paula Catarino

Exploring the Potential of the Outdoors with Digital Technology in Teacher Education 32
Ana Barbosa and Isabel Vale

Computational Simulations in the Construction of Abstract Concepts and in Promoting of Students Autonomy in the 5th Grade 44
Fátima Araújo, J. Bernardino Lopes, Armando A. Soares, and J. Cravino

Instrumental Orchestrations in a Math Teacher's Practices to Enhance Distance Learning of Integral Calculus 61
Carlos Monteiro and Cecília Costa

Using Mathematical Modelling and Virtual Manipulatives to Teach Elementary Mathematics 75
Ricardo Silva, Cecília Costa, and Fernando Martins

BiblioLab Project: Teachers, Parents and Students' Perspectives About the Usability and Usefulness of an Educational Distance Learning Platform 90
J. Rocha, P. Pessoa, J. A. Gomes, X. Sá-Pinto, and B. Lopes

Doing Math with Music - Instrumental Orchestration 111
Ana Silva, J. Bernardino Lopes, and Cecília Costa

Digital Tools Entering the Scene in STEM Activities for Physics Teaching 124
Carla Morais, Luciano Moreira, Mónica Baptista, and Iva Martins

Digital Technologies to Foster Critical Thinking and Monitor Self and Co-regulation of e-learning

Structuring International University Students' Reflection and Meta-reflection Experiences Online . . . 141
Chrysi Rapanta and Carlotta Pisano

Critical Thinking on Mathematics in Higher Education: Two Experiences . . . 156
Vanda Santos and Nuno R. O. Bastos

Cooperative Learning and Critical Thinking in Face to Face and Online Environments . . . 168
Helena Silva, José Lopes, Eva Morais, and Caroline Dominguez

Teaching Strategies to Promote Critical Thinking Skills in an Online Learning Environment . . . 181
Angeliki Lithoxoidou and Catherine Dimitriadou

The Diagnostic Assessment and Achievement of College Skills (DAACS): A Powerful Tool for the Regulation of Learning . . . 193
Elie ChingYen Yu, Angela M. Lui, and Diana Akhmedjanova

Drill-Down Dashboard for Chairing of Online Master Programs in Engineering . . . 203
Anabela Costa e Silva, Leonel Morgado, and António Coelho

Using BPMN to Identify Indicators for Teacher Intervention in Support of Self-regulation and Co-regulation of Learning in Asynchronous e-learning . . . 210
Ceres Morais, Daniela Pedrosa, Vitor Rocio, José Cravino, and Leonel Morgado

Covid-19 Pandemic, Changes in Educational Ecosystem and Remote Teaching

Yes, We Can (?) - A Critical Review of the COVID-19 Semester . . . 225
Gergana Vladova, André Ullrich, Benedict Bender, and Norbert Gronau

Designing Didactic Cycles in a Pandemic Scenario: Facing Challenges as Opportunities . . . 236
Sónia Martins

FuzzyQoI-Based Estimation of the Quality of Interaction in Online Learning Amid Covid-19: A Greek Case-Study . . . 249
Sofia B. Dias, Sofia J. Hadjileontiadou, J. Alves Diniz, and Leontios J. Hadjileontiadis

Design Teaching and Learning in Covid-19 Times:
An International Experience 263
Paulo Ferreira, Filipa Oliveira Antunes, Haroldo Gallo, Marcos Tognon, and Heloisa Mendes Pereira

Communicating Mathematics During Small Groupwork Through
Video-Conferencing Applications 279
Raymond LaRochelle, Michelle Cirillo, and Dawn Berk

Engaging Students During Synchronous Video-Conferencing in COVID19
Times: Preliminary Findings from a Design Study. 287
Ilias Karasavvidis

Social Presence, Satisfaction, and Learning Outcomes in an Undergraduate
Computer Programming Distance Course 301
George Koutromanos, Ioanna Bellou, and Tassos A. Mikropoulos

E-assessment and Academic Integrity: A Literature Review 313
Theologos Tsigaros and George Fesakis

Shifting to Emergency Remote Teaching Due to the COVID-19 Pandemic:
An Investigation of Greek Teachers' Beliefs and Experiences. 320
Athanassios Jimoyiannis, Nikolaos Koukis, and Panagiotis Tsiotakis

Rapid Design and Implementation of a Teacher Development MOOC
About Emergency Remote Teaching During the Pandemic 330
Athanassios Jimoyiannis, Nikolaos Koukis, and Panagiotis Tsiotakis

SciLOET: A Framework for Assessing Digital Learning Objects
for Science Education 340
Tassos A. Mikropoulos and Nikiforos M. Papachristos

Transforming Teaching and Learning Through Technology

The Potential of Audiovisual Online Collaborative Platforms as a Teaching/
Learning Aid of ESP – Testing and Validating a Prototype 351
Tiago da Silva Carvalho

Bring the Social Media to the Classroom of Portuguese as a Foreign
Language in China: Possibilities and Challenges 370
Yuxiong Zhang and António Moreira

Creating Collaborative Research Opportunities at a Distance: From Porto
to Cluj-Napoca 380
Carla Melo, Sandra Vasconcelos, Dália Liberato, Cândida Silva, Paula Amaral, Adina Letiția Negrușa, Smaranda Adina Cosma, and Cristina Fleșeriu

Technology-Supported Collaborative Learning in Language Teaching 389
Giedrė Valūnaitė-Oleškevičienė, Liudmila Mockienė, and Viktorija Mažeikienė

Digital Platforms in the Age of Mobility: A Contribution Towards Language Teaching and Learning 398
Ana Balula, Sandra Vasconcelos, and António Moreira

The Effect of Agency on Cognitive Load in Dyads Learning Physics with a Serious Computer Game 408
Julien Mercier, Ariane Paradis, Ivan Luciano Avaca, and Kathleen Whissell-Turner

Towards Modeling the Psychophysiology of Learning Interactions: The Effect of Agency on Arousal in Dyads Learning Physics with a Serious Computer Game 421
Julien Mercier, Ivan Luciano Avaca, Kathleen Whissell-Turner, and Ariane Paradis

Worker Support and Training Tools to Aid in Vehicle Quality Inspection for the Automotive Industry 432
Ana Teresa Campaniço, Salik Khanal, Hugo Paredes, and Vitor Filipe

Students Drop Out Trends: A University Study. 442
Bruno Silva, E. J. Solteiro Pires, Arśenio Reis, Paulo B. de Moura Oliveira, and João Barroso

Visualization of Scientific Phenomena for Education 451
Roman Rudenko, Arsénio Reis, José Sousa, and João Barroso

Educational Proposals Using Technology to Foster Learning Competences

A Proposal for an Educational Game Platform for Teaching Programming to Primary School Students 463
Andreas Giannakoulas, George Terzopoulos, Stelios Xinogalos, and Maya Satratzemi

Future Teachers Choose Ideal Characteristics for Robot Peer-Tutor in Real Class Environment 476
Anna-Maria Velentza, Sofia Pliasa, and Nikolaos Fachantidis

Creative Process for Designing a Hybrid Game for Nutrition Education. 492
Pedro Reisinho, Cátia Silva, Nelson Zagalo, Mário Vairinhos, and Ana Patrícia Oliveira

Motivating Students to Learn Computer Programming in Higher Education: The SimProgramming Approach 506
Ricardo Rodrigues Nunes, Gonçalo Cruz, Daniela Pedrosa, Ana Margarida Maia, Leonel Morgado, Hugo Paredes, José Cravino, and Paulo Martins

A Proposal of a Classification Scheme to a Survey of Augmented Reality for Education and Training 519
Armando Cruz, Hugo Paredes, and Paulo Martins

Author Index 533

Digital Resources as Epistemic Tools to Improve STEM Learning

Converting Digital Resources into Epistemic Tools Enhancing STEM Learning

J. Bernardino Lopes[1,2](✉) and Cecília Costa[1,2]

[1] UTAD, Universidade de Trás-os-Montes e Alto Douro, Vila Real, Portugal
{blopes,mcosta}@utad.pt
[2] CIDTFF – Centro de Investigação em Didática e Tecnologia na Formação de Formadores, Aveiro, Portugal

Abstract. This study focuses on the problem of the possibility of converting digital resources used by STEM teachers into epistemic tools (ET) to improve the quality of student learning and the role instrumental orchestration can play in this process. Lessons by two STEM teachers from the college teaching were analysed during a period of time in which digital resources (DRs) were used and at some point in the class, the students used these DRs as tools. These classes were described according to the protocol of Multimodal Narratives and are available in a public collection. The research question that is answered is: what instrumental orchestration did teachers use in their classes so that the use of DRs by students would make it possible to use them as an ET? The results show that (a) there are three modes of instrumental orchestration that influence students' use of DRs as ET: time; teacher mediation; articulation between DRs; (b) the most decisive and predictor way of using DR as an ET is the mediation of the teacher (task type, students autonomy provided, epistemic moves and connection between DR and learning); (c) the mode time is decisive especially for the use of DR as ET to a high degree; (d) a more extensive articulation between DRs can favour the use of DR as ET. This article advances in two directions: 1) to characterize instrumental orchestration modes that are effective for using DR as ET; 2) to characterize (three) instrumental orchestration modes instead of instrumental orchestration types.

Keywords: Instrumental orchestration · Epistemic learning · College teaching

1 Introduction

There is a lot of educational research about the use of certain digital resources, such as applets, computer simulations, educative software, augmented reality, virtual reality, etc. Moreover, there is many evidences that digital resources can support teaching, learning, and education in general. Although the research shows that there are various educational resources for science, technology, engineering, and mathematics (STEM) with potential to help teachers create more stimulating and challenging learning environments (e.g., epistemic learning), often teachers fail to obtain educational advantages from their use. Recently several studies have appeared showing how digital resources can be used and

A. Reis et al. (Eds.): TECH-EDU 2020, CCIS 1384, pp. 3–20, 2021.
https://doi.org/10.1007/978-3-030-73988-1_1

orchestrated to improve the quality of students learning, in particular improving epistemic learning [1–13]. These results make it more urgent for teachers to adopt digital resources as epistemic tools. However, this area of research is still recent and there are many aspects to consider and clarify in order to make it possible in a near future for teachers to take effective advantage of digital resources for student epistemic learning. This gives rise to a problem for researchers in education, in particular in STEM education: how can teachers use these digital resources as epistemic tools to improve students' learning in STEM areas. In particular, what is the role of instrumental orchestration in this process?

2 Literature Review

2.1 Digital Resources and Its Impact in STEM Education

ICT offers a considerable variety of digital resources available in different formats and platforms, with different purposes, different degrees of interactivity and different pedagogical qualities [14–16]. We use the expression "digital resources" (DRs) as a synonym for resources that lack the use of a computer, tablet or smartphone (computer technology) [8]. Many DRs are supported in research and others are not. In addition, there is extensive research work on the use of DR in STEM education and that the way they are used, in an educational context, has an influence on the effective learning of students [15, 17–25].

Several studies have devoted attention to determining the effect of the use of DR on the learning of STEM students [17, 22, 24–26]. The results are not unanimous. However, there are meta-analysis studies that show that, globally, the use of DR in STEM subjects positively influences the students' achievement [17, 22, 24, 25]. The same studies indicate that the influence of DR on learning depends on several factors. One of the decisive factors for the influence on learning to be greater or lesser is the teaching approach adopted [15, 17, 21, 27–29]. The influence is greater if DR is used with a constructivist approach to teaching [17, 21].

Another increasingly important aspect due to the increasing availability and variety of DR is whether they change the learning environment [22, 30–32]. It is not entirely correct to assume that DR necessarily enhances the learning environment [27, 32]. In fact, that connection is conditioned by several factors [17, 22] and may have important limitations regarding the development of specific STEM subject skills [24] or depend on the knowledge and skills to be developed in the teacher or the cultural context of the school [29]. On the other hand, it is not clear that the increasing availability and variety of DR has changed social practices in education [27] nor the underlying pedagogical practices [25] despite opening up new perspectives for certain types of students, in particular the most disadvantaged [17, 32].

Taking up the issue of the importance of the teaching approach, and its fundamentals, and the way educators use DR, there are first of all different theoretical perspectives on how to face it. In [33] two theoretical frameworks are presented which could possibly be complementary: one, the TPCK [34], focuses on the knowledge of the teacher; the other, Instrumental Orchestration (IO) [35], focuses on teaching practice. On the issue of the teaching approach, one aspect to consider is the ability of teachers to design their teaching, and whether or not DRs allow it [23].

This is crucial because DR offers teachers the opportunity to design their teaching in a new way and in this way be able to make the learning of their students more effective. Another aspect to consider are the teaching strategies that are adopted [28] and that can change to support more personalised forms of learning [36]. Although some teaching strategies are known to be more effective than others [28] there is a disparity between what is being found in empirical studies, and teaching approaches that have been recognised as optimising the potential of DR to enhance STEM education [21].

The framework we use in this study, both in theoretical and empirical terms, is that of the analysis of the teaching practices of STEM teachers and not their knowledge about the use of DR [14, 33]. In relation to the use of DR in the teaching of STEM, we adopt the perspective of knowing to what extent DR mediates the learning of STEM in specific aspects advocated in [37], which can be concretised in "do STEM", in the perspective of the students, or "learn STEM" (skills or concepts).

Although DRs offer a variety of teaching and learning possibilities and those lacking digital skills, the literature review by [26] shows that 21st-century skills are broader than digital skills and 21st-century skills are not necessarily underpinned by ICT. These results should remind us that the most important thing is not the technology, but the extent to which DRs mediate learning. This gap in research identified by [37] remains current in the research agenda for the use of DR in STEM teaching to which this study intends to contribute.

2.2 Instrumental Orchestration in Teaching to Enhance STEM Learning

Instrumental orchestration is a theoretical approach to frame the use of ICT in educational contexts by focusing on teachers' educational practices [33]. The way in which the notion of IO was developed over time and was used in research practices (from 2002 to 2020) is well studied in [38]. The notion of IO was introduced and defined by [37] thus:

"We will call instrumental orchestration a plan of action, partaking in a didactic exploitation system which an institution (the school institution, in this case) organizes with the view of guiding students' instrumented action. Instrumented orchestration is defined by four components:

- A set of individuals;
- A set of objectives (related to the achievement of a type of task or the arrangement of a work-environment);
- A didactic configuration (that is to say a general structure of the plan of action);
- A set of exploitation of this configuration." (p. 208)

Later [28] he added a fifth component of IO, didactical performance, referring to the decisions that the teacher makes regarding the didactic configuration and set of exploitation to make his intentions effective and which is linked to the temporal dimension of IO. A little later still, [39] they compared the IO theoretical approach with another more popular one at the time (Webding) to verify that they both realized the integration of DR in an educational context, although the former highlighted the teacher and the role he has in that process for the students to learn. From a didactic point of view a theory that gives the teacher an understanding and tools to adjust or change his teaching is more appropriate.

This approach has made efforts to typify the types of IO [33, 38, 40]. These may be more teacher-centred or student-centred [34], but they are all centred on the opportunities that the use of DR provide to STEM students to learn specific aspects [2] which may lead to the teacher having to change their teaching practices in the course of using DR [41].

Although this theoretical framework has developed in the field of mathematics education, we think it can be used in the framework of STEM education as [1] did. What is to be retained from this theoretical framework is that much attention is needed [1–4]: (a) to the task and its objectives; (b) to the mediation of the connections between students' work with DR to perform the task and the learning outcomes in STEM; (c) to the way DR becomes a tool; (d) to the autonomy to be granted to students in a progressive way throughout the task; (e) to the movement from the use of DR in manipulative interactions to the use of DR as an epistemic tool.

2.3 STEM Learning with Epistemic Tools

The notion of IO has not been associated with that of epistemic tool, although some authors have already done so [1]. However, this link is almost obvious, because as [20] says, any artefact, such as DRs, has to be appropriated by the students in order to become tools. This process of appropriation and use of DRs can be taken to the field of epistemic learning and, in this process, artefacts assume the role of epistemic tools [1, 12].

A DR has to fulfil some requirements mentioned in [1, 12, 13] to be used as an epistemic tool: (a) be manipulated in such a way that its use contributes to the students solving the task; (b) allow students to build knowledge from the students' perspective; (c) allow students to take on the role of epistemic agents in the epistemic activity that is taking place during the resolution of the task; (d) support the conversion of representations from one representation system to another.

The epistemic tool concept has been used in engineering education [5, 6] and science education [7], but not in mathematics education. However, the epistemic tool concept is increasingly studied [8] and has already been used across different STEM subjects [1]. As mentioned above, the epistemic tool concept is linked to epistemic practices [5] and epistemic cognition [7], when students solve a task in a given educational context, and to the epistemic moves that teachers make so that students can be the subjects of their own learning [8, 9].

There is no doubt about the increasing role that has been attributed to DRs in STEM learning [11]. DRs have progressively assumed the role of technological representations of the physical world [11]. In the face of this emerging role of DR, STEM teachers have the challenge of addressing DR in their teaching not as transparent and neutral artifact (naïve instrumentalism) and reveal what is "really" there (naïve realism), but as powerful epistemic tools that can help the students represent the reality and build knowledge in the interaction with it [11].

This perspective of viewing DR as epistemic tools poses the challenge for teachers to give pupils a more central role in their teaching efforts, in particular by allowing them to assume their status as epistemic agents [13]. It also opens perspectives for a more integrated learning environment [10]. It is undoubtedly an extension of the theoretical framework "instrumental orchestration" insofar as [1]: (a) it moves from the scope of mathematical education to STEM education, (b) it gives DRs the possibility of becoming not only tools, but also epistemic tools.

2.4 Research Question

The research question to which this study is intended to answer is: what instrumental orchestration did teachers use in their lessons so that the use of digital resources by students would make it possible to use them as an epistemic tool?

3 Description of the Study and Methodological Aspects

3.1 Study Design

We developed an exploratory study with the aim of getting to know the IO that teachers used in their classes so that the use of digital resources (DRs) by students would make it possible to use them as an epistemic tool. We carried out a detailed analysis of teaching and learning practices in the natural classroom environment of two teachers, carrying out a qualitative descriptive and interpretative investigation, based on a multiple case study [42–44].

To do this study we needed two teachers who met the criteria: (a) to have access to a set of teaching practices of teachers in classrooms; (b) to be a Mathematics teacher and another teacher of the Sciences area; (c) to be teachers using DR in classroom during several lessons with the clear intention to use them as artefacts to improve the quality of their students' learning.

In an open science perspective, a Portuguese team [45] created an open source webpage Multimodal Narratives (https://multimodal.narratives.utad.pt), where practices of Science and Technology teaching become public and shareable, preserving its holistic, multimodal and complex nature and are usable by researchers, professionals and the public.

A multimodal narrative (MN) consists of a detailed description of what happened during classes (actions and languages). The teacher (or an external observer) write a MN per lesson, according to a validated protocol [46, 47], based on the data collected and the description of the intentions and decisions of the teacher. A MN is a written document constituted by two parts: (i) a summary of the lesson; and (ii) the detailed narration of the lesson organized in episodes. Each episode begins with a task and ends when new task begins. The summary contains the presentation and contextualization that identifies the theme, objectives, spatial and temporal organization, chronological order of tasks and subtasks and other relevant data of students and school. The detailed narration of all episodes includes several multimodal elements.

The MN is validated by two external researchers that verify the MN compliance with the data collected, its readability and self-contained.

In this open source webpage, we found MNs of two teachers who meet the requirements we needed.

3.2 Data Collection and Participants

As the open source webpage Multimodal Narratives is public, validated and reliable, we use it to get the participants and data. Taking into account the requirements for the choice of teachers already indicated, in the Multimodal Narratives open source webpage we found two teachers from college institutions of the north of Portugal, one of Physics and the other of Mathematics who served our purposes. The information presented in Table 1 is taken from the information made available in the MNs of the two teachers chosen. From the set of MNs available on the webpage, we selected a number of lessons from each teacher so that they were articulated with each other and that in total they had the same duration for both teachers.

Each case is made up of the teacher and his students in a set of lessons and respective teaching and learning practices in the natural environment of classroom.

In Table 1, we characterize the two cases and the participants under analysis:

Table 1. Characterization of cases and participants.

Descriptor	Cases	
	Teacher Mara	Teacher Rafael
Teacher gender	Female	Male
Teacher education	Undergraduate and Master's Degree in Physics and Chemistry TeachingPhD student	Undergraduate and Master's Degree in Mathematics Education PhD student
Teacher experience in research	Six years in education research projects	Without experience in education research projects
Teacher experience using DR	Yes	Yes
Subject area	Physics Science	Mathematics
Topic taught	Heat transfer (processes and laws). Thermal flow and temperature gradient. Thermal Resistance and Analogy with Ohm's law for "thermal circuits"; Coefficient of global thermal transmission. Radiation. Relation of emission and absorption with the colour of the object and its temperature; Stefan-Boltzmann's law	Matrices; operations with matrices Systems of linear equations; Gauss elimination Inverse of a square matrix Linear combination of vectors; generated vector subspace
DR(s)	Slides referring to problematic situation	Slides referring to problematic situation Softwares Scilab and Mathematica Graphical calculator
No. of class members	It varied between 34 and 17 students	It varied between 18 and 16 students
Total time of lessons	5 lessons of 50 min each	3 lessons of about 100 min each
Education level	1st cycle of studies in civil engineering (1st year), discipline of Physics Supplements, students with more than 18 years old	1st cycle of studies in electrical engineering (1st year), discipline of Discrete Mathematics and Linear Algebra, students with more than 18 years old

According to the information made available in the MNs, the data collected were audio recording of the lessons, copies of the students' written records in the notebook, photos of the teachers' written records on the board and the material used (e.g. slides and other DRs), lesson plans, photographs, tasks provided to students and personal teachers notes about their intentions and decisions.

3.3 Data Analysis

The analysis was made from the mentioned MNs (available on the Multimodal Narratives webpage), five of teacher Mara's lessons and three of teacher Rafael's lessons. To answer the research question we use a three-level analysis strategy. In the first level of analysis, the class situations in which DR(s) were used as tools were identified in all MNs, based on the indicators (simultaneously), use of DR(s), autonomous work and existence of task, defined in Table 2.

Table 2. Framework for the first level of analysis.

Dimensions of analysis	Categories	Definition
Indicators of the use of DR(s) as a tool	Use of DR(s)	Individually or in groups students interact with the DR(s) directly or through the teacher or other
	Autonomous work	Students develop autonomous work interacting in a certain way with the DR(s)
	Existence of a task	Resolution by students of a task with some degree of autonomy

Once the situations in which the DR were used as tools (according to Table 2), we moved to a second level of analysis using the two dimensions of analysis: IO used by teachers and the use of DRs as epistemic tool that was done by students. To do so, we analyse what happened in each situation where DRs were used as tools with regard to the two dimensions mentioned. For this purpose, we have defined the dimensions of analysis and categories in Table 3.

Based on the analysis carried out at the two previous levels, the last level of analysis aims to identify relationships between the IOs used and the use of DR as epistemic tools.

Table 3. Framework for the second level of analysis.

Dimensions of analysis	Categories	Definition and codes
Instrumental Orchestration in time **(IO_T)**	A - Length of use	1 less than 1 min 2 between 1 and 3 min 3 between 3 and 7 min 4 between 7 and 15 min 5 more than 15 min
	B - Moment of integration	DR is integrated for 1 introduce concept(s) 2 deepening concept(s) 3 extending concept(s)
Instrumental Orchestration in mediation **(IO_{Med})**	A - Challenge task	Existence of challenging task for students to solve autonomously (yes or no)
	B - Mediation between DR and learning	The teacher mediates the connection between DR use and learning during task resolution (yes or no)
	C - Autonomy granted to use DR	Autonomy granted by the teacher to students to use DR to solve a task (yes or no)
	D - Teacher epistemic moves	Help or suggestions from the teacher for students to use DR as an epistemic tool (yes or no)
Instrumental Orchestration in web **(IO_W)**	A - Type of articulation	1 do not exist 2 sequence 3 web
DR as epistemic tool **(ET)**	A - Epistemic agent	Students have the role of epistemic agents using DR during task resolution (yes or no)
	B - Manipulate DR	The student performs operations (not necessarily physical) with DR to get answers or rehearse solutions to solve the task (yes or no)
	C - Convert representations	DR supports the conversion of representations from one representation system to another made by students (yes or no)

4 Findings

To answer the research question (what instrumental orchestration did teachers use in their lessons so that the use of digital resources by students would make it possible to use them as an epistemic tool?) first the situations in which DRs are used as a tool are identified (Sect. 4.1). Next, we identify the articulation between DRs used throughout the lessons (Sect. 4.2). Finally, the relations between the IOs used by the teacher and the use of DRs as epistemic tools are identified (Sect. 4.3).

4.1 Digital Resources Used as Tools in the Classroom

The analysis made to MNs according to the indicators in Table 2, in simultaneous, allowed the identification in teacher Mara's lessons of 15 situations where DRs are used as tools in the resolution of a task and seven in teacher Rafael's lessons. In Table 4, the results obtained are summarised.

Table 4. Situations where DR is used as a tool

Lesson No.	Teacher Mara					Teacher Rafael		
	1	2	3	4	5	1	2	3
Digital Resources (DRs)	DR1	DR2 DR3	DR4 DR5 DR6	DR7 DR8 DR9 DR10 DR11	DR12 DR13 DR14 DR15	DR1 DR2 DR3	DR4 DR5	DR6 DR7

Label: Teacher Mara, all DRs are slides referring to problematic situation; Teacher Rafael, DR1 is Mathematica; DRs2, 4, 6 are Scilab; DR3 is graphical calculator; DRs5, 7 are slides referring to problematic situation.

In the case of teacher Mara, the DRs are all of the same type (slides referring to problematic situation). In the case of teacher Rafael, there are four different types of DRs (Table 4). As the length of the total of lessons is similar in both cases, the number of situations in which DRs are used as a tool is double in the case of teacher Mara.

The situations in which DRs are used as a tool have an identical distribution in teacher Rafael's three lessons. In the lessons of teacher Mara there is a growing number of situations as the lessons progress, being the 4th lesson the one with more situations of the type under study.

4.2 Articulation Between the Digital Resources Used Throughout the Lessons

The results of the IO in web (IO_W) analysis dimension, category Type of articulation, are presented in Fig. 1 and Fig. 2. The analysis of the articulation of DRs was not done by DR as in other analysis, but in the set of all lessons. We consider that DRs are articulated when there is a relationship between them. This relationship can be direct or indirect. It is considered direct articulation when they use the same subject and the different DRs used are complementary among them and indirect articulation when the subject of one is needed and helps to the subject of the other and the work done with a DR supports the following subject.

In the case of teacher Mara (Fig. 1), we identify four sequences of DRs, one per lesson (except in first lesson), and the third sequence begins in one lesson and continues in the beginning of the next lesson. We also verified that there are several DRs related to each other, not only in sequence, but also in web (DR8 to DR12). Three DRs do not belong to any sequence, i.e. does not exist articulation.

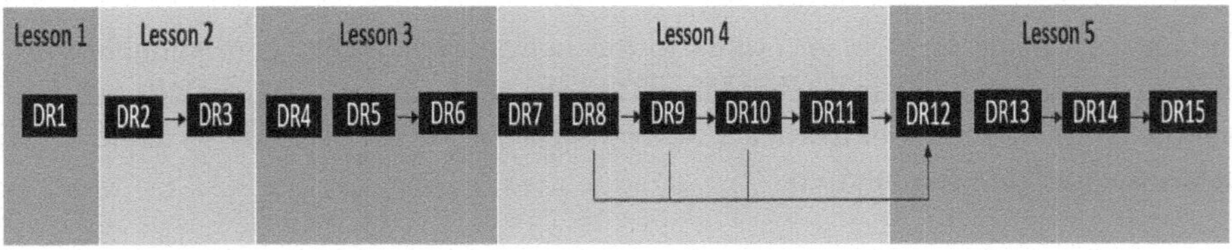

Fig. 1. Type of articulations of DRs used throughout teacher Mara's lessons

In the case of teacher Rafael (Fig. 2), we identify three sequences of DRs, one per lesson. We also verified that there are several DRs related to each other, not only in sequence but also in web and that all DRs belong to some sequence/web. The dotted arrows indicate the existence of an indirect link between the DRs indicated. DR5 recalls the use that was made of DR2 and DR4.

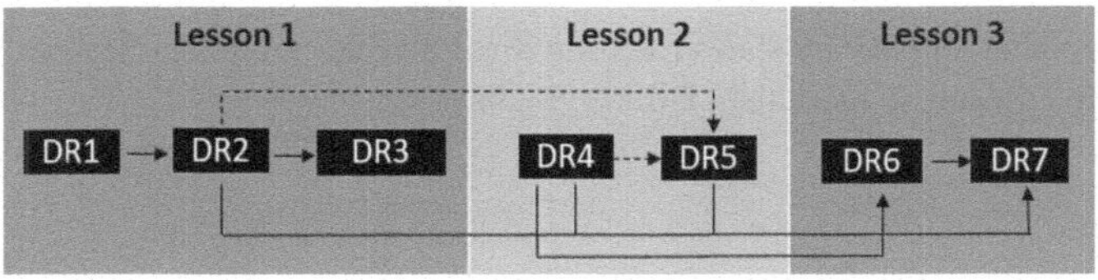

Fig. 2. Type of articulations of DRs used throughout teacher Rafael's lessons

In Table 5, we record the number of articulations of each type identified in the lessons of each of the teachers Mara and Rafael.

Table 5. Number of articulations

IO_W	Teacher Mara	Teacher Rafael
A2 (sequences)	4	3
A3 (web)	1	3

These evidences show that there is articulation of DRs throughout the lessons. The IO in web mode is more extensive (greater number of articulations) and strong (greater number of articulations web type) in the teacher Rafael.

4.3 Instrumental Orchestration and Use of Digital Resources as Epistemic Tools

Based on the codification established in Table 3, we obtained the results for each case, teacher Mara (Annex - Table 7) and teacher Rafael (Annex - Table 8).

The analysis of the last three rows of these tables, which correspond to the use of DRs as epistemic tools, allows us to identify three different cases. There are cases where the three categories occur simultaneously – use of DR as an epistemic tool to a high degree. There are cases where only two categories occur simultaneously – use of DR as an epistemic tool to a medium degree. Moreover, there are cases where either only one or none of the categories occurs – use of DR as an epistemic tool to a low degree or none at all. In Table 6, we present the results of the two cases in study.

Table 6. Number of DRs used as epistemic tools and respective degree of use

Degree of use of DR as ET	Teacher Mara	Teacher Rafael
High	2	3
Medium	9	4
Low	4	0

The conjugation of the results presented in Tables 5 and 6 suggests that a greater articulation between DRs tends to favour their use as epistemic tools.

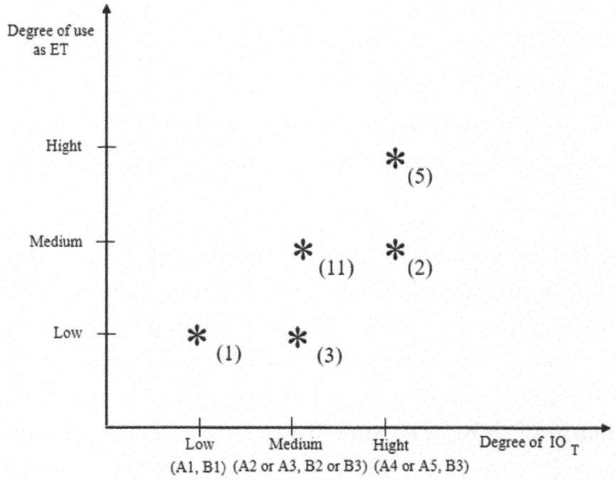

Label: The numbers in brackets indicate the respective occurrences read in tables A and B.

Fig. 3. Relationship between the use of DR as ET and IO in time (IO_T)

The analysis of the upper part of the Tables 7 and 8 (annexed) concerning IO allows us to establish three different levels concerning IO in time and IO in mediation.

Regarding the time dimension of the IO, IO_T, we identify the levels: low, when it occurs simultaneously A1 (length of use less than 1 min) and B1 (DR is integrated for introduce concept(s)); medium, when it occurs A2 or A3 (length of use between 1 and 7 min) simultaneously with B1 or B2 (DR is integrated for introduce or deepening concept(s)); and high, when it occurs A4 or A5 (length of use between 7 and 15 min) simultaneously with B2 or B3 (DR is integrated for deepening or extending concept(s)). The combination of these IO levels in the time category with the use of DRs as epistemic tools is expressed in the scheme of Fig. 3.

As shown in Fig. 3, the way the teacher does IO_T influences the way students use DRs as ETs. As we also see, there are cases where this influence is not decisive.

Regarding the teacher mediation dimension of the IO, IO_{Med}, we identify the levels: low, when it occurs simultaneously A (challenge task) and B (mediation between DR and learning); medium, when it occurs A, B and C (autonomy granted to use DR); and high, when it occurs A, B, C and D (teacher epistemic moves). The combination of these IO levels in the mediation category with the use of DRs as epistemic tools is expressed in the scheme of Fig. 4.

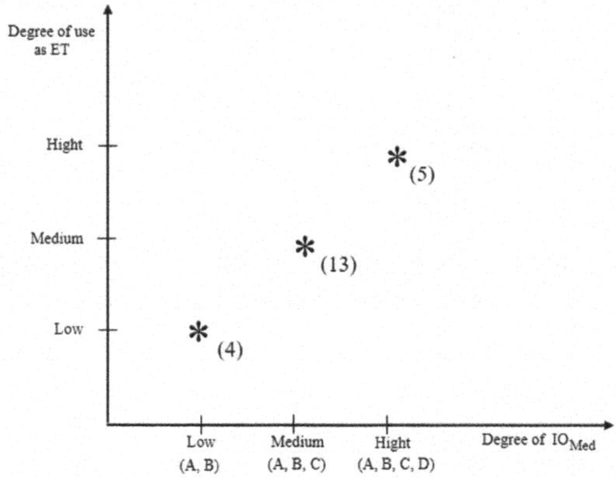

Fig. 4. Relationship between the use of DR as ET and the IO in teacher mediation (IO_{Med})

Figure 4 shows that the higher the epistemic quality of teacher mediation (IO_{Med}) in proposing and dealing with DR, the higher the degree to which students use DR as an ET. There is no evidence that the use of DRs as ET depends on the type of DR used.

The results show that to the students use of DR as ET in medium and high degree it is necessary: (i) to have a challenging task, IO_{Med}/A; (ii) to have teacher mediation between DR and learning, IO_{Med}/B; and (iii) to give students autonomy to use DR to solve the task, IO_{Med}/C. Notice that the existence of a challenging task is assumed by us from the beginning (Table 2).

A detailed analysis of Tables 7 and 8 (annexed) show to use DR as ET in high degree it is necessary, additionally to ones referred above, to have, cumulatively, teacher epistemic moves (IO_{Med}/D) and use of DR longer than 7 min (IO_T/A4 or IO_T/A5). Also, we can verify that the number of all articulations and the quality of articulations (Table 5) influence the quality of the use of DR as ET (epistemic tool in high degree) as can be seen in Table 6.

In summary, in order for a DR to be used by students as an epistemic tool there are *necessary aspects* to exist, *helpful aspects* to this process and *decisive aspects* so that the epistemic use of the tool is of a high-level.

Necessary aspects: to have a challenging task; to have teacher mediation between DR and learning; and to give students autonomy to use DR to solve the task.

Helpful aspects: existence of sequences of DRs, and their articulation.

Decisive aspects (to high-level use): time of use of DR and teacher epistemic moves (in addition to the above).

Finally, we mention the aspects that we consider compromise the use of DR as an epistemic tool: the absence of a challenging task and the very short duration of use (less than 1 min) in conjunction or not with the absence of autonomy for the student to solve the task.

5 Discussion

The contributions made by this study must be understood in the light of the limitations inherent in the context in which it was carried out: (a) only two teachers; and (b) use of DRs in the natural classroom context of higher education.

This study presents two contributions that go further than the established knowledge: (1) characteristics of three IO modes with influence on the use of DR as ET, (2) specification of how each IO mode influences the use of DR as ET. In this study we have clearly chosen to extend the notion of IO presented in [37]. Instead of following the path outlined by several authors in the sense of specifying or extending the types of IO [33, 38, 40], we have chosen to follow the approach followed by other authors in order to specify the importance of certain characteristics of IO [1–4]. Thus, one of the contributions of this study is to specify IO modes that influence the use of DR as ET, focusing on their characteristics that become necessary or decisive. This is a fundamental aspect, since we focus on IO characteristics that are grouped in different modes and can be recognized in various IO typologies. Identifying IO characteristics that may be decisive for certain purposes is what we specify below. In particular, contribution 1 can be formulated as follows:

1. There are three modes of IO important for the use of DR as ET: (a) IO_T, IO regarding the time of use and the moment of insertion of DRs; (b) IO_{Med}, IO regarding the way the teacher introduces, mediates (connection between DR and learning and epistemic moves) and grants autonomy to the student; (c) IO_W, IO regarding the type of articulation between DRs.

As we know the influence that the use of IO has on the learning of STEM [15, 17–21, 23–25], it was important to know what influence the different IO modes had on the use of DRs as ETs (our research question). Although it is known that the teaching approach when using DR is important for learning [15, 17, 21, 27–29], one of them stands out, the constructivist approach to teaching [17, 21], but even so the literature points out several difficulties [21, 28]. The gap identified in [37] is approached by us using the notion of IO [35] trying to identify central characteristics of IO [1–4] that can be decisive for the use of DR as ET [1, 5, 6, 8, 13].

Our results allow us to state the contribution 2 as follows:

2. Any of the IO modes with DRs has an influence on the use of DRs as epistemic tools.

2.1 The IO_{Med} mode has the clearest influence: the more sophisticated IO_{Med} is, the greater the possibility of using DR as an epistemic tool to a high degree. The autonomous resolution of a challenging task using DR with the mediation of the use of DR and learning done by the teacher plays an important role in this. To obtain a high degree of epistemic use of the DR by students beyond the above conditions it is decisive that the time of DR use by the student is significant (more than seven minutes) and that teacher has epistemic moves.

2.2 The IO_T mode has an influence on the use of DR as an epistemic tool, but the relationship is not linear. In any case, the time of use and insertion of the DR is a predictor of use of DR as an ET.

2.3 The IO_W mode can have an influence on the use of DR with epistemic tool. As we only analysed two teachers we cannot state clearly, but IOs used by teachers in their lessons so that students' use of digital resources is as epistemic tool that include sequences/web of interrelated DRs tend to be more productive.

The contribution 2.1 is aligned with the literature in the sense that it points to the importance of the teaching strategy for learning [14, 21], given the availability of DRs [14–16] which does not necessarily imply a change in pedagogical practice [25]. What is new is that it brings together a set of characteristics linked to the mediation of the teacher (task, connection of the use of DR to learning, autonomy granted to students and teacher epistemic moves) which are dispersed in different studies [1–4, 8, 9]. In addition, our study specifies how necessary or decisive some of those characteristics are for DR to be used as ET in a high degree.

Contributions 2.2 and 2.3 are specifications of didactical performance [40]. The didactical performance has a time dimension identified by [33] and what our study specifies as contribution 2.2 referring to the importance of the length of the use of each DR is the moment in which it is inserted in each class for the effective use of DRs as ETs. Contribution 2.3 is new and clearly, it will be necessary to do a more extensive research with more teachers about the importance of how teachers articulate different RDs among themselves.

6 Conclusion

It is possible to create IOs that take advantage of DRs by enabling students to use them as epistemic tools. The important characteristics for an IO to influence the use of DRs as epistemic tools are: (a) the length of their use, the moment of insertion in class; (b) the teacher mediation concerning the task type, students autonomy provided by teacher to students, teacher epistemic moves, and connection between DR use and learning; (c) the way DRs are articulated. The existence of a challenging task is indispensable. The degree of use of DR as an epistemic tool is related with the characteristics of the IO.

6.1 Implications for Teaching Practices

Since the literature points out that a DR when used as an ET increases the quality of learning in STEM, the results of this study have implications for teaching practices of college level in Physics and Mathematics. Our results point to features of IO to be used by the teachers in order to contribute to the use of DRs by students as an ET.

The main points to be consider by teachers in their teaching practices are:

For avoiding compromise the use of DR as an ET, the teacher should structure his/her teaching practices centred on challenging tasks and with at least 7 min of students autonomous activity. In addition, the teacher needs to explain how students can take advantage of DR in relation to the intended learning outcomes.

In order for a DR to be used by students as an epistemic tool the teacher should pay attention to: (i) sequences of DRs and their articulation; and (ii) teacher epistemic moves cumulatively with the previous point.

Annex

Table 7. Teacher Mara

Dimensions / Categories		Le1	Lesson 2		Lesson 3			Lesson 4					Lesson 5			
		DR 1	DR 2	DR 3	DR 4	DR 5	DR 6	DR 7	DR 8	DR 9	DR 10	DR 11	DR 12	DR 13	DR 14	DR 15
Instrumental orchestration (IO)	IO_T/A1															1
	A2									1		1	1			
	A3	1	1	1	1	1			1					1	1	
	A4							1			1					
	A5						1									
	IO_T/B1	1	1	1					1	1				1	1	1
	B2				1	1	1	1			1	1				
	B3												1			
	IO_{Med}/A	1	1	1	1	1	1	1	1	1	1	1	1	1	1	1
	IO_{Med}/B		1	1	1	1	1	1	1	1	1			1	1	
	IO_{Med}/C	1		1	1	1	1	1	1	1	1			1	1	
	IO_{Med}/D						1	1								
Epistemic tool (ET)	ET/A	1		1	1	1	1	1	1	1	1			1	1	
	ET/B	1	1	1	1	1	1	1	1	1	1			1	1	
	ET/C						1	1								

Label: Acronyms are as shown in table 3; the number 1 represents the occurrence of the category

Table 8. Teacher Rafael

		Lesson 1			Lesson 2		Lesson 3	
Dimensions / Categories		DR 1	DR 2	DR 3	DR 4	DR 5	DR 6	DR 7
Instrumental orchestration (IO)	**IO$_T$**/A1							
	A2	1	1					
	A3						1	
	A4			1				
	A5				1	1		1
	IO$_T$/B1							
	B2	1	1		1		1	1
	B3			1		1		
	IO$_{Med}$/A	1	1	1	1	1	1	1
	IO$_{Med}$/B	1	1	1	1	1	1	1
	IO$_{Med}$/C	1	1	1	1	1	1	1
	IO$_{Med}$/D			1	1	1		
Epistemic tool (**ET**)	**ET**/A	1	1	1	1	1	1	1
	B	1	1	1	1	1	1	1
	C			1	1	1		

Label: Acronyms are as shown in table 3; the number 1 represents the occurrence of the category

References

1. Lopes, J.B., Costa, C.: Digital resources in science, mathematics and technology teaching – how to convert them into tools to learn. In: Tsitouridou, M.A., Diniz, J., Mikropoulos, T. (eds.) TECH-EDU 2018. CCIS, vol. 993, pp. 243–255. Springer, Cham (2019). https://doi.org/10.1007/978-3-030-20954-4_18
2. Hollebrands, K., Okumuş, S.: Secondary mathematics teachers' instrumental integration in technology-rich geometry classrooms. J. Math. Behav. **49**, 82–94 (2018)
3. Gueudet, G., Buteau, C., Mesa, V., Misfeldt, M.: Instrumental and documentational approaches: from technology use to documentation systems in university mathematics education. Res. Math. Educ. **16**(2), 139–155 (2014)
4. Tabach, M., Hershkowitz, R., Dreyfus, T.: Learning beginning algebra in a computer-intensive environment. ZDM Math. Educ. **45**(3), 377–391 (2013)
5. Cunningham, C.M., Kelly, G.J.: Epistemic practices of engineering for education. Sci. Educ. **101**(3), 486–505 (2017)
6. Tan, E., Calabrese Barton, A., Benavides, A.: Engineering for sustainable communities: epistemic tools in support of equitable and consequential middle school engineering. Sci. Educ. **103**(4), 1011–1046 (2019)
7. Sezen-Barrie, A., Stapleton, M.K., Marbach-Ad, G.: Science teachers' sensemaking of the use of epistemic tools to scaffold students' knowledge (re) construction in classrooms. J. Res. Sci. Teach. **57**, 1058–1092 (2020)
8. Tang, K.S.: The use of epistemic tools to facilitate epistemic cognition & metacognition in developing scientific explanation. Cogn. Instr. **38**(4), 474–502 (2020)
9. Lindfors, M., Bodin, M., Simon, S.: Unpacking students' epistemic cognition in a physics problem-solving environment. J. Res. Sci. Teach. **57**(5), 695–732 (2020)
10. Chao, J., et al.: Bridging the design-science gap with tools: science learning and design behaviors in a simulated environment for engineering design. J. Res. Sci. Teach. **54**(8), 1049–1096 (2017). https://doi.org/10.1002/tea.21398

11. Oliveira, A., Feyzi Behnagh, R., Ni, L., Mohsinah, A.A., Burgess, K.J., Guo, L.: Emerging technologies as pedagogical tools for teaching and learning science: a literature review. Hum. Behav. Emerg. Technol. **1**(2), 149–160 (2019)
12. Sterelny, K.: Externalism, epistemic artefacts and the extended mind. In: Schantz, R. (ed.) The Externalist Challenge, vol. 2, pp. 239–254. Walter de Gruyter, Berlin (2004)
13. Miller, E., Manz, E., Russ, R., Stroupe, D., Berland, L.: Addressing the epistemic elephant in the room: epistemic agency and the next generation science standards. J. Res. Sci. Teach. **55**(7), 1053–1075 (2018)
14. Roseman, J.E., Fortus, D., Krajcik, J.: Curriculum materials for next generation science standards: what the science education research community can do. In: NARST Annual International Conference, Chicago, IL (2015)
15. Drijvers, P.: Digital technology in mathematics education: why it works (or doesn't). In: Cho, S.J. (ed.) Selected Regular Lectures from the 12th International Congress on Mathematical Education, pp. 135–151. Springer, Cham (2015). https://doi.org/10.1007/978-3-319-17187-6_8
16. El Mhouti, A., Erradi, M., Nasseh, A.: An evaluation model of digital educational resources. Int. J. Emerg. Technol. Learn. (IJET) **8**(2), 29–35 (2013)
17. Li, Q., Ma, X.: A meta-analysis of the effects of computer technology on school students' mathematics learning. Educ. Psychol. Rev. **22**(3), 215–243 (2010)
18. Schwarz, C.V., Meyer, J., Sharma, A.: Technology, pedagogy, and epistemology: opportunities and challenges of using computer modeling and simulation tools in elementary science methods. J. Sci. Teacher Educ. **18**(2), 243–269 (2007)
19. Paris, S.G. (ed.): Perspectives on Object-Centered Learning in Museums. Routledge, NewYork (2002)
20. Monaghan, J., Trouche, L., Borwein, J.M.: Tools and Mathematics. Springer, Cham (2016)
21. Bray, A., Tangney, B.: Technology usage in mathematics education research: a systematic review of recent trends. Comput. Educ. **114**, 255–273 (2017)
22. Cheung, A.C., Slavin, R.E.: The effectiveness of educational technology applications for enhancing mathematics achievement in K-12 classrooms: a meta-analysis. Educ. Res. Rev. **9**, 88–113 (2013)
23. Pepin, B., Gueudet, G., Trouche, L.: Refining teacher design capacity: mathematics teachers' interactions with digital curriculum resources. ZDM Math. Educ. **49**(5), 799–812 (2017)
24. Ibáñez, M.B., Delgado-Kloos, C.: Augmented reality for STEM learning: a systematic review. Comput. Educ. **123**, 109–123 (2018)
25. Curto Prieto, M., Orcos Palma, L., Blázquez Tobías, P.J., León, F.J.M.: Student assessment of the use of Kahoot in the learning process of science and mathematics. Educ. Sci. **9**(1), 55 (2019)
26. Van Laar, E., Van Deursen, A.J., Van Dijk, J.A., De Haan, J.: The relation between 21st-century skills and digital skills: a systematic literature review. Comput. Hum. Behav. **72**, 577–588 (2017)
27. Livingstone, S.: Critical reflections on the benefits of ICT in education. Oxf. Rev. Educ. **38**(1), 9–24 (2012)
28. McKnight, K., O'Malley, K., Ruzic, R., Horsley, M.K., Franey, J.J., Bassett, K.: Teaching in a digital age: how educators use technology to improve student learning. J. Res. Technol. Educ. **48**(3), 194–211 (2016)
29. Spiteri, M., Rundgren, S.N.C.: Literature review on the factors affecting primary teachers' use of digital technology. Technol. Knowl. Learn. **25**(1), 115–128 (2020)
30. Manca, S., Ranieri, M.: Is it a tool suitable for learning? A critical review of the literature on Facebook as a technology-enhanced learning environment. J. Comput. Assist. Learn. **29**(6), 487–504 (2013)

31. Fischer, L., Hilton, J., Robinson, T.J., Wiley, D.A.: A multi-institutional study of the impact of open textbook adoption on the learning outcomes of post-secondary students. J. Comput. High. Educ. **27**(3), 159–172 (2015)
32. Haßler, B., Major, L., Hennessy, S.: Tablet use in schools: a critical review of the evidence for learning outcomes. J. Comput. Assist. Learn. **32**(2), 139–156 (2016)
33. Tabach, M.: A mathematics teacher's practice in a technological environment: a case study analysis using two complementary theories. Technol. Knowl. Learn. **16**(3), 247–265 (2011)
34. Mishra, P., Koehler, M.J.: Technological pedagogical content knowledge: a framework for integrating technology in teacher knowledge. Teach. Coll. Rec. **108**(6), 1017–1054 (2006)
35. Guin, D., Trouche, L.: Mastering by the teacher of the instrumental genesis in CAS environments: necessity of instrumental orchestrations. ZDM Math. Educ. **34**(5), 204–211 (2002)
36. Pepin, B., Choppin, J., Ruthven, K., Sinclair, N.: Digita: curriculum resources in mathematics education: foundations for change. ZDM Math. Educ. **49**(5), 645–661 (2017)
37. Drijvers, P.: Tools and taxonomies: a response to Hoyles. Res. Math. Educ. **20**(3), 229–235 (2018)
38. Drijvers, P., Grauwin, S., Trouche, L.: When bibliometrics met mathematics education research: the case of instrumental orchestration. ZDM Math. Educ. **52**(7), 1455–1469 (2020). https://doi.org/10.1007/s11858-020-01169-3
39. Trouche, L., Drijvers, P.: Webbing and orchestration. Two interrelated views on digital tools in mathematics education. Teach. Math. Appl. **33**(3), 193–209 (2014). https://doi.org/10.1093/teamat/hru014
40. Drijvers, P., Doorman, M., Boon, P., Reed, H., Gravemeijer, K.: The teacher and the tool: Instrumental orchestrations in the technology-rich mathematics classroom. Educ. Stud. Math. **75**(2), 213–234 (2010)
41. Drijvers, P., Tacoma, S., Besamusca, A., Doorman, M., Boon, P.: Digital resources inviting changes in mid-adopting teachers' practices and orchestrations. ZDM Math. Educ. **45**(7), 987–1001 (2013). https://doi.org/10.1007/s11858-013-0535-1
42. Cohen, L., Manion, L., Morrison, K.: Research Methods in Education. Routledge, London (2013)
43. Stake, R.E.: Multiple Case Study Analysis. Guilford Press, New York (2013)
44. Yin, R.K.: Case Study Research: Design and Methods, 3rd edn. Sage, London (2003)
45. Lopes, J.B., Cravino, J.P.: Práticas de Ensino de Ciências e Tecnologia – Acervo de Narrações Multimodais. [Science and Technology Teaching Practices - Multimodal Narratives Collection] Universidade de Trás-os-Montes e Alto Douro, Vila Real (2017). https://multimodal.narratives.utad.pt
46. Lopes, J.B., et al.: Constructing and using multimodal narratives to research in science education: contributions based on practical classroom. Res. Sci. Educ. **44**(3), 415–438 (2013). https://doi.org/10.1007/s11165-013-9381-y
47. Lopes, J.B., Viegas, M.C., Pinto, J.A.: The importance of making teaching practices public, shareable, and usable: the role of multimodal narratives. In: Multimodal Narratives in Research and Teaching Practices, pp. 1–42. IGI Global, Hershey (2019)

The Use of Kahoot, GeoGebra and Texas Ti-Nspire Educational Software's in the Teaching of Geometry and Measurement

Paula Sofia Nunes[1(✉)], Paulo Martins[2], and Paula Catarino[3]

[1] Universidade de Trás-os-Montes e Alto Douro (UTAD), Agrupamento de Escolas de Cabeceiras de Basto, Cabeceiras de Basto, Portugal
[2] Universidade de Trás-os-Montes e Alto Douro & INESC TEC, Vila Real, Portugal
pmartins@utad.pt
[3] Universidade de Trás-os-Montes e Alto Douro, CIDTFF & CMAT-UTAD, Vila Real, Portugal
pcatarin@utad.pt

Abstract. The use of Educational Software (ES) in education has become essential for teachers and students. On the one hand, the effectiveness of its use may facilitate the acquisition of learning and on the other hand, it may enable a better transmission of the contents. In this sense, it is necessary to provide teachers with tools that allow them to develop successful pedagogical actions with appealing and innovative resources, capable of stimulating creativity and motivating students for learning. The aim of this study is to ascertain the knowledge and the use by teachers of ES Kahoot, GeoGebra and Texas Ti-Nspire, in what type of content, activities and what is the impact of their use in the teaching of Geometry and Measurement (GM), whether in teaching practice of teachers, or in the learning of students. The adopted method has a qualitative nature, with characteristics of a case study. Fourteen teachers who teach Mathematics at various schools in Portugal participated. Two questionnaires and a challenge that consisted of the elaboration of tasks were used as instruments. Data analysis was performed using Excel (Office 2016) and content analysis of the answers given, and the tasks developed. The results suggest that of the three ES, Kahoot was the most unknown and was the most chosen by teachers to develop different GM content. The reasons are also described as to why these ES may cause an improvement in the teaching practices of teachers, as well as motivation and student learning.

Keyword: GM teaching · Tasks · ES Kahoot · GeoGebra · Texas Ti-Nspire

1 Introduction

There are several Educational Software's (ES) used in a classroom environment for teaching and learning geometric contents that are part of the Basic and Secondary Education Mathematics program. Currently, several studies show that the use of this type of artifact has a fundamental role in the teaching and learning processes, raising the students' motivation for learning Mathematics. In addition, the use of ES in the teaching of

A. Reis et al. (Eds.): TECH-EDU 2020, CCIS 1384, pp. 21–31, 2021.
https://doi.org/10.1007/978-3-030-73988-1_2

Geometry and Measurement (GM) is considered an excellent tool for the development of pedagogical tasks, where it is possible to work on the acquisition of various skills. Its use in an educational context requires certain knowledge and skills that can be acquired through training.

The use of ES in the field of GM enables the transformation of a Mathematics class into a research environment, where students are involved in the learning process, through manipulation, experimentation, observation, formulation of conjectures, tests and development of explanations for the challenges presented. The use of ES in the GM domain has become almost essential for solving mathematical problems and can be considered as tools that facilitate the transmission of content. With its use, the student gets involved in the cognitive process, through the resolution of complex learning tasks and critical thinking [1]. It is essential to provide teachers with the necessary skills for the effective use of ES, especially at a time when the use of online classes is so used due to the contingencies caused by COVID-19.

The use of free software can cause changes within the Mathematics classroom, which will not only gain space for investigative, critical, and demonstrative exploration, but also, for teacher training courses, enabling the emergence of new pedagogical practices [2].

The aim of this study is to ascertain what knowledge the teachers who teach GM of ES Kahoot, GeoGebra and Texas Ti-Nspire have and what their use in teaching practice is. We also wanted to investigate what kind of activities, as well as what the contents of the GM domain can be developed using the indicated ES. We also wanted to find out what the teachers think about the impact of using these ES in the teaching and learning of GM.

In order to achieve our purposes, a workshop was held for Mathematics teachers with the aim of providing trainees with tools that allow them to use Kahoot, GeoGebra and the Texas Ti-Nspire graphing calculator and to continue their learning independently. A set of practical tasks that could be worked on in the classroom with the use of these three types of software were presented, addressing diverse geometric contents. Then, each trainee was asked to prepare a pedagogical task to develop GM content, using one of the ES Kahoot, GeoGebra or TI-Nsipre and they were also asked what the reasons for choosing the selected software over the others.

This article is structured as follows: in the next section there is the theoretical basis for the use of Kahoot, GeoGebra and Texas Ti-Nspire in the teaching of GM; then, we presented the method of investigation, with the methodological approach, the characterization of the participants, the description of the instruments used and data analysis; the results section and the discussion follow, trying to relate the theoretical perspective with the results obtained; finally, we expose the conclusions, future works and in the end, the references bibliographic are stated.

2 Kahoot, GeoGebra and Texas Ti-Nspire in Teaching Geometry and Measurement

The introduction of modern technology in the education system may cause a greater understanding of the contents, as well as an improvement in the teaching and learning of Mathematics [3]. There are studies that mention evidence that the use of Information and Communication Technologies (ICT) provides effective and inflexible methods for the professional development of teachers [4].

However, there are barriers to the integration of innovative tools in the classroom, which include teachers, students, and schools. Focusing on teachers, we refer to personal factors, such as age, gender, or professional factors, such as the number of years of experience [5], lack of time in its timetable for effective ICT integration, lack of quality software in schools, poor curriculum connections and poor teacher training in these areas [5, 6], among others.

Kahoot is a tool that allows the teacher to develop games, in different areas of Mathematics, including GM, it allows the evaluation of the students' performance, as well as the comparison of the results between the intervening parties [7]. It also provides gamification in the classroom for its characteristics, as it allows clear rules, immediate feedbacks, punctuation, rankings, limited time, reflection, discussion, error inclusion, collaboration, and fun [8]. The use of Kahoot stimulates the development of meaningful learning, since the existence of competition, music, the presence of elements from the games, cause increased motivation, greater involvement of students in the proposed tasks [9], favoring academic success and, consequently, a positive effect on student learning [10].

The activities developed using Kahoot can be used for reviewing and retrieving content [11] make it possible to evaluate students' performance and allow the comparison of results between stakeholders [7].

The implications of using the digital educational game with Kahoot have been studied by several authors [7, 9, 11]. This tool increases motivation, as the sensation of discovery, curiosity, fantasy, and challenge are not only related to the content covered, but also to the process of playing and to the competition. The use of Kahoot promotes the active participation of students and acts as a facilitator of the teaching and learning processes, since the immediate feedback provided in a playful way, through the respective scores, encourages them to redo the activities in search of the correct answer, providing meaningful learning [9].

GeoGebra is an ES where you can work with geometric representations within the scope of the GM domain, but it also can connect with other areas of Mathematics, such as Algebra, Calculus and Arithmetic. The authors Wan Salleh and Sulaiman [12] mention that ES GeoGebra or other similar ones should be used as a teaching tool by teachers, as they help students to acquire an intuitive feeling and properly visualize the mathematical process, also allowing the exploration of a greater variety of functions and stimulating the establishment of connections between symbolic and visual representations, thus contributing to meaningful learning. The use and integration of GeoGebra applets in the teaching of Mathematics and the resulting situations provide a teaching methodology much more effective than the traditional one, as it facilitates the learning of the fundamental concepts to be transmitted by teachers [13].

Texas TI-Nspire calculator also allows you to work in different domains of Mathematics, including GM. It allows the exploration of modeling, simulation and problem-solving activities, linking the various representations, which is fundamental for the consolidation of knowledge [14].

The calculator allows the formulation of hypotheses and conjectures, since the speed with which it performs a given calculation allows freeing up time for that formulation, besides increasing the number of interactions with the calculator in a systematic and sequenced way, it allows to confirm or refuse a certain initial conjecture, this being one of the great advantages of using this graphing calculator [15].

However, for a teacher to propose resources that enrich the students' learning process, a good knowledge of the artifact is necessary. Fact that requires a great deal of individual and teamwork by teachers, computer skills and a calculator for an effective instrumental practice, specific strategies and deep reflections [14].

With this article, we seek answers to the following research questions (RQ):

RQ_1: What knowledge and use of ES Kahoot, GeoGebra and Texas Ti-Nspire do teachers have in teaching GM?
RQ_2: What kind of activities and what GM content can teachers develop using ES Kahoot, GeoGebra and Texas Ti-Nspire?
RQ_3: What is the impact of using ES Kahoot, GeoGebra and Texas Ti-Nspire on GM teaching and learning?

3 Method

In this work, we intend to investigate the knowledge and the use by teachers of ES Kahoot, GeoGebra and Texas Ti-Nspire in the teaching of GM, in what type of activities and content could be used, as well as the impact of the use of these ES in the teaching practice of teachers and student learning.

The adopted methodology is based on a work logic of a qualitative nature and using case study design. Yin [16] defines a case study as an empirical approach that investigates a contemporary phenomenon in depth, in its real context; when the boundaries between certain phenomena and their context are not evident, and in which multiple sources of data are used. This investigation does not intend to generalize, as the object of analysis is unique, our focus is on understanding the phenomenon under study.

According to Ponte [17], a case study is more than a methodology, it is essentially a research design, with its own characteristics, and it is part of a framework of very different methodological paradigms, such as the positivist, the interpretive or the critical. The author states that a case study is an investigation of an empirical nature that relates to fieldwork or document analysis, it is a type of research with a strong descriptive nature; this type of investigation is not experimental, it is used when the researcher does not intend to modify the situation, but to understand it in its essence. His account often takes the form of a narrative that aims to tell a story that adds some interesting novelty to existing knowledge.

This study results from a training course provided to Mathematics teachers on the use of ES Kahoot, GeoGebra and Texas Ti-Nspire in the teaching of GM. The participants trained 14 teachers, who signed up for a workshop, which was part of a Meeting organized by the University of Aveiro, Portugal, alluding to the theme "Mathematics with Life-Different looks on Geometry". All participants were female, 78.6% were aged between 31 and 50 years old and the rest were over 50 years old, from different locations. The majority were teachers of the Grouping Board (64.3%) or of the Pedagogical Zone Board (28.6%), with only 7.1% of teachers being in the Contracted situation. Half of the teachers had between 11 and 20 years of service and the other half between 21 and 30 years of service. All participants were teachers from the 500- Mathematics group, from the third Cycle of Basic and Secondary Education. As for the qualifications, 50% had a bachelor's degree, 35.7% a master's degree and 14.3% a postgraduate degree. The vast majority taught at Basic and Secondary Education levels (from the 7th year to the 12th year), only 14.3% taught only at the third Cycle of Basic Education (7th, 8th, and 9th Years).

Two questionnaires were used as instruments for data collection, one of them was used as a diagnosis, with the objective of verifying the skills that teachers had in the knowledge and use of ES Kahoot, GeoGebra and Texas Ti-Nspire and was applied, via email, before the workshop, to be able to plan and adapt the training to the participants. The second questionnaire was applied at the end of the workshop, whose main objective was to investigate the importance of these tools for teaching GM. Two professors from the University of Trás-os-Montes and Alto Douro (UTAD) validated the questionnaires and their empirical validation was done through their previous application to three teachers, to understand their suitability for the phenomenon under study.

It was also used as data collection a challenge proposed to teachers, during the training, where they had to plan and create a pedagogical task, to develop GM content, with the selection of one of the ES Kahoot, GeoGebra or Texas Ti- Nspire, had yet to justify the reasons for choosing the selected tool. The results obtained in the questionnaires were crossed with the data of the proposed challenge, to collect data from more than one source.

The questionnaire data were analyzed using Excel (Office 2016) and the content analysis of the challenge proposed to teachers was made, as well as the open questionnaire responses.

4 Results and Discussion

Of the three ES presented and explored in the workshop, the most unknown by teachers was Kahoot, 50% knew, however, the vast majority (78.6%) had never used it. Texas Ti-Nspire was known to 71.4% of teachers, but less than half (42.9%) had used it. ES GeoGebra was the best known of teachers (92.9%), however, only 64.3% used GeoGebra in their teaching practice.

We found that the teachers who participated in this study had little knowledge of ES Kahoot (50%), a very satisfactory knowledge of the Texas Ti-Nspire calculator (71.4%) and a good knowledge of ES GeoGebra (92.9%). We found a different situation in the use of ES in teaching practice, as we found that the vast majority did not use these ES: only 21.4% used Kahoot in their classes, less than half (42.9%) used Texas Ti-Nspire in its teaching practice and although GeoGebra is the ES known by the vast majority of teachers, only 64.3% had used it with their students. The barriers to the integration of innovative tools in the classroom by teachers can be justified by several fundamental factors of a personal and professional nature, described by Radović et al. [6] and Nunes et al. [5], namely, the influence of age, gender, length of service and lack of training.

When asked about the reasons that led them to join this training course, the most frequent responses from the participants in this study were the following: acquiring new skills (92.9%) and improving professional performance (78.6%). All participants replied that, after this training course, they would use the knowledge acquired in it for their professional practice. From the answers given, it can be inferred that teachers, despite having some knowledge of the tools Kahoot, Geogebra and Texas Ti-Nspire, use them in a reduced way in their classes, due to the lack of training to integrate these technologies in the classroom. Also, in the study by Nunes et al. [5] it was concluded that most teachers have a weak or reasonable level of ES to apply in the classroom and that having a training in ES is an essential condition for its use in teaching practice.

Of the participants in this study, 74.1% consider that the three tools complement each other, in the teaching of GM, however they subdivided these three tools into two distinct groups and stated several reasons, which we now describe:

- Kahoot: it is interesting and facilitates the assessment/verification of knowledge, it serves to perform tasks such as homework, it is a game that arouses students' motivation.
- GeoGebra and Texas Ti-Nspire: they serve for students to learn and explore the contents, they are particularly interested in the classroom context, they can be used to acquire skills, they both have similar functions and complement each other, they allow different approaches contents.

The type of activities to be developed with the use of the three tools, in the opinion of the teachers, could be: diagnostic assessment, formative assessment, assessment tests [7], deduction and demonstration of properties and theorems [2, 15], exploration/investigation activities and verification of results [1, 12], problem solving [14], content review and recovery [11], content application exercises, consolidation of learning, self-assessment and gamification [8]. Converging opinions with studies carried out by several mentioned authors.

With regard to the content of the GM domain to be developed with the use of ES Kahoot, GeoGebra and Texas Ti-Nspire, the teachers indicated that they could be used in: areas of geometric figures, volumes of solids, geometric places, circumference, properties polygons, analytical geometry, triangles and quadrilaterals, trigonometry, similarity, Pythagorean theorem and isometries. There are also teachers who indicate that these ES can be used in all areas of Mathematics.

Regarding the importance of using Kahoot, GeoGebra and Texas Ti-Nspire tools in improving teachers' teaching practice, the results are shown in Table 1.

Table 1. Teachers' opinion on the contribution of ES to the improvement of teaching practice.

ES \ Opinion	Totally Disagree	Disagree	Neither agree nor disagree	Agree	Totally agree
Kahoot	0%	0%	0%	79%	21%
GeoGebra	0%	0%	0%	43%	57%
Texas Ti-Nspire	0%	0%	7%	43%	50%

We found, therefore, that most respondents *Agree or Totally agree* that the use of these ES in the classroom environment contributes to an improvement in their teaching practice. Opinions in line with studies carried out by other authors, such as Scheffer et al. [2] and Hamidi et al. [4].

It was found that, in the resolution of the challenge proposed in the workshop, where each teacher would have to elaborate the planning of a pedagogical task, with selection of one of the ES Kahoot, GeoGebra or Texas Ti-Nspire, who thought that he contributed in the best way to the improving their teaching practice. The majority selected ES Kahoot (64%) for the elaboration of the task, followed by GeoGebra (29%) and finally Texas Ti-Nspire (7%). The teachers also explained the reasons for choosing the ES to carry out the proposed challenge, described in Table 2.

Table 2. Reasons for choosing the ES

Opinion / ES	Reasons for choosing the ES
Kahoot	ES with less contact and curiosity to explore its potential.
	Strand of gamification is a motivating factor for students.
	Suitable for the distance-learning situation.
	Practical and easy to handle by students.
	Arouses students' curiosity, motivation, and interest.
	It allows self-regulation of students' learning in a playful environment.
	Provides gamification in the classroom.
	Gives immediate feedback on students' knowledge.
	It allows the exportation of results and the verification of questions where students have more difficulties.
	Motivation of students with the idea of competition.
	It allows to approach various contents.
	It provokes dynamic and motivating classes for students familiar with online games.
	Fun and competitive side.
	Allows you to stop the game so that the teacher explains the resolution at the end of each question.
	It allows the analysis of individual student responses.
	Allows individual or group activities.
	You do not need a student registration.
	Gives immediate feedback to students.
	It allows the use of the mobile phone as a tool for working with students.
GeoGebra	Suitable for the age group of students.
	It allows the review of concepts.
	It allows the exploration of different cases and generalization.
	ES easier to access for use in the classroom.
	Suitable for distance learning.
	Arouses students' curiosity, motivation, and interest.
	ES best suited to demonstrate properties of GM content.
	IF you knew better.
Texas Ti-Nspire	Student motivation.
	Be different.
	Familiarization of the graphing calculator for students.

Regarding the opinion of teachers on the impact of using the Kahoot, GeoGebra and Texas Ti-Nspire tools on increasing students' motivation and interest, the results are shown in Table 3.

Table 3. Teachers' opinion on the impact of ES on students' motivation and interest.

ES \ Opinion	Totally Disagree	Disagree	Neither agree nor disagree	Agree	Totally agree
Kahoot	0%	0%	0%	79%	21%
GeoGebra	0%	0%	0%	43%	57%
Texas Ti-Nspire	0%	0%	7%	43%	50%

In relation to the contribution of the use of ES to the improvement of the understanding of the contents and, consecutively, in the learning of contents in the domain of GM, the results of the opinion of the teachers are presented in Table 4.

Table 4. Teachers' opinion on the impact of SE for improving GM learning.

ES \ Opinion	Totally Disagree	Disagree	Neither agree nor disagree	Agree	Totally agree
Kahoot	0%	0%	14%	64%	22%
GeoGebra	0%	0%	0%	43%	57%
Texas Ti-Nspire	0%	0%	7%	43%	50%

From the results obtained, it is concluded that the vast majority of teachers have the opinion that the use of ES Kahoot, GeoGebra and Texas Ti-Nspire in their teaching practice causes students greater motivation and interest, a result similar to the studies carried out by Gozotti- Vallim, et al. [9]. As the students are motivated and interested in the proposed tasks, the teachers consider that the use of these innovative tools in the classroom may lead to an improvement in the learning of GM. Conclusion in line with convergence with investigations carried out by Bature [3], Correia and Santos [10].

Of the teachers who participated in the study, 71.4% say that training in ES Kahoot, GeoGebra and Texas Ti-Nsipre were useful for the exercise of their professional function, while 28.6% considered them very useful. All teachers intend to use the knowledge acquired in their teaching practice, mainly Kahoot and GeoGebra (92.9%).

5 Conclusions and Future Work

The results of this investigation point to some conclusions regarding the application of ES Kahoot, GeoGebra and Texas Ti-Nspire in the teaching and learning of GM:

- we found that the most unknown and least used ES for teachers was Kahoot, which is considered the most appropriate and most interesting of the three presented, for the elaboration of pedagogical tasks to be applied in the classroom, to develop GM content;
- participants subdivided these tools into two distinct groups, according to the most appropriate activities for each ES: Kahoot will be more suitable for diagnostic and formative assessment, for knowledge verification, for sending tasks to be solved at home, for application and content review, consolidation of learning, self-assessment and gamification; GeoGebra and Texas Ti-Nspire have similar characteristics, but complement each other, they will be more suitable for exploring and investigating content, deducing and demonstrating properties and theorems, acquiring knowledge and skills in the classroom and for solving problems;
- the participants in this study considered that the GM content most suitable for carrying out activities using these ES are the following: areas and volumes, geometric places, polygons, triangle, quadrilaterals, analytical geometry, trigonometry, similarity, Pythagorean theorem and isometries;
- The vast majority of teachers consider that the use of these innovative tools in a classroom environment contributes to the improvement of their teaching practices, highlighting Kahoot as the tool that most contributes to this effect, due to its characteristics that provide gamification.

We can also find out reasons, described by the teachers, why the use of ES Kahoot, GeoGebra and Texas Ti-Nspire, provide greater motivation and improvement in student learning, namely: the gamification aspect favors competition among students, they are practical SE and easy to use by students, arouse curiosity and interest, allow self-regulation of learning, enable immediate feedback on student performance, provide more dynamic classes and students do not need any prior registration for their use.

This work is part of a more comprehensive investigation, being considered as a preliminary study on the use of ES in the teaching of GM and what is its impact on the teaching practices of teachers and on students' learning. We intend, therefore, to continue to investigate what characteristics ES should have to promote effectiveness in the teaching of GM and what is the impact of their use in teaching and learning.

As limitations to the study, being a case study, we know that these results are not generalizable however, they work as a piece of a puzzle, which we are building to reach more comprehensive conclusions.

References

1. Kuzle, A.: Delving into the nature of problem solving processes in a dynamic geometry environment: different technological effects on cognitive processing. Technol. Knowl. Learn. **22**(1), 37–64 (2016). https://doi.org/10.1007/s10758-016-9284-x
2. Scheffer, N.F., Bressan, J.Z., Rovani, S.: Possibilidades didáticas de investigação do software gratuito régua e compasso na exploração do triângulo equilátero. Vivências **5**(8), 27–36 (2009)
3. Bature, B.: The role of information and communication technology as a tool for effective teaching and learning of mathematics. J. Appl. Comput. Math. **5**(6), 1–3 (2016). https://doi.org/10.4172/2168-9679.1000333

4. Hamidi, F., Meshkat, M., Rezaee, M., Jafari, M.: Information technology in education. Procedia Comput. Sci. **3**, 369–373 (2011). https://doi.org/10.1016/j.procs.2010.12.062
5. Nunes, P.S., Nascimento, M.M., Catarino, P., Martins, P.: Fatores que Influenciam o Uso de Software Educativo no Ensino de Matemática. REICE: Revista Iberoamericana sobre Calidad, Eficacia y Cambio en Educación **18**(3), 113–129 (2020). https://doi.org/10.15366/reice2020.18.3.006
6. Radović, S., Marić, M., Passey, D.: Technology enhancing mathematics learning behaviours: shifting learning goals from "producing the right answer" to "understanding how to address current and future mathematical challenges." Educ. Inf. Technol. **24**(1), 103–126 (2018). https://doi.org/10.1007/s10639-018-9763-x
7. Sande, D., Sande, D.: Uso do Kahoot como ferramenta de avaliação e ensino-aprendizagem no ensino de microbiologia industrial. HOLOS **1**, 170–179 (2018). https://doi.org/10.15628/holos.2018.6300
8. da Silva, J.B., Andrade, M.H., de Oliveira, R.R., Sales, G.L., Alves, F.R.V.: Tecnologias digitais e metodologias ativas na escola: o contributo do Kahoot para gamificar a sala de aula. Revista Thema **15**(2), 780–791 (2018). https://doi.org/10.15536/thema.15.2018.780-791.838
9. Gazotti-Vallim, M.A., Gomes, S.T., Fischer, C.R.: Vivenciando inglês com kahoot. The ESPecialist **38**(1) (2017). https://doi.org/10.23925/2318-7115.2017v38i1a11
10. Correia, M., Santos, R.: A aprendizagem baseada em jogos online: uma experiência de uso do Kahoot na formação de professores. In: Cristina, P., Juan, M.D., Maria, J.S. (eds.) Atas da Conferência, XIX Simpósio Internacional de Informática Educativa/VIII Encontro do CIED–III Encontro Internacional, pp. 252–257. CIED, Lisboa (2017)
11. Prá, R., Freitas, T.A., de Araújo Amico, M.R.: A análise da ferramenta Kahoot como facilitadora do processo de ensino aprendizagem. Redin-Revista Educacional Interdisciplinar **6**(1) (2017)
12. Wan Salleh, M., Sulaiman, H.: A survey on the effectiveness of using GeoGebra software towards lecturers' conceptual knowledge and procedural mathematics. In: AIP Conference Proceedings, vol. 1522, no. 1, pp. 330–336 (2013). https://doi.org/10.1063/1.4801143
13. Caligaris, M.G., Schivo, M.E., Romiti, M.R.: Calculus & GeoGebra, an interesting partnership. Procedia Soc. Behav. Sci. **174**, 1183–1188 (2015). https://doi.org/10.1016/j.sbspro.2015.01.735
14. Mesquita, J.: A Utilização da Calculadora Gráfica no Estudo das Funções Trigonométricas (Master's thesis). Faculdade de Ciências e Tecnologia da Universidade Nova de Lisboa, Lisboa (2014)
15. Canavarro, A.P.: Ensino e Aprendizagem da Estatística em Estatística e calculadoras gráficas, pp. 159–167. SPE, APM e DEEIO/FCUL, Lisboa (2000)
16. Yin, R.K.: Estudo de Caso: Planejamento e Métodos. 4th edn. Translation: Ana Thorell. Bookman Editora, Porto Alegre (2010)
17. Ponte, J.P.: Estudos de caso em educação matemática. Bolema: Boletim de Educação Matemática **19**(25) (2006)

Exploring the Potential of the Outdoors with Digital Technology in Teacher Education

Ana Barbosa(✉) and Isabel Vale(✉)

Instituto Politécnico de Viana do Castelo, Viana do Castelo, Portugal
{anabarbosa,isabel.vale}@ese.ipvc.pt

Abstract. This paper refers to a study that aims to understand the perceptions of pre-service teachers about the use of digital technology in outdoor mathematics. We followed a qualitative, interpretative approach and collected data through participant observation, questionnaires and photographic records. The participants were forty-eight pre-service teachers, that were enrolled in a Didactics of Mathematics unit course, and they used the MathCityMap app to do a math trail in the city of Viana do Castelo. Results show that they valued the experience, having the possibility to solve realistic problems, developing cooperative work, critical thinking and establishing mathematical connections. They found the app to be user friendly and motivating, mentioning its contribution for students' engagement through active learning, spatial orientation, autonomy and being more interactive than the paper version. As for limitations, the participants highlighted the possible lack of access to Wi-Fi; the fact that students of younger ages normally do not have smartphones; and, in terms of the tasks, the limitation of the answer formats to either a value or multiple choice.

Keywords: Math trails · Digital technology · STEM education · Teacher training

1 Introduction

This paper draws on previous work developed by the authors in the scope of outdoor mathematics education. Several studies conducted in the context of pre-service teacher education [1–3] evidence that the outdoors can be a privileged educational context, that promotes positive attitudes and additional engagement for the study of mathematics. In this type of non-formal context, math trails have great potential in highlighting the connections between mathematics and daily life, particularly with the environment that surrounds us. The focus of these studies has been task design, approaching different aspects of problem posing and problem solving. Being part of the Consortium of the Project Math Trails in School, Curriculum and Educational Environments in Europe (MaSCE3), gave us the opportunity to contact with a different approach to math trails, other than task design, adding the possibility to resort to digital technology, specifically mobile devices. The use of MathCityMap (MCM), a project of the working group MATIS I (IDMI, Goethe- Universität Frankfurt) in cooperation with Stiftung Rechnen, has been reported as having a positive impact in supporting teachers and students in the process

A. Reis et al. (Eds.): TECH-EDU 2020, CCIS 1384, pp. 32–43, 2021.
https://doi.org/10.1007/978-3-030-73988-1_3

of teaching and learning mathematics outside the classroom, acting as a resourceful tool to explore the outdoors in a mathematical perspective [4, 5]. We are convinced that these approaches are extremely relevant in mathematical education and also to the development of a skills expected from students in the 21st century, so it is our purpose in this study to understand the perceptions of pre-service teachers about the use of digital technology in outdoor mathematics. Based on this problem, the following research questions were formulated: 1) Which potentialities and limitations are recognized in MCM by the participants?; 2) How can we characterize the reactions of the participants to a math trail?

2 Conceptual Framework

2.1 Doing Mathematics Outdoors Through Math Trails

School mathematics should be guided by certain principles, specifically providing students with meaningful and authentic learning, that helps them make sense of mathematical ideas [6]. According to Kenderov et al. [7] many students do not get the opportunity to feel and fully appreciate the essence of mathematics and others are even deprived of adequate teaching, hence deprived of significant learning experiences, which can lead to the construction of a negative perspective about mathematics. The same authors draw attention to non-formal education, particularly the outdoors, as a means to complement the work developed inside the classroom with experiences in the scope of outdoor mathematics. This helps students discover and interpret the world beyond the classroom walls and accept that education can take place in different places and contexts. Although the teaching and learning of mathematics is essentially conducted in the classroom, we believe in the importance of diversifying the learning contexts and experiences that are provided to students. Among the various possible experiences and strategies, we may find the math trails.

We consider a math trail to be a sequence of tasks along a pre-planned route (with beginning and end), composed of a set of stops in which students solve mathematical tasks in the environment that surrounds us [3]. The participants of a math trail are challenged to solve interesting mathematical tasks, contextualized by the environment surrounding them, applying acquired knowledge, developing skills such as problem solving, communication and the establishment of a diversity of connections [8].

Due to the atmosphere of discovery that is implied, math trails are stimulating learning situations, that make tasks more significant, challenging and interesting for the participants, requiring an active engagement and can contribute to the improvement of mathematical knowledge [3, 9]. During a math trail the participants contact with realistic problems that illustrate the usefulness of mathematics and amplify the possibility of establishing connections between mathematics and reality. This can be crucial to induce positive attitudes towards this subject, relying specially on curiosity, motivation and interest [7, 10].

As we can infer from the previous ideas, tasks are one of the components of a math trail that most stand out. Tasks are one of the main tools of the teaching practice, if not the most influent, and have great impact in what students learn, however we must be aware of the importance of its careful selection, because tasks with different levels of cognitive demand, induce different learning modes. All students should have the opportunity to engage in meaningful mathematical activity, and it's the teacher's role to unlock their potential, through the choice of adequate tasks and teaching strategies. Although tasks have the power to trigger mathematical activity, they may not be sufficient to implicate mathematical challenge. Teachers must establish a classroom environment that guarantees students' engagement in embracing mathematical challenge [11], aspect that must be contemplated while organizing a trail.

Good tasks are those that are culturally relevant, i.e., those that are related to students' lives raising the possibility of being more meaningful to the student than those that are provided by external sources (e.g. teacher, textbook). So, the environment where students live is a great context to formulate and solve different kinds of tasks that challenge and engage students in its solution. Challenge is important in the mathematics classroom, because students can become demotivated and bored very easily in a "routine" class, and don't learn, unless they are challenged. A mathematical challenge occurs when the individual is not aware of procedural or algorithmic tools that are critical to solve the problem and seems to have no standard method of solution. In this context we privilege *challenging* tasks that can be solved in different ways [11]. The expression *challenging* task is normally used to describe a task that is interesting and perhaps enjoyable, but not always easy to deal with or attain, and should actively engage students, developing a diversity of thinking and learning styles [11]. The solution for the same task may also be scaffolded differently for different students, providing challenges at several levels. Our difficult role and goal as teachers are to engage students with different mathematical backgrounds in different settings so that they can further develop their mathematical ideas, reasoning and problem solving strategies, as well as their enjoyment in solving mathematical tasks.

To organize a math trail, it is necessary to have some planning principles. Richardson [8] proposes the following steps: (1) first comes the selection of the site. It can be anywhere, as long as it is rich in mathematics. The teacher must observe the elements of the chosen context and look for aspects like patterns, shapes, things to measure, count or represent; (2) then, we take photos at each chosen location to later use them in the design of the tasks; (3) select the photos, create a map and identify the chosen places to carry out the tasks in order to verify the distribution of the stops and the distance of the route; (4) formulate the different tasks and the instructions to reach the different stops. These tasks must have different cognitive levels of demand [12] and admit different mathematical approaches. The tasks must be solved with knowledge previously learned in the classroom; (5) whenever possible, it is interesting to establish connections between mathematics and other curricular areas through the tasks. Regarding the task design, Richardson [8] recommends that questions should arouse the curiosity, forcing the students to observe the environment to achieve a successful solution. There are other aspects to consider on a math trail. To complement these ideas, Shoaf, Pollak, and Schneider [9] argue that math trails: should be for everyone, regardless of age and experience, since it is intended that they discuss and compare their reasoning and strategies; require collaboration and not competition; the participants must be able to manage time; participation must be voluntary, given that participants must feel involved and interested; they should be presented in any safe public place, since mathematics is everywhere; and they are temporary, since the places are subject to changes over time.

2.2 Math Trails and Mobile Learning

Digital technology, like mobile, devices is fully integrated in our daily lives and in the lives of students starting from very young ages. Teachers should be aware of this fact and follow this trend using resources of this nature in their teaching practices. Besides this reason, it is also important to state that mobile devices are becoming a resource with great potential in classrooms but also in outdoor learning [13]. This is due to the rapid developments of these devices and also in the creation of a diversity of educational apps, which increases the window of opportunities for teachers to use these tools with their students. Mobile technology is no longer considered just as a functional accessory, among other things, it is an anytime, anywhere device for multimedia, data gathering and data processing. Undeniably there are many advantages of using mobile technology for learning, for example: encouraging anytime anywhere learning, improving social interactions, and enabling a more personalized learning experience [14].

The diversity of learning opportunities offered by this type of technology can make STEM education more interesting, significant and enjoyable for students, enhancing the possibilities for their engagement in STEM subjects, inside but also outside the classroom [13]. Mobile devices may facilitate authentic learning, helping students deal with real-world problems, either by allowing access to virtual contexts, facilitating interactions or collecting/treating/presenting data. In particular, digital technology can help develop a deeper understanding of mathematics, acting as a mind tool that facilitates inquiry, decision making, reflection, reasoning, problem solving and collaboration [15]. The extension of the classroom to the outdoors is facilitated by the portability and wireless functionality of the mobile devices, which presents students with a more authentic and appropriate context, making it easier to explore the surrounding environment [4, 14]. This type of digital tool helps bridge pedagogically designed learning contexts, allowing learning to be situated in a real world context [14].

Recently an app was created to combine the dimensions of outdoors mathematics and mobile learning and that was MathCityMap (MCM). This app, created for mobile devices, allows the user to do math trails previously created in the webportal where the tasks are submitted and published, linked to GPS coordinates. The user accesses the trail guide with the tasks to solve, that are located with the help of the GPS functionality, and introduces the solution in the mobile phone receiving feedback on the correctness of the answer. It is also possible to consult up to three hints to help the user reach the solution when he/she is stuck on a given problem. The hints are formulated as guiding suggestions, without intending to give the solution directly. This digital technology has proven to be useful for outdoors mathematics supporting teachers and students in the teaching and learning process, including in affective-motivational aspects [4].

3 Methodology

Given its nature, this study follows a qualitative and interpretative approach [16]. The choice for an interpretative paradigm is sustained by the fact that the main goal is to understand how the participants regard and perceive a specific situation.

This study was developed during the academic year 2018/2019 and involved the participation of 48 future teachers, that attended a teacher training course in primary education (6–12 years old). The participants were enrolled in a subject of Didactics of Mathematics, which served as context for the data collection. The researchers were responsible for this unit course, fact that facilitated the implementation of the study as well as the contact with the participants.

In order to further contextualize the work developed, first it is important to underline that these pre-service teachers had little or no experience with outdoor mathematics. Given this fact we decided to start by applying Questionnaire I. This questionnaire aimed to access this pre-service teachers' experiences and perceptions regarding teaching and learning mathematics outside the classroom, as well as the possibility of using digital technology in this type of context. After the completion of the first questionnaire, they experienced a math trail in the city of Viana do Castelo using MCM as the main resource. As we had 48 participants, and in order to perform a more focused observation, we chose to divide the group in half, implementing the math trail separately with the pre-service teachers divided in groups of 3 or 4 elements. This math trail was designed and organized by the researchers using the main principles that underly this strategy, considering also the permissions and restrictions of the app regarding task design: select the site and the stops, taking into consideration the opportunities for exploring rich mathematics; take photos of the elements in each stop to include in the webportal of MCM associated with each task; formulate the tasks trying to diversify the contents, have different levels of cognitive demand and establish connection between mathematics and the local environment [8, 11]. While doing the trail each group had a smartphone to access the tasks and insert the answers, an articulated ruler and a calculator. To manage these resources, they had to divide responsibilities within the working group. Questionnaire II was applied after this experience, with the intent to analyze changes in the pre-service teachers' perceptions and know their opinion about the use of MCM.

Data was collected in a holistic, descriptive and interpretative manner through period through participant observation (reactions during the math trail), two online questionnaires, written productions of the participants (solutions of the tasks proposed in the math trail) and photographic records. The researchers accompanied the participants during the math trail, observing in loco the work developed by each group, taking notes about their performance. The questionnaires were designed to access the future teachers' perceptions about outdoors mathematics and the use of digital technologies, before and after the trail experience. These instruments contained mainly open-ended questions, with the intention of getting more in-depth responses, concerning understandings, interpretations and reactions. The photographs taken by the researchers served as a means to visually illustrate specific moments, acting as complementary method of data collection. The tasks solutions performed by each group were requested in order to better understand the future teachers reasoning. For this particular paper we did not consider the written productions concerning the tasks.

Data was analyzed using an inductive approach, recurring to content analysis [17]. After repeatedly reading and consulting information collected with the different methods, the content analysis focused data was categorized to systematize the information regarding the perceptions evidenced by the participants crossed with the evidences emerged from the observation. In this process we reached categories influenced mainly by the research questions, complemented by the theoretical framework and the data collected: reactions to the math trail; potentialities of the MathCityMap app; and limitations of the MathCityMap app.

4 Results and Discussion

In this section we chose to divide the results in three stages, following the chronological timeline of the study.

4.1 Questionnaire I

The first questionnaire was applied at the beginning of the semester. It was completed online so that the researchers could have an easy access to the participants' answers and could more easily analyze the data. Mainly we wanted to be aware of the initial perceptions of the pre-service teachers about: the possibility to teach and learn mathematics outside the classroom; their own experiences as students on outdoors mathematics; and knowledge about digital technology used as resource in this context. As this was a questionnaire with mainly open-ended questions our intention was to perform a content analysis, however we complemented those findings with percentages, as a mere indicator for the reader to notice the trends in the answers presented by the participants. We concluded that the majority of them (about 91%) considered that it is possible to teach and learn mathematics outside the classroom. Several examples were used to illustrate that opinion: tasks related to daily life situations and routines; counting activities; money related tasks; shopping activities; games; competitions; clubs; field trips; observing architecture/artwork/shapes in the outdoors; finding mathematics in nature; doing a trail. Concerning their own experience as students, 87% of the participants stated that they never had the opportunity to experience mathematics outside the classroom, fact that may explain the general and rather vague ideas they had about how to operationalize it from the teacher's perspective. This evidence was important for the researchers to conclude that it is truly important that pre-service teachers experience certain methodologies first hand before they incorporate them in their future practices and this subject (Didactics of Mathematics) was the right context to do it. As for the knowledge about digital technology to use as resource in outdoor mathematics, about 60% of the participants recognized that they did not know any technology with these features. This was not surprising since a significant number of these pre-service teachers assumed the absence of experiences outside the classroom regarding the teaching and learning of mathematics. The other 40% that admitted knowing resources of this nature, mentioned examples like digital games, apps and robots, but none allowed the exploration of the surrounding environment, they only had a playful strand.

4.2 Math Trail with MathCityMap

Prior to the implementation of the math trail, the researchers conducted a session that aimed to present the main features of the MCM app, focusing on the user's perspective, taking the opportunity to download the trail and get acquainted with the route. This session also included some orientations about the dynamics of the math trail.

In the following class, the researchers accompanied the pre-service teachers to the location of the first task and supervised all the activity concerning the trail. The groups were extremely autonomous in managing their work, finding the app user friendly, which can explain the fact that did not evidence noteworthy difficulties at this level. At each stop they accessed the respective task, being able to observe the targeted object and collect data to reach the solution (e.g. making measurements, observing shapes, finding patterns, counting elements). To illustrate the users' perspective we present the layout of a task from this trail as we can see it in the app (Fig. 1):

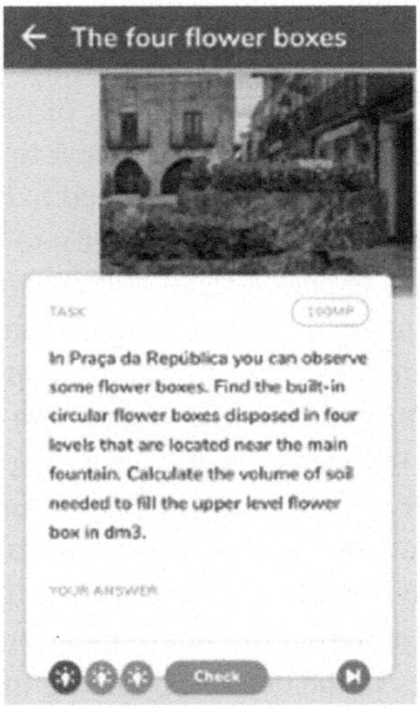

Fig. 1. Example of a task presented through MathCityMap

After reading the task, the groups decided the procedures to apply and came up with the answer to submit. The app had a gamification feature with the attribution of points, depending on the correction of the answer, that is, if the answer was correct they had 100 points, if not, they could still continue to try but the number of points would gradually reduce. The gamification feature of the app was a motivating factor for the future teachers: on one hand it caused excitement when the solution was correct; and implied greater care before the introduction of the answers, because the participants tried to make sure of the validity of the answer discussing it within the groups. The hints on demand were another important feature of the app that the participants showed interest in (Fig. 2). Globally they considered that it could be an asset in cases where users had difficulties in tackling the proposed problem, once again contributing to an autonomous use.

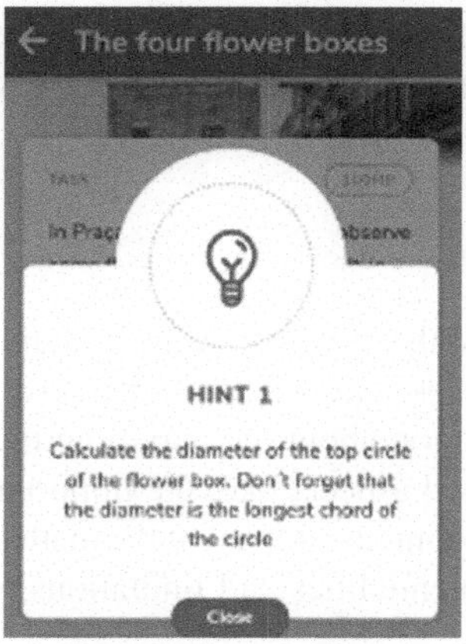

Fig. 2. Example of hint

As for the tasks, we can say that they were diversified in terms of the contents and the cognitive levels of demand (mainly exercises and problems), involving, for example the: determination of the volume of a flower pot; estimate of the length of an avenue based on a pattern of lamps; discovery of the probability of hitting the white area of a no entry sign with a dart; characterization of the rotation symmetries in a stained glass window; solving a word problem using roman numerals; solving process problems; counting intertwined rectangles of different dimensions.

Fig. 3. Example of moments of the trail implementation

It was also evident (Fig. 3) that this dynamic, of the math trail using MCM, triggered collaborative work, intra and inter groups, leading them to share responsibilities (e.g. carry and use the smartphone; measurements; recording data; calculations). We could observe as well the cooperation between different groups having the same goal in mind (e.g. joining several articulated meters to find the measure of a certain length). These pre-service teachers showed enthusiasm along the entire trail, despite considering one or two tasks as being more complex and exhaustive due to the extensive calculations. They sought to achieve the best possible score at the end of the trail, reacting with motivation to each positive feedback after the submission of the answers. Another important aspect that we would like to highlight is the regular verbalization by the participants that it is a good strategy (math trail) and a good resource (MCM) for teaching and learning mathematics.

4.3 Questionnaire II

The second questionnaire was also applied online and after the implementation of the math trail with MCM. In this case, we wanted to perceive changes in the participants' perceptions and also their opinion about the app, pointing out potentialities and limitations. The questions addressed aspects like: the importance of teaching and learning mathematics outside the classroom; the impact of the math trail experience; their opinion about the tasks in the trail; potentialities and limitations of MCM in the teacher's and the user's perspective.

We concluded that all the pre-service teachers, with no exception, recognized the importance of this non-formal context, particularly as a way to complement the traditional mathematics classroom. Unlike the answers in Questionnaire I, they were all convinced of the possibility of teaching and learning mathematics outside the classroom, which means that some of these pre-service teachers changed their opinion after the experience. To sustain their assertions the participants argued that doing a math trail: follows the principles of active learning, promoting intellectual, social and physical engagement; makes learning more meaningful for students because they are directly engaged; increases affective traits like motivation, enthusiasm and curiosity; helps understand the usefulness and applicability of mathematics; makes connections with the cultural and natural heritage visible; facilitates collaborative work and helps develop communication skills, as well as critical thinking; it can lead to the use of technology.

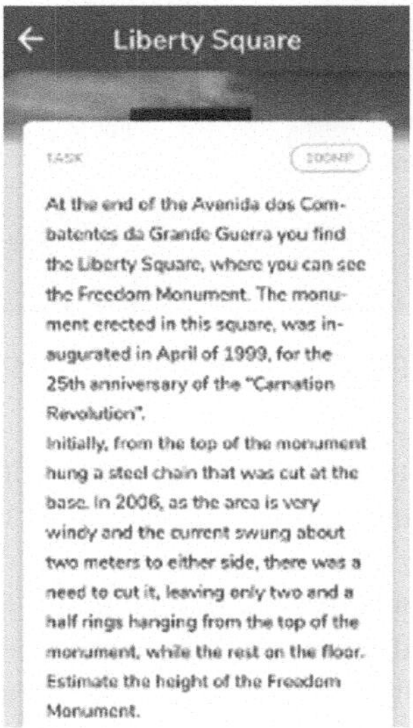

Fig. 4. Example of a task selected as favorite

Most of the participants stated that they have enjoyed solving the tasks in the trail. The ones they highlighted as favorites coincided with the most challenging or the ones that added to their knowledge about historic and cultural aspects about the elements of the city involved in the trail (Fig. 4).

The tasks mentioned as the least favorite by most of the pre-service teachers were the ones involving exhaustive calculations or too many steps to reach the solution, which caused some demotivation (Fig. 5).

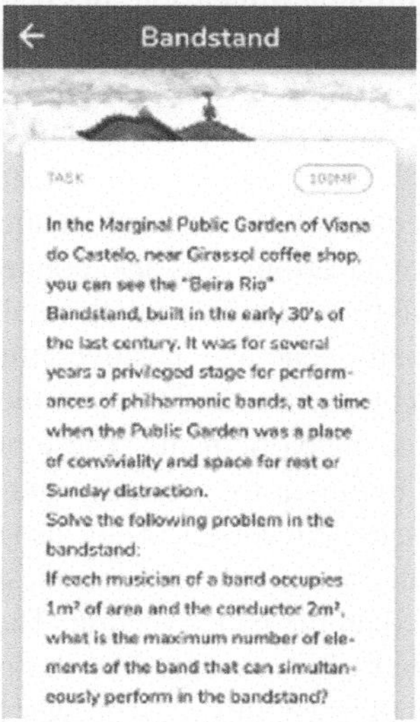

Fig. 5. Example of a task selected as the least favorite

As for the use of MCM and the assessment of the respective features, we started by analyzing the participants' perceptions about the potentialities of the app as users: the possibility to apply knowledge learned in school mathematics; being user friendly and intuitive, promoting autonomy; facilitating cooperation; promote the development of a mathematical eye in the local environment; more interactive than the paper version; getting immediate feedback; and the gamification feature. From the teacher's perspective the potentialities mentioned were: the possibility to design and publish tasks adapted to the local environment; addressing different mathematical contents and promoting interdisciplinary tasks; a way to diversify educational contexts; it allows the teacher to supervise and accompany the work developed by the groups, due to the autonomy it provides the user. Some limitations were pointed to this app, that we chose not to separate in terms of the user's and the teacher's perspective because of the overlaps: the possible lack of access to Wi-Fi; the fact that students of younger ages normally do not have smartphones; and, in terms of the tasks, the limitation of the answer formats to either a value or multiple choice.

5 Conclusions

As previously stated we had the opportunity to conclude on previous studies developed with pre-service teachers [1–3] that the design and implementation of math trails can trigger positive attitudes towards mathematics and facilitate the establishment of connections with the surrounding environment, giving meaning to mathematics. This type of experience develops the mathematical competencies of the trail designers as well as of the trail users [3], bringing out the usefulness and applications of mathematics.

This study focused on a different dimension, the perspective of the trail user and not the trail designer. We intended to understand the perceptions of pre-service teachers about the use of a specific digital tool, the MCM app, in outdoor education. Globally they valued the math trail experience per se as a meaningful strategy to engage students in realistic problem solving [8], and as a means to create a diversity of opportunities for the establishment of connections between mathematics and other content areas, as well as with real life [10]. Active learning was also pointed out by the participants as a fundamental attribute in a math trail, allowing intellectual, physical and social engagement, whose interaction normally generates positive attitudes [3]. MathCityMap was used as tool to present and execute the trail and this was the new dimension of this study, trying to perceive its impact for the participants. These pre-service teachers positively underlined the use of the app, finding it user friendly and motivating, especially due to the gamification feature and the rapid feedback. They also mentioned as positive its contribution for developing spatial orientation, cooperation, students' autonomy and being more practical and interactive than the paper version. The only limitations recognized by the participants were related to constraints like the possible absence of Wi-Fi or smartphones and also the limited possibilities for answer formats.

In conclusion, by implementing the math trail in this manner we recognized an additional motivation associated to the digital and interactive features of the MCM app, which facilitated and made more interesting the exploration of the outdoors [4]. Working with pre-service teachers, the participants gave their opinion as users but also as future teachers, assessing the potential of the strategy (math trail) and the resource (MCM app) and analyzing how could they implement it. Recognizing the importance of keeping up with the technological development and society requirements they considered the possibility of integrating this resource, and the math trail strategy, in their practices.

References

1. Barbosa, A., Vale, I.: Math trails: meaningful mathematics outside the classroom with preservice teachers. JETEN **12**, 49–63 (2016)
2. Barbosa, A., Vale, I.: Math trails: a resource for teaching and learning. In: Gitirana, V., Miyakawa, T., Rafalska, M., Soury-Lavergne, S., Trouche, L. (eds.) Proceedings of the Re(s)sources 2018 International Conference, pp. 183–186. ENS de Lyon, Lyon (2018)
3. Vale, I., Barbosa, A., Cabrita, I.: Mathematics outside the classroom: examples with preservice teachers. Quaderni di Ricerca in Didacttica (Mathematics) **2**(3), 138–142 (2019)
4. Cahyono, A.N., Ludwig, M.: Teaching and learning mathematics around the city supported by the use of digital technology. Eurasia J. Math. Sci. Technol. Educ. **15**(1), 1–8 (2019)

5. Ludwig, M., Jablonski, S.: Doing math modelling outdoors - a special math class activity designed with MathCityMap. In: 5th International Conference on Higher Education Advances (HEAd 2019), pp. 901–909. Editorial Universitat Politecnica de Valencia, Valencia (2019)
6. National Council of Teachers of Mathematics: Principles to Actions - Ensuring Mathematical Success for All. NCTM, Reston - VA (2014)
7. Kenderov, P., et al.: Challenges beyond the classroom—sources and organizational issues. In: Taylor, P., Barbeau, E. (eds.) Challenging Mathematics In and Beyond the Classroom. New ICMI Study Series, vol. 12, pp. 55–96. Springer, Boston (2009). https://doi.org/10.1007/978-0-387-09603-2_3
8. Richardson, K.: Designing math trails for the elementary school. Teach. Child. Math. **11**, 8–14 (2004)
9. Shoaf, M., Pollak, H., Schneider, J.: Math Trails. COMAP-Stake, Lexington (2004)
10. Bonotto, C.: How to connect school mathematics with students' out-of-school knowledge. Zentralblatt für Didaktik der Mathematik **33**(3), 75–84 (2001)
11. Vale, I., Barbosa, A.: Visualization - a pathway to mathematical challenging tasks. In: Leikin, R., Christou, C., Karp, A., Pitta-Pantazi, D., Zazkis, R. (eds.) Mathematical Challenge for All. Springer, Switzerland (in press)
12. Smith, M., Stein, M.K.: Five Practices for Orchestrating Productive Mathematics Discussions. Corwin Press, Thousand Oaks (2011)
13. Sung, Y., Chang, K., Liu, T.: The effects of integrating mobile devices with teaching and learning on students' learning performance: a meta-analysis and research synthesis. Comput. Educ. **94**, 252–275 (2016)
14. Shuler, C.: Pockets of potential – using mobile technologies to promote children's learning. Attn Publications Department, New York (2009)
15. Fessakis, G., Karta, P., Kozas, K.: Designing math trails for enhanced by mobile learning realistic mathematics education in primary education. iJEP **8**(2), 49–63 (2018)
16. Erickson, F.: Qualitative methods in research on teaching. In: Wittrock, M.C. (ed.) Handbook of Research on Teaching, pp. 119–161. Macmillan, New York (1986)
17. Miles, M.B., Huberman, A.M.: Qualitative Data Analysis, 2nd edn. Sage Publications, Thousand Oaks (1994)

Computational Simulations in the Construction of Abstract Concepts and in Promoting of Students Autonomy in the 5th Grade

Fátima Araújo[1](✉), J. Bernardino Lopes[2,3], Armando A. Soares[2], and J. Cravino[2,3]

[1] Agrupamento Gil Vicente, Guimarães, Portugal
[2] Universidade de Trás-os-Montes e Alto Douro, Vila Real, Portugal
{blopes,asoares,jcravino}@utad.pt
[3] CIDTFF-Centro de Investigação em Didática e Tecnologia na Formação de Formadores, Aveiro, Portugal

Abstract. The article refers to an investigation into curricular integration (CI) strategies of computer simulations (CS), level of guidance and teacher mediation on the given tasks when using a CS, in the recognition and conceptual elaboration of the structure of the matter and alterations in the physical state at a microscopic level, in tasks with same degree of orientation and the perception of autonomy by students in the 5th grade. Quantitative and qualitative methods were used. Regarding curricular integration strategies, the class with the best results was the class in which the EXPLORA 1 strategy was applied. With regard to task guidance, the groups submitted to a moderate guidance degree were those who obtained the best learning results. In relations to mediation, the results of mediation are not independent of students' learning and the perception that the student' have about the autonomy and the time they have for the autonomous work. We conclude that autonomy with low guidance can be ineffective and the mediation with a lot of teacher intervention in the context of moderately guidance task can also reduce effectiveness.

Keywords: Physical states of matter · Particulate nature of matter · Computer simulations · Task guidance

1 Introduction

In the pandemic crisis responsible for Covid-19 widespread in more than 193 countries, more than ever Information and Communication Technologies have proved essential for the continuity and completion of the 2019/2020 academic year, at all levels in Portugal both public and private education. In our country, new technologies were being slowly integrated into basic and secondary education. The pandemic could be a driver of access to technologies for all students and new teaching methodologies in STEM (Science, Technology, Engineering and Mathematics), giving the opportunity for greater intervention and student participation in the construction of their learning and knowledge.

A. Reis et al. (Eds.): TECH-EDU 2020, CCIS 1384, pp. 44–60, 2021.
https://doi.org/10.1007/978-3-030-73988-1_4

Although STEM education is recognized by public and educational authorities as a priority in Europe, students' interest in pursuing STEM-related careers and studies has not increased, despite rapid developments in science and technology. The curricular isolation of the STEM disciplines seems to be responsible for the withdrawal of students from scientific and technological areas. Today, it is almost consensual that STEM education is carried out in a more integrated way, opting for multidisciplinary and even transdisciplinary projects. There are a wide variety of tools to support STEM education. The using collaborative technologies can help support collaborative inquiry within science education and can help model how scientists use technology (Donna and Miller 2013). So collaborative tools like Google Docs, and Microsoft OneDrive, are examples of large scale tools and, on a smaller scale, Padlet, make it possible to share documents and create documents, spreadsheets and more. Cloud computing technology can assist teachers' and students' collaborative work and facilitate worldwide interactions. Various software tools like GeoGebra, Minecraft: Education Edition, MakeCode, PORDATA Kids, Etoys, Scratch, Superlogo 3.0, Flora On, labs, video games, mobile app, devices and hardware like smartphones, tablets, robotics and wireless sensors are slowly being introduced to basic education. Computer Simulations can be an important resource for science teaching and the impact of their use has already been documented (Smetana and Bell 2012; Chang et al. 2020; Siiman et al. 2020; Pease et al. 2019). Empirical research has provided evidence of the benefits of CS. These can increase the conceptual understanding of science (National Research Council 2011), they can provide situations of scientific reasoning (Smetana and Bell 2012). They can be used as tools for epistemic practices and procedures (Lopes and Costa 2019) and authentic science tasks (Chinn and Malhotra 2002) and therefore suitable for new teaching methodologies.

2 Research Theoretical Framework

Corpuscular theory (CT), a fundamental theory in chemistry, is important for understanding the contents of physics and chemistry. In Portugal the representation of molecules already appears in school manuals of the 5th year of schooling. However, although they use the representation of molecules, sometimes inserted in other representations, they do not give any explanation about the corpuscular nature of the matter. Some empirical studies (Johnson and Papageorgiou 2008) concluded that a large proportion of students showed gains with the introduction of explanations about the particles and some children from 9 to 11 years old developed a high level of understanding of Corpuscular theory of matter. Metz (1997) is of the opinion that basic education underestimates the ability of students to develop abstract ideas. The CS that are usually used in teaching mostly represent a model of a real or abstract phenomenon or system the student interacts with to perform certain tasks. Thus, they can help students to grow their own mental models of scientific concepts (Treagust et al. 2002) and abstract phenomena by enabling the visualization of models that describe them (Olympiou et al. 2013) and, thus, obtain a deeper understanding (Lopes et al. 2008) of these phenomena. As they are interactive tools, CS are a resource with relevance for the understanding of the abstract corpuscular theory of matter, as they allow to diminish the abstraction, making visible the invisible (Araújo et al. 2017).

The curricular integration of CS has been carried out differently and are used with diversified learning strategies (Ross et al. 2010). Koehler and Mishra (2009) consider that there is no "best way" to integrate technology. This should be designed according to the content in specific classroom contexts. We believe that CS are tools that can, on the one hand, promote greater student autonomy in their learning, and on the other hand, facilitate the student's understanding and abstraction capacity on the corpuscular theory of matter, as they can represent matter at a microscopic level.

Concerning the level of guidance which needs to be given to the student, while learning scientific concepts with the support of CS, Kirschener et al. (2006) argue that a greater orientation of tasks increases learning, by liberating students from making appea to demands of working memory. Chinn and Malhotra (2002) suggested the development of tasks that reflected the cognitive processes and the epistemology of real science. Lopes et al. (2008) consider that the teacher must clarify to the students the purpose of the task and that the language used must be intelligible by the students so that the work performed is effectively what was requested from the students. On the other hand, Akaygun and Jones (2014) concluded that with more oriented tasks, students shifted their attention more towards the structure of the activity in detriment to the exploration of CS. Although many current CSs have already incorporated several types of guidelines (prompts, heretics, scaffolds, etc.), there are still CSs that do not have these attributes and, therefore, it is necessary for the teacher to create guiding guidelines, in paper format, to promote and enhance students' learning. With regard to the autonomy to be provided to the student, from the literature it is known that the learning environments that provide autonomy seem to increase the students' performance, especially the environments that promote the needs of intrinsic motivation and the integration of extrinsic motivations for learning (Vansteenkiste et al. 2004). Students can become discouraged and disconnect from tasks and their learning if teachers interfere with their personal rhythm by giving frequent guidance. Thus, providing students with the experience of exploring CS, to "investigate" the behavior of the matter at a microscopic level, giving it autonomy but also support and adequate guidance to manage and carry out their tasks can satisfy their needs for intrinsic motivation and increase their involvement and consequently the learning of these concepts.

2.1 Research Problem and Objectives

The research is based on the following problem: "It is known, from research, that students have unscientific conceptions about physical phenomena such as changes in the physical state, the constitution of matter and gases' properties. These students' conceptions are related to their macro view of the matter". The CS can support students in understanding the constitution of matter and altering its physical state as well as in understanding the physical properties of each state of matter, since they allow viewing models accepted by the scientific community of physicochemical processes at a microscopic level. They are suitable for research and questioning activities and, being interactive, they can be explored by students either individually or collaboratively. On the other hand, in addition to the task guidance, the way the teacher communicates with his students can influence his autonomy as well as his learning.

Objectives. The main objectives of the study, relating to the teaching of the structure of the matter and the changes in its physical state at a microscopic level are: (1) to evaluate the effectiveness of 4 curricular integration strategies of by using two CS, (2) to evaluate the effectiveness of different degrees of task orientation when students use a CS, (2.1) to know the perception that the student had of the autonomy granted by the teacher in the exploration of the CS. (3) to investigate the influence/effectiveness of the teacher's mediation, in tasks with equal orientation.

Research Questions. This research aims to answer the following questions: Q1- How effective are different strategies for curricular integration (CI) of CS in the recognition and conceptual elaboration of the structure of the subject and changes in physical state at the microscopic level by students in the 5th grade of schooling? Q2- How do different levels of task guidance, provided to students, as help for exploring the CS have an effect on recognition and conceptual elaboration? Q 2.1 - What is the students' perception of the autonomy granted by the teacher in exploring the simulation? Q3 - What actually is the influence or effectiveness of teacher's mediation, as far as tasks with same degree of orientation are concerned, in the recognition and conceptual elaboration of changes in physical status, at the corpuscular level, by students in the 5th grade?

3 Methodology

3.1 Research Design

The research involved two empirical studies carried out in 2016 and in 2017 in a basic school in the Northwest of Portugal. With this first empirical study, it was intended to evaluate the effectiveness of 4 strategies for the curricular integration of two CSs in learning the corpuscular theory of matter and changing of physical state of the matter at the corpuscular level (Table 1). The second empirical study aimed to investigate different degrees of orientation of tasks and mediation of the teacher, in the recognition and conceptual elaboration of the corpuscular structure of the matter, of alterations in physical state, at a microscopic level, by students of the 5th grade (Table 2) and student's perception of the autonomy provided by the teacher. For the 1st study, two PhET CSs were selected, the "states-of-matter basics" and "gas properties". In the second study, only the first CS was used. Pre and post-tests were constructed (the 1st part of the post-test has been withdrawn and adjusted from the literature (Özman and Kenan 2007), which were used in the two empirical studies. Computational simulations of CI strategies to be applied (1st empirical study) and according to the type of guidance desired (2nd empirical study). All students took a pre-test one month before teaching situations (1st study) and five months before teaching situations (2nd study).

In the two groups where the task with moderate guidance was applied, the study of mediation was still carried out to assess its effectiveness (Table 2). In both the first and the second study, convenience sampling was used. 73 students participated in the first study divided into four groups. The second empirical study involved 60 students, also split in four groups. And all of them attending the 5th year of schooling (ages between 9 and 12 years old) in classes of the teacher/researcher in the discipline of Natural Sciences.

Table 1. CI strategies of CS "physical states of matter" and "gas properties"

CI strategies of CS	Group	CS "states-of-matter basics"	CS "gas properties"
EXPLORE 1	D	Guidance task	Task with autonomy
EXPLORE 2	A	Task with autonomy	Guidance task
DEMO 1	C	Demonstration of theory with CS by the teacher	Theory presentation by the teacher
DEMO2	B	Theory presentation by the teacher	Demonstration of theory with CS by the teacher

Table 2. Distribution of the type of task guidance among the groups

Group	Guidance task			Mediation study
	Low	Moderate	High	
1	X			
2		X		X
3		X		X
4			X	

3.2 Data and Data Processing

The common data to the two empirical studies comprise the results of the pre-test and post-test, audio recordings, images of the classes and the students' work carried out in the CS exploration classes. The first study also includes the synthesis of multimodal narrations and the second study the multimodal narrations of classes in which students explored CS with moderate task orientation. In both studies, the percentage of correct answers and the increment obtained in each class/group were determined (data from the 1st part of the pre/ post-test). The relative gains have also been calculated by group of questions (in agreement with the kind of variable referred, that is distance, speed, number and size; along the phase change of the material in the heat transfer or compression) and by class/group. The normalized gains were also calculated by group of questions (in agreement with the type referred). Regarding the 2nd part of the pre/post-test, the descriptions and justifications performed by the students were analyzed. Six response profiles arose from this analysis (Table 3). So when the pupils represents the water in the solid state as an ice cube or when he draws the water flow from a faucet or a river, it is actually describing his visual perception of water. We codify this response profile as profile 1. The answer "Ice is in the solid state" is an instance of this profile. When the pupils refers to the physical states of matter, either by using a drawing or a short answer, referring to the phase change ("It melted and It is in the liquid state, like the waters of the seas"), we assign profile 2. In profile 3 the student already refers to the existence of particles and assigns them the same properties as a sample of matter with a macroscopic dimension ("solid state-particles together (frozen, gaseous state-heated particles").

The student with profile 4 already says that water is formed by particles and describes the phase in which water is found by relating it to a variable ("water in the liquid state, the particles are closer because their temperature is low). The student with profile 5 identifies particles in the three physical states of matter and relates the different states to at least two variables ("When it is in the solid state the particles stay together and the velocity decreases when it is in the gaseous state, the size does not change and the speed increases).

Table 3. Response profiles

Profile	Response profiles
0	Wrong answer and/or alternative design
1	Identifies the states of matter associated with sensory perceptions (visual, tactile aspect)
2	Identifies matter as being formed of particles but with the same properties of matter in the macroscopic dimension
3	Identifies the states of the matter associated to phase change and may or may not be associated with sensory perceptions
4	It identifies particles in the three states but only lists one of the variables (velocity, size, space and distance)
5	It identifies particles in the three states and relates at least two variables to each other (velocity, size, space, and distance)

The classes were recorded in audio. From the audio recordings and the collection of some images in the course of the activities, syntheses (summary with contextual elements and reference to episodes) of multimodal narrations (Lopes et al. 2014; Lopes et al. 2019) were produced, thereby seeking to understand the dynamics used in the classes of the different classes in the first study. In the second study, the Kruskal Wallis test was performed to check if there were significant differences between the groups before classes with CS exploration. The Wilcoxon-Mann-Whitney non-parametric test was used to compare the results of post-tests carried out a few weeks after teaching situations. The mean, median and 75th percentile of the profiles of the 4 groups were calculated. The profiles of students in each group were ordered both in the pre-test and in the post-test. The mediation of the teacher was studied through the content analysis of the multimodal narrations of the CS exploration classes in Groups 2 and 3, who were assigned a task with moderate guidance. At the same time, the dimension of "Student learning" was also analyzed.

In line with Lopes et al. (2010), three categories were defined in the "mediation" dimension: (1) Gives autonomy to students; (2) Promotes student involvement; (3) Provides induction of conceptual elaboration. Each category was further divided into subcategories. Thus, category one (1) was divided into two subcategories. The first concerns the autonomy provided by the teacher in managing the task by the student and the second concerns the autonomy in exploring computer simulation. Category two (2) was divided into three subcategories: contextualization of the task; provides information; simulation orientation. The third category includes two subcategories: "identification" and "understanding" and concerns the type of questions that the teacher asks the student asking (for answers at the level of identification or understanding). Regarding the "Student learning" dimension, three categories were also defined: (1) Student autonomy; (2) Student involvement; (3) Conceptual elaboration. These categories were also divided into subcategories. Thus, the category "Autonomy" includes the subcategory "Task management by the student" and "Exploration of CS". The category "Student involvement" includes the subcategories "Task performance", "Request information" and "Request guidance in CS". The category "Conceptual elaboration" includes the subcategories "Identification" and "Understanding". The mediation dimension of the teacher concerns the connections or conjugations and bonds that are established between the interaction with the epistemic object, the computer simulation, and the interaction with the students. The "student learning" dimension refers to learning and, therefore, to understanding the content that the student is studying. The categories are in alignment with the categories related to the mediation dimension of the teacher.

4 Results

4.1 Results of the 1st Empirical Study

The percentage of students' correct answers in the first part of the post-test (54.3%) was higher than that of the pre-test (36.4%) therefore, a global analysis suggests that there was learning by the students. Comparing outcomes of the pre-test with those of the post-test in each of the groups, it appears that Group D (EXPLORE 1) revealed a higher percentage of correct answers, 61.4%, followed by Group B (DEMO 2) with 60.6%, and group A (EXPLORE 2) with 51.5%. Group C (DEMO 1) had the lowest percentage of correct answers (49.5%).

From the analysis of the results of the pre-test and relative gains by group of questions and by group of students (Table 4), it can be seen that in relation to stratified effectiveness:

Table 4. Pre-test results and relative gains (RG) by group of questions and by students group.

Group	Size issues		Space issues		Number issues		Velocity issues	
	Pré-test	RG	Pré-test	RG	Pré-test	RG	Pré-test	RG
A (EXPLORE 2)	26	0.10	50	0.03	30	0.53	43	0.19
B (DEMO 2)	32	0.12	43	0.39	47	0.64	33	0.36
C (DEMO 1)	20	0.18	50	0.17	37	0.18	30	0.30
D (EXPLORE 1)	16	0.40	49	0.35	40	0.50	40	0.32

a) the EXPLORE 1 strategy (Group D) was effective in the 4 variables;
b) the DEMO 2 strategy (Group B) was effective in three variables (space, number and speed of the particles);
c) the EXPLORE 2 strategy (Group A) and the DEMO 1 strategy (Group C) were effective only on one variable, number of particles and particle speed, respectively.

Analyzing the 2nd part of the pre-test and post-test, it appears that all groups obtained gains in profiles 4 and 5. Groups D and B were the groups with the greatest gains. These results are in agreement with those of the 1st part of the test (multiple choice). However, group C had very reasonable results in the 2nd part of the test as opposed to the results of the first part (Table 5).

Table 5. Results of the descriptive pre-test and class gains (%).

	Group A		Group B		Group C		Group D	
Profile	Pré-test	Gain	Pré-test	Gain	Pré-test	Gain	Pré-test	Gain
0	21	-6	6	5	31	-36	18	-7
1	42	-27	56	-88	52	-33	47	-47
2	26	-28	11	0	19	-7	0	12
3	11	24	28	-9	19	23	35	-21
4	4	0	0	29	6	20	0	14
5	0	5	0	12	0	19	0	41

It appears that in the strategies, from CI to CS, in which the first approach to particulate theory of matter (PTM) had a greater task guidance and a more predominant initial intervention by the teacher (EXPLORE 1 and DEMO 2), the effectiveness was superior to the strategies in which the first approach to PTM had less task guidance and less influential behavior by the teacher (EXPLORA 2 and DEMO 1).

4.2 Results of the 2nd Empirical Study

If we compare the overall outcomes of the first pre-test part with the ones of the post-test in each group, we find out that group 2 obtained a great increase in correct answers (46.1%), followed by group 3 (28.7%). Groups 1 and 4 achieved very close increments, nevertheless smaller than the previous two groups (18.3% and 17.7%, respectively).

It was also realized that the statistics do not show any evidence that allows to state that the groups before the teaching situations are significantly different in the 1st part of the pre-test (Kruskal-Wallis H3 = 6.605, p = 0.086 for $\alpha = 0.05$) and in the 2nd part of the pre-test (Kruskal-Wallis H3 = 6.653, p value = 0.084 for $\alpha = 0.05$).

From the analysis of the relative gains by group and type of question, (Table 6), we can observe that group 2 obtained greater relative gain in the questions "number of particles", (0.80) "size of particles", (0.73), "particle speed", (0.64) followed by group 3. Groups 1 and 4 obtained lower relative gains in all groups of questions.

Table 6. Pre-test results (%) and relative gains by groups of questions and by group of students.

Group	Group of questions							
	Particle size		Space between particles		Particle number		Particle velocity	
	Pre-test	Relative gain	Pre-test	Relative gain	Pre-test	Relative gain	Pre-test	Relative gain
1 (LG)	24	0.30	43	0.19	34	0.38	34	0.30
2 (MG)	15	0.73	51	0.32	32	0.80	29	0.64
3 (MG)	18	0.64	48	0.39	37	0.52	41	0.38
4 (HG)	17	0.28	48	0.23	33	0.43	45	0.27

After the teaching situations, statistics do evidence that in the first part of the post-test the difference between groups 2 and 3 is not meaningful (Mann-Whitney Test U = 73.5 *p value* = 0.105 for α = 0.05) and that Group 2 is different from group 1 in a significative way (Mann-Whitney Test U = 38,000 and *p value* = 0.002 for α = 0.05) and group 4 (Mann-Whitney Test U = 34,500 and *p value* = 0.001 for α = 0.05).

On what concerns the analysis of the 2nd part of the pre-test and post-test, we realized that group 1 and group 3 focus (median) on Profile 1 in the pre-test and groups 2 and group 4 focus on Profile 2. In the post-test, it is evidenced that group 1 remains on Profile 2, group 3 on Profile 3 and groups 2 and 4 on Profile 4. Comparing the 75th percentile of groups in the post-test, it is verified that in group 1 P75 is 2 and in groups 2, 3 and 4 P75 is 4 (Table 7).

Table 7. Descriptive statistics of the second part of the pre and post – tests (profiles).

Descriptive statistics								
Group	1		2		3		4	
	Pre	Post	Pre	Post	Pre	Post	Pre	Post
$\ddot{X}$	1	2	2	4	1	2	2	4
Medium	1	2	2	4	1	3	2	4
P75	2	2	3	4	1	4	3	4

Ordered Profile of Students (Fig. 1). Observing the ordered profile of the pupils in the pre-test and post-test, it is proved that that achieved best outcomes were group 2 (MG) and group 4 (HG), immediately followed by group 3 (MG). Group 1 (LG) achieved the weakest results, therefore, the kind of task guidance (low guidance) used has not been so effective as the others, both in terms of recognition and conceptual elaboration.

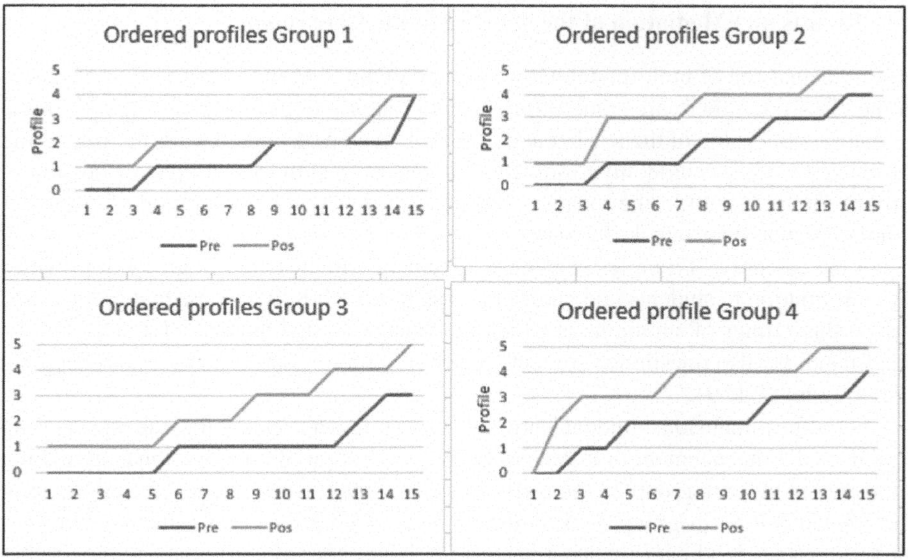

Fig. 1. Ordered student profile

In a global assessment of the outcomes of the 1st. part of the test (multiple choice) and the 2nd. part (descriptions), it appears that the group that achieved weakest results was group 1 (LG).

4.3 Results on the "Perception of the Autonomy Granted by the Teacher"

On what concerns the results of the "classroom environment" questionnaires, groups 1 and 2 are centered on the value 6 and the rest of the groups are close to the value 6 (*I agree*). According to this value, the pupils sensed that they have been given autonomy to explore the simulation. However, groups 3 and 4 sensed that they have been given less autonomy than groups 1 and 2 (Table 8).

Table 8. Classroom environment.

Group	Average scores for individual items			
	1	2	3	4
Average scores	6.1	6.2	5.9	5.6

It was concluded that students sensed that they had autonomy to explore the simulation and that there were no meaningful differences in the quality of the autonomy awarded to them although the groups to whom the teacher gave less autonomy had perceived less autonomy. These results are not only in accordance with the autonomy provided by the teacher or the task, but also with the autonomous working time.

4.4 Results on "Mediation of the Teacher in the Classroom"

From the analysis of multimodal narrations and comparing the number of occurrences in the classroom, there are some differences in relation to groups 2 and 3, both in the mediation dimension of the teacher and in the dimension of student learning. Regarding the category "Gives autonomy to students", it appears that the teacher gave more autonomy to group 2, both in the management of tasks and in the exploration of computer simulation, than in group 3 (Table 8).

In the category "Promotes student involvement", the teacher, in group 3, provides less information to students and guides the task more. Thus, it appears that group 3 had almost three times of situations in which the teacher guided the task (Table 9). On the other hand, he also questioned students in group 3 more in order to induce conceptual elaboration (Table 9).

As for the dimension "Student learning", there is less autonomy for students in group 3, both in the management of tasks and in the exploration of computational simulation compared to those in group 2 (Table 10). In group 2 there is less request for information and guidance than in group 3. Also the number of questions that students answer is higher in group 3, which is in accordance with the number of questions that the teacher asks this group.

Table 9. Number of situations manifested in the classroom regarding the Mediation Dimension.

TEACHER MEDIATION DIMENSION							
GROUP	Empowers students		Promotes student involvement			Provides induction of conceptual elaboration	
	Task management	CS exploration	Task context	Provides information	Task guidance	Identification	Understanding
	Number of situations manifested in the classroom						
2	2	14	2	24	36	55	6
3	1	12	2	17	92	86	7

The number of total interventions by both students in group 3 and the teacher in that group is higher than the total interventions in group 2 (Fig. 2). The number of total interventions is an indicator of the autonomy granted to students (more interventions by the teacher and students means that they dedicate less time to autonomous work).

Table 10. Number of occurrences in the classroom related to student learning.

STUDENT LEARNING							
GROUP	Student autonomy		Student involvement			Conceptual elaboration	
	Task management	CS exploration	Task completion	Request information	Request guidance in -CS	Identification	Understanding
	Number of situations manifested in the classroom						
2	3	19	14	21	7	67	8
3	1	8	14	27	24	88	8

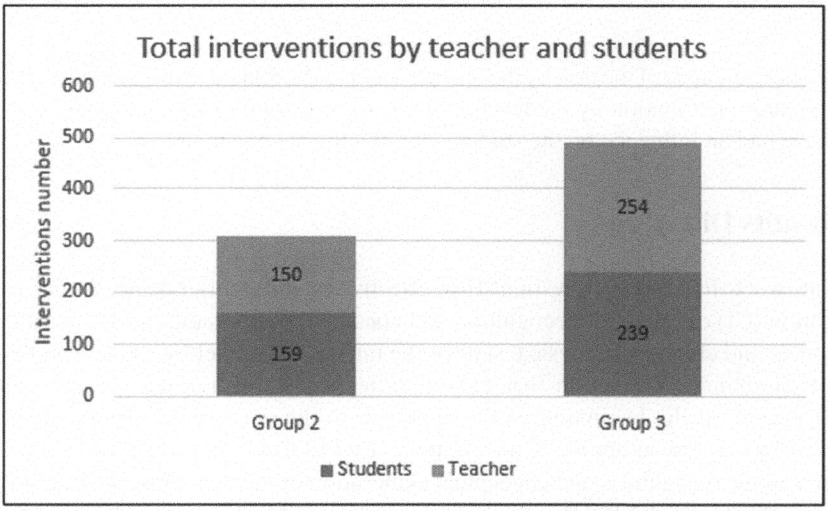

Fig. 2. Total number of oral interventions by students and teacher in both groups.

The global analysis of the results of the students' responses to the tasks allowed us to verify that the performance of the students in group 2 was superior to those in group 3, as can be seen in Fig. 3.

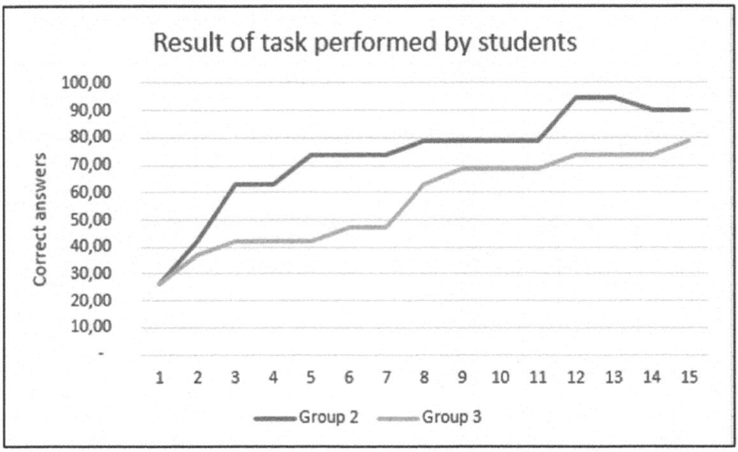

Fig. 3. Results of the tasks of the two groups of students **with** the same task guidance.

Greater guidance of the task by the teacher seems to be related to less student learning. Also, greater intervention by the teacher seems to be related to less autonomy and this may have had an influence on the student's productive involvement.

5 Results Discussion

As an answer to the research question "How effective are different strategies for curricular integration (CI) of CS in the recognition and conceptual elaboration of the structure of the subject and changes in physical state at the microscopic level by students in the 5th year of schooling? "We can say that: (1) the strategies that favor a stronger intervention by the teacher at the beginning of the approach to the corpuscular theory of matter followed by a more autonomous intervention (EXPLORA 1 and DEMO 2) are more effective in the recognition and conceptual elaboration of the than those with an inverse sequence (DEMO 1, EXPLORE 2). Younger students (9 to 12 years old) have little or no knowledge about Corpuscular theory of matter. As already stated by Okumuş et al. (2016), so that students can benefit from the use of CS in their exploration activities, it is necessary that they have prior knowledge of the contents involved in the tasks; (2) within the strategies in which the teacher's intervention is strongest in the beginning, the one that assigns tasks to students with CS exploration (EXPLORA 1) is the most effective. Animations are more effective (Yang et al. 2018) and have a greater impact (Kohen et al. 2019) than static images, in learning and understanding invisible phenomena and in understanding the dynamic behavior of matter. They facilitate the construction of abstract concepts (Olympiou et al. 2013; Araújo et al. 2017).

With regard to the research question "how do different degrees of task guidance, given to students, as support for the exploration of CS influence the recognition and conceptual elaboration?" we claim that tasks with moderate guidance are more effective than tasks with high or low guidance. Low-oriented tasks are the least effective. The tasks with moderate orientation allow the student some autonomy in the exploration of

CS. The design of the activity, in terms of guidance level, may have an impact on pupils learning (Araújo et al. 2019a, b). In line with Gonzalez-Cruz et al. (2003) we found that if students are given some guidance and at the same time freedom and structure to work with CS, they obtain better results in the recognition and conceptual elaboration of the structure of the matter and the alteration of physical states at the microscopic level. In tasks with a high orientation, students can stick to following the task guidelines (Chamberlain et al. 2014) and shift their attention more to the structure of the activity at the expense of CS exploration (Akaygun and Jones 2014). On the other hand, our results show that tasks with low orientation are ineffective for students with little previous knowledge, as advocated by Kirschner et al. (2006). Moderately oriented tasks, with a level of difficulty that can be overcome by students, can stimulate the reasoning that supports learning, understanding and memory (Bjork et al. 2011).

With regard to the research question "What perception did the student have of the autonomy granted by the teacher in exploring the simulation?" we conclude that a greater orientation of the teacher in the exploration of CS by the students is perceived by the students and leads to worse performance in solving tasks and less learning. When the teacher supports the student's autonomy, the intrinsic motivation to perform the tasks is greater (Chang et al. 2016). The association of structure and support for autonomy has a positive effect on intrinsic motivation and student learning outcomes in digital learning tasks (Loon et al. 2012). Thus, the intensity of effort and the frequency with which learning activities are carried out are related to the student's perception of autonomy (Pass and Neu 2014).

Regarding the research question "What is the influence/effectiveness of the teacher's mediation, in tasks with equal orientation, in the recognition and conceptual elaboration of changes in physical status, at the corpuscular level, by students in the 5th year of schooling?" we conclude that mediation that provides more autonomy to students in solving tasks with moderate guidance is more effective than mediation with less student autonomy. Teachers' direct control behaviors have negative effects on students' emotions and involvement (Assor et al. 2005) and tend to decrease their performance (Vansteenkiste et al. 2004). Interfering with students' personal rhythms are behaviors that discourage students who fail to invest effort in learning. Autonomous students show a more efficient and effective learning because they tend to reflect on a more regular basis on their own learning process thus taking control of their own learning (Lan 2018). When the teacher is very interventionist, gives students a lot of information about CS or gives immediate answers to students' questions, depriving them of the opportunity to get the answers themselves, it can lead to situations of non-involvement or reduced involvement students' productive capacity (Cunha et al. 2014). The simple introduction of advanced technologies in educational environments does not guarantee effective and autonomous learning. Appropriate pedagogical approaches must be involved. This has important teaching implications regarding the teacher's behavior in the classroom. What we have shown is that if students are given scripts with moderate task orientation, and if the teacher through his mediation increases the task orientation, thereby removing autonomy from students, this behavior will be reflected negatively in the involvement and in the student learning.

This contribution corroborates the conclusions of Pass et al. (2014). We emphasize the importance of the teacher knowing how to measure his interventions so as not to deprive students of their autonomy so that they have the possibility to develop confidence in themselves, the motivation to learn, set goals, manage and carry out their tasks responsibly.

6 Conclusions

CS are tools that facilitate the construction of abstract concepts (Olympiou et al. 2013; Araújo et al. 2017) and, in some cases, a necessary complement to abstraction - namely as a way to increase "certain types" of abstraction (Törnberg 2019), and therefore can help students aged 9 to 12 to understand concepts such as the corpuscular theory of matter, changes in the physical state of matter at the corpuscular level and the properties of gases. Thus, we conclude that CS in teaching is beneficial for students in learning the referred phenomena and theory. The effectiveness of learning with CS depends on the CI mode of CS (Araújo et al. 2019a, b), the degree of task guidance (Moli et al. 2017) and the mediation of the teacher with regard to guidance in exploring CS and the autonomy provided to students (Araújo et al. 2019a, b). We conclude that autonomy with low guidance can be ineffective and that mediation with a lot of teacher intervention in the context of moderately guidance tasks can also reduce effectiveness.

In the future it would be useful to extend this investigation to a representative sample of students, schools and teachers and to insert controls in the study. Conduct teacher mediation studies in the context of tasks with low guidance and in tasks with high guidance. Longitudinal studies would also make it possible to assess the effects that the early introduction of the corpuscular theory of matter has on students' learning throughout their schooling.

Despite the results and conclusions reached, this investigation has limitations, among them, the fact that no control groups were applied, a convenience sample was used and the number of participating students was reduced.

References

Akaygun, S., Jones, L.: How does level of guidance affect understanding when students use a dynamic simulation of liquid–vapor equilibrium? In: Devetak, I., Glažar, S. (eds.) Learning with Understanding in the Chemistry Classroom, pp. 243–263. Springer, Dordrecht (2014). https://doi.org/10.1007/978-94-007-4366-3_13

Araújo, F., Lopes, J.B., Cravino, J., Soares, A.: Estados físicos da matéria. Simulações computacionais no 5.° ano de escolaridade. [Physical states of matter. Computational simulations in the 5th year of Basic Education]. Comunicações. Piracicaba **24**(1), 35–54 (2017)

Araújo, F.A.A., Bernardino Lopes, J., Soares, A.A., Cravino, J.: Guidance degree of the task in the exploration of a computational simulation. In: Tsitouridou, M., Diniz, J., Mikropoulos, T.A. (eds.) TECH-EDU 2018. CCIS, vol. 993, pp. 319–330. Springer, Cham (2019a). https://doi.org/10.1007/978-3-030-20954-4_24

Araújo, F.M., Lopes, J.B., Soares, A., Cravino, J.: Eficácia da mediação do professor no ensino da estrutura corpuscular da matéria. Comunicações **26**(2), 259–276 (2019b)

Assor, A., Kaplan, H., Maymon, Y.K., Roth, G.: Directly controlling teacher behaviours as predictors of poor motivation and engagement in girls and boys: the role of anger and anxiety. Learn. Instr. **15**(5), 397–413 (2005)

Bjork, E.L., Bjork, R.A.: Making things hard on yourself, but in a good way: creating desirable difficulties to enhance learning. In: Gernsbacher, M.A., Pew, R.W., Hough, L.M., Pomerantz, J.R. (eds.) Psychology and the Real World: Essays Illustrating Fundamental Contributions to Society, pp. 56–64. Worth, New York (2011)

Chamberlain, J.M., Lancaster, K., Parson, R., Perkins, K.: How guidance affects student engagement with an interactive simulation. Educ. Res. Pract. **15**, 628–638 (2014)

Chang, Y.K., Chen, K.W., Chi, L.K.: Effect of autonomy support on self-determined motivation in elementary physical education. J. Sports Sci. Med. **15**, 460–466 (2016)

Chang, C.-J., Liu, C.-C., Wen, C.-T., et al.: The impact of light-weight inquiry with computer simulations on science learning in classrooms. Comput. Educ. **146** (2020)

Chinn, C.A., Malhotra, B.A.: Epistemologically authentic inquiry in schools: a theoretical framework for evaluating inquiry tasks. Sci. Educ. **86**(2), 175–218 (2002). https://doi.org/10.1002/sce.10001

Cunha, A.E., Saraiva, E., Santos, C.A., Dinis, F., Lopes, J.B.: Teacher mediation actions and students' productive engagement during the use of computer simulations in physical science classrooms. Procedia Technol. **13**, 76–85 (2014)

Donna, J., Miller, B.G.: Using cloud-computing applications to support collaborative scientific inquiry: examining pre-service teachers' perceived barriers towards integration. Can. J. Learn. Technol. **39**(3), 1–7 (2013)

Gonzalez-Cruz, J., Rodriguez-Sotres, R., Rodriguez-Penagos, M.: On the convenience of using a computer simulation to teach enzyme kinetics to undergraduate students with biological chemistry-related curricula. Biochem. Mol. Biol. Educ. **31**(2), 93–101 (2003)

Johnson, P.M., Papageorgiou, G.: Explaining melting and evaporation below boiling point. Can software help with particle ideas? Res. Sci. Technol. Educ. **26**(2), 165–183 (2008)

Kirschener, P.A., Sweller, J., Clark, R.E.: Why minimal guidance during instruction does not work: an analysis of the failure of constructivist, discovery, problem-based, experiential, and inquiry-based teaching. Educ. Psychol. **41**(2), 75–86 (2006)

Koehler, M.J., Mishra, P.: What is technological pedagogical content knowledge? Contemp. Issues Technol. Teach. Educ. **9**(1), 60–70 (2009)

Kohen, Z., Amram, M., Dagan, M., Miranda, T.: Self-efficacy and problem-solving skills in mathematics: the effect of instruction-based dynamic versus static visualization. Interact. Learn. Environ. 1–20 (2019)

Lan, Y.J.: Technology enhanced learner ownership and learner autonomy through creation. Educ. Tech. Res. Dev. **66**(4), 859–862 (2018)

Loon, A.M., Ros, A., Martens, R.: Motivated learning with digital learning tasks what about atonomy and structure? Educ. Res. Dev. **60**, 1015–1032 (2012)

Lopes, J.B., Costa, C.: Digital resources in science, mathematics and technology teaching – how to convert them into tools to learn. In: Tsitouridou, M., Diniz, J., Mikropoulos, T.A. (eds.) TECH-EDU 2018. CCIS, vol. 993, pp. 243–255. Springer, Cham (2019). https://doi.org/10.1007/978-3-030-20954-4_18

Lopes, J.B., Viegas, M.C., Pinto, J.A.: The importance of making teaching practices public, shareable, and usable: the role of multimodal narratives. In: Multimodal Narratives in Research and Teaching Practices, pp. 1–42. IGI Global (2019)

Lopes, J.B., Cravino, J.P., Branco, M.J., Saraiva, E.: Mediation of student learning: dimensions and evidences in science teaching. Probl. Educ. 21st Century **9**, 42–52 (2008)

Lopes, J.B., et al.: Constructing and using multimodal narratives to research in science education: contributions based on practical classroom. Res. Sci. Educ. **44**(3), 415–438 (2014). https://doi.org/10.1007/s11165-013-9381-y

Lopes, B., Cravino, J.P., Silva, A.A.: Effective Teaching for intended Learning Outcomes in Science and Technology. Nova Science Publishers, USA (2010)

Metz, K.E.: On the complex relation between cognitive developmental research and children's science curricula. Rev. Educ. Res. **67**(1), 151–163 (1997)

Moli, L., Delserieys, A.P., Impedovo, M.A., Castera, J.: Learning density in Vanuatu high school with computer simulation: influence of different levels of guidance. Educ. Inf. Technol. **22**(4), 1947–1964 (2017). https://doi.org/10.1007/s10639-016-9527-4

National Research Council. Learning Science Through Computer Games and Simulations. The National Academies Press, Washington, DC (2011)

Okumuş, S., Lewis, L., Wiebe, E., Hollebrands, K.: Utility and usability as factors influencing teacher decisions about software integration. Educ. Tech. Res. Dev. **64**(6), 1227–1249 (2016). https://doi.org/10.1007/s11423-016-9455-4

Olympiou, G., Zacharias, Z., de Jong, T.: Making the invisible visible: enhancing students' conceptual understanding by introducing representations of abstract objects in a simulation. Instr. Sci. **41**, 575–596 (2013)

Özman, H., Kenan, O.: Determination of the Turkish primary student's views about of the particulate nature of matter. In: Asia-Pacific Forum on Science Learning and Teaching, vol. 8, no. 1 (2007)

Pass, M.W., Neu, W.A.: Student effort: the influence of relatedness, competence and autonomy. Acad. Educ. Leadersh. J. **18**(2), 1–1 (2014)

Pease, M., Pérez-Lapeña, B., Lant, C.: Energy and water resource simulations for U.S. geography undergraduates. J. Geogr. High. Educ. **43**(1), 40–55 (2019). https://doi.org/10.1080/03098265.2018.1554629

Ross, S.M., Morrison, G.R., Lowther, D.L.: Educational technology research past and present Balancy rigor and relevance to impact school learning. Contemp. Educ. Technol. **1**(1), 17–35 (2010)

Siiman, L.A., Rannastu-Avalos, M., Maeots, M.: Developing smart device friendly asymmetric simulations for teaching collaborative scientific inquiry. In: 2020 IEEE 20th International Conference on Advanced Learning Technologies (ICALT), pp. 130–131 (2020)

Smetana, L.K., Bell, R.L.: Computer simulations to support science instruction and learning: a critical review of the literature. Int. J. Sci. Educ. **34**(9), 1337–1370 (2012)

Törnberg, A.: Abstractions on steroids: a critical realist approach to computer simulations. J. Theory Soc. Behav. **49**(1), 127–143 (2019)

Treagust, D.F., Chittleborough, G., Mamiala, T.L.: Students' understanding of the role of scientific models in learning science. Int. J. Sci. Educ. **24**(4), 357–368 (2002)

Vansteenkiste, M., Simons, J., Lens, W., Sheldon, K.M., Deci, E.L.: Motivating learning, performance, and persistence: the synergistic effects of intrinsic goal contents and autonomy-supportive contexts. J. Pers. Soc. Psychol. **87**(2), 246–260 (2004)

Yang, C., Jen, C., Chang, C., Yeh, T.: Comparison of animation and static-picture based instruction: effects on performance and cognitive load for learning genetics. J. Educ. Technol. Soc. **21**(4), 1–1 (2018)

Instrumental Orchestrations in a Math Teacher's Practices to Enhance Distance Learning of Integral Calculus

Carlos Monteiro[1(✉)] and Cecília Costa[2,3]

[1] Agrupamento de Escolas D. Sancho II, Alijó, Portugal
cjpmonteiro@gmail.com
[2] School of Sciences and Technologies, Universidade de Trás-Os-Montes e Alto Douro, Vila Real, Portugal
mcosta@utad.pt
[3] CIDTFF - Research Centre Didactics and Technology in Education of Trainers, Aveiro, Portugal

Abstract. Due to the confinement by Covid-19, teachers were forced to teach at a distance, which necessarily leads to a change in their teaching practices. Using Trouche's theoretical instrumental orchestration framework, this case study shows that this framework continues to be valid in this type of teaching, it presents the similarities and differences found in these instrumental orchestrations in the case of distance learning, using a teacher's teaching practice 12th year math class in the chapter on antiderivative and integral calculus. A new type of orchestration has been found.

Keywords: Instrumental orchestrations · Distance learning · Mathematics · Antiderivative and integral

1 Introduction

During the Covid-19 pandemic period in Portugal, teachers had to resort to distance learning. This change was sudden, with little preparation time. Somehow the teachers had to use technology. How did they do it? What instrumental orchestrations [1] used and what similarities and differences did they have in relation to those used in presential education to which they were used? Several studies have characterized instrumental orchestrations in classroom situations [1, 2]. The research problem we pose is related to realizing that changes in instrumental orchestrations in distance learning situations suffer, in a resource situation. Thus, it is important to reflect on the practices that have been carried out in this type of teaching. In this case study, the teaching practice of a secondary school mathematics teacher was analysed under the theme "calculating antiderivatives and integrals". The research questions that guide this study are as follows:

i) What are the characteristics of the didactic configurations and the modes of exploitation used by a teacher in the approach of antiderivative who, due to Covid-19, is forced to move from classroom teaching to distance learning?

A. Reis et al. (Eds.): TECH-EDU 2020, CCIS 1384, pp. 61–74, 2021.
https://doi.org/10.1007/978-3-030-73988-1_5

ii) What types of instrumental orchestration does a teacher in the approach of antiderivative who, due to Covid-19, is forced to move from classroom teaching to distance learning?
iii) What differences can be identified in didactic configurations, modes of exploitation and types of instrumental orchestration from classroom teaching to distance learning?

2 Theoretical Background

2.1 Non-classroom Teaching

It can be argued that distance learning has always existed. In ancient times, teachers who travelled great distances existed, attracting students and disseminating knowledge. Ancient educators used various means to transmit their knowledge on parchments, letters or books. Although this type of education can go a long way, it is not always distance learning. In some cases, the teacher and the student occupy the same space and time. In distance education, there is usually a difference in space and, often, time [3].

According to King et al. [4], there are two main types of distance education - synchronous and asynchronous. Synchronous teaching requires the simultaneous participation of the teacher and all students. The advantage of synchronous instruction is that the interaction is done in "real time" and immediate. Asynchronous teaching does not require the simultaneous participation of teachers and students. Asynchronous instruction is more flexible than synchronous instruction, but experience shows that time limits are necessary to maintain focus and participation.

The existing research studies related to distance learning refer mainly to university education, where more and more different institutions offer training through this medium. Martin, Sung and Westine [5] conducted a study where they review papers on teaching and learning online from 2009 to 2018, finding 506 studies on higher education and only 53 on K-12 education. Thus, what happened in mass distance learning in all teaching cycles that occurred this year due to the pandemic escapes published literature.

Adapting the existing literature, a simple definition may be implicit in the binary contrast between face-to-face and distance learning [6], but if we try to categorize the type of distance learning, the similarities between online learning, e-learning and m-learning make it difficult to define these terms. For Traxler [6], these terms are apparently synonymous and interchangeable. Vagarinho [7] distinguishes these types of teaching taking into account the characteristics and sub-characteristics (see Table 1).

Sadeghi [8] listed the most relevant advantages and disadvantages of non-classroom teaching. Enumerating the advantages, the student can study from anywhere, anytime (in the case of asynchronous teaching), can save money, does not need to travel, has the flexibility to choose any educational institution, can save time, may have a job while attending an educational institution. As disadvantages it identifies the great probabilities of distraction, the technology can be complicated, the lack of social interaction, the difficulty in maintaining contact with teachers and the job market tend not to accept degrees from courses taken online.

Table 1. Characterization of Distance Learning, E-Learning e M-Learning (Vagarinho, 2018, p. 277)

Characteristic	Sub-characteristic	Distance learning	E-learning	M-learning
Technology	Access devices	Paper, radio and TV	Desktop computer	iPod, iPhone, iPad, PDA, laptops[a], MP3 and tablets (that is, mobile devices[b])
	Transmission mode	Postal mail, fax, television, video/audio tapes	internet or intranet (cable)	GPRS, GSM, Wireless, WI-FI, Bluetooth, 3G, 4G
Course	Type	Higher and professional courses	Higher education, MBAs, ALV, MOOC, others	Higher education, MBAs, ALV, MOOC[c], other
Accessibility	Technological platform, tools and content	Does not exist	Exist	Needs adjustments
Adaptability	Learning	Does not exist	Exist	Needs adjustments[d]
Communication	- Form - Type - Link - Learning	- Asynchronous - No interaction - Does not exist - Isolated	- Asynchronous and Synchronous[e] - Interactive - Momentary - Collaborative	- Asynchronous and synchronous - Spontaneous - Permanent - Networked
Flexibility	- Local - Time - System (technology and communication with participants)	- Static - Any - Does not exist	- Static - Any - Advanced/Advanced	- Dynamic - Any - Medium[f]/Advanced

SOURCE: organized by the author.
[a]As long as they are connected to the network GPRS, GSM, Wireless, WI-FI, Bluetooth, 3G, 4G.
[b]It also has limitations in terms of hardware, i.e. battery capacity, limitations on storage.
[c]Not all MOOC learning platforms allow viewing in mobile applications for all operating systems.
[d]Older students who do not master mobile technology have some difficulties.
[e]Asynchronous mode is the most used. Synchronous mode is limited to the availability of other participants.
[f]Due to the limitations it still has as printing and storage.

Despite the promises and advantages of distance learning, there are problems that need to be solved. These problems include the quality of teaching and learning, especially of students with more difficulties or special needs, improper use of technology and the attitudes of teachers and students.

2.2 Artifacts and Tools

The concepts of artifact and tool in the classroom context are the object of study by several researchers [9, 10]. However, and in the context of this study, among the definitions present in [9], we adopted the definition presented by John Monaghan that artifact is the material object, usually something made by humans for a specific purpose, for example, a pencil.

An artifact becomes a tool when it is used by an agent, usually a person, to do something. The compass becomes a tool when it is used to draw a circle (which is the purpose of a compass); the same artifact becomes a different tool if used to measure distances. This establishes, according to the author, a link between the agent, the purpose and the artifacts; it is not possible to answer "is it a good tool?", without considering the user and the purpose. After being used as a tool (for any purpose), the compass becomes an artifact again. An artifact does not have to be something physical. For example, an algorithm is an artifact and is material in the sense that it can be written or programmed on a computer.

2.3 Instrumental Orchestration

An instrumental orchestration is defined as the teacher's intentional and systemic organization and the use of various artifacts to, in a learning environment and given a situation with a mathematical task, guide students' appropriation of these artifacts, transforming them in tools [1].

According to this author, instrumental orchestration is constituted by the didactic configuration and the mode of exploitation. Drijvers, Doorman, Boon, Reed e Gravemeijer [2], add to these two elements the didactic performance, as the orchestration is prepared in advance and partly created while teaching. The didactic configuration is the arrangement of artifacts in the environment, in other words, it is the configuration of the teaching environment and the artifacts involved in it [2]. Using the orchestra's musical metaphor (introduced by Trouche [1]), the didactic configuration can be compared to choosing the musical instruments to include in the band and arranging them in the space so that the different sounds result in polyphonic music that, in a mathematics class, may correspond to convergent mathematical discourse. The mode of exploitation is the way the teacher decides to explore her/his didactic configuration for the benefit of her/his didactic intentions. This includes decisions on how the task is introduced and worked on, about possible roles that artifacts can take and the schemes and techniques to be developed and established by students [2]. Finally, the didactic performance involves the ad hoc decisions taken while teaching and how the chosen didactic configuration and the mode of exploitation are really carried out: what question to ask now, how to attend (or not) a student's intervention, how to deal with an unexpected aspect of the mathematical task or a technological tool, or of unforeseen events that arise [2].

Eight types of instrumental orchestration that emerge in classes taught in environments rich in technology are identified [2]. Tabach [11, 12] adds some types of orchestrations and organizes them. Mazza, Ligorio and Cacciamani [13] extend these concepts to a distance learning platform, adding more orchestrations. Thus, the orchestrations present in the literature are summarized in Table 2, completed from the Tabach table [12].

Table 2. Orchestration types identified – (Completed from Tabach [12], p. 3)

Type of instrumental orchestration	Didactical configuration	Didactical exploitation
Technical-demo (Drijvers et al. 2010)	Whole-class setting, one central screen	The teacher explains the technical details for using the tool
Explain-the-screen (Drijvers et al. 2010)	Whole-class setting, one central screen	The teacher's explanations go beyond techniques and involve mathematical content
Link-screen-board (Drijvers et al. 2010)	Whole-class setting, one central screen	The teacher connects representations on the screen to representations of the same mathematical objects that appear either in the book or on the board
Discuss-the-screen (Drijvers et al. 2010)	Whole-class setting, one central screen	Whole-class discussion guided by the teacher, to enhance collective instrumental genesis
Spot-and-show (Drijvers et al., 2010)	Whole-class setting, one central screen	The teacher brings up previous student work that he/she had stored and identified as relevant for further discussion
Sherpa-at-work (Trouche 2004)	Whole-class setting, one central screen	The technology is in the hands of a student, who brings it up to the whole class for discussion
Work-and-walk-by (Drijvers 2012)	Students work individually or in pairs with computers	The teacher walks among the working students, monitors their progress and provides guidance as the need arises
Not-use-tech (Tabach 2011)	Whole-class setting, one central screen	The technology is available but the teacher chooses not to use it
Discuss-the-tech-without-it (Tabach 2013)	Whole-class setting, one central screen	Discuss the technology without the technology being present in that moment
Monitor-and-guide (Tabach 2013)	Each student has an electronic element	Teacher interacts with students from a distance by sending messages rather approaching them
Collaborative (Mazza et al. 2018)	Online platform	Use of a platform for the exchange of materials and ideas and for a comparison both between students and between teacher and students
Based-on-content (Mazza et al. 2018)	Internet	Search for information online
Experimental (Mazza et al. 2018)	Online platform	Focused on laboratory and experimental activities, where the platform constitutes a support tool for their realization

3 The Study

This work is a qualitative research study based on a case study [14, 15]. The chapter "calculation of antiderivatives and integrals" was taught in May 2020 and 7 classes of 2 × 50 min were used in synchronous mode. Data were collected through recording classes, student work and researcher's notes (the teacher was also one of the researchers). To record the lessons, the Freecam 8 software was used (through screen recording).

3.1 The Setting

In this subsection we proceed to the description of the technological apparatus and its instrumental orchestration used in distance learning. In Fig. 1 we present the configuration used by the teacher. Firstly, we refer to the material requirements for distance learning. In addition to a computer, webcam, microphone (a portable computer usually contains these three components) and a good connection to the internet, there are two more peripherals that complement and help in this teaching: a second monitor and a drawing tablet. The second monitor allows you to perform another task while the main one is with the teaching platform.

Fig. 1. Configuration used

The drawing tablet allows you to have all the capabilities of an interactive whiteboard. It also allows correcting students' exercises as if it were on paper (Fig. 2).

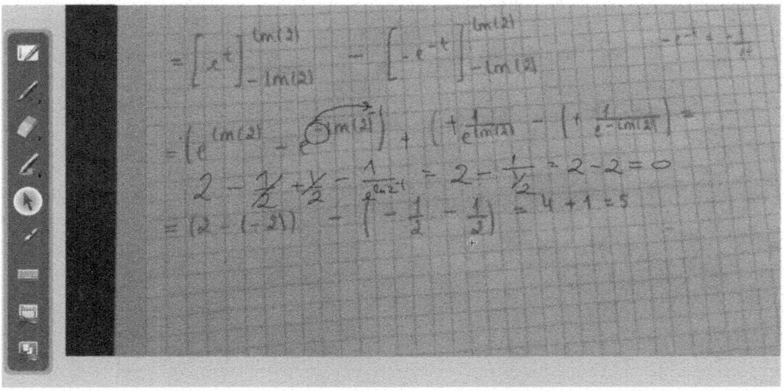

Fig. 2. Example of exercise correction using the drawing tablet

Secondly, we refer to the software. In this type of teaching it is important to have a distance learning platform that, in addition to video conferencing, concentrates all the resources and activities proposed. At the school where the study was conducted, since it uses Microsoft's Office 365, the platform used was Teams. This platform incorporates Onenote, where each student has a folder to place her/his work, sharing it with the teacher. Microsoft Whiteboard and Openboard were used for the drawing tablet. Sometimes it was necessary to use the Paint.NET software to correct students' exercises, since they were images. We also used software for presentations (Powerpoint), the digital platform of the adopted manual (20 Digital Classroom) and the Virtual School[1]. In Powerpoint,

[1] These are online platforms to support study and distance learning, provided by publishers that contain various teaching materials including school manuals.

images and animations prepared in Geogebra were included. This Powerpoint has been prepared by the teacher for use in face-to-face classes (it has not been changed for distance learning). During the teaching of this chapter, the students were in contact with some computer games, developed by the teacher, to consolidate the learning of the antiderivatives.

Finally, the Freecam 8 software was used to record the teacher's screen and occasionally the students' screens.

It is our opinion that, in this context, this entire setting can be considered didactic configuration, as these are the artifacts that will be used in distance learning.

3.2 The Participants

This study was implemented in a 12th year class of Mathematics A (the last year of secondary school) of a Portuguese public school in the north of the country. The class consisted of 20 students, 10 boys and 10 girls, aged between 16 and 18 years old, with an average age of 16.6 (with reference to the beginning of the school year). One student attended the Socio-Economic Sciences course and the rest the Science and Technologies course. Mathematics is the discipline chosen by 9 students as the one with the most difficulties and for 8 of them, Mathematics is the one with the least difficulties. All students attend the course of Computer Applications B, therefore having some abilities for the use of technologies.

The teacher has been teaching for 18 years, and 10 of them in the same school, always in secondary level. He always was fond of technologies. The teacher started the distance teaching period 15 days earlier, than the one officially established due to having made a trip abroad during the carnival school break, which led him to voluntary confinement. During this period, he taught at a distance, with students and an educational assistant in the classroom, and the teacher at home. This additional period allowed the teacher to prepare the non-presential teaching practice, anticipating the closure and generalization of the distance learning that came to be verified.

4 Results

Taking into account the characteristics of the teaching provided, following the designations of Vagarinho [7], we are facing an e-learning or m-learning situation, given that the teacher uses a desktop computer technology or laptops, using the internet (fixed or mobile), with mostly synchronous and interactive communication.

In the teaching of the chapter "calculation of antiderivatives and integrals", the methods of exploitation used by the teacher were diverse, which led to several types of instrumental orchestrations. As a basic didactic configuration, PowerPoint was used to present and explain the contents (Fig. 3) and the Whiteboard, to solve exercises (Fig. 4).

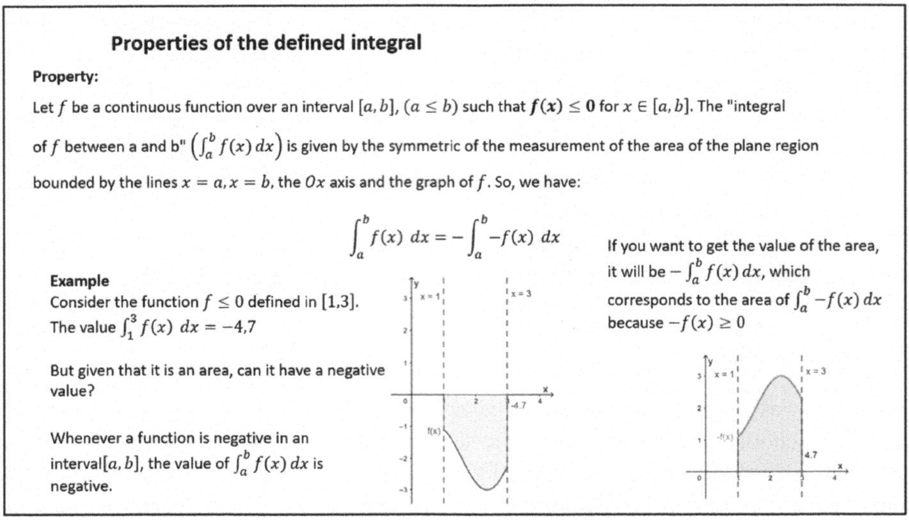

Fig. 3. Example of a PowerPoint slide used by the teacher to present theoretical content

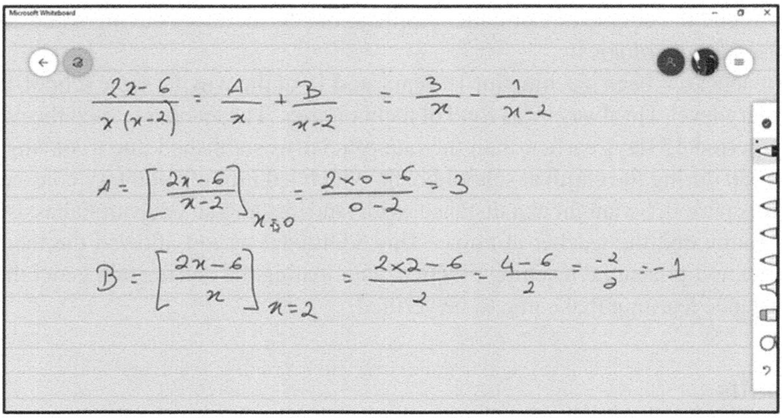

Fig. 4. Example of the use of Whiteboard by the teacher to solve an exercise

The type of *technical-demo* orchestration was initially used to explain the functioning of the Teams platform. Later, in the operation of the Onenote, which is integrated in Teams (see Fig. 5) and also in the use of Freecam 8. Finally, in the application of games, so that students become familiar with its operation.

A Teams channel was created where the materials used were placed. The students, in turn, watched the Powerpoint presentation (previously made available on the channel), identifying a situation of *Collaborative orchestration*, asking their questions and solving exercises in the adopted manual.

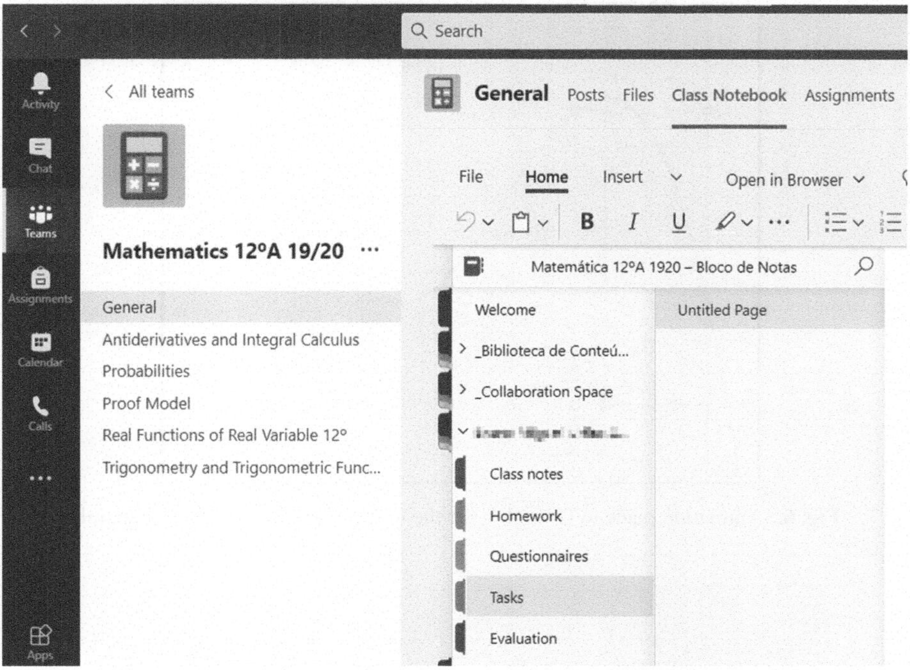

Fig. 5. Typical organization of Onenote, integrated in Teams

In the classes taught (which were initially prepared to be taught in person through Powerpoint), the predominant orchestration was *Explain-the-screen*, where the teacher, through the successive presentation of the various slides, presents and explains the contents to be taught.

This type of orchestration is interspersed with the *Discuss-the-screen* where the teacher asks the class to comment on a given situation.

The type of *link-screen-board* orchestration was used when explaining the intuitive notion of defined integral, where an animation made in Geogebra (Fig. 6) was used, emphasizing its relationship with the symbolism $\int f(x)\,dx$.

Spot-and-show was occasionally present, when the teacher used exercises solved by students, both to emphasize some different reasoning and to illustrate typical errors to correct (Fig. 7).

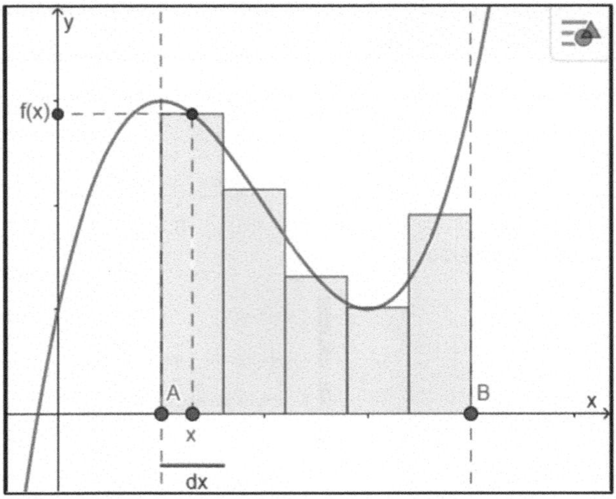

Fig. 6. Animation made in Geogebra for the intuitive notion of definite integral

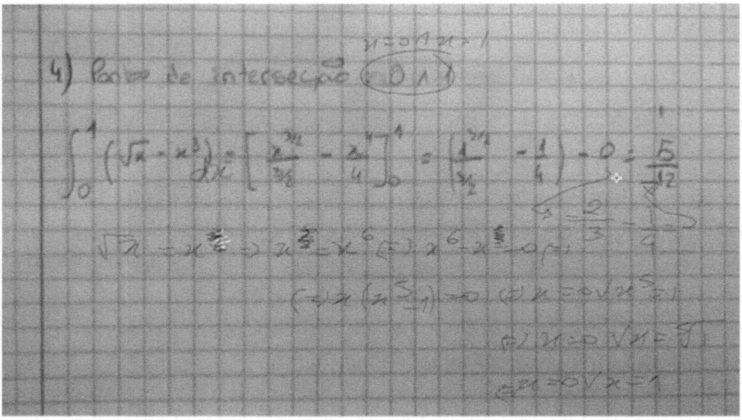

Fig. 7. *Spot-and-show* example - The student had not calculated the points of intersection between the curves and the teacher showed the student's resolution explaining the mistake made.

Regarding *Work-and-walk-by*, given that the teacher cannot walk among students as he usually does in face-to-face teaching, it was not identified as defined. However, the teacher resorted to the strategy of randomly asking some students, asking them to share their work, which is accepted by almost all students (Fig. 8). Not corresponding to the *work-and-walk-by* orchestration, it was decided to designate it *work-ask-for-show*.

Not present in this work were the *Sherpa-at-work*, *Discuss-the-tech-without-it*, *Based-on-content* and *Experimental* orchestrations.

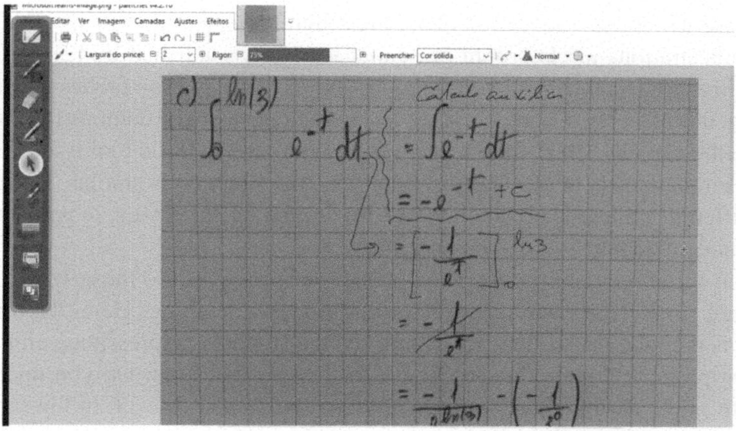

Fig. 8. *Work-and-ask-for-show* example

5 Discussion

Regarding the question of the type of distance learning used, as Traxler [6], neither to us is relevant the distinction between *e-learning* and *m-learning*. In the work developed, some students used a desktop computer, others a laptop. Some of them used a fixed internet, others a mobile one. When everyone is at home, is there a distinction between the type of non-presential education? On the other hand, even though students had a webcam, they preferred to use the mobile phone to take a picture of their exercises, as it is of a higher quality. So, are we facing m-learning? Clearly, all of these concepts need more precise definitions which fall outside the context of this work.

Trouche's notion of didactic configuration [1] in this context, that is, the configuration of the teaching environment and the artifacts involved in it, has to be adapted. Evidently, there is no physical environment, nor common material objects, since each participant of the class is (most likely) at home, in front of her/his computer. However, there remains a need for the teacher to organize the distance learning environment and non-material artifacts to be used.

The first element to take into account is how the communication is insured. Teams includes the whiteboard application, which allows, on the one hand, the teacher to teach in a traditional way, being able to easily include images from the book, for instance, or use drawing tools, and on the other hand, allows the different participants (teacher and students) to collaborate in solving an exercise, for instance - of course, this participation is only feasible if everyone has drawing tables or touch screens. The teacher can follow the resolution of exercises in the notebook of each student (through the Onenote). You can organize the materials to be made available in folders, for all students. Many other applications can be integrated, leading to a richer experience. The platform, and the available means, condition the organization we offer. Regarding the mode of exploitation, the way the teacher decides to explore her/his didactic configuration for the benefit of her/his didactic intentions, we were able to find several orchestrations present in the literature.

Next, we will make a reflection about the differences identified by us in the instrumental orchestrations in classroom presential teaching, stablished by [2] and in non-presential teaching, stablished by [13]. As for the *Technical-demo* orchestration, it can be said that it is not a big difference. If the technological tool to be demonstrated is on the computer, the explanation is simple, just sharing the screen. If the tool is a device with computer emulators, as in the case of calculators, the situation is similar. The situation may be different if there is no emulator for the technological device, in which case the teacher can demonstrate it to the camera.

Explain-the-screen and *Link-screen-board* orchestrations are those where the differences are smaller between face-to-face and distance learning. Here, the difference identified is the fact that the teacher cannot see the students' expressions, immediately identifying possible doubts. You will have to trust the question: Do you understand? Being 12th grade students, they will be more autonomous however, in lower years of schooling this problem will be greater.

Regarding the *Discuss-the-screen* orchestration, the organization of the discussion is conditioned by the distance learning environment. The teacher launches the discussion, but she/he will have to be careful to organize the interventions. The platforms allow interventions both written in a chat or oral. To avoid confusion, the platforms have a tool for a student to ask for the word, "raising her/his hand" and also a way to turn off the microphone of a given student or all students. Thus, whoever is managing the discussion will have to be careful to take into account written interventions while oral interventions are taking place. On the other hand, the teacher has the possibility to give voice to only one student, silencing all the others, something that can be more complicated to do in person.

With the teacher able to collect interesting work from the students, the *Spot-and-show* orchestration also seems to be easy to implement.

As for the *Sherpa-at-work* orchestration, although not present in this work, it is possible in synchronous distance learning, if the student in question only shares her/his screen (or camera, depending on the technology), showing her/his work or actions requested by the teacher. In the orchestration *Discuss-the-tech-without-it*, not taking into account the distance learning platform, it is also possible to implement.

The *Work-and-walk-by* orchestration will be the orchestration where the transition to distance learning will be more delicate. It is possible to create small work groups (with two students or more) on the distance learning platforms, but how can the teacher go through the classroom, helping students? If technology is available (that is, if students have touch screens or drawing tables), it is possible for the teacher to monitor the resolution of the exercises through each student's Onenote notebook.

As there was none in the case analysed, the path followed was to ask students chosen at random to send their answers in order to be corrected before the whole class. Thus, when requested by the teacher, a student would take a photo of her/his work to be corrected/commented on by the whole class, through screen sharing and using software for interactive whiteboards or image editing. Of course, it is not the same as going through the room and checking the development of students' reasoning and quick intervention when there are difficulties, but it is a possible alternative within the context.

It can be said that this new orchestration *work-ask-for-show* results from the crossing of *work-and-walk-by* with *spot-and-show*.

As for the *Not-use-tech* orchestration [11], it can be seen from two perspectives in the context of distance learning. On the one hand, technology is a necessary condition for teaching to work at a distance, so it is always present. However, if the teacher in person does not use technology, and in distance learning uses the same strategies, it does not seem to us that we are able to say that technology was used.

Finally, in all distance learning, the teacher interacts with students at a distance. Thus, the *Monitor-and-guide* orchestration [13] will not make sense in distance learning exclusively.

6 Conclusions

In this study we obtained the main characteristics of the didactic configurations and the modes of exploitation used by a teacher in the approach of antiderivative when he has to make the transition from classroom teaching to distance learning. We found that through the technological setting, on the one hand, the teacher tried to reproduce the classroom conditions, namely the blackboard with the drawing tablet, and on the other hand, used the potential of the Distance Learning Platform. The types of orchestration used are similar to those established by the literature for classroom teaching with the use of technology. Differences in use are the main contribution of this study. We can affirm that the majority of instrumental orchestrations, for teaching using technology, remains valid for distance learning, with slight adaptations. *Technical-demo*, *Explain-the-screen*, *Link-screen-board*, *Discuss-the-screen*, *Spot-and-show* and *Collaborative* situations were found. No *Sherpa-at-work*, *Based-on-content* and *Experimental* situations were found, but they are feasible to happen in the context of distance learning. In distance learning, *Monitor-and-guide* orchestration does not make sense.

As for the *work-and-walk-by* orchestration, since there is no physical space to cover, it is difficult to implement and can be adapted, however, requiring additional technology for each student. In our study we identified a new type of instrumental orchestration that we called *work-ask-for-show* which replaces in distance learning the work-and-walk-by orchestration and can be characterized by the teacher requesting at a random student to take a photo of her/his work to be corrected/commented on by the whole class, through screen sharing and using software for interactive whiteboards or image editing.

References

1. Trouche, L.: Managing the complexity of human/machine interactions in computerized learning environments: guiding student's command process through intrumental orchestrations. Int. J. Comput. Math. Learn. **9**, 281–307 (2004)
2. Drijvers, P., Doorman, M., Boon, P., Reed, H., Gravemeijer, K.: The teacher and the tool: instrumental orchestrations in the technology-rich mathematics classroom. Educ. Stud. Math. **75**, 213–234 (2010)
3. Johnston, J.: Creating better definitions of distance education. Online J. Distance Learn. Adm. **XXIII**(2) Summer (2020)

4. King, F., Young, M., Drivere-Richmond, K., Schrader, P.: Defining distance learning and distance education. AACE J. **9**(1), 1–14 (2001)
5. Martin, F., Sun, T., Westline, C.: A systematic review of research on online teaching and learning from 2009 to 2018. Comput. Educ. **159**, 17 (2020)
6. Traxler, J.: Distance learning—predictions and possibilities. Educ. Sci. **8**(35) (2018)
7. Vagarinho, J.: What should we consider to correctly define the terms distance learning, e-learning, and m-learning? Educar em Revista **34**(68), 269–287 (2018)
8. Sadeghi, M.: A shift from classroom to distance learning: advantages and limitations. Int. J. Res. Engl. Educ. **4**(1), 80–88 (2019)
9. Monaghan, J., Trouche, L., Borwein, J.: Tools and Mathematics. Springer, Cham (2016)
10. McDonald, G., Le, H., Higgins, J., Podmore, V.: Artifacts tools, and classrooms. Mind Cult. Activity **12**(2), 113–127 (2005)
11. Tabach, M.: A mathematics teacher's practice in a technological environment: a case study analysis using two complementary theories. Tech. Know. Learn. **16**, 247–265 (2011)
12. Tabach, M.: Developing a general framework for instrumental orchestration. In: The Eighth Congress of the European Society for Research (2013)
13. Mazza, S., Ligorio, M., Cacciamani, S.: Orchestrazione strumentale per l'inserimento di "Aule Virtuali" a scuola. Qwerty **13**(2), 49–65 (2018)
14. Cohen, L., Manion, L., Morrison, K.: Research Methods in Education. Routledge, New York (2007)
15. Yin, R.: Case Study Research: Design and Methods, 5th edn. Sage, London (2014)

Using Mathematical Modelling and Virtual Manipulatives to Teach Elementary Mathematics

Ricardo Silva[1,2,3(✉)], Cecília Costa[1,2], and Fernando Martins[3,4]

[1] Universidade Trás-os-Montes e Alto Douro (UTAD), Vila Real, Portugal
mcosta@utad.pt
[2] CIDTFF - Centro de Investigação Didática e Tecnologia na Formação de Formadores, Vila Real, Portugal
[3] Instituto Politécnico de Coimbra, ESEC, NIEFI , Coimbra, Portugal
{rjpsilva,fmlmartins}@esec.pt
[4] Instituto de Telecomunicações, Covilhã, Portugal

Abstract. The acronym STEM has been gaining prominence in discussions around the future of Education. With the growing importance of mathematics and technology in the STEM context, it is important that initial teacher education can respond to this challenge. Participation in STEM teaching experiences, which make an appropriate integration of technology, promote the development of professional teaching knowledge related to the TPACK dimensions and motivate pre - service teachers to adopt these teaching practices. We seek to contribute to this discussion with an intervention proposal, implemented during the practice component of pre-service teacher training, which combined Mathematical Modelling as a learning environment with the use of Virtual Manipulatives. A set of tasks supported by the TPACK conceptual model were designed to assist a group of 1st year elementary school to overcome difficulties detected in their learning related to elementary arithmetic operations. Through a qualitative research of interpretative nature and action research design, the analysis of the pre-service teacher performance identified the teaching practice characteristics that contributed to the creation of favourable conditions for self-regulation and co-regulation of students' mathematical learning.

Keywords: STEM · Pre-service teachers · Virtual manipulatives · Mathematical Modelling

1 Introduction

Science Technology Engineering and Mathematics (STEM) fields are identified by the OECD [23] as important indicators for innovation and economic development. However, these areas of knowledge are not the most sought after by Higher Education students [23]. Worldwide STEM promotion has been used with different objectives, either to equip future generations with skills considered essential to leverage economic growth or

A. Reis et al. (Eds.): TECH-EDU 2020, CCIS 1384, pp. 75–89, 2021.
https://doi.org/10.1007/978-3-030-73988-1_6

as a strategy to improve student outcomes in STEM disciplines [16]. This issue has been thoroughly monitored by the scientific community [6, 29, 35], which seeks to understand the contribution of a STEM approach in teaching and learning processes [11], as well as the role to play in the in-service teachers' professional development [3, 18] and also in the pre-service teachers [2].

Lacking initial training is identified by teachers as one of the obstacles to proficiently implement STEM teaching, as well as to the improvement of positive attitudes towards STEM learning [20]. There are several challenges that teachers in training programs face in the field of STEM, particularly regarding the integration of technology [19] and its articulation with learning trajectories [24]. Thus, the proficient use of these tools by teachers for the promotion of meaningful mathematical learning becomes more important [21].

In the specific case of computational tools, it is necessary that teaching strategies develop skills that foster conceptual understanding of the mathematics used by these tools while solving tasks [14]. To be able to do so, pre-service teachers should have the opportunity to develop their professional knowledge in learning environments that intentionally integrate technology [19, 21]. The inclusion of problem-solving tasks that promote mathematical discussion in these learning environments contributes to both teacher and student development of STEM fields knowledge [20].

There are known advantages to the Interdisciplinary STEM approach [11], such as the use of Mathematical Modelling (MM) for the teaching and learning of mathematical concepts [3], a fundamental characteristic of the proposal presented here. Part of a broader study [26, 31, 32], it was designed to create settings that would allow a group of students to overcome a set of difficulties identified in their mathematical learning. In view of the context of this group, we designed an intervention, which sought to understand how the integration of Virtual Manipulatives (VM) in classroom practices, using Mathematical Modelling as a Learning Environment (MMLE), generates positive impacts in the construction of students' knowledge related to the development of the meaning of addition and subtraction.

Adding to previous works, focused on student learning, we discuss here the characteristics of the teaching practice, devised with the purpose of contributing to the creation of favourable settings for self-regulation and co-regulation [27] of students' learning and allowing them to take an active role in the construction of their mathematical knowledge related to elementary arithmetic operations.

2 Literature Review

The MMLE enhances the construction of mathematical knowledge [28]. In this context, the use of computers assists students to establish multiple mathematical connections, fostering the holistic development of mathematical understanding [25] and its concepts [7].

2.1 Mathematical Modelling

MM is a bidirectional translation process between the real world and mathematics [5]. There are in the literature different proposals of MM cycles [12] and each of its stages represents potential cognitive barriers for students [15]. The specific characteristics of the teaching and learning processes associated with MM present challenges to teachers and students, requiring the former a set of skills [12] that allow them to maintain a balance between minimal teacher guidance and maximal students' independence [15]. In order to achieve this flexible form of teaching, it is important that the MM tasks are structured in such a way as to allow students co-constructive group work, time for their resolution [12] and that they respect five criteria [13]: 1) meaning of the modelling task; 2) realistic age appropriate context; 3) question incitement; 4) stimulation of holistic forms of learning and 5) adequate language level.

By making MM an integral part of mathematical education, learning environments are created [9]. In these, teachers as mediators of the educational process, help students to establish connections between mathematical and extra-mathematical knowledge through contextualized pedagogical activities [28]. In this type of teaching performance, scaffolding gains an increased importance since it is supported by the diagnostic evaluation of the students' mathematical knowledge [15]. By resorting to real contexts, the MMLE prompts the active participation of students in tasks, creating conditions for meaningful learning [4].

2.2 Virtual Manipulatives

"An interactive, technology-enabled visual representation of a dynamic mathematical object, including all of the programmable features that allow it to be manipulated, that presents opportunities for constructing mathematical knowledge" [22].

The use of VM in mathematics education is not an unknown practice, with a remarkable technological evolution in recent years [22]. Their integration into the classroom, chosen carefully for an intended purpose and according to their constraints and specificities, is pointed out as beneficial for the understanding of mathematical concepts [30, 34]. For this, it is important that the teacher is able to help students to establish connections between manipulation and mathematical concepts, needing to understand and being able to position themselves in each of the dimensions of the TPACK [33].

Using VM as a MM tool gives students immediate feedback and ensures that mathematical concepts are correctly reinforced [10, 19]. Students' motivation for tasks, and immediate validation of the task by the applet, allow greater autonomy for students, enabling self-regulation of learning and creating favourable conditions for differentiated monitoring by the teacher.

The digital skills needed to operate VM can be challenging for students. Obstacles that can be overcame with teacher scaffolding, taking advantage of immediate feedback from VM on student error [33]. In a study with pre-service teachers, Suh [33] presents evidence that the participants recognized the importance of understanding how to use technology in order to provide greater equity in the teaching and learning process, while trying to help students overcome shortcomings in their mathematical knowledge. Also focused on pre-service teachers, Martins et al. [19] argue that the use of VM helps future teachers to feel confident and prepared for proper integration of technology in the teaching of elementary mathematics content.

3 Study's Investigation and Context Description

This study was carried out with a class of 1st year of the 1st Cycle of Basic Education in a school in Coimbra (central Portugal), in the school year 2017/2018, during the practice of pre-service teacher training. The pre-service teacher, with a background in Electrotechnical and Computer Engineering, was comfortable using technology. The 26 students who were part of the class participated in the study, grouped into 13 pairs according to the conditions of the Zone of Proximal Development (ZDP) [36], whose levels of optimal discrepancy were established according to the results of the tasks performed by the students in the initial phase (subsection Initial Phase).

Through participant observation, difficulties were diagnosed in solving tasks related to the meanings of addition and subtraction. Given the context of the class – using computer tools was a common habit inside and outside the classroom – an intervention was put into practice to help overcome the diagnosed difficulties. We present and discuss representative results that allow us to depict the teaching practice and its contribution to the construction of the learning environment.

3.1 Methodological Options

The chosen methodology followed the principles of a qualitative research of interpretative nature and action research design [8]. We sought to create an intervention proposal based on the conceptual model TPACK [17], since this approach allows structuring didactic sequences that stem from the established curriculum, with student-centred learning and proper technology integration in the teaching and learning processes.

Interventions

The intervention proposal was composed of a set of distinct phases which are set out below:

Initial Phase. Individually, each student solved a set of written tasks, composed of problematic situations relating to each of the meanings of the operations addition (add and join) and subtraction (remove, compare, and complete). The analysis of the students' productions made it possible to map out their difficulties, to seek improvements in the action plan and to form pairs according to ZDP conditions.

Intervention Phase. A set of six weekly sessions supported by MMLE in which VM were used, held in the school library where there was a computer for each pair of students. The first session was dedicated to the exploration of the VM by the students, to picture these tools as a positive input and not an obstacle to learning. The remaining five sessions were dedicated to each of the meanings of addition and subtraction. The tasks were solved in a collaborative way between the pre-service teacher and the students. The pre-service teacher supported students' work, through dialogue and questioning, always with the aim of helping the students' research and discovery. After the task's conclusion, their discussion took place – time allocated for the groups to explain what they did, justifying the steps taken – followed by the student's evaluation of the session. This final part took place in an informal area of the library where there are sofas and poufs.

The data collected in each session was analysed at its end. This made possible to redesign the next session lesson plan, seeking improvements to students' learning and autonomy, pre-service teacher differentiated instruction skills associated with the pedagogical use of VMs in the MMLE.

Final Phase. Identical to the initial phase. The students written productions were analysed to assess their progression regarding the comprehension of the meanings of addition and subtraction.

3.2 Procedures

The choice of VM was made considering the affordances and restrictions of each one, the specific context of the class, the curricular contents to be addressed, what the pre-service teacher knows about them and the tasks to be implemented.

For this study, applets with a structured number line[1] were created by the research team according to the principles of didactic engineering [1] – since it was not possible to find a freeware and Portuguese option that served the objectives of the study. Taking into account the characteristics of the group and the pre-service teacher's knowledge of the software GeoGebra, we decided to create a VM that: allows visualization of the mathematical concepts that are involved, through the manipulation of the slide bar; restraining the number line to the numbers already known to the students, and reinforces the importance of precision in the construction of a number line; encourages the use of mathematical terms suitable to the students language, by taking advantage of the specific affordances and constraints of the VM [31]. We also used the VM Base Blocks, Base Blocks Addition and Base Blocks Subtraction, from the repository of the National Library of Virtual Manipulatives[2] (NLVM).

The data collection resorted to participant observation, field notes, audio recordings, documentary analysis of the students' written productions and screen recordings captured with the software Flashback Express Recorder.

4 Results

The following presentation of results is structured in six sections corresponding to each one of the intervention phase sessions. Diachronic results related to the characteristics of the teaching performance during the Intervention phase are presented in the form of student/student and teacher/student interactions.

4.1 Exploration Session

The first tasks were supported by the NLVM Base Blocks applet (to represent numbers) and the NLVM Base Blocks addition applet (to represent and solve additions, with and without composing of a superior order unit).

[1] https://www.geogebra.org/m/scwjXjee; https://www.geogebra.org/m/g2k4PYT9.

[2] https://nlvm.usu.edu/.

The sharing of students' discoveries allowed the class to understand the functioning and mechanics of the applets. The comment made by student M is an example of this ("it goes like this, here we have 4 + 6, then we have to look for the result and put it here, after that I don't know…"), or the one made by student E, upon discovering that after composing a superior order unit, he should move the bar to the column of the tens ("Oh, I get it. So, we make a square, get a bar and drag it there"). The mechanics of the grouping of units needed to be demonstrated by the pre-service teacher, since the manipulation of the mouse was complicated to apprehend and execute by the students.

During the evaluation of the session, the students expressed their satisfaction with the environment of exploration and collaborative learning:

1. "it's like, S and I messed up a little bit at first, but then he said we needed to pull into the tens and we managed to do it" – student R, describing the discovery process of composing superior order units with the Base Blocks Addition applet;
2. "I liked it because it was more difficult and I also liked it because after we could do the adds we wanted" – student A, referring to the moment of free exploitation, in which they could create and solve operations autonomously, outside the obligation of the task script;
3. "I had never used a computer, but H helped me, and I did it!" – student G, valuing the pair's help in being able to use a computer for the first time.

4.2 Add Session

The first task of the session consisted of a set of additions to solve with the number line applet. While observing the class the pre-service teacher identifies a common obstacle, how to represent numbers in the applet. Opting for a collective intervention, the pre-service teacher asks: "How can we represent the value of the first addend on the computer?".

Challenged by the pre-service teacher's question, student C explores the desktop with the mouse pointer. Noticing the change of shape of the pointer when passing over the slide bar addend, clicks until he gets 3 units (Fig. 1). After discovering the manipulation of the slide bar, he represents the value corresponding to the second addend, a task made difficult by the manipulation of the mouse. Student C relates the structure of the manipulative with the structure of the addition and manipulates the slide bar sum to represent the value read in the number line, the value of the addition of the two addends (Fig. 2), sharing the discovery with the pair "You see, the bunny is the sum".

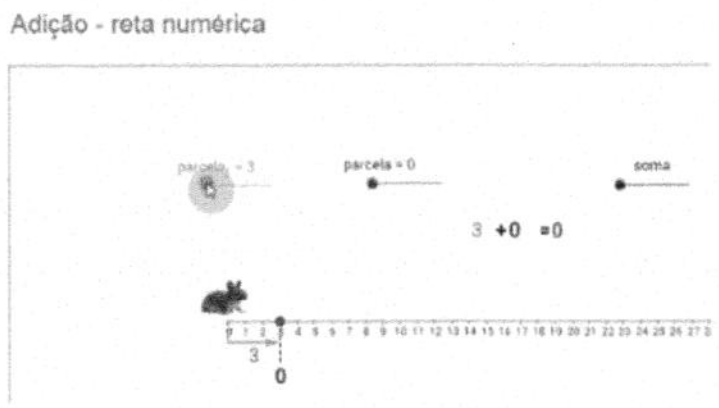

Fig. 1. Manipulation of the 1st addend

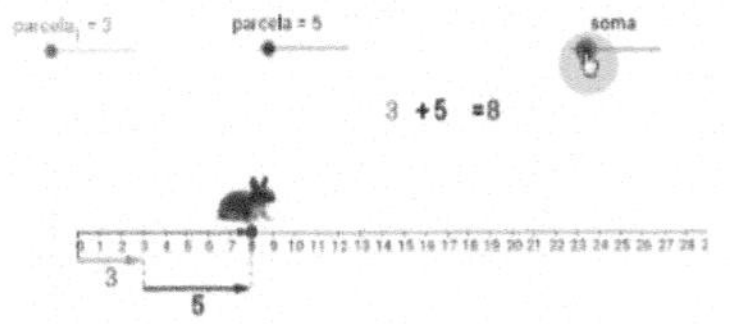

Fig. 2. Manipulation of the sum

The remaining additions are carried out with ease, with students C and D taking turns in mouse manipulation. In the first additions (3 + 5 and 9 + 7) student D insists on confirming the results by counting his fingers, starting to rely on the manipulative by encouragement of the pair: "Look, the number line is always right". In the next addition (25 + 18), student D, after representing the values of both addends, immediately reads the number line – Wow, 43! –, showing that he now relies on the manipulative (Fig. 3).

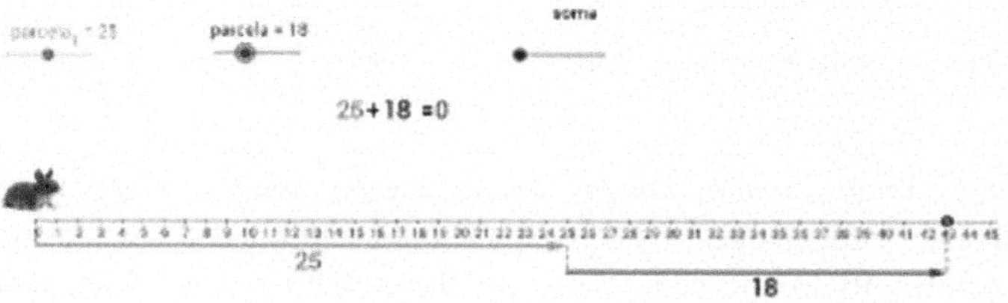

Fig. 3. Interpretation of student D

This event exemplifies some of the characteristics of the learning environment, namely exploration and collaborative learning.

4.3 Remove Session

Supported by the Base Blocks Subtraction applet, the first task in the session consisted of a set of subtractions. After representing the quantities indicated in the task script (23-9) and starting the resolution of the subtraction (Fig. 4), student B decomposes a superior order unit. Being an exploratory manipulation, without mathematical intention, the student goes from "I already know how it works", to "Why is it crossed out here? Look, you try. I don't understand." After deleting what she did, hands the manipulation over to student A. After a few more unsuccessful attempts at resolution, they ask the teacher for help:

Student A: I did it like this… And then I put one of these like this and it fell apart (Fig. 5).

Pre-service teacher: But when it fell apart, what happened to the ten?

Student B: It was like this – pointing to the screen.

Pre-service teacher: The ten turned into?

Student B: Units.

Pre-service teacher: Exactly, it decomposed into units.

The pre-service teacher's help allowed unblocking the situation. By establishing connections between the manipulation and the mathematical concepts involved, the pre-service teacher helped the students to overcome the obstacle and successfully complete the task.

4.4 Complete Session

This session was supported by the number line applet. Through the analysis of the recordings of the previous sessions, the pre-service teacher identified a problem with

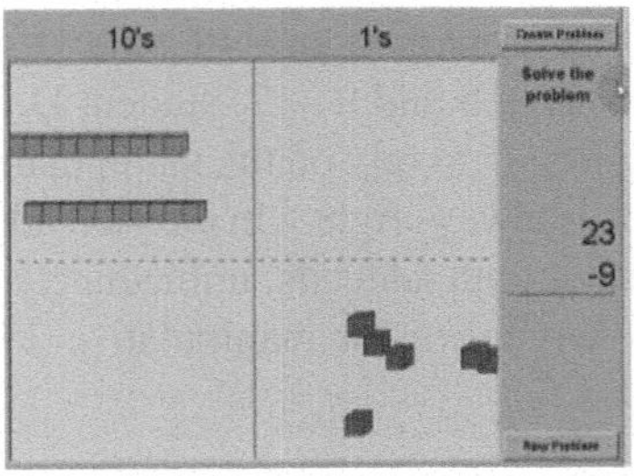

Fig. 4. Subtraction with decomposition

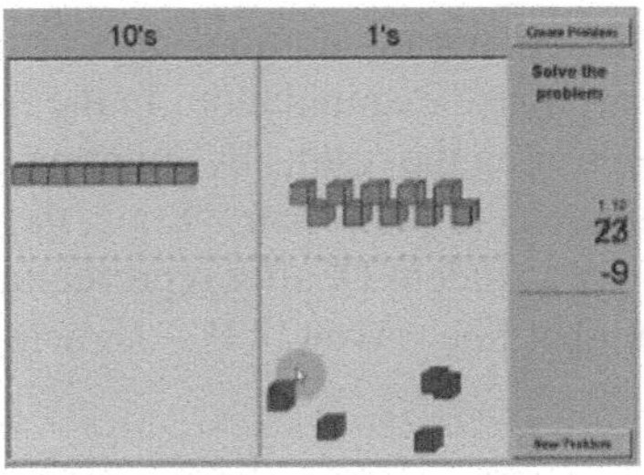

Fig. 5. Student B manipulation

one of the groups. Only one of the students was doing the manipulation of the applets. The pre-service teacher kept an eye on the group the next session, waiting for an appropriate window of opportunity to intervene. As usual, the applet was manipulated by student F at the beginning of the session. Student F's discontent was growing throughout the task:

Student F: "Watch, watch and learn, because you don't want to do".

Student M: "I do, I do, but it makes me feel funny".

This discussion was the moment chosen by the pre-service teacher to intervene. After a talk between the pre-service teacher and the students, it was agreed that the next subtraction (83-44) would be made by the student M, with the pre-service teacher remaining alongside the students to assist with the difficulties of manipulating the mouse, in order to help explore the task. It was necessary to demonstrate how to manipulate the mouse to obtain representations in the applet, the next attempt of student M was more fruitful. The prompt help of student F, suggested that the group was again on the path of mutual help and sharing, allowing the pre-service teacher to move away, keeping an eye on the performance of these students. With the help of student F, student M was able to represent the additive, the subtractive and the difference read in the number line (Fig. 6), while still expressing the difficulty felt: "this makes the tummy feel colder than I thought", student M.

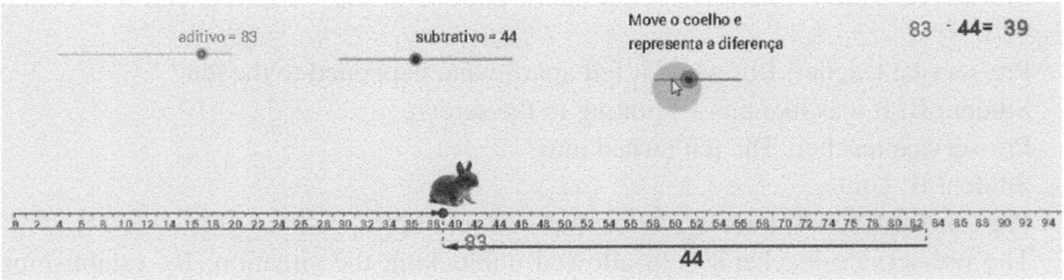

Fig. 6. Student M manipulation of the applet

The analysis of the recordings allowed the pre-service teacher to identify specific difficulties of each group and adjust his intervention in subsequent sessions. The pre-service teacher differentiated instruction contributed to overcoming obstacles and enhancing students' collaborative learning and autonomous work.

During the discussion of task 2 (Fig. 7), the group composed by students A and B asked to speak:

2 – It's time to plan another field trip. We need to decide who is going on each bus. The blue bus has 42 seats. Twenty-six students of the 1st A are going. How many students from 1st B can still get on this bus?

Fig. 7. Word problem created for task 2

Pre-service teacher: What did we want to know?
Student B: How many could still go on the bus.
Pre-service teacher: And for that we needed to know the number of seats…
Student B: All… May we say our answer?
Pre-service teacher: Yes.
Student A: From 1st only 16 students can go.
Pre-service teacher: And why only 16?
Student A: Because most of the 1st A is going – referring to the whole class, 26 students –, which leaves only a few seats free.

The moments of task discussion compel students to verbalize their reasoning. This feature of the intervention proposal, combined with the recordings analysis, allows the pre-service teacher a thorough perception of the understanding of students' mathematical concepts. It also allows the design of different intervention strategies for each group and orchestrate the discussions to diagnose difficulties, systemize learning or overcome obstacles to learning.

4.5 Compare Session

Like the previous one, this session was also supported by the number line applet. During the task consisting in solving a problematic situation (Fig. 8), a side conversation begins between two groups:

1- The 1st A class did a study on water consumption. At Ricardo's house, 56 litres of water are used up every day. What is the difference between litres of water spent in Ricardo's house and in your house?

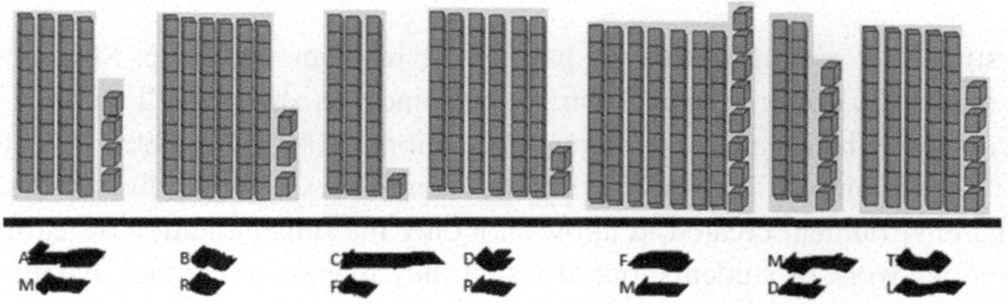

Fig. 8. Word problem created for task 1

Student E: Our bill is higher – referring to the value of water consumption.

Student C: That's bad, they spend a lot of water, but those spent almost nothing – referring to another group with a very low water consumption.

This small dialogue highlights the importance of using problem situations based on reality.

The following episode also occurred during the word problem task (Fig. 8). The interpretation of the word problem raised a doubt in the group: which of the data corresponds to the additive and subtractive. Student A suggests that the additive is 57 because "it comes first", student B disagrees. They cannot reach a consensus and the conflict escalates until student A hurts student B. In view of this situation, student A did not participate in the completion of the task.

Student B is unable to interpret the word problem and requests the help of the teacher, who questions her about the possibility of the information she needs to be somewhere else on the worksheet. Alerted to the presence of the graphic information, she can proceed. Once the data is obtained, she represents the quantities referring to the additive and the subtractive to then interpret the number line and represent the difference in the applet (Fig. 9).

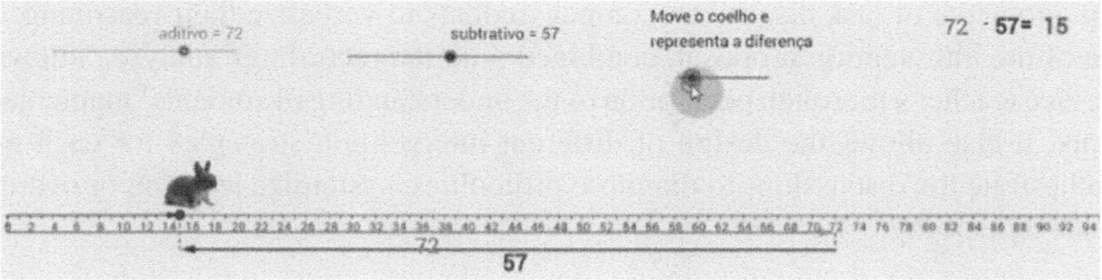

Fig. 9. Student B manipulation of the applet

After finishing the first task, student B is dedicated to the next, which consists in creating and solving subtractions. Without any difficulty, student B solves all the subtractions created (10 − 49 = 51; 36 − 16 = 20; 55 − 54 = 1; 100 − 100 = 0). She is, however, surprised by some values that differ from its estimate, evidence that reinforces the affordance of the applet to allow to put to test hypotheses through the instant feedback and immediate validation of the tasks, while allowing the autonomous work of the students.

After student A apologized to his partner, he resumes his place. Student B suggests that student A do three more subtractions, since, as she says, "I've done many." Like his colleague, he creates and solves subtractions (100 − 1 = 99; 81 − 18 = 63; 13 − 5 = 8) without difficulty. This episode exemplifies some of the advantages of the learning environment created. It allows not only the self-regulation of learning and the autonomous work of students, but also that they manage relational dynamics with minimal intervention of the pre-service teacher.

4.6 Join Session

The last session of the Intervention phase, supported by the Base Blocks Addition applet, was dedicated to the meaning join of addition. Students C and D started the first task with the representation of the addends in the applet. Although they no longer fully remember the mechanics of the applet, they explore several options, changing the arrangement of objects, to no avail. Since they cannot remember how to compose a superior order unit, they decide to ask the pre-service teacher for help. Noticing that this is a common problem to most groups, the pre-service teacher chooses to address the entire class:

Pre-service teacher: there are many boys and girls asking how to do next. It is normal, the last time we worked with this applet was a long time ago. Can you look at the screen, please? Look at the units. How many units do you have D?

Student D: All in all?

Professor: Yes.

Student D: 12.

Pre-service teacher: 12. And can you have 12 units?

All class at the same time: Yes/No.

Pre-service teacher: Who thinks so? (some students answer by raising their arm) who thinks not? (some students answer by raising their arm) Why can't we have 12 units?

Student M: After 10 units is a ten.

Pre-service teacher: Did you hear what M said? From the moment we have 10 units, it becomes a…

All class at the same time: Ten (in chorus).

Pre-service teacher: And how do we turn 10 units into a ten? Do you still remember? Do you remember that we need to group them together?

This moment of horizontal dialogue was enough to unblock the situation. The use of VM in the classroom allows students to develop autonomous work, freeing the pre-service teacher to individually follow each group, being able to grasp what they are doing in order to decide for different instructions for each group or, as in this case, guide moments of large group discussions.

5 Discussion of the Results

The use of screen recording allowed the pre-service teacher to analyse what was said and done by the students, as well as how the teaching intervention helped them to overcome difficulties. This practice enabled an adaptation and search for improvements in the lesson planning and tasks, as well as in the differentiated instruction of the pre-service teacher [15].

The evidence presented corroborates Shu [33] findings, regarding the importance of the teacher being able to help students establish connections between mathematical concepts and the manipulation of applets. By creating conditions for differentiated instruction, with individual and collective moments, the learning environment allowed student's autonomous work and minimalist guided intervention of the pre-service teacher [15]. These settings fostered situations of self-regulation and co-regulation cognition, behaviour, motivation, and emotions by the students [27].

The design and implementation of the tasks [12], relating curricular contents with real situations, whose implications and relationships are known to the students [4], associated with the characteristics of the VM used [10, 30, 34], contributed to the motivation and involvement of the students in the tasks. These results are consistent with what Martins et al. [19] report in their study.

What is presented here refers to a study with a specific context regarding students and pre-service teacher. There was a predisposition of the pre-service teacher to seek an appropriate integration of technology in the teaching and learning processes.

Regardless of the teacher's technological knowledge [17], we consider it particularly important for future teachers to experience learning environments that promote an appropriate integration of technology [19, 21]. By doing so, initial teacher training can help future teachers to be more prone and proficient to use STEM teaching [20].

6 Conclusions

It is indisputable the importance of digital technologies in current education systems. Therefore, an appropriate integration of technology in teaching and learning processes is increasingly relevant. The STEM approach, in teaching contexts, allows students opportunities to express themselves creatively, allowing them to build transferable skills to other areas of knowledge.

As such, we believe to be important that initial teacher education includes the STEM approach in its curricula with theoretical and practical components. In this way, the pre-service teacher can participate and conduct teaching experiences, duly accompanied by competent experts, thus creating conditions for them to develop their professional teaching knowledge and become more prone to adopt STEM teaching practices.

In the specific context of this study, we sought to create a didactic sequence in which tasks were planned based on the conceptual model TPACK. This decision allowed designing a didactic sequence that started from the established curriculum, placing the student at the centre of learning, and adequately integrating technology in the teaching and learning processes. The integration of VM, considering its affordances and restrictions, using MMLE contributed to the creation of favourable conditions for self-regulation and co-regulation of students' learning related to elementary arithmetic operations. For this, it was important the pre-service teacher differentiated instruction, supporting the students' autonomous work with minimal teacher guidance, helping them to establish connections between mathematical concepts and the manipulation of the applets. These characteristics of the teaching performance were enhanced by pedagogical decisions in the tasks design. Grounded on a recursive principle of analysis of previous sessions for the preparation and reformulation of subsequent sessions, the pre-service teacher intervention helped students overcome obstacles and diminish shortcomings in their learning.

Regarding the students, we highlight the motivation and strong enthusiasm in the involvement of the tasks, fondness of the discovery process and sharing of solutions found for the challenges presented.

Acknowledgment. This work is funded by FCT/MCTES through national funds and when applicable co-funded EU funds under the project UIDB/50008/2020 and also financially supported by

National Funds through FCT – Fundação para a Ciência e a Tecnologia, I.P., under the project UID/CED/00194/2020.

References

1. Artigue, M.: Didactic engineering in mathematics education. In: Lerman, S. (ed.) Encyclopedia of Mathematics Education, pp. 202–206. Springer, Cham (2018)
2. Akaygun, S., Aslan-Tutak, F.: STEM images revealing stem conceptions of pre-service chemistry and mathematics teachers. Int. J. Educ. Math. Sci. Technol. **4**(1), 56–71 (2016). https://doi.org/10.18404/ijemst.44833
3. Baker, C.K., Galanti, T.M.: Integrating STEM in elementary classrooms using model-eliciting activities: responsive professional development for mathematics coaches and teachers. Int. J. STEM Educ. **4**(1), 1–15 (2017). https://doi.org/10.1186/s40594-017-0066-3
4. Blum, W.: Quality teaching of mathematical modelling: what do we know, what can we do? In: Cho, S.J. (ed.) The Proceedings of the 12th International Congress on Mathematical Education, pp. 73–96. Springer, Cham (2015). https://doi.org/10.1007/978-3-319-12688-3_9
5. Blum, W., Ferri, R.B.: Mathematical modelling: can it be taught and learnt? J. Math. Model. Appl. **1**(1), 45–58 (2009)
6. Bozkurt, A., Ucar, H., Durak, G., Idin, S.: The current state of the art in STEM research: a systematic review study. Cypriot J. Educ. Sci. **14**(3), 374–383 (2019). https://doi.org/10.18844/cjes.v14i3.3447
7. Confrey, J., Maloney, A.: A theory of mathematical modelling in technological settings. In: Blum, W., Galbraith, P.L., Henn, H.-W., Niss, M. (eds.) Modelling and Applications in Mathematics Education, pp. 57–68. Springer, Boston (2007). https://doi.org/10.1007/978-0-387-29822-1_4
8. Creswell, J.: Research Design: Qualitative, Quantitative, and Mixed Methods Approaches, 4th edn. Sage, Thousand Oaks (2014)
9. D'Ambrosio, U.: Mathematical modeling: cognitive, pedagogical, historical and political dimensions. J. Math. Model. Appl. **1**(1), 89–98 (2009)
10. Durmus, S., Karakirik, E.: Virtual manipulatives in mathematics education: a theoretical framework. Turkish Online J. Educ. Technol. **5**(1), 117–123 (2006)
11. English, L.D.: Advancing elementary and middle school STEM education. Int. J. Sci. Math. Educ. **15**(1), 5–24 (2017). https://doi.org/10.1007/s10763-017-9802-x
12. Ferri, R.: Learning How to Teach Mathematical Modeling – In School and Teacher Education. Springer, New York (2018)
13. Ferri, R.: Estabelecendo conexões com a vida real na prática da aula de Matemática. Educação e Matemática **110**(5), 19–25 (2010)
14. Gravemeijer, K., Stephan, M., Julie, C., Lin, F.-L., Ohtani, M.: What mathematics education may prepare students for the society of the future? Int. J. Sci. Math. Educ. **15**(1), 105–123 (2017). https://doi.org/10.1007/s10763-017-9814-6
15. Kaiser, G.: Mathematical modelling and applications in education. In: Lerman, S. (ed.) Encyclopedia of Mathematics Education, pp. 553–561. Springer, Cham (2020). https://doi.org/10.1007/978-3-030-15789-0_101
16. Kelley, T.R., Knowles, J.G.: A conceptual framework for integrated STEM education. Int. J. STEM Educ. **3**(1), 1–11 (2016). https://doi.org/10.1186/s40594-016-0046-z
17. Koehler, M., Mishra, P.: What is technological pedagogical content knowledge? Contemp. Issues Technol. Teach. Educ. **9**(1), 60–70 (2009)

18. Margot, K.C., Kettler, T.: Teachers' perception of STEM integration and education: a systematic literature review. Int. J. STEM Educ. **6**(1), 1–16 (2019). https://doi.org/10.1186/s40594-018-0151-2
19. Martins, N., Martins, F., Lopes, B., Cravino, J., Costa, C.: The use of applets in understanding fundamental mathematical concepts in initial teacher's training. In: Tsitouridou, M., Diniz, J.A., Mikropoulos, T.A. (eds.) Technology and Innovation in Learning, Teaching and Education: First International Conference, TECH-EDU 2018, pp. 307–318. Springer, Cham (2019). https://doi.org/10.1007/978-3-030-20954-4_23
20. McClure, E.R., et al.: STEM starts early: grounding science, technology, engineering, and math education in early childhood. The Joan Ganz Cooney Center at Sesame Workshop, New York (2017)
21. Milner-Bolotin, M.: Nurturing creativity in future mathematics teachers through embracing technology and failure. In: Freiman, V., Tassell, J.L. (eds.) Creativity and Technology in Mathematics Education. MEDE, vol. 10, pp. 251–278. Springer, Cham (2018). https://doi.org/10.1007/978-3-319-72381-5_10
22. Moyer-Packenham, P.S., Bolyard, J.J.: Revisiting the definition of a virtual manipulative. In: Moyer-Packenham, P.S.S. (ed.) International Perspectives on Teaching and Learning Mathematics with Virtual Manipulatives. MEDE, vol. 7, pp. 3–23. Springer, Cham (2016). https://doi.org/10.1007/978-3-319-32718-1_1
23. OECD: Education at a Glance 2019: OECD Indicators. OECD Publishing, Paris (2019). https://doi.org/10.1787/f8d7880d-en
24. Okita, S.Y.: Social components of technology and implications of social interactions on learning. In: Kuhl, et al. (eds.) Developing Minds in the Digital Age: Towards a Science of Learning for 21st Century Education, OECD Publishing, Paris (2019). https://doi.org/10.1787/78511afd-en
25. Pead, D., Ralph, B., Muller, E.: Uses of technologies in learning mathematics through modelling. In: Blum, W., Galbraith, P.L., Henn, H.-W., Niss, M. (eds.) Modelling and Applications in Mathematics Education, pp. 309–318. Springer, Boston (2007). https://doi.org/10.1007/978-0-387-29822-1_32
26. Pratas, R., Martins, F., Rato, V.: Modelação matemática como prática de sala de aula: o uso de manipulativos virtuais no desenvolvimento dos sentidos da adição. In: Canavarro, A., Borralho, A., Brocardo, J., Santos, L. (eds.) Atas do EIEM 2016, Encontro em Investigação em Educação Matemática, vol. 1, pp. 35–48. SPIEM, Évora (2016)
27. Räisänen, M., Postareff, L., Lindblom-Ylänne, S.: University students' self- and co-regulation of learning and processes of understanding: a personoriented approach. Learn. Individ. Differ. **47**, 281–288 (2016). https://doi.org/10.1016/j.lindif.2016.01.006
28. Rosa, M., Orey, D.C.: A modelagem como um ambiente de aprendizagem para a conversão do conhecimento matemático. Boletim de Educação Matemática, Bolema, pp. 261–290 (2012)
29. Ritz, J.M., Fan, S.-C.: STEM and technology education: international state-of-the-art. Int. J. Technol. Des. Educ. **25**(4), 429–451 (2014). https://doi.org/10.1007/s10798-014-9290-z
30. Shih, W.-C.: Enhancing virtual manipulatives for after-school tutoring in the subtraction unit. In: Gen, M., Kim, K.J., Huang, X., Hiroshi, Y. (eds.) Industrial Engineering, Management Science and Applications 2015. LNEE, vol. 349, pp. 439–449. Springer, Heidelberg (2015). https://doi.org/10.1007/978-3-662-47200-2_47
31. Silva, R.: Modelação matemática como ambiente de aprendizagem: o uso de manipulativos virtuais no desenvolvimento dos sentidos da adição e da subtração. Relatório Final de Mestrado em Ensino do 1.º CEB e de Matemática e Ciências Naturais no 2.º CEB, ESE do IPC (2018)
32. Silva, R., Martins, F., Rato, V., Raimundo, I.: TPACK: uma proposta de integração da tecnologia na aula de matemática. Exedra: Revista Científica (1), 167–181 (2019)

33. Suh, J.M.: Ambitious teaching: designing practice-based assignments for integrating virtual manipulatives into mathematics lessons. In: Moyer-Packenham, P.S.S. (ed.) International Perspectives on Teaching and Learning Mathematics with Virtual Manipulatives. MEDE, vol. 7, pp. 301–321. Springer, Cham (2016). https://doi.org/10.1007/978-3-319-32718-1_13
34. Suh, J., Moyer-Packenham, P.: How affordances and constraints of physical and virtual manipulatives support the development of procedural fluency and algorithmic thinking in mathematics. Int. J. Res. Math. Educ. **6**(2), 245–265 (2016)
35. Thibaut, L., et al.: Integrated STEM education: a systematic review of instructional practices in secondary education. Eur. J. STEM Educ. **3**(1), 02 F (2018). https://doi.org/10.20897/ejsteme/85525
36. Vygotsky, L.: Mind in Society: The Development of Higher Psychological Processes. Harvard University Press, Cambridge (1980)

BiblioLab Project: Teachers, Parents and Students' Perspectives About the Usability and Usefulness of an Educational Distance Learning Platform

J. Rocha[1,2(✉)], P. Pessoa[1,2], J. A. Gomes[3], X. Sá-Pinto[1], and B. Lopes[1,2]

[1] CIDTFF, Research Centre Didactics and Technology in the Education of Trainers, Aveiro, Portugal
blopes@utad.pt
[2] UTAD, University of Trás-os-Montes e Alto Douro, Vila Real, Portugal
[3] ESE-IPP, Polytechnic Institute of Porto - School of Education, Porto, Portugal
jam.gomes@netcabo.pt

Abstract. The dialogue between science education and literary education increases the interest of students and promotes the development of skills essential for the learning process. Despite its potential for fostering learning, this articulation - science and literature - is scarce in schools. In this context BiblioLab appears as a platform that intends to articulate these two areas of knowledge, fostering skills such as creativity, critical thinking, collaboration and communication. In this study we report the development of BiblioLab, a platform that offers Open Educational Resources (OER) developed through a design science research methodology to be used by teachers, parents and students. Students, parents and teachers were invited to use BiblioLab and to provide us feedback during the entire development process. Also, after exploring and completing one activity, teachers, parents and students were invited to complete a questionnaire and an interview. With this, we aim to understand how what we observed throughout this first phase of implementation supports the usability of the platform, and to detect the main difficulties and co-construct solutions to overcome these. Our results suggest that: students, teachers and parents have enjoyed using BiblioLab and consider that its platform and associated OER, achieve good levels of functionality and usability. The results also highlight the need to find additional solutions to foster autonomous and collaborative work in science and literary education (at distance) in primary schools.

Keywords: Educational platform · Open educational resources (OER) · Autonomy · Collaboration · Science education and literary education

1 Introduction

According to the National Research Council [1] and the Next Generation Science Standards [2] of the United States of America, science education should be meaningful to

A. Reis et al. (Eds.): TECH-EDU 2020, CCIS 1384, pp. 90–110, 2021.
https://doi.org/10.1007/978-3-030-73988-1_7

students so that they can learn scientific contents, engage in scientific practices, understand how scientific knowledge is developed and apply this knowledge in real situations. This process should begin as early as possible and throughout children's lives. In this context, literary education may provide a good opportunity for articulation, introducing topics close to students' reality, increasing interest and curiosity for sciences, promoting science content knowledge, autonomy, as well as reading, argumentative, and other skills and fostering discovery, exploration, cognition, emotion and imagination [3, 4]. [5] argues that literature stimulates observation and imagination in science classes. Considering that literature is a discourse in which different cultural discourses intersect (and this includes the scientific ones) and according to [6] literary education is essential as it helps students to develop skills for the analysis and interpretation of increasingly complex texts, to communicate literally and to write with literary intent.

Some studies also support the potential of this articulation, for promoting a sense of admiration and enthusiasm for science, for getting students involved in scientific tasks, ideally that promote epistemic practices which enable students to build knowledge with reference to Science and Technology practices in the context of their production [28], and in presenting solutions and ideas for action regarding problems that are proposed to them [3, 5, 7]. Despite this [8] suggests that it is difficult for teachers to articulate science and literary education in an educational context making these teaching dynamics scarce. This highlights the need to rethink the dynamics of interdisciplinarity and to improve it to strengthen students' learning outcomes.

There are also some positive effects in these interdisciplinary approaches that lead to the development and fast spread of approaches like STEAM (Science, Technology, Art, Engineering and Math) and more recently STREAM (Science, Technology, Reading, Art, Engineering and Math). These approaches are usually used with the purpose of engaging diverse students and developing their problem-solving skills and creativity, integrating science and arts and language-rich experiences [9, 10]. Moreover, these approaches usually lack clear learning goals for artistic education, prioritizing Science, Technology, Engineering and Math learning goals [10].

According to [11] and [12], the impacts of Covid-19 in the field of education highlighted the need to create OER to the entire educational community. [11] argue that to address teacher/students' isolation and keep students engaged, teachers should build their courses around OER. These can provide a range of innovative pedagogical options that allow both educators and learners, to become more participant in educational processes and creators of contents. [12] argue that OER are powerful tools because they provide content that can be downloaded and saved, or retained for later use, as well as adapted or remixed to better meet the needs of the global user. According to these authors, the content within the resource can also be customized and personalized to a classroom, allowing for greater cultural inclusivity than commercial materials. [13] says that the use of digital resources by students requires not only that they master the technology, but mainly a greater knowledge of contents involved in the task, as well as a number of advantages in terms of visualization, interaction, cognitive and sensory experiences. [14] also defend that the reconfiguration of the school is the inclusion of video-game objects as didactic resources in teaching practices, for the improvement of distance learning.

The BiblioLab project (https://bibliolab.pt) arose in the context of the social isolation imposed by Covid-19, and from the need for OER that could be used not only by teachers, but also by parents and students. The main objective of this platform of OER is to develop interdisciplinary didactic activities that articulate scientific education and literary education to be applied in elementary schools and that can be explored by students in a playful and autonomous way, promoting the development of literary and scientific skills.

In this context, we propose the following research question: *What is the perception of teachers, parents and students about: i) the usability and usefulness of the BiblioLab educational platform?; ii) its potential to foster autonomous learning?; iii) its potential to foster collaborative learning?; iv) the pleasure they get while exploring the BiblioLab OER?*

2 Research Methodology

2.1 Research Design

The methodology that best fits this research is design science research, which implies the contextualization of a problem, the creation of an artifact that will help to understand the problem and the execution of iteration cycles to fine-tune the problem and the artifact, which is reflected in theoretical enrichment [15]. This process is important because it allows us to reformulate the resource as the needs arise and based on the feedback we receive from the participants involved. According to the authors previously mentioned and as can be seen in Fig. 1, below, this methodology is useful to conceive an educational resource as an artifact and for this it is necessary first to identify the problem and its relevance. According to these authors it is also important to progress, through successive approaches, in the understanding of the problem, requiring at least two cycles executed to fine-tune the problem, the artifact to solve the problem that will lead to theoretical enrichment. So, we follow these phases and describe the BiblioLab platform development process in the following chapter.

2.2 Development of the Educational Resource

Once the didactic and pedagogical intention of the project was outlined, we began by researching what would be the necessary requirements for the BiblioLab platform to achieve its goals. [16] defends that artifacts and objects can be used as tools if they are used for a certain purpose. [17] argues that an artifact becomes in this case a tool and when it is used by users (students, teachers and parents) with a specific purpose: make available activities, as an OER, must fulfil an idealized level of functionality and usability, which fosters the articulation of literary education and science education, collaborative work, autonomous learning, and pleasure when using BiblioLab resources.

Therefore, we started designing a testable solution by creating activities for the 1st cycle of Portuguese basic education (from 6 to 10 years old) that would combine the teaching of science with the teaching of literature and by defining the structure for each activity constructed, based on the article in prep. by [18]. Hence, each activity was

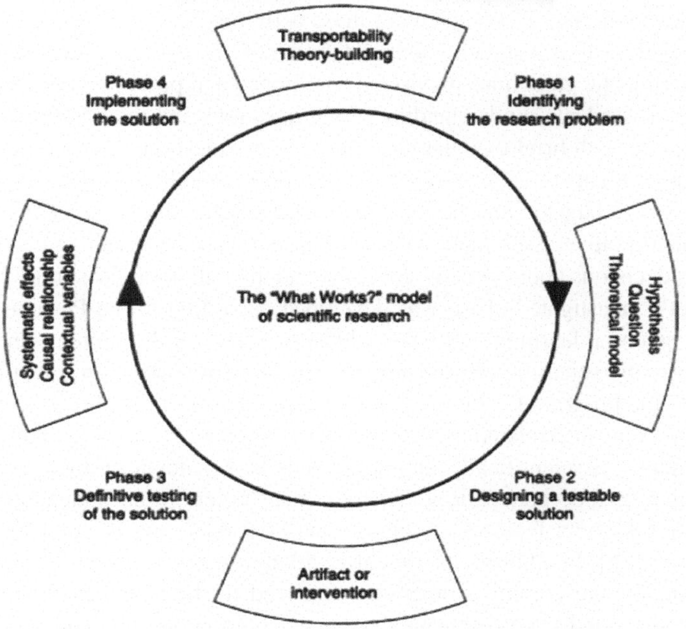

Fig. 1. Basic Model of Scientific Research in Education [13].

conceived according to three phases: "Let's read and understand", "Let's investigate" and "Let's create". This structure, based on [18], was based in the theoretical framework for art integration in science teaching of [8], where the link between science and art (literature) is made through an activity, and it was also based on the work already developed by some authors such as [3–5, 7] that rely on a quality literary book to explore a scientific topic, making the link between these two areas.

The "Let's read and understand" phase was developed according to the guidelines of the didactic materials elaborated in the National Program for the Teaching of Portuguese [19] and the essential learning for basic education of Directorate General of Education in Portugal [20]. The selected literary book must be in the Portuguese National Reading Plan (https://www.pnl2027.gov.pt/np4/home) or be written by an author that critics and literary history consider important. All the terms and literary contents presented in the activities are defined according to the e-dictionary of literary terms by [21]. Also the whole didactic structure is based on the principles of [22, 23] that highlight the importance of investing in a line of preparation for an appreciation of literature that can be valued and oriented in the sense of becoming a source of pleasure, with a double integrating character: learning to interpret and learn to value and appreciate the creations of the aesthetic literary sign. For example, in the case of our first activity "How does Jack's beanstalk grow?", as it is based on the narrative text "Jack and the beanstalk", we have established as a reading learning objective to develop specific skills of understanding narrative texts of folk tradition, where children can hear and read texts expressing ideas, feelings and points of view raised by the story worked. To achieve this, we proposed students to listen to an expressive reading of the tale, and then to train and record their own expressive reading. To complement these activities, we asked students to fill in a quiz with questions to test students' understanding of the text. All these questions were based on the didactic guidelines previously mentioned and presented constructive feedback to support students' understanding of the questions and the possibility to rethink their answers through brief explanations and guiding questions. According to [4], this strategy helps students to better analyse the questions, enabling them to understand the lessons and to recall the lessons they've learned. [24] argues that these surveys also serve as a form of formative assessment by providing the instructor with valuable feedback that informs decisions about content coverage and allocation of class time.

The "Let's investigate" phase was developed according to the Portuguese official guidelines "essential learning" for basic education [20]. All the contents and resources were supported by scientific and didactic theory and aim to develop scientific literacy. According to the Program for International Student Assessment (PISA), scientific literacy comprises four interrelated aspects: contexts, knowledge, skills and attitudes [25]. The performance of scientifically literate citizens is dependent on their knowledge of science, which include epistemic knowledge, that "refers to an understanding of the constructs and defining features of science and how these can be used to justify scientific claims" [26]. In addition [27] identify 5 key aspects of epistemic performance: "engaging in reliable cognitive processes that lead to the achievement of epistemic aims, adapting epistemic performance to diverse situations, metacognitively regulating and understanding epistemic performance, caring about and enjoying epistemic performance, and participating in epistemic performance together with others". Hence, this phase has been developed according to these theoretical constructs and aims to involve students in scientific, technological and ethical practices and discussions, designated in the literature as epistemic practices, which could be for example: describe phenomena, recognise phenomena in their context, represent physical phenomena, change empirical language into conceptual language and predict what happens based on conceptual knowledge [28].

The "Let's create" phase was developed in accordance with the official guidelines of "essential learning" for basic education [20] and the Program for Basic Education of Directorate General of Education in Portugal (DGE).

Therefore, at the end of each activity, we present a questionnaire with open and closed questions for students to answer and receive feedback on their answers with the aim of stimulating autonomy. In the stage "Let's investigate" we created a self and hetero evaluation grid for students to work in collaboration with their peers in order to develop their experimental plans more autonomously [29, 30], and we also suggested using the Slack platform which allows teachers to follow their students' work and facilitates communication, work sharing and feedback between students [31–33].

While we created and defined the activities structure and characteristics, we have been developing the BiblioLab platform. Initially, the platform was created using Webnode, a platform for creating and editing websites, and was organized in two sections: the activities section that intends to challenge teachers and students to develop activities that articulate literature and science in the most autonomous way possible and the reading suggestions section that intends to stimulate students to read literature, with the intention of stimulating the pleasure of reading. In this section we sometimes also present, associated with the reading suggestion, scientific, artistic and literary challenges to encourage children's creativity.

The next phase was to implement and test all the resources on their usability and feasibility, for the definitive testing of the solution. Teachers, students and parents' feedback was collected and used for the OER reformulation. However, after a few weeks, the initial platform was no longer able to respond to the public demands. The number of students, teachers and tutors/parents accessing the BiblioLab platform started to increase, exceeding the monthly traffic limit, and the available storage capacity for the creation of activities and other contents was close to the limit allowed by the free Webnode plan, no longer responding to the project's needs. For this reason, it became necessary to change and create a new platform, we needed to start using a Linux hosting and the WordPress content management system, to allow a greater influx of users and a greater storage capacity.

Regarding the implementation of the project in school, initially, two classes (33 students in total from the 3th and 4th grade) were invited to pilot BiblioLab, one in the context of regular activities and the other in the context of supplementary activities. "How does Jack's beanstalk grow?" activity was the first that became available in BiblioLab platform and which was piloted. We presented the activity divided in the three moments already mentioned. The first moment presented the following tasks: reading the story "How does Jack's beanstalk grow?", listening to the story, expressive reading of the story, sharing of the readings by the students and quiz with questions of interpretation of the story. The second moment challenged students to watch a video that encouraged them to reflect on a moment in history that helped them identify an investigable problem to be explored through an experimental activity. After that moment, we also presented one video that explained how to make experimental plans, observations and records and reach conclusions, and one video that explained how to give good suggestions of peer improvement. Students would then have to carry out the experimental plan divided into two parts (the first part where they identify the problem-issue, variables, records and observations, necessary materials, procedure and forecasts, and the second part where they record their observations and the data collected during the experiment and answer the problem-issue, also recording the conclusions they reached according to the data) and individually, then sharing it with a colleague to make good suggestions. To do this, we developed a grid of self and hetero-evaluation of the experimental plan to foster their learning autonomy [34]. The third and last moment of this activity, asked students to create a Comics recreating the "Jack and the beanstalk" story but integrating the results of the scientific activity developed in the previous moment. For that, we created a video providing guidelines on how to build a Comics strip story.

During the entire piloting phase, teachers, students and parents identified problems and proposed solutions that resulted in changes and modifications on this activity that are detailed in the results section.

After the piloting of the first activity, we started to develop the second proposal of activity, according to the same process and made it available on the platform. During this period a Facebook page, a Twitter account and a YouTube channel were created, as strategies and channels to promote the project's activities to the community and to give visibility to scientific and literary productions created by students and activities proposed by teachers. In addition, to further engage parents in the project we created a section entitled "family challenges" which aims to present suggestions for playful activities that articulate science and literature to be carried out with the family.

2.3 Assessment of Teachers', Parents' and Students' Perceptions

In order to assess students', teachers' and parents' perceptions regarding the BiblioLab platform, a questionnaire was developed. To ensure that only people who have participated in the activities or used the BiblioLab resources would answer the questionnaire, the first section of the questionnaire asks people: i) to identify what they are (students, teachers or parents), ii) if they have used BiblioLab or not, iii) in case they have used, what activities they have explored/completed and iv) in case they have not used, it asks them to identify the causes of the non-use. If they have used BiblioLab, the questionnaire continues, if they have not used it the questionnaire ends. The questions in the second section of this questionnaire were adapted and designed based on [35] to assess their perceptions regarding six topics that we aimed to appraise: platform functionality (refers to the accurateness of the functions), platform usability (refers to the perceived usability, questions adapted from [36]), perceived students' learning outcomes, perceived students' autonomy, group work opportunities and pleasure felt by the users while using the platform. The questions in the questionnaire were adapted to the person filling it (teachers, parents and students). The questionnaire includes items measured on a five-point Likert scale (1- 'strongly disagree' to 5- 'strongly agree' and 1- 'never' to 5- 'very frequently') and open-ended questions (see Appendix I) conducted with the intention of deepening users' ideas regarding the Bibliolab. The first question was to assess which of the activities had been worked on by the users. Next, we presented the following questions to the students: "What were the three most important things that you learned in BiblioLab?"; "What were the three things that you liked the most in BiblioLab?", "What were the three things that you liked the least about BiblioLab?", "What would you change in BiblioLab?", adapting them to parents and teachers.

After the questionnaire was developed, we contacted the teachers and asked them to answer it and to share it with their students and respective parents, for them also to complete it.

To complement the data collected, we conducted an interview with a teacher who used BiblioLab resources, but did not provide us feedback during the development stage. We also conducted an interview with four of the students from the piloting groups. Analysis categories have been constructed based on the answers floating reading to analyse the open-ended questions and interviews [37]. All the answers have been translated and are transcribed in Appendix II: https://bit.ly/3j3IffL.

3 Research Results

3.1 BiblioLab Platform

The BiblioLab platform presents activities and challenges that articulate science with literature. Nowadays, the platform menu contains nine pages:

1) **BiblioLab**, the home page of the site where we highlight the latest information added to the site;
2) **About**, where we describe the project, our mission and objectives;
3) **Activities**, with educational activities for students where the tasks are described and all the necessary documents and resources for the development of the activities are available;
4) **Reading Suggestions**, where literary works for childhood and youth with a certain emphasis of scientific nature are suggested with the intention of promoting reading habits and the pleasure of reading;
5) **Family Challenges**, that aims to present suggestions for playful activities to be carried out with the family. These activities present writing tasks with literary intention and/or activities that stimulate creativity, associated with scientific tasks;
6) **News,** where we present news related to the project objectives and the work of the BiblioLab team;
7) **Teachers**, where we present the advantages of exploring our activities and offer support to teachers that want to implement them;
8) **Team**, where we present the team members;
9) **Contacts**, where we provide our contacts and a contact form.

With regard to the OER developed we highlight the following: *i)* a set of two didactic videos to explain how an experimental science plan is prepared, where all the information that should be included in each field of the experiment plan and terms used in scientific practices are explained and where a possible filling in is exemplified by an example of a research question, *ii)* a set of two videos to explain how to give good suggestions to peers, where the feedback purposes, what aspects to take into account to give constructive feedback to a colleague, and two ways of proceeding to send feedback are explained, *iii)* one video with a Comics writing challenge, where the challenge is explained and questions are raised to trigger students' creativity in the Comics story creation, *iv)* one exploration guide for writing folk-like poems, where the necessary steps for writing folk-like poems are explained, such as planning, writing and reviewing, and *v)* one video that teaches children to observe, where the characteristics of a scientific method observation are explained and practical examples are given of how to observe, record and communicate them.

As a result of teachers', parents' and students' feedback the BiblioLab activities have been modified and adjusted as necessary. Here we will list the changes made in the first activity, "How does Jack's beanstalk grow?", as an example. During the development of the second activity, which is already available on the BiblioLab platform, we took into consideration all the suggestions and modifications applied in the first activity.

The first activity is organized in the three phases previously described in Sect. 2.2, but one of the teachers thought that the different tasks within each phase should be clearly enumerated and visually explicit so each phase is currently subdivided into enumerated tasks and marked with a distinctive visual element.

When it comes to open educational resources available in the platform, we have developed so far: a quiz about the story "Jack and the beanstalk" with questions of interpretation and reflection on the story; a didactic video, splitted into two parts, explaining how an experimental science plan is prepared; a video, splitted into two parts, that explains in a visual way how to give good suggestions to peers through the Slack channel; a video with a Comics writing challenge, an explanatory page with the terms and concepts of Comics and an exploration guide with guidelines for creating Comics. Until now we have shared two activities ("How does Jack's beanstalk grow?" and "Where do shadows live?"), twelve reading suggestions, one family challenge and six news. In this way, we also created an exploration guide for writing folk-like poems and a video with the scientific explanation for hot air balloons to fly. We also offer a video with an expressive reading of a poem about shadows, a challenge of reading in Google Forms with questions about this poem, the game "who is who of the shadows"; a video that encourages questioning about the shadows topic; a video that teaches children to observe and register sheets for observation, a video and an exploration guide that explains how to create dramatized poetry with shadows.

3.2 Teachers', Parents' and Students' Perceptions

Subsequent paragraphs, however, are indented. Through the questionnaire we collected the answers from 5 students, 2 teachers and 8 parents. In the interviews we collected answers from 4 students and 1 teacher. So, this gives a total of 9 students, 3 teachers and 8 parents. The results obtained in the questionnaire's Likert scale questions, designed to assess the students', teachers' and parents' perception of functionality, usability, learning, autonomy, development of group work and pleasure can be found in Appendix I. In the following Figs. (3, 4, 5, 6, 7 and 8) presented in the Appendix II) we select and present the results of each topic analysed. The answers to the questionnaire's open-ended questions and the interviews can be found in Appendix II: https://bit.ly/3j3IffL.

When we asked the students what were the three most important things they learned from the BiblioLab activities, they mentioned learning goals related to: plant ecology and reproduction ($n = 5$), write lines, dialogues or subtitles for Comics ($n = 3$), scientific practices ($n = 2$), Information and Communications Technology skills ($n = 2$), write little poems ($n = 2$), intraspecific biodiversity ($n = 1$), factors that influence the shadow of an object ($n = 1$), collaborative skills ($n = 1$), read and listen literary texts ($n = 1$) and dramatize literary texts ($n = 1$).

When we asked students, teachers and parents what they liked most in BiblioLab, we found the dimensions presented in Fig. 2.

When we asked students, teachers and parents what they liked the least about BiblioLab, three students, one teacher and the majority of parents ($n = 6$) said they have nothing to report. The remaining six students indicated: "That the white beans did not grow.", "The online classes; filling out questionnaires.", "I just didn't like so many questions about the tales…", "I didn't like the style of online classes because as I had done things before I wasn't doing anything…", "I liked almost everything. I was disappointed that plants withered when I went on holiday. The questions I wasn't sure about: reading quiz

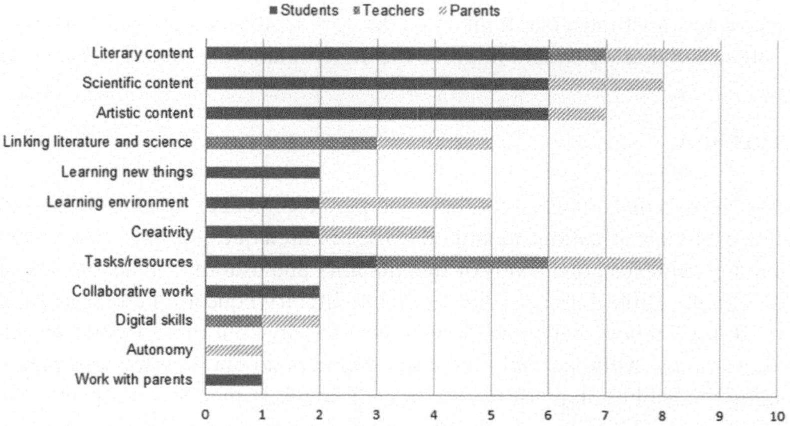

Fig. 2. Results obtained in the questionnaire open-ended questions and interviews about the three things that students (n = 9, 5 questionnaire students + 4 interview students), teachers (n = 3, 2 questionnaire teachers + 1 interview teacher) and parents (n = 8) liked most about BiblioLab; x-axis: number of users who indicated each dimension.

questions", and "Go to a platform that didn't work.". The two remaining parents indicated: "There could have been a better explanation of the process of seed germination.", and "Website organization.". The two remaining teachers wrote: "Disorganisation in the sending of answers by students; few online quizzes (to guide students in developing their experiments)." and "The work was conditioned by the situation of confinement precluding more direct monitoring of the students".

When we asked students, teachers and parents what they would change in BiblioLab, in the questionnaire two students indicated that BiblioLab should have more activities and challenges, one student suggested that we should have stories for each age, another preferred face-to-face classes and another student suggested making the videos available on Youtube Kids. In the interview, the students said: "Nothing. I like everything the way it is. I just would change the things in the texts on the site (for example, in the section activities) and put more emphasis on that (colour and images)", "I would put the videos on Youtube kids", "I like everything, I wouldn't change anything. But I would add a task: I would pose a challenge to all the people who use the BiblioLab for them to plant two trees!", and "I wish that in BiblioLab… I'd like to present a challenge, we could do it: we launched a theme and suggested different things on the site, we could make a game about what we're talking about, a file with game and final video saying what we learned. I'd like a BiblioLab question game about the theme of a story". Teachers suggested "To have questionnaire answers' bank/platform collecting system, i.e. each participant would download the forms and load the replies in their space on the platform. Trainers can access these documents.", "I think that the use of the literature proposed for Literary Education could be a way to attract teachers' attention.", and "I would suggest some activities with fewer steps for students to work autonomously and with less demand and mention the school grades to which each activity applies to". Two parents answered that they wouldn't change anything, two parents suggested that we should improve autonomy dimension, one that we should use more the new technologies, one that we should use a clearer message sometimes, one thinks that the peer feedback does not work very well and one suggested that we should improve the dissemination of the BiblioLab platform.

4 Discussion

Our results showed that students, teachers and parents consider that the BiblioLab platform achieves the specifications identified in the research question. More precisely, they consider that it achieves good levels of functionality and usability. Teachers and parents recognise that the BiblioLab activities articulate literary education and science education, and all users report that students were able to carry out the activities and use the proposed resources. Although only three interviewees do not mention any suggestions for changing the BiblioLab platform, six of the remaining mentioned aspects related to functionality and usability that are useful to further improve the platform.

Regarding the perceptions of students' autonomy, students showed the least positive result and teachers the most positive when we asked if students were able to carry out the tasks without help. However, when we asked teachers and parents how often they needed to help the students, teachers indicated "occasionally" and "very frequently" and the majority of parents indicated "occasionally". Several factors may be influencing these results, namely: i) the fact that students and teachers were not previously used to use these kinds of resources ii) the piloting stage of the OER that were explored which was later adjusted according to the feedback received; iii) the students' reduced digital skills, which teachers consider to be limited to watching videos or playing games [38, 39]. Nevertheless, the teachers agree that the students will be able to carry out the activities in a more autonomous way after the first experience. These results are in accordance to [40, 41] who state that, targeted self-learning materials are of great significance to promote students' autonomous learning, but acknowledge that, for these resources to be useful, they require an initial guidance by teachers or counselling agencies.

Perception of group work opportunities was the dimension that achieved the least positive results. In fact, most students, parents and teachers "neither disagree nor agree" with "students' group work in the BiblioLab activities" and a large percentage of parents responded "strongly disagree". These outcomes may result from the fact that we only proposed group work in the "let's investigate" phase, although it is the phase that occupied most of the students' time. Moreover, during the implementation of the activities, which took place at the Covid-19 social confinement, teachers and students reported difficulties in establishing connections with some elements of the groups (personal communication from the teachers piloting the activities). According to [42] considering the practice of social distancing in this new era, group working approaches, might just be modified or reduced, if not eliminated, from the options for teaching methods. However, the students who were interviewed showed that they enjoyed engaging in group work, supporting the importance of developing new strategies to foster group work in future activities, finding other solution than Slack [43] which teachers have decided not to use, and to make clear the advantages of its use in the tasks we propose.

Regarding the perception of pleasure felt by users while using the platform, the majority of students, teachers and parents "agree" and "strongly agree" with the statements related to this topic, such as "I enjoyed learning science from stories and poetry",

"It was fun to do the BiblioLab activities", and "The students enjoyed the BiblioLab activities". When we asked what aspects of the BiblioLab they liked most, we found several positive points as shown in Fig. 2. For example, students said: "make the bean experiment"; "make the Comics"; "work with peers in the computer" and "videos were cool". Parents said: "the articulation between contents"; "opportunity to make experiments" and teachers added: "the articulation of Science and Literature"; "enhance digital skills"; "quality of resources and videos". When we asked what aspects of the BiblioLab they least liked half of the twenty interviewees did not mention any aspect. The remaining answers, (Appendix II: https://bit.ly/3j3IffL), refer to issues related with the organisation of the site and of the group work, dissatisfaction with the outcome of the experimental work, the need for better student follow-up at some activity phases, the fact that monitoring has been conditioned by the social distancing state and the mandatory learning at a distance. All this information will serve to improve the BiblioLab platform.

All students identified what they had learned from BiblioLab activities and that they are able to ask new questions about the activities they have done. The majority of students also indicated that they can explain to a colleague what they had done. These results are in line with [44] findings, which demonstrate significant impacts on students' learning performance during distance learning, regarding computing, autonomous learning and critical thinking skills, and with [45] who consider OER to be widely regarded as a cost-effective option from which students take important benefits.

In the future, it is our intention to improve resources and activities according to the perspectives and opinions of teachers, parents and students. BiblioLab intends to carry out research on the resources created and on how to promote the training of teachers and teachers in training. In addition, we intend to expand the team in order to make it even more complete and diverse. This study also has its limitations: although we have complemented the data from the questionnaire with the interviews, we would like to have more answers to the questionnaire in the future. We also focus more on the activities and don't know how useful the different dimensions of the website were, so we intend to evaluate this in the future.

5 Conclusions/and Implications

We concluded that the BiblioLab platform achieves good levels of the idealized specifications, such as platform functionality, platform usability, students' learning outcomes, students' autonomy, group work opportunities and pleasure felt by the users while using the platform. However, some of these dimensions have reached lower levels, such as autonomy and group work, highlighting the need for the development of alternative strategies to improve these dimensions to achieve the desired goal. We highlight that the BiblioLab platform was considered functional and useful by parents, students and teachers, and also that all users enjoyed the activities and challenges presented, taking pleasure from the use they made of the platform.

In the future, the BiblioLab project intends to expand the team in order to make it engage people with skills complementary to those already available on the team, to co-construct the resources with teachers with the aim of improving the platform, broadening the range of resources available and adapting them better to the needs and challenges that arise from their users' experiences.

Acknowledgements. This work is financed by national funds through FCT – Fundação para a Ciência e a Tecnologia, I.P., under the doctoral scholarships: SFRH/BD/141159/2018 and 2020.05634.BD and in the scope of the framework contract foreseen in the numbers 4, 5 and 6 of the article 23, of the Decree-Law 57/2016, of August 29, changed by Law 57/2017, of July 19. This work was also financially supported by FCT under the project UID/CED/00194/2019.

Appendix I

Questions included in the students', teachers' and parents' questionnaires to assess each topic and the Likert scale questions results.

Topic	Interviewed	Questions	Answer				
			·SD *N	·D *R	·DA *O	·A*F	·SA *VF
Functionality	Teachers (n=2)	· The BiblioLab activities articulate literary education with science education.	0	0	0	2	0
	Parents (n=8)	· The BiblioLab activities articulate Portuguese Language teaching with Science.	0	0	2	4	2
Usability	Students (n=5)	· I was able to carry out the tasks that were proposed in the BiblioLab activities.	0	0	1	1	3
		· I was able to see the videos and use all the materials provided necessary to perform the tasks.	0	0	0	3	2
		§ What would you change in BiblioLab?					
	Teachers (n=2)	· The students were able to carry out all the tasks of the activity(ies) explored.	0	0	1	1	0
		§ What would you change in BiblioLab?					

	Parents (n=8)	· My child was able to accomplish all the tasks of the activity(ies) explored.	0	0	0	5	3
		§ What would you change in BiblioLab?					
Learning	Students (n=5)	· I learned new things from the videos and materials available.	0	0	0	1	4
		· I can explain to a colleague of mine what I have done in the tasks I have explored.	0	0	2	1	2
		· I can ask new questions about the activities I have done.	0	0	0	2	3
		§ What were the three most important things you learned from BiblioLab?					
Autonomy	Students (n=5)	· I was able to carry out the tasks without help.	0	1	2	1	1
	Teachers (n=2)	· The majority of students are able to carry out their tasks autonomously.	0	0	0	2	0
		· I believe that after the first experience, students will be able to carry out the activities in a more autonomous way.	0	0	0	2	0
		*I had to help my students during the development of the BiblioLab activities.	0	0	1	0	1

	Parents (n=8)	· My child carried out the tasks autonomously.	1	1	0	6	0
		*I had to help my child during the development of BiblioLab activities.	0	1	5	1	1
Group work	Students (n=5)	· I worked in groups with my classmates in the BiblioLab activities.	0	1	2	1	1
	Teachers (n=2)	· The BiblioLab activities promoted group work.	0	0	1	1	0
	Parents (n=8)	· My child did group work in the BiblioLab activities.	3	0	3	2	0
Pleasure	Students (n=5)	· I enjoyed learning science from stories and poetry.	0	1	0	0	4
		· It was fun to do the BiblioLab activities.	0	0	1	1	3
		§ What were the three things that you liked most about BiblioLab?					
		§ What were the three things you least liked about BiblioLab?					
	Teachers (n=2)	· The students enjoyed the BiblioLab activities.	0	0	0	1	1
		· I liked the activities proposed by BiblioLab.	0	0	0	0	2
		§ What were the three aspects that you liked most about BiblioLab?					
		§ What were the three aspects you least liked about BiblioLab?					

	Parents (n=8)	· My child enjoyed the BiblioLab activities.	0	0	0	3	5
		· I liked the activities proposed by BiblioLab.	0	0	0	5	3
		§ What were the three aspects that you liked most about BiblioLab?					
		§ What were the three aspects you least liked about BiblioLab?					

Legend: · - questions measured on a five-point Likert scale, where SD- strongly disagree, D- disagree, DA- neither disagree nor agree, A- agree and SA- strongly agree; * - questions measured on a five-point Likert scale, where N- never, R- rarely, O- occasionally, F- frequently and VF- very frequently; § - open-ended questions.

Appendix II

Results obtained in the Likert scale questions of each topic analysed: functionality perception, usability perception, learning perception, autonomy perception and group work perception.

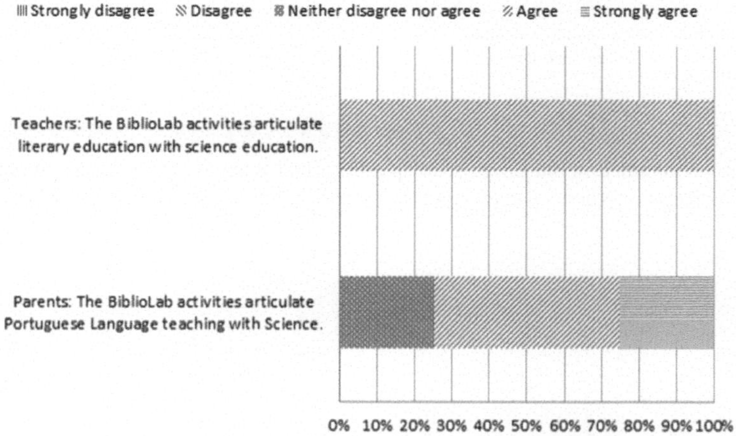

Fig. 3. Results obtained in the Likert scale questions that intend to evaluate the teachers' (n = 2) and parents' (n = 8) functionality perception; x-axis: percentage of people that choose each of the options in the Likert scale.

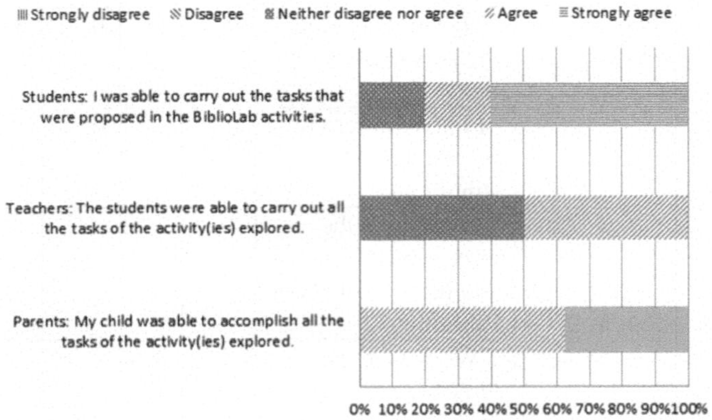

Fig. 4. Results obtained in the Likert scale questions that intend to evaluate the students' (n = 5), teachers' (n = 2) and parents' (n = 8) usability perception; x-axis: percentage of people that choose each of the options in the Likert scale.

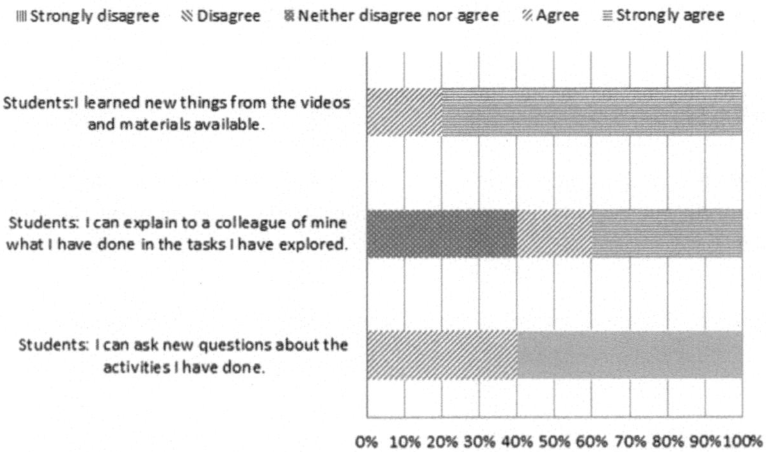

Fig. 5. Results obtained in the Likert scale questions that intend to evaluate the students' (n = 5) learning perception; x-axis: percentage of people that choose each of the options in the Likert scale.

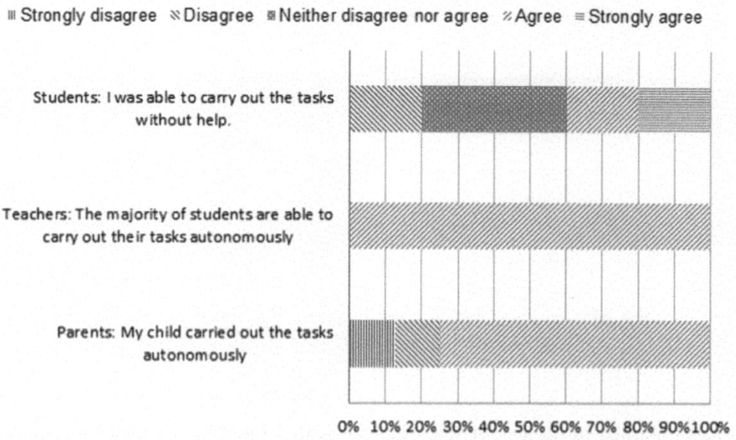

Fig. 6. Results obtained in the Likert scale questions that intend to evaluate the students' (n = 5), teachers' (n = 2) and parents' (n = 8) autonomy perception; x-axis: percentage of people that choose each of the options in the Likert scale.

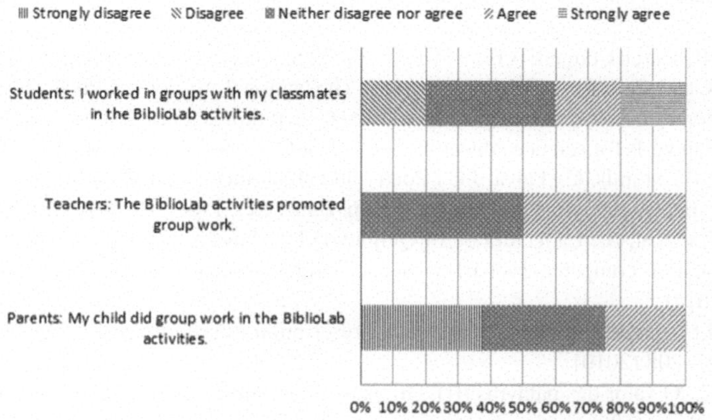

Fig. 7. Results obtained in the Likert scale questions that intend to evaluate the students' (n = 5), teachers' (n = 2) and parents' (n = 8) group work perception; x-axis: percentage of people that choose each of the options in the Likert scale.

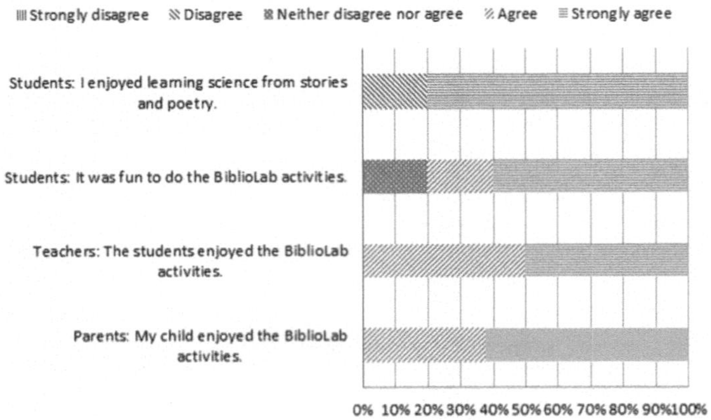

Fig. 8. Results obtained in the Likert scale questions that intend to evaluate the students' (n = 5), teachers' (n = 2) and parents' (n = 8) pleasure perception; x-axis: percentage of people that choose each of the options in the Likert scale.

References

1. National Research Council: A Framework for k-12 Science Education. Practices, Crosscutting Concepts, and Core Ideas. Washington, DC: The National Academies Press (2012)
2. Next Generation Science Standards: Final Next Generation Science Standards Released State-created standards for science education in the 21st Century. Washington, DC (2013)
3. Araújo, J.L., Morais, C., Paiva, J.C.: Poetry and alkali metals: building bridges to the study of atomic radius and ionization energy. Chem. Educ. Res. Pract. **16**, 1–10 (2015)
4. Franco-Mariscal, A.: La lectura de El Quijote de La Mancha como estratégia metodológica para trabajar las competencias básicas en educación secundaria. Perfiles Educativos **37**(148), 83–99 (2015)
5. Watts, M.: Science and poetry: passion v. prescription in school science? Int. J. Sci. Educ. **23**(2), 197–208 (2010)
6. Lomas, C.: O valor das palavras (II). Gramática, literatura e cultura de massas na aula. Asa Editores, Porto (2006)
7. Godínez-Sandí, A., et al.: Converging science and literature cultures: learning physics via The Little Prince novella. Phys. Educ. **53**(6), 065006 (2018). https://doi.org/10.1088/1361-6552/aad721
8. Turkka, J., Haatainen, O., Aksela, M.: Integrating art into science education: a survey of science teachers' practices. Int. J. Sci. Educ. **39**(10), 1403–1419 (2017)
9. Mayer, E.: Bilingual STREAM: Inquiry of Water through Science and Engineering. A thesis submitted in partial satisfaction of the requirements for the degree Masters. University of California, San Diego (2018)
10. Perignat, E., Katz-Buonincontro, J.: STEAM in practice and research: an integrative literature review. Think. Skills Creativity **31**, 31–43 (2019). https://doi.org/10.1016/j.tsc.2018.10.002
11. Huang, R., Tlili, A., Chang, T.-W., Zhang, X., Nascimbeni, F., Burgos, D.: Disrupted classes, undisrupted learning during COVID-19 outbreak in China: application of open educational practices and resources. Smart Learn. Environ. **7**(1), 1–15 (2020). https://doi.org/10.1186/s40561-020-00125-8
12. Allen, J., Katz, S.: Teaching with OER during pandemics and beyond. J. Multicultural Educ. 2053-535X (2020). https://doi.org/10.1108/JME-04-2020-0027

13. Lopes, J., Costa, C.: Digital resources in science, mathematics and technology teaching – how to convert them into tools to learn. In: Tsitouridou, M., Diniz, J., Mikropoulos, T.A. (eds.) TECH-EDU 2018. CCIS, vol. 993, pp. 243–255. Springer, Cham (2019). https://doi.org/10.1007/978-3-030-20954-4_18
14. Rodríguez, Gómez, Suelves, Rodríguez: Materiales didácticos digitales y coronavirus en tiempos de confinamiento en el contexto español. Práxis Educativa, vol. 15, e2015776, p. 1, 20 (2020)
15. Kelly, A., Lesh, R., Baek, J.: Handbook of Design Research Methods in Education Innovations in Science, Technology, Engineering and Mathematics Learning and Teaching. Routledge, Taylor & Francis, New York (2008)
16. Lopes, J.B.: Visual representation artifacts used as epistemic tools to improve the quality of mathematics and science teaching practices. Teaching Practices - Implementation, Challenges and Outcomes. Nova Science Publishers, New York (2019)
17. McDonald, G., Le, H., Higgins, J., Podmore, V.: Artifacts, tools, and classrooms. Mind Cult. Activity **12**(2), 113–127 (2005). https://doi.org/10.1207/s15327884mca1202_3
18. Rocha, J., Sá-Pinto, X., Lopes, J.: From stories to science: an exploration guide to promote epistemic practices in primary school (in prep.)
19. Buesco, H., et al.: Programa e metas curriculares de português do ensino básico. Ministério da Educação e Ciência. Portugal, Lisboa (2015)
20. Martins, G., et al.: Perfil dos Alunos à Saída da Escolaridade Obrigatória. Ministério da Educação/DGE, Lisboa (2017)
21. Ceia, C.: E-dicionário de termos literários (2018). https://edtl.fcsh.unl.pt/
22. Fillola, A., Valero, A., Lobo, I., Padrino, J., Garcia, R.: Literatura Infantil en la Escuela. Alicante: Universidad de Alicante (2000)
23. Compagnon, A.: Para que serve a literatura? Deriva, Porto (2010)
24. Anderson, J.: Frequent feedback through Google forms. Primus **29**(2), 124–137 (2019)
25. OECD: Draft PISA 2015 science framework. Paris: OECD (2013). https://www.oecd.org/pisa/pisaproducts/pisa2015draftframeworks.htm
26. Yang, F.Y., et al.: High-School students' epistemic knowledge of Science and its relation to learner factors in Science learning. Res. Sci. Educ. **48**(2), 325–344 (2018)
27. Barzilai, S., Chinn, C.A.: On the goals of epistemic education: promoting apt epistemic performance. J. Learn. Sci. **27**(3), 353–389 (2018)
28. Lopes, J.B., et al.: Instrumentos de Ajuda à Mediação do Professor Para Promover a Apredizagem dos Alunos e o Desenvolvimento Profissional dos Professores. Revista do Centro de Investigação e Inovação em Educação **2**(1), 125–171 (2012)
29. Goldin, I.M.: A focus on content: the use of rubrics in peer review to guide students and instructors (Doctoral dissertation, University of Pittsburgh) (2011)
30. Tasker, T.Q., Herrenkohl, L.R.: Using peer feedback to improve students' scientific inquiry. J. Sci. Teacher Educ. **27**(1), 35–59 (2016)
31. Moore, C., Teather, S.: Engaging students in peer review: feedback as learning. Issues Educ. Res. **23**(2) (2013)
32. Wang, W.: Students' perceptions of rubric-referenced peer feedback on EFL writing: a longitudinal inquiry. Assess. Writ. **19**, 80–96 (2014)
33. Brookhart, S.M.: How to give effective feedback to your students. ASCD (2017)
34. Bosch, J., Wilbert, J.: Contrast and assimilation effects on self-evaluation of performance and task interest in a sample of elementary school children. Front. Educ. **4**, 165 (2020). https://doi.org/10.3389/feduc
35. Restivo, M.T., et al.: Augmented reality in electrical fundamentals. Int. J. Online Biomed. Eng. **10**(6) (2014)
36. Lewis, J.R.: Measuring perceived usability: the CSUQ, SUS, and UMUX. Int. J. Hum. Comput. Interact. **34**(12), 1148–1156 (2018)

37. Bardin, L.: Análise de conteúdo [Content analysis]. Lisboa: Edicões 70 (2015)
38. Warih, M.P., Rindarjono, M.G., Nurhadi, N.: The impact of parental education levels on digital skills of students in urban sprawl impacted areas. JPhCS **1469**(1), 012071 (2020)
39. Heinz, J.: Digital skills and the influence of students' socio-economic background. An exploratory study in German elementary schools. Ital. J. Sociol. Educ. **8**(2) (2016)
40. Xie, Z., Yang, J.: Autonomous Learning of Elementary Students at Home during the COVID-19 Epidemic: A Case Study of the Second Elementary School in Daxie, Ningbo, Zhejiang Province, China (2020)
41. Xie, Z.: Effectiveness of autonomous learning materials for students during the COVID-19 pandemic: a case study of the Daxie Second Elementary School in Ningbo, Zhejiang China. Sci. Insight Educ. Front. **6**(1), 613–624 (2020)
42. Cahapay, M.B.: Rethinking education in the new normal post-COVID-19 era: a curriculum studies perspective. Aquademia **4**(2), ep20018 (2020)
43. Teckchandani, A.: Slack: A Unified Communications Platform to Improve Team Collaboration (2018)
44. Almanar, M.A.: The shifting of face to face learning to distance learning during the pandemic Covid-19. Globish: Engl.-Indonesian J. Engl. Educ. Cult. **9**(2), 111–118 (2020)
45. Eau, G., Judah, K., Shahid, H.: How can adaptive platforms improve student learning outcomes? A case study of open educational resources and adaptive learning platforms. A Case Study of Open Educational Resources and Adaptive Learning Platforms (October 30, 2019) (2019)

Doing Math with Music - Instrumental Orchestration

Ana Silva[1](✉), J. Bernardino Lopes[2,3], and Cecília Costa[2,3]

[1] Escola Secundária Celorico de Basto, Braga, Portugal
[2] UTAD, Universidade de Trás-os-Montes e Alto Douro, Vila Real, Portugal
{blopes,mcosta}@utad.pt
[3] CIDTFF – Centro de Investigação em Didática e Tecnologia na Formação de Formadores, Aveiro, Portugal

Abstract. The use of artefacts by mathematics teachers in their classroom while teaching practices can play an important role in the quality of teaching. The selection of these artefacts depends on the type of intervention carried out in an educational context and on the mathematical concepts to be worked on. The aim of this study is to understand how artefacts are orchestrated when interventions are made where math is done with music, as well as to understand how these artefacts become epistemic tools for students. Therefore, a case study was developed, with a class of the 7th grade, during an academic year, covering the areas of mathematics: numbers and operations; algebra and functions. The results suggest that it is possible to do mathematics with music, using artefacts orchestrated among themselves. They also suggest that the orchestrated artefacts allow to create a context in which the student's learning is active, where the artefact has the status of an epistemic tool.

Keywords: Mathematics · Music · Artefacts · Technologies

1 Introduction

The current context is shaping the future of education. This includes adopting new tools and requiring new approaches to education to meet the needs of students and society. Nowadays and henceforward students need to acquire competence through self-regulated learning to face the uncertain and changing world [1].

The present study emphasizes the value of creativity and learning based on the arts, more specifically in music, articulating artefacts, in an educational context, in the teaching of mathematics. The future of innovative thinking in STEM subjects depends on breaking the distinction between subjects traditionally seen as "creative", such as the arts or music, and STEM ones traditionally seen as rigid or logical-mathematical [2].

2 State of the Art

2.1 Mathematics and Music

Since the first civilizations, mathematics and music have been linked. This relationship between knowledges was evidenced, for the first time, by Pythagoras (6th century BC).

A. Reis et al. (Eds.): TECH-EDU 2020, CCIS 1384, pp. 111–123, 2021.
https://doi.org/10.1007/978-3-030-73988-1_8

Pythagoras created an artefact, the monochord, and established relationships between the length of the extended string and the sound emitted when played. This artefact enabled to relate musical intervals and introduce the concept of fractions. Two thousand years after Pythagoras, great mathematicians and musicians appeared: Marin Mersenne, Descartes, Fermat and Napier. Everyone contributed intensively to the musical understanding, but it was Mersenne who left a valuable legacy in his work "Harmonie Universelle", dated 1636.

Several studies refer to the benefits of music in students' mathematical learning [3–8].

Turkka, Haatainen and Aksela refer, from the examples they analysed, that the integration of art in the classroom does not include the expression of emotions often associated with art. They add that teacher training should provide activities that allow critical assessment and reflection on the emotions of students and teachers. The integration of art should address the role of emotions more explicitly rather than waiting for it to happen naturally [9].

Investigations that privilege the potential of music for the purpose of teaching mathematics still emerge. For example, Quinn et al. dedicated themselves to the study of transformations of trigonometric functions in secondary education [10]. Wilhelmi and Montiel extend this type of experience to future teachers, during their initial training [11]. Mannone mentions the importance of this type of approach, emphasizing the aesthetic pleasure that can be obtained in the sciences seen as more "creative", and therefore can help students find motivation to face difficulties that may arise during the study of sciences traditionally seen as more rigid [12].

According to Edelson and Johnson, teachers can use music to improve children's pleasure and understanding of difficult maths concepts and skills. Children need learning experiences, in meaningful contexts, to develop thinking and problem-solving skills. The idea of a pattern is powerful and is not only essential for mathematics and music, it also cuts across all other curriculum areas [13].

Considering the mathematical-music relationship, classroom experiences and activities have increased significantly in recent years. It is already possible to find web spaces where teachers and researchers publish and share different experiences, such as the European Music Portfolio.

In this context, "doing maths" by students is an approach to mathematics with an attitude that is both playful and serious, with a focus on working on the edge of knowledge, "breaking maths" and making mistakes as a crucial aspect of doing maths [14].

2.2 Technologies in an Educational Context

Emerging technologies, such as touchscreen tablets, are bringing sensorimotor interaction back to mathematical learning activities, promoting the discovery of mathematical concepts through electronic manipulators [15]. There has been a growing interest in how to theorize mathematics learning when digital technologies are involved. Researchers were initially interested in comparative studies - do students learn better with digital technologies than without it? - there was a shift towards trying to understand how digital technologies were implicated in learning and what they changed about mathematics and how it was learned [16].

An example of integration of the arts, using technologies, was presented by Quinn et al., using the shape of sound waves to help students explore the relationship between period and frequency. We highlight the use of guiding tasks provided to students in order to generate a touch for a smartphone, thus combining music, mathematics and technology [10].

Teaching mathematics and computer concepts, including coding, music and art was presented by Shamir, using an effective learning tool to teach maths and computer science concepts, using the creative learning environment Scratch 2.0. According to the author, there was a significant improvement of students in mathematics (and also in computer science), as well as an increase in students' interest in STEM classes [17].

2.3 Artefacts and Epistemic Tools

Lopes and Costa consider that an artefact is an entity or product of human creation. As the authors refer, a piece of wood is not an artefact, it is an object. However it can be used as a hammer, becoming a tool. Likewise, when an artefact is used to solve a problem, it becomes a tool. On one hand, the use of an artefact must have a purpose which gives it the status of a tool. On the other hand, its use in the classroom can allow the creation of a context in which the student's learning is active, and thus, the artefact has the status of an epistemic tool [18].

When it is intended that students are able, for example, to identify in music a mathematical object, the role of artefacts becomes central. Let us use the example of a piano. The purpose of a piano can be different: learn to play, give concerts, use as a decorative object. The piano itself does not teach mathematics. But the piano can be seen as an artefact that makes it possible to recognize a mathematical object in music. The way in which this piano is used, using a task (another artefact) requires that it is created and equipped with a set of characteristics that enable to convert music into a mathematical object. Furthermore, it is necessary to convert this recognition into mathematical knowledge (using another task - another artefact). The articulation of this set of artefacts (piano and tasks) must be done in a careful way (through a guide - another artefact) to ensure that the student has made the learning and has managed to solve the various challenges that are proposed [18]. The professor appears as an artefact orchestrator.

It is known that the use of artefacts by mathematics teachers in their teaching practices in the classroom can play an important role in the quality of teaching. Although teachers use them, they do not make the most of their use, even if they know how to work with these artefacts easily [19].

The use of artefacts in the classroom enriches the form of communication between the teacher and the student. According to Lerman, from the point of view of cultural, discursive psychology, students are provided with mathematical language, meanings, connections, strategies, artefacts such as diagrams, graphs, physical artefacts (rulers, calculators). Students are able to "read", with the help of teachers and colleagues, thus collecting tools with which they think and speak mathematically. The child is not expected to structure itself mathematically. Learning mathematics at school is nothing more than initiation into the practice of school mathematics, hence the central role of the initiator, the teacher. While you are learning maths or learning to think mathematically, you are learning to speak mathematically. The classroom should provide a context, an activity, a power and knowledge to the student so that he is oriented to communicate and act. On one hand, the use of artefacts incorporated in mathematics teaching activity should aim at the student's active participation in the construction of his knowledge, leading him to reflect on the action being carried out. On the other hand, it encourages teachers to create their own artefacts, articulating mathematics with other areas of knowledge, contributing significantly to their professional development [20].

According to Lopes, the use of artefacts in classrooms by teachers can promote students' learning in three different ways: (i) in a "superficial way", without making use of their potential; (ii) making use of the potential of the artefact; (iii) making use of the artefact as an epistemic tool for thinking and learning. The author stresses that the quality of learning increases as artefacts become epistemic tools. That is, the use of artefacts as tools in mathematics teaching practices can improve the quality of teachers' teaching practices. This happens whenever they are used as tools [19].

In order to understand when an artefact is used as an epistemic tool, the following three criteria are applied: autonomous work, making conversions and learning mathematics [18, 21, 22].

2.4 Instrumental Orchestration

Learning mathematics with and through technology is not evident and requires a process of instrumental genesis, that is, the subtle processes of appropriation of digital tools for the teaching of mathematics [23]. Instrumental genesis is a psychological construction that describes the process of how an artefact becomes an instrument, illuminates the ways in which technological tools support the learning of mathematics. Teachers have vital roles in creating appropriate tasks, helping students to make connections between their work with the artefact and the mathematics they are learning [24].

Guin and Trouche define an instrumental orchestration as an action plan, participating in a didactic exploration system that an institution (the school institution, in this case) is organized with the objective of guiding students in instrumented action. Instrumented orchestration is defined by four components: a set of individuals; a set of objectives (related to the accomplishment of a type of task or the organization of a work environment); a didactic configuration (that is, a general structure of the action plan); a set of exploration of this configuration [25]. This same definition of Instrumental Orchestration is used by other authors [23, 26].

The availability of technology in the maths classroom challenges teachers to orchestrate students learning [27].

2.5 Research Question

With this study we intend to answer the following research question: what characteristics should have the artefact orchestration that allows students to use them as epistemic tool to do mathematics with music?

3 Interventions in an Educational Context

3.1 Study Design

Based on a case study, the goal of this study is to understand how artefacts are used in interventions in an educational context, which enable to do mathematics with music, that is, to understand what characteristics these artefacts have and how they are articulated with each other, like they are outlined in Fig. 1.

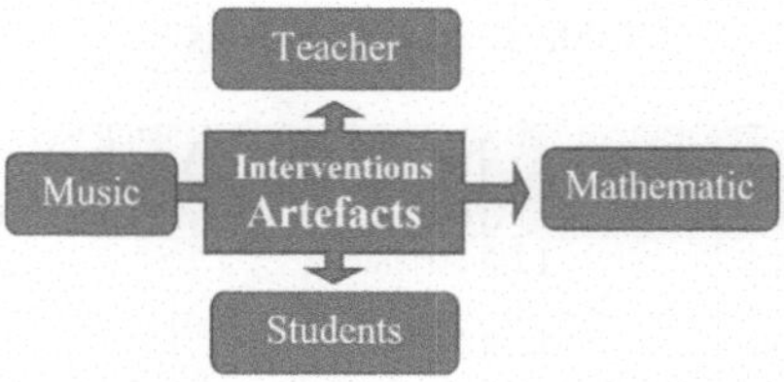

Fig. 1. General scheme of interventions.

Classroom interventions follow the scheme in Fig. 2. Artefacts were created, with well-defined goals. In a first step, artefacts are used in order to allow the student to be able to identify the mathematical object (Math.Obj) in the music. In a second step, the artefact must allow mathematical learning (Math.Lear), starting from the mathematical object previously identified, through a scientific approach, using reason and logical knowledge. In the chosen approach, conditions are created for students to do mathematics, with music as their object. The artefacts constructed (and combined with others already existing) cover the following areas of mathematics: numbers and operations; algebra and functions. Therefore, methodologically Design Science Research was used.

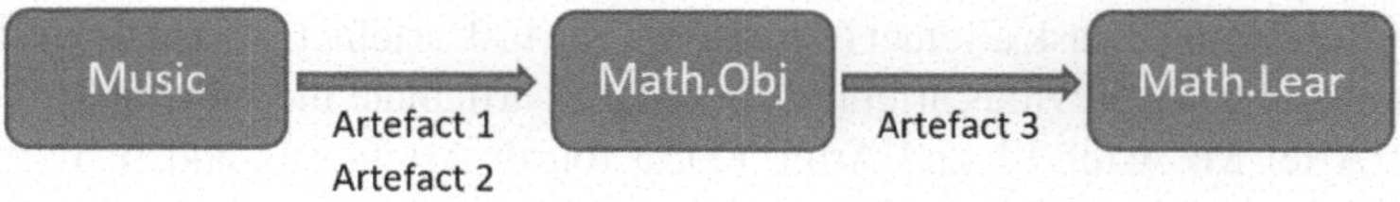

Fig. 2. Scheme that operationalizes the way of doing mathematics with music.

The interventions were made during an academic year, in a class attending the 7th year of schooling, in a basic and secondary school, in the northern region of Portugal. Interventions were carried out within the scope of the aforementioned approach: doing mathematics with music, using articulated artefacts.

It is important to mention that "know how to read music" is not a necessary condition, for the various interventions to occur with benefit to students. The artefacts, in the various interventions, include a way to solve this musical gap that students may demonstrate.

3.2 Interventions in an Educational Context

Over the course of an academic year, three interventions took place, each focusing on a mathematical theme. In each one, different artefacts were articulated: intervention artefacts and reserve artefacts. Intervention artefacts are a set of constructed/selected artefacts for a particular intervention. The reserve artefacts are a set of resource ones and are used if necessary, replacing some intervention artefact. Each intervention has a set of artefacts indexed to it, as summarized in Table 1.

Table 1. Set of artefacts.

	Intervention Artefacts			
	Artef-M	**Artef-T1**	**Artef-T2**	**RO**
Intervention I	Digital Piano (mobile application)	Task-Artefact "As Pombinhas da Catrina"	Task-Artefact "Melodia das Dízimas"	Guide n.° 1
Intervention II	Digital Piano (mobile application)	Task-Artefact "Transformando uma música – Parte A"	Task-Artefact "Transformando uma música – Parte B"	Guide n.° 2
Intervention III	Digital Piano (mobile application)	Task-Artefact "Completando a partitura de uma música"	Task-Artefact "Resolvendo Equações"	Guide n.° 3
	Reserve Artefacts (**Artef-R**)			
	Recorded Audios (various interventions) Smartphone + Speaker (Sound Link Mini – Bose)			

The first intervention addressed the issue of Numbers and Operations: rational numbers; decimal expansion; repeating decimal and irrational numbers. The second intervention addressed the theme of Functions: correspondences; function definition; domain and codomain of a function; objects and images. The third intervention addressed the theme of Equations: notion of equation; solution of an equation; solving linear equations.

Each intervention always starts with music. It is here where the intended mathematical object is identified. Generally, two artefacts are used simultaneously: a musical artefact (Artef-M) and a task artefact (Artef-T1). The task artefact (Artef-T2) follows the context created by the previous artefacts. In order to articulate the previously described Artefacts (Artef-M, Artef-T1 and Artef-T2), a fourth Artefact is added: Exploratory Guide (RO).

The Exploratory Guide consists of three parts: before class, during class and after class. The one before class includes: target audience; duration; necessary content and material. One of the necessary materials is Artef-M - digital piano, which will be installed, in a first phase, on the student's mobile phone or tablet. The during class phase includes the five steps of the classroom intervention. The after-class phase includes the analyses to be carried out on the work developed.

As an example, Intervention III is presented in detail, which addresses the theme of equations: notion of equation; solution of an equation; solving linear equations. Focusing on this intervention during the class, the first step is to present to the students, in a global way, the intervention that is intended to be done, the goals of the same and the way it will work. Subsequently, in a second step, the Artef-T1 is distributed: "Completando a partitura de uma música" (see Table 1), letting students explore the challenges with the application on their mobile phone, manipulating the Artef-M: Digital piano (mobile application). If students are not familiar with the melodies of the songs presented, the audios can be used, using the reserve Artefacts (Artef-R), guiding students if they show difficulties (see Table 1). The third step consists on interacting with students, reflecting on the proposed challenges, exploring the concept of equation, in a holistic way - identification of the mathematical object. The presentation of Artef-T2 follows: "Resolvendo Equações" (see Table 1), where mathematical equation is defined, unknown and solution of an equation. In the fourth step, students are presented with the mathematical challenges presented in Artef-T2. At the end, a synthesis/conclusion is made with the students, remembering how the mathematical object was identified in the music, as well as the mathematical learning was achieved later. It ends by inviting students to play the songs proposed in the initial challenges (fifth step).

3.3 Data Collection

During the three interventions, in a total of 6 classes, audio records, photographic records of moments of the class, records on the blackboard and copies of the students' notebooks were made. The complete Multimodal Narration (NM) of these classes was proceeded with. This instrument was used to organize the data collected from teaching practice according to the protocol presented by Lopes et al. [28]. It facilitates the research work, since it brings together in a single document the various aspects that can be observed in the classroom.

3.4 Data Analysis

In order to analyse how the artefacts were orchestrated, the time dimension was privileged [26] and the didactical performance dimension in terms of how artefacts interconnect [27]. Analysing the NM, the time intervals used by each artefact in each intervention were identified. After identification, they were organized in the form of a timeline, in order to allow the articulation between the various artefacts to be seen during the classes of the three interventions.

In order to organize the evidence that allows us to verify when students use artefacts as an epistemic tool, criteria were defined to know whether artefacts are being used with epistemic tools [18, 21, 22] and subsequently identified throughout the interventions, comparing the results obtained by the students in each challenge/task.

The following criteria/indicators were defined based on [18, 21, 22]:

C1.1 - Students solve the challenge/task autonomously.
C1.2 - Students solve the challenge/task with some autonomy.
C1.3 - Students do not solve the challenge/task with autonomy.
C2 - Students show conversion of representations, that is, students move from a musical representation to a mathematical representation (there is identification of the mathematical object).
C3 - Students show conversions between mathematical languages (natural; symbolic; algebraic; graphic).
C4 - Students show mathematical learning.
C5 - Students demonstrate mathematical learning beyond the concepts that were the objective of the intervention.

4 Results

Table 2 and Fig. 3 show results that show how the teacher orchestrates the different artefacts in each intervention and from intervention to intervention. In Fig. 3, these results are presented schematically, using a timeline of the different artefacts used in the three interventions. The percentage of time used by each artefact by intervention was calculated (see Table 2).

Table 2. Percentage of use of the artefact by intervention

	Artefacts				
	RO	Artef-M	Artef-T1	Artef-R	Artef-T2
Intervention I	100%	42,1%	35,5%	---	56,3%
Intervention II	100%	30,2%	67,2%	28,8%	30,1%
Intervention III	100%	29,0%	54,8%	0,4%	40,2%

It is observed that the guide (RO) accompany the whole of the classes, as they have the function of articulating with each other the other artefacts present, by intervention.

The musical artefacts (Artef-M) and the reserve artefacts (Artef-R) are articulated with each other and with the task artefact: Artef-T1. The task artefacts (Artef-T1 and Artef-T2) never coincide during the interventions. However, the articulation between artefacts is not made only when artefacts coexist in time. This articulation comes from the fact that Artef-T2 is based on Artef-T1, using its results.

Table 3 shows results that allow to identify when students use artefact as an epistemic tool. The challenges/tasks worked on are presented for each intervention. Also presented are the artefacts used by challenge/task, as well as the criteria/indicators identified in the resolution of that challenge/task.

The students present in almost the majority of the challenges/tasks some degree of self-nomination, except for the last challenge of the third intervention. In all interventions there is a conversion of representations, from musical to mathematics or between mathematical languages, as well as mathematical learning. In one of the interventions there are mathematical learnings in addition to those initially foreseen (challenge 3, from intervention III), corresponding to criteria C5. It is also possible to observe that in interventions I and II there are challenges/tasks that correspond simultaneously to criteria C2 and C4, that is, there is identification of the mathematical object in music and this identification translates into mathematical learning. These cases correspond all with situations identified also with the criteria C1.2 (students who reveal some autonomy). In intervention III, criteria C2 and C4 do not occur simultaneously. In this intervention, criteria C1.1 predominates, the self suggests that this intervention provides a greater level of autonomy to students. Criteria C3 and C4 occur, in all interventions, only in the challenges where Artf-T2 is present.

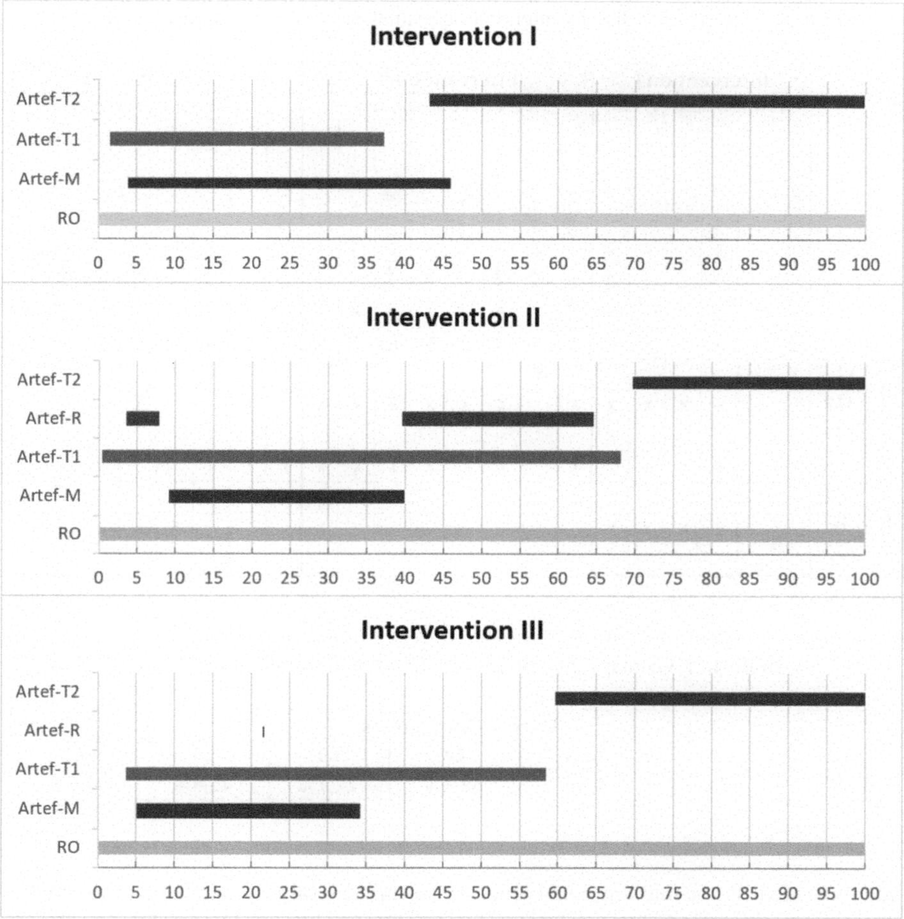

Fig. 3. Temporal scheme of the different artefacts used in the three interventions (scale in % of the total time of each intervention).

Looking at Table 4, it can be seen that, as far as autonomy is concerned, it has a greater expression in criteria C1.2 (63.6%), that is, students reveal some autonomy in solving the challenges/tasks in opposition 31.8% of criteria C1.1, where students reveal full autonomy. Overall, 95.4% of the challenges/tasks, the students presented resolutions with autonomy, in contrast to the 4.5% (corresponding to a challenge) in which the students were limited to "receiving" the information from the teacher (criteria C1.3).

Analysing Table 5 and Fig. 3 together, it seems that mathematical learning occurs with a certain degree of student autonomy (doing mathematics), when artefacts are used as epistemic instruments. In general, these moments are preceded by the use of artefacts as epistemic tools, although with a more modest degree of sophistication. Now these periods of mathematical learning are preceded (Intervention II) or preceded and concomitant with the use of musical artefacts or their reserve (Intervention I and III). In other words, the orchestration that is done around musical artefact becomes central for

Table 3. Criteria identified by intervention to analyse how each artefact was used.

		Intervention I						Intervention II								Intervention III							
		Artefacts by Challenge / Task						Artefacts by Challenge / Task								Artefacts by Challenge / Task							
		Ro; Artef-M; Artef-T1	Ro; Artef-M; Artef-T1	Ro; Artef-M; Artef-T2	Ro; Artef-T2	Ro; Artef-T2	Ro; Artef-T2	Ro; Artef-R; Artef-T1	Ro; Artef-M; Artef-T1	Ro; Artef-M; Artef-R; Artef-T1	Ro; Artef-R; Artef-T1	Ro; Artef-R; Artef-T1	Ro; Artef-R; Artef-T1	Ro; Artef-T2	Ro; Artef-T2	Ro; Artef-M; Artef-T1	Ro; Artef-M; Artef-R; Artef-T1	Ro; Artef-T1	Ro; Artef-T2	Ro; Artef-T2	Ro; Artef-T2	Ro; Artef-T2	Ro; Artef-T2
		1	2	3	4	5	6	1	2	3	4	5	6	7	8	1	2	3	4	5	6	7	8
Criteria / Indicators	*C1.1*	X	X						X							X		X	X		X		
	C1.2			X	X	X	X	X		X	X	X	X	X	X		X			X		X	
	C1.3																						X
	C2			X	X	X		X		X	X	X	X	X	X	X	X	X					
	C3			X	X									X							X	X	
	C4			X	X	X	X							X	X				X	X	X	X	
	C5																	X					

Table 4. Percentage, by criteria, identified in the total interventions.

Criteria/Indicators						
C1.1	C1.2	C1.3	C2	C3	C4	C5
31,8%	63,6%	4,5%	59,1%	22,7%	45,4%	4,5%

students to identify the mathematical object (criteria C2 – Table 3) and learn mathematics with a certain degree of autonomy with it.

Table 5. Use of artefacts with epistemic tool and their relationship with mathematical learning

	Intervention I						Intervention II								Intervention III							
	Artefacts by Challenge / Task						Artefacts by Challenge / Task								Artefacts by Challenge / Task							
	Ro; Artef-M; Artef-T1	Ro; Artef-M; Artef-T1	Ro; Artef-M; Artef-T2	Ro; Artef-T2	Ro; Artef-T2	Ro; Artef-T2	Ro; Artef-R; Artef-T1	Ro; Artef-M; Artef-T1	Ro; Artef-M; Artef-R; Artef-T1	Ro; Artef-R; Artef-T1	Ro; Artef-R; Artef-T1	Ro; Artef-R; Artef-T1	Ro; Artef-T2	Ro; Artef-T2	Ro; Artef-M; Artef-T1	Ro; Artef-M; Artef-R; Artef-T1	Ro; Artef-T1	Ro; Artef-T2	Ro; Artef-T2	Ro; Artef-T2	Ro; Artef-T2	Ro; Artef-T2
	1	2	3	4	5	6	1	2	3	4	5	6	7	8	1	2	3	4	5	6	7	8
Epistemic Tool (high grade)			X	X	X								X	X			X			X	X	
Epistemic Tool (low grade)						X	X		X	X	X	X			X	X		X	X			
Mathematical learning																						

The analysis of Table 3 shows that the three criteria for an artefact to be used as an epistemic tool (autonomy, conversion of representations and learning) occur simultaneously or with the presence of two criteria as shown in Table 5.

5 Discussion

The orchestration of artefacts allows students to use them as an epistemic tool, doing math with music. The instrumental orchestration used has the following main characteristics:

- The existence of an artefact that articulates all others - the exploratory guide - throughout each intervention.
- The musical artefact (Artef-M) must be easily manipulated and used individually;
- The task artefacts (Artef-T1) used must make it possible to transform enjoyed music into a mathematical object;
- The task artefacts (Artef-T2) used must allow that the mathematical object identified in the music, transform into mathematical knowledge. The task artefact (Artef-T2) must follows the context created by the previous task artefact (Artef-T1).
- Students must solve the challenging task with autonomy.

The manipulation of technological artefacts - mobile phone and the application with the digital piano, promoted the discovery of mathematical concepts, taking advantage of the sensorimotor interaction in the proposed challenges/tasks, as defended by Botza-kis [15].

The use of artefacts allowed to create a context in which the student's learning was active, and thus, the artefact started to have the status of an epistemic tool, that is, it was used as a tool for thinking and learning, which according with Lopes increases the quality of learning [19].

It is also known that a certain orchestration of the artefacts used in mathematics classes has positive effects on learning [25]. However, the main contribution of this study was to show that it is possible for students to do mathematics from music, as long as the artefacts made available to students are used as epistemic tools and for that it is necessary to have an orchestration of artefacts in two dimensions: articulation between artefacts throughout the intervention and articulation between artefacts at a given stage of the intervention.

6 Conclusion

The use of artefacts, in an educational context, promotes mathematical learning from music as long as the teacher orchestrates the artefacts that in the first phase allow students to use them as epistemic tools even in a modest degree and in a second phase it allows to work the mathematical object using the artefacts as epistemic tools in a higher degree, in particular making conversions between types of mathematical languages.

The students presented autonomy in solving the vast majority of the proposed challenges/tasks, thus transforming the artefacts involved in these challenges/tasks into epistemic tools. To make it possible, the instrumental orchestration among the artefacts need to have the following traces: (i) a musical artefact easily manipulated by each student, (ii) a task artefact to transform enjoyed music into a mathematical object, (iii) a task artefact allowing that the mathematical object identified in the music, can be transformed into mathematical knowledge.

The teaching approach presented does not have as a necessary condition the obligation of students and teachers to have musical knowledge, which covers this approach of the universal application characteristic.

References

1. Hernandez-de-Menendez, M., Escobar Díaz, C., Morales-Menendez, R.: Technologies for the future of learning: state of the art. Int. J. Interact. Des. Manuf. (IJIDeM) **14**(2), 683–695 (2019). https://doi.org/10.1007/s12008-019-00640-0
2. Henriksen, D.: Full STEAM ahead: creativity in excellent STEM teaching practices. STEAM J. **1**(2), 15 (2014)
3. Hodges, D.A.: Why study music? Int. J. Music Educ. **23**(2), 111–115 (2005)
4. An, S.A., Kulm, G.O., Ma, T.: The effects of a music composition activity on Chinese students' attitudes and beliefs towards mathematics: an exploratory study. J. Math. Educ. **1**(1), 91–108 (2008)
5. Viladot, L., et al.: The integration of music and mathematics education in Catalonia and England: perspectives on theory and practice. Music Educ. Res. **20**(1), 71–82 (2018)
6. Chao-Fernández, R., Román-García, S., Chao-Fernández, A.: Art, science and magic: music and math the classroom. In Proceedings of the 5th International Conference on Technological Ecosystems for Enhancing Multiculturality, p. 77. ACM (2017)
7. Gardiner, M.F., Fox, A., Knowles, F., Jeffrey, D.: Learning improved by arts training. Nature **381**, 284 (1996)
8. Graziano, A.B., Peterson, M., Shaw, G.L.: Enhanced learning of proportional math through music training and spatial-temporal training. Neurol. Res. **21**(2), 139–152 (1999)
9. Turkka, J., Haatainen, O., Aksela, M.: Integrating art into science education: a survey of science teachers' practices. Int. J. Sci. Educ. **39**(10), 1403–1419 (2017)
10. Quinn, C.M., et al.: Music as math waves: Exploring trigonometry through sound. J. Math. Arts **13**(1–2), 173–184 (2019). https://doi.org/10.1080/17513472.2018.1552822
11. Wilhelmi, M.R., Montiel, M.: Integrated music and math projects in secondary education. In: Montiel, M., Gomez-Martin, F., Agustín-Aquino, O.A. (eds.) MCM 2019. LNCS (LNAI), vol. 11502, pp. 390–393. Springer, Cham (2019). https://doi.org/10.1007/978-3-030-21392-3_35
12. Mannone, M.: Have fun with math and music! In: Montiel, M., Gomez-Martin, F., Agustín-Aquino, O.A. (eds.) MCM 2019. LNCS (LNAI), vol. 11502, pp. 379–382. Springer, Cham (2019). https://doi.org/10.1007/978-3-030-21392-3_33
13. Edelson, R.J., Johnson, G.: Music makes math meaningful. Child. Educ. **80**(2), 65–70 (2003)
14. Mun, R.U., Hertzog, N.B.: Teaching and learning in STEM enrichment spaces: from doing math to thinking mathematically. Roeper Rev. **40**(2), 121–129 (2018)
15. Botzakis, S.: Websites and apps for teaching and learning mathematics. J. Adolesc. Adult Lit. **5**(60), 597–600 (2017)
16. Sinclair, N.: Generations of research on new technologies in mathematics education. Teach. Math. Appl. Int. J. IMA **33**(3), 166–178 (2014)
17. Shamir, M., Kocherovsky, M., Chung, C.: A paradigm for teaching math and computer science concepts in k-12 learning environment by integrating coding, animation, dance, music and art. In: 2019 IEEE Integrated STEM Education Conference (ISEC), pp. 62–68. IEEE, March 2019

18. Lopes, J.B., Costa, C.: Digital resources in science, mathematics and technology teaching – how to convert them into tools to learn. In: Tsitouridou, M., A. Diniz, J., Mikropoulos, T.A. (eds.) TECH-EDU 2018. CCIS, vol. 993, pp. 243–255. Springer, Cham (2019). https://doi.org/10.1007/978-3-030-20954-4_18
19. Lopes, J.B.: Visual representation artefacts used as epistemic tools to improve the quality of mathematics and science teaching practices. In: Vogler, B. (ed.) Teaching Practices - Implementation, Challenges and Outcomes, pp. 45–74. Nova Science Publishers, New York (2019). ISBN 9781536159011
20. Lerman, S.: Cultural, discursive psychology: a sociocultural approach to studying the teaching and learning of mathematics. Educ. Stud. Math. **46**(1–3), 87–113 (2001). https://doi.org/10.1023/A:1014031004832
21. Sterelny, K.: Externalism, epistemic artefacts and the extended mind. In: Schantz, R. (ed.) The Externalist Challenge, vol. 2, pp. 239–254. Walter de Gruyter, Berlin (2004)
22. Miller, E., Manz, E., Russ, R., Stroupe, D., Berland, L.: Addressing the epistemic elephant in the room: epistemic agency and the next generation science standards. J. Res. Sci. Teach. **55**(7), 1053–1075 (2018)
23. Drijvers, P., Grauwin, S., Trouche, L.: When bibliometrics met mathematics education research: the case of instrumental orchestration. ZDM **52**(7), 1455–1469 (2020). https://doi.org/10.1007/s11858-020-01169-3
24. Hollebrands, K., Okumuş, S.: Secondary mathematics teachers' instrumental integration in technology-rich geometry classrooms. J. Math. Behav. **49**, 82–94 (2018)
25. Guin, D., Trouche, L.: Mastering by the teacher of the instrumental genesis in CAS environments: necessity of instrumental orchestrations. ZDM **34**(5), 204–211 (2002). https://doi.org/10.1007/BF02655823
26. Tabach, M.: A mathematics teacher's practice in a technological environment: a case study analysis using two complementary theories. Technol. Knowl. Learn. **16**(3), 247–265 (2011). https://doi.org/10.1007/s10758-011-9186-x
27. Drijvers, P., Doorman, M., Boon, P., Reed, H., Gravemeijer, K.: The teacher and the tool: instrumental orchestrations in the technology-rich mathematics classroom. Educ. Stud. Math. **75**(2), 213–234 (2010). https://doi.org/10.1007/s10649-010-9254-5
28. Lopes, J.B., et al.: Constructing and using multimodal narratives to research in science education: contributions based on practical classroom. Res. Sci. Educ. **44**(3), 415–438 (2014). https://doi.org/10.1007/s11165-013-9381-y

Digital Tools Entering the Scene in STEM Activities for Physics Teaching

Carla Morais[1], Luciano Moreira[2(✉)], Mónica Baptista[3], and Iva Martins[3]

[1] CIQUP, Unidade de Ensino das Ciências, Departamento de Química e Bioquímica, Faculdade de Ciências, Universidade do Porto, Rua do Campo Alegre, 4169-007 Porto, Portugal

[2] CIQUP, Departamento de Engenharia Informática, Faculdade de Engenharia, Universidade do Porto, Rua Dr. Roberto Frias, 4200-465 Porto, Portugal
lucianomoreira@fe.up.pt

[3] Instituto de Educação da Universidade de Lisboa, Alameda da Universidade, 1649-013 Lisbon, Portugal

Abstract. This paper focuses on the problematic role of digital tools in STEM activities for Physics teaching. A group of 47 teachers of Physics and Chemistry, from middle and secondary education, attended a continuous professional development training course during the academic year 2019/2020 that aimed to promote the development, adaptation, and implementation of STEM activities, centered on various topics in Physics (sound, electricity, kinetic and potential energy, mass and weight, gravitational pendulum and free fall) in teachers' practices. Most of the activities already had an integration proposal for digital tools. Results revealed that teachers' options range from adding specific and unspecific tools to implement STEM activities. In most cases, they only replace other non-digital tools. This work contributes to foster the action and reflection related to teachers' knowledge and experience to introduce digital tools productively, amplify their options, and explore other related areas.

Keywords: STEM · Physic teaching · Digital tools

1 The STEM Horizon

1.1 he Decline of the Occidental Genius

Along with the economic, technological, and scientific development, societies are confronted with new demands in a global and competitive world. Despite the growing influence of science and technology in every realm of human activity, occidental, economically developed societies do not seem to be capable of attracting young generations to pursue careers in such areas.

Given this scenario, several reports and programs were developed, particularly since the '80s, to assess and fulfill human capital needs in science, technology, engineering, and mathematics [e.g., 1, 2, 3]. A line of proposals was embodied, in the '90s, in the creation of the acronym STEM (Science-Technology-Engineering-Mathematics), initially SMET, by the National Science Foundation (NSF) [4]. Since then, STEM Education is

A. Reis et al. (Eds.): TECH-EDU 2020, CCIS 1384, pp. 124–137, 2021.
https://doi.org/10.1007/978-3-030-73988-1_9

unquestionably related to the need to captivate students and future professionals for these scientific areas. Several studies aim to understand the influence of STEM programs on students' interest, motivation, and attitudes towards these scientific areas [5–7]. These investigations point to several benefits and effects on motivation and students' choice for STEM careers.

Moreover, learning by using the STEM approach provides learners training to integrate each STEM acronym component at once. That learning process will shape the knowledge of the subject more understandably. In physics learning, STEM allows learners to use technology and assemble an experiment based on engineering aspects that can prove a law or science concept considering mathematic formulations. "The physics learning [...] using the STEM approach effectively improves students' learning competencies includes knowledge, attitudes, and skills" [8].

1.2 On the Dawn of a New Day – Digital Tools as a Panacea or a Poison

When one thinks of technology, it is hardly a pen or a book that comes to mind. Technology is now intimately connected with digital media, and, after a process of industrialization, society seems to go through a digitalization process. Schools and education are included. However, the way digital tools integrate education practices is far from being a straightforward process.

Against the promise of a world of benefits, opportunities, and profound change, the coming of age of digital media is asking for a reflection on the roots and wings of how we educate younger generations rather than offering a ready-made solution for its challenges [9, 10].

STEM only makes the challenge of integrating digital media in education more acute. Simó et al. [11] ask the right questions: what opportunities do digital tools give to STEM education, and what opportunities does STEM education give to digital education?

Acting on four fronts (Science, Technology, Engineering, and Mathematics), STEM strategies need to find focus and balance. By finding focus, we refer to the need to specify if digital tools are being used as a means or as an end. Contrary to other educational technologies, such as the pencil, that have become specific, stable, and transparent, digital technologies are protean, unstable, and opaque [12]. Therefore, digital literacy, or the capacity to cope with digital technologies, need to be taught [13]. Digital literacy can be developed in other educational experiences, but it might – and sometimes need – to be an end of its own right. However, it seems that as digital media becomes transparent – now in Jenkins et al. [14] sense and not in Mishra and Koehler [12] – educators want to use it merely as a means to address other contents. Thus, often, digital media connection with each of the four fronts of STEM is overlooked. With rare exceptions, both teachers and students use software and machines without understanding its components and functioning: they become transparent because they are used without awareness [14] and simultaneously opaque because they are like black boxes for the users [12].

By balance, we mean that after realizing how digital tools are being used in a STEM strategy – either as a means or as an end – it is necessary to find the right dosage to connect with the different fronts. Besides, the integration of digital media onto pedagogical tasks activates a set of representations and stereotypes –gender-related and content-related – that are still far from being mapped. The salience of its connection with each of the STEM areas might vary. Whereas the connection to Engineering and Technology might be obvious, its link to mathematics and science might be less visible. It is a pharmacological question in Stiegler's [15] sense. The dosage and manner of usage might intoxicate or heal. To give but a simple example, the Higher Education panorama in Engineering or Science areas in Portugal shows a severe gender gap and distortion despite the programs' relatively good capacity of attraction [16].

In this paper, we explore the problematic role of digital tools in the STEM project, primarily focused on Physics.

2 Methods

2.1 Context of the Study

This study is part of the research project GoSTEM [17], which aims to assess the impact of a STEM approach on students' motivation to learn science, their interest in STEM careers, and their learning. During the program, the project team developed together with teachers of Physics and Chemistry STEM activities focused on various Physics topics (sound, electricity, kinetic and potential energy, mass and weight, gravitational pendulum, and free fall) using technologies.

The work with the teachers took place during the academic year 2019/2020, in the first edition of the training program. The program took place at the Instituto de Educação da Universidade de Lisboa and the Faculdade de Ciências da Universidade do Porto, lasting 50 h. This training program intended to train teachers for the development, adaptation, and implementation of STEM activities in their teaching practice to promote the teaching of Physics. In its initial planning, the training program would occur between January and July of 2020 but, due to the global pandemic by Covid-19, the face to face sessions were interrupted in the middle of March. This situation affected the training program and teachers' practice at schools, and a distance learning regime was adopted.

2.2 Participants

Participants in this study were a group of 47 teachers of Physics and Chemistry of Middle and Secondary Education (43 females and four males), with the following ages: four with ages between 30–39 years old, 20 with ages between 40–49 years old, 21 with ages between 50–59 years old and 2 with 60 or more years old. These teachers belong to school clusters in the Lisbon and Porto region and participated in the training program described in the previous section.

2.3 STEM Activities' Description

STEM activities were aligned with the national curricula (8th to 12th grades) and were developed according to the framework proposed by Thibaut et al. [18] regarding instructional practices in STEM education. The proposed model is aligned with the social constructivist learning theory and contemplates five fundamental principles: 1) integration of STEM content, that requires the "explicit assimilation of learning goals, content and practices from different STEM disciplines" [18]; 2) problem-centered learning, that involves students in authentic, real-world problems; 3) inquiry-based learning, that engages students in the different processes that enable them to solve the initial problem, to learn new concepts and to develop new skills; 4) design-based learning, related to engineering design processes and practices, with the implementation of hands-on design challenges, that allows students to deepen their knowledge about core ideas; and 5) cooperative learning that promotes teamwork and communication.

A brief description of the activities, and integration of digital tools, is presented in Table 1.

Table 1. Description of STEM activities and suggestions for digital tools integration.

Activity (grade)	Students' tasks	Digital tools
Mass and Weight – Reverse Engineering (7th)	*Objectives* - Understand how a simple analogic scale works - Understand the difference between mass and weight - Build an innovating scale *Students' tasks* - Draw up a scheme of the components and operation of a simple analogic scale - Disassemble the balance, observe, analyze, and explain how it works - Plan and execute an experiment to answer the question: "What does a scale measure?" - Plan and build an innovative scale	No suggestion

(continued)

Table 1. *(continued)*

Activity (grade)	Students' tasks	Digital tools
Sound (8th)	*Objectives* - Measure the sound level at various locations in the school - Organize an awareness campaign on excessive noise - Build a soundproofed school radio studio model *Students' tasks* - Construction of a school noise map based on exemplary noise maps of the locality (Portuguese Environment Agency): plan the measurements to be carried out - Use of a sound meter app - Gather information on the impact of noise on human health and organize an awareness campaign - Build a model of the school's radio studio, justifying the materials used (acoustic comfort and cost-benefit) - Build a robot for measuring the noise level (optional)	Mobile Apps: · *Science Journal App* · *Phyphox App*
Electricity – Reverse Engineering (9th)	*Objectives* - Assemble simple electrical circuits - Identify conductive and insulating materials - Perform measures (U and I) in simple electrical circuits *Students' tasks* Describe how a mystery box (without opening the box) worked in a Reverse Engineering approach - Build a mystery box, similar to the one presented, but with an innovative modification - Plan an activity to answer the question: "What are the materials that conduct electric current?" Simulate the electrical circuit assembly: measurements with ammeter and voltmeter and identify the electric current's real and conventional direction	· Online simulator (PhET): *Circuit Construction Kit: DC* [19]

(continued)

Table 1. (*continued*)

Activity (grade)	Students' tasks	Digital tools
The Race of Rubber Band Cars-E(lastic) Formula (9th)	*Objectives* - Understand energy transformations (elastic potential energy and kinetic energy) *Students' tasks* - Construct a rubber car prototype (inspired by Formula E(lastic) competitions, which take place at several universities) that moves in a straight line for at least 3 m (selection and justification of the materials to be used) - Test the prototypes and measure their average speed by utilizing the Science Journal Google App, which works as a photogate - Construction of a poster that explains the stages of construction of the prototype	· Utilization of mobile App: *Science Journal App*
Free Fall (11th)	*Objectives* - Construction of equipment that allows determining the value of gravity acceleration with 97% accuracy *Students' tasks* - Conduct research to demonstrate that all athletes reach the water with the same acceleration (contextual inspiration in the news about the Red Bull Cliff Diving World Series competition) Plan and build equipment that allows the determination of gravity acceleration's value with 97% accuracy - Use the equipment to collect the data required to determine the value of the gravitational acceleration - Identify error sources and ways to overcome them - Make a video on the process steps and publish it online	· Internet to conduct the research · Use of a video editor and a publishing platform

(*continued*)

Table 1. (*continued*)

Activity (grade)	Students' tasks	Digital tools
Gravitational Pendulum (12th)	*Objectives* - Determine the mathematic expression for the period of a gravitational pendulum - Construction of a gravitational pendulum *Students' tasks* Reflect on the variables that influence the gravity pendulum (inspired by the historical context of the pendulum's utilization as an instrument for measuring time) - Plan and construct a pendulum to test the variables previously indicated - Use of an online simulator (PhET) to study the influence of gravity acceleration in the pendulum period - Deduct the expression for the period of the pendulum - Conduct experiments with pendulums located in different latitudes, using the e-lab remote laboratory	· Online simulator (PhET): *Pendulum Lab* [20] · Remote laboratory: e-lab [21]

The teachers selected the STEM activities proposed according to the school year they were teaching and the syllabus they were going to teach. At the end of the training program, the participant teachers elaborated a final reflection, in the form of a written report, describing and reflecting on how the implementation of the activities with their students took place. It should be noted that the process of implementing these activities was, in some cases, interrupted by the suspension of classroom activities due to the Covid-19 pandemic.

2.4 Data Collection and Analysis

Data were collected from the reflections written by the teachers at the end of the STEM program. The analysis of the written reports was carried out to ascertain the number of teachers who implemented the activities in the classroom, in a face to face modality, or through the distance learning regime and, within this last group, whether the selected activities already suggested the specific integration of some digital tools. Additionally, the content analysis of the reports was directed to find out how many teachers interacted with the digital tools, distinguishing those who use these digital tools as proposed in the STEM activity and those who integrated the digital tools modified by them. Suggestions for modifications regarding the integration of digital tools in STEM activities were also subject to analysis.

3 Results

To know how many teachers used activities with digital tools, a list of the selected and implemented activities, with the indication of the frequency in each case, is presented in Table 2. As we referred before, the STEM activities selection took into account the school year and the syllabus that the teachers would teach. It should be noted that three teachers chose to implement more than one activity.

The Sound activity was the most chosen (16) and implemented (11) by the teachers, followed by the activity The Race of Rubber Band Cars- E(lastic) Formula (12 teachers selected and of these nine implemented). The Electricity - Reverse Engineering activity was chosen by 11 teachers and implemented by seven; Mass and Weight activity was selected by six teachers selected and implemented by five; the Gravitational Pendulum was selected and implemented by four; and, finally, the Free Fall activity was selected by two teachers but was not implemented in any of the cases. The Mass and Weight activity was the only one in which digital tools' integration was not suggested. In the remaining activities, digital tools were suggested as: i) auxiliary means of data collection, as is the case of the activities of Sound and The Race of Rubber Band Cars- E(lastic) Formula; ii) a way of simulating physical phenomena by manipulating variables in the simulated system, as is the case with the Gravitational Pendulum and Electricity - Reverse Engineering activities; iii) assistants in organizing and communicating the results obtained, as in the case of the Free Fall activity.

In total, 51 activities were selected; 36 were implemented either directly in the classroom or using distance classes. Table 2 also indicates actions of implementing STEM activities by teachers related to integrating digital tools, defining three categories of analysis. In the implementation of the activity without introducing changes in digital tools, we observe 26 occurrences. In this category, it is noteworthy that the activity The Race of Rubber Band Cars, Formula E(lastic) (8), followed by the activity of Sound (6), and Mass and Weight (5) were the ones that registered the least changes for the teachers. If we analyze the following category results regarding changes in how digital tools should be integrated, there are 11 occurrences in total. It is precisely the Sound activity that has undergone the most significant number of changes (7). Besides the ones initially suggested in the activity, the addition of other digital tools occurred only once and took place in the case of The Race of Rubber Band Cars- E(lastic) Formula activity. Concerning suggestions for changes related to the digital tools, there were 12 suggestions, eight from teachers who implemented STEM activities, and four from teachers who did not have the opportunity to implement the activity but still, in a prospective and grounded manner in their experience, provide suggestions for future optimization. The suggestions presented aimed at all activities except the Gravitational Pendulum activity. The activities with the highest record of suggestions were the activities of the Race of Rubber Band Cars, E(lastic) Formula (4), Sound and Electricity - Reverse Engineering (each with three suggestions).

In order to understand what did the teachers change in their activities in what concerns digital tools, the following categories of analysis were used: i) implementation of STEM activities with changes in the integration of digital tools; ii) implementation of STEM activities with additions in the integration of digital tools; and iii) suggestions for the

Table 2. Presence of digital tools (DT), frequency of selection (S), and implementation (I) of STEM activities; actions to implement the activities: no changes (NC), changes (C), additions (A), and suggestions.

STEM activities				Implementation and integration			Suggestions	
Designation	DT	S	I	NC	C	A	S	I
Sound	Yes	16	11	6	7	-	3	-
The Race of Rubber Band Cars, E(lastic) Formula	Yes	12	9	8	2	1	1	3
Electricity – Reverse Engineering	Yes	11	7	4	1	–	2	1
Mass and Weight –Reverse Engineering)	No	6	5	5	–	–	1	–
Gravitational Pendulum	Yes	4	4	3	1	–	–	–
Free Fall	Yes	2	–	–	–	–	1	–

integration of digital tools in STEM activities. Excerpts from the teachers' records are encoded as follows: Px (teacher), m/f (sex), P/L (city).

3.1 Implementation of STEM Activities with Modifications in the Integration of Digital Tools

The main changes introduced by the teachers are related to the way of recording, organizing, and disseminating results, using for this purpose non-specialized digital tools for the area of Physics, such as PowerPoint.

> "Students were asked to organize the collected data in a table and to build an appropriate bar graph; iii) the students were asked to prepare a ppt, with a maximum of 5 slides, with all the work they have done". (P1fL)
>
> "[...]students [...] made video recordings and proceeded to the acquisition of data with CBR sensor, in order to elaborate a speed-time and position-time graphs. This was the only change [...]since it would be interesting to use real data from the prototype built by the students and to study not only the conversion of potential energy into kinetic energy but also to review the concepts associated with uniform and uniformly varied motion." (P2fP)

The calculation of the physical quantities under study, such as speed, was also carried out using the mobile phone application suggested in the activity guide but complemented by the analog calculation:

"[...] some of the groups calculated the speed using the mobile phone application suggested in the activity guide and others calculated the average speed through the distance traveled and the time it took to travel that distance". (P3fL)

3.2 Implementation of STEM Activities with Additions in the Integration of Digital Tools

Regarding the addition of digital tools, the integration of collaborative and online tools stands out, as happened in the activity The Race of Rubber Band Cars, E(lastic) Formula, where the Software Tracker was introduced. This free software allows for video analysis and modeling to be used in Physics education and Padlet, an information organizer with many applications.

"The alternative found so that groups that had not yet carried out any measurements could complete the project, was to carry out video analysis using the Software Tracker. [...] a Padlet was prepared, replacing the poster suggested [...] project, but fulfilling the same objectives". (P2fP)

In the Sound activity, teachers suggested integrating generic platforms to design floor plans for buildings based on which studies on the acoustic conditions of spaces would be made. Its free and easy installation was highlighted:

"I also gave them an indication of various platforms that allow them to draw plans in 2D or 3D. These applications are available on the internet, and many are free and easy to install". (P4fL)

3.3 Suggestions for the Integration of Digital Tools in STEM Activities

In what concerns the main suggestions to improve the activities, these refer essentially to more explicit and fruitful use of remote access laboratories, as is the case with e-lab and virtual laboratories.

"[...] to do something similar to what they showed us in the first training session, related to the gravitational pendulum, in which, through the e-lab application, the student has access to a real laboratory, and where from a distance he could program and observe the fall of the sphere in real-time, as well as record all necessary measurements." (P5fP)

"This activity could also be complemented with the use of online digital laboratories in which students simulated this experience [Energy Transformations (kinetic energy and potential energy)]." (P6fP)

Optimizations of STEM activities were also suggested, as in the case of the Sound activity, related to the training of students for the Arduino programming language:

"For the study of the sound, I had planned a series of activities [...] the students divided themselves into small groups to create, from well-known songs [for example of the song "Happy birthday to you" is mentioned], the notes and the corresponding times to be inserted in Arduino." (P7mP)

In the suggestions made by the teachers, the mention of the inclusion of educational games and computer simulations is also frequent:

> "[...] in the awareness campaign, one can try to disseminate it through interactive multimedia tools, such as a question and answer game on Scratch about noise pollution, applied to the school context and the obtained results". (P7mP)

> "The changes I propose [...] are the use of educational games/simulations in which students could even create the game with the content of the activity". (P6fP)

4 Discussion

In this paper, we wanted to analyze teachers' choices–who underwent a continuous professional development course to promote a STEM program focused on Physics contents–on what digital resources to integrate and how to integrate them. Such accounts about how teachers adopted the course's activities give us exciting clues about digital media's STEM role.

We must start the discussion with some lines about the project team's reflection on the activities' design. Right since the beginning of the project, designing activities to respond to four fronts was a challenge. If Physics was an end on its own right, we observed that sometimes the other fronts were thought of as serving to reach that end or seen as byproducts. This is true despite our efforts to follow a framework for creating STEM activities [18]: addressing real-life problems centered in Physics and integrating or using contents from other areas (Technology, Mathematics, and Engineering). However, this is especially true–if possible–when the digital tools entered the scene: more or less interesting characters but still with secondary roles aimed at amusing the audience or facilitating the plot's development, but never leading. Why?

It seems, first, that we are before the problem of transparency, one of the significant challenges of digital culture [14]. The inner mechanisms of the digital are hidden from the end-user eyes by interfaces that are more and more intuitive as they become more and more coercive: choices are limited for the sake of simplicity and rapidity at expenses of complexity and depth. Between brackets, we should note that the problem is acquiring unforeseen dimensions, as deep learning functioning is hidden even from engineers and computer scientists' eyes. How can we expect science teachers to go beyond the smokescreen of interfaces and explore the code, algorithms, or logic that runs behind? Because some do, a simple strategy consisting of doing the math aside and comparing results. As we have seen, one teacher computed the average speed by other means that not the application. Trusting in the correction of the calculations provided by applications need to be discussed. If the gap between practitioners (teachers) and programmers become too deep, how can teachers enlighten their students when facing a mismatch in the calculation?

One thing is clear so far. The role of digital tools in this context was that of a means rather than an end. And its relation to the other STEM areas was not that of content. In the educational political turmoil, with endless reforms, one after another, changing nothing and everything, there is yet no room for digital media education, except for some hours of Informatics and Communication Technology. The rest is left to schools' own initiative, including some programs on computing or robotics. The flexibility and autonomy afforded to schools by the Decree-Law 55/2018 July 6th did not solve the problem; neither did the document on students' profile [22] or essential learning goals [23]. On the contrary, switching from contents to skills makes it possible to identify digital media contents even far away.

As a means, digital tools were thought to give more options to teachers at school, but they would work differently: some would replace existent options (replacement function) whereas others would extend teachers agency (amplification function) [24].

For example, simulators would do the job instead of laboratory equipment, whereas the e-lab offered them a chance to gather and analyze that from several places of the world, introducing their students to international research complexity. Training mirrored these options. Understanding the functioning of the e-Lab would require more time and expertise: we were fully aware that teachers needed to learn how to use the e-Lab. In other words, e-lab turned out to be a specific, stable, even if an opaque system, showing that the qualities ascribed by Koehler and Mishra [12] do not apply to all digital tools. Perhaps they apply only to computing and coding, to the languages at work behind the scenes. Digital tools, as always happens with tools, are subverted by the users or–to use another expression–co-construed by the users during domestication [25]. However, teachers need to be taught some techniques to identify digital media contents and reverse – here and there – foreground and background. This reversal is an urgent need as science is today made with and through digital media. STEM is more and more digitalized.

The same applied to free fall. It loaded teachers with the need to develop materials. Only four teachers selected pendulum and two free fall. In addition to what was previously mentioned about the criteria teachers adopted for choosing STEM activities, these activities were seldom selected because: a) in the case of pendulum activity, it was directed towards the 12th year, and in the group of teachers who did the training, few taught 12th year of physics; b) in another case, the free fall activity, for the 11th year, the students have a national examination as a condition to enter University, and often teachers are less open to pedagogical novelties in their practices.

As for other digital tools, such as internet usage for searching or simulators, teachers are more acquitted with them. They not only implemented the activities as they changed or suggested modifications to the script. However, still much is to be known about how teachers use internet affordances [26] in connection with STEM activities. Actually, against the shared representation of the internet as an unlimited field of resources, teachers report a limited, recursive number of sources they use, PhET, Casa das Ciências, and publishing houses online manuals [27].

When we observe teachers' written accounts, some tensions seem to be at work. Teachers' options range from adding specific and unspecific tools as a means to implement the activity. In most cases, they only replace other non-digital tools. We are before a replacement vs. displacement paradigm. Digital tools are used not because they add up but because they do the same differently. We might evoke many reasons: perceived usefulness and perceived ease of use [28] or pedagogical beliefs about the motivational contribution of digital tools for students. In the end, digital tools remain opaque.

The other tension is skills vs. contents. Schools are, perhaps, neglecting that their mission is to transmit a body of selected, precious contents that were trusted to them by society [9, 10]: such heritage should be endlessly transmitted if we are to keep a sense of history and belonging, but also of genius and rationality. The task is also endless, to select at the light of times which contents should be transmitted. There are no competencies in a vacuum.

5 Conclusion

If one thing became evident with the Covid crisis is that nobody was prepared to move to distance learning, and that distance learning can ever replace schools. Because if competencies do not exist in a vacuum, neither do contents. Teachers embody knowledge. The role of digital tools problematic because teachers are expected to move beyond their expertise as if they should know how to integrate and explore digital tools. We understood that teachers need to be knowledgeable to introduce digital tools productively: to amplify their options and explore other related areas.

Funding. This work was financed by national funds through FCT - Fundação para a Ciência e a Tecnologia, I.P., within the scope of the PTDC/CED-EDG/31480/2017 project also within project UIDB/00081/2020.

References

1. AAAS: Benchmarks for Science Literacy. Oxford University Press, New York (1993)
2. NCTM: Curriculum and evaluation standards for school mathematics, Reston, VA (1989)
3. NRC: National Science Education Standards. The National Academies, Washington, DC (1996)
4. Sanders, M.: STEM, STEM education, STEMmania. Technol. Teach. **68**, 20–27 (2009)
5. Martinez Ortiz, A., Rodriguez Amaya, L., Kawaguchi Warshauer, H., Garcia Torres, S., Scanlon, E., Pruett, M.: They choose to attend academic summer camps? A mixed methods study exploring the impact of a NASA academic summer pre-engineering camp on middle school students in a latino community. J. Pre-Coll. Eng. Educ. Res. (J-PEER) **8**, Art. 3 (2018)
6. Julià, C., Antolí, J.Ò.: Impact of implementing a long-term STEM-based active learning course on students' motivation. Int. J. Technol. Des. Educ. **29**(2), 303–327 (2018). https://doi.org/10.1007/s10798-018-9441-8
7. Luo, T., Wang, J., Liu, X., Zhou, J.: Development and application of a scale to measure students' STEM continuing motivation. Int. J. Sci. Educ. **41**, 1885–1904 (2019)
8. Selisne, M., Sari, Y.S., Ramli, R.: Role of learning module in STEM approach to achieve competence of physics learning. J. Phys. Conf. Ser. **1185**, 012100 (2019)
9. Kambouchner, D., Meirieu, P., Stiegler, B., Gautier, J., Vergne, G.: L'école, le numérique et la société qui vient. Mille et une nuits (2012)
10. Stiegler, B.: Taking Care of Youth and the Generations. Stanford University Press, Palo Alto (2010)
11. Victor López, S., Digna Couso, L., Cristina Simarro, R.: Educación STEM en y para el mundo digital. Revista de Educación a Distancia (RED) 20 (2020)
12. Koehler, M.J., Mishra, P.: What is technological pedagogical content knowledge? Contemp. Issues Technol. Teach. Educ. **9**, 60–70 (2009)
13. Ng, W.: Can we teach digital natives digital literacy? Comput. Educ. **59**, 1065–1078 (2012)

14. Jenkins, H., Purushotma, R., Weigel, M., Clinton, K., Robison, A.J.: Confronting the Challenges of Participatory Culture: Media Education for the 21st Century. MIT Press, Chicago (2009)
15. https://arsindustrialis.org/vocabulaire-pharmakon-pharmacologie
16. Torres, M., Ferreira, S., Sousa, A., Moreira, L., Torres, R.: Welcome to engineering: gender equality in learning and integration among first year students. Int. J. Eng. Educ. **34**, 45–55 (2018)
17. https://gostem.ie.ulisboa.pt/
18. Thibaut, L., et al.: Integrated STEM education: A systematic review of instructional practices in secondary education. Eur. J. STEM Educ. **3**, 2 (2018)
19. https://phet.colorado.edu/en/simulation/circuit-construction-kit-dc
20. https://phet.colorado.edu/sims/html/pendulum-lab/latest/pendulum-lab_en.html
21. https://e-escola.tecnico.ulisboa.pt/elab.asp
22. Martins, G.d.O., et al.: Perfil dos alunos à saída da Escolaridade Obrigatória (2017)
23. https://www.dge.mec.pt/aprendizagens-essenciais-0
24. Greenhow, C., Robelia, B., Hughes, J.E.: Learning, teaching, and scholarship in a digital age. Educ. Res. **38**, 246–259 (2009)
25. Haddon, L.: Roger silverstone's legacies: domestication. New Media Soc. **9**, 25–32 (2016)
26. Wallace, R.M.: A framework for understanding teaching with the internet. Am. Educ. Res. J. **41**, 447–488 (2004)
27. Vilaça, P.: Perfis e práticas de integração do multimédia por professores de ciências: contributos para a construção de um espaço de afinidade. Faculdade de Engenharia. Universidade do Porto (2020)
28. Davis, F.D.: A technology acceptance model for empirically testing new end-user information systems: theory and results. Ph.D. Massachusetts Institute of Technology, Cambridge, MA (1985)

Digital Technologies to Foster Critical Thinking and Monitor Self and Co-regulation of e-learning

Structuring International University Students' Reflection and Meta-reflection Experiences Online

Chrysi Rapanta[1(✉)] and Carlotta Pisano[2]

[1] Faculty of Social Sciences and Humanities, Universidade Nova de Lisboa, Avenida de Berna 26, 1069063 Lisbon, Portugal
crapanta@fcsh.unl.pt

[2] International Mobility Office, Universidade Nova de Lisboa, Campus de Campolide, 1099085 Lisbon, Portugal

Abstract. The recent emergency remote teaching experiences caused by the Covid-19 pandemic have placed a forced attention on existing online pedagogical tools and intelligent ways of combining them to reinforce student presence in the learning environment. In higher education, where students' autonomy is even more desired, the design of online learning experiences that focus on reflective thinking has always been a principal focus, due to the relation between reflection and self-regulated learning. This study focuses on a technically non-demanding way of combining two existing online tools and appropriating their use towards a two-fold pedagogical goal: (a) students' creation and sharing of reflective narrations on their experience of a practice-oriented social science methods introductory course using JustPaste.it; and (b) their subsequent meta-reflection on these narrations using the course's online Discussion Forum. The study highlights two main factors in the success of this combination, namely the importance of structuring guidelines and prompts for both reflection and meta-reflection to take place, and taking into account the age (average 17 years old) and multiple national backgrounds of the participants. An assessment rubric for students' reflective and meta-reflective texts was also designed and tested as part of the study.

Keywords: Reflective narration · Meta-reflection · Online teaching · Hybrid course design

1 Introduction

During the Spring Semester of the 2019–2020 academic year, educational institutions around the world, including universities, have been forced to an emergency remote teaching and learning experience due to the Covid-19 pandemic. The subsequent year (2020–2021) started within uncertainty, and with hybrid learning experiences [1] already available to be tested or reinforced. This study presents the online assessment part of a hybrid learning experience designed for international students at a large public Portuguese university.

A. Reis et al. (Eds.): TECH-EDU 2020, CCIS 1384, pp. 141–155, 2021.
https://doi.org/10.1007/978-3-030-73988-1_10

Students' autonomy and self-regulation have always been on the spot for higher education researchers and practitioners. Autonomy defined as learners' capacity to control and manage their own learning [2] is a necessary ingredient of successful online learning experiences [3, 4] as it allows students to find their own space, time and ways to organize what and how they learn. Although many times it is treated in the distance education literature in an atheoretical [5] and *de facto* manner (e.g. online learners are or must be autonomous, without explaining how or why), autonomy is indeed an operationalizable attitude composed of several self-regulatory mechanisms. Among these, Lynch and Dembo [5] identify the following: goal orientation, experience in Internet technologies, time management, study environment management, and learning assistance management skills.

Relevant to the personal goal orientation and motivation are the critical reflection skills. Reflection, a primary component of critical thinking [6], is defined as a "turning back" on experience [7]. Although it is often perceived as a requirement or stimulator for critical thinking skills [8, 9], studies focusing on learners' autonomy view critical thinking and reflection as two highly interconnected competences, with one "feeding" the other [10]. The view on reflection adopted in this paper is based on this interconnection. We view constructive critique as a productive context to support reflection, and reflective experience as a constructive context to embrace critique. Taking into consideration the vast critique that the experiential learning cycle models have attracted for being unrealistically linear and therefore no representative of how reflection actually takes place [11, 12], we opted for adopting two approaches that have been used in more realistic, professional learning environments (see Sect. 2) and for adapting them to our particular, from several points of view, study's context (see Sect. 3).

2 Theoretical Background

The "father" of reflection as an educational experience is John Dewey. In his seminal work "How we think" [13], he defines the following characteristics of reflective thought:

(a) It is consecutive, not merely a sequence.
(b) It aims at knowledge, at beliefs about facts or in truths.
(c) It considers the basis and consequences of knowledge and beliefs. For Dewey [13], reflective thought is "active, persistent and careful consideration of any belief or supposed form of knowledge in the light of the grounds that support it, and the further conclusions to which it tends" (p. 6).

Decades later, Donald Schön [14, 15] expanded the idea of reflective thought into reflective practice, and made the distinction between reflection-in-action and reflection-on-action. For Schön [15], reflection-in-action is a process consisting of a sequence of four components, namely: routinized action, encounter of surprise, reflection, and new action. In line with Dewey's idea of consecution rather than a mere sequence, these four components (re)produce each other in a flow, which can be interrupted, responded to, and re-established. Reflection-in-action always takes place within a practice, which for Schön is situated in a professional context, and it is embedded, engaged and embodied within social interaction. Although for Schön, participation in a community of practitioners is an essential element of his definition of practice, he does not offer any evaluative theorizing it terms of knowledge and beliefs change as result of participating in a community of practice. This gap in his theory was later addressed by other scholars. Here we offer a brief view by Yanow and Tsoukas [16] who explain that (p. 1344):

> Practices are constituted by certain collective self-understandings that situate practitioners relative to particular standards of excellence and to obligations, held both collectively within the practitioner community which individuals aspire to join or to which they belong. These self-understandings cannot be qualitatively neutral: they are articulated through contrasts (e.g. of right and wrong uses of concepts) and, hence, entail an evaluative component (Taylor, 1985, p. 19). Both self-understandings and evaluative components are learned through engaging in and with the practice, not through thinking about them.

Therefore, engagement in practice implies engagement with a continuous evaluation and contrast of self-understandings with the collective understanding acquired within the community. At the same time, because of the different self-understandings of its members, a community's collective understandings and standards of knowledge may change. It is this mutuality between the individual and the community that forms part of the social learning [17] and it is also expressed with the term "accountability" [17, 18]. Through participating in a community, the learner-participant becomes gradually accountable to knowledge, standards of reasoning, and the other learners [18].

Such accountability implies criticality [19], meaning that the more learners participating in a community confront themselves with the knowledge and learning standards and norms developed within the community, the more critical they become in their thinking, action, and reflection. As the focus of this paper is on reflection, we are interested in the passage marked from a simple reflection to a critical reflection. To explain this passage, we will draw on Mezirow's [7, 20] transformative learning theory, and its particular implications for reflection. Early in his theory development, Mezirow [20] made a distinction between ordinary reflection and critical reflection, with the former being the act of "intentional assessment of the nature and consequences" (p. 44) of learning to justify one's beliefs, ideas and feelings, and the latter being any attempt of connecting between the circumstances of origin of those learnings with their nature and consequences. This connection between circumstances, learnings and consequences is what forms the premise reflection, a necessary ingredient of critical reflection, as opposed to content and process reflection. Mezirow [20] gives the following example to distinguish between these three types of reflection (p. 45):

> If the problem is to assess whether George is bad, *content reflection* might cause us to reassess those bad things George has done. *Process reflection* might ask whether we have generalized about George's bad behavior from too limited a number of observations (…) *Premise reflection*, on the other hand might cause us to ask why we have to judge George bad or good in the first place.

This premise reflection, later renamed as Critical Reflection of Assumptions [7], "involves critique of a premise upon which the learner has defined a problem" (p. 186) and it can be of two types: an objective reframing or a subjective reframing of assumptions. The main difference between the two is that although the objective reframing includes either a narrative or an action critical reflection of assumptions, the subjective reframing refers to critical self-reflection on, rather than of, assumptions (for examples of each type see [21]). What we keep here is the following: for a reflection to be considered as critical reflection a certain degree of meta-language [22] is necessary for both reflection-in-action and reflection-on-action processes. This meta-language aims at revealing connections between the events, meanings of these events for oneself, and reconstruction of the event-meaning relationship as result of the reflective experience.

However described and operationalized, reflection *in* and *on* action requires an immersion in specific practices that characterize a specific community of learners. Immersion in learning activities aiming at thinking like a professional are in the heart of inquiry-based learning. Inquiry-based learning, as opposed to top-down instruction, is a pedagogical method based on not only revealing what we know, but also and mainly how we know, and why we believe. Placing its emphasis on learners' active participation and responsibility in discovering knowledge that is new to them, inquiry-based learning activities aspire to engage learners in authentic processes of knowledge construction, similar to the ones experienced by professionals [23]. Due to its strong relationship with self-regulated learning and learning how to learn, it has been successfully applied in higher education contexts [24]. Therefore, its adaption for a Social Science Methods (SSM) undergraduate course, as explained below, is well-justified, also because SSM is a meta-language discipline [25], implying deep reflection on how and why social science is done, and which method serves an issue better than another.

The goal of this study is to design and test a hybrid inquiry-based course on Social Science Methods having reflection in the core of its learning and assessment activities. The rationale behind this is to foster young university students' critical thinking and self-regulation skills, due to the connection of reflection to both, as previously explained. Structuring the contents and activities of a hybrid university course having reflection as the core expected learning outcomes is the main challenge addressed.

3 Study Context

The study was part of a Pre-University Semester (PUS) program of a large public university in Portugal. The PUS is designed for students worldwide who have concluded the high school and they wish to start their university studies in Portugal. The average age of participants is between 17 and 19 years old. Through a specific multidisciplinary and bilingual program, the PUS's main objectives are to upgrade the technical and linguistics skills of the participants from several different countries so that they subsequently join university as undergraduate students in one of the offered programs. Being part of this versatile and international opportunity allows students to directly participate in the transition into a European way of education, through acquiring more autonomy and discovering new studying methods.

Within the year of the study (2020–2021), the PUS counted with 33 students from 17 different countries, six of whom only participated as online participants due to travel restrictions. Moreover, because of the Covid-19 precaution measures, a hybrid model was designed to protect both the students and teachers, according to which: students were meeting face-to-face once per week for each course; this class was synchronously attended by the online participants (i.e. the ones who did not manage to come to Portugal as explained before); each week both face-to-face and online students were also invited to assist either a video-recorded expository class on the contents of the week, or to participate in an asynchronous online activity on the same topics.

For the needs of this study, only the experiences and online activities designed for one of the PUS courses will be described, namely the Introduction to the Social Science Methods course. What follows is the description of the design of the learning experience for that specific course and its alignment with the course's contents and structure.

4 Design of the Learning Experience

The inspiration of the design of the learning experience presented in this paper lies in a lack already identified back in the '90s:

> "What a sad comment on modern educational systems that most learners neither value nor practise active, critical reflection. They are too busy studying to stop and think. Sadder still, many educators don't reflect either. They must be too busy ´teaching´" ([26] p. 163).

Notwithstanding the increasing focus on the use of web-based learning environments that foster students' reflexivity [27, 28], the question of how critical reflection can/should be worked out within higher education hybrid courses is still an open issue [29]. In this paper we address this gap by making explicit the design rationale of an inquiry-based, hybrid learning course on Social Science Methods within the particular study context presented in Sect. 3. After explaining the overall design of the course, we focus on the reflection and meta-reflection activities situated within it, and how they were designed in a way to also inform students' assessment.

4.1 Overall Design and Course Objectives

The "Introduction to Social Science methods" course for international pre-university students was designed within a frame facilitating and fostering critical reflection. Since the first class, the course sought to exploit any opportunity for students to reflect on the meaning and methods implicit in social science research practice. During the first two weeks of classes, the concept and nature of social sciences and social science issues was explored, through conversationally establishing distinctions between social and exact science, and between social science problems and social science research issues. In its face-to-face form, this was achieved through teacher-guided whole-class question-directed discussions. In its online component, students were guided through an individual reflection about whether social sciences can/should be considered sciences or not (multimodal sources supporting one or another view were made available for this scope). They were also invited to participate asynchronously in an online ideas' sharing environment (www.padlet.com) twice, once for brainstorming what is social science and once for offering examples of social science issues under five different disciplinary areas, namely Sociology, Anthropology, Geography, Communication, and Political Science. At the end of the second week, students formed teams according to their interest for one social science sub-field or another. They were also asked to identify an issue they would like to address during the course from the adopted disciplinary field. Therefore, groups of aspiring sociologists, anthropologists, geographers, communication, and political scientists were formed. During off-class teamwork discussions, assisted by the teacher at least once, either face-to-face or online, each group defined a specific research issue which had all the characteristics explained in the face-to-face class, namely it was: resolvable, addressable, questionable, and related to a social problem or phenomenon.

In the following seven weeks, students were introduced to three main social science research methods, namely interviews, surveys and focus groups. The three different teaching modalities (face-to-face classes, video-recorded power-points, and asynchronous activities) were used for different purposes: (a) Video-recorded power-point presentations were used to share basic content about each one of the three methods and were shared with the students before the face-to-face classes; (b) the face-to-face classes were used to showcase how each of the three methods can be used in practice, with each data collection method being designed in situ for an issue selected for this scope; and (c) finally, asynchronous activities aimed at guiding students' implementation of each social science research method, with each group at the end choosing to implement one of the three presented methods, the one which was considered most adequate by the group with the teacher's help. The teaching style of both video-recorded presentations and face-to-face classes was "conversational, oriented to experience, rather than seeking the complexity and sophistication of traditional academic discourse" ([30], p. 538).

The last two weeks were held for group presentations of how they designed/implemented the taught method, and any challenges they faced during planning and implementation. For the groups choosing to use interview and surveys, these had to be planned and implemented before the group presentation. In the case of Focus Groups Discussions, the group(s) having opted for this method had to do a real-time implementation with the rest of the class. After each group finished the presentation/implementation of their chosen method, a peer-evaluation discussion session was held, guided by the instructor, during which constructive critique was encouraged focusing on pre-defined quality criteria presented for each method.

Overall, the course objectives, and main steps of how these were met, were the following:

- Understand the differences and similarities between social and exact sciences: students were asked to *reflect* about what is social science and how social science methods are compared to the scientific method.
- Identify a social science issue and distinguish it from a social science problem: students were gradually guided to understand what a social science issue is, and to *reflect* on the difference between an issue and a problem.
- Apply knowledge related to the main social science methods of interview, survey, and focus group discussion: students were asked to discuss, *reflect*, and decide in groups which of the methods would be more adequate for addressing the chosen issue, and to implement it within the course duration limits, so they were able to present the main

outcomes of the method's design and/or implementation in the last two weeks of the course.
- *Reflect* on the utilities and limitations of each method and argue about the applicability of one or another as the most adequate for addressing a particular issue: the final class was dedicated to do an overall *reflection* on the methods learnt and how they addressed specific issues, the pros and cons of each method, and their usability as research tools.

As seen from the explanations given above about how each goal was met, reflection was an essential part of the pedagogy adopted throughout the course. In addition to this, explicit design decisions towards reflection and meta-reflection were also taken as explained in the next section.

4.2 Reflection and Meta-reflection as Part of the Course Design

As the course followed the inquiry-based instruction paradigm, much of the students' off-class time was devoted to work on their group projects focusing on a collectively chosen issue and method to address it. For such work to be "self-in-social-setting regulated" ([31], p. 276), a guiding structure is necessary both for the coregulation processes emerging in interaction, and for the individual reflection afterwards. For the first reflection-in-action [14, 15] to take place, we asked groups to assign metacognitive regulation roles which team members had to carry on during each group meeting. These roles were [32]: monitoring and evaluating the process (e.g. how well we are doing as a group), task understanding monitoring (e.g. how well we have understood what we are supposed to do, task goal discussion (e.g. what we are supposed to do in general and with this meeting), and ideas' and strategies' sharing (e.g. how we can carry out the general task goal and the meeting goal in particular). This last role was always preserved for the group-assigned leader (subset to change for every group meeting), whereas the other three roles were distributed among the remaining team members. In addition to this metacognitive role assignment, each student was asked to take diary notes, when possible, during the group discussions. These notes were aimed at revealing important information regarding the self-regulated learning strategies implemented by the students.

The in-action diary note taking was also aimed at serving the writing of on-action reflective narrative reports by the students throughout the course project. Again, structuring of reflection was considered necessary. Among the available models that can be used to prompt and structure reflection on experience (https://www.ed.ac.uk/reflection/reflectors-toolkit/reflecting-on-experience), we have chosen the 5R Framework for reflective writing [33], consisting of five interlinked stages, namely: Reporting, Responding, Relating, Reasoning and Reconstructing. Students were guided to take diary notes during the reflection moments described below, answering the following questions:

1. What happened? What are the key aspects of this situation? Who was involved? What did I do? (Reporting)
2. How did what happened make me feel? What did I think? What made me think and feel this way? (Responding)
3. Have I seen this before? What was similar/different then? Do I have skills and knowledge to deal with this? (Relating)

4. What was the most important aspect of this situation and why? How did it relate to my emotions, knowledge, and previous experiences? What made this specific situation memorable? (Reasoning)
5. How would I need to do this differently in the future? What might work and why? Are there different options? (Reconstructing)

Finally, we prompted students to reflect on at least three course moments, where critical incidents for reflection were possible to take place: (a) on group discussions taking place as part of the course inquiry-based learning structure; (b) on peer assessments taking place after each group presented their work to their classmates or "used" their classmates as part of their group work presentation (in the case of the Focus Group discussions); and (c) on their method implementation, either off-class (in the case of interviews and surveys) or in-class (in the case of focus groups).

Each time a student finished a reflective narration (concrete deadlines were given for each one of the three texts), (s)he would share this online with the teacher and the other students using the online text sharing tool JustPaste.it (www.justpaste.it). The tool, together with other platforms, was recently criticised as for being largely used by the Islamic state supporters to disseminate propaganda among their followers [34]. However, as the tool's creator Mariusz Zurawek claims, the use of a tool for wrong purposes is not the tool's fault. Given the technical easiness of the tool, its accessibility (it can work with very low internet coverage), and the extreme protection measures that were taken to protect users from being faces with inappropriate content [34], we considered it as a good option for students to share their texts with each other in the form of a sequential multiple-authored online diary.

In addition to the reflective writing text sharing, a forum of discussion was also created for the course's scope, and in particular for supporting the activity of meta-reflection. Meta-reflection, i.e. the reflection about the reflective experience, is not an easy task, as it requires continuous self-evaluation [35]. For our course case study, the meta-reflective activity was designed to take place in an online forum, already available within the course's learning management system. Participation in asynchronous discussion boards is shown to enhance students' agency and collective reflexivity [28]. Nonetheless, as Rausch and Crawford [36] observe, "just making discussion forums available does not result in effective use" (p. 177). Therefore, to foster students' meta-reflective participation in the discussion forum, two types of prompt structures were created: pre-discussion prompts, referring to rules of participation in the forum, as explained below, and within-discussion prompts, referring to instructors' ways of intervening in the discussion to prevent non-reflective comments from expanding, and to foster reflective comments to appear.

Pre-discussion Prompts. The students were informed that the discussion forum will open on the day after their first reflective narration submission was due. They were also informed that each one had to create at least one reflective post about another student's reflective text, previously shared on JustPaste.it, and to react towards someone else's reflective post. Both creation and reaction of/to discussion posts had to follow the same norms of participation, which were the following: (a) I respect the other and his/her opinions, experiences, and ideas as if they were mine; (b) I show maturity by reflecting before writing and before reacting to a critical comment by one of my colleagues; (c) I accept that every critique is positive as long as it is sufficiently justified with reasons; (d) I do not in any way offend others and their understanding of the world, the course and the activities; (e) I contribute in the discussion in ways that can be an opportunity for the others to get to know my ideas, my personality, and my "best self." Although the idea of classroom discussion norms is not new [37], its adaptation for university students and for online discussions was an innovative aspect of the course design.

Within-Discussion Prompts. As Dennen [38] affirms, "generating true learning dialogue as opposed to a collection of loosely affiliated posted messages on a class discussion board can be challenging" (p. 127). To address this challenge, the instructors participated in the forum with a twofold intention: (a) to prevent one-sided, uncritical and non-reflective commenting from going on and on, once a post revealing some of these characteristics was added in the forum. Immediately after this happened, the instructor intervened with comments of the type: "Thank you for your contribution. It is true that sometimes X happens. However, other aspects also need to be taken into consideration. Who has any idea of what these aspects can be? Can you justify your opinion?" and (b) to create triggers for reflective comments to become more critical. These were prompts such as: "Why do you say so? Are you based on what types of experiences? How do you know that these experiences relate to X? What would somebody who disagrees with you say to you? How would you respond?". These metacognitive prompts aiming at critical thinking and reflection were based on the work of Deanna Kuhn [39, 40, 41].

4.3 Assessment of Students' Critical Reflection Skills

Assessing students' reflective narrations and meta-reflections, and identifying what part of this reflection is critical, is considered an ongoing challenge. The greatest difficulty lies in "the lack of an overarching framework for how to operationalize critical reflection" ([42], p. 23), the inclusion and assessment of emotions as reflective experiences, and the avoidance of a coding scheme that what grasps is not students' reflection skills but their ability to express their thoughts in writing.

To address the above challenges, we constructed a flexible scheme for assessing students' critical reflection skills as manifested both in their shared narratives and their discussion posts. This scheme was based on two criteria namely criticality and reflexivity. The assumption behind was that a text (ranging from an extended narration to a simple comment) could be of four types, as per the combination of the two criteria: critical and non-reflective, reflective and critical, non-critical and reflective, and non-critical and non-reflective. Situating a textual contribution in one category or another depended on the score that each text received in the following assessment statements. The assessment statements were five for each criterion (see Table 1), and they were used altogether as an assessment rubric for the written reflective texts shared online among the students.

The construction of the assessment statements presented in Table 1) was based on a combination of the theoretical frameworks of Dewey [13], Schön [14, 15], and Mezirow [7, 20] previously presented in Sect. 2). More precisely, we combined the following ideas as evidence that reflection takes place as part of students' narrative and meta-narrative texts:

Table 1. Reflective narration assessment rubric.

1. Reflexivity criterion assessment statements
1.1 Did the textual contribution manifest any positive or negative surprise experienced in the narrated or meta-narrated event? (1 = not at all, 5 = absolutely)
1.2 Did the textual contribution manifest any effort to reconciliate the surprise, either through adding to it, or resolving the conflict, adopting in both cases a "yes and" attitude? (1 = not at all, 5 = absolutely)
1.3 Did the textual contribution contain any reference to similar reconciliation strategies used in the past in similar situations? (1 = not at all, 5 = absolutely)
1.4 Did the student opt for adding any information on how the social environment reacted to his/her surprise resolution strategies? (1 = not at all, 5 = absolutely)
1.5 Did the student offer an overall estimation of how this experience has contributed in his/her learning? (1 = not at all, 5 = absolutely)
2. Criticality criterion assessment statements
2.1 Did the textual contribution explain the reason for an experienced surprise? (1 = not at all, 5 = absolutely)
2.2. Did the surprise resolution strategies were described in detail making references to personal or socially shared experiences? (1 = not at all, 5 = absolutely)
2.3 Did the text contain any hint on how this particular situation was similar or different to others experienced in the past? (1 = not at all, 5 = absolutely)
2.4 Did the student take into consideration the social environment's reaction to his/her surprise resolution strategies? (1 = not at all, 5 = absolutely)
2.5 Was any conflict between one's own living the experience and others' perception of or reaction to it solved? (1 = not at all, 5 = absolutely)

- As part of his reflection-in-action paradigm, Schön [14, 16] places a particular attention on the **element of surprise**, and how it reads to turning and talking back to experience. Surprise can be of several types, either positive (e.g. an "aha!" experience) or negative (e.g. a communication breakdown). What was important for us, though, was the recognition of surprise elements by students as part of their inquiry-based learning activities, and in particular, of working in small groups on the several social science methods projects. The ability to let oneself be surprised and to recognize the power of uncertainty as a learning mechanism is the basis of thinking critically [43]. It therefore formed the primary focus of assessing students' reflection. In addition, we assessed students' capacity to reconstruct a lived learning experience as a casual sequence of events (see Dewey, [13]), to which they reacted, in relation to the place, time, and others (see assessment statements 1.3 and 1.4).
- Responding to the surprise both constructively and critically is an ability showing that the learner **becomes accountable for his/her actions** [18], and (s)he is in a position to justify those using personal or socially shared information as evidence [39]. Although Dewey has not used the word 'accountability' himself, a careful reading of his works reveals the importance he pays to each one of us, as learners, becoming accountable "to

the democratic structure of society, to our own need for growth, to the consideration of a plurality of ideas" ([44], p. 10). Such accountability becomes relevant in each step of the 5R Reflection Framework [33], which was used as part of this study. In the Reporting stage, becoming accountable refers to being able to explain the reason of the surprise (assessment statement 2.1). In the Responding stage, accountability equals to the degree of improvisation [16] the learner implements to constructively reply to the surprise (assessment statement 1.2). In the Relating stage, accountability is expressed through the learner's capacity to situate the experience within the palette of his/her learning repertoire (assessment statements 2.2, 2.3). In the Reasoning stage, the learner is able to justify how the experience actually led to his/her learning (assessment statement 1.5). In the Reconstructing stage, the learner recognizes not only the impact of this experience on his/her personal growth, but also how the social environment reacts or forms part of this transformation (assessment statements 2.4, 2.5).

- Overall, the idea behind the assessment rubric presented in Table 1 is that in order to be able to evaluate learners' **passage from non-critical to critical reflexivity**, as assessed by their reflective texts, their use of parts of this narrated experience as basis for justifying the impact of the narrated event(s) on their own learning is essential. The importance of the explicit use of self-narrated facts as evidence for one's own arguments about how his/her learning experience actually took place is supported by recent research (e.g. [45]) focusing on the interconnections between narration and argumentation, as two discursive genres serving critical thinking aims in a complementary way.

5 Final Considerations

Although reflection forms an essential part of students' electronic Portfolios commonly used for distance learning assessment [46], it is not a common practice for hybrid learning environments where traditional (teacher-centered) and innovative (student-centered) pedagogical methods often overlap. This study focused on the use and usability of critical reflection as an assessment method for an introductory social science methods course for international students.

In particular, we focused on two online assessment methods which aimed at accessing and fostering learners' reflection and meta-reflection skills: the first was the construction and sharing of reflective narrations using an online text editing tool, and the second was the guided reflection on those reflective texts by the learners themselves and their peers. This online pedagogical assessment experiment was situated within an active, inquiry-based, multicultural learning environment combining face-to-face/synchronous and online/asynchronous classes for incoming first year students from all over the world (i.e. Portugal, Brazil, India, Angola, United States, Vietnam etc.). Due to the variability of the pedagogical methods and environments, on one hand, and the diversity of the students, on another, the following design aspects were taken into consideration, based on the framework recently proposed [47] in light of the recent remote teaching needs for online instruction pedagogical content knowledge:

- **Interactivity:** The question regarding whether reflection is an individual or a social activity is a difficult one to answer, as reflection is always about a social (or others-mediated) event. Therefore, introducing the reflective narration activity without a previous highly interactive learning context would not make much sense.
- **(In)dependence:** As the participants were young (average 17 years old) and without any structured higher education learning experience yet, taking any existing autonomy for granted would have been erroneous. This was also strengthened by the fact that they were coming from so different educational systems that no uniformity in previous experience with self-regulated activities could be expected. Therefore, a balance between dependence, inter-dependence and independence was sought for. Participants were dependent on the learning instructions gradually guiding their participation in the hybrid, inquiry-based learning environment; at the same time they were inter-dependent as in order to be able to follow the learning contents and activities they had to engage in intense systematic reflective groupwork throughout the course; and also they were independent, as they were asked to choose on which of these social learning experiences they would like to reflect on and which peers' reflective narration to critically comment on.
- **Mediation:** Mediation refers to the actions that the instructor takes to facilitate learners' relation with the tools/resources and the tasks assigned for a learning objective. In the case of our pedagogical experiment, this mediation served the additional goal of assessment: although learners had as an explicit goal to first construct and then reflect on shared reflective narratives regarding their course experience, there was also the implicit goal of assessing whether certain critical reflection skills were acquired, necessary for the subject of the course (social science methods). To fulfill this twofold scope, the mediation techniques used focused on guiding the learning process using existing structures from the reflection assessment literature. Translating these structures into specific learning instructions (in the case of the reflective narrations) and interaction prompts (in the case of the meta-reflection forum-mediated activity) was a main design contribution of our experiment. Moreover, due to the direct connection between mediation and assessment, the problem of assessing students' reflective and meta-reflective texts as part of the course's evaluation was also addressed.

6 Conclusion

Reflection, however necessary for autonomous learning based on critical, metacognitive skills, is not an easy activity to engage with, as it implies self-motivation and the ability to reflect deeply and critically. In our study with pre-university students from all over the world, we aimed at: (a) boosting their self-motivation to reflect on their learning experiences through implementing an inquiry-based instruction framework within a social-science research-based course; and (b) guiding them through individual and team face-to-face and online activities towards writing and sharing reflective and meta-reflective texts as part of the course assessment. Students' perception of this whole reflective assessment enterprise as well as of the hybrid learning environment, that formed the context of the reflected experience, would also be valuable to examine, as previous studies show that students' relation to both influences on the quality of their learning [48, 49].

References

1. O'Byrne, W.I., Pytash, K.E.: Hybrid and blended learning: modifying pedagogy across path, pace, time, and place. J. Adolesc. Health. **59**(2), 137–140 (2015). https://doi.org/10.1002/jaal.463
2. Stefanou, C., Stolk, J.D., Prince, M., Chen, J.C., Lord, S.M.: Self-regulation and autonomy in problem-and project-based learning environments. Act. Learn. High. Educ. **14**(2), 109–122 (2013). https://doi.org/10.1177/1469787413481132
3. Lee, E., Pate, J.A., Cozart, D.: Autonomy support for online students. TechTrends **59**(4), 54–61 (2015). https://doi.org/10.1007/s11528-015-0871-9
4. Seiver, J.G., Troja, A.: Satisfaction and success in online learning as a function of the needs for affiliation, autonomy, and mastery. Distance Educ. **35**(1), 90–105 (2014). https://doi.org/10.1080/01587919.2014.891427
5. Lynch, R., Dembo, M.: The relationship between self-regulation and online learning in a blended learning context. Int. Rev. Res. Open Distrib. Learn. **5**(2) (2004). https://doi.org/10.19173/irrodl.v5i2.189
6. Sanders, M.: Embracing critical thinking as a model for professional development: creating CTB-FLCs on your campus. Inquiry: Critical Thinking Disciplines **26**(1), 29–37 (2011). https://doi.org/10.5840/inquiryctnews20112615
7. Mezirow, J.: On critical reflection. Adult Learning Quarterly **48**, 185–198 (1998). https://doi.org/10.1177/074171369804800305
8. Gupta, T., Burke, K.A., Mehta, A., Greenbowe, T.J.: Impact of guided-inquiry-based instruction with a writing and reflection emphasis on chemistry students' critical thinking abilities. J. Chem. Educ. **92**(1), 32–38 (2015). https://doi.org/10.1021/ed500059r
9. Naber, J., Wyatt, T.H.: The effect of reflective writing interventions on the critical thinking skills and dispositions of baccalaureate nursing students. Nurse Educ. Today **34**(1), 67–72 (2014). https://doi.org/10.1016/j.nedt.2013.04.002
10. Ghanizadeh, A.: The interplay between reflective thinking, critical thinking, self-monitoring, and academic achievement in higher education. High. Educ. **74**(1), 101–114 (2016). https://doi.org/10.1007/s10734-016-0031-y
11. Seaman, J.: Experience, reflect, critique: the end of the "learning cycles" era. J. Experiential Educ. **31**(1), 3–18 (2008). https://doi.org/10.5193/jee.31.1.3
12. Stewart, M.: Understanding learning: theories and critique. In: Hunt, L., Chalmers, D. (eds.) University Teaching in Focus: A Learning-Centred Approach, pp. 3–20. Routledge, London (2012)
13. Dewey, J.: How We Think. D.C. Heath, Boston (1910)
14. Schön, D.A.: The Reflective Practitioner: How Professionals Think in Action. Basic Books, New York (1983)
15. Schön, D.A.: Educating the Reflective Practitioner. Jossey-Bass, San Francisco (1987)
16. Yanow, D., Tsoukas, H.: What is reflection-in-action? A phenomenological account. J. Manag. Stud. **46**(8), 1339–1364 (2009). https://doi.org/10.1111/j.1467-6486.2009.00859.x
17. Wenger, E.: Communities of practice and social learning systems: the career of a concept. In: Blackmore, Ch. (ed.) Social Learning Systems and Communities of Practice, pp. 179–198. Springer, London (2010)
18. Michaels, S., O'Connor, C., Resnick, L.B.: Deliberative discourse idealized and realized: accountable talk in the classroom and in civic life. Stud. Philos. Educ. **27**(4), 283–297 (2008). https://doi.org/10.1007/s11217-007-9071-1
19. Rapanta, C.: Argumentation as critically oriented pedagogical dialogue. Informal Logic **39**(1), 1–31 (2019). https://doi.org/10.22329/il.v39i1.5116

20. Mezirow, J.: Transformation theory of adult learning. In: Welton, M.R. (ed.) Indefence of the Lifeworld, pp. 39–70. SUNY Press, New York (1995)
21. Kitchenham, A., Chasteauneuf, C.: An application of Mezirow's critical reflection theory to electronic portfolios. J. Transform. Educ. **7**(3), 230–244 (2009). https://doi.org/10.1177/1541344610383287
22. Esposito, G., Freda, M.F., Picione, R.D.L.: Reflexivity or "reflexivities" in higher education: conceptualizing unique reflexive process. In: Freda, M.F., González-Monteagudo, J., Esposito, G. (eds.) Working with Underachieving Students in Higher Education, pp. 58–68. Routledge, London (2016)
23. Pedaste, M., et al.: Phases of inquiry-based learning: definitions and the inquiry cycle. Educ. Res. Rev. **14**, 47–61 (2015). https://doi.org/10.1016/j.edurev.2015.02.003
24. Aditomo, A., Goodyear, P., Bliuc, A.M., Ellis, R.A.: Inquiry-based learning in higher education: principal forms, educational objectives, and disciplinary variations. Stud. High. Educ. **38**(9), 1239–1258 (2013). https://doi.org/10.1080/03075079.2011.616584
25. Diana, P., Catone, M.C.: E-learning in an undergraduate course in research methods for the social sciences: reflections on teaching. Italian J. Sociol. Educ. **8**(2), 110–142 (2016)
26. Hammond, M., Collins, R.: Self-directed Learning: Critical Practice. Kogan Page, London (1991)
27. George, S., Michel, C., Ollagnier-Beldame, M.: Favouring reflexivity in technology-enhanced learning systems: towards smart uses of traces. Interact. Learn. Environ. **24**(7), 1389–1407 (2016). https://doi.org/10.1080/10494820.2015.1016532
28. Kahn, P., Everington, L., Kelm, K., Reid, I., Watkins, F.: Understanding student engagement in online learning environments: the role of reflexivity. Educ. Tech. Res. Dev. **65**(1), 203–218 (2016). https://doi.org/10.1007/s11423-016-9484-z
29. Mumford, S., Dikilitaş, K.: Pre-service language teachers reflection development through online interaction in a hybrid learning course. Comput. Educ. **144**, 103706 (2020). https://doi.org/10.1016/j.compedu.2019.103706
30. Walker, P., Finney, N.: Skill development and critical thinking in higher education. Teach. High. Educ. **4**(4), 531–547 (1999). https://doi.org/10.1080/1356251990040409
31. Jackson, T., Mackenzie, J., Hobfoll, S.E.: Communal aspects of self-regulation. In: Boekaerts, M., Pintrich, P.R., Zeidner, M. (eds.) Handbook of Self-regulation, pp. 275–300. Academic Press, San Diego (2000)
32. Hadwin, A.F., Järvelä, S., Miller, M.: Self-regulation, coregulation, and socially shared regulation: exploring perspectives of social in self-regulated learning theory. In: Zimmerman, B.J., Schunk, D.H. (eds.) Handbook of Self-regulation of Learning and Performance, pp. 65–84. Routledge, New York (2011)
33. Bain, J.D., Ballantyne, R., Mills, C., Lester, N.C.: Reflecting on Practice: Student Teachers' Perspectives. Post-pressed, Flaxton, Qld (2002)
34. Shehabat, A., Mitew, T.: Black-boxing the black flag: anonymous sharing platforms and ISIS content distribution tactics. Perspect. Terrorism **12**(1), 81–99 (2018). https://doi.org/10.1080/1356251990040409
35. Mortari, L.: Learning thoughtful reflection in teacher education. Teachers Teaching **18**(5), 525–545 (2012). https://doi.org/10.1080/13540602.2012.709729
36. Rausch, D.W., Crawford, E.K.: Cohorts, communities of inquiry, and course delivery methods: UTC best practices in learning—the hybrid learning community model. J. Contin. High. Educ. **60**(3), 175–180 (2012). https://doi.org/10.1080/07377363.2013.722428
37. Hofmann, R., Ruthven, K.: Operational, interpersonal, discussional and ideational dimensions of classroom norms for dialogic practice in school mathematics. Br. Edu. Res. J. **44**(3), 496–514 (2018). https://doi.org/10.1002/berj.3444

38. Dennen, V.P.: From message posting to learning dialogues: factors affecting learner participation in asynchronous discussion. Distance Educ. **26**(1), 127–148 (2005). https://doi.org/10.1080/01587910500081376
39. Kuhn, D.: The Skills of Argument. Cambridge University Press, New York (1991)
40. Kuhn, D.: A developmental model of critical thinking. Educ. Res. **28**(2), 16–46 (1999)
41. Kuhn, D.: How do people know? Psychol. Sci. **12**(1), 1–8 (2001)
42. Lundgren, H., Poell, R.F.: On critical reflection: a review of Mezirow's theory and its operationalization. Hum. Resour. Dev. Rev. **15**(1), 3–28 (2016). https://doi.org/10.1177/1534484315622735
43. Burbules, N.C.: Aporia: Webs, passages, getting lost, and learning to go on. Philos. Educ. Archive 33–43 (1997)
44. Breault, R.: Accountability: to whom, for whom, and by whom? In: Breault, D.A., Breault, R. (eds.) Experiencing Dewey: Insights for Today's Classroom, pp. 9–12. Routledge & Kappa Delta Pi, New York (2014)
45. Surrain, S., Duhaylongsod, L., Selman, R.L., Snow, C.E.: Using narrative thinking in argumentative writing. In: Veneziano, E., Nicolopoulou, A. (eds). Narrative, Literacy and Other Skills: Studies in Intervention, pp. 151–172. John Publishing, Amsterdam (2019)
46. Jenson, J.D.: Promoting self-regulation and critical reflection through writing students' use of electronic portfolio. Int. J. ePortfolio **1**(1), 49–60 (2011)
47. Rapanta, C., Botturi, L., Goodyear, P., Guàrdia, L., Koole, M.: Online university teaching during and after the Covid-19 Crisis: refocusing teacher presence and learning activity. Postdigital Sci. Educ. **2**(3), 923–945 (2020). https://doi.org/10.1007/s42438-020-00155-y
48. Jackson, M.J., Helms, M.M.: Student perceptions of hybrid courses: measuring and interpreting quality. J. Educ. Bus. **84**(1), 7–12 (2008). https://doi.org/10.3200/joeb.84.1.7-12
49. White, J.V.: Students' perception of the role of reflection in leadership learning. J. Leadership Educ. **11**(2), 140–157 (2012). https://doi.org/10.12806/v11/i2/rf8

Critical Thinking on Mathematics in Higher Education: Two Experiences

Vanda Santos[1(✉)] and Nuno R. O. Bastos[2,3]

[1] Research Centre on Didactics and Technology in the Education of Trainers (CIDTFF), University of Aveiro, Aveiro, Portugal
vandasantos@ua.pt
[2] Polytechnic Institute of Viseu, Viseu, Portugal
nbastos@estgv.ipv.pt
[3] Center for Research & Development in Mathematics and Applications (CIDMA), University of Aveiro, Aveiro, Portugal

Abstract. Critical thinking (CT) helps us to distinguish between good and bad arguments, to recognize information that has value from that which is essential, to find well-founded conclusions, to create alternatives, to improve communication and, finally, to have our own thinking and acting accordingly.

Mathematics makes it possible to reinforce CT as it develops a constant search for truth through precise and exact techniques. Besides the active, collaborative and participative methodologies of learning, the uses of information and communication technologies enhance a set of advantages at the pedagogical level, namely the GeoGebra and Socrative at CT.

The participants in this study were undergraduate students of Business Management and postgraduate students of Pre-service Teachers from two Portuguese public higher education institutions. The aim of the study is to investigate students in problem solving on sequences and geometry reasoning and the CT skills and dispositions (truth seeking, creativity, inquisitiveness) developed or not.

Qualitative data findings have suggested that students exhibit CT skills and dispositions for arithmetic and geometric sequences. Another result, the study identified issues dealing with geometric constructions through a dynamic geometry system (DGS), they found it was easier to solve problems with "pencil and paper" instead of using DGS.

Keywords: Critical Thinking · Information and Communications Technolgy · Mathematic · Problem Solving

1 Introduction

The foundations of the Bologna Process are based on the assumptions of the needs of a knowledge society, gifted with cultural, scientific and technological development.

One of the great current concerns of society is the promotion of an education that leads to the development of skills that are essential to the exercise of an interventional and critical citizenship with capacities to adapt to different situations.

A. Reis et al. (Eds.): TECH-EDU 2020, CCIS 1384, pp. 156–167, 2021.
https://doi.org/10.1007/978-3-030-73988-1_11

A greater number of citizens should be encouraged to study subjects where skills are scarce. In addition, all students need to acquire transversal skills and advanced essential skills that will enable them to succeed in active life. These skills include advanced digital and numeracy skills, as well as critical thinking (CT) and problem-solving skills [8]. There is also a great need for flexible and innovative teaching and learning techniques, planned to make education more effective. In fact, the development of skills presupposes the acquisition of knowledge, which is subsequently put to the service of practical purposes, with CT having the mission of supporting the selection of important information according to our intentions. On the other hand, the important role that information and communications technology (ICT) plays in today's society is undeniable, not only for facilitating access to information and its management, but also for making the user the (co) author of his productions, because he shares them with the community, and those of others, for being able to modify them. In this process, various skills are developed, including the CT itself. More and more, teachers feel the need to resort to ICT, to facilitate the management of their work and the interaction with other stakeholders in Education [3, 7].

The education in today's world with new information and communication technologies, is becoming complex and full of challenges. ICTs become a fundamental ally for educators, since their use will allow the development of skills and abilities that can be applied directly in the formation process to stimulate CT.

According to [8], CT is developing skills to identify or formulate problems and solve them, evaluate information and use it, test ideas based on relevant criteria, recognize your own judgments and put them to the test of new arguments, and communicate effectively with others.

Achieving this type of thinking involves some activities such as analyzing, judging, criticizing, evaluating, contrasting, comparing and evaluating actions that teachers should try to develop in their teaching-learning sessions. What better alternative to carry out these actions than the use and application of ICT, for training activities to educate in an agile way.

The CT should be stimulated in different areas of knowledge, namely that of Mathematics. The scientific area of Mathematics is, without a doubt, the science that best allows analyzing the work of the mind and developing a reasoning applicable to the study of any subject or theme. However, perhaps because mental habits were created that we can hardly get rid of, there are many difficulties that young people encounter in their study. Mathematics makes it possible to reinforce CT as it develops a constant search for truth through precise and exact techniques [9].

One of the branches of mathematics is geometry. Geometric representation has a lot to do with intuitive and even appealing representation. One way of working with geometry is to use the dynamic mathematics software, GeoGebra. The use of the dynamic geometry system (DGS), GeoGebra [4], can assist in teaching and learning mathematical content, allowing students to visualize, experiment, formulate hypotheses, building mathematical ideas, providing reflections and CT in the learning process [6].

Another digital tool is Socrative[1] which is a classroom app that allows for educators to engage students through numerous interactive lessons.

---

[1] www.socrative.com.

Socrative can be used to implement different strategies, such as the Think-Pair-Share (TPS) model [5]. This learning strategy promotes the students participation by encouraging the collaborative/cooperative evolving by peers in discussion of an idea. This strategy provides an opportunity for all students to share their thinking with at least one other student which, in turn, increases their sense of involvement in classroom learning. Activities available include instant polling, quizzes and quick questions. Space race visuals allow for students to compete during quizzing keeping the student engaged as they track their progress. Educators upload their own content making it possible to include higher level, CT and problem-solving questions. Since formative assessment is viewed instantly the educator has the opportunity to give immediate feedback to the students to clarify subject matter or open discussion to further promote CT.

2 Methodology

The research presented in this article is of a qualitative nature [1], and intends to contribute to the reflection on CT, supporting the development of future experiences by higher education teachers.

The investigation was carried out during the 1st and 2nd semester of the academic year 2019/2020 in two public higher education institutions, University of Aveiro and Polytechnic Institute of Viseu, with graduated and undergraduate students.

3 Study Description

The participants in this study were 7 students from the maste's programme for Pre-service Teachers, MSc for Training of Teachers for the 1st to 6th grades with emphasis on Mathematics and Natural Sciences at the University ofAveiro and 25 students from undergraduate programme, BSc in Business Management at the Polytechnic Institute of Viseu.

Postgraduate Students. The postgraduate students of Pre-service Teachers worked in concepts on geometry, namely Euclidean geometry. These students had previously contacted, in other curricular units, the DGS GeoGebra. The activities consisted of constructing regular polygons, individually, with the use of GeoGebra. The activities were proposed in class and the class teacher had the role of mediator of the reflections and questions that arose during the class. These proposed polygons were triangles and squares. In the activity on the construction of triangles, they were asked to build, with a ruler and compass (i.e. without using the polygon tool available in GeoGebra), isosceles, equilateral and scalene triangles. They were also asked to build the square with a ruler and compass. One of the objectives was to recall the properties of these polygons. The other were an exercise in analyzing the possible contribution of teaching to the development of CT in students. In terms of CT, the student has to appeal to his/her interpretation, analysis and explanation skills.

Undergraduate Students. The undergraduate students of Business Management worked with sequences (arithmetic and geometric). Mostly of these students never learn anything about arithmetic and geometric sequences. In these activities (two different quizzes) were used Socrative and the TPS technique. The students have answered questions in two different moments and conditions: first, they think and answer (THINK) individually (questions with the odd number) and then, without teacher's feedback, they discuss in groups (PAIR) of two or three students (with the teacher's guidance when it is asked for), they turn to answer individually, again. In terms of CT, during the debate, the student has to appeal to his/her interpretation, analysis and explanation skills.

After they answer the same question in two different moments, the teacher selects a particular student (or a pair of students) and asks that student to explain how he or she got the results (SHARE).

4 Results and Discussion

In this section we will analyze the problem solving on sequences and geometry reasoning and the CT skills and dispositions developed or not at these two higher education institutions.

Postgraduate Students. In the data analysis collected from the activities was found that students construct the equilateral triangle and isosceles well (see Fig. 1 and Fig. 2), it was a consensual response among the students' constructions. Their knowledge of the properties of an equilateral triangle and isosceles triangle allowed them to be constructed with the "ruler and compass".

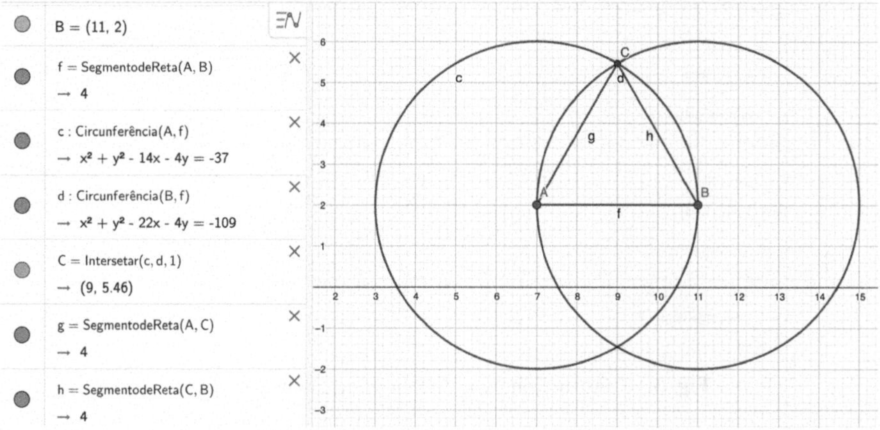

Fig. 1. Construction by a student of an equilateral triangle.

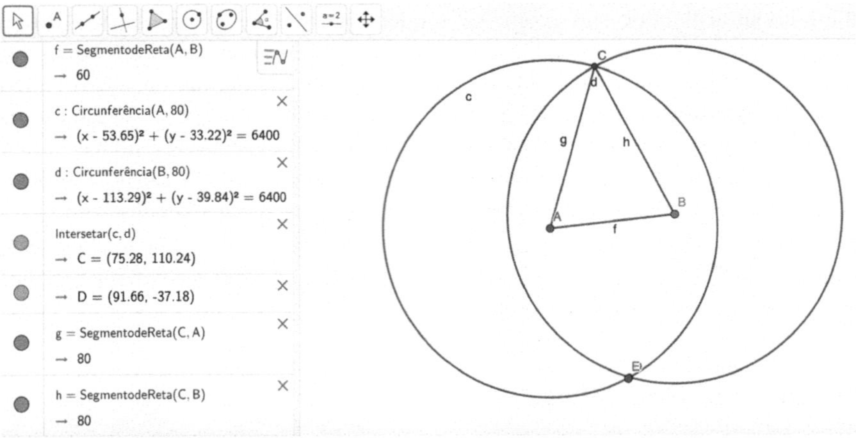

Fig. 2. Construction by a student of an isosceles triangle.

The difficulty starts with the construction of a scalene triangle (see Fig. 3) and a square (see Fig. 4).

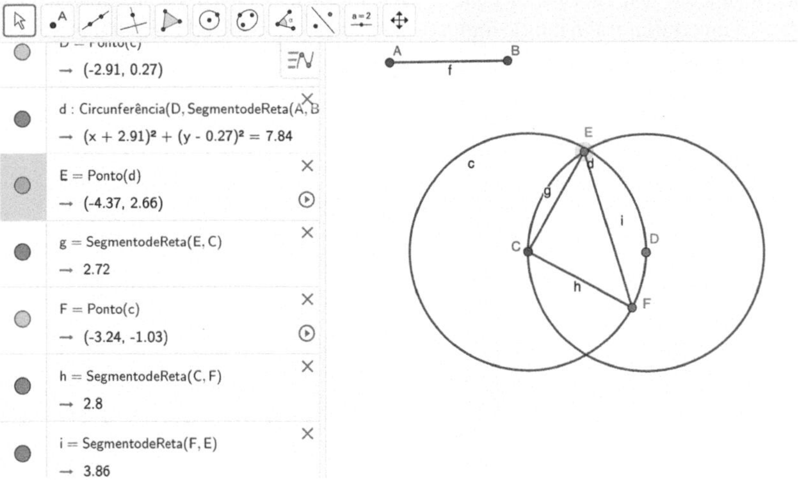

Fig. 3. Construction by a student of a scalene triangle.

At Fig. 3 there are some difficulties about the construction, because we can observe when the point F coincides with point D, we have an isosceles triangle.

At Fig. 4 we can observe two different constructions of a square, with ruler and compass. At classroom it was evident their doubts to use ruler and compass to construct this polygon. They reveal some creativity to construct the square, but with no success.

The cognitive skills that underlie CT with Pre-service Teachers demonstrated a clear understanding of the purpose of the activity, they clearly defined the problem, and were able to accurately identify the central issues and problems inherent in the activity, namely

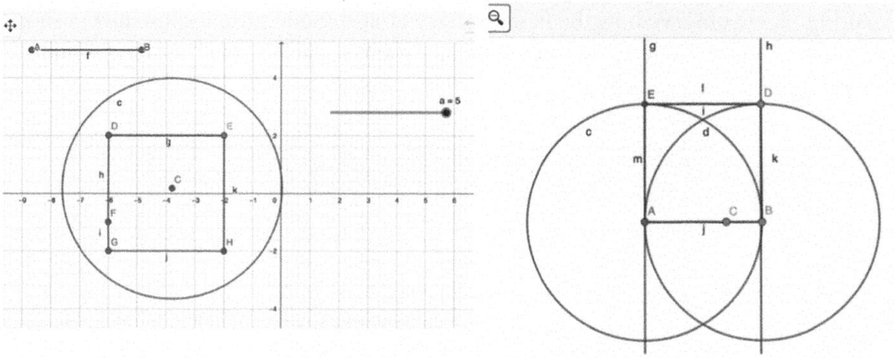

Fig. 4. Construction by two students of a square.

the dynamism of the DGS. They accurately identified and explained the relevant key concepts and made assumptions that are consistent and reasonable.

The way in which this activity relates to ICT also helped us to identify some of its strengths:

- Effectively placing the student at the center of the process, in which the use of ICT is essential to develop the activity, reflect on concepts and essential principles for the construction of polygons and confront their opinions with those of other colleagues, present and discuss ideas with the teacher;
- Sensitize students to the possible use of these technologies in the teaching/learning of mathematics.

At the end of the activity, some written questions were asked, by email, requesting feedback about the experiment to understand their difficulties. Regarding the use of DGS they find it easy to use when they know the properties to be built, but the construction of a square they felt was a higher level of difficulty. One of the students says that, in fact, she had already done this same activity before with GeoGebra, but at that moment she felt difficult to construct. Another, student says, she had some difficulties in building the figures because they are used to doing it on paper, however, by remembering the properties of the requested figures, they were able to build them.

Undergraduate Students. The data collected from quizzes show that, after discussion with their pairs, the number of students that obtain the correct answer have improved (see Fig. 7 and Fig. 9).

From the experience we observed that Socrative help teacher to improve, more quickly, students CT skills through keeping students more engaged with the material, allowing the student to get immediate feedback [2], by making students defend their answers and share results with their pairs.

In the first stage the teacher launches the quiz with the following settings in Socrative: teacher paced, requiring names and shuffle answers. Then students' access to the quiz through https://b.socrative.com/login/student/ by introducing first the room name indicated by the teacher and then her/his name.

At Fig. 5, we observe how the first question of arithmetic progression quiz is shown to the student and at Table 1, we can see the questions regarding to arithmetic sequences quiz.

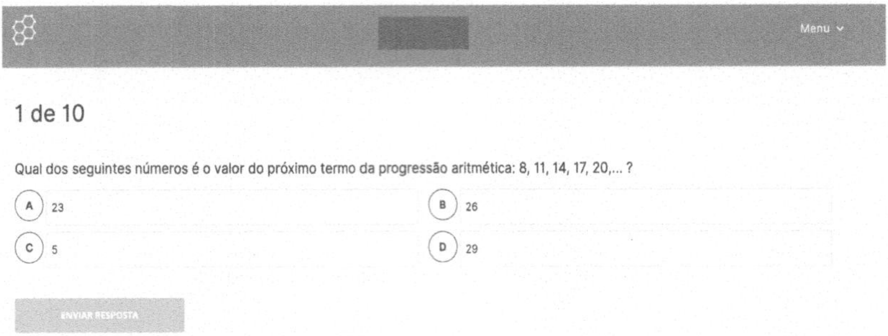

Fig. 5. First question of arithmetic sequences at Socrative.

Table 1. Arithmetic sequences quiz.

Question number	Question
1 & 2	Which of the following numbers is the value of the next term in the arithmetic progression: 8, 11, 14, 17, 20, ...? 5 23 26 29
3 & 4	Fill in the blank in the following sentence in order to make a statement true: "170 is the ____ term of the arithmetic sequence -4, 2, 8, ...
5 & 6	A teenager has 100 teddy bears and decides that each birthday she will offer 2 bears to a children's hospital. What is the general term of this arithmetic sequence? u(n)=100+(n-1)-2 u(n)=100+(n-1)*(-2)
7 & 8	In the following arithmetic sequence, two consecutive values are missing: 11, ____, ____, 32. What values are these respectively?
9 & 10	Knowing that x, y, z and w are the first 4 terms of an arithmetic progression write w as a function of x, y and z.

After all the students answer individually, the teacher looks at the results, forms groups and tells students to debate their answers in groups along 10 min. After the 10 min, teacher ask to students answer again to the questions and the final results are shown to the classroom (see Fig. 6).

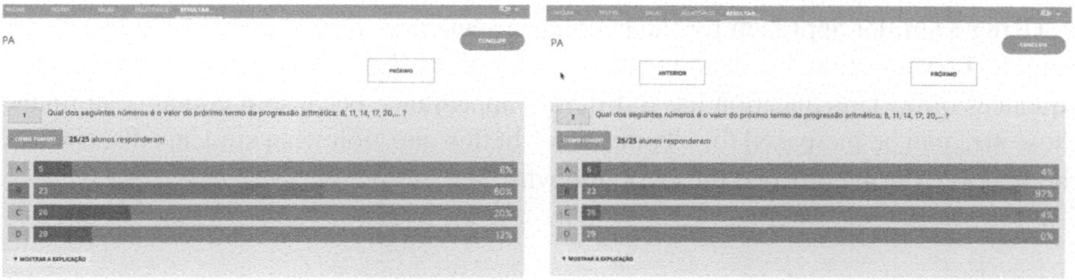

Fig. 6. Results obtained before and after group discussion, respectively.

At Fig. 7, we have a board with the final results of the arithmetic sequences quiz, and we can observe that from the first moment, where students answer before discussion (questions with the odd numbers) to the moment after discussion, questions with the even numbers was always an improvement. We can also observe that although the final questions are more complex after the discussion, the results are also very positive.

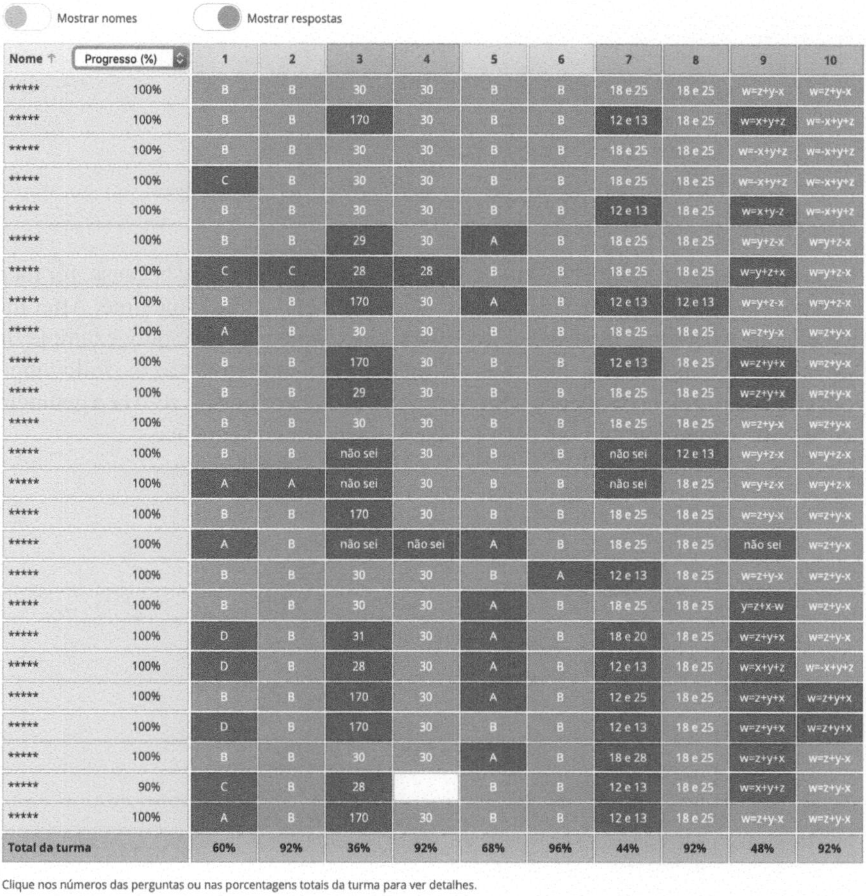

Mostrar nomes   Mostrar respostas

Nome ↑	Progresso (%)	1	2	3	4	5	6	7	8	9	10
*****	100%	B	B	30	30	B	B	18 e 25	18 e 25	w=z+y-x	w=z+y-x
*****	100%	B	B	170	30	B	B	12 e 13	18 e 25	w=x+y+z	w=-x+y+z
*****	100%	B	B	30	30	B	B	18 e 25	18 e 25	w=-x+y+z	w=-x+y+z
*****	100%	C	B	30	30	B	B	18 e 25	18 e 25	w=-x+y+z	w=-x+y+z
*****	100%	B	B	30	30	B	B	12 e 13	18 e 25	w=x+y-z	w=-x+y+z
*****	100%	B	B	29	30	A	B	18 e 25	18 e 25	w=y+z-x	w=y+z-x
*****	100%	C	C	28	28	B	B	18 e 25	18 e 25	w=y+z+x	w=y+z-x
*****	100%	B	B	170	30	A	B	12 e 13	12 e 13	w=y+z-x	w=y+z-x
*****	100%	A	B	30	30	B	B	18 e 25	18 e 25	w=z+y-x	w=z+y-x
*****	100%	B	B	170	30	B	B	12 e 13	18 e 25	w=z+y+x	w=z+y-x
*****	100%	B	B	29	30	B	B	18 e 25	18 e 25	w=z+y+x	w=z+y-x
*****	100%	B	B	30	30	B	B	18 e 25	18 e 25	w=z+y-x	w=z+y-x
*****	100%	B	B	não sei	30	B	B	não sei	12 e 13	w=y+z-x	w=y+z-x
*****	100%	A	A	não sei	30	B	B	não sei	18 e 25	w=y+z-x	w=y+z-x
*****	100%	B	B	170	30	B	B	18 e 25	18 e 25	w=z+y-x	w=z+y-x
*****	100%	A	B	não sei	não sei	A	B	18 e 25	18 e 25	não sei	w=z+y-x
*****	100%	B	B	30	30	B	A	12 e 13	18 e 25	w=z+y-x	w=z+y-x
*****	100%	B	B	30	30	A	B	18 e 25	18 e 25	y=z+x-w	w=z+y-x
*****	100%	D	B	31	30	A	B	18 e 20	18 e 25	w=z+y+x	w=z+y-x
*****	100%	D	B	28	30	A	B	12 e 13	18 e 25	w=x+y+z	w=-x+y+z
*****	100%	B	B	170	30	A	B	12 e 25	18 e 25	w=z+y+x	w=z+y+x
*****	100%	D	B	170	30	B	B	12 e 13	18 e 25	w=z+y+x	w=z+y+x
*****	100%	B	B	30	30	A	B	18 e 28	18 e 25	w=z+y+x	w=z+y-x
*****	90%	C	B	28		B	B	12 e 13	18 e 25	w=x+y+z	w=z+y-x
*****	100%	A	B	170	30	B	B	12 e 13	18 e 25	w=z+y-x	w=z+y-x
Total da turma		60%	92%	36%	92%	68%	96%	44%	92%	48%	92%

Clique nos números das perguntas ou nas porcentagens totais da turma para ver detalhes.

Fig. 7. Overall results from quiz about arithmetic sequences (green cells signify right answers while red cells mean wrong answers). (Color figure online)

Using a similar approach for the geometric sequences quiz we can see at Fig. 8, for example, how question 3 is shown to the student. At the Table 2 we can see the geometric sequences quiz. This question has a different appearance because it contains an image whose size can be increased for a better view. In this question what students discuss was who makes (Marika or Lori) the error and why.

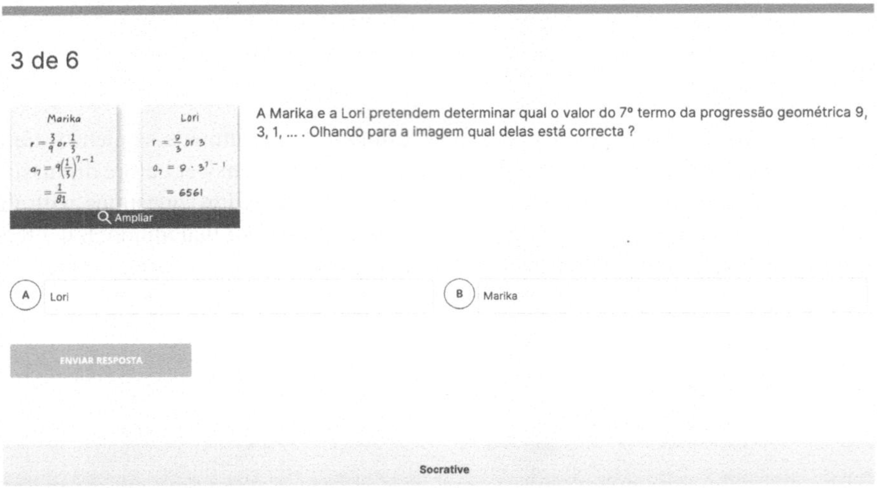

Fig. 8. Third question of geometric sequences at Socrative.

To answer question number 5, students need to discuss more time because, for them, it's strange that a sequence can be geometric and arithmetic at the same time. After they discuss and answer again, the teacher asks for real examples and the only example that they gave was the constant sequence. The justification that they gave was the following: if we consider an arithmetic sequence with common difference equal to zero or a geometric sequence with a common ratio of 1 we get the same constant sequence.

Table 2. Geometric sequences quiz.

Question number	**Question**
1 & 2	Which of the following is the next term of geometric sequence 8, 20, 50, 125, ...? A. 75 B. 200 C. 250 D. 312.5
3 & 4	Marika and Lori intend to determine the value of the 7th term of the geometric sequence 9, 3, 1, ... Looking at the image which one is correct? 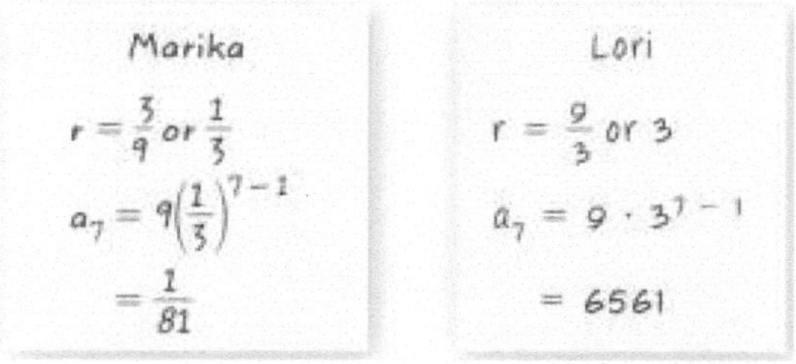 A. Marika B. Lori
5 & 6	The logical value of the following sentence "There is no succession that is simultaneously an arithmetic and a geometric sequence "is: A. true B. false

At Fig. 9, we have a board with the final results of the geometric sequences quiz, and we can observe, as in the arithmetic quiz, that from the first moment, where students answer before discussion (questions with the odd numbers) to the moment after discussion, questions with the even numbers was always an improvement.

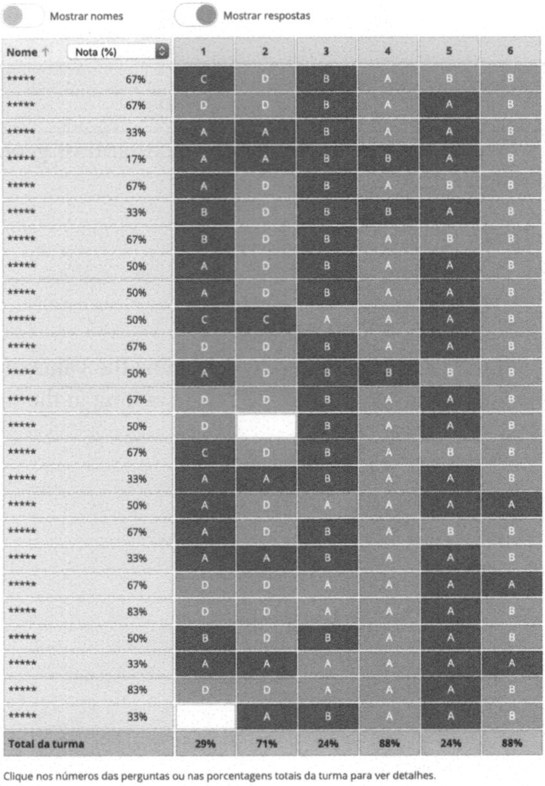

Mostrar nomes Mostrar respostas

Nome ↑	Nota (%)	1	2	3	4	5	6
*****	67%	C	D	B	A	B	B
*****	67%	D	D	B	A	A	B
*****	33%	A	A	B	A	A	B
*****	17%	A	A	B	B	A	B
*****	67%	A	D	B	A	B	B
*****	33%	B	D	B	B	A	B
*****	67%	B	D	B	A	B	B
*****	50%	A	D	B	A	A	B
*****	50%	A	D	B	A	A	B
*****	50%	C	C	A	A	A	B
*****	67%	D	D	B	A	A	B
*****	50%	A	D	B	B	B	B
*****	67%	D	D	B	A	A	B
*****	50%	D		B	A	A	B
*****	67%	C	D	B	A	B	B
*****	33%	A	A	B	A	A	B
*****	50%	A	D	A	A	A	A
*****	67%	A	D	B	A	B	B
*****	33%	A	A	B	A	A	B
*****	67%	D	D	A	A	A	A
*****	83%	D	D	A	A	A	B
*****	50%	B	D	B	A	A	B
*****	33%	A	A	A	A	A	A
*****	83%	D	D	A	A	A	B
*****	33%		A	B	A	A	B
Total da turma		29%	71%	24%	88%	24%	88%

Clique nos números das perguntas ou nas porcentagens totais da turma para ver detalhes.

Fig. 9. Overall results from quiz about geometric sequences (green cells signify right answers while red cells mean wrong answers). (Color figure online)

The students demonstrated a clear understanding of the purpose of the activity and during the moments of discussion, in the activities, they identify and evaluate relevant significant points of view. The use of Socrative as a responsive system encourages deeper level learning/CT in the classroom with focus on reasoning skills.

5 Conclusions

The study showed that students have an objective view on their level of CT, when they understand their activities and think about them with creativity and truth-seeking.

The use of ICTs such as GeoGebra and Socrative can improve and enhance students' knowledge and skills, such as critical, creative and innovative thinking [2, 6].

There are studies in which teachers believe that the introduction of ICT in the educational curriculum helps students to achieve their strengths and weaknesses, indicates methods to develop new strategies in order to achieve learning objectives and helps students to acquire knowledge through involvement and autonomous behavior [3]. In this study we identified these beliefs, with Pre-service Teachers, when one student said when remembering the properties of the requested figures, they were able to build them, this revealed that the students, through their autonomous behavior, can think critically on their learning objectives to achieve their purposes.

To create critical thinkers is developing personalities. They have to be partners in teaching and have to become partners in professional discussions, mathematical knowledge and CT appear as crucial to the autonomy of each student.

Acknowledgements. The first author was supported by National Funds through FCT – Fundação para a Ciência e a Tecnologia, I.P. under the projects UIDB/00194/2020, and in the scope of the framework contract foreseen in the numbers 4, 5 and 6 of the article 23, of the Decree-Law 57/2016, of August 29, changed by Law 57/2017, of July 19.

The second author was supported by Portuguese funds through the CIDMA - Center for Research and Development in Mathematics and Applications, and the Portuguese Foundation for Science and Technology (FCT-Fundação para a Ciência e a Tecnologia), within project UIDB/04106/2020.

References

1. Cohen, L., Mannion, L., Morrison, K.: Research Methods in Education, 7th edn. Routledge, New York (2011)
2. Dakka, S.M.: Using Socrative to enhance in-class student engagement and collaboration. arXiv preprint arXiv:1510.02500 (2015)
3. Giavrimis, P., Papanis, E., Papanis, E.M.: Information and communication technologies and development of learners' critical thinking: primary school teachers' attitudes. Int. Educ. Stud. **4**(3), 150–160 (2011)
4. Hohenwarter, M.: GeoGebra - Ein Software system für dynamische Geometrie und Algebra der Ebene. Master thesis, University of Salzburg (2002)
5. Kaddoura, M.: Think pair share: a teaching learning strategy to enhance students' critical thinking. Educ. Res. Q. **36**(4), 3–24 (2013)
6. Kim, K.M., Md-Ali, R.: GeoGebra: towards realizing 21st century learning in mathematics education. Malaysian J. Learn. Instruction 93–115 (2017)
7. Luić, L., Glumac, D.: The role of ICT technology in the knowledge society. In 2009 9th International Conference on Telecommunication in Modern Satellite, Cable, and Broadcasting Services, pp. 310–313. IEEE (2009)
8. Paul, R., Elder, L.: The miniature guide to critical thinking concepts and tools (ed.). J. Korean Soc. Des. Sci. *19*(3), 17 (2003).
9. Su, H.F.H., Ricci, F.A., Mnatsakanian, M.: Mathematical teaching strategies: pathways to critical thinking and metacognition. Int. J. Res. Educ. Sci. **2**(1), 190–200 (2016)

Cooperative Learning and Critical Thinking in Face to Face and Online Environments

Helena Silva[1,2](✉), José Lopes[1,2], Eva Morais[1,3], and Caroline Dominguez[1,4]

[1] University of Trás-os-Montes e Alto Douro, Vila Real, Portugal
{helsilva,jlopes,emorais,carold}@utad.pt
[2] CIIE (Centre for Research and Intervention in Education), Faculty of Psychology and Education Sciences, University of Porto, Porto, Portugal
[3] CMAT (Centre of Mathematics), University of Minho, Braga, Portugal
[4] LabCTD-CIDTFF (Research Centre on Didactics and Technology in the Education of Trainers), University of Aveiro, Aveiro, Portugal

Abstract. The importance of developing higher order skills in higher education students is a recommendation of several international organizations, so that they are able to respond to the challenges of 21st century society. The literature mentions several methodologies with these potentialities, including Cooperative Learning (CL), especially in presential learning environments. This study aims at comparing the effectiveness of CL in the development of Critical Thinking (CT) skills of higher education students in Portugal in two learning environments: face-to-face and distance learning. A quasi-experimental study was implemented, with pre and posttest, using the Critical and Creative Thinking Test (1.Revista Lusófona de Educação 44:173–189) with 32 students of the 3rd year of the Basic Education Program, distributed in two groups: 1) the presential group (academic year 2018/19) and 2) the distance learning group through synchronous sessions and virtual rooms in small groups (academic year 2019/20). The results show that there are no statistically significant differences in the total score of the Critical and Creative Thinking Test or with regard to the different skills assessed by the Critical and Creative Thinking Test: interpretation, analysis, explanation, evaluation, synthesis and creativity. In line with recent research, these results, to be confirmed at a larger scale, point out that CL is equally effective in promoting CT for students in face-to-face or in distance synchronous learning environments.

Keywords: Cooperative Learning · Critical thinking · Online Learning Environment

1 Introduction

The global challenges of the 21st century demand active professionals and citizens capable of thinking critically about the different and complex problems at stake in order to find sustainable alternatives. The role of the educational institutions to prepare students

A. Reis et al. (Eds.): TECH-EDU 2020, CCIS 1384, pp. 168–180, 2021.
https://doi.org/10.1007/978-3-030-73988-1_12

to think critically, creatively and systematically and to be able to integrate multiple perspectives is thus reinforced [2]. Not only students have to learn how to deal with the overwhelming (and fast) information that needs processing and interpretation, but they also must know how to communicate their ideas and opinions in an effective way and to integrate the social and ethical dimensions of the situations they are confronted with [3, 4].

Together with international economic and political bodies like the World Economic Forum [5] or the Council of Europe [6] and professional bodies like the Accreditation Board for Engineering and Technology [7], Higher Education Institutions (HEI) and educational bodies have come to build a consensus on the importance to effectively develop Critical Thinking (CT) in students, putting CT as a primary goal of undergraduate and graduate degrees [8]. Thus, diverse initiatives like the European funded project Crithinkedu [9], are gradually being implemented to include in the HEIs' curricula, strategies which support CT development [10, 11] through active pedagogies. In general, these are grounded in the social constructivist learning theory [12, 13] that favors a learning environment in which students move away from a passive position to one in which higher order skills like critical thinking are fomented. Vygotsky's theory [12] stresses the role that social and cultural interactions play in the learning process putting the emphases on the idea that knowledge is co-constructed and that individuals learn from one another, being engaged in the learning process.

More than eventual disagreement between authors, the variety of existent CT definitions [14] shows that this conceptual construct has multiple facets, each author choosing to focus more on one or some in particular. For Norris and Ennis [15, p. 3] CT is "a rational and reflective thought, centered on defining what to believe or what to do". According to Halpern [16, p. 450] "it is the use of cognitive skills or strategies that increase the probability of obtaining desired results" stressing the characteristic of being an intentional process. Facione ([17], p. 2) defines it as "the intentional, self-regulated judgment that results in interpretation, analysis, evaluation and inference as well as an explanation of the evidence and conceptual, methodological, criteriological or contextual considerations on which the judgment was based". Broadly speaking, CT can be defined as "a superior form of thinking integrating cognitive skills and dispositions, 'made to measure', as it is applied on a daily basis depending on the situation to increase the possibility of achieving the intended objective" [18, p. 21]. When defining CT, authors generally describe it as a higher-order thinking component that combines several cognitive dimensions: knowing how to analyze, explain, interpret, make inferences, evaluate, decide what to believe, solve problems effectively, exercise in-depth questioning, being able to detect weaknesses in their way of thinking, among others [19]. For many authors [19–21], CT includes dispositions and attitudes, like communication, empathy, open-mindedness, truth seeking, systematicity necessary for a positive integration of students in their professional life and as active citizens.

One of the strategies that has been pointed out as being effective to promote CT skills and dispositions by a significant body of literature, more recently at the HEI level, is Cooperative Learning (CL) [22–26]. It refers to students working together in an attempt to achieve a shared learning goal [22]. The five characteristics of well-structured CL groups (positive interdependence, group and individual accountability, promotive interaction, appropriate social skills, and group processing) enable the promotion of CT [27]. Through CL students are exposed to intellectual diversity and thus confronted with different ways of processing information and points of views. Through the interaction, they have many opportunities to debate ideas, defend or question arguments, synthesize information and evaluate solutions [28] coming up with a better understanding and a shared knowledge [29].

If the literature is abundant on the reasons why CL promotes cognitive development in face to face learning environments, with the increase of the use of distance learning, some authors have more recently started investigating the influence of online technologies on the learning outcomes and more specifically on the development of CT (e.g. [30, 31]) with the use of online Cooperative learning (e.g. [32]).

Adding to the recent literature at the Higher Education (HE) level on active teaching/learning strategies which support CT development [10, 33], still scarce and little systematized [34], this study intends to contribute from an empirical point of view, to the discussion about the development of CT through CL as a promising and effective learning approach in HE.

Besides the advantages pointed out by the literature on using online cooperative learning like handling increasing number of students in classroom, spreading sense of community, making learning and teaching a shared experience and obtaining a cost efficient way of delivering education [35], CL used in an online environment seems to show the potential to effectively promote Critical Thinking skills [36] although some literature suggests that more studies are needed in order to identify if some factors, like race, social origins influence its outcomes [37].

Based on current trends in education which point toward increased use of distance learning and according to research on the benefits of cooperative learning, this study will reflect more specifically on the effects of an online CL environment on CT development compared to a face to face CL learning environment, adding to the recent studies both on CT (e.g. [30, 31]) and on CL (e.g. [32]) in online environments.

As the Horizon report Higher Education Edition states [38], with the increased emphases on CT and a steady growth in the use of educational technologies, online learning environments are here to stay. In the authors' view, it is valuable to add to the experimental research in order to evaluate if the format of learning (face to face and/or online) has an influence on CT development, and in particular if CL in an online environment helps develop CT through CL.

The goal of this study is thus to verify if the CL methodology is as effective in the promotion of CT in virtual learning environments as in face-to-face ones.

2 Methodology

2.1 Research Methodology

A quasi-experimental design was used with two experimental non-randomized groups with 3rd year undergraduate students [39]. The Group 1 consisted in 14 students learning in presential classes during the 2018/19 academic year and Group 2 consisted in 18 students in a distance learning environment during the academic 2019/20 year.

Students had to respond to the Critical and Creative Thinking (CCT) test elaborated by the authors [1] which evaluates CT skills proposed in the reviewed Bloom's taxonomy and some of the Facione's one [17, 40] (Table 2), the total score ranging from 0 to 25. The inter-judge reliability of the test (Cohen kappa coefficient) ranged between 0.76 and 0.93 [1].

In the face-to-face scenario, data were collected using the pen-and-paper method in the form of a questionnaire. In the online scenario, the questionnaire was filled in a digital way (Google Forms). Pre and Post Test questionnaires were filled at the same moments of the semester for both groups (at the beginning and at the end).

The collected data were analyzed through descriptive statistics and inferential analysis using IBM SPSS Statistics 25.

2.2 Pedagogical Context

At the beginning of the semester the following activities were done: 1) the teacher organized heterogeneous groups of four to five students; and 2) different roles were assigned to each member of the group, on a rotating basis and adjusted to the objectives of the activities. Throughout the 13 classes: 3) students in the cooperative groups analyzed pedagogical scenarios, which involved problem solving (classroom situations related to learning problems, indiscipline, lack of motivation) in which students had to answer questions aimed at developing the CT skills that the test evaluates; 4) students read and analyzed articles on teaching-learning methods; 5) works were exchanged between groups to give and receive feedback between peers; 6) the teacher gave feedback to the work of each group after feedback given by their colleagues; 7) students improved their work, incorporating feedback from colleagues (feedback from peers) and from the teacher; 8) each small group made a final oral presentation to the whole class; and 9) each group periodically developed a reflection on the functioning of the group (group process), namely in relation to the strengths, weaknesses and possible improvement strategies.

The two groups had the same teacher, the course corresponded to 13 lessons of 120 min and the same intervention took place during each academic semester. The students of the two experimental groups worked in cooperative groups of 3 to 4 elements. In these groups, students were involved in pedagogical analysis scenarios that involved problem solving and the analysis of articles on teaching and learning methods, on which they also had to elaborate concept maps and exercise, intentionally and explicitly, critical and creative skills. Table 1 summarizes the information of the groups involved in the research.

Table 1. Information about the groups and respective pedagogical settings

	Group 1: Presential classes	Group 2: Virtual classes / Distance learning
Academic degree	Primary School Teaching (Basic Education, 1st cycle degree)	Primary School Teaching (Basic Education, 1st cycle degree)
Course year	3rd year	3rd year
Academic year	2018/19	2019/20
Number of students	N = 14	N = 18
Methodology	Cooperative learning, using Think-Pair-Share and Jigsaw methods	Cooperative learning, using Think-Pair-Share and Jigsaw methods
Groups	Heterogeneous, organized by the teacher, with 3 to 4 students	Heterogeneous, organized by the teacher, with 3 to 4 students
Teaching platform		Zoom (main room and breakout rooms) and Padlet – synchronous sessions
Number of sessions	13	13
Session duration	120 min	120 min
Learning tasks	Analysis of pedagogical scenarios and scientific articles Written feedback between peers and written and oral feedback from the teacher Presentation and discussion of group work	Virtual common room: Presentation and discussion of group work; oral feedback from the teacher and students Simultaneous virtual rooms: Analysis of educational scenarios and scientific articles. Written feedback between peers and oral and written feedback from the teacher (in Padlet)
CT assessment	CCT test Pretest: beginning of the semester Posttest: end of the semester	CCT test Pretest: beginning of the semester Posttest: end of the semester

Students worked in cooperative groups applying 2 types of cooperative learning techniques: Think-Pair-Share [41] and Jigsaw [42]. These techniques were used in order for the students to learn the basic principles of cooperative learning mentioned previously.

For the Think-Pair-Share technique, the goal was to build consensus regarding the teacher's questions. With the Jigsaw, the final and mutual goal consisted in all members reaching an understanding of the whole material, provided that each member of the group understood his/her part first (going through the process of learning it in the "experts' group") and explained it clearly later to the other members.

Students in Group 1 carried out the above described tasks in face-to-face (presential) classes. Students in Group 2 performed the same activities on the Zoom platform. Activities 1 and 2 were promoted by the teacher in the main room with all students, as well as activities that involved the presentation of works by each group (activity 8). The remaining activities that involved working in small groups were carried out in breakout rooms (for the online environment). During these activities (3–7, 9) the teacher stayed in the main room and interacted with the students in the virtual rooms whenever requested, giving the necessary support for them to carry out the activities. The collaborative Padlet platform was used to help students and teachers perform the feedback activities in the online environment [43].

All students took the pretest in the first class of the semester (on paper for the presential group and online for the other). In the last class of the semester, in 2018/19 students took the posttest in a classroom, whereas in 2019/20 students took the posttest online. The tests lasted about 30 min to be completed.

3 Results

The subjects of this study were 14 students of a class of the Primary School Teaching course (Basic Education, 1st cycle degree) in the academic 2018/19, and 18 students of a class of the same course of the 2019/20 academic year. The majority of the students in each class were female (12 students in 2018/19, (85.7%); 16 students in 2019/20, (88.9%)) and almost all students ages ranged between 19 to 21.

Regarding the scoring of the CCT tests, the results showed high inter-rater reliabilities (0.95).

The basic descriptive statistics of the scores in the CCT test are presented in Tables 2, 3 and 4.

Table 2. Statistics of the scores in the CCT test in the academic year 2018/2019 (N = 14).

Dimension		Median	Mean	SD
Interpretation	Pretest	1	.71	.47
	Posttest	1	1.14	.54
Analysis_a (identification of solutions that imply making inferences)	Pretest	2	2.0	0
	Posttest	2	2.29	.47
Analysis_b (comparison and contrasting of solutions)	Pretest	1	.93	.48
	Posttest	1	1.07	.62
Explanation	Pretest	2	1.57	.76
	Posttest	1.5	1.64	.74
Evaluation	Pretest	1	1.0	.88
	Posttest	1	1.29	.73
Synthesis	Pretest	.5	1.14	1.35
	Posttest	3	2.36	1.15
Creativity – Fluency	Pretest	1	.93	.48
	Posttest	1	1.5	.76
Creativity – Flexibility	Pretest	1	.93	.48
	Posttest	1	1.36	.50
Creativity – Originality	Pretest	1	1.14	.86
	Posttest	1	1.79	.98
Total CCT test	Pretest	10.5	10.36	3.30
	Posttest	15	14.43	2.79

Table 3. Statistics of the scores in the CCT test in the academic year 2019/2020 (N = 18).

Dimension		Median	Mean	SD
Interpretation	Pretest	1	.78	.81
	Posttest	1	1.0	.97
Analysis_a (identification of solutions that imply making inferences)	Pretest	2	2.0	0
	Posttest	3	3.22	.55
Analysis_b (comparison and contrasting of solutions)	Pretest	1	.93	.48
	Posttest	1	1.22	.55
Explanation	Pretest	1	.89	.47
	Posttest	2	2.0	.77
Evaluation	Pretest	1	1.17	.51
	Posttest	2	1.56	.78
Synthesis	Pretest	1	1.33	1.41
	Posttest	3	2.06	1.26
Creativity – Fluency	Pretest	1	1.0	.34
	Posttest	1	1.22	.43
Creativity – Flexibility	Pretest	1	1.06	.42
	Posttest	1	1.39	.50
Creativity – Originality	Pretest	2	1.94	.54
	Posttest	2	2.17	.38
Total CCT test	Pretest	11	11.33	2.66
	Posttest	15.5	14.61	2.95

Table 4. Differences between the mean score in the posttest and the mean score in the pretest.

	Group 1: Presential classes	Group 2: Virtual classes / Distance learning
Interpretation	.43	.22
Analysis_a (identification of solutions that imply making inferences)	.29*	1.22
Analysis_b (comparison and contrasting of solutions)	.14	.29
Explanation	.07	1.11*
Evaluation	.29	.39
Synthesis	1.22*	.73
Creativity – Fluency	.57*	.22
Creativity – Flexibility	.43*	.33*
Creativity – Originality	.65*	.23
Total CCT test	4.07	3.28

* Significant differences (level .05) according to the results of the Wilcoxon signed-rank tests.

The normality assumption and the homogeneity of variances were checked in the total score in the pretest and in the posttest for each academic year. Thus, an independent samples t-test indicates that the scores weren't significantly different between the two groups ($t(30) = -.928$, $p = .361$, $d = .324$). Therefore, we consider that the two independent groups were equivalent at the beginning of each semester.

As for the evolution of students during the semester, there was a significant increase in the score of students in the face-to-face class in 2018/19 ($t(13) = -6.183$, $p < .001$, $d = 1.333$) and in the online environment in 2019/20 ($t(17) = -4.818$, $p < .001$, $d = 1.167$). These results indicate that the percentile gains were similar for the two groups: 41 points for the first group and 38 points for the second group [44].

In order to analyze if the two groups had significantly different scores for each dimension measured by CCT test at the end of the semester, as the normality assumption was not verified for all dimensions, we used the Mann-Whitney to explore if there were significant differences between the medians in the posttest. The results of these analysis are presented in Table 5.

Table 5. Analysis of the differences between the two groups posttest scores.

Dimension	Mann-Whitney test statistic U	p
Interpretation	104	.419
Analysis_a (identification of solutions that imply making inferences)	90	.180
Analysis_b (comparison and contrasting of solutions)	110.5	.561
Explanation	88.5	.122
Evaluation	101	.298
Synthesis	107	.404
Creativity – Fluency	105	.310
Creativity – Flexibility	122	.856
Creativity – Originality	90	.137
Total CCT test	120	.817

These results show there are no significant differences between the two groups for the total score of the CCT posttest, which is confirmed by a t test ($t(30) = -.178$, $p = .860$, $d = .065$). Regarding the dimensions evaluated by the CTT test, the results in Table 5 show that there are no significant differences between the two groups also for each dimension in the posttest. However, although the differences between the two groups are slight in the posttest, the results in Table 4 show that the group with presential classes had significant gains in Analysis (identification of solutions that imply making inferences), Synthesis and Creativity, and the group with virtual classes had significant gains in the dimensions of Explanation and Creativity (Flexibility).

4 Discussion and Conclusions

There is an increasing literature (e.g. [10, 11, 45]) which focuses on the outcomes of pedagogical practices promoting critical thinking in HE. This paper had the goal to verify if the CL methodology is as effective in the promotion of CT in virtual environments as in face-to-face, through a quasi-experimental research at the HE level. Both groups in either environment increased significantly the total score in the CCT test, and slight differences were noted in the improvement of the CT specific skills evaluated by the CCT test.

In line with one of the first studies comparing online and face-to-face CT outcomes [46] and with a more recent work targeting CT development in online and face-to-face environments (comparing grades, assignments and the pre and post CCTST test) [30], the main conclusion of this study is that there are no significant differences in pre and post CCT test, between the results on CT skills development among students of the same course in a face-to-face environment and the online one, using CL. This result confirms the literature review showing that CT can be promoted online through diverse pedagogical strategies [30]. Therefore, it asserts that online CL can be a relevant methodology for teachers to use for CT development [47]. The analysis of the collected data showed that the CL online learning strategy has enabled the development of CT (significant increase of the mean score of the CCT test) and that there were no significant differences in the gains for the assessed skills using the CCT test between the face-to-face or the online learning environments.

Since our study shows that the use of CL approaches, both in face-to-face or in online environments, enable the development of CT skills, it is interesting to focus on the factors related to the functioning of cooperative learning groups that can explain these results. The first one is the characteristics of the CL groups of this study [48] whether in online or in face-to-face learning environments, like: 1) small heterogeneous groups, 2) positive interdependence (although each element of the group has a different role, they have a common objective that they can achieve only if all together work toward it; 3) face-to-face interaction (this is possible in some virtual platforms like Zoom), 4) individual and group responsibility, 5) group process evaluation (regular evaluation of how the group functions), 6) use and mastery of social skills like mutual help, effective communication, etc…

The second aspect refers to the potential that CL groups entail through their regulated learning dynamic characteristic [49]. As social systems, the cooperative groups enable the sharing and discussion of beliefs and knowledge [13], thus facilitating the regulation and the broadening of perspectives as well as the development of skills like analysis, evaluation, etc. [29]. The use of CL as a learning method lies on the premise that the interaction between students in their groups and the confrontation of ideas often lead to a cognitive and socio-cognitive conflict and to an epistemic thawing [49, 50] which turn students curious to know more or question their own beliefs and knowledge. As students must justify their position and detect strengths and weaknesses in others' points of view, CL facilitates the development of critical thinking skills like analysis, evaluation, argumentation, etc. [51].

The third aspect is related to the effectiveness of the cooperative learning techniques that were used (reported in the Pedagogical context subsection). In line with some authors, the Think-Pair-Share and Jigsaw techniques were found effective in increasing the interaction between students as they had more opportunities to share their ideas and what they had learnt with their peers, accomplishing the tasks together. Therefore, the students' active participation was also enhanced and helped to sharp the thinking and problem-solving skills [52, 53], among others.

In short, the constructivist learning approach at the basis of CL, the techniques used and the online features of Zoom (possibility to work in small groups in simultaneous virtual rooms) and of Padlet (possibility of giving written feedback between groups), provided the conditions for the development of CT skills, taking in account that the characteristics of CL groups stated above were met. In line with other authors, it is not the environment (online or face to face) which matters, but the learning approach [32].

Along with explicit, clear and measurable goals, another factor that the literature points out to as being determinant for the success of the learning process, is the role of the teacher, more specifically in the case of an online environment, the so called "teacher's presence" [54]. Online group facilitation is challenging, as several authors have noted, because of often students' hidden identities, absence of non-verbal cues and limited verbal communication [55, 56]. Thus, teacher's presence, in face-to-face groups, but more so in an online environment, is the "teacher's ability to engage with each learner on an intellectual as well as on an empathic level of understanding, towards meeting the intellectual and cognitive needs of the learner" (p. 20) [57]. The teacher's presence enhances students' comfort, confidence and willingness to participate, establishing an instructional environment, not only based on technical procedures, but also which demonstrates humanness, reflexiveness and acknowledged vulnerability of all involved.

Taking this last point into consideration, in future work, the authors of this article suggest that a perception survey on the teacher's presence should be applied to students (in face-to-face and in online environment) in order to evaluate the influence on the results and better characterize what "teacher's presence" means in an online environment whose primary goal is to foment Critical Thinking.

Also, due to the limitation of the small number of students involved in this research, and in order to validate the present results, the authors intend to test their results in a larger sample of students, and evaluate if results might be similar in different courses (for example in STEM degrees versus social sciences and humanities).

References

1. Lopes, J., Silva, H., Morais, E.: Teste do Pensamento Crítico e Criativo para estudantes do ensino superior. Revista Lusófona de Educação **44**(44), 173–189 (2019)
2. UNESCO: Educación para la ciudadanía mundial. Preparar a los educandos para los retos del siglo xxi. París: Organización de las Naciones Unidas para la Educación, la Ciencia y la Cultura (2016)
3. Ananiadou, K., Claro, M.: 21st Century Skills and Competences for New Millennium Learners in OECD Countries. OECD Education Working Papers, 41, OECD Publishing, Paris (2009)
4. OECD: Future of education and skills. Education 2030 (2018). https://www.oecd.org/education/2030-project/
5. World Economic Forum: New vision for education - Fostering Social and Emotional learning through Technology (2016). https://www3.weforum.org/docs/WEF_New_Vision_for_Education.pdf
6. Council of Europe: Competences for Democratic Culture - Living together as equals in culturally diverse democratic societies (2016). https://go.coe.int/yJqEd

7. ABET: Criteria for accrediting engineering programs (2015). https://www.abet.org/wp.../2015/05/E001-15-16-EAC-Criteria-03-10-15.pdf. Accessed 3 Oct 2020
8. Oliver, B., St. Jorre, T.J.: Graduate attributes for 2020 and beyond: recommendations for Australian higher education providers. Higher Educ. Res. Dev. **37**(4), 821–836 (2018)
9. CRITHINKEDU. https://crithinkedu.utad.pt/pt/what-is-crithinkedu/. Accessed 07 Oct 2020
10. Dominguez, C. (coord.): A European review on Critical Thinking educational practices in Higher Education Institutions. UTAD, Vila Real (2018)
11. Elen, J., Jiang, L., Huyghe, S., Evers, M., Verburgh, A.: Promoting critical thinking in European higher education institutions: towards an educational protocol. In: Dominguez, C., Payan-Carreira, R. (eds.) UTAD, Vila Real (2019)
12. Vygotsky, L.: Mind and Society. Harvard University Press, Cambridge (1978)
13. Hadwin, A.F., Järvelä, S., Miller, M.: Self-regulation, co-regulation, and shared regulation in collaborative learning environments. In: Schunk, D.H., Greene, J.A. (eds.) Handbook of Self-regulation of Learning and Performance, 2nd edn. Routledge, New York (2018)
14. Sternberg, R., Roediger, H.L., III., Halpern, D.: Critical Thinking in Psychology. Cambridge University Press, New York (2007)
15. Norris, S., Ennis, R.: Evaluating Critical Thinking. Midwest Publication, Pacific Grove (1989)
16. Halpern, D.: Teaching critical thinking for transfer across domains: Dispositions, skills, structure training, and metacognitive monitoring. Am. Psychol. **53**(4), 449–455 (1998)
17. Facione, P.: Critical thinking: A statement of expert consensus for purposes of educational assessment and instruction (The Delphi Report). The California Academic Press, Millbrae, CA (1990)
18. Franco, A.: Pensamento crítico: Desenvolvimento e mediação no quadro das experiências académicas no Ensino Superior. Universidade do Minho, Tese de doutoramento. Braga (2016)
19. Paul, R., Elder, L.: The Miniature Guide to Critical Thinking-Concepts and Tools, 5th edn. Foundation for Critical Thinking Press, Dillon Beach (2008)
20. Facione, P.A., Sanchez, C.A., Facione, N.C., Gainen, J.: The disposition toward critical thinking. J. General Educ. **44**(1), 1–25 (1995)
21. Ennis, R.H.: Critical thinking: a streamlined conception. In: Davies, M., Barnett, R. (eds.) The Palgrave Handbook of Critical Thinking in Higher Education. Palgrave Macmillan, New York (2015)
22. Johnson, D.W., Johnson, R.T., Smith, K.A.: Active learning: Cooperation in the college classroom. Edina, MN: Interaction (1991)
23. Silva, H., Lopes, J., Dominguez, C.: Enhancing College Students' Critical Thinking Skills in Cooperative Groups. In: Tsitouridou, M., A. Diniz, J., Mikropoulos, T.A. (eds.) TECH-EDU 2018. CCIS, vol. 993, pp. 181–192. Springer, Cham (2019). https://doi.org/10.1007/978-3-030-20954-4_13
24. Burbach, M., Matkin, G., Fritz, S.: Teaching critical thinking in an introductory leadership course using active learning strategies: A confirmatory study. Coll. Student J. **38**(3), 482–494 (2004)
25. Laal, M., Ghodsi, S.M.: Benefits of collaborative learning. J. Proc.-Soc. Behav. Sci. **31**, 486–490 (2012)
26. Klimovienė, G., Urbonienė, J., Barzdžiukienė, R.: Developing critical thinking through cooperative learning. Stud. Lang. **9**, 77–85 (2006)
27. Johnson, D.W., Johnson, R.: Learning Together and Alone: Cooperative, Competitive, and Individualistic Learning, 5th edn. Allyn & Bacon, Boston (1999)
28. Paul, R.W.: Critical thinking: How to prepare students for a rapidly changing world. Library of Congress, Santa Rosa, CA (1995)
29. Mitchell, J., Johnson, D.W., Johnson, R.T.: The impact of academic controversy on subsequent conflict resolution and relationships among students. J. Res. Educ. **13**(1), 73–78 (2003)

30. Derwin, E.B.: Critical thinking in online vs. face-to-face higher education. Media Psychol. Rev. **2**(1), 20 (2009)
31. Leston-Bandeira, C.: Using e-learning to promote critical thinking in politics. Enhancing Learn. Soc. Sci. **1**(3), 1–4 (2009)
32. Kupczynski, L., Mundy, M.A., Goswami, J., Meling, V.: Cooperative learning in distance learning: a mixed methods study. Int. J. Instr. **5**(2) (2012)
33. Bezanilla, M.J., Fernández-Nogueira, D., Poblete, M., Galindo-Domínguez, H.: Methodologies for teaching-learning critical thinking in higher education - the teacher's view. Thinking Skills Creativity **33**, 100584 (2019)
34. Ennis, R.H.: Critical Thinking Across the Curriculum - A Vision. Topoi **37**, 165–184 (2018)
35. Chandrasekaran, S., Badwal, P.S., Thirunavukkarasu, G., Littlefair, G.: Collaborative learning experience of students in distance education. In: PAEE/ALE 2016: 8th International Symposium on Project Approaches in Engineering Education and 14th Active Learning in Engineering Education Workshop, pp. 90–99. PAEE, University of Minho, Braga (2016). https://www.researchgate.net/publication/305983309_Collaborative_Learning_Experience_of_Students_in_Distance_Education. Accessed 23 Sept 2020
36. Guillier, J., Durndell, A.: Peer interaction and critical thinking: Face-to-face or online discussion? Learn. Instruct. **18**(2), 187–200 (2008)
37. Loes, C.N., Pascarella, E.T.: Collaborative learning and critical thinking: Testing the link. J. High. Educ. **88**(5), 726–753 (2017)
38. Alexander, B., et al.: EDUCAUSE Horizon Report: 2019 Higher Education Edition. EDUCAUSE. https://www.k12blueprint.com/sites/default/files/2019horizonreport.pdf
39. Fraenkel, J.R., Wallen, N.E., Hyun, H.H.: How to Design and Evaluate Research in Education, vol. 7. McGraw-Hill, New York (1993)
40. Anderson, L., Krathwohl, D. (eds.): A Taxonomy for Learning, Teaching, and Assessing: A Revision of Bloom's Taxonomy of Educational Objectives. Longman, New York (2001)
41. Lyman, F.: Think-pair-share: An ending teaching technique. MAA-CIE Cooperative News **1**(1), 1–2 (1987)
42. Sharan, S.: Cooperative learning in small groups: Recent methods and effects on achievement, attitudes, and ethnic relations. Rev. Educ. Res. **50**(2), 241–271 (1980)
43. Rathakrishnan, M., Ahmad, R., Choi, L.J.: Padlet online discussion in enhancing students' macro critical thinking skills. Int. J. Latest Res. Humanit. Soc. Sci. IJLRHSS **1**(03), 121–126 (2018)
44. Marzano, R.J.: Designing & Teaching Learning Goals & Objectives. Solution Tree Press (2010)
45. Cruz, G., Payan-Carreira, R., Dominguez, C.: Critical thinking education in the Portuguese higher education: A systematic review of educational practices. Revista Lusófona de Educação **38**, 43–61 (2018)
46. Huff, M.T.: A comparison study of live versus interactive television for teaching MSW students. Res. Soc. Work Practice **10**(4), 400–416 (2000)
47. Lengua Cantero, C., Bernal Oviedo, G., Florez Barboza, W., Velandia Feria, M.: Tecnologias emergentes en el proceso de ensenanza-aprendizaje: Hacia el desarrollo del pensamiento critico. Revista Electrónica Interuniversitaria de Formación del Profesorado **23**(3), 83–98 (2020)
48. Johnson, D.W., Johnson, R.T.: An educational psychology success story: Social interdependence theory and cooperative learning. Educ. Res. **38**(5), 365–379 (2009)
49. Fransen, J., Weinberger, A., Kirschner, P.A.: Team effectiveness and team development in CSCL. Educ. Psychol. **48**(1), 9–24 (2013)
50. Morais, T., Silva, H., Lopes, J., Dominguez, C.: Argumentative skills development in teaching philosophy to secondary school students through constructive controversy: An exploratory study case. Curriculum J. **28**(2), 249–265 (2017)

51. Lopes, J., Silva, H.: A Aprendizagem Cooperativa na Sala de Aula. Um guia prático para o professor [The cooperative learning in the classroom. A practical guide for the teachers]. Lidel, Edições Técnicas, Lda, Lisboa (2009)
52. Devi, A.P., Musthafa, B., Gustine, G.G.: Using cooperative learning in teaching critical thinking in reading. Engl. Rev.: J. Engl. Educ. **4**(1), 1–14 (2015)
53. Saputra, M.D., Joyoatmojo, S., Wardani, D.K., Sangka, K.B.: Developing critical-thinking skills through the collaboration of Jigsaw model with problem-based learning model. Int. J. Instr. **12**(1), 1077–1094 (2019)
54. Thomas, G., Thorpe, S.: Enhancing the facilitation of online groups in higher education: A review of the literature on face-to-face and online group-facilitation. Interactive Learn. Environ. **27**(1), 62–71 (2019)
55. Baran, E., Correia, A.P., Thompson, A.D.: Tracing successful online teaching in higher education: Voices of exemplary online teachers. Teach. Coll. Rec. **115**(3), 1–41 (2013)
56. Chang, B., Kang, H.: Challenges facing group work online. Distance Educ. **37**(1), 73–88 (2016)
57. Crawford, C.M.: Instructor immediacy and authenticity: Engaging in cognitive vulnerability within the online instructional environment. In: D'Agustino, S. (ed.) Creating Teacher Immediacy in Online Learning Environments, pp. 15–36. Information Science Reference, Hershey (2016)

Teaching Strategies to Promote Critical Thinking Skills in an Online Learning Environment

Angeliki Lithoxoidou(✉) and Catherine Dimitriadou

University of Western Macedonia, Florina, Greece
{alithoxoidou,adimitriadou}@uowm.gr

Abstract. Distance learning at undergraduate level has not been applied in Greek Higher Education Institutions so far. However, during the quarantine period due to corona virus pandemic, distance learning by the use of online platforms was applied for the semester continuation. On this occasion, a mixed-methods research was conducted aiming at exploring students' motivation, learning strategies and Critical Thinking skills. In particular, the research focused on students' potential to develop their Critical Thinking skills in the context of the course "Teaching Methodology", since due to distance learning they would have been offered the chance for student-centered instruction according to the push model of teaching. Slideshows, pictures conveying underlying messages, scenarios, case studies of unexpected events and search through various online and printed sources were used in order to promote Critical Thinking skills. Two questionnaires with close- and open-ended questions were administered to 45 participants regarding their opinions before and after the course completion. According to the results, participants seem to have developed particular CT skills while their answers offer further insights regarding the teaching process during distance learning.

Keywords: Critical thinking skills · Distance learning · Contemporary teaching approaches

1 Introduction

The new coronavirus (COVID-19) pandemic caused unprecedented conditions worldwide since many countries introduced several measures to control the spread of the disease including self-isolation and quarantine [1]. Lockdowns in response to COVID-19 were followed by nationwide school closures which lasted for a considerable time period [2]. According to UNESCO [3] on 2nd April 2020, 192 countries have imposed country-wide closures impacting 91% of student population worldwide. Thus, COVID-19 has caused major turbulence and disruption to the education system in combination with the health, economic and social effects [4]. Higher Education was also negatively affected since universities had to close all campus activities and events such as workshops while face-to-face lectures had to be replaced with distance learning [2, 5]. In other

A. Reis et al. (Eds.): TECH-EDU 2020, CCIS 1384, pp. 181–192, 2021.
https://doi.org/10.1007/978-3-030-73988-1_13

words, universities were forced to transform their instructional and teaching practices into distance learning in a really short time [6].

Even though distance learning is not a new approach [7], this shift in the teaching process due to the hygiene crisis was a rather unexpected and unplanned situation which probably indicates that students and professors did not have the appropriate time to get accustomed to the new reality which violated their daily routine [4].

Furthermore, another impact of the pandemic was a mass production of fake news for COVID-19 ranging from health to religious references which spread online [8] – especially on social media– and could be characterized as an infodemic [9]. Therefore, it seems that Higher Education Institutions should diligently focus on developing Critical Thinking (CT) skills so that students can be enabled to evaluate and filter deceiving and fake information. Under this rationale, CT infusion in the course curriculum seems to arise. CT can be potentially infused in a course curriculum with the promotion of critical dialogue and provided that the teaching process is organized in this direction, it simultaneously aims at transferring these skills to a broader scope of situations [10].

1.1 The Research Background

The research presented in this paper was conducted in the context of the BSc course "Teaching Methodology" in the Department of Primary Education of the University of Western Macedonia, Greece. During the spring semester, the course was switched to synchronous online learning with the use of Zoom. Students being in their first year of studies had never attended an online course before; thus it was considered that their insights and perceptions regarding the new teaching approach would probably offer valuable information for the orchestration and planning of online courses in the future.

A major concern regarding the course organization was related to the promotion of students' CT since in the case of distance learning and in comparison to traditional lectures, the development of CT should be meticulously orchestrated by the professor with the integration of innovative and constructivistic approaches such as active or team-based learning activities [11].

According to American Philosophical Association, CT is defined as following: "*We understand CT to be purposeful, self-regulatory judgement which results in interpretation, analysis, evaluation, and inference, as well as explanation of the evidential, conceptual methodological, criteriological, or contextual considerations upon which that judgment is based. CT is essential as a tool of inquiry. As such, CT is a liberating force in education and a powerful resource in one's personal and civic life.*" [[12], p. 3].

In the APA Delphi Report [12] six skills were conceptualized: interpretation, analysis, evaluation, inference, explanation and self-regulation. Interpretation refers to the ability of understanding and expressing the concept or importance of a set of experiences, data or situations in terms of categorizing and clarifying potential ambiguities. Analysis stands as the skill to trace and recognize relationships between different meanings and concepts in the framework of examining ideas and arguments. Evaluation is based on the assessment of arguments, statements and claims while inference is defined as the extent to which particular elements may lead to secure conclusions through investigatory reasoning. Explanation correlates with one's ability to thoroughly justify statements in concrete arguments according to meticulous methodology and criterion selection. Finally, self-regulation stands as the ability to monitor cognitive abilities while detecting and recognizing potential distractions or interventions in this process. Thus, self-regulation probably constitutes a process of self-examination and self-correction [[12], pp. 13–19, 13].

Metacognitive self-regulation is considered a CT skill playing a significant role in learning since students are able to assess their process and strategies [14]. Moreover, students who adopt an active and responsible –in terms of their learning– role by exhibiting and applying self-regulatory strategies also tend to be characterized by higher self-efficacy [14]. Especially in an online learning setting, self-regulation is considered to be a strong predictor regarding students' academic achievement [15]. This is probably the reason why in this type of instruction professors should actively support and scaffold students' learning by promoting interaction and group activities [15]. Motivation also seems to correlate with metacognitive self-regulation in terms that learning and academic achievement are not only influenced by a student's personality characteristics or classroom climate [16]. On the contrary, students may exhibit self-regulation as far as it concerns their motivation and behavior [16]. This finding may also successfully address the problem of students' lack of motivation which frequently appears in Higher Education [17].

2 Method

The research presented in this paper adopted a mixed-methods approach combining qualitative and quantitative elements in order to thoroughly examine as well as robust its findings [18]. At the beginning of the research which coincided with the semester beginning, an initial test was administered to students regarding their motivation and learning strategies while there was also an open-ended question included aiming at tracing students' CT skills. The infusion of CT into the course curriculum was approached in online setting so that comparisons could be enabled in students' answers before and after the course and enhancements in this field could be traced. The teaching process (2.2 The teaching process) included contemporary approaches which operated bilaterally for: a) the optimum infusion of CT skills in the course and b) stimulating students' interest in online setting since it was considered that their active participation may be hindered. This perception was adopted since learning usually derives from interdependence and communication between the professor and the students as a "social process" which may be restricted in distance learning in comparison to face-to-face teaching [19, p. 26]. At the end of the semester, a final questionnaire was administered to students aiming at tracing their satisfaction, interaction and engagement during the course. The questionnaire also consisted of a final open-ended question which was once again analyzed in the light of CT skills.

Based on the above rationale, the following research questions were set:

- To what extent does self-regulation correlate with motivation and learning strategies during the course "Teaching Methodology" in online setting?
- To what extent were students' CT skills developed after the course "Teaching Methodology"?

- To what extent does self-regulation correlate with specific learning components such as satisfaction and learner interaction during the course "Teaching Methodology" in online setting?

2.1 Participants

One hundred and forty freshmen of the Department of Primary Education, University of Western Macedonia were enrolled in the course. However, 45 students (40 female and 5 male) completed the online questionnaires since participation in the research was voluntary.

2.2 The Teaching Process

The course "Teaching Methodology" is a core course of the Department of Primary Education and aims at familiarizing students with the concept of teaching; different teaching practices; modern curricula; teaching orchestration and assessment. Students are to comprehend and compare a variety of teaching models as well as to be introduced to the psychological and sociocultural aspects of teaching.

Given the conditions, plenary sessions were carried out with the use of Zoom. However, the whole teaching process was organized in the direction of enhancing students' CT skills and stimulating their motivation to learn. Hence, every lesson included case studies of unexpected events to support speculation and further discussion [20], pictures with underlying meanings or double connotations for students to identify and interpret them [21], scenarios and examples to robust decision-making in the framework of opinion plurality and contradiction between students [22]. During the course, memorization was avoided while questioning techniques were activated so that students could be able to assess and analyze the information given while they could also be successfully led to problem solving skills and decision making [23]. More particularly, questioning techniques emphasized on higher-cognitive questions which required students to analyze and evaluate facts (e.g. *How would you deal with an unexpected event such as an earthquake during your lesson as a future in-service teacher? Would that be an opportunity for the teaching process?*) instead of lower-cognitive questions requiring memorization [24]. Students were also assigned activities as homework which were later discussed with specific references to contemporary literature in combination with students' reflection on each issue so that they could able to make judgements on problems that could be characterized as "complex, messy and ill-defined" [25, p. 451]. For example, students were assigned to design and describe a project that would cross-curricularly approach island formation so that it could be potentially applied to primary school classes.

Fire-up questions (e.g. *Can you recall a teaching approach your primary school teacher employed –when you were pupils– that may have included elements of non-formal education?*) referring to students' personal experiences from their primary school years as pupils also set the stage for critical reflection and the formation of new ideas regarding the school settings. That way, through experiential learning [26, 27] and by following constructivism as a teaching approach, students were the protagonists of the class being able to reconstruct meanings, question previous beliefs and attitudes and as a result be transformed into reflective practitioners [28] instead of passive knowledge receivers [29, 30]. Another important element of the course organization was that students were assigned a final paper which had to be written and presented in pairs. That way, cooperation and interaction between students could be promoted.

2.3 Data Collection

Due to the mandatory social distancing measures while the research was being conducted, the data were collected with the use of Google forms. Two questionnaires were used in order to facilitate the research's aims and scope. In detail, for the first stage of the research students' motivation and learning strategies were examined before the beginning of the course, while –in the second stage– the research aimed at tracing students' satisfaction and interaction as these were assessed by students themselves after the end of the course. Regarding these two questionnaires, results were validated with the use of Cronbach's alpha (2.4 Data Assessment).

In particular for the first stage of the research, the Motivated Strategies for Learning Questionnaire (MSLQ) [31] translated in Greek was administered to students as an initial test. More specifically, the questionnaire consists of two sections: a) the motivation and b) the learning strategies. In each section, there are different scales that can be used together or singly. The statements contained in each scale are close-ended and are assessed through a 7-point Likert Scale. For the research, regarding the motivation section the scales: a) Intrinsic goal orientation (4 items), b) Extrinsic goal orientation (4 items), c) Task value (6 items), d) Control of learning beliefs (4 items), and e) Self-efficacy for learning and performance (8 items) were used. Each scale used is described in the two following paragraphs.

In detail, Intrinsic goal orientation concerns the extent to which students perceive their participation in a course or activity by approaching it with curiosity or genuine interest. Extrinsic goal orientation refers to students' perceptions regarding their participation in terms of grades, assessment and rewards. Regarding Task value, students are asked to express their opinion on the course or task they participate in. As far as it concerns Control of learning beliefs, it has to do with students' beliefs regarding their efforts and the potential positive outcome of the course. Self-efficacy for learning and performance includes students' perceptions regarding their ability and confidence to successfully participate in the course.

For the Learning Strategies part, the scales: a) Metacognitive self-regulation (11 items), b) Time and study environment (8 items), and c) Peer learning (3 items) were included in the research. Metacognitive self-regulation refers to students' skills such as planning and goal setting in combination with monitoring and self-assessment. Time and study environment consists of statements regarding students' perceptions of their planning and time management as well as the organization of realistic studying schedules. Finally, Peer learning scale refers to cooperation and collaboration between students in the direction of achieving better academic performance in the course [31]. At the end of the MSLQ, an open-ended question was included in order to trace students' perceptions regarding online courses in the light of the pandemic: *Do you think that online courses can be useful taking into consideration the current worldwide condition? If yes, why? If no, why not?*

As far as it concerns the final stage of the research, students were invited to complete the Student Learning and Satisfaction in Online Learning Environments Instrument (SLS-OLE) [32]; translated in Greek. The questionnaire was administered to students after authors' written permission was granted. The questionnaire consists of different scales which include close-ended statements assessed with a 6-point Likert scale. For the research, the scales: a) Learner interaction (7 items), b) Student engagement (5 items), c) Student satisfaction (4 items), and d) Perceived learning (5 items) were used. Each scale used is described in the following paragraph.

Regarding Learner interaction, the scale included statements which refer to students' communication and active learning during the course. The second scale, Student engagement concerns students' participation in the course in terms of synchronous sessions and assignments. The third scale, Student satisfaction includes statements referring to the degree to which students feel satisfied with their learning and experience through the course. Regarding Perceived learning, students were asked to assess the extent to which their learning expectations were fulfilled during the course. At the end of the final questionnaire, an open-ended question was included for students to assess the online course in the light of reflection: *In your opinion, what are the major advantages and disadvantages of online learning during the course "Teaching Methodology?"*.

It should be noted, though, that the open-ended questions for each questionnaire were different since they were tailor-made in accordance with each questionnaire's aims. For the initial questionnaire, before the beginning of the course, students' perceptions of online courses were to be traced, while in the final questionnaire, students' reflection on the course, after its completion, was examined. Simultaneously, the open-ended questions were to be utilized as means of assessing students' CT skills. However, students were not directly asked regarding their perceptions in this field so that results could not be biased.

2.4 Data Assessment

Data collected from the close-ended questions were assessed quantitatively while the qualitative approach was followed for the open-ended questions. In detail, the close-ended questions were assessed with the use of IBM SPSS Statistics Version 22. A mean for each participant's answer in every scale was calculated. Additionally, to study internal consistency of the measures, Cronbach's alpha was calculated in each scale both for the initial and the final questionnaire and is displayed in Table 1.

Regarding the qualitative data as they arose through the open-ended questions, they were analyzed with the use of direct approach to content analysis [33], utilizing the six skills included in Facione's research tool (1.1 The Research Background). Students' answers were assessed in the light of their CT skills though a deductive approach with the use of theory-driven categories [34] in an attempt to extract elements that correlate with the particular skills, while they were commenting on the two open-ended questions. In detail, six categories were used for the qualitative analysis which arose from Facione's theory; one for every skill [33]. Before the final coding, two research assistants classified 20% of students' answers into the six categories. According to Cohen's kappa, the inter-rater agreement was medium for both the initial ($\kappa = 0{,}74$ (95% CI, 0,60 - 0,88), $p <$ 0,05.) and the final questionnaire ($\kappa = 0{,}72$ (95% CI, 0,59 - 0,85), $p < 0{,}001$.) and was increased to excellent after discussion with the authors.

Table 1. Cronbach's alpha for each scale.

Scale	Cronbach's alpha
Intrinsic goal orientation (Initial questionnaire)	.751
Extrinsic goal orientation (Initial questionnaire)	.770
Task value (Initial questionnaire)	.915
Control of learning beliefs (Initial questionnaire)	.779
Self-efficacy for learning and performance (Initial questionnaire)	.870
Metacognitive self-regulation (Initial questionnaire)	.753
Time and study environment (Initial questionnaire)	.669
Peer learning (Initial questionnaire)	.734
Learner interaction (Final questionnaire)	.811
Student engagement (Final questionnaire)	.729
Student satisfaction (Final questionnaire)	.830
Perceived learning (Final questionnaire)	.850

3 Results

In this section, results will be presented according to each measure and the analysis followed. Regarding the close-ended questionnaires, correlations were traced between the scales as well as between the two questionnaires with the use of Pearson correlation coefficient.

3.1 Initial Questionnaire Results

Motivated Strategies for Learning Questionnaire (MSLQ) Results. There was a statistically significant positive correlation between Meta-cognitive self-regulation and the following scales: a) Intrinsic goal orientation ($r = .469$, $p = .005$), b) Task value ($r = .699$, $p = .005$), c) Control of learning beliefs ($r = .506$, $p = .005$), d) Self-efficacy for learning and performance ($r = .641$, $p = .005$) and e) Time and study environment ($r = .351$, $p = .005$).

Open-ended Question Results. As the content analysis of students' answers reveals, they seem to exhibit four out the six CT skills while commenting on the usefulness of online courses. Eleven students seem to exhibit interpretation since they recognize the significance of participating in this type of instruction in a time of crisis *(e.g. "I believe that taking into consideration the current condition, distance learning is useful so that we can understand the course in a better way"*, Student_1). Through their answers, analysis is also exhibited by thirteen students since they seem to acknowledge the potential offered through online courses in terms of ameliorating their computer literacy; thus, they recognize the contribution of the course to their future careers and professional role (e.g. *"It is a challenge and a chance since we are going to acquire skills that* *will be useful to us in the future, living in an e-learning era"*, Student_43). Fifteen students also seem ready to evaluate the new form of instruction by comparing it to the traditional one while expressing their belief that it can only stand as a conditional substitute which cannot replace face-to-face teaching since human contact may be lost and/or technical issues may arise (e.g. *"Face-to-face teaching is irreplaceable since there are problems regarding the internet quality, the sound or the camera. This is why it (face-to-face teaching) can be of better quality"*, Student_31). Finally, six students exhibit self-regulation as they recognize the contribution of distance learning in their following a study schedule and managing to be alerted while remaining at home (e.g. *"Yes, these lessons are useful because they keep students alerted and they do not fall behind with their schedule"*, Student_38).

3.2 Final Questionnaire Results

Regarding the correlations between the scale Metacognitive self-regulation and the scales measured through the final questionnaire, it should be noted that no statistically significant correlations were traced. The same applies for correlations between every other scale of the initial and the final questionnaire. However, the scales of the final questionnaire were separately analyzed and are described underneath.

Student Learning and Satisfaction in Online Learning Environments Instrument (SLS-OLE) Results. Statistically significant positive correlations were revealed between the scales in the final questionnaire. More specifically, the scale Learner interaction positively correlates with the following scales: a) Student engagement ($r = .671$, $p = .005$); b) Student satisfaction ($r = .669$, $p = .005$) and c) Perceived learning ($r = .534$, $p = .005$). A statistically significant positive correlation was found between the scale Student engagement and a) Student satisfaction ($r = .688$, $p = .005$) as well as b) Perceived learning ($r = .599$, $p = .005$). Finally the scale Student satisfaction also correlates with the scale Perceived learning ($r = .755$, $p = .005$).

Open-Ended Question Results. In contrast to students' answers in the open-ended question of the initial questionnaire, their answers in the final questionnaire seem to reveal that they exhibit six CT skills. Given that this particular question stands as an evaluation regarding the advantages and disadvantages of distance learning in the course, six students exhibit the evaluation skill by positively assessing the teaching practices applied (e.g. *"The lesson was direct and comprehensible while we could ask questions and get immediate answers by the professor"*, Student_24). Five students also tend to be analytic in their arguments as they try to identify the difficulties or the problems that they faced during the course referring to awkward feelings regarding the camera or microphone use (e.g. *"I sometimes felt awkward having my camera and microphone on"*, Student_22). Eleven students also try to interpret the importance of distance learning since it offered them the opportunity to remain safe at home setting while they were simultaneously able to continue their studies (e.g. *"We could stay home safe without discontinuing our studies"*, Student_43). The inference skill is exhibited by seven students since they draw conclusions and refer to side-effects that are not directly related to the learning process but rather concern the issue of socialization during their first year of studies (e.g. *"We really missed our socialization and interaction with other students"*, Student_35). These conclusions are drawn in the light of reflection so seven students seem ready to explain their perceptions as well as their concerns with certain arguments by setting examples such as the issue of practicum that cannot be realized through distance learning (e.g. *"Practicum is considered to be necessary in a lot of departments and the same goes for ours...however it cannot be organized and realized online"*, Student_14). Finally, in the light of self-regulation, nine students also seem to reflect on their own practices during the course since they feel that face-to-face learning may significantly contribute to their attention and concentration (e.g. *"I would say that it is rather easy for students to be distracted and not pay attention during distance learning"*, Student_28).

4 Discussion and Conclusion

Regarding the first research question, the findings of the research indicate that self-regulation, which was examined as a scale in the initial questionnaire and also stands as a CT skill, correlates with almost every other scale included in the initial questionnaire. In detail, the finding that self-regulation correlates with other motivation and learning strategies namely: a) Intrinsic goal orientation, b) Task value, c) Control of learning beliefs, d) Self-efficacy for learning and performance and e) Time and study environment probably highlights the importance of emphasizing this skill while infusing CT into the curriculum. This is probably the case since meta-cognitive self-regulation may mediate students' academic performance and achievement. Since metacognitive self-regulation indicates students' control over their learning and learning processes as well, the aforementioned correlations seem to indicate students' assertiveness that they can successfully conduct and participate in tasks or activities in the particular course [35] even when it is carried out in online setting. More importantly, self-regulatory practices define a task's result and quality [36].

Regarding the second research question, besides the fact that the aforementioned motivation and learning strategies seem to stand as predictors of CT, it is possible that classroom climate as well as the teaching process may also foster the development of students' CT skills [37]. This is probably highlighted by the qualitative data of the research. Students exhibited four CT skills (interpretation, analysis, evaluation, self-regulation) at the first stage of the research, which increased to six at the final stage with inference and explanation being added. This finding may indicate the influence of the teaching process since it was tailor-made in the direction of fostering students' CT skills with the employment of contemporary teaching practices in the light of constructivism through which cooperation and further discussion would be promoted even in online setting. Taking into consideration the fact that students had never before participated in distance learning courses, it can be inferred that –according to their answers– even though they sometimes faced technical problems, they could simultaneously secure their active learning and attendance in an organized and meticulous manner. The finding that students' CT skills increased after the course seems to be of major importance for their professional role as future primary school teachers. Their CT skills may be infused in their classrooms with the creation of educational material and the employment of particular strategies, so that primary school pupils could also cultivate CT skills through teamwork, problem-solving and decision-making techniques [38].

Regarding the third research question, the research did not trace correlations between Metacognitive self-regulation and specific learning components as: a) Learner interaction, b) Student engagement, c) Student satisfaction, d) Perceived learning. More particularly, regarding students' engagement, the findings of the research may differentiate from previous research according to which self-regulation was significantly correlated with engagement [39]. However, regarding student satisfaction, the findings coincide with the study of [40] in which student satisfaction does not correlate with self-regulation while learner-content interaction seems to contribute to students' satisfaction. This finding seems to indicate the importance of learner interaction during an exclusively online course as a predictor of academic performance. Additionally, the aforementioned correlations seem to highlight the importance of integrating authentic tasks that promote cooperation and draw on information from realistic content that lies in students' interest and experiences in distance learning courses.

Finally, the research offers insights regarding the course organization and design in distance learning emphasizing the importance of the teaching process focusing on cooperation and interaction through which students' academic performance is promoted and the stage for CT skills development is set. These findings can offer further implications for the future distance learning editions of this course according to which a constructivist approach should be the foundation of the teaching process and careful orchestration is probably needed for students to be activated so that their motivation could be stimulated. In these terms, academic performance may be ameliorated and learning results will be probably safeguarded.

5 Research Limitations

Although the research questions of this research were answered and its aims were achieved, some limitations should be noted. Firstly, the number of participants was restricted. Therefore, a larger number of participants would need to be involved so that generalizations of the results could arise. Finally, even though students' CT skills seem to have developed, further research would be necessary in order to trace the transfer of these skills in other university courses or future semesters.

References

1. Bedford, J., et al.: COVID-19: towards controlling of a pandemic. Lancet **395**, 1015–1018 (2020). https://doi.org/10.1016/S0140-6736(20)30673-5
2. Scheicher, A.: The impact of Covid-19 on education: Insights from education at a glance 2020. https://www.oecd.org/education/the-impact-of-covid-19-on-education-insights-education-at-a-glance-2020.pdfAccessed 7 Oct 2020
3. UNESCO Homepage. https://en.unesco.org/covid19/educationresponse. Accessed 10 Oct 2020

4. Ratten, V.: Coronavirus (Covid-19) and the entrepreneurship education community. J. Enterprising Communities: People Places Global Economy (2020). https://doi.org/10.1108/JEC-06-2020-0121
5. Sahu, P.: Closure of universities due to Coronavirus Disease 2019 (COVID-19): impact on education and mental health of students and academic staff. Cureus **12**(4) (2020). https://doi.org/10.7759/cureus.7541
6. Liguori, E., Winkler, C.: From offline to online: challenges and opportunities for entrepreneurship education following the COVID-19 pandemic. Entrepreneurship Educ. Pedagogy **3**(4), 346–351 (2020). https://doi.org/10.1177/2515127420916738
7. Schneider, S.L., Council, M.L.: Distance learning in the era of COVID-19. Arch. Dermatol. Res. 1–2 (2020). https://doi.org/10.1007/s00403-020-02088-9
8. Al-Zaman, S.: Covid-19-related fake news in social media. https://ssrn.com/abstract=3644107. Accessed 7 Oct 2020. https://doi.org/10.2139/ssrn.3644107
9. Cinelli, M., et al.: The covid-19 social media infodemic. arXiv preprint arXiv:2003.05004 (2020). https://arxiv.org/ct?url=https%3A%2F%2Fdx.doi.org%2F10.1038%2Fs41598-020-73510-5&v=5c44ac78
10. Halpern, D.: Thought and Knowledge: An Introduction to Critical Thinking, 5th edn. Psychology Press, New York and London (2014)
11. Saadé, R.G., Morin, D., Thomas, J.D.: Critical thinking in E-learning environments. Comput. Hum. Behav. **28**(5), 1608–1617 (2012). https://doi.org/10.1016/j.chb.2012.03.025
12. American Philosophical Association: Critical Thinking: a statement of expert consensus for purposes of educational assessment & instruction, The Delphi Report: research findings & recommendations prepared for the committee on pre-college philosophy. P. Facione, (Project Director), ERIC Doc. No. ED 315–423 (1990)
13. Facione, P.A., Sanchez, C.A., Facione, N.C., Gainen, J.: The disposition toward critical thinking. J. General Educ. **44**(1), 1–25 (1995)
14. Uzuntiryaki-KondakÇi, E., Çapa-Aydin, Y.: Predicting critical thinking skills of university students through metacognitive self-regulation skills and chemistry self-efficacy. Educ. Sci.: Theory Practice **13**(1), 666–670 (2013)
15. Cho, M.H., Shen, D.: Self-regulation in online learning. Distance Educ. **34**(3), 290–301 (2013). https://doi.org/10.1080/01587919.2013.835770
16. Pintrich, P.R.: A conceptual framework for assessing motivation and self-regulated learning in college students. Educ. Psychol. Rev. **16**(4), 385–407 (2004). https://doi.org/10.1007/s10648-004-0006-x
17. Pintrich, P.R., Zusho, A.: Student motivation and self-regulated learning in the college classroom. In: Smart, J. C. , Tierney, W.G. (eds.) Higher Education: Handbook of Theory and Research, vol. 17. Agathon Press, New York (2002)
18. Schoonenboom, J., Johnson, R.B.: KZfSS Kölner Zeitschrift für Soziologie und Sozialpsychologie **69**(2), 107–131 (2017). https://doi.org/10.1007/s11577-017-0454-1
19. Zacharis, N.Z.: Fostering students participation in online environments: focus on interaction, communication and problem solving. J. College Teach. Learn. (TLC) **6**(2), 25–34 (2009). https://doi.org/10.19030/tlc.v6i2.1169
20. McDade, S.A.: Case study pedagogy to advance critical thinking. Teach. Psychol. **22**(1), 9 (1995). https://doi.org/10.1207/s15328023top2201_3
21. Hattwig, D., Bussert, K., Medaille, A., Burgess, J.: Visual literacy standards in higher education: new opportunities for libraries and student learning. Portal: Libr. Acad. **13**(1), 61–89 (2013). https://doi.org/10.1353/pla.2013.0008
22. O'Brien, F.A.: Scenario planning–lessons for practice from teaching and learning. Eur. J. Oper. Res. **152**(3), 709–722 (2004). https://doi.org/10.1016/S0377-2217(03)00068-7
23. Snyder, L.G., Snyder, M.J.: Teaching critical thinking and problem solving skills. J. Res. Bus. Educ. **50**(2), 90 (2008)

24. Gall, M.D., Rhod, T.: Review of research on questioning techniques. In: Wilen, W.W. (ed.) Questions, Questioning Techniques, and Effective Teaching, pp. 23–48. National Education Association, Washington, D.C. (1987)
25. Halpern, D.F.: Teaching critical thinking for transfer across domains: disposition, skills, structure training, and metacognitive monitoring. Am. Psychol. **53**(4), 449–455 (1998). https://doi.org/10.1037/0003-066X.53.4.449
26. Kolb, A.Y., Kolb, D.A.: Learning styles and learning spaces: enhancing experiential learning in higher education. Acad. Manag. Learn. Educ. **4**(2), 193–212 (2005). https://doi.org/10.5465/amle.2005.17268566
27. Kolb, D.A., Boyatzis, R.E., Mainemelis, C.: Experiential learning theory: previous research and new directions. In: Sternberg, R.J., Zhang, L.F. (eds.) Perspectives on Thinking, Learning, and Cognitive Styles, pp. 227–247. Lawrence Erlbaum, New Jersey (2000)
28. Schön, D.: The reflective practitioner: how professionals think in action. Basic Books, New York (1983)
29. Hyslop-Margison, E.J., Strobel, J.: Constructivism and education: misunderstandings and pedagogical implications. Teach. Educ. Q. **43**(1), 72–86 (2007). https://doi.org/10.1080/08878730701728945
30. Jones, M.G., Brader-Araje, L.: The impact of constructivism on education: Language, discourse, and meaning. Am. Commun. J. **5**(3), 1–0 (2002)
31. Pintrich, P.R., Smith, D.A.F., Garcia, T., McKeachie, W.J.: A manual for the use of the Motivated Strategies for Learning Questionnaire (MSLQ). National center for research to improve postsecondary teaching and learning, Technical Report No. 91-B-004 (1991)
32. Gray, J., DiLoreto, M.: Student satisfaction and perceived learning in online learning environments: the mediating effect of student engagement. In: Annual Meeting of the National Council of Professors of Educational Leadership, Washington, DC (2015)
33. Hsieh, H.-F., Shannon, S.E.: Three approaches to qualitative content analysis. Qual. Health Res. **15**(9), 1277–1288 (2005). https://doi.org/10.1177/1049732305276687
34. Mayring, P.: Qualitative content analysis. Forum: Qual. Res. Anal. **1**(2) (2000)
35. Gurcay, D., Ferah, H.O.: High school students' critical thinking related to their metacognitive self-regulation and physics self-efficacy beliefs. J. Educ. Training Stud. **6**(4), 125–130 (2018). https://doi.org/10.11114/jets.v6i4.2980
36. Bandura, A.: On the functional properties of perceived self-efficacy revisited. J. Manag. **38**(1), 9–44 (2012). https://doi.org/10.1177/0149206311410606
37. Phan, H.P.: Relations between goals, self-efficacy, critical thinking and deep processing strategies: a path analysis. Educ. Psychol. **29**(7), 777–799 (2009). https://doi.org/10.1080/01443410903289423
38. Dimitriadou, C., Vrantsi, A., Lithoxoidou, A., Seira, E.: Teachers' critical thinking dispositions through their engagement in action research projects: an example of best practice. In: Tsitouridou, M., A. Diniz, J., Mikropoulos, T.A. (eds.) TECH-EDU 2018. CCIS, vol. 993, pp. 166–180. Springer, Cham (2019). https://doi.org/10.1007/978-3-030-20954-4_12
39. Sun, J.C.Y., Rueda, R.: Situational interest, computer self-efficacy and self-regulation: their impact on student engagement in distance education. Br. J. Edu. Technol. **43**(2), 191–204 (2012). https://doi.org/10.1111/j.1467-8535.2010.01157.x
40. Kuo, Y.C., Walker, A.E., Belland, B.R., Schroder, K.E.: A predictive study of student satisfaction in online education programs. Int. Rev. Res. Open Distrib. Learn. **14**(1), 16–39 (2013). https://doi.org/10.19173/irrodl.v14i1.1338

The Diagnostic Assessment and Achievement of College Skills (DAACS): A Powerful Tool for the Regulation of Learning

Elie ChingYen Yu[1](✉), Angela M. Lui[2](✉), and Diana Akhmedjanova[3](✉)

[1] University at Albany–State University of New York, Albany, NY 12222, USA
cyu5@albany.edu

[2] Rutgers, The State University of New Jersey, New Brunswick, NJ 08854, USA
angela.lui@rutgers.edu

[3] Westminster International University in Tashkent, 12 Istkbol Street, Tashkent 100047, Uzbekistan

Abstract. The Diagnostic Assessment and Achievement of College Skills (DAACS) is an open-source diagnostic assessment tool that measures students' college readiness and is designed to promote success through feedback and resources. Evidence for the validity and reliability of the four DAACS assessments (reading, writing, mathematics, and self-regulated learning) have been addressed, which further supports the use of DAACS with our targeted population. Empirical studies have shown that the DAACS improves the prediction accuracy of students' performance, which allows DAACS to be used to identify at-risk students. Students who use DAACS feedback and resources are more successful than those who do not. Various behavioral nudges were sent to students as reminders to complete and use the DAACS, which resulted in a significant increase in the use of feedback and resources. DAACS is not just a tool but a system that facilitates the self and co-regulation of learning. Since the DACCS is now being implemented in new settings and contexts, further validation will be needed. The future of DAACS will involve expansion from use at the institutional level to the instructor level, where DAACS could be maximized to support students' SRL development and academic achievement.

Keywords: Self-regulated learning · Co-regulation of learning · Feedback

1 Overview of DAACS

The Diagnostic Assessment and Achievement of College Skills (DAACS) is an open-source diagnostic assessment tool designed to measure newly enrolled college students' reading, writing, mathematics, and self-regulated learning skills and provide instant, individualized feedback and resources that students can use to become better prepared for college. The online DAACS system has four primary components: (1) diagnostic assessments of self-regulated learning, reading, writing, and mathematics; (2) instant feedback with recommendations and links to open educational resources (OERs); (3) a

A. Reis et al. (Eds.): TECH-EDU 2020, CCIS 1384, pp. 193–202, 2021.
https://doi.org/10.1007/978-3-030-73988-1_14

dashboard for academic advising, and (4) predictive modeling. The first three components were designed to directly influence student functioning, while the fourth is intended for institutional use.

The diagnostic assessment of self-regulated learning (SRL) and the SRL Lab, an OER created for DAACS, aligns with the vision of the Special Track because they are tools for monitoring the Self and Co-Regulation of e-Learning (SCReL): DAACS can raise learners' awareness and promote the use of SRL to facilitate students' learning in an e-learning context. The diagnostic SRL survey is a practical, freely accessible, and actionable SRL assessment. The survey focuses on three aspects of SRL known to be associated with success in college [1–3]: (1) motivation, which measures students' mastery orientation, test anxiety, self-efficacy, and mindset; (2) learning strategies, which measures students' help seeking behaviors and ability to manage their understanding, time, and environment; and (3) metacognition, which measures students' ability to plan, monitor, and evaluate their learning. The SRL survey contains a psychometrically sound number of items but is short enough to encourage its use. In addition, the survey is designed for instructional purposes. Each scale, subscale, and item is explicitly linked to actionable feedback that can help students help themselves become more academically successful.

The purpose of the present paper is to describe the work that has been done to develop and refine the DAACS as a powerful tool and system for the self- and co-regulation of learning. We first describe a theoretical model of how the DAACS can be used by students to regulate their learning. Then, we provide a summary of the key empirical research that has been conducted on the validity and reliability of DAACS assessments, the efficacy of DAACS, and the efficacy of nudges designed to encourage use of the DAACS. The paper concludes with future directions for research and practice.

1.1 DAACS in the Context of Self- and Co-regulation of Learning

In addition to providing diagnostic assessment results, DAACS supports self-directed learning with immediate, individualized feedback intended to increase students' awareness of discrepancies between their current and desired skill levels and provide suggestions about how to improve. Included in the feedback also provides learners with links to relevant online educational resources such as the SRL Lab (https://srl.daacs.net). This SRL online Lab provides students with detailed information about what self-regulated learning is, how it is related to success in college, task-specific strategies students can use, and case scenarios that demonstrate their value and utility. The availability of information and resources encourages autonomy in learning.

For example, many students decide to work on time management, which is one of the sub-domains of the learning strategies domain. Students can go to the SRL Lab and easily navigate to the time management section, where they can learn more about what time management is and why it is important for college success. The Lab includes descriptions of and likely outcomes for people who often, sometimes, or rarely manage their time. Students can then read a brief case scenario about a hypothetical student and his struggles with learning before he managed his time, the actions he took to improve his time management, and the positive effects these improvements had. Students are then provided with six effective time management strategies, each of which they can click on to learn more about.

Figure 1 summarizes the DAACS system, grounded in Bronfenbrenner's bioecological systems theory [4]), that highlights the reciprocal and transactional relationship between the students and their interrelated ecological environment. With the DAACS-generated individualized diagnostic assessment, students become more informed about themselves as learners. Thus, a more intentional behavioral change could be planned, directly and indirectly, with the support of their academic advisors and institutions that students interact with as a part of their educational setting: Trained advisors can use DAACS information in advising, and institutions can use DAACS data in predictive models.

The objective of DAACS is in line with that of SCReL since it not only raises students' awareness of themselves as learners through the individualized feedback, but it also encourages and develops students as a self-directed learner through the self and co-regulation of learning: taking advantage of the OERs in DAACS as well as interacting with the resources in their immediate learning environment. DAACS is not just a tool but also a system that immerses students in the process of self-regulation and co-regulation of learning.

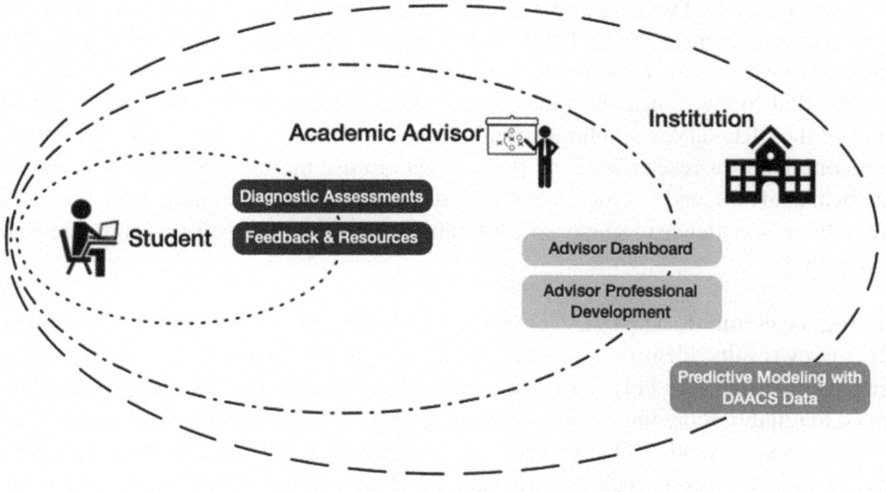

Fig. 1. DAACS framework and components

2 Empirical Findings

Several empirical studies have been conducted using DAACS: In 2016, DAACS was administered to students to collect validity evidence regarding inferences made from results of the four DAACS assessments (SRL, writing, reading, and mathematics). In 2017, DAACS was implemented as an intervention in a randomized controlled trial experiment to examine the efficacy of DAACS on student achievement and retention. In

2019, we developed DAACS nudges in response to findings from the DAACS efficacy study, and conducted two randomized controlled experiments to investigate the effects of DAACS nudges on student achievement.

Data for these studies were collected from incoming undergraduate students at two private, nonprofit, online liberal arts colleges (Excelsior College [EC] and Western Governors University [WGU]). These institutions serve predominately non-traditional, first-generation college students with an average age in the mid-30s. In this section, we briefly summarize these empirical efforts, key findings, and implications.

2.1 Validity and Reliability of DAACS Assessments

SRL Survey. The SRL survey consists of 62 Likert-type items adapted from established SRL measures [5–9]. The items are organized in three domains: (1) motivation, which measures students' mastery orientation, test anxiety, self-efficacy, and mindset; (2) learning strategies, which measures students' help seeking behaviors, as well as the ability to manage their understanding, time, and environment; and (3) metacognition, which measures students' ability to plan, monitor, and evaluate their learning. The SRL survey has excellent internal consistency ($\alpha = .79$–$.91$).

To establish validity evidence regarding internal structure, exploratory factor analysis (EFA) was conducted with a sample of 682 students from EC and WGU, which resulted in our measurement structure [10]. Confirmatory factor analysis ($n_{WGU} = 6{,}644$) was then used to validate the measurement structure derived from EFA, and the instructional structure that follows our conceptual organization of the three domains and 11 subdomains of the SRL survey. Findings revealed acceptable model fit for the two structures; we recommend for researchers and practitioners to use the measurement structure for statistical analyses, and instructional structure for teaching and learning purposes. Altogether, there is evidence to support the inferences drawn from the survey scores are valid and reliable.

Writing Assessment. The DAACS writing assessment asks students to summarize their SRL survey results, identify specific strategies for improving their SRL, and commit to using them. LightSide [11], an open source, automated essay scoring program was trained to reliably score the writing assessments in terms of nine criteria related to effective college-level writing [12] and provide students with feedback within one minute [13]. The scoring rubric includes criteria related to content, organization, paragraphs, sentences, and conventions, with subdomains focused on summary, suggestions, structure, transitions, focus on a main idea, cohesion, correct sentence structure, and complex sentence structures.

To examine inter-rater reliability, the first 1,093 essays written by students from WGU were scored by human raters; 597 (55%) were double scored and adjudicated. The essays and their scores were used to train LightSide. Exact percent agreement between human raters ranged from 55% to 63%; exact percent agreement between human and LightSide ratings range from 47% to 74%. Confirmatory factor analysis with the same sample suggests that the factor structure of the scores generally conform to our conceptual framework as represented by the rubric [13].

Although agreement was often unsatisfactory, LightSIDE and human scorers rarely disagreed by more than one level on the three-level rubric. In a poll of students, 38 of 40 (95%) said the writing assessment was mostly or completely accurate. In order to increase the accuracy of machine-scored essays, we have scored a new sample of 500 essays and are preparing to train the new, Python-based system known as BERT.

Mathematics and Reading Assessments. The DAACS mathematics assessment includes over 180 items that cover word problems, geometry, variables and equations, numbers and calculations, and lines and functions. Using a computer adaptive testing framework, students see a stratified random selection of 18 to 24 items among the five domains, with item difficulty tailored to the individual student. The DAACS reading assessment includes 30 passages of varying difficulty levels with six items per passage. The items assess students' understanding of the ideas, language, purpose, and structure of written passages, as well as their ability to make inferences. Students see a random selection of three to four passages with difficulty levels tailored to their performance on the first selection. Cronbach's alphas are 0.67 for math and 0.69 for reading assessments, respectively.

Convergent and discriminant validity evidence were examined to gather validity evidence regarding relations to other variables. Intercorrelations reveal that, at both institutions ($n_{\text{EC}} = 5{,}141$, $n_{\text{WGU}} = 6{,}536$), reading total scores correlated more highly with the reading subdomains ($r = .52$ to .82; convergent) and less with mathematics total score ($r_{\text{EC}} = .37$ and $r_{\text{WGU}} = .44$) and its subdomains ($r = .15$ to .38; discriminant validity). The same is true for mathematics: Mathematics total scores correlated higher with its subdomains ($r = .57$ to .70) than with reading subdomains ($r = .15$ to .38).

2.2 Efficacy of the DAACS

We used randomized controlled trials (RCT) to examine the efficacy of DAACS intervention on students' academic progress and achievement. Academic progress was operationalized as on-time progress: At EC, where most students are part-time, *on-time* was defined as completing at least three credits within six months, while at WGU, where all students are full-time, on-time was defined as earning at least 12 credits within six months. Academic achievement was operationalized as credit acquisition rate (ratio of credits earned to credits attempted).

Student participants were incoming, mostly non-traditional (i.e., adult students, often transferring in credits, in fully online programs) undergraduates enrolled at the two institutions ($n = 23{,}467$) in 2017. All incoming students were expected to complete an institution-specific, required zero-credit online orientation to college before beginning coursework. Students ($n = 23{,}467$) were randomly assigned to one of two versions of the orientation course at each institution: Students in the treatment group ($n = 11{,}667$) took all four DAACS assessments, received individualized feedback and suggestions based on their results, and were assigned a DAACS-trained advisor ($n = 350$). Students in the control group ($n = 11{,}790$) attended the same orientation but without DAACS: They did not take the DAACS assessments, did not receive DAACS feedback, and were assigned to advisors who had not been trained to use DAACS during advising.

Although the results of the RCT revealed overall null effects of DAACS on on-time progress and credit acquisition, post-hoc correlational analyses of DAACS usage data for the treatment condition revealed a pattern of statistically significant differences between subgroups. Figures 2 and 3 illustrate the associations between DAACS and on-time progress for subgroups: Students who (1) took the assessments but did not view the feedback (assessments only), (2) took the assessments, viewed the feedback, and/or clicked at least one link to a recommended open educational resource (assessments + feedback), (3) were advised by an advisor who viewed the students' DAACS results (assessments + advisor), (4) took the assessments, viewed the feedback, and whose advisor viewed the students' results (assessments + feedback + advisor), and (5) did not do orientation. Conditions three and four were in place only at WGU (Fig. 3), due to restructuring of advising services at EC at the time of the study. Furthermore, Condition five was evident only at EC, but in both treatment and control groups, because while orientation was required, some students still elected not to complete it.

Figures 2 and 3 reveal a clear trend: The more DAACS was used by students and advisors, the more likely students were to pass a course and earn the credits they attempted within six months (EC: $\chi 2 = 503.32$, $p < 0.001$; WGU: $\chi 2 = 60.93$, $p < 0.001$). The results were identical for credit acquisition (EC: $F(4, 10280) = 170.8$, $p < 0.001$, $p < 0.001$; WGU: $F(5, 13176) = 14.31$, $p < 0.001$).

Because accurately identifying students at risk of academic failure is of great importance to administrators in higher education [14], we also investigated the extent to which the DAACS assessment data (reading, mathematics, writing, and SRL scores) could improve the accuracy of prediction models of student success. Parametric and non-parametric methods were used, including logistic regression, classification trees, and random forests: The model with the highest accuracy was retained. The addition of DAACS assessment data to baseline student predictor variables (demographics, transfer credits, etc.) improved prediction accuracy of on-time progress by up to 6.9% [15]. Administrators at the participating institutions considered this a significant improvement in predictive power.

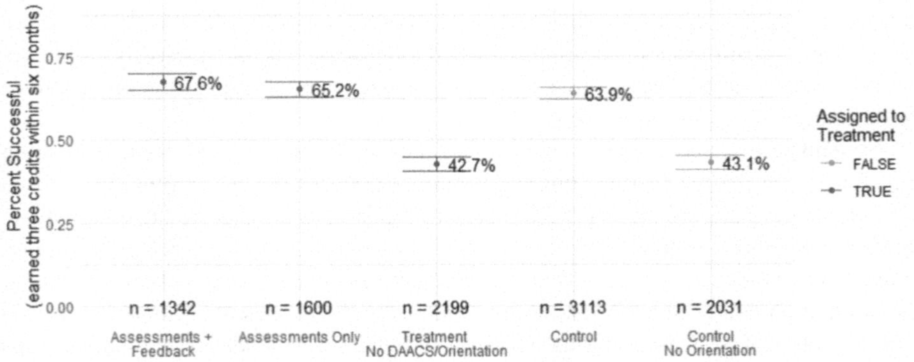

Fig. 2. Percent of Excelsior College students making on-time progress at six months

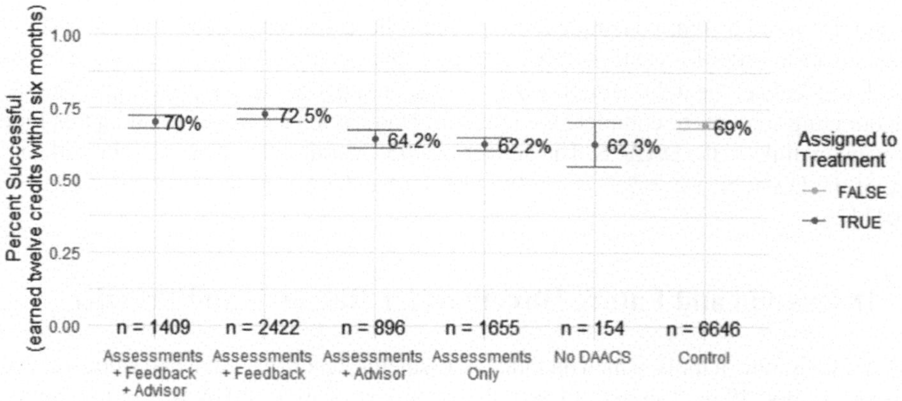

Fig. 3. Percent of WGU students making on-time progress at six months

2.3 Efficacy of the DAACS Nudges

A major finding from the efficacy study indicated that DAACS is only helpful to students who choose to not only take the assessments, but also access the feedback and resources (see Figs. 2 and 3). In response to these findings, we developed and tested nudges in 2019 to encourage more students to take advantage of the wealth of information and resources available to them via the DAACS. Two randomized controlled trials – one focused on nudging students to complete the DAACS ($n = 5{,}057$); the other focused on nudging students to review DAACS feedback ($n = 1{,}255$) – were conducted concurrently to examine the effects of two types of nudges: reminders and social norm nudges.

To nudge is "to alert, remind, or mildly warn another" [16]. The nudges were informed by studies that demonstrated their effectiveness in influencing behavior. For example, the U.K. Nudge Unit sent letters to individuals who had not paid their taxes, the most effective of which read, "Nine out of ten people in the U.K. pay their taxes on time. You are currently in the very small minority of people who have not paid us yet." Within 23 days, there was an increase of 15% in the number of people paying their taxes [17]. Similar nudges based on social norms have been shown to be effective in improving organ donor registrations [16], decreasing cigarette smoking on college campuses [18], and increasing elementary school students' use of deliberate practice [19].

Reminders are a type of nudge that prompts students to turn their attention to a particular problem or task, gives them easy access to information, and/or reminds them of the benefits of completing a task [20]. These types of nudges have had a positive effect on several educational outcomes, including college enrollment for low income and first-generation students [21]. Informational nudges aim to improve student outcomes by providing information about their behavior and ability, or by encouraging students to overcome barriers [20]. Informational nudges aimed at improving students' grit [22], planning [23, 24], goal setting [22, 23], and time management [23, 25] have had positive effects on academic outcomes.

Two of our nudges reflect social norms: They inform students of either the percentage of students from their school who have completed DAACS or the higher success rate of students who use DAACS. We also developed three reminder and informational nudges, including one that reminds students to re-read the essay they wrote for the writing assessment in order to recall the SRL strategies they committed to using; one that has a link to feedback on a domain on which they scored particularly low or high; and one encouraging students to complete the DAACS. Nudges were sent via email and include convenient links to the DAACS. The nudges resulted in a significant increase in students' use of the DAACS ($\chi2 = 7.7$, $p < 0.05$) and the feedback it provides ($\chi2 = 14.2$, $p < 0.01$) [26].

3 Discussion and Future Directions for Research and Practice

DAACS is a suite of tools, which includes assessments, feedback, advisor dashboard, and predictive modelling. The initial research on implementation of DAACS at two online colleges identified evidence of acceptable psychometric qualities of all four assessments. While the overall efficacy of DAACS indicated a null effect, a closer examination of the results revealed that students who took all four assessments, accessed feedback, and discussed their DAACS results with their advisors were more likely to earn the credits than students in other comparison groups. Furthermore, adding DAACS data along with other student predictor variables improved prediction accuracy of on-time progress by up to 6.9%. Finally, nudging students to use DAACS resulted in a significant increase of their use of DAACS and feedback.

DAACS is still being implemented at EC and WGU, as well as at a new site, which is a traditional research university. There has also been international interest in DAACS, including from Denmark and Taiwan. As we expand the use of DAACS nationally and internationally, this assessment and feedback system will need to be revalidated. The efficacy and predictive power of the DAACS should also be examined at each new institution. In addition, analyses of outcomes by institution-specific subgroups must be conducted, in order to determine who benefits most from DAACS, and why.

One of the future goals of DAACS is to permit course instructors at the individual level, rather than only at the institutional level, to use DAACS with their students. We plan to research the ways in which students, advisors, and instructors use DAACS by examining trace data, as well as by conducting interviews and observations. These data will reveal how DAACS can best serve practitioners in order to support students' self-regulated learning and achievement.

Acknowledgments. This work was supported by the U.S. Department of Education under grant #P116F150077. The contents do not necessarily represent the policy of the U.S. Department of Education, and endorsement by the Federal Government should not be assumed.

References

1. Efklides, A.: Interactions of metacognition with motivation and affect in self-regulated learning: the MASRL model. Educ. Psychol. **46**(1), 6–25 (2011). https://doi.org/10.1080/00461520.2011.538645

2. Winne, P.H., Hadwin, A.F.: Studying as self-regulated engagement in learning. In: Hacker, D., Dunlosky, J., Graesser, A. (eds.) Metacognition in Educational Theory and Practice, pp. 277–304. Lawrence Erlbaum Associates, New Jersey (1998)
3. Zimmerman, B.J.: Attaining self-regulation: a social-cognitive perspective. In: Boekaerts, M., Pintrich, P., Zeidner, M. (eds.) Self-regulation: Theory, Research, and Applications, pp. 13–39. Academic Press, Cambridge (2000)
4. Bronfenbrenner, U.: The Ecology of Human Development: Experiments by Nature and Design. Harvard University Press, Cambridge (1979)
5. Cleary, T.: The development and validation of the self-regulation strategy inventory—self-report. J. Sch. Psychol. **44**(4), 307–322 (2006). https://doi.org/10.1016/j.jsp.2006.05.002
6. Driscoll, R.: Westside Test Anxiety Scale Validation. ERIC Digest (2007). https://files.eric.ed.gov/fulltext/ED495968.pdf
7. Dugan, R., Andrade, H.L.: Exploring the construct validity of academic self-regulation using a new self-report questionnaire - the survey of academic self-regulation. Int. J. Educ. Psychol. Assess. **7**(1), 45–63 (2011). https://scholarsarchive.library.albany.edu/edpsych_fac_scholar/1
8. Dweck, C.S.: Mindset: The New Psychology of Success. Random House, New York (2006)
9. Schraw, G., Dennison, R.S.: Assessing metacognitive awareness. Contemp. Educ. Psychol. **19**(4), 460–475 (1994)
10. Lui, A., et al.: Validity evidence of the internal structure of the DAACS self-regulated learning survey. Future Rev. Int. J. Trans. Coll. Career Success **1**(1), 1–8 (2018)
11. Mayfield, E., Rosé, C.P.: LightSIDE: Open source machine learning for text. In: Shermis, M., Burstein, J. (eds.) Handbook of Automated Essay Evaluation, pp. 146–157. Routledge, Abingdon (2013)
12. Yagelski, R.: The Essentials of Writing: Ten Core Concepts. Cengage Learning, Boston (2015)
13. Akhmedjanova, D., Lui, A.M., Andrade, H.L., Bryer, J.: Validity and reliability of the DAACS writing assessment. Paper presentation, Annual Meeting of the National Council on Measurement in Education (NCME), Toronto, Canada, 4–8 April 2019
14. Ekowo, M., Palmer, I.: Predictive analytics in higher education: five guiding practices for ethical use. Education Policy, 6 March 2016. https://www.newamerica.org/education-policy/reports/predictive-analytics-in-higher-education/
15. Bryer, J., Lui, A.M., Andrade, H.L., Franklin, D., Cleary, T.: Efficacy of the diagnostic assessment and achievement of college skills on multiple success indicators. Roundtable presentation, Annual Meeting of the American Educational Research Association (AERA), Toronto, Canada, 5–9 April 2019
16. Thaler, R.H., Sunstein, C.R.: Nudge: Improving Decisions About Health and Happiness. Penguin Group, New York (2008)
17. Halpern, D.: Inside the Nudge Unit: How Small Changes Can Make a Big Difference. Penguin Random House, New York (2015)
18. Perkins, H.W.: The Social Norms Approach to Preventing School and College Age Substance Abuse. Jossey-Bass, San Francisco (2003)
19. Eskreis-Winkler, L., Gross, J.J., Duckworth, A.L.: GRIT: sustained self-regulation in the service of superordinate goals. In: Vohs, K.D., Baumeister, R.F. (eds.) Handbook of Self-regulation: Research, Theory and Applications, 3rd edn., pp. 380–396. Guilford, New York (2016)
20. Damgaard, M.T., Nielsen, H.S.: Nudging in education. Econ. Educ. Rev. **64**, 313–342 (2018). https://doi.org/10.1016/j.econedurev.2018.03.008
21. Castleman, B.L., Page, L.C.: Parental influences on postsecondary decision making: evidence from a text messaging experiment. Educ. Eval. Policy Anal. **39**(2), 361–377 (2017). https://doi.org/10.3102/0162373716687393

22. Alan, S., Boneva, T., Ertac, S.: Ever failed, try again, succeed better: results from a randomized educational intervention on grit. Q. J. Econ. **134**(3), 1121–1162 (2019). https://doi.org/10.1093/qje/qjz006
23. De Paola, M., Scoppa, V.: Procrastination, academic success and the effectiveness of a remedial program. J. Econ. Behav. Organ. **115**, 217–236 (2015). https://doi.org/10.1016/j.jebo.2014.12.007
24. Yeomans, M., Reich, J.: Planning prompts increase and forecast course completion in massive open online courses. In: Proceedings of the Seventh International Conference on Learning Analytics & Knowledge Conference, ACM, New York, pp. 464–473 (2017). https://doi.org/10.1145/3027385.3027416
25. Bettinger, E.P., Baker, R.B.: The effects of student coaching: an evaluation of a randomized experiment in student advising. Educ. Eval. Policy Anal. **36**(1), 3–19 (2014). https://doi.org/10.3102/0162373713500523
26. Franklin, D., Bryer, J., Akhmedjanova, D., Lui, A.M., Andrade, H.L.: The effects of nudges on students' use of the diagnostic assessment and achievement of college skills. Roundtable presentation, Annual Meeting of the American Educational Research Association (AERA), San Francisco, CA, USA (Conference Canceled), 17–21 April 2020

Drill-Down Dashboard for Chairing of Online Master Programs in Engineering

Anabela Costa e Silva[1(✉)], Leonel Morgado[2], and António Coelho[3]

[1] Faculty of Engineering of the University of Porto, Porto, Portugal
up201506034@fe.up.pt

[2] Universidade Aberta and INESC TEC, Coimbra, Portugal
Leonel.Morgado@uab.pt

[3] Faculdade de Engenharia, Universidade do Porto / INESC TEC, Porto, Portugal
acoelho@fe.up.pt

Abstract. Online masters' program chairs need up-to-date information to monitor efficiently and effectively all the courses in the program for which they are responsible.

Learning Management Systems supporting the operation of the online programme collect vast amounts of data about the learning process. These systems are geared to support individual teachers and students, not program chairs.

This article presents the process that led to the development of a Dashboards for program chairs, based upon an analysis of their regular supervision tasks, decision-making information needs, and available data in the learning management system, Moodle.

The information presented via the dashboard is aggregated and contextualised for all students enrolled in the program, in all its courses, contributing to improve decision-making in program chairing.

The dashboard prototype is presented as a concrete outcome of this process, which can be replicated to achieve more advanced and updated versions, hopefully contributing to better program chairing.

Keywords: Learning management systems · Dashboards · Program chairing · Program direction · Program coordination

1 Introduction

Recently, Learning Dashboards use and research surged significantly. Nevertheless, their application to support the role of masters' program chairs (also known as program directors or, in the non-English speaking world, program coordinators) has not been the focus of much analysis.

A program chair must ensure that students enrolled in the program have the support they need to be successful. They monitor the individual and collective learning process of the whole cohort to forecast student failure, and act to prevent it. The role of a program coordinator is also to cater for the resources and structure needed so that the program is successful.

A. Reis et al. (Eds.): TECH-EDU 2020, CCIS 1384, pp. 203–209, 2021.
https://doi.org/10.1007/978-3-030-73988-1_15

Most current tools aim to encourage the learning process, but focused on the role of students or teachers [10]. A program chair needs to consider several courses in parallel, not a single one. In the case of online programs, since educational activities take place in a Virtual Learning Environment (VLE) most commonly a structured one known as Learning Management System (LMS), there is plenty of data about occurrenes. However, this is mostly structured by individual or course, not by program. Similarly, data views and reports available in these VLE/LMS present information in suited for individual students and teachers, not chairs. From the viewpoint of program chairs, the information is scattered, lacking cohort context, course-comparison context, and hard to interpret.

This paper approached this problem by analysing the roles of program chairs in the context of Engineering Master Programs in Portugal, establishing available data in the context of online programs developed with the Moodle LMS, ascertaining the available data accessible via public Web services or log exports, and prototyping a sample dashboard to support some of the chairs' roles using those available data.

2 Background: Dashboards for Masters Program Chairs

A literature review of the use of dashboards by masters program chairs was conducted. The search was performed on the 14th of August 2020 and using Harzing's Publish or Perish software [3] to rank results from Google Scholar. We searched for "dashboard AND ("learning analytics" OR "educational data mining" OR "educational datamining") AND (master OR graduate) AND (administ* OR coordinat* OR advis* OR chair)", limiting the search for results from the year 2015 onward. This search string was used to compensate for different nomenclatures used for this position, like program chair or advisor. The first 19 results were selected. Two of these ([11] and [14]), were not peer-reviewed works and were discarded, and one ([5]) was unavailable. In total 16 articles were read and analysed for this review.

Only two paper discussed in any way the role of masters program chairs. Strang [12] relates different approaches of employing Learning Analytics (LA) in Moodle, distinguishing between Course-level and Organizational-level information. Uskov et al. [13] provide a larger analysis of these various levels of depth, two of which are related to master program chairs: "Concentration/minor program level" and "Departmental/program of study/curriculum level". In their case, the master program chair has an analogous role to that of a department chair.

Overall, there was little specifically on program chairing support with dashboards. Possible reasons are that little has been written about existing dashboards for chairs, that there are few such dashboards, or that there is yet another nomenclature to describe them besides those we employed in this review.

3 Problem Statement

Moodle and other LMS have vast amounts of information about the education environment events. Nonetheless, they are geared towards supporting actions of individual teachers and students, and structure data and information by courses, dispersing the data and information required by program chairs for decision-making. Our aim was to create a dashboard-development process that can overcome this lack of information for program chairs. This process includes the analysis of program chairing tasks, of the decision-making associated with then, of the required information to support those decisions, of the available data towards those information in the LMS, and of the accessibility of those data from external systems.

4 Methodology

Design Science Research (DSR) seeks to learn from creating new and innovative artefacts and values learning by doing [4]. By applying DSR, researchers aim to create effective or useful artifacts, and learn from that creation process, generating knowledge from the adequacy analysis of the artifacts in concert with the principles employed in their design. Decision-support systems, such as dashboards, are a common artifact in DSR, as are modelling tools, governance strategies, or evaluation methods [2].

> The fundamental questions for design-science research are, "What utility does the new artefact provide?" and "What demonstrates that utility?" [4].

We followed a DSR process with six activities or steps [6] to design and evaluate the dashboard prototype.

5 Tasks Required of Master Program Chairs

In Portugal, the functions of program chairs are specified in the statutes of each university. Their main function is, usually, to ensure the well-governance of the program. In the statutes of the University of Porto, the first duty of a program chair is to ensure the normal functioning of the program as well as to safeguard its quality [8]. However, the specific requirements and tasks vary between universities. Both the University of Porto's and the University of Trásos-Montes and Alto Douro's statutes specify that other tasks may be added [1, 9]. At Universidade Aberta, its pedagogical model includes other functions in the role of program chairs [7].

To better understand and prioritize the task details of what master program chairs do, we interviewed 5 chairs. With the results of these interviews, 8 tasks were identified as having higher priority for chairs.

These tasks were spread unevenly throughout the academic year or semester. Task "Review and Rank Candidates' Applications" is done yearly at the beginning of the academic year; "Review the Courses' Reports" and "Register Dissertation Plans" are repeated at the beginning of each semester; "Oversee Absenteeism", "Prevent Dropout", and "Create and Review Student Results" are done regularly throughout the semester; "Review Satisfaction Surveys" is done at the end of each semester; and "Review Program Evaluation Reports" is done at an undefined by delimited time frame, dependent on data availability from academic services.

Do to their time dispersion and recurring nature, the tasks "Oversee Absenteeism", "Prevent Dropout", and "Create and Review Student Results", were selected for this dashboard prototype. The rationale was that the other tasks, due to their more restricted time frame, would be less critical, since chairs could devote a more focused effort for that short time span, rather than year-round.

6 Prototype

Following the DSR process, iterative prototyping was done to design and develop the prototype. The final code is publicly available at https://github.com/AnabelaSilva/DISSFEUP-20192020. Three iterations were made, the last one being analysed by 5 master program chairs, who were interviewed regarding the prototype relevance and adequacy.

The prototype dashboard contains three views: program-wide, student-wide, and course-wide.

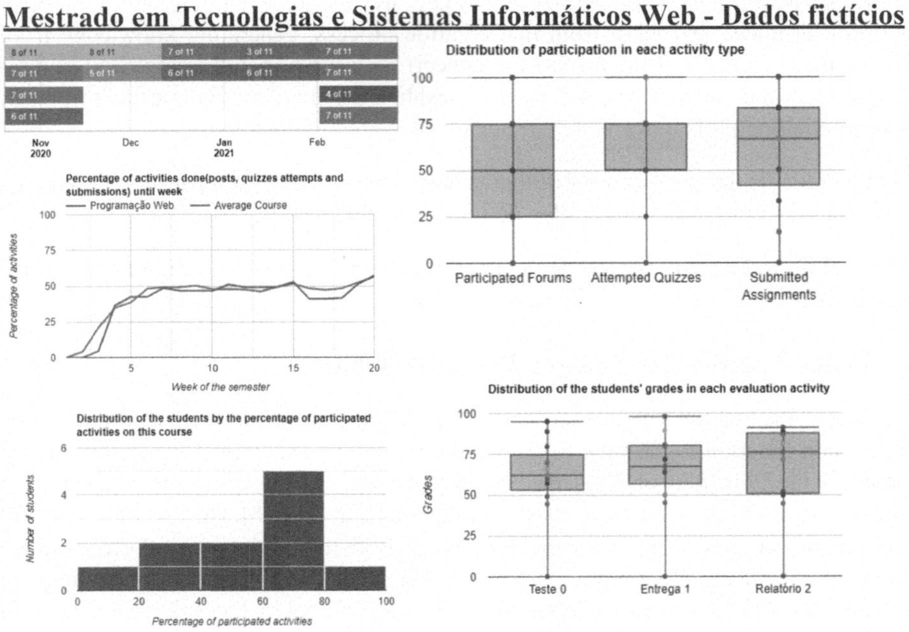

Fig. 1. Final prototype: screenshot of the course-wide view

The program-wide view is composed of four different displays that help the master program chair oversee the whole program: all students in all courses. Figure 3 depicts a screenshot of this view.

The student-wide view is composed of four different displays that allow the master program chair to see how a particular student is behaving in the program, in all courses, Fig. 2 depicts a screenshot of this view.

The course-wide view is composed of five different displays that allow the master program chair to see how a particular course is developing, with all students, in the context of the other courses. Figure 1 depicts a screenshot of this view.

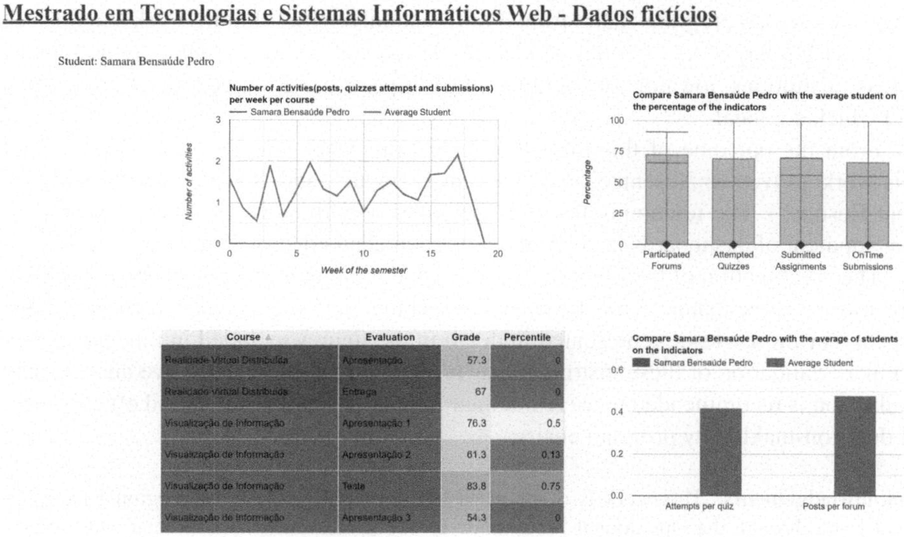

Fig. 2. Final prototype: screenshot of the student-wide view

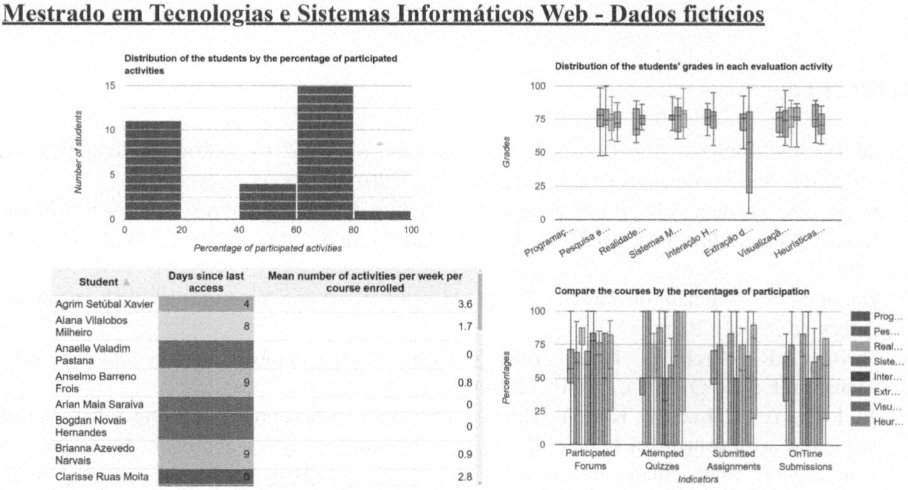

Fig. 3. Final prototype: screenshot of the program-wide view

7 Conclusions and Future Work

Herein we presented the process by which a dashboard was developed to support online master program chairing, resulting from the work developed for a master dissertation by the first author and her supervisors. The identification of the role and tasks of masters program chairs is a fist process step. Although the nomenclature and required tasks vary between institutions, some tasks are common to many chairing positions and can be useful for a wider audience. To conduct this first step, we used a literature review and interviews with 5 program chairs from 3 different universities. Future work should seek to establish a larger set of common chairing tasks, and compare distinct requirements across institutions, towards ascertaining which aspects are more generic in application and which are local.

From the outcome of this first step, three tasks were selected to be the focus of this work: "Oversee Absenteeism", "Prevent Dropout", and "Create and Review Student Results"). The remaining tasks are potential opportunities for future research on development of dashboards in support of program chairs decision making.

The combination of the interviews data with the literature review enabled the identification of three distinct view for decision-making, and of particular instruments and aspects for those views, represented in detail in the figures included in this paper. Preliminary validation of these instruments is promising, but more extensive analysis and evaluation is recommended to ascertain their impact on actual quality and effectiveness of decision-making by program chairs.

Acknowledgements. This work is co-financed by the ERDF – European Regional Development Fund through the Operational Programme for Competitiveness and Internationalization - COMPETE 2020 and the Lisboa 2020 under the PORTUGAL 2020 Partnership Agreement, and through the Portuguese National Innovation Agency (ANI) as a part of project CHIC POCI-01-0247-FEDER-024498.

References

1. de Trás-os-Montes e Alto Douro, U.: Regulamento nº 570/2018. Diário da República no. 161/2018, Série II de 2018-08-22. Accessed 5 Dec 2019
2. Gregor, S., Hevner, A.R.: Positioning and presenting design science research for maximum impact. Manag. Inf. Syst. Q. **37**(2), 337–355 (2013). https://doi.org/10.25300/MISQ/2013/37.2.01
3. Harzing, A.: Publish or Perish (2007). https://harzing.com/resources/publish-or-perish. Accessed 29 July 2020
4. Hevner, A.R., March, S.T., Park, J., Ram, S.: Design science in information systems research. Manag. Inf. Syst. Q. **28**(1), 75–105 (2004)
5. Jo, I.-H., Yu, T., Lee, H., Kim, Y.: Relations between student online learning behavior and academic achievement in higher education: a learning analytics approach. In: Chen, G., Kumar, V., Kinshuk, Huang, R., Kong, S.C. (eds.) Emerging Issues in Smart Learning. LNET, pp. 275–287. Springer, Heidelberg (2015). https://doi.org/10.1007/978-3-662-44188-6_38
6. Peffers, K., et al.: The design science research process: a model for producing and presenting information systems research. In: Proceedings of First International Conference on Design Science Research in Information Systems and Technology DESRIST, Claremont, California, USA, pp. 83–106 (2006)
7. Pereira, A., Mendes, A.Q., Morgado, L., Amante, L., Bidarra, J.: Modelopedagógico virtual da Universidade Aberta: para uma universidade do futuro. Universidade Aberta, Lisboa, Portugal, ISBN 978-972-674-493-1 (2007). https://hdl.handle.net/10400.2/1295
8. do Porto Reitoria, U.: Regulamento n.º 699/2018. Diário da República n.º 203/2018, Série II de 2018-10-22. Accessed 25 Jan 2020
9. do Porto Reitoria, U.: Regulamento n.º 706/2018. Dia´rio da República n.º 204/2018, Série II de 2018-10-23. Accessed 05 Dec 2019

10. Schwendimann, B.A., et al.: Perceiving learning at a glance: a systematic literature review of learning dashboard research. IEEE Trans. Learn. Technol. **10**(1), 30–41 (2015). https://doi.org/10.1109/TLT.2016.2599522
11. Sclater, N.: Learning Analytics Explained. Taylor & Francis, New York (2017).ISBN 9781317394563
12. Strang, K.D.: Do the critical success factors from learning analytics predictstudent outcomes? J. Educ. Technol. Syst. **44**(3), 273–299 (2016). https://doi.org/10.1177/0047239515615850
13. Uskov, V., et al.: Building smart learning analytics system for smart university. In: Uskov, V.L., Howlett, R.J., Jain, L.C. (eds.) SEEL 2017. SIST, vol. 75, pp. 191–204. Springer, Cham (2018). https://doi.org/10.1007/978-3-319-59451-4_19
14. West, D., et al.: Learning analytics: assisting universities with student retention, Case studies. Technical report, Australian Government Office for Learning and Teaching (2015). Project outcome of Final Report

Using BPMN to Identify Indicators for Teacher Intervention in Support of Self-regulation and Co-regulation of Learning in Asynchronous e-learning

Ceres Morais[1(✉)], Daniela Pedrosa[2,3], Vitor Rocio[1,4], José Cravino[2,5], and Leonel Morgado[1,4]

[1] INESC TEC, Porto, Portugal
ceres.g.morais@inesctec.pt, {vjr,leonel.morgado}@uab.pt
[2] CIDTFF, Aveiro, Portugal
dpedrosa@ua.pt, jcravino@utad.pt
[3] University of Aveiro, Aveiro, Portugal
[4] Universidade Aberta, Lisbon, Portugal
[5] University of Trás-dos-Montes e Alto Douro, Vila Real, Portugal

Abstract. We used BPMN diagrams to identify indicators that can assist teachers in their intervention actions to support students' self-regulation and co-regulation in an asynchronous e-learning context. The use of BPMN modeling, by making explicit the tasks and procedures implicit in the intervention of the e-learning teacher, also exposed which data were available for developing decision-support indicators, as well as the relevant moments for carrying out interventions. Such indicators can help e-learning teachers focus their interventions to support self-regulation and co-regulation of learning, as well as enabling the creation of live data dashboards to support decision-making for those interventions, thus this process can contribute to devise better instruments for teacher intervention in support of self-regulation and co-regulation of student learning.

Keywords: Self-regulation · Co-regulation · Indicators · BPMN · Dashboards · e-learning

1 Introduction

Teaching support for self and co-regulation of learning (SCRL) is crucial for the academic success of students as well as to prevent dropout during their studies. In e-learning contexts, occasions for synchronous contact between teacher and students are limited or absent, which is a further challenge to identify needs to support students' SCRL.

We used a business process improvement technique to explain and reveal the activities of the stakeholders in an e-learning engineering course: visual modeling with the graphic notation BPMN (Business Process Model and Notation) [1]. This contributed to the course planning, clarifying teaching actions, and revealing opportunities to intervene in support of self and co-regulation of learning [2].

A. Reis et al. (Eds.): TECH-EDU 2020, CCIS 1384, pp. 210–222, 2021.
https://doi.org/10.1007/978-3-030-73988-1_16

Using the BPMN models, we matched the intervention opportunities with the data available on e-learning platforms. This allowed us to identify relevant indicators to support the teacher's intervention towards self and co-regulation of students' e-learning. Such indicators can be used to create live monitoring tools, thus streamlining teachers' decision-making process for intervening in this regard.

2 Related Work

Improving processes requires awareness of their realities and context. In human contexts, processes are typically complex and negotiated, relying on both explicit and implicit rules, expectations, and assumptions. While this reliance means human-involving processes are rich, diversified, and versatile, it also means their improvement is cumbersome, conflicting, and hard. A common technique employed to tackle this difficulty is rendering explicit what is implicit, so that assumptions and contradictions can be visualized and addressed. BPMN is a commonly-used notation employed in business and organizations in general for this purpose.

In educational planning and learning design, several techniques have been used over time to render explicit the implicit, such as descriptive narratives, planning templates or forms (e.g. tabular/matrix representations), conceptual maps (e.g. mind maps and other dendrograms), and several types of diagrams, detailing workflows, actor participation, or other dimensions [3]. More formal approaches employ instructional design languages, with the IMS LD model being the most common [4]. These are detailed and powerful, able to express the pedagogical activities, as tested by researchers at the Open University of the Netherlands [5]. However, their focus is mostly in automating the generation and tracking of the online activities, rather than supporting human-led analysis and improvement of processes involving humans, such as teacher decision-making in support of student actions, such as SCRL.

Self-regulated learning (SRL) is considered as a meta-process in which students have control of their behaviour, emotion, motivation and cognition through the use of personal strategies to achieve the goals they have established [6, 7], and are proactive in managing their learning. In its turn, co-regulated learning (CRL) is understood as a social regulation of learning, in which students regulate their cognition, behaviour, motivation and their emotion in coordination of regulation between the student and other people (teachers or peers) [8]. CRL helps understand the SRL process [9].

Distance Learning (DL) courses present higher dropout rates, indicating greater hurdles [10]. The plan, development, and adequate use of SCRL skills are some of the difficulties faced by DL students [11, 12]. Also, they lack immediate support, in a context of potential social isolation [11–14], which are challenges for teacher development of effective pedagogical strategies [15]. Author's earlier work [14] identified some of these challenges: reduced cooperation, gradual missing of deadlines, prioritization of SCRL aspects; development of processes and tools to promote SCRL in teaching-learning of programming, engaging students on effective planning, organizing and management of their learning methods, and creating socialization opportunities. Teachers also found it difficult to gain awareness of class dynamics and provide immediate feedback. These support the relevance of developing pedagogical and instructional design techniques supporting student development of SCRL strategies [16].

A literature review [17] identified the need to create models that allow students to combine their activity with the tools that allow them to monitor the use of SRL strategies in online platforms. However, existing tools have not offered sufficient detail about students' activities and mechanisms to support SRL strategies. Thus, it is essential that in the design process phase of the tools, the relationships that are established between the student's activities, the SRL strategy to be developed and how this tool accompanies and supports these activities can be clarified through indicators. Since they identified the gap "that there is no guide for the design, implementation and evaluation of this type of tools." (ibid.) In addition, evidence from Learning Analytics to support teaching is rarely reported [18].

The literature on learning analytics recommends that inferences about learners' SRL and metacognitive control should be supported by trace data (e.g., logs) and shown as "observable indicators" [19]. For that, an analytics system must perform calculations based on action tracing and generate indicators leading to recommendations for change. Three dimensions should be considered when analyzing SLR traces in asynchronous online learning environments [20]:

1. *Time investment in content learning:* indicators such as how students allocate and spend time. Teachers must adopt strategies that lead students to define their learning goals and assess their performance. Associated indicators are: the student's learning time and attention level, as found in log traces.
2. *Study regularity and time management strategy:* indicators such as the regularity of access to the e-learning platform, the student's learning status, and time devoted to studying. Time management is promoted by maintaining regular contact and communication between teachers and students. This includes e-mailing to encourage students' progress monitoring and revising of their planning.
3. *Activate help-seeking:* indicators such as questions asked by students, students reading questions placed by their colleagues, and reading of the teacher's replies. Complementary aspects include the number of messages, time and frequency of reading and/or interaction. Reading metacognitive feedback is also an indicator supporting help-seeking skills.

While the first dimension is the foremost one, the others, related to students' ability to follow the discussion flow, enable adjustment and monitoring of their performance and learning objectives. Students self-monitoring through such indicators of tracking log data are able to check their learning progress and compare it with their peers.

Approaches bringing into e-learning process-improvement techniques from businesses and organizations, have thus been emerging. BPMN is a case of one such technique showing promise for improvement of educational processes, for instance by modelling collaboration activities in massive online courses [21]. BPMN's ability to represent alternative pathways instead of a single, strict e-learning process, documenting the rich and dynamic nature of e-learning processes, enabled researchers to get enhanced feedback on e-learning processes from a variety of stakeholders and experts [22]. BPMN has also been used to combine activities of different users, modelling a learning path with associated goals and activities [23].

3 Detecting Opportunities for Teacher Support of SCRL of e-learning Activities Using BPMN

We have employed BPMN diagrams in the planning of an asynchronous e-learning course on software engineering at Universidade Aberta (UAb) - Portugal, to expose the foreseen teaching and learning activities of course participants, mediated by the e-learning platform [2]. Being an asynchronous course, there is no required schedule for students to meet online with the lecturer. Instead, discussions and other dynamics take place by posting messages in forums or similar platforms, or by separately editing/commenting on shared media during a set period for completion of activities.

The joint involvement of lecturer and researchers in the development of the BPMN diagrams clarified the implicit activities of teachers in this asynchronous environment, rendering them explicit. Those activities stem from the virtual pedagogic model of UAb [24], which foresees that teachers must support student-centered learning with adequate guidance, as a facilitator of the learning process, promoting reflection and sharing within the group of students, and moderating interactions. UAb also requires that teachers be aware of the needs and difficulties expressed by students, responding to their queries within 48 h of working days [25].

An example is provided in Fig. 1, detailing one of the first course activities: reading and debating the syllabus (PUC, "Plano de Unidade Curricular"), suggesting possible adjustments. The BPMN process, involving the lecturer throughout, yielded this explicit rendering of teaching activities, enabling us to detect opportunities for teaching intervention in support of self- and co-regulated learning.

The model in Fig. 1 has three pools (labelled rectangles identifying participants' actions): Students, Platform, and Teacher. The online activities of the students are recorded in the platform, hence its central placement as a mediator participant.

The core activity, from a student perspective, is plain: read the syllabus (PUC), and discuss it in the appropriate course forum. This can occur at any moment during a given period at the beginning of the semester For this lecturer, this was two weeks.

However, from a teacher's perspective, one must consider the university's pedagogic model and its requirements, as above. Since teachers must respond within 48 h of working days, it makes sense to use this period for checking up on class status for intervention needs. The need to render explicit this check/intervention process revealed that it was not identical throughout the two-week period:

1. **Milestone 1.** Early in the process, the teacher was more concerned with awareness of overall class dynamics, rather than individual students, due to their demographics: being working students, many would plan for weekend study rather than moonlight study. Thus, it's too early for the teacher to provide unrequested individualized self-regulation support, which might be understood as undue pressure. Instead, considering the overall class dynamic could be more significant, providing class-level encouragement. This encouragement can be motivational, self-regulation advice, or promoting co-regulation, and being provided at a class level will reach those that may benefit from it, without undue pressure on those that don't. Individual feedback is due, however, for students who have already engaged in the activity (debating the syllabus). This led to **Realization 1**: the need to consider two different teacher

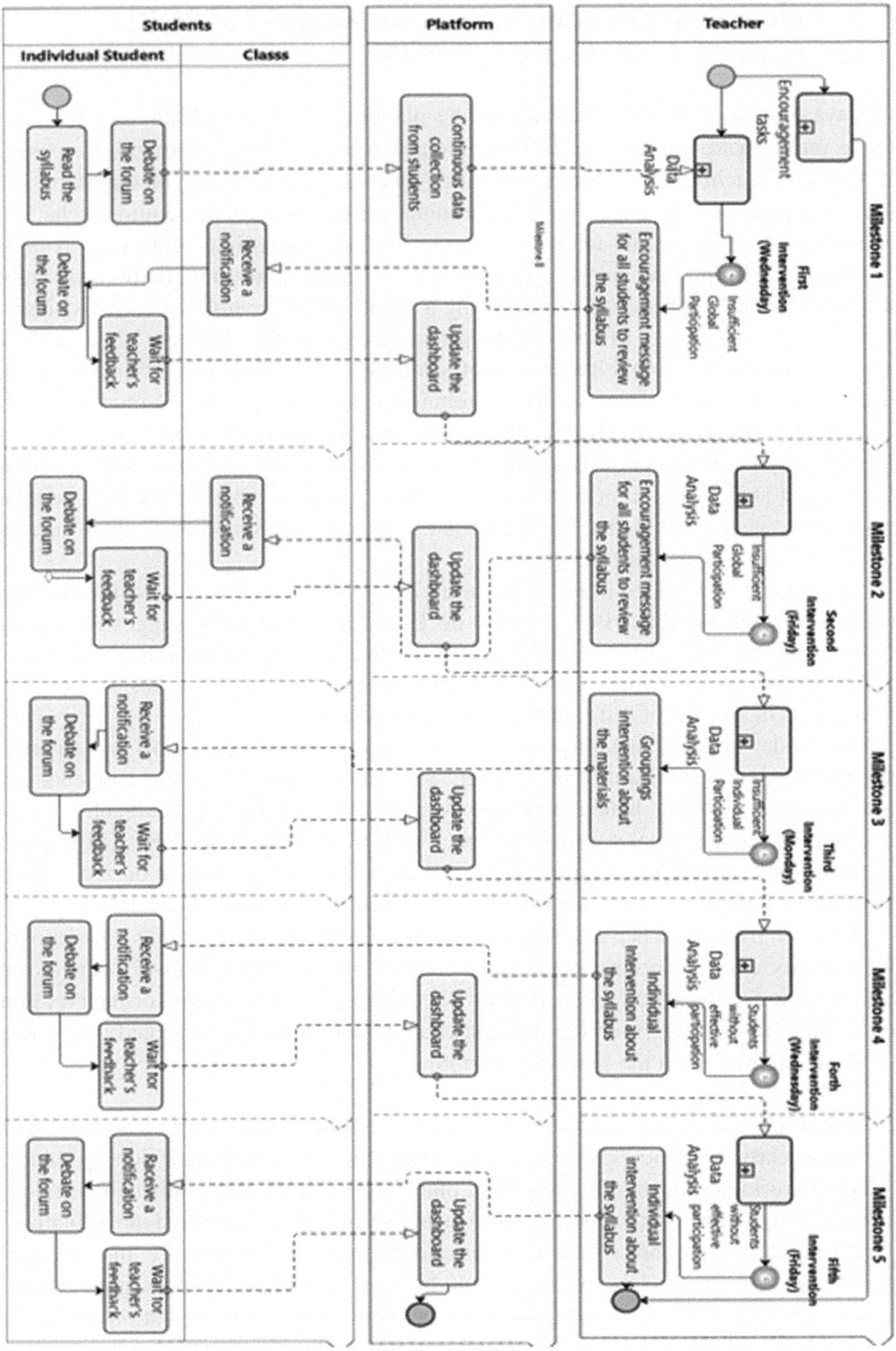

Fig. 1. BPMN diagram of tasks for visualization and participation in the syllabus forum

awareness approaches, reflected in two BPMN swimlanes within the Students pool: Individual Students and Class.

2. **Milestone 2**. The teacher reckoned that when checking up just before the weekend, an adequate intervention in support of self-regulation and co-regulation was to remind students that a prime occasion for study might be due. This led to **Realization 2**: Each intervention stemming from a check-up might lead to a different opportunity for self-regulation and co-regulation, identified as BPMN milestones.
3. **Milestone 3**. Once the first weekend has elapsed, the teacher intervention changes from class dynamics to groupings of individuals: any student who has not participated is now having less opportunities to do so. Specific analysis is due, to identify categories of individual situations: which students have not even accessed the syllabus? which have but did not contribute in the forum? which did but only inconsequential remarks? etc. While individuals in these categories need to be approached by personal messages, these can still be customized to the larger category context, since a full week is still available for student participation. This led to **Realization 3**: teacher interaction opportunities in week 2 shift in focus from co-regulation to self-regulation, but individuals are still part of groupings.
4. **Milestone 4:** midway through the final week of the topic, students who still have not achieved adequate participation require further support, and this led to **Realization 4:** the teacher interaction focus must shift to the individual, with personalized messages.
5. **Milestone 5:** before the final weekend of the topic, which for some students will be the last chance to participate within the allocated time frame, the teacher intervention must be tailored to specific situations of any remaining individuals. This led to **Realization 5:** the final interaction must consider not just individualized messages, but any personal student history details that may be useful to encourage use of this last chance for participation.

4 Identifying Data in Support of Teacher Interventions

The realizations of BPMN modelling, described in the previous section, point towards different levels of informational needs in support of teacher's decision-making for intervening in support of students' self- and co-regulation of learning.

Depending on each institution's choice of e-learning platform, different data sources may be available to provide that information. At Universidade Aberta, the Moodle e-learning platform is used. Table 1 matches the informational needs of the teacher of this course to guide teaching interventions at each milestone, with the available data in Moodle to provide that information.

The data required to perform the activities of milestones 1 to 5 can be obtained through Moodle's Web Services, according to Moodle's Application Programming Interface (API) [26]. They can also be obtained by having teachers manually export them using Moodle's log export features. These sources are clarified in Tables 2 and 3, below.

Table 1. Teacher information needs at each milestone, and available Moodle data

Milestone	Teacher information needs	Available Moodle data
1	Overall level of class participation (syllabus access and forum posting/debating, level of peer interaction) Contributions of students who have already engaged in debating the syllabus	List of students who accessed each page of the syllabus; Threads initiated by students (date, hour, author, and content); Replies to current threads (date, hour, author, and content); Individual reading (viewing) of threads (author, date and hour)
2	Idem	Idem
3	Groupings of students by category of participation, with relative prevalence of each grouping	Idem
4	Individual students with insufficient participation and contribution	Idem
5	Individual students with insufficient participation and contribution, and their personal student history	Idem. + each individual student's history of access to prior resources, participation in prior forums, and submission of prior assignments

Table 2. Web services to obtain data for Milestones 1–4

Data	WebService/Log export	Description
List of students who accessed the syllabus	Log export	Get records on resource (book) use by students
Threads initiated by students (date, hour, author, and content)	mod_forum_get_forum_discussions	Get a list of forum threads, with date, hour, author and content
	mod_forum_get_forum_discussion_posts	Get the list of forum posts for a given thread
	mod_forum_get_discussion_post	Get a thread's opening post with date, hour, author and content
Replies to current threads	mod_forum_get_discussion_posts	Gets a list of posts for a thread
	mod_forum_get_discussion_post	Get a specific post with date, hour, author and content
Individual reading (views) of threads	Log export	Get records on thread (discussion) access by students

Table 3. Web services to obtain specific data for Milestone 5

Data	WebService/Log export	Description
Student's history of access to prior resources	Log export	Get the student's history of access to prior resources with date, hour, author and resource accessed
Student's history of participation in prior forums	Log export	Get the student's history of access to prior forums
Student's history of submission of prior assignments	mod_assign_list_participants	Get the list of students who participated in an assignment, with grading status

5 Indicator for Teacher Intervention in Support of SCRL

The identification of necessary information, using the BPMN notation process, and the identification of available data to provide that information, done in Table 1, and of the feasibility of lifting those data from the learning platform, shown in Tables 2 and 3, enabled us to ascertain indicators towards teachers' process of decision-making. By considering the live status of these indicators, an e-teacher can intervene with greater focus in support of students' self and co-regulation of learning. Table 4 showcases how the indicators can be drawn from the available data.

With these indicators, one aims to promote teacher awareness: "the sense of the perceptual processes in order to assess how the learning situation evolves" [27]. In particular, to identify and address students' need for support in their self-regulation processes [28]. A typical approach is to present these indicators visually as dashboards, instead of having to analyze raw data on a daily basis on the e-learning platform itself. Since the teacher already has multiple tasks to develop throughout a course, providing a tool that streamlines this analysis can be transformative. From the perspective of SRL, dashboards are enablers, contrasting goals vs. Current state [29]. Research that supports the effects of learning analysis dashboards concludes that such tools contribute to student self-reflection and strategic action for establishing SRL [28].

In addition to checking the students' self-regulation status, it is possible to check how students interact within the e-learning platform with each other, to identify their co-regulation status. This can reveal progress and potential problems. Moreover, process-oriented feedback would help teachers and students improve engagement and task performance [30], supporting students' co-regulation. To further the analysis, dashboards should be taken into account as decision-making tools, amplifying or directing cognition, and capitalizing on human perceptual capacities [31].

Table 4. Indicators per milestones

Milestone	Indicators	Data
1	Percentage of students who accessed the syllabus	#(list of students who accessed the syllabus)/Total students in the class
	Percentage of students who accessed all pages of the syllabus	#(list of students who accessed all pages of the syllabus)/Total students in the class
	Percentage of students who did not access all pages of the syllabus	(Total students in the class - Size of the list of students who accessed all pages of the syllabus)/Total students in the class
	Percentage of students taking the initiative to start threads	Count different authors in {Number of threads initiated by students}/Total students in the class
	Percentage of students who read the threads	Number of different students reading threads/Total students in the class
	Percentage of students who replied to other's threads	Count different authors in {for each thread, list different authors in replies that are not the original post's author}/Total students in the class
2	Idem	Idem
3	Percentage of students per participation category (from no access to resources and no contributions; up to access to all resources and contribution both by creating threads and by responding to other students' threads)	Number of different students in each category/Total students in the class
4	List of students per lower participation categories	List of students in each category expunged of students in higher participation categories
5	Idem Milestone 4 +	Idem. 4 +
	Relative access to prior resources of each individual student in lower participation categories for the current activity	Student's history of access to prior resources/Average of class access to prior resources
	Relative participation in prior forums of each individual student in lower participation categories for the current activity	Student's history of participation in prior forums/Average of class participation in prior forums
	Relative participation in prior assignments of each individual student in lower participation categories for the current activity	Student's history of submissions to prior assignments/Average of class submissions to prior assignments

6 Discussion

The starting point for discovering opportunities in which the teacher can interact with students to support them in the process of self and co-regulation was given through the BPMN modeling developed with the teacher. The modeling allowed us to be aware of actual activities demanded by the different actors of the process, whether students, teachers or the e-learning platform itself, corroborating prior research [23].

The definition of participation milestones was one of the aspects that emerged from this aspect. It enabled us to clarify, at each one, what teacher interventions were being considered, what would determine them, and how to proceed to assist the self and co-regulation of students. This clarity helps minimize one of the challenges reported, the need for timely feedback from the teacher and intervention [14, 15].

The novel aspect of this work is identifying what data needs to be extracted from the e-learning environment to carry out these interventions: their consideration, decision-making, and actual process. For example, one can consider the 3 dimensions recommended by Kim et al. [20]: time investment in content learning, study regularity and time management strategy, and activate help-seeking. With the identified data indicators above, one can use these dimensions at each of the specified milestones. For example, by using indicators for Milestone 1 from Table 4, one can ascertain whether the class has started to invest time in content learning; with the same indicators for Milestone 2, one can ascertain if more time was invested or not. And similar analysis can be made with other indicators at other milestones, moving from class-level analysis to individuals'.

7 Conclusions

Indicators such as the ones we identified for the activity analyzed in this paper can help e-learning teachers guide their interventions in support of SCRL: with them indicators, a more aware teacher has more latitude to decide how to support the students, considering pedagogical strategies [16] to promote students SCRL strategies [6, 7]. Awareness aspects promoted by the indicators include time management (time students devoted to carrying out tasks); focus of students' learning (initiative for initiation of threads vs. Passive status); and student's contact/interaction with colleagues and the teacher (reading of threads, replying to threads).

The visualization and interpretation of student participation data can be streamline by automation, using tools such as dashboards. This can contribute to the dissemination of these benefits throughout courses, programs, and even entire institutions. Identifying indicators for such tools is a major aspect of their development, even mentioned as the major gap in tools to support self-regulation [17]. The process herein, of using BPMN to identify information needs, and then follow from those to assess available data and construct indicators towards those needs, is a method for the design, implementation and evaluation of such tools.

To validate the relevance of these (or other) indicators obtained via this method, actual instruments should be developed to provide teachers with this information in real time, so that an analysis of their impact on teacher interventions can be pursued. We plan on creating dashboards to guide teacher interventions in support of their students'

SCRL, as a means to analyze the relevance of these indicators, refine them, or identify new ones. The ultimate goal is contributing to teachers' and students' learning success.

Acknowledgements. This work is co-financed by the ERDF – European Regional Development Fund through the Operational Programme for Competitiveness and Internationalization - COMPETE 2020 and the Lisboa 2020 under the PORTUGAL 2020 Partnership Agreement, and through the Portuguese National Innovation Agency (ANI) as a part of project CHIC POCI-01–0247-FEDER-024498. And also by national funds through the FCT – Fundação para a Ciência e a Tecnologia, I.P., as part of project UID/CED/00194/2019, SCReLProg.

Daniela Pedrosa wishes to thank Fundação para a Ciência e Tecnologia (FCT) and CIDTFF (UID/CED/00194/2019) - Universidade de Aveiro, Portugal, for Stimulus of Scientific Employment – CEECIND/00986/2017 Individual Support 2017.

References

1. OMG - Object Management Group: Business Process Model and Notation (BPMN), Version 2.0 (2011)
2. Morais, C., Pedrosa, D., Fontes, M.M., Cravino, J., Morgado, L.: Detailing an e-Learning course on software engineering and architecture using BPMN. In: Queirós, R., Portela, F., Pinto, M., Simões, A. (eds.) First International Computer Programming Education Conference (ICPEC 2020), pp. 17:1–17:8. Schloss Dagstuhl–Leibniz-Zentrum für Informatik, Dagstuhl, Germany (2020)
3. Caeiro-Rodriguez, M.: Making teaching and learning visible: how can learning designs be represented? In: Proceedings of the Seventh International Conference on Technological Ecosystems for Enhancing Multiculturality, pp. 265–274. ACM, León Spain (2019)
4. Savić, G., Segedinac, M., Milenković, D., Hrin, T., Segedinac, M.: A model-driven approach to e-course management. Aust. J. Educ. Technol. (2017). https://doi.org/10.14742/ajet.3124
5. van Es, R., Koper, R.: Testing the pedagogical expressiveness of IMS LD. Educ. Technol. Soc. **9**, 229–249 (2006)
6. Zimmerman, B.J.: From cognitive modeling to self-regulation: a social cognitive career path. Educ. Psychol. **48**, 135–147 (2013). https://doi.org/10.1080/00461520.2013.794676
7. Panadero, E.: A review of self-regulated learning: six models and four directions for research. Front. Psychol. **8**, 422 (2017). https://doi.org/10.3389/fpsyg.2017.00422
8. Panadero, E., Järvelä, S.: Socially shared regulation of learning: a review. Eur. Psychol. **20**, 190–203 (2015). https://doi.org/10.1027/1016-9040/a000226
9. Harley, J.M., Taub, M., Bouchet, F., Azevedo, R.: A framework to understand the nature of co-regulated learning in human-pedagogical agent interactions. In: SRL@ET (2012)
10. Bowers, J., Kumar, P.: Students' perceptions of teaching and social presence: a comparative analysis of face-to-face and online learning environments. Int. J. Web-Based Learn. Teach. Technol. **10**, 27–44 (2015). https://doi.org/10.4018/ijwltt.2015010103
11. Dabbagh, N., Kitsantas, A.: Personal learning environments, social media, and self-regulated learning: a natural formula for connecting formal and informal learning. Internet High. Educ. **15**, 3–8 (2012). https://doi.org/10.1016/j.iheduc.2011.06.002
12. Broadbent, J.: Comparing online and blended learner's self-regulated learning strategies and academic performance. Internet High. Educ. **33**, 24–32 (2017). https://doi.org/10.1016/j.iheduc.2017.01.004
13. Broadbent, J., Poon, W.L.: Self-regulated learning strategies & academic achievement in online higher education learning environments: a systematic review. Internet High. Educ. **27**, 1–3 (2015). https://doi.org/10.1016/j.iheduc.2015.04.007

14. Pedrosa, D., et al.: Challenges implementing the simprogramming approach in online software engineering education for promoting self and co-regulation of learning. In: 2020 6th International Conference of the Immersive Learning Research Network (iLRN), pp. 236–242. IEEE, San Luis Obispo (2020)
15. Kebritchi, M., Lipschuetz, A., Santiague, L.: Issues and challenges for teaching successful online courses in higher education: a literature review. J. Educ. Technol. Syst. **46**, 4–29 (2017). https://doi.org/10.1177/0047239516661713
16. Sharp, L.A., Sharp, J.H.: Enhancing student success in online learning experiences through the use of self-regulation strategies. J. Excell. Coll. Teach. **27**, 57–75 (2016)
17. Pérez-Álvarez, R., Maldonado-Mahauad, J., Pérez-Sanagustín, M.: Tools to support self-regulated learning in online environments: literature review. In: Pammer-Schindler, V., Pérez-Sanagustín, M., Drachsler, H., Elferink, R., Scheffel, M. (eds.) EC-TEL 2018. LNCS, vol. 11082, pp. 16–30. Springer, Cham (2018). https://doi.org/10.1007/978-3-319-98572-5_2
18. Viberg, O., Khalil, M., Baars, M.: Self-regulated learning and learning analytics in online learning environments: a review of empirical research. In: Proceedings of the Tenth International Conference on Learning Analytics & Knowledge. pp. 524–533. Association for Computing Machinery, New York (2020)
19. Winne, P.: Learning analytics for self-regulated learning. In: Lang, C., Siemens, G., Wise, A.F., Gaševic, D. (eds.) The Handbook of Learning Analytics. pp. 241–249. Society for Learning Analytics Research (SoLAR), Alberta (2017)
20. Kim, D., Yoon, M., Jo, I.-H., Branch, R.M.: Learning analytics to support self-regulated learning in asynchronous online courses: a case study at a women's university in South Korea. Comput. Educ. **127**, 233–251 (2018). https://doi.org/10.1016/j.compedu.2018.08.023
21. Hassani, A., Ghanouchi, S.A.: Modeling of a collaborative learning process in the context of MOOCs. In: 2016 Third International Conference on Systems of Collaboration (SysCo), pp. 1–6. IEEE, Casablanca (2016)
22. Hammad, R., Odeh, M., Khan, Z.: Towards a generalised e-learning business process model. In: BUSTECH 2017 : The Seventh International Conference on Business Intelligence and Technology, pp. 20–28. IARIA, Athens (2017)
23. Subramanian, V.: Towards business process management based workplace e-learning. In: 2016 IEEE 16th International Conference on Advanced Learning Technologies (ICALT), pp. 555–557. IEEE, Austin (2016)
24. Pereira, A., Mendes, A.Q., Morgado, L., Amante, L., Bidarra, J.: Universidade Aberta's pedagogical model for distance education: a university for the future. Universidade Aberta, Lisbon, Portugal (2008)
25. Guia Informativo - Ensino Aprendizagem - Orientações Metodológicas. https://www2.uab.pt/guiainformativo/detailmenu.php?content=24
26. Web Service API Functions. https://docs.moodle.org/dev/Web_service_API_functions
27. Prieto, L.P., Asensio-Pérez, J.I., Muñoz-Cristóbal, J.A., Jorrín-Abellán, I.M., Dimitriadis, Y., Gómez-Sánchez, E.: Supporting orchestration of CSCL scenarios in web-based distributed learning environments. Comput. Educ. **73**, 9–25 (2014). https://doi.org/10.1016/j.compedu.2013.12.008
28. Grann, J., Bushway, D.: Competency map: visualizing student learning to promote student success. In: Proceedings of the Fourth International Conference on Learning Analytics and Knowledge, pp. 168–172. Association for Computing Machinery, New York (2014)
29. Kim, J., Jo, I.-H., Park, Y.: Effects of learning analytics dashboard: analyzing the relations among dashboard utilization, satisfaction, and learning achievement. Asia Pac. Educ. Rev. **17**(1), 13–24 (2015). https://doi.org/10.1007/s12564-015-9403-8

30. Gašević, D., Dawson, S., Rogers, T., Gasevic, D.: Learning analytics should not promote one size fits all: The effects of instructional conditions in predicting academic success. Internet High. Educ. **28**, 68–84 (2016). https://doi.org/10.1016/j.iheduc.2015.10.002
31. Sedrakyan, G., Malmberg, J., Verbert, K., Järvelä, S., Kirschner, P.A.: Linking learning behavior analytics and learning science concepts: designing a learning analytics dashboard for feedback to support learning regulation. Comput. Hum. Behav. **107**, 105512 (2020). https://doi.org/10.1016/j.chb.2018.05.004

Covid-19 Pandemic, Changes in Educational Ecosystem and Remote Teaching

Yes, We Can (?) - A Critical Review of the COVID-19 Semester

Gergana Vladova[1,2(✉)], André Ullrich[1], Benedict Bender[1], and Norbert Gronau[1]

[1] Chair of Business Informatics, Processes and Systems, University of Potsdam, Karl-Marx-Str. 67, 14482 Potsdam, Germany
{gergana.vladova,andre.ullrich,benedict.bender, norbert.gronau}@wi.uni-potsdam.de

[2] Research Group Education and Training in the Digital Society, Weizenbaum Institute for the Networked Society, Hardenbergstr. 32, 10623 Berlin, Germany

Abstract. The COVID-19 crisis has caused an extreme situation for higher education institutions around the world, where exclusively virtual teaching and learning has become obligatory rather than an additional supporting feature. This has created opportunities to explore the potential and limitations of virtual learning formats. This paper presents four theses on virtual classroom teaching and learning that are discussed critically. We use existing theoretical insights extended by empirical evidence from a survey of more than 850 students on acceptance, expectations, and attitudes regarding the positive and negative aspects of virtual teaching. The survey responses were gathered from students at different universities during the first completely digital semester (Spring-Summer 2020) in Germany. We discuss similarities and differences between the subjects being studied and highlight the advantages and disadvantages of virtual teaching and learning. Against the background of existing theory and the gathered data, we emphasize the importance of social interaction, the combination of different learning formats, and thus context-sensitive hybrid learning as the learning form of the future.

Keywords: COVID-19 · Higher education · Virtual learning · Digital learning · Subject differences

1 Exogenous Shock Changes Teaching and Learning Environment

The COVID-19 pandemic has changed the way societal processes take place and how individuals perceive and treat each other. It has had a directly observable impact on educational processes, since the shutdown of in-person education at such short notice had a radical effect [1]. Even though new educational technologies have been in development for decades, they have not yet had a real transformative effect on the education sector. During the worldwide lockdown, their no-alternative deployment became a reality overnight. Educational institutions began to shift their activities into a virtual space, which was simply the only alternative to a complete standstill.

Before the crisis, it was necessary to promote the professional development of teachers and improve academic digital literacy [2]. Students had access to a range of digital

A. Reis et al. (Eds.): TECH-EDU 2020, CCIS 1384, pp. 225–235, 2021.
https://doi.org/10.1007/978-3-030-73988-1_17

tools and were willing to use digital media for academic learning. When the outbreak led to the government-ordered shutdown of universities, lecturers and staff had, in some cases, just two or three days to convert content and formats from classic classroom teaching to virtual lectures, seminars, and exercises. This situation fostered both students' technology usage and their twenty-first century skills, which generation Z does not innately possess at the appropriate level [3–5]. Considering the lecturers, competence gaps in handling digital technologies and methods for goal-oriented transfer of content became apparent. After four months of online teaching, student voices called for face-to-face meetings with lecturers in person [6]. This tendency toward a need regarding in-person or hybrid courses is an important issue for further research.

The COVID-19 crisis has proved to be an enabler for implementing digital technologies in the context of university teaching. The digitalization of educational processes inherits several challenges and interdependencies for students, teachers, and administratiors. On the contrary, digitalization of processes and virtual learning provides a toolbox for revolutionizing university teaching and learning and is thus an enormous opportunity. Suitability for virtual learning depends, however, on each teaching discipline and its applied teaching format [6]. Hybrid forms, in which in-person meetings are complemented by virtual knowledge transfer or vice versa, are a promising approach since learning is a social process and humans rely on interaction. In particular, the latter fosters reflective capability and thus supports the creation of action-competent and self-determined humans in the sense of the Humboldtian educational ideal.

This paper introduces and discusses four theses in the context of the digitalization of university education during the COVID-19 crisis and argues for context-sensitive hybrid learning as a learning and teaching form of the future. We discuss the theses based on theory but also build on results from a survey conducted with more than 850 students, who answered questions on acceptance, expectations, and attitudes regarding the positive and negative aspects of virtual teaching during the first fully digital semester due to the COVID-19 pandemic. Thereby, an analysis of discipline-specific differences between information systems (IS) and music and arts students (M & A) is discussed. The following section introduces our data-gathering approach. Afterwards, the individual theses are discussed. Selected study results are presented to illustrate our theses.

2 Empirical Study in Universities

We conducted a quantitative empirical study in four German universities using an online survey to capture students' perceptions of digital learning throughout the Spring-Summer semester 2020 (COVID-19 semester). To identify potential differences between disciplines, we gathered responses from universities with varied subjects taught. In university 1, we gathered responses from master's students in information systems. Assuming that the level of technology penetration of the subjects would impact students' perception of digital learning, we included three universities where courses are part of the M & A curriculum.

Throughout the semester, for the duration of four months, we gathered 875 responses, of which 246 were from information systems students and 629 from arts and music students. From the responses, 59% (513) were received from females, 35% (310) from males, and the rest specified other sex or provided no information. We used LimeSurvey for survey administration. Data preparation and analysis were conducted in R with the Stats package in version 3.6.1. Incorrect encoding and values were filtered.

We asked questions about the following main areas: attitudes toward the positive and negative aspects of digital learning (with questions based on theories of benefits and disadvantages of e-learning), acceptance toward digital learning (using the Technology Acceptance Model—TAM [7]), trust in the learner (based on the Technological Pedagogical Content Knowledge (TPACK)-Model [8]), technical equipment at home, digital tools used during the semester, and demographics.

3 Lessons Learned—Four Theses for Virtual Teaching and Learning

In the following section, four theses on digital learning at universities are presented, based on the results of a literature review on digital learning and knowledge transfer, with supporting data from our survey.

Thesis 1: Students Need Social Interaction to Develop Competences and Acquire Specific Types of Knowledge
Learning is a social process in which a learner processes content by internalization, externalization, or socialization. Therefore, learning depends on interaction with other learners and with lecturers. Research on applied social psychology in educational contexts, such as social comparison theory [9] or cooperative learning methods [10], shows the positive impact of interaction within the classroom on academic performance. Constructivist [11, 12], cognitive [13, 14], and subject-oriented learning theories and models [15, 16] and theories and models of knowledge dynamics [17, 18] point out that social entities are necessary for learning and gaining a deep understanding of knowledge objects. In addition, purely virtual lessons using digital media do not provide sufficiently high levels of skills [19], such as negotiation, teamwork, and soft skills, which ultimately lead to the creation of a self-determined and competent individual.

Learning with digital media relates to a lack of direct social interaction and a personal touch and has the potential to socially isolate the learner or at least to negatively influence the social aspects of learning processes [20–22]. In research, the negative influence of socially isolated learning on the development of learners' communication skills and the changed communication conditions is emphasized, e.g., the lack of support through non-verbal cues or by observing the interactions of others [23]. Furthermore, learners are insecure about their learning in the absence of regular contact with teachers. The social and cognitive presence and involvement of the teacher is perceived as very important, whereby interaction is an important variable in online learning and the teacher's feedback is perceived as a motivating and instructional tool [23].

In our study, all students confirmed the high importance of social exchange during the lockdown period. Both, study-specific exchange (among themselves and with lecturers) and interpersonal social interaction in general were emphasized. Social interaction could be identified as a significant influencing factor on the perceived usefulness of the learning format. Considering social interaction in combination with the subject studied, a high influence was also observed. The M & A students perceived social isolation more negatively than the IS students and considered it a deficit of digital teaching. The perceived benefit of digital teaching depends on the extent of social interaction. Table 1 presents the analysis results of the perceived usefulness of digital teaching with a focus on social isolation.

Table 1. Estimation of perceived usefulness with a focus on social isolation.

Variable	Estimate	Std. Error	t-value	Pr (>|t|)
(Intercept)	3.44733	0.07726	44.62	< 2e−16***
Social_Isolation	0.31254	0.02493	12.54	< 2e−16***
Social_Isolation: SubjectMusic and Arts	−0.22902	0.01852	−12.37	< 2e−16***

Signif. Codes: 0 '***' 0.001 '**' 0.01 Multiple R-squared: 0.189, F-statistic: 98.01 on 2 and 841 DF, p-value: < 2.2e−16.

In summary, we vouch for a mixture of learning formats; that is, different learning formats that should be used. However, it must be considered that greater effort needs to be put into preparing different formats for gaining better learning results. Thereby, and in accordance with non-behavioral understanding of learning and the Humboldtian education ideal, we advocate for addressing each learner individually as much as possible and creating framework conditions that fulfil the need for individual as well as cooperative learning in terms of a social process.

Thesis 2: Exclusively virtual teaching Leads to Less Student Focus Toward the Content

The benefits of virtual teaching and learning, such as cost efficiency, flexibility (time and place), time saved in traveling to the learning location, access to learning materials, and the potential to offer personalized learning according to the learner's specific needs, have been widely discussed in the literature [22–27]. The possibilities of creating video presentations and databases with material as well as sustaining the quality and usefulness of the learning material for a longer period are further advantages of virtual learning and teaching [20].

However, virtual learning environments require learners to have self-motivation, proper time management, self-directed learning, and organizational skills [22, 26, 28, 29]. According to [23], these requirements arise partly from social isolation and lack of direct social interaction, which means that the learner must have relatively strong motivation to mitigate these effects. To be an online learner, students feel the need for structure and the need for learning (i.e., to be self-directed and autonomous) [29].

A major issue perceived during the COVID-19 semester at most higher education institutions was the challenge that lectures are less binding for the students. Many lectures were available as recordings. This time- and place-independent repeatability led to less focus since the students seemed more prone to distractions [30]. The anonymity of the virtual classroom, in extreme cases with no video on the student's side, e.g., to preserve internet capacity or similar arguments, created a new situation of less interaction, which could not be controlled by teachers with the usual procedures like direct verbal requests to answer questions. Considering the technologies, although virtual tools can contribute massively to conveying content and attaining learning goals, their usefulness is also limited [31]. They cannot be applied to every kind of knowledge conveyance, tacit and experience-based knowledge, in particular, needs to be handled differently. Furthermore, the lack of human interaction can lead to uncertainties on both students' and lecturers' sides.

To assess the advantages and disadvantages of the virtual teaching format from the students' point of view, various questions were asked in our survey. The increase in the potential for distraction under digital teaching conditions was assessed by all students as rather negative. However, the students considered it positive that digital learning conditions required self-discipline. Table 2 shows the study results of the perceived usefulness of digital teaching with a focus on the usage of digital media. They show that the perceived usefulness of digitally-mediated learning decreased with increasing usage of digital media, which conflicts with the aim of the lessons—to impart knowledge, skills, and competences. Thus, exclusive use of virtual learning formats should be critically reviewed, as perceived usefulness also influences learning success.

Table 2. Estimation of perceived usefulness with a focus on usage of digital media.

Variable	Estimate	Std. Error	t-value	Pr (>|t|)
(Intercept)	4.94073	0.07607	64.95	< 2e−16***
Usage_Digital_Media	−0.22943	0.01640	−13.99	< 2e−16***

Signif. Codes: 0 '***' 0.001 '**' 0.01 Multiple R-squared: 0.1874, F-statistic: 195.8 on 1 and 849 DF, p-value: < 2.2e−16.

In summary, we find the non-binding nature of the virtual lecture particularly problematic, and it must be handled with caution. In addition, a mixture of virtual and non-virtual teaching and learning formats is recommended. Learning formats should be adapted to the respective learning goals to ensure students' focus and learning success. It is advisable to introduce netiquette for the event, including basic rules of behavior (e.g., turning the camera on, showing reactions with certain signs, etc.). It should be considered that in such a lesson, a new culture of learning together is created. Cultures (in this case learning cultures) need norms and rules to subsequently establish appropriate values. If these are clearly defined and clearly communicated, uncertainty among teachers and learners disappears. Furthermore, it is advisable to increase students' motivation by requiring them to participate interactively. This common approach for fully digital learning formats, such as online courses, can also be successfully established in hybrid learning formats.

Thesis 3: Exclusively virtual Teaching Confronts Teachers with New Pedagogical, Content-Related, and Technological Challenges to Develop Suitable Learning Concepts
To educate students about digitization, teach digital literacy, or use digital media to engage professionally or prepare lessons, teachers need a wide range of digital competencies [32]. In terms of professional engagement, this includes, for example, organizational communication, professional collaboration, reflective practice, and digital continuous professional development (compare also in the following [32]). Additionally, it is necessary to develop competences in digital resources, including selection, creation, modification, management, protection, and sharing. The teaching and learning competence area covers specific competences for teaching and guidance as well as the support and enhancement of collaborative learning and self-regulated learning. To enhance assessment with digitalization, teachers need specific assessment strategies and competences in analysis evidence and in feedback and planning. Teachers' digital competence also includes the ability to empower learners through digital strategies. Thus, teachers need to use digital technologies for accessibility and inclusion, differentiation and personalization, and for actively engaging learners.

In our study's context, the students' perceptions regarding their teachers' competencies to master the learning process was most important. Students generally rely on the pedagogical skills of their teachers in familiar learning environments. However, e-learning teaching environments—as well as the emergency situation during the COVID-19 semester in particular—bring new challenges for teachers, both through the use of technology and through the students' motivation to learn. A major challenge for teachers who use technology in the learning process is the right connection between content, pedagogical, and technology knowledge [8]. To capture how the teachers dealt with this challenge during the COVID-19 semester, we investigated students' perceptions of and trust in their teachers' knowledge by adapting the TPACK model [8].

Although IS students were much more confident than M & A students that their teachers could choose the right didactic formats and media, our survey, and especially the open questions, also show that all students believed that not all content in their subject could be successfully taught digitally. Furthermore, all the students pointed out that classroom teaching is indispensable for exercise formats, laboratory work, group work, experiments, etc. In general, students said that face-to-face teaching is associated with more commitment, more exchanges with each other and with the lecturers, and more variety in everyday life. They also mentioned the fact that spontaneous exchanges on random topics often adds value to their learning processes, the conscious journey to the university as a place of study, and the relevant structure. What the digital world of learning brings with it is much more focused on the subject and more planned. Regarding the students' trust in their teachers (use of appropriate teaching tools and selection of appropriate methods and assessment), our data show that trust in the teacher was negatively influenced by the usage of digital media (highly significant). More specifically, the students had less trust in their teachers' concepts and evaluation methods in digital teaching (Table 3).

We conclude that university learning is associated with an institution that fulfils different tasks in students' lives. Besides their teaching tasks, teachers are understood

Table 3. Estimation of trust in teachers concept.

Variable	Estimate	Std. Error	t-value	Pr(>|t|)
(Intercept)	5.53906	0.11533	48.03	< 2e−16***
Trust in Teacher	−0.25875	0.02486	−10.41	< 2e−16***

Signif. Codes: 0 '***' 0.001 '**' 0.01 Multiple R-squared: 0.1127, F-statistic: 108.3 on 1 and 853 DF, p-value: < 2.2e−16

by their students as authorities that are not only valid for the individual learner but for the whole social and teaching environment in the classroom. Such psychological and social effects are part of a socially constructed reality for which there is no comparable construct in the virtual world. The first teaching units during the lockdown served as orientation and gave the teachers additional technical security. After this, questions came to light that went beyond the use of the tools, not only to the appropriate way of using them to teach the content but also to create a familiar learning atmosphere. Questions of what could be expected of the learners under the new circumstances also arose. For this reason, suitable ways of exploiting the advantages of digital learning should be found without abandoning universities as places of learning. Teachers usually have a wide range of content, pedagogy, and technology knowledge and should use it to develop an optimal mix of learning combinations. What is needed is a combination in which digital content is addressed by appropriate pedagogical concepts and on-site teaching also remains a part of university teaching.

Thesis 4: Students' Acceptance of Virtual Teaching and Learning Formats Depends on the Subject of Study

Current students represent a generation of digital natives for whom a steady switch from the real to the virtual world should not pose any operational challenges [33–35]. However, research indicates that students show differences according to discipline, such as subject matter [36] or facets of digital literacy and competency [37], which should be taken into consideration when developing virtual learning environments and approaches.

The teaching formats applied prior to COVID-19 differed between subjects. Given the different virtual classroom formats and the tendency for people to adopt familiar formats more easily, the corresponding acceptance varies between subjects [38]. Whereas, for example, IS students are more familiar with virtual environments, it is assumed that they are more likely to accept and manage the switch to fully virtual learning formats. In contrast, M & A students, who are generally assumed to be less familiar with virtual environments, may show less acceptance of related formats. Moreover, the appropriateness of virtual teaching and learning may generally vary among subjects. However, personal interaction may not be fully substituted through virtual formats. While some may argue that the acceptance of virtual learning formats is similar for all students of a similar age, we argue for consideration of their familiarity and competences with related technologies as well as their technological affinity, which varies among subjects [6].

Our survey data unveiled differences between the IS and M & A participants, with the IS students' acceptance toward virtual teaching and learning being higher (cf. Fig. 1).

Among other things, the IS students have more fun using digital technologies and more clearly intend to apply this to teaching in the future. Indications of this can also be found in the answers to the question of what relationship between digital teaching and classroom teaching is considered optimal. Here, the median for IS students is approximately a 60% share of digital teaching compared to approximately 40% for arts students. However, all students were uncertain whether teaching and learning in virtual classrooms would worsen their performance. The two subgroups showed highly significant differences in their behavioral intentions (i.e., their attitude toward the future use of digital learning opportunities.

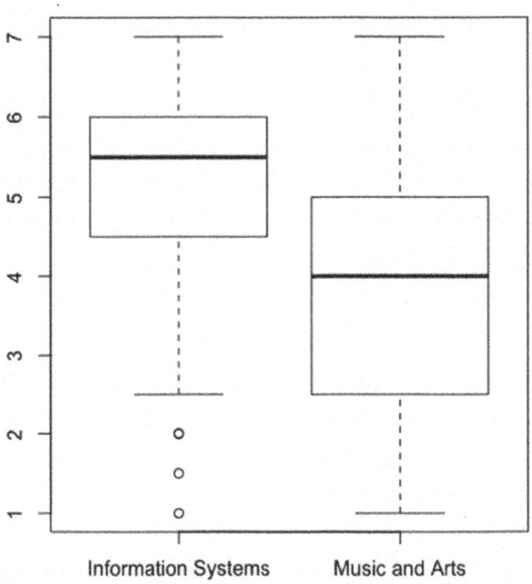

Fig. 1. Acceptance (from high 7 to low 1) of digital learning: Two Sample t-test → Results: t = 67.721, df = 966.23, p-value < 2.2e–16.

To summarize, our survey and prior literature suggest differences between students' subjects of study regarding their expectations and acceptance of virtual teaching and learning. We assume higher acceptance is a result of familiarity with virtual learning formats, appropriateness for the subjects' content, students' confidence that the content of their lectures can be conveyed digitally, and their openness toward digital learning. Therefore, customized approaches, which differ in their respective shares of online and offline teaching and learning formats, should be considered for students of different subjects.

4 Mastering the Crisis Means Learning from the Crisis

One debate in the context of COVID-19 has concerned labelling the situation as a "black swan" (shaped by Nassim Taleb) or a "gray rhino" (introduced by Michele Wucker). Both describe the occurrence of events with enormous consequences, in the first case unexpected and in the second predictable. Regarding the digitalization of education, the situation has the character of a curse and a blessing at the same time, but it is anything other than unforeseeable. From a global point of view, the process of digitalization in this field is progressing irreversibly. The exclusivity and uniqueness of the COVID-19 situation as a concrete backdrop for digital learning is also questionable—after all, this is the sixth time the World Health Organization has declared such a public health emergency of international concern, all since the turn of the millennium. It is a question of time until digital education has found its place as an equivalent alternative or at least as a well-designed solution for crisis situations.

The biggest live experiment in online learning in the Spring-Summer semester 2020 offered university teachers and students a unique opportunity to practice digital teaching without any alternatives and to learn more about its opportunities, limits, benefits, and risks in a practical context. The good news is that most universities were able to offer digital teaching within a very short time. Detailed studies on this will bring more clarity.

Our study highlights some critical aspects to be considered, such as differences between subjects. Even if digital learning formats have proven to be much more suitable for IS students, we need to look again at the social nature of learning and the specifics of the knowledge to be taught. In our opinion, hybrid learning, combining digital assets with personal elements, will be the future form of learning. To succeed in the field of virtual learning, three conditions for the related stakeholders need to be fulfilled. First, students need to have the technical equipment to participate in virtual learning formats and the required skills for self-organization. Second, virtually adapted or totally newly developed learning concepts are required to appropriately address the virtual conditions for maximum learning success [39]. Moreover, teachers need to be skilled in the respective technologies and format specifics to adapt their teaching. Finally, the technical and supportive infrastructure in higher education needs to be designed accordingly [40].

For educational technology (EdTech) companies, important learning effects result from direct user feedback in this study. The role played by differences in the field of study when knowledge is transferred in an academic environment has become even clearer. This can be addressed by short- and long-term solutions and lead to innovative concepts and products.

The limitations of our study's results should be considered. First, it was conducted under the special circumstances of complete social isolation in every area of life, which, among other things, influenced the results. Furthermore, we summarized the M & A group in the evaluation and did not pay attention to the differences within it (i.e., music, theatre, architecture, and visual communication).

Our further research focuses on the evaluation of the data with regard to the investigation of acceptance in orientation to the TAM model, the analysis of the relationships between the positive and negative aspects of e-learning and acceptance, and the evaluation of the qualitative data from the open questions [6].

Acknowledgments. This work has been funded by the Federal Ministry of Education and Research of Germany (BMBF) under grant no. 16DII127 ("Deutsches Internet-Institut").

References

1. Crawford, J., Butler-Henderson, K., Rudolph, J., Glowatz, M.: COVID-19: 20 countries' higher education intra-period digital pedagogy responses. J. Appl. Teach. Learn. (JALT) **3**(1), 1–20 (2020)
2. Bond, M., Marín, V.I., Dolch, C., Bedenlier, S., Zawacki-Richter, O.: Digital transformation in German higher education: Student and teacher perceptions and usage of digital media. Int. J. Educ. Technol. High. Educ. **15**(1), 1–20 (2018). https://doi.org/10.1186/s41239-018-0130-1
3. Akçayır, M., Dündar, H., Akçayır, G.: What makes you a digital native? Is it enough to be born after 1980? Comput. Hum. Behav. **60**, 435–440 (2016)
4. Barak, M.: Are digital natives open to change? Examining flexible thinking and resistance to change. Comput. Educ. **121**, 115–123 (2018)
5. Henderson, M., Selwyn, N., Aston, R.: What works and why? Student perceptions of useful digital technology in university teaching and learning. Stud. High. Educ. **42**(8), 1567–1579 (2017)
6. Vladova, G., Ullrich, A., Bender, B., Gronau, N.: Students' acceptance of technology-mediated teaching – how it was influenced during the COVID-19 pandemic in 2020: a study from Germany. Front. Psychol. **12**, 69 (2021)
7. Davis, F.D.: A technology acceptance model for empirically testing new end-user information systems: theory and results. Ph.D. Thesis. Massachusetts Institute of Technology (1985)
8. Mishra, P., Koehler, M.J.: Technological pedagogical content knowledge: a framework for teacher knowledge. Teach. Coll. Rec. **108**(6), 1017–1054 (2006)
9. Festinger, L.: A theory of social comparison processes. Human Relat. **7**(2), 117–140 (1954)
10. Slavin, R.E.: Cooperative Learning: Theory, Research, and Practice. Englewood Cliffs (1990)
11. Hein, G.: Constructivist learning theory. Institute for Inquiry (1991). https://www.exploratorium.edu/ifi/resources/constructivistlearning.htmlS. Accessed 12 Nov 2020
12. Bada, S.O., Olusegun, S.: Constructivism learning theory: a paradigm for teaching and learning. J. Res. Method Educ. **5**(6), 66–70 (2015)
13. Tennyson, R.D., Rasch, M.: Linking cognitive learning theory to instructional prescriptions. Instr. Sci. **17**(4), 369–385 (1988). https://doi.org/10.1007/BF00056222
14. Nagowah, L., Nagowah, S.: A reflection on the dominant learning theories: behaviourism, cognitivism and constructivism. Int. J. Learn. **16**(2), 279–285 (2009)
15. Holzkamp, K.: Learning: subject-scientific foundation (In German), Frankfurt (1995)
16. Teichmann, M., Ullrich, A., Gronau, N.: Subject-oriented learning - a new perspective for vocational training in learning factories. Procedia Manuf. **31**, 72–78 (2019)
17. Nissen, M.E., Bordetsky, A.: Leveraging mobile network technologies to accelerate tacit knowledge flows across organisations and distances. In: Trentin, G. (ed.) Technology and Knowledge Flow: The Power of Networks, pp 1–25. Chandos Publ, Sawston (2011)
18. Nonaka, I.: A dynamic theory of organizational knowledge creation. Organ. Sci. **5**(1), 14–37 (1994)
19. Dung, D.T.: The advantages and disadvantages of virtual learning. IOSR J. Res. Method Educ. **10**(3), 45–48 (2020)
20. Becker, K., Newton, C., Sawang, S.: A learner perspective on barriers to e-learning. Aust. J. Adult Learn. **53**(2), 211 (2013)
21. Bell, J.: E-learning: your flexible development friend? Dev. Learn. Organ.: Int. J. **21**(6), 7–9 (2007)
22. Hameed, S., Badii, A., Cullen, A.J.: Effective e-learning integration with traditional learning in a blended learning environment. In European and Mediterranean Conference on Information Systems, pp. 25–26 (2008)

23. Al-Qahtani, A.A., Higgins, S.E.: Effects of traditional, blended and e-learning on students' achievement in higher education. J. Comput. Assist. Learn. **29**(3), 220–234 (2013)
24. Brown, L., Murphy, E., Wade, V.: Corporate eLearning: Human resource development implications for large and small organizations. Hum. Resour. Dev. Int. **9**(3), 415–427 (2006)
25. Hill, N.S., Wouters, K.: Comparing apples and oranges: toward a typology for assessing e-learning effectiveness. In: Research in Personnel and Human Resources Management, vol. 29, no. 201 (2010)
26. Jefferson, R.N., Arnold, L.W.: Effects of virtual education on academic culture: perceived advantages and disadvantages. Online Submiss. **6**(3), 61–66 (2009)
27. Welsh, E.T., Wanberg, C.R., Brown, K.G., Simmering, M.J.: E-learning: emerging uses, empirical results and future directions. Int. J. Train. Dev. **7**(4), 245–258 (2003)
28. Klein, D., Ware, M.: E-learning: New opportunities in continuing professional development. Learn. Publ. **16**(1), 34–46 (2003)
29. Tomasson, J.: Learners and E-learning. https://digitalrepository.unm.edu/oils_sp/1. Accessed 12 Nov 2020
30. Winter, J., Cotton, D., Gavin, J., Yorke, J.D.: Effective e-learning? Multi-tasking, distractions and boundary management by graduate students in an online environment. ALT-J **18**(1), 71–83 (2010)
31. Murugaiah, P., Yen, S.H.: Navigating the shortcomings of virtual learning environments via social media. Int. J. Virtual Pers. Learn. Environ. (IJVPLE) **9**(2), 1–4 (2019)
32. Vladova, G., Renz, A., Heuts, A.: Ready to inovate? A self-assessment tool for schools on the edge towards digital education. In: ISPIM Innovation Conference – Innovation in the Times of Crisis, Berlin, Deutschland (2020)
33. Berk, R.A.: Multimedia teaching with video clips: TV, Movies, YouTube, and mtvU in the college classroom. Journal of Technology in Teaching & Learning **5**(1), 1–21 (2009)
34. Carlson, S.: The net generation in the classroom. Chron. High. Educ. **52**(7), 34–37 (2005)
35. Jones, C., Ramanau, R., Cross, S., Healing, G.: Net generation or digital natives: is there a distinct new generation entering university? Comput. Educ. **54**(3), 722–732 (2010)
36. Biglan, A.: The characteristics of subject matter in different academic areas. J. Appl. Psychol. **57**(3), 195–203 (1973)
37. Nelson, K., Courier, M., Joseph, G.W.: An investigation of digital literacy needs of students. J. Inf. Syst. Educ. **22**(2), 95–110 (2011)
38. Janssen, J., Erkens, G., Kirschner, P.A., Kanselaar, G.: Influence of group member familiarity on online collaborative learning. Comput. Hum. Behav. **25**(1), 161–170 (2009)
39. Richards, C.: The design of effective ICT-supported learning activities: exemplary models, changing requirements, and new possibilities. Lang. Learn. Technol. **9**(1), 60–79 (2005)
40. Alzaza, N.S., Yaakub, A.R.: Students' awareness and requirements of mobile learning services in the higher education environment. Am. J. Econ. Bus. Adm. **3**(1), 95–100 (2011)

Designing Didactic Cycles in a Pandemic Scenario: Facing Challenges as Opportunities

Sónia Martins(✉)

University of Madeira, Campus Universitário da Penteada, 9020-105 Funchal, Portugal
soniam@staff.uma.pt

Abstract. Following Vygotsky's seminal idea of semiotic mediation, the theoretical framework of Theory of Semiotic Mediation is used in this research to create and implement learning activities that can possibly allow future teachers to analyse semiotic potential of several technological artefacts, namely applets, identifying the knowledge and the mathematical procedures produced with their use. Because of the global pandemic, it was necessary and imperative to shift from in-person classes to online classes. In this line, new research' challenges have been posed in educational environments. In this paper, an overall reflection is presented about how these challenges were faced as new opportunities for the understanding of pre-service teachers' learning in this new reality.

Keywords: Applets · Educational research · Mathematics · Semiotic potential

1 Introduction

The study of mediation using technologies, based mainly on the work of Vygotsky [1], has promoted several reflections that contributes to the understanding of the use of technology in the perspective of instrumented and socially constructed situations of knowledge [2]. More recently, with the spread of the Internet and the use of mobile devices, there has been a growing interest in understanding the contributions offered by the use of digital applications - applets - for teaching and learning mathematics [3, 4].

The term applet usually refers to a small and supplemental program that is used within a main program to provide it an additional functionality. Typically, applets are embedded in web browsers and are designed to perform specific tasks using less code. This makes a web page more dynamic, once provides interaction between the user and the contents in the web page (sound, animation, graphics, simulations, etc.).

The present research has its backgrounds in previous research focused in understanding the role of technological artefacts in the learning of mathematics' contents and procedures [5–9]. More recently [10] the main interest relies specifically in the study of the complexity of the teacher's role in orchestrating the teaching and learning process when that process is mediated by applets.

Following Vygotsky's seminal idea of semiotic mediation, the theoretical framework of Theory of Semiotic Mediation developed Bartolini Bussi and Mariotti [11] is used in this research to create and implement learning activities that can possibly allow future

A. Reis et al. (Eds.): TECH-EDU 2020, CCIS 1384, pp. 236–248, 2021.
https://doi.org/10.1007/978-3-030-73988-1_18

teachers to analyse semiotic potential of applets, identifying the knowledge and the mathematical procedures produced with their use. The construction of mathematical meanings cannot be easily achieved through a direct use of technology, needing a careful didactic design of tasks to exploit the use of artefacts [12]. According to this, this research, developed with pre-service elementary teachers, in a the University of Madeira in Portugal, uses the Theory of Semiotic Mediation both to the design of the tasks and in the analyses of the processes by which participants explore the semiotic potential of technology for mathematics' learning.

Because of the global pandemic, it was necessary and imperative to shift from in-person classes to online classes. So, new research' challenges were posed: How the research should be conducted in the online environment? How to design and carry out research activities when the context in which those activities are developed is no longer available in the form in which the research activities were previously designed? How to collect data in this new scenario? How to analyse these data? From these perspectives, the present paper intends to present a reflection about how these challenges were faced as new opportunities for the understanding of pre-service teachers' learning in this new reality.

2 Changing Research Methods: Facing Challenges as Opportunities

This research adopts the assumptions of a design research [13] insofar as it intents, in an interventionist way, to study an emerging situation in the educational field, such as the use of applets as a tool to teach and to learn mathematics. The study is conceived in a research dynamic, both 'in' and 'by' action, in Amado's [14] perspective. This option was due to the fact that, with the study, it is intended to face three challenges: produce knowledge (research objectives), introduce changes (innovation objectives) and develop competences by the participants (training objectives).

The main purpose of the present research is to characterize the practice developed with the use of applets by fifteen pre-service elementary teachers in the curricular unit of Didactic of Mathematics. The data were collected between March and May 2020. Because of the pandemic scenario, all the interactions between the students (pre-service teachers) and the teacher (researcher) were yield in online environment, with synchronous and asynchronous moments.

The synchronous moments were developed in the Zoom platform. This platform allowed different forms of communication such as video, voice, content sharing and chat. When students were developing activities in small groups, the 'Breakout rooms' function was used to split the Zoom meeting in separate sessions. By doing this, the teacher/researcher had the opportunity to work separately with students' groups and analyse how they were accomplishing the tasks.

For the asynchronous interactions it was used the Moodle platform. In this platform it was integrated the learner's activities and resources. The discussion forums were used to promote collective and collaborative discussions about the subjects under analysis. Students works and perspectives were posted in the forums conversation and all the participants could comment. Also, messaging was enabled for participants (teacher and students) to contact each other via real-time chat - if they are online - or message - if they are offline.

Since the signs that emerge from the use of an artefact by the subject are individual, data were collected and analysed considering the pre-service teachers' schemes of utilization [17] with the applet. That schemes are based in the procedures that are used by pre-service teachers to accomplish the task with the applet. To perceive that procedures, all the synchronous sessions were recorded and all asynchronous interactions in Moodle platform (written dialogues and uploaded files) were also considered.

Since most interaction in this virtual setting was in text (chats and forums messages), audio and video format (from the recorded online sessions), qualitative data analysis techniques such as discourse analysis and content analysis were necessary. But once the empirical field has shift to an online setting, based on the engagement on virtual discussions among the pre-service teachers and among them and the researcher (teacher), it was a concern that the credibility of the findings should be established through using multiple new data sources, as the ones explained above, and cross validation.

The theoretical framework of Theory of Semiotic Mediation [11] is used in this research to create and implement didactic cycles [15] that allow future teachers to analyse semiotic potential applets, identifying the knowledge and the mathematical procedures produced with their use. The main research question is posed in the following way: How to design and implement didactical cycles to exploit semiotic potential of applets with pre-service elementary teachers?

According to Mariotti [16] the semiotic potential of an artefact is associated with its '(…) evocative power, stressing the distinction between meanings emerging from the activity with the artefact and the math meanings evoked by such activity' (p. 442). In other words, it is related to the potential for math meanings to emerge whilst participants solve a mathematical task, following a certain didactic cycle. Following this core idea, the qualitative methods are used to interpret how participants, in this case pre-service elementary teachers, construct their own meaning about the semiotic potential of some applets, which they work with.

Participant observation was a fundamental instrument in data collection. It allowed the researcher to holistically perceive the practice of using applets in the social context under analysis, but also represented an important method so that he could always maintain a degree of interaction with the studied situation, affecting it and being affected by it.

For the purposes of this study, the researcher' participation in the synchronous and asynchronous activities allowed him to intervene in the process of renegotiating the meanings of the participants with regard to the use of applets and providing the emergence of new needs for future teachers who developed their activities in this specific context.

According to Mariotti and Maffia [15] the identification of the semiotic potential of a certain artefact constitutes the necessary ante fact of its use in the classroom, however the effectiveness of its use needs the careful design of the teaching intervention. So, the didactical approach should take a central role. The mentioned authors [15] present the didactical cycle, as shown in Fig. 1, as a teaching sequence designed to exploit the semiotic potential of the artefact. Each cycle is constituted by specific activities each type of activity contributes differently, but complementarily, to the developing of the complex process of semiotic mediation.

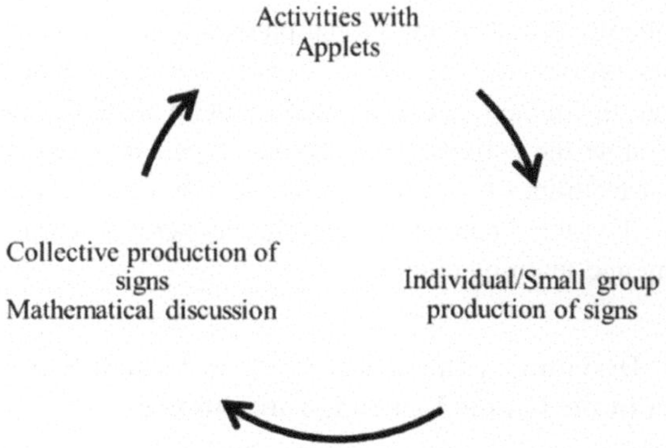

Fig. 1. Didactical Cycle (adapted from [15], p. 53)

The 'Activities with the artefact' [15] constitute the start of any didactical cycle and are based on asking learners to carry out a task involving the use of the artefact, with the aim of promoting the emergence of individual signs whose meanings refers to the use of the artefact but are also in connection with the mathematical meanings that are planned to be learned. Spontaneous production of signs emerges during the activities with the artefact, so in the next moment of the didactical cycle, different semiotic activities are proposed, asking individual production and elaboration of signs, related to the previous phase. In the 'Activities of individual production of signs' [15] a crucial role is played by written texts, because of their nature and unlike other signs, like gestures, written signs start to be isolated from the contingency of the situated action. Those written productions can become objects of discussion in the following moment of the didactic cycle. In 'Collective Discussion' plays an essential part in the teaching-learning process and according to [15] constitutes the core of the semiotic mediation process. The entire class is involved: several strategies and conclusions are discussed collectively, students' written texts or other texts are collectively analyzed, commented, discussed. Students' interventions are coordinated by the teacher with the purpose of fostering the emergence and appropriation of mathematical meanings, exploiting the semiotic potentialities coming from the use of the artefact.

In a pre-pandemic scenario, didactical cycles were designed and implemented with pre-service teachers with the purpose to collect data that allow to interpret their learning trajectory about semiotic potential of applets. In in-person classes this model is followed to design learning activities to be implemented with pre-service teachers, in which tasks are proposed to be developed, individually or in small groups, with the artefact, followed by moments of collective discussion. It was intended that those moments contribute to the production of mathematical signs, based on the personal signs produced by pre-service teachers with the use of the artefact in the performance of tasks. The moments of collective discussion were also guided by a concern to foster discussion about the contribution of the artefact to the production of the aforementioned mathematical signs, that is, to encourage participants to analyse the semiotic potential of the artefacts used in the different tasks.

So, the first challenge posed by the global pandemic arises from not being face-to face with the students (pre-service teachers) designing and implementing those didactical cycles, and moreover, the didactical cycles should not be designed and implemented in the same way, once now the activities will be developed in a virtual environment. In this sense, this paper examines how the research design was modified to face the new challenges raised by the global pandemic, namely the fact that it was necessary to shift to an online teaching and learning context.

2.1 Challenge #1: Designing a Didactical Cycle to Exploit Semiotic Potential of This Applet in the Online Learning Environment

The Theory of Semiotic Mediation is constructed on two key elements: the notion of the semiotic potential of an artefact and the notion of a didactic cycle. The concept of a didactic cycle is about the design of the teaching-learning process, especially describing semiotic processes: "(i) activities with artefact (students work in pairs or in small groups), (ii) individual production of signs and (iii) collective production of signs" ([11], pp. 754–755).

The activity with the artefact is the first activity of any cycle and is based, in this specific case, on asking pre-service teachers to carry out a task involving the use of the artefact, with the aim of promoting the emergence of signs (words, sketches, gestures, …) whose meanings are linked to the use of the artefact but are also in connection with the mathematical meanings that are the purpose of the teaching intervention.

Thinking in this first step of the cycle, in which students in pairs or small groups are involved in solving a certain task with an applet, it seems clear that a shift to an online environment requires adjustments in the didactical approach previously adopted.

As described by [15] in in-person classes, pre-service teachers solved the task using the applet and the researcher intend to perceive the evolution from the emergence of personal meanings related to the accomplishment of a task to the collective development/construction of shared signs related to both the artefact's use and the mathematics to be learnt. The drawings, sketches, calculations, discourses, etc. made by pre-service teachers were analysed to understand how that process occur. Besides that, it was also important to promote collective reflection with pre-service teachers about the contributions offered by the applet and by the didactical approach in that evolution.

Changing to an on-line environment implied that the proposed activities with applets needed to be adjusted. It was necessary to perceive how pre-service teachers constructed individual signs by accomplishing the task using the applet in the online environment and how they engage in mathematical discussions that contribute to a collective production of mathematical signs. To do that, it was important to create a supportive online environment in which all students (pre-service teachers) feel comfortable participating and interacting with each other virtually. To better discuss this subject, a designed and implemented didactical cycle will be analysed. The used applet is available in: https://apps.mathlearningcenter.org/geoboard/.

In a didactical cycle to promote the analysis of the semiotic potential of the digital geoboard it was proposed to the pre-service teachers, the following task, divided into three parts:

1st Part:

1. Start by drawing three squares (A, B and C) in the digital geoboard. Those squares must have the following features:

   i) Square A must be connected to square B only by one apex.
   ii) Square B must be connected to square C only by one apex.
   iii) Square C must be connected to square A only by one apex and also connected to square B by another apex.

   In Fig. 2. You can see an example of three square with the given conditions.
2. Find three sets of squares that are constructed following the given conditions. In a Microsoft Word document paste your constructions and identify those sets of squares as Fig. 1, 2 and 3, respectively.
3. What kind of polygons can you identify in your constructions?

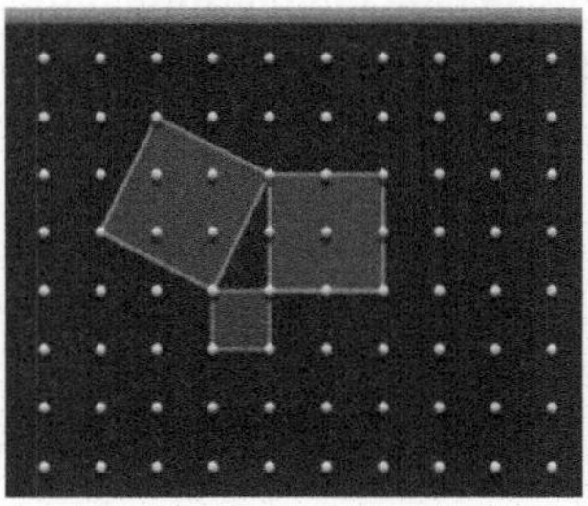

Fig. 2. Three squares constructed with the applet, under the given conditions.

2nd Part:

4. Let us assume that the unit of area is the smallest square constructed in the geoboard, as you can see in Fig. 3. Calculate the area of the squares in your constructions.
5. Analyse all the constructions made by your colleagues. Is there any pattern related with the squares' areas when we have a right triangle in the construction?
6. The same happens when the triangles are acute or obtuse?

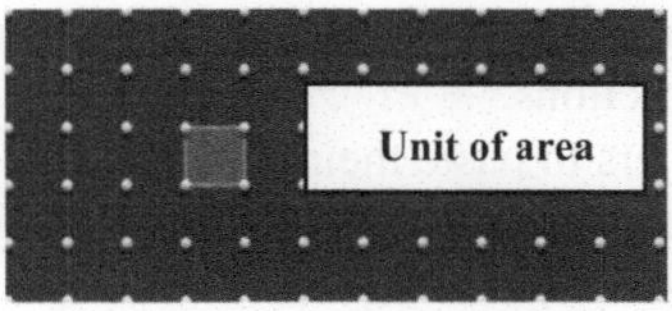

Fig. 3. Unit of area in the virtual geoboard.

3rd Part:

7. What mathematical knowledge does come into play with this task? Does the applet help a student to perceive that mathematical knowledge?
8. Which educational level do you consider suitable for this task to be implemented at and why?
9. What are the main difficulties that a student might find when solving this task?
10. Do you have any suggestion to improve this task?
11. Do you recognize any didactical potential of using this applet or do you think the task could be developed with another one (e.g. a physical geoboard)?

The first part of the task was designed to pre-service teachers explore the possibility offered by the applet to construct the asked polygons, according to the given conditions. In the first moment, the task was presented in a synchronous online meeting/class in Zoom.

Pre-service teachers used the applet individually to construct the squares with the given conditions and the researcher helped to run a virtual discussion among them, providing opportunities for them to engage thoughtfully with the task. Pre-service teachers were required to interact by showing their work, posing their doubts, or helping others to clarify some aspects related with involved mathematical concepts or related with specific features of the applet.

The second part of the task was presented to pre-service teachers in a synchronous moment, but they should solve it and discuss it in an online forum, created in the Moodle platform. All students (pre-service teachers) and teacher (researcher) were enrolled in the online forum and all could upload and download resources, create discussion' topics, etc.

The third part of the task was developed synchronously. This moment was designed to pre-service teachers analyse the semiotic potential of the given applet.

According to Mariotti and Maffia [15] the didactic use of an artefact has a dual nature: on the one hand it is directly used by the students as a mean to accomplish a task; on the other hand, it is indirectly used by the teacher as a mean to achieve specific educational goals, in this case, the learning of mathematical contents and procedures.

The questions in the third part of the task were posed in order to collect data related with pre-service teachers' perceptions about the mathematical signs that emerged from using the applet and about the didactical approach that they eventually use if they implement the mentioned task.

Some changes were made in the previously task, developed in a pre-pandemic scenario. In in-person classes the constructions made in the applet were usually reproduced by students in a proper paper. In Fig. 4. Bellow we show an example of a paper used by students to draw their constructions.

Asking pre-service teachers to paste their constructions and conclusions in a Word document and promoting the online synchronous and asynchronous discussion changed the way they usually expressed their strategies.

In the next images we can see analyse how pre-service teachers present their work in an online discussion forum.

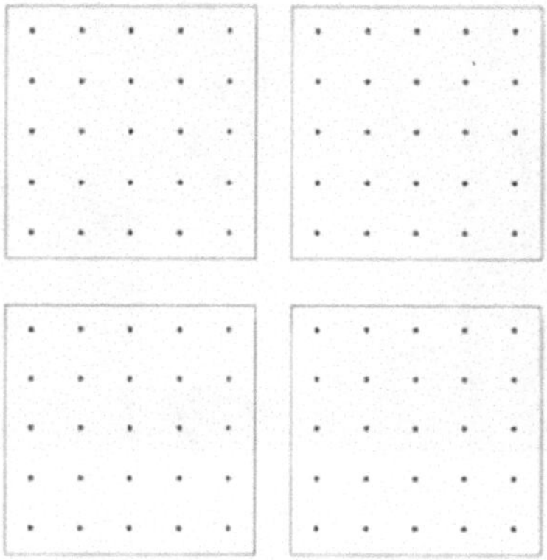

Fig. 4. Paper to draw students' constructions.

In Fig. 5 teacher_1 explains how it is calculated the area of the yellow square (square that is adjacent to triangle's hypotenuse). That yellow square is decomposed into other figures (small squares and triangles), for which it is possible to easily calculate their areas. The small squares have area equals to one and the triangles have the same area of a half of a unit. By doing that this pre-service teacher explain their procedures to calculate this specific area.

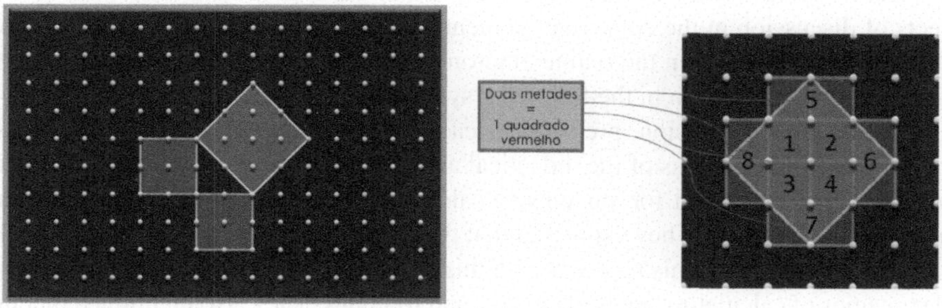

Fig. 5. Pre-service teacher_1 explains how calculates yellow square area.

In Fig. 6, we can examine another procedure to express the strategies used to calculate the area of the squares in a pre-service construction.

The large square was also decomposed into other figures (small squares and triangles). The small squares obtained are also squares that measures a unit of area, but the triangles are not the same that the ones used in the above example. In this specific case, pre-service teacher_2 used triangles that have area equals to 1,5 once they are half of rectangles that have an area that measures 3 units.

These two examples from these two pre-service teachers bring us evidences of how they express the mathematical signs in the online environment. Different ways of calculating square areas were presented and discussed in this context and by doing that, participants constructed different mathematical approaches to the same task.

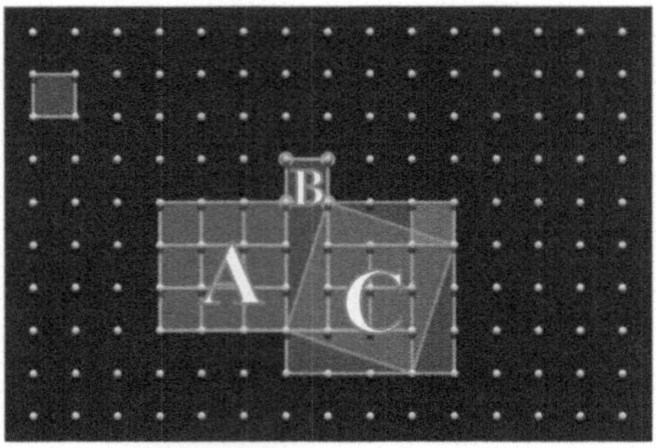

Área do Quadrado A = 9 unidades de medida

1+1+1+1+1+1+1+1+1= 9

Área do Quadrado B = 1 unidade de medida

=1

Área do Quadrado C= 4 unidades de medida e 4 metades de retângulo, cuja área é igual à de 2 retângulos com área de 3 unidades de medida, ou seja, 6 unidades de medida.

= 1+1+1+1+1,5+1,5+1,5+1,5

= 4+6= 10

Fig. 6. Pre-service teacher_2 strategies explanation

According to Mariotti and Maffia [15] these individual productions should become objects of discussion in the collective moments. In fact, once all the constructions and strategies were available in the online environment, they were analyzed and discussed in the collective discussion in the following synchronous moment.

In a collective discussion, pre-service teachers also analyzed the potential of this applet and the effectiveness of the didactical approach. They mentioned that the applet was a very important tool for students to calculate square areas by decomposing the shapes they constructed. They expressed that they usually think in area calculating only by using formulas. With this task and with this applet children could explore new ways and strategies of calculating areas of squares and triangles. They also mentioned that the opportunity they had to analyze and to reflect about others' strategies was important for they to improve their own work and to see different approaches to the same task. Their opinion is that also children must have this opportunity to analyze others' strategies and to reflect about their own work.

2.2 Challenge #2: Collecting and Analysing Representative Data that Allows to Comprehend How Pre-service Teachers Construct Their Own Meaning About the Semiotic Potential of the Applet

The didactical cycle above described was designed to collect data related with the comprehension of two important aspects about the recognition of the semiotic potential of the applet by the participants (future teachers). On the one hand, it was important to comprehend how the future teachers identified the mathematical knowledge that was evocated with the use of the applet to accomplish the task. On the other hand, was important to collect evidence about their reflection about the didactic approach used in the development of the task with the applet.

The resources that pre-service teachers uploaded in the Moodle platform and the collective discussion occurred in Zoom sessions provide important evidence about the mathematical contents that were invocated when pre-service teachers were engaged in this task with the applet. But one of the challenges faced in this research by shifting to the online learning environment is to comprehend pre-service teachers' engagement in this new context. It became very important in this research to consider what such change might mean for the understanding about online engagement.

In this sense, it was important to consider an interdisciplinary conceptual framework designed specifically for reflecting on online participant engagement. The framework proposed by Redmond, Heffernan, Abawi, Brown and Henderson [18], presented in Fig. 7, is an important theoretical tool to achieve this purpose:

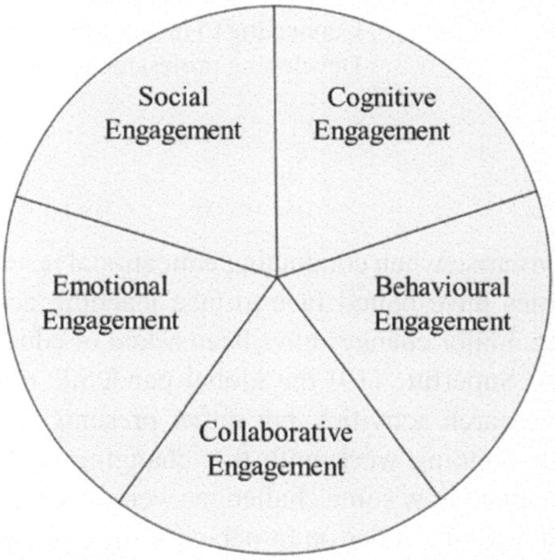

Fig. 7. Online engagement framework overview (in [18], p. 189).

The authors [18] argue that the online engagement framework presented here is a multidimensional construct with interrelated elements that impact on student engagement in online settings.

In this specific moment of this research, the pre-service teachers' engagement is being analysed according to the indicators related with three of these elements: Social engagement, Cognitive engagement, and Collaborative engagement. Those indicators can be found in Table 1 further down. The reason for not being considered the indicators for Behavioural engagement and Emotional engagement it is because it does not seem to be related with the research problem in this specific study.

Table 1. Online engagement framework for higher education [18].

Online engagement element	Indicators (illustrative only)
Social engagement	Building community Creating a sense of belonging Developing relationships Establishing trust
Cognitive engagement	Thinking critically Activating metacognition Integrating ideas Justifying decisions Developing deep discipline understandings Distributing expertise
Collaborative engagement	Learning with peers Relating to faculty members Connecting to institutional opportunities Developing professional networks

3 Conclusions

Numerous considerations arise when conducting educational research during this global pandemic. As universities have halted face-to-face teaching activities and moved to online forms of working, major changes have been asked of educational researchers.

According to Castro Superfine [19] the global pandemic does not mean we have to put a pause on our research activities, but rather presents an opportunity for us as researchers to align our ongoing work with this changing and pressing reality. This paper offers a reflection about how some challenges were faced in this specific scenario.

Qualitative research typically relies on in-person settings for data collection through interviews, focus groups and presential field work. This paper discusses how this specific topic was addressed when it was needed to shift to an online setting. The theoretical approach is used in this research to design didactical cycles to exploit semiotic potential of applets. Shifting to an online learning environment posed some questions about the design of these didactic cycles, about the nature of the collected data and how that data should be analysed to answer the research question.

This pandemic is guiding researchers to reflect on how things could and must be done. Researchers should take time to pause and reflect on whether data collection is possible and if so, in which conditions. In this sense this paper tries to bring some light about how can be possible continue to carry out research activities making the possible and necessary adjustments.

Acknowledgments. The author acknowledges the financial support from the FCT grant with reference project UIDB/04083/2020.

References

1. Vygotsky, L.S.: Mind in Society. The Development of Higher Psychological Processes. Harvard University Press, Cambridge (1978)
2. Peixoto, J., Carvalho, R.: Mediação Pedagógica Midiatizada pelas Tecnologias? Teoria e Prática da Educação. **14**, 31–38 (2011)
3. Daher, W.: Preservice teachers' perceptions of applets for solving mathematical problems: need, difficulties and functions. Educ. Technol. Soc. **12**(4), 383–395 (2009). ISSN 1436-4522
4. Terrel, R.: Applets for mathematical learning. In: Habre, S. (ed.) Enhancing Mathematics Understanding through Visualization: The Role of Dynamical Software, chap. 8, pp. 145–152. Information Science Reference, Hershey (2013). https://doi.org/10.4018/978-1-4666-4050-4
5. Fernandes, E., Lopes, P.C., Martins, S.: Learning Scenarios with Robots Leading to Problem-Solving and Mathematics Learning. In: Amado, N., Carreira, S., Jones, K. (eds.) Broadening the scope of research on mathematical problem solving: Focus on Technology, Creativity and Affect, pp. 129–152. Springer, New York (2018). https://doi.org/10.1007/978-3-319-99811-9-16
6. Fernandes, E., Martins, S.: Learning scenarios with robots for the learning of STEM. In: 11th Annual International Conference of Education, Research and Innovation, pp. 5811–5817. IATED, Seville (2018). https://doi.org/10.21125/iceri.2018
7. Martins, S.: Learning sciences through a robotics project. In: Costa, M.F., Dorrío, B.V. (eds.) Hands-on Science. Growing with Science. Hands-on Science Network, pp. 123–128 (2017). ISBN 978-84-8158-737-1
8. Martins, S., Fernandes, E.: Aprender Matemática num projeto interdisciplinar com robots. Revista Tecnologias na Educação. **7**(13), 1–12 (2015). ISSN 1984-4751
9. Martins, S., Fernandes, E.: Robots na Aprendizagem das STEAM. In: Duarte A.C., Cristóvão, N. (eds.) Educação, Artes e Cultura: Discursos e Práticas, pp.188–202. CIE-UMa, Funchal (2020). ISBN 978-989-54390-3-4
10. Martins, S.: Applets como artefactos de mediação semiótica na formação inicial de professores na Licenciatura em Educação Básica. Quadrante. **29**(1), 74–96 (2020). ISSN 2183-2838
11. Bartolini Bussi, M.G., Mariotti, M.A.: Semiotic mediation in the mathematics classroom: artefacts and signs after a Vygotskian perspective. In: English, L., Bartolini Bussi, M., Jones, G., Lesh, R., Tirosh, D. (eds.) Handbook of International Research in Mathematics Education, 2nd revised edition, pp. 746–783. Lawrence Erlbaum, Mahwah (2008). ISBN 978-0805858761
12. Mariotti, M.A.: ICT as opportunities for teaching–learning in a mathematics classroom: the semiotic potential of artefacts. In: Tso, T.Y. (ed.) 36th Conference of the International Group for the Psychology of Mathematics Education, vol. 1, pp. 25–35. PME, Taipei (2012)
13. Bereiter, C.: Design Research for Sustained Innovation. Cogn. Stud. Bull. Jpn. Cogn. Sci. Soc. **9**(3), 321–327 (2002). https://doi.org/10.11225/jcss.9.321
14. Amado, J.: Manual de Investigação Qualitativa em Educação, 3rd ed. Imprensa da Universidade de Coimbra, Coimbra (2017). https://doi.org/10.14195/978-989-26-0879-2
15. Mariotti, M.A., Maffia, A.: From using artefacts to mathematical meanings: the teacher's role in the semiotic mediation process. Didattica della matematica. Dalle ricerche alle pratiche d'aula. **3**, 50–63 (2018). https://doi.org/10.33683/ddm.18.3
16. Mariotti, M.A.: Introducing students to geometric theorems: how the teacher can exploit the semiotic potential of a DGS. ZDM Math. Educ. **45**(3), 441–452 (2013). https://doi.org/10.1007/s11858-013-0495-5
17. Rabardel, P.: Les hommes et les technologies – Approche cognitive des instruments contemporains. Armand Colin, Paris (1995). ISBN 978-2200215699

18. Redmond, P., Heffernan, A., Abawi, L., Brown, A., Henderson, R.: An online engagement framework for higher education. Online Learn. J. **22**(1), 183–204 (2018). https://doi.org/10.24059/olj.v22i1.1175
19. Castro Superfine, A.: Conducting research in the time of pandemic: a pause or an opportunity? J. Math. Teach. Educ. **23**(5), 429–431 (2020). https://doi.org/10.1007/s10857-020-09478-w

FuzzyQoI-Based Estimation of the Quality of Interaction in Online Learning Amid Covid-19: A Greek Case-Study

Sofia B. Dias[1(✉)], Sofia J. Hadjileontiadou[2], J. Alves Diniz[1], and Leontios J. Hadjileontiadis[3,4]

[1] CIPER, Faculdade de Motricidade Humana, Universidade de Lisboa, Cruz Quebrada Dafundo, Portugal
{sbalula,jadiniz}@fmh.ulisboa.pt

[2] Department of Primary Education, Democritus University of Thrace, Alexandroupolis, Greece
schatzil@eled.duth.gr

[3] Department of Electrical Engineering and Computer Science, Department of Biomedical Engineer, Khalifa University of Science and Technology, Abu Dhabi, UAE
leontios.hadjileontiadis@ku.ac.ae

[4] Department of Electrical and Computer Engineering, Aristotle University of Thessaloniki, Thessaloniki, Greece
leontios@auth.gr

Abstract. In the beginning of 2020, the coronavirus (Covid-19) pandemic has raised significant challenges for the Higher Education Institutions (HEIs) worldwide. Due to Covid-19 outbreak, HEIs were forced to close due to social lockdown, placing online teaching-learning environments/modalities to the foreground of the educational settings. In an effort to examine how this 'new normal' has affected users' Quality of Interaction (QoI) within the Learning Management System (LMS) Moodle, a modeling approach based on fuzzy logic (FuzzyQoI), was used here and applied to LMS Moodle data, drawn from an undergraduate discipline, offered by a public Greek HEI during the Covid-19 period. The results have shown the ability of the FuzzyQoI model to express the time-depended dynamics of the users' QoI and associate it with the societal effects of Covid-19. Clearly, these findings shed light upon the way users interact with a LMS online learning when societal disruptors, such as Covid-19, come in to play, informing HEIs' policy makers for monitoring and re-examining online (teaching-learning) practices.

Keywords: FuzzyQoI · Covid-19 · Societal disruptors · Quality of interaction · Fuzzy logic · Moodle learning management systems · Higher education institutions · Online learning

1 Introduction

With the Covid-19 outbreak, the human daily habits have been altered across the globe in a very short time period, with significant effects in many sectors, such as economy,

A. Reis et al. (Eds.): TECH-EDU 2020, CCIS 1384, pp. 249–262, 2021.
https://doi.org/10.1007/978-3-030-73988-1_19

health and education [1–4]. In fact, until October 2020, approximately 600 million learners across the Globe have been impacted[1]. Actions, like partial and/or full lock-down, have caused educational disruption that calls for remedy actions. The latter stem from UNESCO's Education 2030, Incheon declaration and framework for action, which describes a new vision for the Education until 2030 [5], proposing alternative modes of learning and education, bridging programmes to ensure flexible learning in both formal and non-formal settings. Flexibility denotes an educational environment where learning choices are offered to the student along with customizations, in order to meet his/her needs [6]. In fact, this is a student-centered approach, which is even further sustained and enhanced with options provided by the use of the information and communication technologies (ICTs).

Among other choices in online learning environments (OLEs), flexible learning can also be supported by applying formative feedback to the student/learner, as reports or dashboards, on the basis of analysis of his/her digital traces, while interacting with the learning system, i.e., Learning Management Systems (LMSs) [6]. However, Ryan and Tilbury [7], believe that apart from the student, flexibility refers also to the educational strategies employed at the institution level. Considering the emergency condition that was imposed by the Covid-19, institutions like Higher Education Institutions (HEIs) exposed the ability to adapt to the new situation on the basis of online learning and, thus, exhibiting flexibility and customization attributes towards the student/learner needs.

In a flexible OLE, the ability of combining different delivery methodologies is needed, in order to foster optimization both in the development of learning and costs and time deployment [8]. In this vein, the quality of interaction (QoI) can contribute to the evaluation of the quality of the learning experience within an OLE, considering effective technological integration [9]. The latter can be combined with amalgamation of strategic decisions that take into consideration all the necessary and available resources to increase the efficiency of the online learning, sustaining online learning communities [10–13]. In this vein, the latter could be expressed via the QoI of the learner, within the LMS, and based on proper design within the OLE, interactions towards learning can be activated and sustained. Using these interactions with learning resources at a user and/or group basis, specific learning patterns can be identified related with personalized learning [14].

In the view of the aforementioned, the aim of this work is to examine how the 'new normal' due to Covid-19 has affected users' QoI within LMS Moodle, in terms of QoI dynamics and association with the societal effects of Covid-19. To achieve this, the structure and functionality of a previously validated fuzzy logic-based modeling approach, i.e., FuzzyQoI model [15], was adopted here and applied to LMS Moodle data, drawn from an undergraduate discipline, offered by a public HEI during the Covid-19 period. The interpretation of the findings reveals the way users interact with a LMS online learning when societal disruptors, such as Covid-19, come in to play. Apparently, this can be used to inform HEIs' policy makers in an effort to extract useful information about monitoring and re-examining online (teaching-learning) readiness practices, especially when the societal disruptors exhibit resurgences (e.g., Covid-19s wave).

[1] https://en.unesco.org/covid19/educationresponse (accessed 23/10/2020).

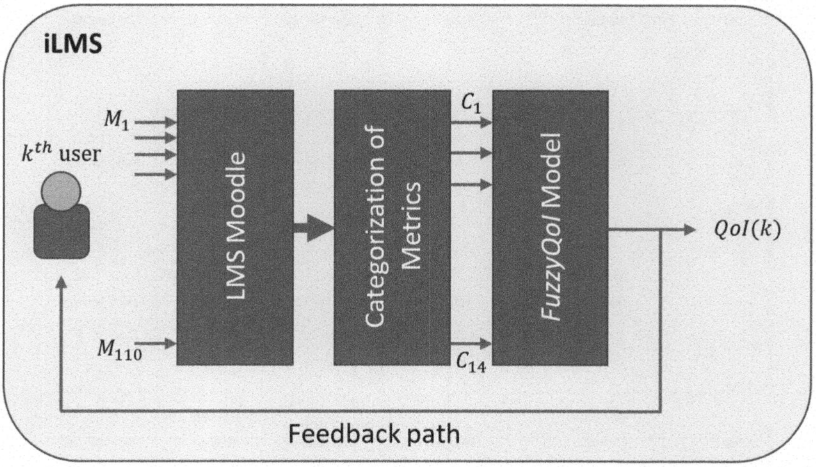

Fig. 1. A block diagram of the intelligent LMS (iLMS) functionality, with the LMS Moodle user's interaction metrics ($M1, \ldots M110$) included, and the related 14 input parameters ($C_1, \ldots C_{14}$) fed to the *FuzzyQoI* model [15], resulting in an estimation of QoI(k)(k) at instance k, triggering the user's feedback path

2 The FuzzyQoI Model

Towards the development of a system to successfully evaluate users' QoI with the LMS, intelligent LMS (iLMSs) may be a key-factor. In this line, the FuzzyQoI model was introduced [15], structured on a series of nested Mamdani-type [16] Fuzzy Inference Systems (FISs), that is able to inference upon input data. These data include the key metrics concerning the use of the LMS Moodle employed within an OLE, and, based on these, the FuzzyQoI model quantitively inferences the user's overall QoI [15].

The schematic representation of the FuzzyQoI model is represented in Fig. 1, showing the users' interaction with the iLMS. In particular, 110 metrics that come from the LMS Moodle are corresponded to 14 categories which are the FIS structure inputs [15]. These include C_1: Journal/Wiki/Blog/Form; C_2: Forum/Discussion/Chat; C_3: Submission/Report/Quiz/Feedback; C_4: Course Page; C_5: Module; C_6: Post/Activity; C_7: Resource/Assignment; C_8: Label; C_9: Upload; C_{10}: Update; C_{11}: Assign; C_{12}: Edit/Delete; C_{13}: Time Period; C_{14}: Engagement Time [15]. For the construction of the knowledge base of the FuzzyQoI model, an expert in the field of analyzing Moodle LMS data was engaged and assisted in the formation of the fuzzification of the expert's knowledge, in terms FIS membership functions and related IF/THEN fuzzy rules, as depicted in Fig. 2. As shown in the latter, three-level trapezoid membership functions (Low, Medium and High values), were used for the FIS1-FIS4, whereas five-level trapezoid membership functions (Very Low, Low, Medium, High and Very High values) were implemented for the final FIS5. Figure 3 depicts the output surfaces for all combinations of inputs of the FIS4 (left column) and FIS5 (right column). More details about the structure of the FuzzyQoI model are available in [15].

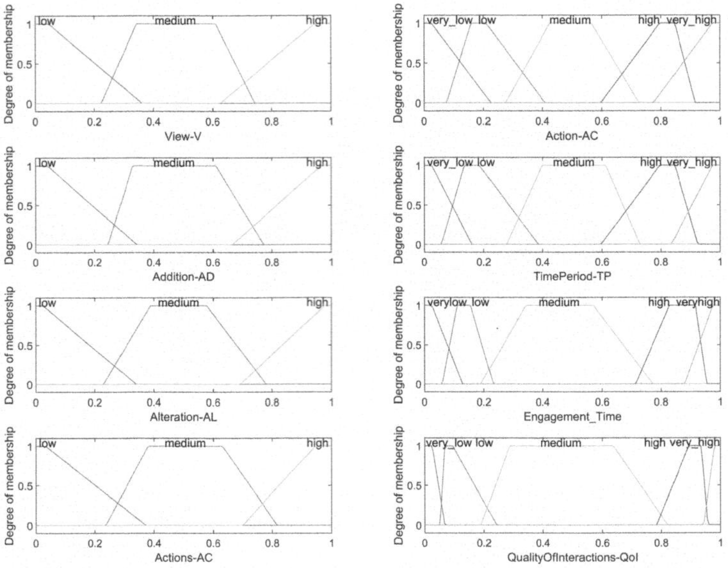

Fig. 2. Membership functions (indicative examples) used in FIS4 for View (V), Addition (AD), Alteration (AL) and Actions (AC) (left column) and FIS5 for Action (AC), Time Period (TP), Engagement Time (ET) and Quality of Interaction (QoI) (right column).

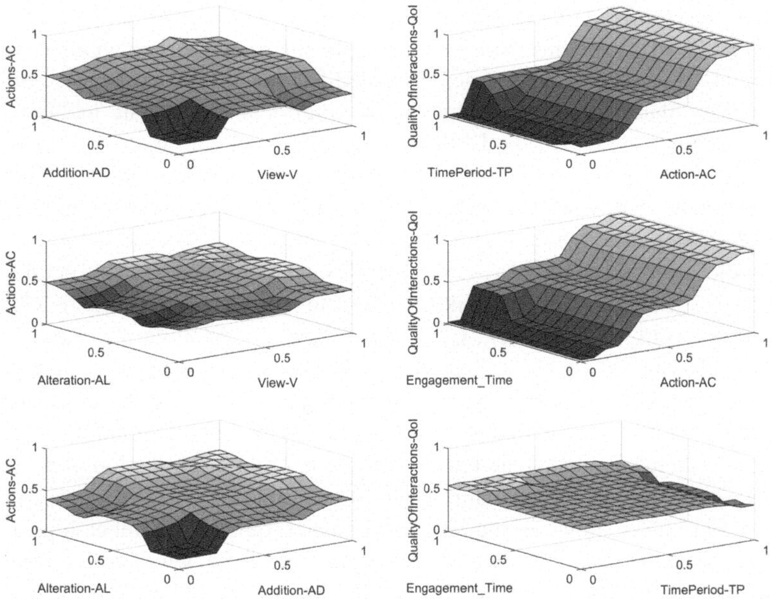

Fig. 3. The surfaces that correspond to the outputs of FIS4 (left column) and FIS5 (right column), for all combinations of inputs.

3 Experimental Dataset

The validation of the FuzzyQoI model was based on LMS Moodle data drawn from an OLE related to the undergraduate "Advance Signal Processing" discipline, offered by a Greek Public HEI (Department of Electrical and Computer Engineering (ECE), Aristotle University of Thessaloniki (AUTH), Thessaloniki, Greece). The users of the LMS Moodle were both students (52 at their 4th year of ECE studies) and two professors; the acquired LMS Moodle usage data correspond to a time-period of 26-week (29/3–25/9/2020 (181 days)). The main focus of this discipline is the introduction of efficient advanced signal processing techniques/algorithms to be used as background knowledge for efficiently solving research problems; this discipline was supported by two Professors.

Table 1. Demographics and LMS contributions of the participants from 29/3–25/9/2020 (181 days).

Users	No	Sex (Male/Female)	Age/Age range (yrs) (mean ± std)	LMS interactions
Professors	2	2/0	40, 54 (47 ± 9.8)	683
Students	52	32/20	22–25 (23.2 ± 1.2)	26373
Total	**54**			**27056**

Table 2. The segmentation periods of the whole examined time-period and the corresponding Covid-19 effects in Greece.

Distinct periods of online courses	Week (date)	Societal Covid-19 effect
Spring Semester 2020 Lectures Start	1 (29.3.20)	Lockdown ON
Lectures Continue	6 (4.5.20)	Lockdown OFF
Lectures End	11 (6.6.20)	Curfew after 00:00
Summer Course Exams End	18 (27.7.20)	Curfew after 00:00
Fall Exams Period Starts	23 (1.9.20)	No general restrictions
Fall Course Exams End	26 (25.9.20)	No general restrictions

Table 1 tabulates the demographics and LMS contributions of all participants. For each online user, a normalization process of all derived input variable values per week to the corresponding maximum value across the analysed total time-period, i.e., 26 weeks was involved, taking into consideration that all input and output variables of the FuzzyQoI model range within [0, 1]. Moreover, the societal effects of Covid-19 at distinct dates within the examined duration were considered for further segmentation of the analysed time-period (see Table 2). This segmentation allowed for the identification of the dynamics of the estimated QoI by the FuzzyQoI model across different periods and the exploration of any causality due to the related societal Covid-19 triggers. The whole analysis was implemented in Matlab 2020a (The Mathworks, Inc., Natick, USA), resulting in .fis and .m formatted files (all available for free upon reasonable request from the last author).

4 Societal Covid-19 Effects in Greece

On 30th January 2020, Covid-19 was declared by the World Health Organization (WHO) as a global public health emergency of international concern [17]. In Greece, the Covid-19 appeared for the first time on the 26th of February 2020. After the verification of the first three cases, several local measures were gradually taken. On March, Covid-19 was spread in many areas of Greece and further measures at the national scale were introduced. In particular, on the 11th of March, the public and private educational sectors were closed. This path was gradually followed by other sectors, like places for cultural events (on the 12th of March), bars and restaurants (on the 13th of March), up to the 23rd of March when a national lockdown was decided. The latter lasted until the 4th of May and from this day on, gradually, different sectors restarted their operation.

More specifically, concerning the educational sector, on the 11th of May schools opened only for the last grade of secondary education, whereas kindergartens and elementary schools restarted on the 1st of June. In particular, the HEIs managed to successfully complete the Spring semester, which was extended until the end of July, by shifting amidst the Covid-19 outbreak in Greece, to online learning solutions. These included LMS (e.g., Moodle, e-class) for the asynchronous communication and various platforms (e.g., Skype for Business, WebEx, Zoom) for the synchronous one. Yet, the laboratory lessons were postponed from the 11th of March and were offered again face-to-face (F2F) from the 25th of May until the end of the Spring semester. During September 2020, the HEIs run examinations following online learning solutions again and from 5th of October 2020 initiated the Fall semester combining online learning solutions for large audiences (>50 students) and face to F2F for the small ones (<50 students). This situation revealed that blended learning could not be followed as before and the focus was put on online learning solutions.

5 Results

Figure 4 shows the FuzzyQoI model results (in terms of contour plots) for the case of 52 students across the 26 weeks. In particular, the normalized ET input to the FS5 is depicted in Fig. 4(a), whereas the estimated outputs View (V), Addition (AD) and Alteration (AL), derived from FIS1, FIS2 and FIS3 [15], are illustrated in Figs. 4(b)–(d), respectively. Considering the way high ET values of Fig. 4(a) are distributed across time, it is evident that a sufficient time was spent by the students interacting with the LMS Moodle during the Spring semester, immediately after lectures start (weeks 2–11), and in the path towards the final exams period (weeks 18–26). On the other hand, as expected, less estimated ET is observed at end of lectures period (weeks 11–18). In general, a unified pattern across the students is seen in the normalized ET estimates, as sustained ET values above middle and towards high levels, i.e., $ET \in [0.5, 1]$, are exhibited by many students and for many consecutive weeks (see for instance Student #4 in Fig. 4(a)).

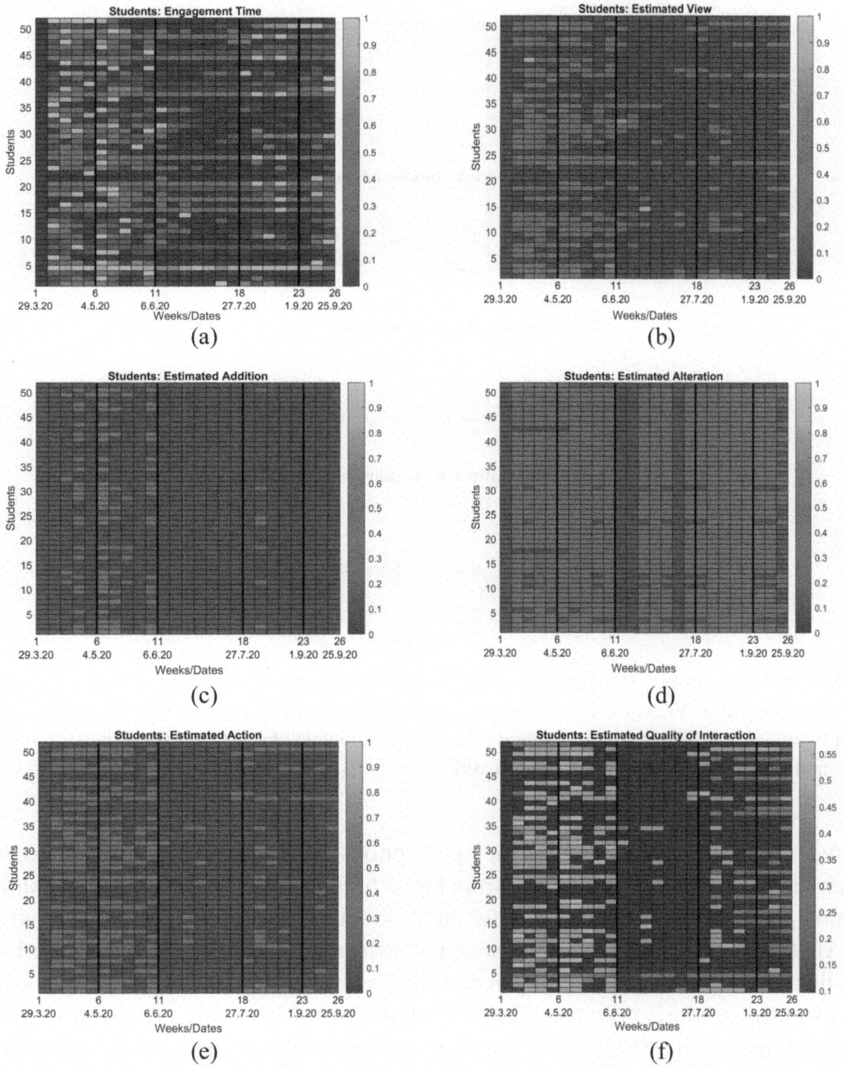

Fig. 4. The normalized Engagement Time input of the fuzzy inference system FIS5, along with the estimated fuzzy outputs from FIS1-FIS5 for the students across the examined time period (26 weeks), (a) Normalized Engagement Time, (b) View, (c) Addition, (d) Alteration, (e) Action, and (f) Quality of Interaction. The specific weeks/dates that define the time-period segmentation (Table 2) are shown as vertical lines.

As illustrated in Figs. 4(b)–(d), the estimated V, AD and AL covered almost all range of [0.1, 1]; this reveals the existence of diverse interaction with the LMS Moodle across

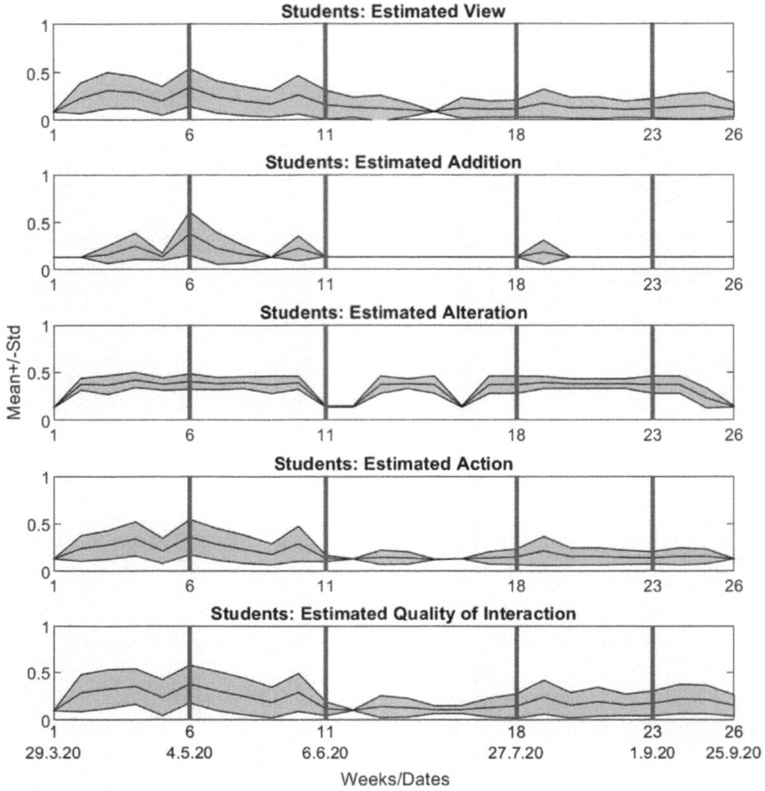

Fig. 5. The mean value (solid middle line) ± std (gray area) of the estimated fuzzy outputs (from top to bottom: View, Addition, Alteration, Action, and Quality of Interaction), of FS1-FS5, respectively, averaged across the students. The specific weeks/dates that define the time-period segmentation (Table 2) are shown as vertical lines.

the students and, hence, a variety in their perception of LMS Moodle as a supportive tool in their learning activities. Moreover, from Fig. 4(b) it seems that the estimated V exhibits the most distributed high values across the 26 weeks, followed by the AL (Fig. 4(d)), and AD (Fig. 4(c)). This places the students' primary focus upon the use of the LMS Moodle as a monitoring learning system, followed by its view as a material update and addition one. Curiously, a concentration of AL medium-high values is noticed across all examined time-period (Fig. 4(d)), revealing a continuous commitment with the online environment across all the semester (weeks 2–26).

Figure 4(e) depicts the estimated output AC from the FIS4 [15] spanning values, within [0.1, 0.65], mainly concentrated in the first weeks (weeks 2–11). Generally, the estimated AC values follow a pattern similar to the one seen in the estimated V and AD, showing a significant lack of interaction (even null for AD) after the end of the lectures (week 11) and most of them just returning for the Summer Course Exams period (week 19).

Finally, Fig. 4(f) illustrates the estimated output QoI from the FIS5 [15], with values within [0.1, 0.58]. From this figure, in several cases, a distribution of the students' estimated QoI around 0.50 is noticeable; moreover, in some cases QoI values exceed 0.55 (e.g., week#6: students #2, 5, 7, 10, 16, 19, 24, 26, 28, 34, 43, 46, 47); however, other students get lower values of QoI (<0.25) (e.g., week #22: students #16, 18, 21, 26, 30, 38, 39, 45, 49). In spite of that, in many cases, a sustained QoI values for more than one week across students could be identified, mostly at the end of the lectures period (weeks 2–11) and during exams period (weeks 18–23). Clearly, the estimated QoI values (Fig. 4(f)) can be considered as a tool for dynamic monitoring of the QoI per student, capturing the variations across the examined learning period. These could be used for students' feedback and metacognitive triggers that could contribute to increased efficiency of the LMS Moodle in their activities as learners.

The five subplots of Fig. 5 show the mean value (solid middle line) ± std (grey area) of the estimated fuzzy outputs of FS1-FS5, respectively, averaged across the students, as a means to express the QoI from a group-like perspective. A moderate-towards-low interaction is noticeable from Fig. 5 (all mean values within [0.1, 0.4]) considering also the time-period segmentation (see Table 2).

Focusing upon the estimated QoI (Fig. 5-botom), which is the final output of the FuzzyQoI model (see Fig. 1), an increase at the beginning of the semester (week 3) along with a gradual reduction at the end of the lectures (after week 11) are seen. Moreover, a global peak of the mean QoI lies around week 6 (with a simultaneous increase of the std values) that generally exhibits a reduction tendency towards the Fall course exams period (week 26) with smooth, though, oscillations.

From the above it is clear that the dynamic nature of the students' attitude as a group, regarding their effective interaction with the LMS Moodle, Clearly, the estimated mean (±std) QoI could well monitor the dynamic nature of the students' attitude as a group when interacting with the LMS Moodle across the whole time-period, forming an overview of the students' interaction trend as LMS-mediated learners.

Clearly the number of Professors involved in the data analysis is low (2); for conformity with Fig. 5 results, however, Fig. 6 shows the group-like tendency across the professors (mean value (solid middle line) ± std (grey area) across the 26 weeks) of the estimated fuzzy outputs of FS1-FS5., averaged. From Fig. 6 it is visible that, as a group, the professors show a moderate-towards-low interaction (mean value lies within [0.1, 0.3]), considering also the time-period segmentation (see Table 2).

6 Discussion

Combining the findings with the time segmentation reported in Table 2, some insights for the QoI dynamics and its association with the societal Covid-19 effects in Greece (see §3 and Table 2) can be explored. In particular, From Fig. 5 it can be noticed that almost a similar trend of periodicity can be observed, as far as the outputs of the FIS1 (V), FIS2(AD), FIS4(AC) FIS5(QoI) is concerned. In particular, in the period of lockdown (1–6 weeks), a steeper upwards change is detected with the highest values by the end of it. As the National lockdown was already running from when the Spring Semester Lectures Start (see Table 2), it seems that the students showed a very quick adaptation from F2F

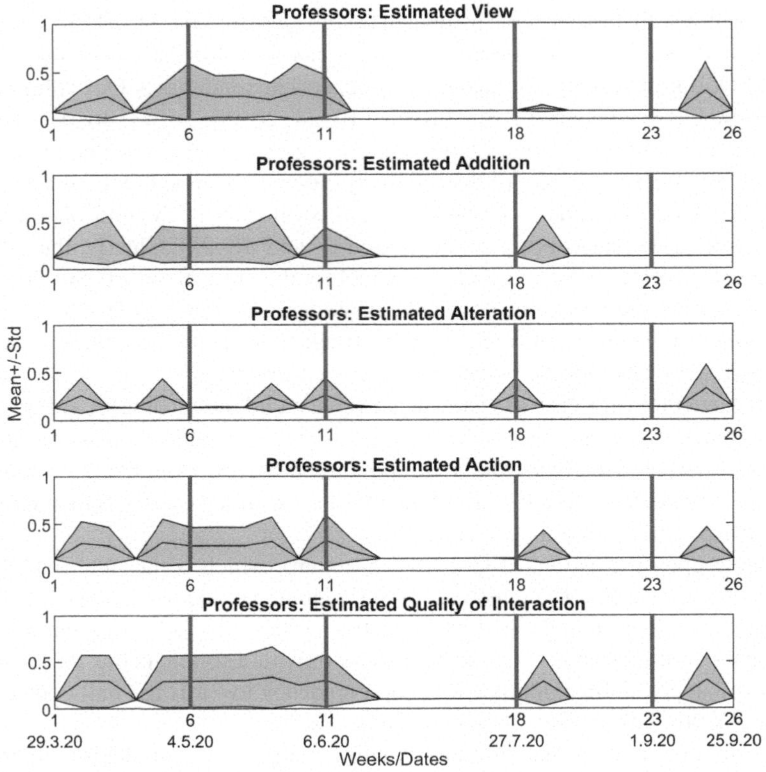

Fig. 6. The mean value (solid middle line) ± std (gray area) of the estimated fuzzy outputs (from top to bottom: View, Addition, Alteration, Action, and Quality of Interaction), of FS1-FS5, respectively, averaged across the professors. The specific weeks/dates that define the time-period segmentation (Table 2) are shown as vertical lines.

to online learning right from the beginning and kept being engaged increasing their V, AD, AC and QoI during this period. This can be characterized as a positive side effect of the Covid-19 confinement on higher education students, and it has been also reported in other performance contexts, e.g., improvement of autonomous learning using e-learning material and tests [18]. Moreover, according to [19], there is a positive social influence on students' behavioral intention to use LMS, in both voluntary and mandatory settings [20], whereas [21] found that social isolation has positive and significant relationship to behavioral intention towards the use of LMS, which in turn lead to the LMS use behavior. Another psychological aspect is considered by [21], i.e., the fear of the Covid-19 pandemic, who found that it moderates the relationship between social isolation and the behavioral intention towards the use of LMS.

Within the aforementioned framework, it is notable that although the students were under the National lockdown, the sociocultural impact of the Easter Holidays was also detected by the FuzzyQoI model, as the values V, AD, AC and QoI in Fig. 5 fall down in this period (weeks 4–5), revealing possible minimization of the fear and the need to follow socially established alteration of workflow during holidays, even in the lockdown situation.

In the next period (6–11 weeks), as the National lockdown was gradually released, the LMS interaction was on average declined in smaller values of V, AD, AC and QoI, yet smoother than the previous one. In this period, due to optimistic reports about the Covid-19 management that resulted after the lockdown in Greece, it seems like the fear about the Covid-19 pandemic also withdraws along with the social isolation. However, towards the end of this period, the external stimuli of the forthcoming period of the Summer Course Exams mobilized the students.

The next period (11–18 weeks) was devoted to the Summer Course Exams. These exams normally finished at the most until the 10th of July, but this academic year due to Covid-19 this period was extended. A lot of effort was put by the stakeholders and the technical staff in the HEIs to decide the appropriate technology and support students and teaching staff to shift to online exams, making appropriate alterations. In the case that is presented, the Professors of this lesson extended the date for the submission and presentation of the final assignment by the end of week 18. This impact of Covid-19 sustained interactions with the LMS even at low values for V, AC and QoI.

The next period (18–23weeks) was normally devoted to the summer holidays. This period there were only dispersed local restrictions and the Covid-19 situation seemed under control. Yet, another fear appeared, i.e., the contribution of tourism and generally of travelling in the dispersion of Covid-19. This year, half of Greeks went on holidays for a few days. Within this framework it is very interesting to realize that the students kept interacting with the LMS during this period. This activity although at lower values for V, AC and QoI, was kept stable until the end of the last period (23–26 weeks), i.e., the Fall Course Exams.

From Fig. 5 it is interesting to realize in particular that the V value is inferred upon the use of the LMS tools that support the social presence of the user in the LMS (e.g., wiki, forum, feedback) [15]. It seems that the social presence of the students was established in the LMS upon feelings of companionship, motivation and solidarity [22], almost in the middle of the lockdown period (1–6 weeks) and lasted until the end of the 26 weeks. It is interesting to notice that these feelings were diffused in the society due to Covid-19, especially during the lockdown period). Moreover, after the Lectures End (week 11), the AD value is zero almost until the end, i.e., the actions upon it is inferred by FIS3 (module, post/activity, resource/ assignment and label) [15] were not triggered. Also, along the whole duration of the 26 weeks, the AL values remain at high level, almost stable, with low $\pm$ std. As presented in [15], the AL value is inferred upon the actions upload, update, assign and edit/delete that seem to be sustained. As the V, AD and AL served as inputs to FIS4 [15], their characteristics resulted in the AC output that is sustained almost during the whole period of the 26 weeks.

Although just the behaviour of two professors is shown in Fig. 6, the general monitoring of QoI alterations (mean QoI $\pm$ std) across the whole time-period can reveal the underlying group-like attitude of the professors, regarding their effective LMS Moodle interaction. Following Fig. 6, the Professors present continuous and stable values of V, AD, AC and QoI along the Lectures period (1–11 weeks), whereas at the rest periods a more sporadic presence is detected in the LMS.

From the overall examination of the mean values in Figs. 5 and 6 a periodicity is recorded that reflects, along the examined period of 26 weeks, possible impacts of the Covid-19 emergency situation on the case lesson, e.g., psychological, managerial, organizational, as were captured by the FuzzyQoI model. This reinforces the use of the estimated QoI as a means to support flexible learning and provide meaningful interpretation in the context of adaptation of the online learning/teaching offerings under emergencies, such as Covid-19 pandemic.

What Covid-19 revealed is the focus of online learning as a new form of educational disruptor. Nevertheless, the view of the online learning value proposition is different as it was before, when the technological innovation gradually started entering the word of education as a form of disruptive innovation [23]. Nowadays, in a new decade of innovation that is still powered by technology, the reiteration of online learning at the foreground has less to do with just transforming how students *learn*; the focus now is in the alteration of how they *connect to and interact with*—experts, mentors, and peers. This affects the learning behavior, as new ways of connections become feasible in circumstances where students lack access to relationships. In fact, students are helped to accrue the so-called *social capital*—that is, the value contained in our networks. Using measures that could capture the dynamics and social aspects of such interactions, e.g., QoI across time/peers, pandemic effects, such as hysteresis in education induced by HEIs closures, could be identified, informing corrective policies by HEIs.

6.1 Limitations and Practical Implications

The presented case served as a test-bed for the efficacy of the FuzzyQoI model to depict the impact of the Covid-19 emergency on the QoI of the students and professors when interacting with LMS. Is seemed that a trend of periodicity was detected in intermediate indicators and also in the QoI that was outputted upon them [15]. This trend follows a timeline segmentation that coincides with social and psychological dimensions due to Covid-19. However, possible triangulation of these results with other measures like (questionaries and/or interviews with sample of the participants) may contribute the verification of this coincidence. Moreover, the use of the FuzzyQoI model with larger LMS databases amid Covid-19 might allow for statistical generalization of its results. Yet, towards this direction more open databases (diminishing the ethics constrains) from the Covisd-19 era might contribute.

The efficacy of the FuzzyQoI model to monitor the users' QoI while interacting with LMS has been verified [15] and could contribute to HEIs towards their move to new models for online programs as declared in the 2020 Horizon report [24], irrespectively from Covid-19. However, due to Covid-19 pandemic, a challenge for HEIs worldwide has emerged to engage students/learners and make them actively participate in the online teaching-learning process. Though Covid-19 had a severe impact on established educational progress, HEIs can take this unexpected opportunity to reformulate and rethink about online education practices through the integration of innovative course content by using efficient teaching-learning management systems [25]. The emergency situation put the focus on the technological aspect of the adaptation to the new situation and a lot of effort was placed to the technological knowledge. However, the presented approach, by means of the FuzzyQoI model, revealed that the pandemic situation may influence the

QoI while interacting with LMS. Thus, it provides the teachers with practical indicators to interpret the student's QoI with the LMS. Moreover, it contributes to the awareness of sociocultural and psychological issues that might disrupt QoI with LMS during online learning during emergency situations like Covid-19. The latter contribution, based on data from the first wave of Covid-19, may inform online learning community for remedy actions towards possible next waves.

7 Conclusions

A more enhanced shift of HEIs to online learning was anticipated in the forthcoming years, yet it was accelerated due to Covid-19. The present work aimed at monitoring the QoI with LMS amid Covid-19. Towards this direction, a Greek HEI's course was used as a case study to monitor the QoI of the participating 52 students and 2 Professors for a total duration of 26 weeks amid Covid-19. On the basis of the alterations of official measures that were taken for the protection against Covid-19 in Greece, a segmentation of the total duration of the monitoring period was performed in specific periods. By means of the FuzzyQoI model and for each time period, intermediate indicators concerning the participants' interactions with Moodle LMS were extracted upon which the QoI indicator was also calculated. Indices of periodicity for all the indicators were detected and when "translated" with the lenses of Covid-19, sociocultural and psychological issues were surfaced from possible impacts of the Covid-19 era to the QoI. Although the present conclusions are based on a case, the work attempts to reveal other aspects, than the mere technological adaptation to the emergency situation, that have to be considered towards sustainable online learning.

Acknowledgments. The authors would like to thank the eLearning Administrators of AUTH for their assistance in LMS Moodle access.

References

1. Shahzad, A., Hassan, R., Aremu, A.Y., Hussain, A., Lodhi, R.N.: Effects of COVID-19 in E-learning on higher education institution students: the group comparison between male and female. Qual. Quan. 1–22 (2020). https://doi.org/10.1007/s11135-020-01028-z
2. Dhawan, S.: Online learning: a panacea in the time of COVID-19 crisis. J. Educ. Technol. Syst. **49**(1), 5–22 (2020)
3. Johnson, N., Veletsianos, G., Seaman, J.: US faculty and administrators' experiences and approaches in the early weeks of the COVID-19 pandemic. Online Learn. **24**(2), 6–21 (2020)
4. Bisht, R.K., Jasola, S., Bisht, I.P.: Acceptability and challenges of online higher education in the era of COVID-19: a study of students' perspective. In: Asian Education and Development Studies (2020). https://doi.org/10.1108/AEDS-05-2020-0119. Accessed 16 Sept 2020
5. UNESCO (nd.): Education 2030, Incheon declaration and framework for action for the implementation of Sustainable Development Goal 4. https://unesdoc.unesco.org/ark:/48223/pf0000245656. Accessed 8 Oct 2020. Accessed 16 Sept 2020
6. Huang, R.H., Liu, D.J., Tlili, A., Yang, J.F., Wang, H.H., et al.: Handbook on facilitating flexible learning during educational disruption: the Chinese experience in maintaining undisrupted learning in COVID-19 outbreak. Smart Learning Institute of Beijing Normal University, Beijing (2020)

7. Ryan, A., Tilbury, D.: Flexible Pedagogies: New Pedagogical Ideas. Higher Education Academy, London (2013)
8. Oliver, M., Trigwell, K.: Can 'blended learning' be redeemed? E-learn. Digit. Media **2**, 17–26 (2005)
9. Garrison, D.R., Kanuka, H.: Blended learning: Uncovering its transformative potential in higher education. Internet High. Educ. **7**, 95–105 (2004)
10. Anderson, T., Liam, R., Garrison, D.R., Archer, W.: Assessing teaching presence in a computer conferencing context. J. Asynchronous Learn. Netw. **5**, 1–7 (2001)
11. Kidd, T.: Key aspects affecting students' perception regarding the instructional quality of online and web-based courses. Instr. Technol. Dist. Learn. **2**(10), 55–61 (2005)
12. Lim, C., Lee, S.: Pedagogical usability checklist for ESL/EFL e-learning websites. J. Converg. Inf. Technol. **2**, 67–76 (2007)
13. Grant, M.R., Thornton, H.R.: Best practices in undergraduate adult-centered online learning: mechanisms for course design and delivery. J. Online Learn. Teach. **3**, 346–356 (2007)
14. Sheard, J.I., Albrecht, D.W., Butbul, E.: ViSION: visualizing student interactions online. In: Proceedings of the Eleventh Australasian World Wide Web Conference, pp. 48–58. Southern Cross University, Lismore (2005)
15. Dias, S.B., Diniz, J.A.: FuzzyQoI model: a fuzzy logic-based modelling of users' quality of interaction with a learning management system under blended learning. Comput. Educ. **69**, 38–59 (2013)
16. Tsoukalas, H.L., Uhrig, R.E.: Fuzzy and Neural Approaches in Engineering. Wiley, New York (1996)
17. Cucinotta, D., Vanelli, M.: WHO declares COVID-19 a pandemic. Acta Bio-Medica: Atenei Parmensis **91**(1), 157–160 (2020)
18. Gonzalez, T., et al.: Influence of COVID-19 confinement on students' performance in higher education. PLoS ONE **15**(10), e0239490 (2020)
19. Fidani, A., Idrizi, F.: Investigating students' acceptance of a learning management system in university education: a structural equation modeling approach. In: ICT Innovations 2012 Web Proceedings, pp. 311–320 (2012)
20. Gruzd, A., Staves, K., Wilk, A.: Connected scholars: examining the role of social media in research practices of faculty using the UTAUT model. Comput. Hum. Behav. **28**(6), 2340–2350 (2012)
21. Raza, S., Qazi, W., Khan, K., Salam, J.: Social isolation and acceptance of the learning management system (LMS) in the time of COVID-19 pandemic: an expansion of the UTAUT model. J. Educ. Comput. Res. **59**(2), 183–208 (2020). https://doi.org/10.1177/0735633120960421
22. Tomei, J., Beaufait, P., Lavin, R.: Identity in online education. In: Proceedings of Education for a Digital World: Advice, Guidelines and Effective Practice from Around the Globe, pp. 461–474. BCampus and Commonwealth of Learning, Vancouver (2015)
23. Christensen, C.M., Horn, M.B., Johnson, C.W.: Disrupting Class: How Disruptive Innovation will Change the Way the World Learns. McGraw Hill, New York (2011)
24. Brown, M., et al.: 2020 Educause Horizon Report Teaching and Learning Edition. EDUCAUSE (2020)
25. Sun, L., Tang, Y., Zuo, W.: Coronavirus pushes education online. Nat. Mater. **19**(6), 687–687 (2020)

Design Teaching and Learning in Covid-19 Times: An International Experience

Paulo Ferreira[1(✉)], Filipa Oliveira Antunes[1], Haroldo Gallo[2], Marcos Tognon[2], and Heloisa Mendes Pereira[2]

[1] Lusófona University, Lisbon, Portugal
paulo.ferreira@ulusofona.pt
[2] Campinas University (UNICAMP), Campinas, Brasil

Abstract. The present article is about the academic partnership between the University of Campinas (Campinas, Brazil) and the Lusófona University (Lisbon, Portugal) for the adoption of a distance-learning methodology to students in the first year of Architecture and Urbanism at UNICAMP during COVID-19 lockdown. The contents from the online course "Drawing for Graphic Diary" were made available to UNICAMP students with minor adaptions.

Three didactic practices were implemented to face the pandemic restrictions: 1) biweekly tasks to be done in the LusofonaX – Digital Academy LMS environment; 2) online advice to students to resolve doubts; 3) online synchronous classes with course teachers detailing the exercises and visual expressive modalities.

The course design assessment was done through questionnaires that were carried out to students using Google Forms at two different moments: 1) before the course, to identify pre-existing skills and available knowledge about drawing concepts. For this, the authors depart from the following eight concepts as indicators of pre-existing competences for drawing: conic projection, two-dimensionality, surface, three-dimensionality, vanishing point, perspective construction, visual field and visual expression. After the course (2), to assess the perceived evolution of these same concepts through self-reported measures about the perceived knowledge acquired by students. Final student evaluation for the course was accessed with the Net Promoter Score (NPS). Results from the t-Tests and the NPS point to the success of the course methodology to deliver distance learning in the subject of design teaching compared to regular classes.

Keywords: Drawing · Remote education · Covid19 · NPS · Online education · Open edx · MOOC's

1 Introduction

Through an existing partnership of institutional cooperation, between the University of Campinas - UNICAMP (Brazil) and Lusófona University (Portugal), a group of lecturers and graduate students of both countries was created to apply the remote teaching system from the course "Drawing for Graphic Diary" into the UNICAMP course degree. This research aims to describe the methodology used to adopt the already existing course

A. Reis et al. (Eds.): TECH-EDU 2020, CCIS 1384, pp. 263–278, 2021.
https://doi.org/10.1007/978-3-030-73988-1_20

Drawing for Graphic Diary [5] and to evaluate the scope, objectives and needs for use it for teaching the *AP211 – Artistic Drawing for Architecture and Urbanism course* at UNICAMP. Additionally, this research also pretends to evaluate the results based on three metrics: (1) the completion rate, (2) the self-reported measures from students about their perceived knowledge and, finally, (3) the will to recommend the course to others. This research results also from the resilience of the teaching staff and students from both HEI's in making it possible during the period of social isolation and suspension of academic activities from March to July 2020.

The first metric, the MOOC completion rate is one of the most widely used metrics to evaluate the success of a MOOC [13]. According to the available literature on MOOCs, the average completion rate is about 5%, which means that only five students in 100 finish the course after enrolment. There are possibly several reasons for it. Rai and Chunrao [14] identify four possible reasons for this. These four characteristics are (1) learners as information viewers, or collectors rather than active users, (2) minimum learning by doing, (3) lack of personal support and human intervention, and (4) high difficulty level and lack of Self-Motivation, uncontrolled and undisciplined environment.

The courses of the undergraduate program in Architecture and Urbanism, which require significant in-person learning activities, such as live projects and workshops, artistic and technical drawing, laboratories in general, etc., were immediately impacted. This gave rise to the high risk that teachers would not be able to meet their objectives, if they taught remotely, on Internet-based platforms. It should be highlighted that both students and teachers, particularly the latter, were ill-prepared conceptually, methodologically and technologically to deal with this unexpected and unprecedented situation. If the impact education, in general, was enormous, it was more intense in the contexts where the tradition of the trainer – trainee *intimate* relationship as well as mimetic and repetitive practices are more intense, as is the case of teaching and learning in artistic areas, such as in drawing, painting, music, among others.

A critical factor in a teaching and learning process is the mutual knowledge that is usually shared among students about the work they produce. Available literature about MOOCs success identifies the feeling of community and human feedback as an important factor for distance course design [13]. This collaborative approach [16] not only generates a comparative framework of shared competences and vocations but also fosters active reciprocity among participants, developing a necessary academic interaction of open collaboration among all.

The second element for increasing the success rate was applying learning by doing methodology. Learning by doing has always been present in the field of Architecture [1, 4]. Rai and Chunrao [14] identify the lack or minimum of learning by doing approach as one of the key factors for low MOOCs success rate. Since drawing is an operative action, that speaking is not teaching, nor is listening is learning: learn to draw demands doing it, besides, of course, reflecting on what was done [11]. Therefore, the purpose of this course was to break initial barriers, eliminate inhibitions and fears associated with the act of drawing through its practice. As Rai and Chunrao [14] affirm "modern innovate education tools help students to understand what to learn, but fail to produce enough interest on how to learn, and also fail to produce critical thinking among students." Our research tries to overcome these difficulties pushing the practice to the centre of the learning process supported in close collaboration between all the agents [6].

In this way, the remote drawing course "Drawing for Graphic Diary", available before the outbreak of the pandemic, offered a learning structure that was, simultaneously, characterized by a linear set of classes, videos, exercises, questionnaires and for peer-review assignments for each course module. The peer-review assignments were taken from the UNICAMP course design version since teachers would review and evaluate each final student exercises and be present for assignment review and to given support through live sessions.

The self-reported measures from students about their perceived knowledge before and after the course were build based on the framework proposed by Ching and Juroszek for teaching drawing [15]. The authors developed a teaching framework based on three phases: (1) drawing from observation, that introduces the graphic elements that constitute the vocabulary of drawing - line, shape, tone, form and space, (2) formal systems for representing three-dimensional objects and space, and (3) speculative manner to stimulate the design process. From the proposed framework, and from the experience of the authors of this research in teaching drawing for students in higher education institutions, the authors elected eight critical concepts that would be considered as elementary units of knowledge for the process of drawing.

The concepts were:

1. **Conic projection**: concept and practice by doing;
2. **Two-dimensionality**: concept and practice by doing;
3. **Surface**: concept and practice by doing;
4. **Three-dimensionality**: concept and practice by doing;
5. **Vanishing Point**: concept and practice by doing;
6. **Perspective Construction**: concept and practice by doing;
7. **Visual Field**: concept and practice by doing;
8. **Visual Expression**: concept and practice by doing.

The student perceived knowledge about these concepts will be used as metrics to evaluate the student's evolution before and after the course.

2 The UNICAMP Online Course Adaption

2.1 Research Methodology

With the goal to identifying each students' level of knowledge in the eight concepts presented bellow, questionnaires were applied to participants in two distinct stages: (1) before the course, to identify existing self-reported competences and knowledge in the area of artistic drawing; (2) after the course, to evaluate the evolution of these same competences and knowledge acquired.

The questionnaires were developed by the research team, and among others, specific questions were included to assess the initial and end levels each of the eight concepts that were considered to evaluate the teaching/learning process.

In the two questionnaires used in this study, the level for each of these concepts was assessed by a 7-point scale, where one (1) corresponds to "I know nothing about it" and seven (7) to "I understand this concept very well". For measuring each competence, the students were asked to self-rate their perceived knowledge: "Rate your present level of understanding of the concept of..." followed by the name of the competence. For example, for Conic Projection, the question was: *Rate your present level of understanding of the concept of Conic Projection.*

Finally, for accessing the overall course satisfaction, the Net Promotor Score scale was applied in the same questionnaire.

2.2 Objectives and Implemented Didactic Practices

This research departs from this framework for implementing the course version for UNICAMP students. This was a unique opportunity, since the course available regularly at LusofonaX [17] lack some of the characteristics presented above for staff availability reasons (the course is usually offered live on campus, with LusofonaX being only a support system for the learning process).

Teaching drawing concepts and practice in the first years of an architect's training is and has always been a great challenge. It requires the deployment and acquisition of not only critical theoretical concepts but also of a body of resources that include practical methods and stances to be applied by students to each exercise. With the COVID-19 lockdown, we were all faced with a more significant challenge. In the Architecture and Urbanism undergraduate programme, the courses relating to the practice of drawing, be it artistic, technical, and project-oriented, require the comprehension of an indispensable set of competences and knowledge. Developing and acquiring forms of expression that are relevant in architecture and urbanism requires important self-expression from of its author's identity, their ideas, their creative universe that is needed to communicate an idea, a concept, an emotion.

The traditional methods of teaching drawing have always been based on three critical didactical principles, from the Accademia del Disegno [12], founded by Giorgio Vasari in Florence in 1563. These principles are (1) the progressive and consequent application, in difficulty and ability, of exercises of manual skill and expression; (2) the systematic monitoring by the teachers at every result obtained, allowing corrections, improvements, and finally (3) mastering the various nuances of the graphic language, between the subjective and the adopted conventions for an objective interpretation, for instance, of technical projects.

The global framework of the Covid-19 pandemic imposed social lockdown, and consequent interruption of all face-to-face activities, the activities in all Architecture schools in Brazil (as in the world) were abruptly interrupted. In Brazil, the interruption happened a few weeks into the new academic year.

The nature of the course "Unicamp – drawing for graphic diary" is to serve as an introduction to artistic drawing for students of the first year of the bachelor's degree in architecture and urbanism. Its prime objective is to foster the development of "visual thinking", along with the acquisition of specific competencies, by learning different modalities of graphic expression, using multiple manual techniques and materials.

The different exercises and contents were through didactical videos, produced with the intent to show the process of drawing in real-time, highlighting their development with the application of a mix of techniques and audio comments. This approach contributes to debunking the idea that drawing is merely the result of a "natural gift".

Overcoming the absence of conviviality and teacher supervision during the training activities required from both the teams to change the presentation of concepts procedures, exercises and techniques but also to create a class routine and activities schedule. This new routine should enable the daily monitoring of the results achieved by the students, as alternative means for the acquisition of the competencies required by academic training.

Thus, aiming to achieve these objectives and methods, a framework was designed that could provide and ensure the dynamics needed among all involved. The course framework was developed as follows:

1. Each module was made available every two weeks with tasks to be carried out within the environment of LusofonaX;

   a. Each module contains several recorded video lessons for each unit showing the teacher applying in real time the specific technique and materials, a quiz and an optional practice assignment to students for each unit;

2. Online supervision to students, by e-mail and personal individual and group counselling scheduled via Google Meet, to deal with queries;

   a. The team from UNICAMP was responsible for all the support to students, be it through the online forum available on LusofonaX, Google Meet or email.

3. Online classes with teachers of the course, detailing the exercises and modalities of graphic expression;

   a. At the end of each module live classes took place, with UNICAMP students and the teachers from UNICAMP and Lusofona;
   b. This live lessons through Google Meet were recorded and made available later through LusofonaX LMS
   c. In the different live sessions, the current module assignment was draw live and explained by the teachers so students could take any doubt they had.
   d. After the drawings, each teacher explain different approaches possible and materials;
   e. Finally a period of Q&A for students was available.

Conducting these three practices at the same time, allowed regular and consistent interaction between students and teachers. The hourly workload previewed for the online course was higher than defined for the face-to-face course. The online course staff determined a minimum of 6 h per week based on the workload expected when the regular course is of 3 h per week. The final course structure with the different modules and assigments is presented in following table (Table 1).

Table 1. Modules and course assignments for each module / unit

Module/Unit	Assignment	Type
01/Box 2D|Two-dimensionality, orthogonal projection: Plan and view	Produce the front and side view of an object at hand scale, without the aid of ruler, with rigor and proportion, taking into account invisible lines, intersections and limits	Optional
01/Box 3D|Three-dimensionality, axonometric and conic projection;	Produce an axonometric perspective and a conical perspective of an object scale, starting from a front elevation in true grandeur, without ruler aid, with rigor and proportion, taking into account the lines invisible, intersections and limits	Optional
01/Box Surfaces|Conic with textures and conic with shadows	Represent two conical perspectives with two vanishing points from an object to scale of the hand, without the aid of a ruler, with rigor and proportion, taking consideration the texture of visible surfaces and the proper and projected shadows	Optional
01/Module Assignment	Represent a set of steps using the methodology of the perspective with the graphic marking of the different surfaces through the stain, with different shades depending on the direction and light	Compulsory for course grading
02/Interior space|Perspective construction with 1 and 2 vanishing points;	Draw two conical perspectives with one and two vanishing points from one architectural space, without the aid of a ruler, with rigor and proportion, taking into consideration the perspective convergence of parallel elements and the expressiveness of the fundamental traces	Optional
02/Exterior space|Perspective construction;	Draw a conical perspective with a vanishing point from an outer space (street), without the help of a ruler, with rigor and proportion, taking into account the perspective of the elements and the expressiveness of the outlines and fundamental surfaces	Optional

(*continued*)

Table 1. (*continued*)

Module/Unit	Assignment	Type
02/Exterior space|Perspective construction with human figure	Draw a conical perspective with a vanishing point of a space outside (street), without the help of ruler, with rigor and proportion, taking considering the notion of scale by the positioning of several figures in the different planes of the drawing (1st, 2nd planes and background)	Optional
02/Module Assignment	Students should design a space with a sense of depth using a progressive perspective grid	Compulsory for course grading
03/Graphite sticks|Gradation;	Draw a space, without the aid of a ruler, with rigor and proportion, taking into considering the notion of scale by the positioning of the various elements in the different planes of the drawing [**]. The values should be taken into account expressive removed from textures, shadows… or background, registering the full and the empty	Optional
03/Water-colour|Transparencies;	[**] The values should be taken into account expressive from the transparencies and chromatic densities of the watercolor, registering the configurations in black ink at the end	Optional
03/Water-colour brush pens|structure; - Water-colour pencils|over-lapping	[**] The values should be taken into account expressions taken from the transparencies and chromatic overlays of the pencil watercolourable, registering at the beginning the regulatory outlines of configuration	Optional
03/Module Assignment	Select an object to draw. It should represent the volume and the respective double-colored sparkles (two opposite colors) in dachina paint, coffee, pastel or watercolor. Finish with a black pen at the limit of various components	Compulsory for course grading
04/Coffee|Volume;	[**]The values should be taken into account expressive from the singular pigment of coffee, registering in the beginning the fundamental stains for understanding the volume, and only at the end of regulatory traces of the entire contrast setting (negative / positive)	Optional

(*continued*)

Table 1. (*continued*)

Module/Unit	Assignment	Type
04/China ink|High contrast; - Pastel|Background	[**]The values should be taken into account significant figures taken from the density of the Chinese ink, recording only the fundamental stains for understanding depth and height contrast, without defining strokes, only surfaces	Optional
04/Module Assignment	Select an outer space to draw. The Design must be initiated by coloring with one of the materials used, such as watercolor or the pencils, and at the end it will be outlined with the main components using different thicknesses of black pen	Compulsory for course grading

Carrying out such practices had the collaboration of all the teachers involved, who had access to and full control of the digital platforms used and could steer all the methods quickly minimizing any possible harm of a remotely-taught course. It was also necessary to give training to the group of UNICAMP students and teachers in the use of the LusofonaX platform. First, the team from Lusofona defined a training plan to the UNICAMP teachers staff. After that, the UNICAMP team did initial training for students remotely. The training presentations were recorded and then made available to students so that they could refer back to it whenever necessary. Generally, students did not report to the UNICAMP team any problems using the LusofonaX LMS.

It should be emphasized that UNICAMP University is a public, free University, and part of its students comes from low wage aggregates, as derived from its inclusive social policies. For this reason, some of the students did not possess the necessary equipment, namely personal computers, needed for the course. For them, the Rectory provided immediately a computer loan system, which some students joined.

2.3 The Course Framework

The course was carried out using two digital platforms: the environment of LusofonaX Learning Management System (powered by OpenedX), provided by Lusófona University, and Google Meet, made available by Unicamp.

LusófonaX hosted the contents and materials for the course. The original course design structure was developed by the Lusófona University team. Then it was adapted for UNICAMP students following a learning plan divided into bimonthly sections. Small adjustments were made to the initial setup, mainly regarding the evaluation method so that the course could be delivered to a class of regular students at the bachelor's degree in Architecture and Urbanism of Unicamp. The final curriculum was structured in the following sections (Fig. 1):

- Introdutcion and course materials;

- Introductory live session;
- Module 01 – Codification of the Visual Field - Objects;
- Module 02 – Codification of the Visual Field - Space;
- Module 03 – Codification of Expression – Part 1;
- Module 04 – Codification of Expression – Part 2;
- Module 05 – Drawing at home – Final Exercise;
- Design Labs.

In the first section, “Welcome note”, students had access to a presentation of the course, including the identification of objectives, methods, evaluation elements and an introductory lecture on “Media, materials and techniques”. The following section was “Course Lives” which offered the live classes taught by the lecturers, so that, even when the student was unable to participate in the activity, the content was available to be accessed later. In this way, the loss of the mimetic effect in the teaching process was minimized. There was a need to adjust the schedules of the activities, making them flexible to enable the participation of people from two different continents.

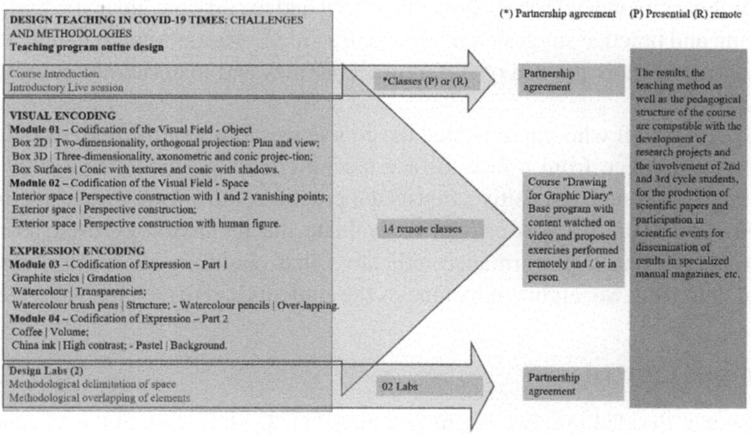

Fig. 1. Course framework outline design

The main didactic load, where most of the contents and development of competences could be found, was distributed between modules 1 to 4. These modules were composed of different subsections in which the subject matter was conveyed by video and text, followed by a quiz and a mid-term exercise for retention and practice. At the end of each module, there was a subsection with a problem and a submission for the final drawing for evaluation of the student in each module. Module 05, the final one, consisted of the proposal for the course’s final assignment (Fig. 2).

Finally, this learning roadmap also included two extra contents, which were made available to students of the course as experimental laboratories to enrich the experience further. These laboratories were composed by two additionally recorded videos that addressed two particular topics, relevant to the practice of artistic drawing: (1) the

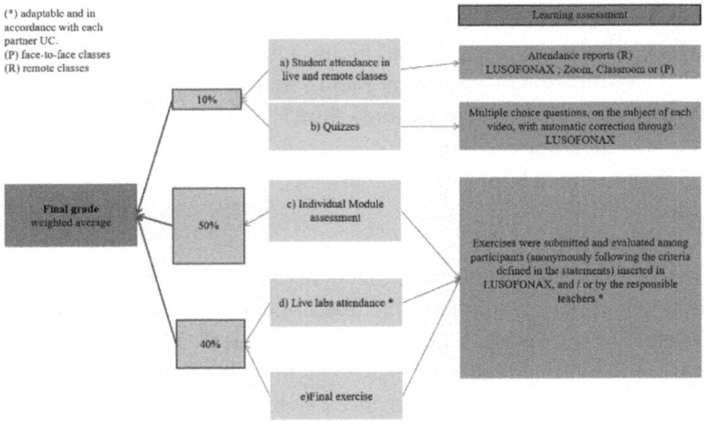

Fig. 2. General course assignment division

methodological delimitation of space, and (2) the methodological overlapping of elements. For this extra video lessons students did not had to carry out any extra assignment. The viewing and practice suggested in these extra videos was optional for students. They were produced to show the use of different techniques and material not covered in the course curriculum.

The teaching staff who implemented the course was aware of the high risks involved in the *(forced)* change from a face-to-face teaching/learning model to a fully remote mode, especially in such a sensitive area as the practice of drawing. Therefore, measure the outputs of the course was critical to evaluate the methodology used. For it was fundamental to identify performance indicators that could enable us to measure the success of our effort. So, eight competencies the students had to develop were identified.

2.4 Contents Covered

The course was divided into two learning topics: (1) “Codification of the Visual Field”, further divided into object and space, and (2) “Codification of the Expression”, subdivided into part 1 and part 2. In the codification of the visual field and, later, regarding expressive codification, drawing assumes the position that technical knowledge leads to a connotative value, not merely a descriptive and denotative one, of the object in time and in space.

We present below the list of specific topics of the course which were addressed in the core modules of the learning roadmap:

- Module 01 – Codification of the Visual Field - Object
  - Box 2D|Two-dimensionality, orthogonal projection: Plan and view;
  - Box 3D|Three-dimensionality, axonometric and conic projection;
  - Box Surfaces|Conic with textures and conic with shadows.
- Module 02 – Codification of the Visual Field - Space

  - Interior space|Perspective construction with 1 and 2 vanishing points;
  - Exterior space|Perspective construction;
  - Exterior space|Perspective construction with human figure.

- Module 03 – Codification of Expression – Part 1

  - Graphite sticks|Gradation;
  - Water-colour|Transparencies;
  - Water-colour brush pens|structure; - Water-colour pencils|overlapping.

- Module 04 – Codification of Expression – Part 2

  - Coffee|Volume;
  - China ink|High contrast; - Pastel|Background.

Each of the course units explores at least one of the eight concepts that are part of the course pedagogical plan. Some course units mix several concepts in the same unit. The following table (Table 2) illustrates the correspondence between each course unit and at least one of the concepts embedded in it.

Table 2. Correspondence between concepts and course units

Concept	Course unit
Conic projection	Module 1, 2
Two-dimensionality	Module 1
Surface	Module 1, 2
Three-dimensionality	Module 1, 2
Vanishing point	Module 1
Perspective construction	Module 2
Visual field	Modules 1, 2, 3 and 4
Visual expression	Module 3, Module 4

3 Results

The purpose of the course was to stimulate students to develop their drawing language grounded in concrete graphic representation concepts and techniques, regardless of the medium in which the learning process takes place. Under the pretext made possible by COVID-19, we aimed to evaluate the ability to successfully implement the practical teaching of drawing in a remote mode.

The assessment of the students' evolution, and consequently of the pedagogic methodology chosen for the course, was achieved in two ways: one, by applying questionnaires to the students; and two, by the individual evaluation of the drawings by the teachers.

The individual evaluation per module carried out by the lecturers was characterized by being implemented in interaction with the students. In this way, all students' drawing presentations, as well as their interpretation of their colleagues' work was taken into account, in a creative and highly fruitful process. Thus, at the end of each module, the drawings were brought together and presented, anonymously, to the class. This cross-feedback enriched the students' repertoire, as they were able to observe other interpretations of the same exercise. This approach encouraged them to revise their drawings and seek new forms, or readings, to improve the final product, and at the same time starting to discover and identify their unique and individual way of *seeing*.

For the analysis of the self-reported values for each question, the mean and the standard deviation (SD) for each one of the 8 questions were calculated. Besides the mean distribution for each question, the variation percentage between moment 1 (before the course) and moment 2 (after the course) was also calculated. The obtained data is summarised in Table 3 below.

Table 3. Summary with mean, standard deviation and variation rate in the response value

#	Competence	Pre-course		Post-course		V%	t
		Mean	SD	Mean	SD		
1	Conical projection	3.40	1.73	6.53	1.14	92%	**−11.03*****
2	Two-dimensionality	5.21	1.64	6.60	1.17	27%	**−5.73*****
3	Surface	4.85	1.59	6.62	1.15	37%	**−7.51*****
4	Three-dimensionality	5.19	1.57	6.67	1.09	28%	**−6.68*****
5	Vanishing point	5.17	1.69	6.69	1.13	29%	**−5.71*****
6	Perspective construction	4.43	1.87	6.47	1.25	46%	**−7.03*****
7	Visual field	4.30	1.61	6.31	1.23	47%	**−8.10*****
8	Visual expression	3.83	1.72	6.31	1.23	65%	**−9.60*****
	Total	**4.55**		**6.53**		**46%**	**−9.470*****

*p-value $\leq .05$, **p-value $\leq .01$, ***p value $\leq .001$

The mean values for each answer vary considerably, and their variation rate is a good indicator of the increase in perception reported on the acquisition of the expected outcomes defined for the course. In particular, we deem it important to mention the 92% variation in the competence conic perspective. For the total percentage variation, we observe an average increase of 46% between the answer values at the moment 1 and the answers at the moment 2. To test the hypothesis that the variation in answers between the two moments is indeed statistically significant, we conducted a t-Test: Paired Two Sample for Means which resulted in a significance value of $P(T \leq t)$ two-tail of 0.000, lower than 0.001, which indicates a statistically significant difference for the values of the means between moment 1 and moment 2 (Alpha of 0.05). Likewise, the t-tests applied individually to each of the individual measures (see Table 1) all obtained significant values for $p \leq .001$, which reinforces the hypothesis for the existence of differences in the self-reported measures by the students in the two moments considered. Based on these results, we can affirm with some degree of certainty that students' perception of their levels of competence between moment 1 and moment 2 has changed. The average value of the responses recorded at time 2 and the results of the general and individual t-tests applied to each question, allow us to conclude that the levels of competence perceived by students have increased considerably.

Finally, the student's drawings were evaluated by the teachers on a scale between 0–100. The evaluation was performed based on a set of pre-defined criteria. The final score is a weighted average of the grades of the quizzes, the interim exercises and the end exercise of each module, plus the final drawing assignment. From the 47 students who started the course, only two dropped, while the remainder of the class had pass scores, with performance averages ranging between 79 and 96.

It was observed by the authors that, as they advanced in the learning programme, students achieve better results in their evaluations. In some cases, the development and improvement in the student's skills regarding their critical ability vis-à-vis their drawing and graphic expression was quite clear (Fig. 3). This perception is reinforced by the results of the self-reported measures, which indicates a statistically significant difference between existing competencies at the moment 1 and those at the moment 2.

3.1 Developing a Critical Thinking Approach Through Peers and Teachers

Although we all regret the absence of direct contact with students in teaching drawing, its techniques, and materials, we can see some significant gains for students concerning the remote modality with continuous tutoring.

There are at least three factors that we assess through the results and the weekly follow-up, which allows us to evaluate positively the didactic experience proposed by our course in facing the limitations imposed by Covid-19.

First, the responsibility of the students in fulfilling each of the tasks on time. This can be assessed easily through the course success rate (98%). More, the intense use of their newly acquired skills and spatial references for the making of the exercises and the real-time interaction between the teacher's goals and the student's results for each activity. Course staff and teachers could receive meaningful feedback from students that allow improving the course in almost real-time.

The **second** was the creativity required for students to make their materials feasible, especially their graphic expression resources that are unusual in the presential classroom: porous tip pens, coffee water-colour pencils, and other natural pigments, pencils of different hardness, which required from all of us constant requirements reassessing. Although the design instruments and resources are variables that contribute to the result of excellence in professional work, creativity can be exercised and expressed through alternative and, sometimes, unusual tools.

The **third** reason, and probably the most significant factor of all this unprecedented experience due to the pandemic was the increase in the students' capacity to think

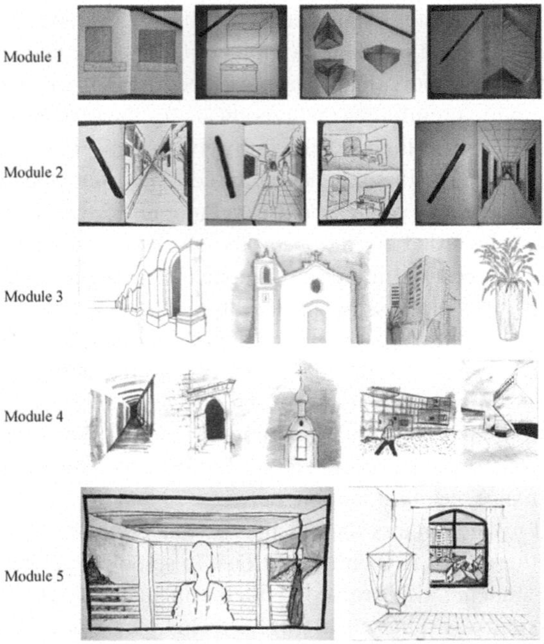

Fig. 3. Evolution of the drawings of three students. Left, final drawings of Module 01, Right, final drawings of Module 05. Source: Course collection.

critically and positively about their work, about their expression capacity in relation with other's work [2]. This was achieved mainly by confronting their results with those of their colleagues and with those presented by the teachers. The increase in students' critical thinking can be observed from the results that arise from individual student work, at each successive stage of the course, which allowed them to better understand the use of colours, textures, and to handle media more freely, such as notebooks or loose sheets, for the execution of the expected drawings.

These three factors together generated significant personal and academic gains, with growing responsibility for their training, self-discipline about work time and space, and their dedication and effort. Also, greater autonomy to be able to complete the rules of observation and analysis exercises more harmoniously, and thus demonstrate a full understanding of what was requested by the teachers. Finally, greater self-confidence to walk the path of a very demanding course, which required concrete progress in the development of expressive graphic skills essential for future architects and urban planners, all this in a very complex context for all the parts involved.

The efficiency of this set of new didactic practices adopted was acknowledged by the students themselves during the end-of-semester evaluation of the bachelor's degree at Unicamp.

3.2 Applying the Net Promoter Score (NPS) to Assess Course Satisfaction

The Net Promoter Score [10] is a measure widely used in the industry to evaluate customer satisfaction. Still, it's not common in the literature to use it to evaluate higher education courses. The NPS is a one-item scale with just one question to score the likelihood of a customer to recommend a service. The one-item question is measured through a 10 point Likert scale. Respondents should choose from "not at all Likely" to "Extremely likely" to the question "How likely is it that you would recommend our company/product/service to a friend or colleague". The NPS score range from -100 (worst) to 100 (best). A NPS above 0 is considered "good", above 50 is "excellent", and from 70 to 100 is considered "best in class" [10]. The design course scored 84 on the NPS, which is very good. The NPS is not a common metric for measuring student satisfaction in the higher education context. Nevertheless, a growing number of studies can be found where the use of NPS for academic purposes is used [3, 7, 8], namely in the assessment of MOOCs [9]. The growing market orientation of higher education institutions in an ever more competitive global market is pushing the need of looking to students as regular customers. The score of 84 could be a good initial indicator, but it lacks detail about what worked and what didn't work about the course.

4 Conclusions and Future Research

We conclude that a student-oriented course design approach in close interaction with the students is fruitful, and despite the physical distance, did not impede the success of the teaching/learning process. Provided that the experience is designed and implemented with rigour and aimed at distance learning, this type of initiatives, now fostered by COVID-19, may constitute moments of tremendous growth for all the involved. The course framework followed for this research, with focus on learning by doing approach, shared ways of doing and active monitoring allowed the team envolved in the course design to achieve a completion rate of 95%. Additionally, the importance given to the acquisition of creative and operational in drawing skills was fundamental, in the sense of the physical practice of the stroke allied to the reading, or decoding, of reality. Additionally, eight drawing concepts units were identified and were used to evaluate the course design. The analysis of the resulting data reveals a statistically significant difference that reinforces our belief about the apparent student's evolution. Also, the NPS rate of 84 is a valuable indicator of student satisfaction with the course methodology.

However, we should notice that the results presented in this article are based on the students' perception of the learning process, that is, the perceived learning and not the real learning output. Additional research should try to clarify where this perceived difference is real. Developing a research design based on A/B methodology could shed more light on the success of this course design methodology.

References

1. Ching, F.D.: Desenho para Arquitetos-2. Bookman Editora (2012)
2. D'Alessio, F.A., Avolio, B.E., Charles, V.: Studying the impact of critical thinking on the academic performance of executive MBA students. Think. Skills Creat. **31**, 275–283 (2019)

3. Dvorakova, L., Faltejskova, O.: Net promoter score use at university education sector. In: International Multidisciplinary Scientific Conference on Social Sciences & Arts SGEM, pp. 567–577 (2014)
4. Frampton, K., i Ramió, J.R.: Historia crítica de la arquitectura moderna. Gustavo Gili (2009)
5. Ferreira, P., Catarino, F.: Graphic diary mooc: developing a slow and learning by doing approach to drawing through graphic diaries. In: EDULEARN2020 (2020)
6. Gallo, H.: O croqui como instrumento de conhecimento. Registro de uma experiência internacional em arquitetura e urbanismo. Arquitextos, São Paulo, ano 19, n. 224.01, Vitruvius, Disponível em (2019). https://www.vitruvius.com.br/revistas/read/arquitextos/19.224/7273
7. Grisaffe, D.B.: Questions about the ultimate question: Conceptual considerations in evaluating Reichheld's net promoter score (NPS). J. Consum. Satisf. Dissatisf. Complain. Behav. **20**, 36 (2007)
8. Lee, S.: Net promoter score: using NPS to measure IT customer support satisfaction. In: Proceedings of the 2018 ACM SIGUCCS Annual Conference, pp. 63–64 (2018)
9. Palmer, K., Devers, C.: An evaluation of mooc success: net promoter scores. In: EdMedia+ Innovate Learning, Association for the Advancement of Computing in Education (AACE), pp. 1648–1653 (2018)
10. Reichheld, F.F., Covey, S.R.: The Ultimate Question: Driving Good Profits and True Growth, vol. 211. Harvard Business School Press, Boston (2006)
11. Ennis, R.H.: A concept of critical thinking. Harv. Educ. Rev. **32**, 81–111 (1962)
12. Jack, M.A.: The accademia del disegno in late renaissance florence. Sixteenth Century J. **7**, 3–20 (1976)
13. Henderikx, M., Kreijns, K., Kalz, M.: To change or not to change? That's the question… on MOOC-success, barriers and their implications. In: Delgado Kloos, C., Jermann, P., Pérez-Sanagustín, M., Seaton, D.T., White, S. (eds.) EMOOCs 2017. LNCS, vol. 10254, pp. 210–216. Springer, Cham (2017). https://doi.org/10.1007/978-3-319-59044-8_25
14. Rai, L., Chunrao, D.: Influencing factors of success and failure in MOOC and general analysis of learner behavior. Int. J. Inf. Educ. Technol. **6**(4), 262 (2016)
15. Ching, F.D., Juroszek, S.P.: Design Drawing. Wiley, Hoboken (2010)
16. Sein-Echaluce, M., Fidalgo-Blanco, Á., García-Peñalvo, F.: Adaptive and cooperative model of knowledge management in MOOCs. In: Zaphiris, P., Ioannou, A. (eds.) LCT 2017. LNCS, vol. 10295, pp. 273–284. Springer, Cham (2017). https://doi.org/10.1007/978-3-319-58509-3_22
17. https://cursos.lusofona-x.pt

Communicating Mathematics During Small Groupwork Through Video-Conferencing Applications

Raymond LaRochelle(✉), Michelle Cirillo, and Dawn Berk

University of Delaware, Newark, DE 19716, USA
rlaroche@udel.edu

Abstract. The Covid-19-induced closure of schools forced many instructors throughout the world to develop ways to deliver instruction online. Video-conferencing applications became one prominent tool for instructors to continue instruction. We report the perceptions of undergraduate mathematics students and preservice mathematics teachers who interacted in online "workshops." In the online workshops, students worked on mathematics problems in small groups while preservice teachers supported their work. Two rounds of semi-structured interviews with both groups were conducted, wherein participants compared and contrasted their experiences with in-person and online group work. Analyses revealed three challenges with respect to online communication: (a) limited access to one another's written mathematical work, (b) limited ability to have one-on-one conversations, and (c) the tendency for students to leave their cameras turned off during the workshops. In particular, we emphasize that the multimodal nature of mathematics requires extra attention to strategies for sharing symbolic, diagrammatic, gestural, and other non-verbal ways of communicating mathematics.

Keywords: Mathematics · Online Communication · Discourse · Active Learning

1 Introduction

At the undergraduate level, professional organizations strongly encourage mathematics instructors to engage students in groupwork, authentic problem solving, and other active-learning activities to support their learning [1, 2]. When the Covid-19-induced closure of schools began, many instructors around the world had to quickly adapt their instruction to an online setting [3, 4]. This shift presented unique challenges for instructors implementing active learning, particularly in mathematics, which is a multimodal subject. Consequently, it is worthwhile to understand what affordances and constraints

This material is based upon work supported by the National Science Foundation (NSF; Collaborative Award #1726364, PI: Michelle Cirillo). Any opinions, findings, and conclusions or recommendations expressed in this material are those of the authors and do not necessarily reflect the views of the NSF.

A. Reis et al. (Eds.): TECH-EDU 2020, CCIS 1384, pp. 279–286, 2021.
https://doi.org/10.1007/978-3-030-73988-1_21

video-conferencing applications provide for supporting synchronous online mathematics groupwork. We describe three challenges that were identified by undergraduate students related to engaging in groupwork in a foundational mathematics course over the Zoom application (v 5.4.2), a currently prevalent video-conferencing application [4, 5].

The study presented here is set in a section of a precalculus course at a doctoral-granting institution in the United States. After the online shift, the precalculus instructors at this university endeavored to continue implementing groupwork activities in online "workshops," hosted through Zoom. In addition, this precalculus section was hosting an early field experience for preservice secondary mathematics teachers (i.e., preservice teachers training to teach students of age 12 – 18) who assisted small groups during the workshops [6].

In prior work, we reported the perceived benefits of continuing the early field experience after the online shift, as reflected by the stakeholders involved in the course [6]. Here, we focus on one type of reflection that consistently emerged during interviews with the precalculus students and preservice teachers regarding their experiences with groupwork in the course - reflections on the challenges of communicating mathematics over Zoom. Our research question is: *What difficulties with regard to communicating mathematics through a video-conferencing platform are identified by precalculus students who engaged in online groupwork activities and by preservice teachers who supported those students during the online groupwork activities?*

2 Literature Review: Communicating Mathematics During Online Groupwork

An important goal for instructors of all disciplines is to help students develop appropriate ways to communicate within their domain [7]. Mathematics is no exception, and researchers have become increasingly aware of the important and complex ways that language supports mathematical engagement and learning [7–9]. In particular, teachers must support students' development of the *mathematics register*, which not only includes learning mathematical vocabulary, but also learning unique grammar, syntax, and sentence structures for expressing mathematical ideas. In addition, there are many different modes of communicating mathematics beyond language that students must learn, such as mathematical symbols, diagrams, tables, graphs, and gestures; and each mode has its own sets of affordances and constraints [7, 9]. For example, mathematical notation allows one to condense meanings and generalized relationships into fewer symbols than what language allows. As another example, a mathematical diagram allows one to convey meanings and relationships along multiple spatial dimensions, which is not feasible through language and mathematical notation. Hence, mathematical notation and mathematical diagrams provide distinct (and complex) avenues for communicating mathematical ideas. For these reasons, mathematics has been described as a "multimodal, semiotic enterprise, the outcome of using language, symbolic notation and mathematics images to describe and predict patterns in space, number, quantity and arrangement" (p. 72) [9].

Research about synchronous computer mediated content-focused communication focuses heavily on text-based communication (e.g., chat, email) in foreign language courses [10]. Our study contributes to the literature by investigating the use of a video-conferencing application in an online mathematics course. Because mathematics is a "multimodal, semiotic enterprise," implementing effective authentic groupwork activities in an online environment requires an online tool that allows students to not only discuss ideas with one another, but also to easily share written words, gestures, notation, and diagrams with one another [7, 9, 11].

Of the papers we reviewed regarding synchronous computer-mediated communication in mathematics classrooms, most studies considered dynamic whiteboards, chat forums, and email [12–14]. Only one of these papers discussed the use of video-conferencing applications for online synchronous teaching, and these researchers focused on ways teachers can learn from each other to develop best practices for teaching in online environments [15]. We did not find articles about the affordances and constraints of video-conferencing applications for communicating mathematics during online groupwork. Hence, here we share some of the challenges of video-conferencing applications for supporting synchronous online groupwork in mathematics, as expressed by participants in the groupwork activities.

3 Methods

Data presented here comes from a larger study focused on an innovative model of early field experience for preservice teachers, which takes place in an undergraduate precalculus course designed to provide students with opportunities to engage in active learning of mathematics [16]. In this paper, we focus on students' comments about communicating mathematics during groupwork over Zoom, the video-conferencing application used for the shift to online instruction [5]. Because the shift happened mid-semester, and because the planned groupwork activities continued to be implemented, the precalculus students (PCSs) and preservice secondary mathematics teachers (PSTs) experienced the same course/setting with the same instructor/field supervisor, classmates, and mathematical activities in both in-person and online settings. Hence, the online shift allowed us to investigate affordances and constraints of Zoom for communicating mathematics while controlling for several variables. It is important to note that we are treating Zoom as a proxy for all similar video-conferencing applications, and, even though we consistently refer to Zoom throughout the paper, we believe our results are applicable for other similar video-conferencing platforms.

3.1 Participants and Classroom Context

Participants were recruited from one section of a precalculus course at a U.S. university. The precalculus course was designed to include opportunities for active learning. In total, there were 44 PCSs in this section. Eight PCSs participated in the first round of interviews, and eight participated in the second round of interviews, including two PCSs who participated in both rounds. In the first round, PCSs were selected based on a range of course grades. In the second round, we endeavored to select PCSs who had consistently attended class and thus experienced groupwork both in-person and online. In addition, this section of Precalculus hosted an innovative early field experience for

PSTs. An important part of the early field experience was that the PSTs were required to sit at tables with PCSs during instruction and assist during groupwork activities, assuming a teacher-like role [6]. There were 12 PSTs in this section, and six of these students participated in both rounds of interviews. These six were representative of the larger group in terms of gender and course grades.

After the university shifted to online instruction, the precalculus instructors modified instruction in two ways in order for it to be delivered online. First, they created videos to deliver the course material, which PCSs were asked to view asynchronously. Second, each instructor hosted optional online Zoom "workshops" for their respective sections wherein PCSs worked on problem-solving tasks in small groups. The precalculus instructor allowed the PSTs to continue their early field experience by working with PCSs in the workshops. Hence, when classes resumed for online instruction, the instructor, PCSs, and PSTs met twice weekly to work on problems together over Zoom.

3.2 Data Collection and Analysis

Data was collected in two rounds of semi-structured interviews. Interviews were conducted and recorded over Zoom. Interviews focused on the shift to online instruction (Round 1), and on comparing and contrasting online and in-person experiences in the class (Round 2). PCSs were asked to share their thoughts about their opportunities to learn mathematics over Zoom (e.g., How do you feel about your experiences learning mathematics in an online platform?). PSTs were asked their thoughts about PCSs' opportunities to learn over Zoom as well as their own opportunities to learn about teaching (e.g., How do you feel about your experiences teaching PCSs in an online platform?).

Data analysis involved phases similar to those described by Creswell and Poth [17]. In Phase I, all three authors watched a subset of the interviews and took notes on patterns and themes in the data. In Phase II, the team met to propose codes and develop an initial codebook. In Phase III, the codebook was refined by applying, revising, and re-applying the codes to additional interviews until we agreed on a final set of codes. For the research question discussed in this paper, we focus on one code that was developed from the larger codebook: *communicating mathematics online*. This code applied to any talk turn (i.e., a participant's response to an interviewer's question) where the PST or PCS described a difficulty related to communicating mathematics over Zoom. To answer our research question, the first author used Transana (v 3.32) [18] to code the full data set using this code. Finally, the clip-making feature of Transana was used to compare and contrast all episodes and identify themes related to students' perceived difficulties with communicating over Zoom. Results reported here are preliminary.

4 Results

Results are organized around three key challenges identified by PSTs and PCSs about communicating mathematics over Zoom: (a) limited access to one another's written mathematical work; (b) limited ability to have one-on-one conversations; and (c) the tendency for some students to leave their cameras turned off during the workshops. For each challenge, we describe how the challenge specifically affected PCSs and PSTs and share illustrative quotations from the interviews. Common speech fillers used in American English such as "um," "like," and repeated words were removed from all quotations to improve readability.

It is important to note that the findings reported here are participants' *perceptions* of the difficulties of communicating mathematics over Zoom. Hence, these challenges do not represent absolute features of Zoom. Instead, participants' perceptions highlighted important aspects of communicating mathematics in person that were valued and missed by both PCSs and PSTs after shifting to the online platform.

4.1 Limited Access to One Another's Written Mathematical Work

All research participants reported the challenge of sharing written mathematical work with one another; some students were more concerned about this challenge than others. For PCSs, this difficulty caused problems with sharing their thinking and understanding what their peers were saying. For example, PCS-05 (i.e., Precalculus Participant #5) said, "We have to communicate a lot better…We can't just say, 'Oh, I did this' and then show them. You have to describe each part of the problem a little bit more in-depth so that everyone understands." Similarly, PCS-09 said, "It's harder to verbalize math than it is just to show it… Someone would be like 'Oh, you just do this, this, and this,' and I'd be like [confused expression]." These comments indicated that the PCSs recognized some of the challenges of communicating mathematics without the aid of written work, notation, and graphs. Without the visual medium readily available for communicating, PCSs had to make heavier use of the mathematics register. Problematically, many PCSs were still developing this register for precalculus. Consequently, limited access to written work coupled with a limited ability to use the mathematics register created challenges for communicating mathematics, which many students reported.

The PSTs also reported that they missed being able to easily see PCSs' written work, and all of them recognized that limited access to written work made communicating mathematical ideas more challenging. They too recognized that everyone had to be more specific and thorough when sharing mathematical ideas through the online medium. For example, PST-04 recounted an experience where a PCS attempted to describe a nonlinear graph: "I remember that the student was just like, 'Okay. And then it makes a line like this and that.'…It just wasn't great to have to annotate [the shared whiteboard], not always fully understanding what it was that they meant." Hence, PST-04 also noticed that the lack of access to written work and the PCSs' limited ability to use the mathematics register created compound difficulties for communicating mathematical ideas. Many of the PSTs reported that they spent more time eliciting PCSs' thinking because they could not simply "look over [the PCSs'] shoulders" at their written work.

4.2 Limited Ability to Have One-On-One Conversations

Another significant challenge perceived by both PCSs and PSTs was the limited ability for one-on-one conversations to happen during groupwork. In particular, PSTs and PCSs reported that, even though they were in Zoom breakout rooms during groupwork, it was not feasible to have smaller one-on-one conversations, which is something they could do in person. Zoom does have a chat feature that allows attendees to communicate privately to one another, but this was not used by PCSs or PSTs. So, for example, PCS-10 said, "It's easier to talk in person than over the Zoom.... You could just go to the partner next to me [*sic*] and just be like, 'Hey I missed that' or 'How'd you get that?'" PCS-10 also recognized that he might disrupt others' thinking with these small questions, and thus was hesitant to ask them over Zoom.

PSTs also recognized that trying to have small one-on-one conversations over Zoom might be uncomfortable for PCSs. For example, PST-06 noted, "So I know some students would work with the person sitting next to them if they got stuck. But then when online learning happened, that wasn't really as possible.... They might find it awkward. They might feel uncomfortable saying [their question] out loud because then everybody [in their group] would hear it." Similarly, PST-01 said, "Sometimes you feel like if you say something, it has to be substantial or worth you saying it and trying to get that communication across." Hence, some PSTs recognized that PCSs might not feel comfortable sharing if they perceived their questions or ideas to be less substantial.

4.3 Tendency for PCSs to Leave Their Cameras Off During Groupwork

Students were given a choice as to whether or not to turn their web-cameras on; many students chose not to. Both PCSs and PSTs found it difficult to communicate with PCSs who had their cameras off. In particular, talking to a blank screen felt uncomfortable to many participants. For example, PCS-07 said, "I think [turning your camera on] makes you feel a little more comfortable seeing your peers' faces, as opposed to just a voice, and it makes you a little more comfortable to share all your stuff." PCS-01 reported, "It really helped if that student had their camera [turned on], and they were interacting and participating, as opposed to muting it or talking every now and then [with] no face or anything like that." In addition to feeling more comfortable when cameras were turned on, PSTs recognized that they missed non-verbal cues, such as gestures, body language, and facial expressions when cameras were turned off. For example, PST-03 said, "I couldn't see how they were feeling by their body language...[with cameras off] I just see their name and a colored background. That's not exactly helpful."

5 Discussion

We reported preliminary findings related to challenges undergraduates perceived when engaging in active learning over Zoom, a currently prominent video-conferencing application [4]. Whereas other studies about synchronous online groupwork focused on affordances and constraints of chat forums, discussion boards, and dynamic whiteboards [cf., 11–14], we add to the literature by identifying challenges of using video-conferencing applications for synchronous online groupwork in mathematics. Three key challenges were identified: (a) limited access to one another's written mathematical work, (b) limited ability to have one-on-one conversations, and (c) the tendency for PCSs to leave their cameras turned off during groupwork. These findings provide insight into aspects of communicating mathematics in person that became salient to PCSs and PSTs because of the shift to online instruction. In particular, the multimodal nature of mathematics makes it difficult to verbally communicate symbolic and diagrammatic representations of mathematical ideas. In addition, even though both PCSs and PSTs were undergraduate students, because the PSTs undertook the role of teacher in the small groups, these results provide information about both learners' and teachers' perspectives of using video-conferencing applications to engage in synchronous online groupwork. Herein we discuss ideas for addressing these challenges.

When considering each challenge, it is important to remember that these were *perceived* challenges rather than absolute features of Zoom or other video-conferencing applications. For example, with respect to the first challenge, there certainly are ways to share written work quickly with others over Zoom, such as by holding up written work to the camera, sharing electronic notes, or using Zoom's shared whiteboard feature. However, our results indicate that instructors may need to teach students how to make better use of the technology during groupwork. Focused discussions about the affordances and constraints of video-conferencing applications could help address the other two challenges as well. In addition to learning how to make better use of the technology, instructors may need to negotiate new groupwork norms specific to the video-conferencing platform in order to support a more seamless groupwork experience. For PSTs, discussions about the limited access to students' written work might lead into discussions about the multi-semiotic nature of mathematical communication and what it means to develop the mathematics register [7–9]. Mathematics teacher educators might also support PSTs by facilitating discussions about other ways to gain access to students' thinking in this new environment.

In this paper we identified three potential challenges with communicating mathematics over video-conferencing platforms, and some ideas for addressing these challenges. However, our data indicate that it may still be vital to develop new tools, technologies, and applications that allow for seamless communication of mathematical ideas and expressing those ideas through all possible modalities of communication. For example, while it is possible to hold up written work to the camera, PCSs in this study also commented that this was not a very effective way to show one's work, and that there were issues with video-quality and figuring out where to hold one's paper.

We end with a limitation and possible future directions. In particular, because we focused on PCSs' perceptions, we do not have access to what actually happened during the workshops. Future research might include analyses of the groupwork sessions, which could also provide insight into ways in which students and teachers work around these challenges in the moment.

References

1. Conference Board of the Mathematical Sciences (CBMS): Active learning in post-secondary education (2016). https://www.cbmsweb.org/2016/07/active-learning-in-post-secondary-mathematics-education/
2. Saxe, K., Braddy, L.: A common vision for undergraduate mathematical sciences programs in 2025. Mathematical Association of America (2015)
3. Trust, T., Carpenter, J.P., Krutka, D.G., Kimmons, R.: #RemoteTeaching & #RemoteLearning: educator tweeting during the COVID-19 pandemic. J. Technol. Teach. Educ. **28**(2), 151–159 (2020)

4. Stefanile, A.: The transition from classroom to zoom and how it has changed education. J. Soc. Sci. Res. **16**, 33–40 (2020)
5. Zoom Video Communications Inc.: Security guide. Zoom Video Communications Inc. (2016). https://d24cgw3uvb9a9h.cloudfront.net/static/81625/doc/Zoom-Security-White-Paper.pdf
6. Cirillo, M., LaRochelle, R., Arbaugh, F., Bieda, K.N.: An innovative early field experience for preservice secondary teachers: early results from shifting to an online model. J. Technol. Teach. Educ. **28**(2), 353–363 (2020)
7. Schleppegrell, M.J.: The linguistic challenges of mathematics teaching and learning: a research review. Read. Writ. Q. **23**(2), 139–159 (2007)
8. Morgan, C., Craig, T., Schuette, M., Wagner, D.: Language and communication in mathematics education: an overview of research in the field. ZDM **46**(6), 843–853 (2014). https://doi.org/10.1007/s11858-014-0624-9
9. O'Halloran, K.L.: The language of learning mathematics: a multimodal perspective. J. Math. Behav. **40**, 63–74 (2015)
10. Martin, F., Ahlgrim-Delzell, L., Budhrani, K.: Systematic review of two decades (1995 to 2014) of research on synchronous online learning. Am. J. Dist. Edu. **31**(1), 3–19 (2017)
11. Gadanidis, G., Graham, L., McDougall, D., Roulet, G.: On-line mathematics: visions and opportunities, issues and challenges, and recommendations. In: White Paper based on The Fields Institute for Research in Mathematical Sciences Mathematics Online Working Meeting. Fields Institute (2002)
12. Hodges, C., Hunger, G.: Communicating mathematics on the internet: synchronous and asynchronous tools. TechTrends **55**(5), 39–44 (2011). https://doi.org/10.1007/s11528-011-0526-4
13. Smith, G.G., Torres-Ayala, A.T., Heindel, A.J.: Disciplinary differences in E-learning instructional design: the case of mathematics. Int. J. E-Learn. Dist. Educ. **22**(3), 63–88 (2008)
14. Montiel, M., Bhatti, U.B.: Advanced mathematics online: assessing particularities in the online delivery of a second linear algebra course. Online J. Dist. Learn. Adm. **13**(2) (2010). https://www2.westga.edu/~distance/ojdla/summer132/montiel_bhatti132.html
15. Henriksen, D., Creely, E., Henderson, M.: Folk pedagogies for teacher education transitions: approaches to synchronous online learning in the wake of COVID-19. J. Technol. Teach. Educ. **28**(2), 201–209 (2020)
16. Bieda, K.N., Arbaugh, F., Cirillo, M.: Collaborative research: investigating early field experiences for prospective mathematics teachers through the university teaching experience model (DRL #s 1725910, 1725920, 1726364) [Grant]. National Science Foundation (2017-2021)
17. Creswell, J.W., Poth, C.N.: Qualitative Inquiry and Research Design: Choosing Among Five Approaches. Sage Publications, Thousand Oaks (2016)
18. Woods, D.: Transana Multiuser v3.32d (2019). https://www.transana.com. Spurgeon Woods LLC

Engaging Students During Synchronous Video-Conferencing in COVID19 Times: Preliminary Findings from a Design Study

Ilias Karasavvidis(✉)

University of Thessaly, 38221 Volos, Greece
ikaras@uth.gr

Abstract. This paper explores student engagement in an undergraduate course during the pandemic-induced emergency remote teaching in the spring of 2020. Fifty preschool education students participated in a course in which synchronous video-conferencing was used. The design study that is outlined in this work focuses on the effect of an instructional approach on the rate and patterns of student engagement. The instructional approach involved questioning in multiple communication channels, chief among which was the chat. The findings indicate that despite the principled design, student engagement varied considerably. A small group of students were very active, systematically participating in the chat and answering all quizzes. Still, the large majority of students exhibited lower engagement rates as they reacted to a few posts on the chat and failed to participate in many of the quizzes assigned. Overall, the study results suggest that the patterns of student engagement identified in the study tend to approximate the ones that characterize face-to-face settings.

Keywords: e-learning · Synchronous video-conferencing · Student engagement · Chat · Quiz

1 Introduction

1.1 The Road to Microsoft Teams

In the spring of 2020 the covid19 pandemic forced higher institutions world-wide to switch to fully online teaching. The emergence of the pandemic led the Greek central government to take prompt measures, leading to the general lockdown issued on March the 10th 2020. Much like all other instructors at my home institution, I was required to teach the courses that had been assigned to me using a video-conferencing platform. More specifically, after the central educational authority signed a contract with Microsoft Corporation, all higher education institutions were offered access to Microsoft Teams (MST). In the present study MST was used as one-way video-conferencing application. The adoption of MST complimented the use of e-class, a custom Learning Management System (LMS) developed by the Greek Ministry of education and widely adopted in Greek academia. E-class had already been used in all existing courses at the institution

A. Reis et al. (Eds.): TECH-EDU 2020, CCIS 1384, pp. 287–300, 2021.
https://doi.org/10.1007/978-3-030-73988-1_22

at the onset of the pandemic. As the MST was used for synchronous e-learning and e-class was used for asynchronous e-learning, there was no integrated platform for the courses. This meant that with the exception of the videoconferencing lectures, all other typical online resources (e.g. course syllabus, lecture slides, and all other materials) were available through the e-class LMS. Following the announcement about the institution-wide adoption of MST, the IT department staff created the respective course team on the MST platform on March the 16th 2020. Then, the IT staff also created MST accounts for all the students who had enrolled in the course. Finally, I communicated the course access code through e-class by sending an email to all registered students.

What is particularly interesting in this context is that there was essentially no preparation or planning involved in the switch to fully online teaching. Thus, this is a case of emergency remote teaching [20]. In fact, when the switch occurred, the course was well under way as 4 out of the 13 lectures had already been given in the classroom. Due to the sudden and unplanned switch to synchronous e-learning, the overall experience was not exactly expected to be as easy as falling off a log for two main reasons. First, the students in the study were only accustomed to traditional learning. Even though e-class was widely used in the courses taught in the department, it served a supportive function (i.e. disseminate online resources, lecture slides and presentations, assignments etc.). Consequently, going from traditional learning to fully synchronous e-learning – without any former preparation or planning – was expected to be a challenge for both students and instructors. For instance, meta-analyses indicate that students tend to find blended learning more difficult than traditional learning [28]. Moreover, the course involved primarily video-conferencing and qualitative studies [28] report that student ratings of synchronous web-conferencing sessions were very low.

Second, one of the major criticisms of initial e-learning approaches is that they have tended to replicate the traditional practices online [16, 17]. The problem with such approaches to teaching and learning is that they adopt a transmissionist model of teaching resulting in passive learners. In fact, passive learning has been seen as the Achilles heel of traditional education. For instance, a recent comprehensive meta-analysis of 225 studies by [14] indicated that students who are attending classes in which active learning approaches are adopted tend to perform better compared to students in traditional lecturing classes. Typically, one of the main routes through which to foster active learning is to engage students in the learning process.

As teaching large introductory courses often involves expository teaching, my main concern with the switch to synchronous e-learning was to avoid teaching that could lead to passive forms of learning. My main goal was to establish and maintain high levels of student engagement throughout the video-conferencing sessions, thereby promoting active learning.

At first sight, synchronous video-conferencing might naturally map directly to transmissionist approaches to learning. After all, a traditional lecture in class is replaced with a high-tech, distance video-lecture by the same instructor: both are characterized by instructional approaches that can be described as information delivery. Interestingly, modern e-learning platforms offer an impressive array of tools through which student engagement can be achieved. For instance, to ask a question in class a student needs to be granted permission to speak. However, a simple tool such as the chat enables students to ask questions whenever they come to mind. Moreover, unlike questions that students ask in class which are temporal, questions asked in a chat are more permanent and can be revisited at a later point in time. In this context and in addition to video-conferencing, I turned to the chat – among other tools – as a means of fostering student engagement. This paper reports the findings of a design study that aimed to examine student engagement in synchronous video-conferencing.

1.2 Student Engagement in Online Settings

Engagement can be broadly defined as an investment of time and effort in learning activities. Several conceptualizations and models of engagement have been advanced in the literature (e.g. [5, 12]). Engagement is seen as essential for learning as the empirical evidence indicates that it is strongly associated with higher levels of academic achievement [11].

Novel, technology-based learning environments are believed to have the potential to advance new, active forms of learning. Hence, Information and Communication Technologies (ICTs) are considered as one of the most promising tools through which student engagement can be fostered. Several studies have examined student behavioral engagement in online learning environments eg [18]. Typical forms of online engagement include clicks, page views, document downloads, forum views and posts, assignment uploads, and chat participation.

As far as asynchronous e-learning is concerned, the evidence indicates that active engagement in online courses is a predictor of student achievement. For instance, student behavioral engagement in online environments (such as page views, watching video, assignment completion and participation in online forums) has been linked with higher performance [2, 4, 12, 15, 22, 23, 25, 32]. Similar findings regarding engagement are reported for MOOCs. [26] found that students who demonstrated active learning performed better than those who did not. In particular, certain student participation patterns, such as posting to the discussion forum, trying an assignment, submitting an assignment, and responding to forum posts, were positively correlated with performance.

Considerably less attention has been given to student engagement in synchronous e-learning settings. A comprehensive literature search returned a handful of studies that examine student engagement through the use of tools such as the chat. On the one hand, a few studies have investigated the use of chat indirectly in the context of synchronous e-learning.

In some studies the chat is examined as an auxiliary tool. [10] examined synchronous discussions in the chat that took place in the context of an audio-conference course. In this study the chat was used to mitigate audio-conferencing problems, functioning as an additional support layer to address technical issues rather than conceptual understanding. In other studies researchers explored the use of online chatting tools for community building purposes (e.g. [14] who focused on the #EdChat community on Twitter).

Another set of studies have specifically examined how chatting contributes to learning. For example, in a study of 23 online courses, [21] found that the quality of interpersonal interaction within a course is positively correlated with student performance. High-interpersonal interaction was defined as involving instructors who posted frequently, invited student questions, responded to student queries quickly, and solicited and incorporated student feedback in their responses. In another study that took place in a graduate seminar, [33] implemented an online discussion in the regular class period. They report that elaborating (i.e. clarifying, narrowing, specifying, expanding or refining prior knowledge) (24%) and resisting (14%) (namely challenging an idea providing counter arguments) were the most prevalent manifestations of learning in the chat.

On the other hand, some studies have specifically examined how the chat ihas been linked with higher performancempacts engagement. [27] concluded that synchronous class sessions can be used to promote student engagement. The authors examined the engagement of 27 undergraduates in a synchronous class section that was held once a week for a period of 6 weeks. They found that the vast majority (87%) of the student interactions were student-instructor interactions. Furthermore, they reported that intellectual instructor prompts (leading questions, make declarations, suppositions, and modeling intellectual processes) were highly positively correlated with active and collaborative learning, with instructor interactions and enriching academic experiences.

[36] examined student engagement in two settings, experimental and naturalistic respectively (real-life academic courses). They identified five main instructional interaction types: instructor's presentation (direct instruction and content explanations by the instructor), student as instructor (students explain content and share their understanding or artifacts), instructor-student interaction (the instructor explicitly encourages student participation), student-instructor interaction (students ask the instructor questions or make comments) and interaction among peers (students interact with each other.). They concluded that the instructor-student interaction style dominated over all other four types of interactions. On the one hand, the number of words uttered by the students and the respective frequency were low in the case of teacher presentation. On the other hand, more words were spoken in instructor-student interactions compared to all other interaction types. Interestingly, they found that participation frequency was higher when participants were explicitly encouraged by the instructor to ask questions.

1.3 Study Objective and Research Questions

As the aforementioned studies suggest, the chat can be a potentially useful tool in promoting student engagement in synchronous e-learning. However, none of these studies has specifically examined the use of the chat during synchronous video-conferencing sessions. In all these studies the use of the chat involved setups that did not take place during lecturing. Hence, there is a knowledge gap concerning the use of synchronous e-learning tools to establish and maintain high levels of student engagement. Using a design research approach [1, 6, 7, 31], the study described in this paper attempts to fill this gap through the examination of how a specific instructional intervention influenced student engagement.

1.4 Rationale of the Instructional Approach

The instructional techniques and technological tools that comprise the rationale that I adopted to promote student engagement are briefly analyzed below (see Table 1). The overall instructional approach is rooted in the Learning Sciences in general (e.g. [3]) and in Sociocultural Theory in particular [8, 34, 35].

Table 1. Outline of the instructional approach used

id	Steps	Description
1	Introduction	Use questions and problems to introduce the concept
2	Functionality	Examine why the concept was developed, what purpose it serves, providing further explanations and elaborations as needed
3	Application	Apply the concept in practice using various tasks and problems
4	Assessment	Check student conceptual understanding using questions, quizzes, and tasks
5	Feedback	Give feedback based on student responses, provide further examples and explanations to remedy poor understanding, address potential misconceptions

The approach was meant to invoke student participation, providing opportunities for thinking, reflection, practice, and feedback. Questioning played a significant role in this approach. More specifically, I used questions to make the student experience interactive and engage students as much as possible. This decision was based on (a) findings reported by [27, 36, 37] involving the use of chat that were reviewed above and (b) a large body of research indicating that questioning can be an effective technique for advancing learning. For instance, in the case of traditional classrooms, research indicates that interpolating lectures with memory tests leads to higher information retainment than plain lectures [29, 30]. This pattern of findings also appears to be replicated in online settings. In particular, the meta-analysis by [28] indicated that quizzes positively affect both the effectiveness and the attractiveness of blended learning. Similar findings are reported by [19] who concluded that interpolated tests help students stay focused.

Three specific technological tools provided by MST, the audio channel, the chat and the quiz were instrumental in implementing this instructional approach. Questions were asked and answered in these three channels.

To facilitate communication and establish a concrete workflow, a specific set of ground rules were established at the beginning of the video-conferencing lessons. These rules were meant to be followed throughout the synchronous video-conferencing sessions (see Table 2).

First, the video-conferencing channel would be used for introduction, functionality, and application (steps 1–3 above). The students were not allowed to activate their cameras (strict privacy directives issued by the administration), thus this channel was primarily occupied by the instructor. The audio channel was meant to be used by both the instructor and the students. To maintain control and avoid potential technical problems (e.g. echo, overlapping talk etc.), however, the students were advised to raise their hand using the specific button on the MST client. When they were called upon to speak, they could unmute their microphone and talk. They could ask a question, answer a question or make comment. Thus, the audio-visual channel afforded only regulated participation for the students.

Second, the students were alerted to the fact that the chat was going to be a main two-way communication channel. I communicated up front that, in addition to the video-conferencing channel, the chat was meant to be the main online reference space. The chat could be used by the students without any constraints whatsoever. As opposed to participating in the audio channel, the chat afforded complete and unregulated freedom. The students could ask questions, answer questions, make comments, share thoughts and feelings about the course topics. This intended functionality of the chat was presented to the students who were strongly encouraged to use the chat to ask, comment, and communicate anything related to the lecture.

The chat also offered certain affordances to the instructor. In particular, I used the chat to ask questions, answer questions, make comments, share information (e.g. links to YouTube videos, links to quizzes in Microsoft Forms). Of particular interest is the fact that I also used the chat to either stress the importance of certain questions (e.g. repeat a question asked in the video-conference channel in the chat to make it more accessible) or simply make them more permanent (e.g. writing the question in the chat alleviated students from the burden of having to remember the question or the need to write it down). In this sense, some questions, problems or tasks that were presented during the video-conference were also repeated in the chat by the author.

Finally, I periodically used the chat to summarize important concepts that were introduced and discussed in the video-conferencing channel (e.g. outline important concepts, provide written definitions or highlight information that was critical in understanding the concepts).

Table 2. Major communication channels and forms of engagement

Engagement	Video	Audio	Chat	Quiz
Present information	I	I	I	–
Share information	I	I	I,S	–
Ask question	I	I,S*	I,S	I
Answer question	I	I,S*	I,S	S
Comment	I	I,S*	I,S	–

Note: I: instructor, S: students, S* = students after raising the hand and being called upon by the instructor

The main objective of the study was to determine how the specific instructional approach outlined above influenced the levels of student engagement in the given course setting. In particular, the following research questions are addressed:

RQ1: What is the rate of student engagement?

RQ2: What are the main forms of student engagement?

2 Method

2.1 Participants and Design

This study involves 83 students (77 female, 6 male) who enrolled in an undergraduate course on Digital Media at the authors' host institution. The large majority (67.46%) were freshmen, all others were simply repeating the course because it was a required one.

This study can be broadly categorized as a design study as I set out to promote student engagement and took measures to sustain it. Due to the approach, the study also has an ethnographic and auto-ethnographic dimension - at least as far as my perspective both as a participant and as instructor is concerned. I provide a comprehensive and holistic account that involves both me, as a critical agent in this context, and the dynamic interactions that emerged among the students, the tools, the conventions (ground rules), and myself. While this is a design study, due to space limitations only a portion of the data is reported. Thus, an account of the problems that surfaced and the successive measures that were taken to resolve them are not presented in this work.

2.2 Measures

For the purposes of this study, engagement was broadly operationalized as the rate of student participation in the various channels. Both quantitative and qualitative data were collected. Regarding the former, the log files from the MS Teams platform were used to extract the following measures:

- participants: number of students who were logged in during the scheduled video-conferencing hours
- identity of each video-conferencing session: dates, times, titles, channels, duration, and participants
- chat: total number of exchanges in the chat tool were initially tallied and then summed to compute the final value. This value was based on the detailed chat statistics per session that MST provides (It should be noted that this does not include responses that were not explicitly typed, such as clicking on the thumbs-up icon to react to a chat post).
- quiz: total number of quizzes used, type of quizzes, and number of students who took each quiz. These values were derived from MS Forms, which provide detailed statistics about the quiz participants and their selections.

Regarding the latter, qualitative data collection involved my own observations and notes taken after each video-conferencing session, informal communications with students through email, telephone or video-conference about problems they faced and experiences with the whole video-conferencing process. Due to space limitations and the fact that the data analysis is not completed, this paper draws largely on the quantitative measures. For the purposes of this paper, the analysis is descriptive, in an attempt to convey the overall picture of student engagement in the online course space.

2.3 Results

Overview of Video-Conferencing Sessions

Before focusing on the research questions per se an overview of video-conferencing sessions and other related information is provided (session type, dates held, duration, and attendance per session). This information is provided in the 5 leftmost columns of Table 3 below. As the table shows, the course video-conferencing sessions started at the end of March and ended in the beginning of July 2020. In total, 13 video-conferencing sessions were held, 11 of which were course lectures. The remaining 2 sessions were not formal lectures and involved course review and summary and final project instructions. While the last two sessions were not initially planned, the students requested them.

Next we turn to an examination of student participation rates. This is important for the readers to know because for instance the absolute value of the total number of chat exchanges might take on different meanings depending on the number of participants. That is, 100 chat messages might suggest a relatively high participation rate if 10 students are involved while a relatively low rate if 200 students are involved. While 83 students had enrolled in the course, the number of students who attended the online sessions was much smaller. Student attendance varied considerably, from as low as 19% up to 60% of the registered students. Even though at first sight the percentage of the students who enrolled but did not participate might seem high (40%), it should be noted that this reflects the typical classroom attendance rates of pre-covid19 semesters. Therefore, in terms of attendance the online class was not substantially differentiated from a typical face-to-face class.

On average, about 36 students participated per video-conferencing session (SD: 10.71). The maximum number of students who logged in during any of the videoconferencing sessions (namely 50) was used as reference to compute attendance rates. Using this value as a reference, student participation did hit a low (32%) in the session held on June 15th. However, attendance in almost all other sessions was fair, ranging from 46% to 100%. As Table 3 shows, in terms of absolute numbers the student participation tended to drop throughout the semester.

Table 3. Main video-conferencing statistics

id	Video-conferencing event	Date	Duration (min)	Participants N (%)	Chat exchanges	Quizzes
1	Lecture	30 March	182	36 (43.4)	515	6
2	Lecture	06 April	202	50 (60.2)	367	2
3	Lecture	08 April	161	50 (60.2)	228	3
4	Lecture	27 April	156	46 (55.4)	104	4
5	Lecture	04 May	232	44 (53.0)	102	2
6	Lecture	11 May	202	41 (49.4)	131	1
7	Lecture	18 May	191	42 (50.6)	97	2
8	Lecture	25 May	196	37 (44.6)	155	0
9	Lecture	15 June	194	16 (19.3)	70	1
10	Lecture	17 June	174	26 (31.3)	79	1
11	Lecture	19 June	215	23 (27.7)	60	0
12	Recap/review	3 July	182	28 (33.7)	382	1
13	Final project	8 July	165	31 (37.3)	91	1

2.4 RQ #1: What is the Rate of Student Engagement?

Chat

The first major dependent variable of the study was student participation in the chat. In total, the 13 video-conferencing sessions involved 2381 chat exchanges. The average exchange rate across all sessions was 183.15. It should be noted, however, that the variance was very high (SD 146.22). More specifically, the last video-conferencing session (lecture) on June the 19th included 60 chat exchanges, while the first session held on March the 30th was by far the one characterized by most interactions as it included 515 exchanges.

Table 3 shows an overall decline in the absolute number of chat interactions throughout the course. The specific peak observed during the course end is due to the purpose of the specific video-conferencing session.

In particular, the second higher number of exchanges occurred during the second last video-conferencing session (on July 3rd) that involved a review of the main concepts and was characterized by high participation and interactivity. This was because the students wanted to test their understanding of the concepts and get feedback on their responses.

It should be noted that, as the analysis is currently in a preliminary stage, it is not sufficiently fine-grained to allow for a low-level representation of engagement such as likes on posts.

Overall, student participation rates in the chat were below expectations. As this was the first time that the author tried emergency online teaching, there is no reference against which such participation rates could be compared. Nevertheless, my expectations of participation were much higher than what was eventually recorded.

Quiz

The second major dependent variable of the study involved student participation in the course quizzes. The distribution of quizzes throughout the video-conferencing sessions can be seen in Table 3. Twenty-four quizzes were created using Microsoft Forms and were shared through the chat. On average, 1.85 quizzes were posted per video-conferencing session. Variability was high, ranging from no quizzes (in two of the video-conferencing sessions on 25th of May and 19th of June) to 6 quizzes during the first video-conferencing session (30th of March). The number of quizzes that were made available decreased as the semester progressed.

Four different types of quizzes were used. Twelve of the quizzes (50%) were content-related, 9 (37.50%) targeted presentation format and rate, 2 quizzes (8.33%) were used to make administrative decisions (e.g. decide the dates on which to host the review/summary and final project instruction sessions). Finally, one quiz was used in the first session as an ice-breaker activity, so as to familiarize the students with the process of taking quizzes (i.e. sharing the quiz link in the chat, take the embedded quiz, and view the responses inline on the chat).

Overall, the student quiz taking participation rates were also low: about half of the quizzes had participation rates lower than 60%.

2.5 RQ #2: What are the Main Forms of Student Engagement per Channel?

Overall, the data analysis indicated that engagement varied from no engagement whatsoever to full engagement. This engagement pattern is presented in Table 4 as a function of response type per engagement channel.

The first column indicates the level of engagement, with 0 meaning no engagement and 4 indicating high engagement. The level 0, which corresponds to the lowest form of engagement, practically suggested no involvement at all: the students logged in on time but did not exhibit any form of activity throughout the session. They ignored prompts, questions, quizzes, and tasks in the course of the session. The next form of engagement (1) involved a simple mouse click. The students did engage, but this form of engagement is relatively low – especially in the case of the chat where it simply meant clicking on an emoticon to respond to a statement of any form by the instructor or fellow students. For instance, the author would post the following in the chat: "r u guys still out there?" and the students would react to this post by clicking on one of the available post emoticons such as a smiley (i.e. smiley face). The next form of engagement that was observed involved typing an emoticon to the chat in response to some prompt by the instructor or other students. As this was considered to be fairly similar to clicking on an emoticon with the mouse it was assigned the same code (1). The last 3 forms of engagement were considered to be of higher level. In particular, the clicking on a quiz option indicated that the student needed to think about one of the available options and pick one (code 2). Compared to the previous 3 levels, this reflects deeper cognitive processing as the students needed to think through the options and make a decision. The next engagement level (code 3) was the second highest observed in the study as it involved typing in the chat. Regardless of the actual length of the post, this behavior indicates that the student was actively following the presentation and reacted to it either when prompted (e.g. the instructor asked a question and the student typed an answer) or not (e.g. the student took the initiative and typed a question or comment without being explicitly prompted to do so). Finally, the highest form of cognitive engagement (level 4) involved using the MS Teams video-conference channel: raise hand, being called upon, and engage in a conversation with the instructor (i.e. ask a question, request explanation, make a comment etc.).

Even though data analysis is on-going, preliminary findings indicated that the students could be categorized in three major subsets: (a) high engagement by a small group of students (levels 1 through 4), (b) low engagement by the large majority of students (levels 1–3), and (c) no engagement by a small student group (level 0). It is expected that more specific engagement patterns will be identified when data analysis is completed.

Table 4. Outline of the main forms of engagement during the video-conferencing sessions

Level	Type of response	Channel	Description
0	No response	–	Students were logged in but there was no discernible participation whatsoever
1	Mouse click – emoticons	MS Teams chat	Clicking on emoticon to react to a chat post
1	Typing - emoticon	MS Teams chat	Reacting to a post by typing/Posting an emoticon
2	Mouse click – quiz	MS Forms	Participating in a quiz by selecting one of the available options
3	Typing – text	MS Teams chat	Typing in reaction to an instructor prompt, task etc.
4	Speaking – audio	MS Teams video-conference channel	Unmuting the microphone and interacting with the instructor on the channel

3 Discussion

Much like every course instructor in higher education in the spring of 2020, I was required to undertake emergency remote teaching [20]. The sudden switch to fully online teaching was expected to be challenging for two reasons. On the one hand, student ratings of web-conferencing sessions are reported to be very low [28] and the course was meant to be taught using synchronous video-conferencing (see also [9]). On the other hand, synchronous video-conferencing could easily replicate traditional transmissionist practices and lead to passive learning [16].

The present study aimed to determine how a specific instructional approach that was based on questioning and was mainly materialized through the chat influenced student engagement during the synchronous video-conferencing sessions. Overall, the findings of the study indicate that a very small group of students interacted with me in the audio channel, systematically participated in the chat, answered all quizzes assigned, and were very active throughout the course. On the other hand, the large majority of students were relatively silent on the audio channel, failed to participate in many of the quizzes, and reacted to a few posts on the chat. Finally, a small group of students failed to engage, as they were logged in throughout the videoconferencing sessions but reacted to none of the multiple stimuli. As the course instructor I must confess that I consider this level of engagement achieved to be very low. Furthermore, I consider that – despite best intentions – I had failed to establish and maintain the desired engagement levels that I had set out to.

While this pattern of engagement agrees with the patterns reported by other studies in the literature (e.g. [24, 27, 36]), the specific intervention failed to lead to levels of engagement that I would consider acceptable. It appears that engagement is not easily attainable for the majority of students even when the instructor adopts an approach that is explicitly aimed at fostering it. Interestingly enough, the affordances offered by the chat for engaging students were not utilized.

Such a pattern of engagement might appear similar to the one that characterizes typical classrooms, where only a small number of students are active participants. However, it should be born in mind that the tools offered by modern synchronous e-learning platforms can accommodate high engagement levels for all students rather than a small sub-set of them.

This study has two main limitations. First, the study is not balanced in terms of gender because the participants were overwhelmingly female. It is not known whether the same pattern of findings will emerge with different gender ratios. Second, the study does not capture the student perspective and experience regarding engagement. While the study outlines my perspective both as a designer of the course and the course instructor, it does not examine how the students experienced remote teaching.

To conclude, there is hardly any published research documenting engagement patterns particularly in such emergency remote teaching settings involving synchronous e-learning. The present study made a modest contribution to this direction by examining the rate and patterns of student engagement. Future research needs to explore more systematically other instructional approaches, tools, and tool combinations to determine how to best foster student engagement in synchronous video-conferencing settings.

References

1. Barab, S., Squire, K.: Design-based research: putting a stake in the ground. J. Learn. Sci. **13**(1), 1–14 (2004)
2. Barba, P.G., Kennedy, G.E., Ainley, M.D.: The role of students' motivation and participation in predicting performance in a MOOC. J. Comput. Assist. Learn. **32**(3), 218–231 (2016)
3. Bransford, J.D., Brown, A.L., Cocking, R.R.: How People Learn: Brain, Mind, Experience, and School. National Academy Press, Washington DC (2000)

4. Chen, P.S.D., Lambert, A.D., Guidry, K.R.: Engaging online learners: the impact of web-based learning technology on college student engagement. Comput. Educ. **54**(4), 1222–1232 (2010)
5. Chi, M.T., Wylie, R.: The ICAP framework: linking cognitive engagement to active learning outcomes. Educ. Psychol. **49**(4), 219–243 (2014)
6. Cobb, P., Confrey, J., diSessa, A., Lehrer, R., Schauble, L.: Design experiments in educational research. Educ. Res. **32**(1), 9–13 (2003)
7. Collins, A., Joseph, D., Bielaczyc, K.: Design research: theoretical and methodological issues. J. Learn. Sci. **13**(1), 15–42 (2004)
8. Daniels, H.: Vygotsky and Pedagogy. Routledge, Abingdon (2016)
9. De Jong, N., Verstegen, D.M., Könings, K.D.: The role of the e-tutor in synchronous online problem-based learning: a study in a Master Public Health Programme. Br. J. Educ. Technol. **49**(3), 385–397 (2018)
10. Earnshaw, Y.: Navigating turn-taking and conversational repair in an online synchronous course. Online Learn. J. **21**(4), 315–336 (2017)
11. Finn, J.D., Zimmer, K.S.: Student engagement: What is it? Why does it matter? In: Christenson, S.L., Reschly, A.L., Wylie, C. (eds.) Handbook of Research on Student Engagement, pp. 97–131. Springer, Boston (2012). https://doi.org/10.1007/978-1-4614-2018-7_5
12. Fredricks, J.A., Blumenfeld, P.C., Paris, A.H.: School engagement: potential of the concept, state of the evidence. Rev. Educ. Res. **74**(1), 59–109 (2004)
13. Freeman, S., et al.: Active learning increases student performance in science, engineering, and mathematics. Proc. Natl. Acad. Sci. **111**(23), 8410–8415 (2014)
14. Gao, F., Li, L.: Examining a one-hour synchronous chat in a microblogging-based professional development community. Br. J. Educ. Technol. **48**(2), 332–347 (2017)
15. Giesbers, B., Rienties, B., Tempelaar, D., Gijselaers, W.: Investigating the relations between motivation, tool use, participation, and performance in an e-learning course using web-videoconferencing. Comput. Hum. Behav. **29**(1), 285–292 (2013)
16. Gros, B., García-Peñalvo, F.J.: Future trends in the design strategies and technological affordances of e-learning. In: Spector, M., Lockee, B., Childress, M. (eds.) Learning, Design, and Technology, pp. 1–23. Springer, Cham (2016). https://doi.org/10.1007/978-3-319-17727-4_67-1
17. Henderson, M., Selwyn, N., Aston, R.: What works and why? Student perceptions of 'useful' digital technology in university teaching and learning. Stud. High. Educ. **42**(8), 1567–1579 (2017)
18. Hew, K.F., Cheung, W.S.: Attracting student participation in asynchronous online discussions: a case study of peer facilitation. Comput. Educ. **51**(3), 1111–1124 (2008)
19. Hew, K.F., Qiao, C., Tang, Y.: Understanding student engagement in large-scale open online courses: a machine learning facilitated analysis of student's reflections in 18 highly rated MOOCs. Int. Rev. Res. Open Distrib. Learn. **19**(3), 1–26 (2018)
20. Hodges, C., Moore, S., Lockee, B., Trust, T., Bond, A.: The difference between emergency remote teaching and online learning. Educause Rev. **27**, 1–12 (2020)
21. Jaggars, S.S., Xu, D.: How do online course design features influence student performance? Comput. Educ. **95**, 270–284 (2016)
22. Macfadyen, L.P., Dawson, S.: Mining LMS data to develop an "early warning system" for educators: a proof of concept. Comput. Educ. **54**(2), 588–599 (2010)
23. Milligan, C., Littlejohn, A., Margaryan, A.: Patterns of engagement in connectivist MOOCs. J. Online Learn. Teach. **9**(2), 149–159 (2013)
24. Parkes, M., Stein, S., Reading, C.: Student preparedness for university e-learning environments. Internet High. Educ. **25**, 1–10 (2015)

25. Peters, L., Shmerling, S., Karren, R.: Constructivist pedagogy in asynchronous online education: examining proactive behavior and the impact on student engagement levels. Int. J. E-Learn. **10**(3), 311–330 (2011)
26. Phan, T., McNeil, S.G., Robin, B.R.: Students' patterns of engagement and course performance in a Massive Open Online Course. Comput. Educ. **95**, 36–44 (2016)
27. Shoepe, T.C., McManus, J.F., August, S.E., Mattos, N.L., Vollucci, T.C., Sparks, P.R.: Instructor prompts and student engagement in synchronous online nutrition classes. Am. J. Distance Educ. **34**, 1–17 (2020)
28. Spanjers, I.A., et al.: The promised land of blended learning: quizzes as a moderator. Educ. Res. Rev. **15**, 59–74 (2015)
29. Szpunar, K.K., Jing, H.G., Schacter, D.L.: Overcoming overconfidence in learning from video-recorded lectures: implications of interpolated testing for online education. J. Appl. Res. Mem. Cogn. **3**(3), 161–164 (2014)
30. Szpunar, K.K., Khan, N.Y., Schacter, D.L.: Interpolated memory tests reduce mind wandering and improve learning of online lectures. Proc. Natl. Acad. Sci. **110**(16), 6313–6317 (2013)
31. The Design-Based Research Collective: Design-based research: an emerging paradigm for educational inquiry. Educ. Res. **32**(1), 5–8 (2003)
32. Thompson, J.R., Klass, P.H., Fulk, B.M.: Comparing online and face-to-face presentation of course content in an introductory special education course. Tech. Educ. Spec. Educ. **35**(3), 228–242 (2012)
33. Vogler, J.S., Munsell, S.E., Knutson, D.: LOLsquared: when laughing-out-loud and learning-on-line intermingle in a computer-mediated classroom discussion. Comput. Educ. **140**, 103597 (2019)
34. Vygotsky, L.S.: Mind in society: the development of higher psychological processes. In: Cole, M., John-Steiner, V., Scribner, S., Souberman, E. (eds.) (trans.). Harvard University Press (1978)
35. Vygotsky, L.S.: The collected works of L.S. Vygotsky. In: Rieber, R.S., Carton, A.S. (eds.) Minick, N. (trans.) Vol. 1. Problems of General Psychology. Plenum Press, New York (1987)
36. Weiser, O., Blau, I., Eshet-Alkalai, Y.: How do medium naturalness, teaching-learning interactions and Students' personality traits affect participation in synchronous E-learning? Internet High. Educ. **37**, 40–51 (2018)
37. Zanjani, N., Edwards, S.L., Nykvist, S., Geva, S.: The important elements of LMS design that affect user engagement with e-learning tools within LMSs in the higher education sector. Australas. J. Educ. Technol. **33**(1), 1–13 (2017)

Social Presence, Satisfaction, and Learning Outcomes in an Undergraduate Computer Programming Distance Course

George Koutromanos[1](✉), Ioanna Bellou[2], and Tassos A. Mikropoulos[2]

[1] Department of Primary Education, National and Kapodistrian University of Athens, Athens, Greece
koutro@primedu.uoa.gr

[2] Department of Primary Education, University of Ioannina, Ioannina, Greece
{ibellou,amikrop}@uoi.gr

Abstract. This study investigated the social presence, satisfaction and learning outcomes of undergraduate students based on their participation in an emergency remote online course entitled "Educational Programming Environments" during the COVID-19 pandemic. Instruction was delivered using a student-centered design and discovery learning to teach computer programming problem solving. Data were collected from 39 students who did not undertake prior preparation for engaging in distance education. Social presence, learning outcomes and satisfaction towards the course were measured by previous well-established scales, respectively. The students' learning outcomes were evaluated through their code development. At the end of the course, the students filled out an online questionnaire which measured these three variables. The results of this study showed that all three variables were evaluated as satisfactory by the students. The results also indicated that social presence and code development were positively associated with satisfaction. Moreover, the results of the regression analysis indicated that social presence and code development were critical factors affecting students' satisfaction. Together, these two factors explain 39.9% of the variance of satisfaction. Social presence alone contributed about 32.3% of this variance, suggesting that it may be very important in predicting satisfaction. This study could prove useful to instructors in understanding which factors may influence the design and implementation of distance learning in higher education.

Keywords: Distance learning · Social presence · Satisfaction · Learning outcomes · Undergraduate students

1 Introduction

The coronavirus disease 2019 (COVID-19) has caused a global health crisis, with immense economic [1], psychological [2] and social consequences [3, 4]. In addition, the COVID-19 pandemic has led to some swift changes in the higher education landscape. Traditional classroom instruction abruptly shifted from face-to-face to remote teaching through the use of Information and Communication Technologies (ICT).

A. Reis et al. (Eds.): TECH-EDU 2020, CCIS 1384, pp. 301–312, 2021.
https://doi.org/10.1007/978-3-030-73988-1_23

Consequently, academics have been forced to use specific systems and distance learning platforms to completely rethink their teaching methods and adapt to pandemic conditions. Examples of these systems and platforms include Learning Management Systems such as Moodle [5] and Blackboard, as well as commercial systems such as ZOOM and Microsoft Teams. However, throughout the period in which they were being used, various issues arose concerning the nature of computer mediated communication (CMC). These issues are generally related to distance learning. For example, a common concern is how students interact with and relate to others in CMC. Distance learning technologies provide a varying degree of social interaction, which is dependent on their technical and social affordances. In addition, social interaction with peers and instructors is a complex process that is influenced by academics' knowledge of technical skills and learning strategies [6, 7].

Furthermore, in recent years' research interest has focused particularly on socio-psychological factors concerning how students interact with and relate to others in distance learning technologies. To this end, various models and theories have been developed, such as Social Presence Theory [8] and the SIPS model (Sociability, Social Interaction, Social Presence, Social Space) [9]. According to these models, one of the main factors that leads to an effective online and distance learning interaction is social presence. There is evidence in the literature suggesting that this factor is crucial to students' satisfaction [10], which is defined as "the individuals' perceptions of the extent to which their needs, goals, and desires have been fully met" [11], (p. 364). Similarly, previous findings show social presence to be associated with students' perceived learning outcomes [10].

Despite much research about how social presence relates to satisfaction and perceived learning [10], there is a lack of empirical studies focusing on social presence among undergraduate students in emergency remote online learning environments during COVID-19. This form of emergency remote online learning differs from conventional distance education [12]. It took place suddenly, without university faculty and students having obtained the necessary technical and pedagogical skills and knowledge. These students needed more support in order to be successful in online learning. Therefore, it is important to examine whether social presence is associated with satisfaction and learning outcomes, particularly in emergency remote online learning environments during COVID-19.

Within this framework, this study took place during the pandemic and focused on an emergency remote online course in which the instructors sought interaction with the students and an increase of social presence through student-centered approaches. This study supports the belief that social presence depends not only on technological affordances, but primarily on the instructor's ability to form the appropriate learning conditions for interaction. Understanding students' social presence, satisfaction and learning outcomes are important factors for improving emergency remote online courses during future periods of crisis that will resemble COVID-19.

Therefore, this research investigated the social presence, satisfaction and learning outcomes of undergraduate students based on their participation in a course entitled "Educational Programming Environments," which took place during the COVID-19 pandemic. The learning outcomes were evaluated through the context of code development by the students. The objectives of the study were: (a) to measure the students' social presence, code development and satisfaction; (b) to examine if there was any relationship between social presence, code development and satisfaction; and (c) to examine the effects of social presence and code development on the students' satisfaction.

2 Social Presence

The Social Presence Theory is one of the main theories that guide the development of effective online learning interaction. It was first introduced in the work of Short et al. [8]. They define social presence as "the degree of salience of the other person in the interaction and the consequent salience of the interpersonal relationships" (p. 65). According to Dahlstrom-Hakki et al. [13] "social presence describes the extent to which we view other individuals in a technology mediated interaction as real people, and as a result the extent to which we view our interactions with them as authentic social interactions" (p. 2). Gunawardena and Zittle [14] support that the degree of social presence a student perceives depends on the quality of each medium. More specifically, it depends on the ability possessed by each medium to transfer certain information that contributes to the sense of social presence, such as facial expression, direction of gaze, posture, and other nonverbal cues. Gunawardena and Zittle [14] define two key concepts of social presence. The first concept is immediacy, which refers to the "measure of the psychological distance that a communicator puts between himself or herself and the object of his/her communication" (p. 9). The second concept is intimacy, which refers to the psychological closeness between communicators. Immediacy depends on verbal and nonverbal codes such as gesturing, smiling and using humor, whereas intimacy depends on factors such as eye contact, physical distance and smiling.

Social presence has been studied in different learning environments, such as in a blended learning environment [15, 16], a social web-based environment [17], video-centric online learning platforms [18] and a virtual environment [19]. Additionally, it has been studied on different samples, such as university students [14, 16, 20], students with disabilities [13], customers [21], employees [22] and adults [18].

Currently, the study of social presence can be divided into three categories. The first category of studies relates to how social presence, together with other variables, can better explain students' social interaction. For example, together with the elements of sociability and social space, social presence served as the basis for the theoretical framework developed by Kreijns et al. [23] for research on social interaction in computer-supported collaborative learning (CSCL) environments. More recently, social presence was used in the SIPS model in order to better explain the social interaction exhibited by users in a distance learning environment. The second category of research examines the impact of adding social and technical features (e.g., personal profiles) to online environments in order to facilitate students' perceptions of social presence (e.g., [20, 24]). For instance, recent research by Weidlich & Bastiaens [20] found that enriching the learning environment with social affordances (e.g., profile pictures, a list indicating users' online/offline status, easy sharing of documents and materials) can improve perceptions of students' social presence. The third category of research deals with the relationship between social presence and other variables. Recent meta-analytic evidence from Richardson et al. [10] shows that social presence influences important concepts of online and distance education, such as student motivation and participation, actual and perceived learning, course and instructor satisfaction. Additionally, the link between social presence, satisfaction and perceived learning has been confirmed from more recent studies (e.g., [25]).

Criticism regarding social presence [9] relates to its various definitions (see [10], p. 404) and the different questionnaires used to measure it (e.g., [14, 26, 27]). In general, the conclusion arising from the literature is that social presence is the most popular variable used to understand how students and academics socially interact in online learning environments. The study of this variable during the pandemic and its relation to university students' satisfaction and learning outcomes presents particular interest. This study will seek to cover this parameter.

3 Method

This study was conducted during the 2020 spring semester, which coincided with the COVID-19 period. Data were collected using an online questionnaire addressing multiple items regarding social presence, code development and satisfaction. This section describes the participants, the course content and procedure, instrument development, and data analysis.

3.1 Participants

Data in this study were collected from 39 undergraduate students, training to be future teachers, taking the elective course "Educational Programming Environments" at the Department of Education of the University of Ioannina, Greece. Their ages ranged from 22 to 32 years old (Mean = 23.4, SD = 0.7) and most of them were females (89.7%).

3.2 Course Content and Procedure

The course "Educational Programming Environments" is offered in the final (eighth) semester of the Department's curriculum. The course consists of a theoretical background regarding the values of computer programming in education, the basic programming structures, educational robotics, various programming environments, and block-based programming environments. The environment on which the students work is code.org; especially the section for educators entitled "teach your students". Instruction followed a student-centered design and discovery learning to teach computer programming problem solving. The course delivered over 13 lessons. The duration of each lesson was three hours. After the first three lessons, lockdown was imposed in Greece. Consequently, the other 10 lessons were conducted via the MS-Teams platform that is available through the University. The educational material for the course is available on the University's Content Management System (Moodle based). Sixty-two students attended the course. After the last lesson, three anonymous questionnaires were available to the students through Google forms. Thirty-nine questionnaires were filled over a period of one week.

3.3 Instruments

The questionnaire included three scales of items derived from earlier studies. For social presence, we used the 14-item scale by Gunawardena and Zittle [14]. For satisfaction, we used the 10-item scale also based on the study of Gunawardena and Zittle [14]. The code development scale was based on the questionnaire proposed by Richardson and Swan [28]. This scale measures the overall perceptions of learning outcomes that were obtained through the code development activities in which students were engagement. The above tools were properly modified for the purpose of our study and adapted accordingly to suit the nature of the computer programming course. The questionnaires were translated from English into Greek by two researchers successively who agreed at a degree of 95%. Each statement was measured on a 5-point Likert scale ranging from 1 (strongly disagree) to 5 (strongly agree). The questionnaire scales are presented in Tables 1, 2, and 3.

3.4 Data Analysis

SPSS (version 25) was used for the statistical analysis of the empirical data. Data were analyzed using descriptive statistics (means and standard deviations analysis). Reliability was examined using Cronbach's α values for each factor. In addition, Pearson correlation coefficients among the variables of social presence, code development and satisfaction were conducted. A stepwise linear regression analysis was also used in order to examine the effects of social presence and code development on satisfaction.

4 Results

4.1 Internal Consistency and Descriptive Analysis

The Cronbach's α of each factor was as follows: social presence = 0.724; code development = 0.882; satisfaction = 0.837. All these values are above 0.70, which is a commonly acceptable level.

Tables 1, 2, and 3 present descriptive statistics (minimum and maximum value, means, and standard deviations) for social presence, code development and satisfaction respectively. Table 1 shows that the overall mean of the social presence scale was 3.22 (SD = .485), indicating that the 39 undergraduate students perceived relatively satisfactory levels of social presence. The mean for the 14 items ranged from 2.13 (see item 9) to

4.05 (see item 7). The items which had high mean scores (higher than 4.00) related to the role of instructors (see items 7 and 8). Items 2, 9 and 14 were rated low (lower than 3.00) and related to the role of discussions in MS-Teams, the role of CMC as a medium of social interaction, and students' personal contact with some classmates.

Table 1. Questionnaire items in the social presence scale.

	Min	Max	Mean*	SD
1. Messages on MS-Teams were impersonal**	1	5	3.26	1.251
2. CMC is an excellent medium for social interaction	1	5	2.85	1.159
3. I felt comfortable conversing through chats	1	5	3.38	1.067
4. I felt comfortable introducing myself on MS-Teams	1	5	3.08	1.109
5. The introductions enabled me to form a sense of online community	1	5	3.31	1.030
6. I felt comfortable participating in discussions on MS-Teams	1	5	3.18	1.023
7. The instructors created a feeling of online community	2	5	4.05	.686
8. The instructors facilitated discussions within the framework of the course	2	5	4.03	.811
9. Discussions using the medium of MS-Teams tend to more impersonal than face-to-face discussions**	1	5	2.13	1.128
10. Discussion on MS-Teams are more impersonal than audio teleconference discussions**	2	5	3.44	.968
11. Discussions on MS-Teams are more impersonal than video teleconference discussions**	1	5	3.08	.957
12. I felt comfortable interacting with other classmates using MS-Teams	1	5	3.28	1.050
13. I felt that my point of view was acknowledged by my classmates on MS-Teams	1	5	3.18	1.048
14. I was able to have personal contact with some classmates even though we communicated only via a text-based medium	1	5	2.87	1.128
Overall scale	2	4	3.22	.485

*Likert scale used: 1 = Strongly Disagree, 2 = Disagree, 3 = Uncertain, 4 = Agree, 5 = Strongly Agree. **These items in the questionnaire were reverse coded for analysis purposes.

Table 2 shows that the overall mean of code development was 3.65 (0.666). This indicates that students' level of perceived learning regarding code development was satisfactory. Inspection of the means and the standard deviations per item indicate that item 7 (i.e., The instructors facilitated the activities) had the highest mean score (Mean = 4.10, SD = .882) and item 3 (i.e., Distance learning serves as an excellent medium for social interaction based on how it was conducted with the activities) the lowest (Mean = 2.95, SD = 1.169).

Table 3 shows that the overall mean of satisfaction scale was 3.59 (SD = .667). As we can see in this table, the mean for most satisfaction items (9 of 10 items) ranged from 3.38 (see item 7) to 4.18 (see item 6). These results indicate that students tended to agree that they were satisfied with their participation in the emergency remote online course entitled "Educational Programming Environments".

Table 2. Questionnaire items in the code development scale.

	Min	Max	Mean*	SD
1. The quality of learning for the coding activities was excellent	2	5	4.05	.793
2. I felt comfortable discussing the activities	1	5	3.51	.997
3. Distance learning serves as an excellent medium for social interaction based on how it was conducted with the activities	1	5	2.95	1.169
4. The activities enabled me to form a sense of online community	1	5	3.56	.912
5. The instructors created a feeling of online community through the activities	1	5	4.05	.857
6. I felt comfortable participating in the activities	1	5	3.79	.978
7. The instructors facilitated the activities	1	5	4.10	.882
8. I felt comfortable interacting with others during the activities	1	5	3.54	1.047
9. I felt that my point of view was acknowledged by other classmates	1	5	3.23	.902
10. I was able to get a sense of some of my classmates' impressions during the activities	1	5	3.67	.982
Overall scale	2	5	3.65	.666

*Likert scale used: 1 = Strongly Disagree, 2 = Disagree, 3 = Uncertain, 4 = Agree, 5 = Strongly Agree.

4.2 Pearson Correlation Analysis

Table 4 presents the results of the Pearson correlation coefficients between three scales. The results showed a positive and large correlation between social presence, code development ($r = +.586$, $p < 0.01$) and satisfaction ($r = +.584$, $p < 0.01$). In addition, the results showed a positive and large correlation between code development and satisfaction ($r = +.585$, $p < 0.01$).

Table 3. Questionnaire items in the satisfaction scale.

	Min	Max	Mean*	SD
1. I was able to learn through the distance learning system MS-Teams	2	5	3.87	.833
2. I was able to learn from MS-Teams discussions	1	5	3.69	.977
3. I was stimulated to do additional reading or research on topics discussed in MS-Team	1	5	3.90	.852
4. I learned to value my classmates' points of view	1	5	3.95	.944
5. As a result of my experience in this course, I would like to participate in other distance learning courses in the future	1	5	3.41	1.251
6. This course delivered through MS-Teams was a useful learning experience	3	5	4.18	.644
7. Distance learning courses like this enhance face-to-face on-campus courses	1	5	3.38	1.206
8. As a result of my participation in this course, I made acquaintances electronically with others	1	5	2.44	1.231
9. The diversity of topics discussed in this course prompted me to participate in the discussions	1	5	3.44	1.095
10. I put in a great deal of effort to learn the MS-Teams system to participate in the course	1	5	3.64	1.246
Overall scale	2	5	3.59	.667

*Likert scale used: 1 = Strongly Disagree, 2 = Disagree, 3 = Uncertain, 4 = Agree, 5 = Strongly Agree.

Table 4. Correlation analysis.

	Social presence	Code development	Satisfaction
Social presence	1	.586*	.584*
Code development		1	.585*
Satisfaction			1

*Correlation is significant at the 0.01 level (2-tailed).

4.3 Regression Analysis

Table 5 presents the results of stepwise regression analysis. These results showed that the variables of social presence and code development influence students' satisfaction significantly. Specifically, in Model 1, social presence (b = .584) explained 32.3% (F = 5.753, p = .000, p < .05) of the variance in students' satisfaction. When the code development was added to regression Model 2, the explained variance increased from 32.3% to 39.9% (F = 13.613, p = .000, p < .05). Code development was the strongest of the predictors of satisfaction (b = .371), and social presence was the second strongest (b = .366).

Table 5. Regression analysis of social presence and code development on students' satisfaction.

Dependent variable: satisfaction	Adjusted R^2	Independent variable	Beta	*t*	*p*
Model 1	.323	Social presence	.584	4.371	.000*
Model 2	.399	Social presence	.366	2.359	.024*
		Code development	.371	2.387	.022*

*Significant ($p < .05$).

5 Conclusions

In this empirical study, we examined undergraduate students' social presence, learning outcomes through code development and satisfaction from their participation in an emergency remote online course that took place during the COVID-19 pandemic. The results of this study showed that all three variables were evaluated as satisfactory by the students. These results are particularly significant considering that students' participation in this course was sudden and took place under the difficult circumstances caused by the pandemic, without them undertaking any prior preparation for engaging in distance learning. Similar measurements regarding the mean values for social presence and satisfaction were found in previous studies, where students were more familiar with distance learning compared to the sample in this study (e.g., [14, 20]).

Furthermore, the results from this study concerning the sense of social presence and learning outcomes may be due to the role of the instructors. As mentioned earlier, the course was designed by instructors to feature a student-centered design and discovery learning in computer programming problem solving. The significance of the instructors' role in the course is also apparent from the fact that the items related to them presented the highest mean scores in Tables 1 and 2.

The results also indicated that social presence and code development were positively associated with satisfaction. These positive correlations mean that when students feel that social presence and learning outcomes increase from their participation in distance learning course, their satisfaction also increases. These findings are consistent with previous studies that found social presence to be associated with perceived learning outcomes and satisfaction [14, 25].

The results of the regression analysis indicated that social presence and code development are critical factors affecting students' satisfaction. Together, these two factors explain 39.9% of the variance of satisfaction. Code development was the first strongest predictor of students' satisfaction. Nonetheless, the results of the stepwise regression analysis showed that social presence alone contributed about 32.3% of this variance. This suggests that social presence may be a very strong predictor of satisfaction. Furthermore, it suggests that by improving students' social presence, it should be possible to enhance satisfaction from their participation in distance learning courses. This finding is similar to that of a previous study by Gunawardena and Zittle [14] that indicated the importance of social presence in the prediction of satisfaction.

The findings presented in this study have one major implication for the use and the design of emergency remote online courses in universities. These courses should take into account the need to encourage a positive sense of social presence, particularly for those students who may not be experienced in distance education. For instance, the students in this study may need different learning activities and social presence support compared to those enrolled in distance education courses prior to the COVID-19 pandemic. The instructor can play an important role in this. Through his or her technological and pedagogical/instructional training, the instructor must be in a position to evaluate the affordances of platforms contributing to more active engagement among students in both synchronous and asynchronous teaching, and ultimately, to student-centered and constructive approaches. These issues lead us to suggest that professional development in the pedagogical use of distance learning courses should be mandatory for all university instructors, regardless of their subjects, ICT skills and experience in using digital technologies in their teaching.

5.1 Limitations

The present study has two limitations. The first relates to the size of this study's sample (N = 39). It is important to note that previous studies in the area of social presence have used small samples and showed reliable results (e.g., see the sample of 50 in [14]). Nevertheless, the results must be interpreted cautiously. The second limitation relates to the measurement of social presence, code development and satisfaction. These factors were measured using self-reports. The gathering of additional quantitative and qualitative data using other instruments as well (e.g., interviews, course analytics, diaries) may be able to help us better understand the quality and type of interaction between students, as well as with instructors.

5.2 Future Research

The limitations as well as the findings of this study have indicated the following areas for further research. First, future research should include a larger sample. Second, future research should investigate possible demographic (e.g., gender, ICT knowledge and skills) differences in students' social presence, learning outcomes and satisfaction. Third, future research should be designed to investigate whether social presence, learning outcomes and satisfaction are influenced by other factors (e.g., a platform's ease of use, usefulness) in order to increase the percentage of the explained variance of satisfaction. Finally, future research should collect longitudinal data to examine probable changes in social presence, learning outcomes and satisfaction at particular times, as well as if these changes are related to the instructor's role.

References

1. Shafi, M., Liu, J., Ren, W.: Impact of COVID-19 pandemic on micro, small, and medium-sized Enterprises operating in Pakistan. Res. Global. **2**, 100018 (2020)

2. Islam, S.M.D.-U., Bodrud-Doza, M., Khan, R.M., Haque, M.A., Mamun, M.A.: Exploring COVID-19 stress and its factors in Bangladesh: a perception-based study. Heliyon **6**(7), 04399 (2020)
3. Kye, B., Hwang, S.J.: Social trust in the midst of pandemic crisis: implications from COVID-19 of South Korea. Res. Soc. Stratif. Mob. **68**, 100523 (2020)
4. Dwivedi, Y., et al.: Impact of COVID-19 pandemic on information management research and practice: transforming education, work and life. Int. J. Inf. Manag. **55**, 102211 (2020)
5. Moodle: Moodle Learning Management System. https://moodle.org/. Accessed 14 Sept 2020
6. Liu, Q., Geertshuis, S., Grainger, R.: Understanding academics' adoption of learning technologies: a systematic review. Comput. Educ. **151**, 103857 (2020)
7. Wang, Y.-H.: Design-based research on integrating learning technology tools into higher education classes to achieve active learning. Comput. Educ. **156**, 103935 (2020)
8. Short, J., Williams, E., Christie, B.: The Social Psychology of Telecommunications. Wiley, London (1976)
9. Weidlich, J., Bastiaens, T.J.: Explaining social presence and the quality of online learning with the SIPS model. Comput. Hum. Behav. **72**, 479–487 (2017)
10. Richardson, J.C., Maeda, Y., Lv, J., Caskurlu, S.: Social presence in relation to students' satisfaction and learning in the online environment: a meta-analysis. Comput. Hum. Behav. **71**, 402–417 (2017)
11. Mohammadi, H.: Investigating users' perspectives on e-learning: an integration of TAM and IS success model. Comput. Educ. **45**, 359–374 (2015)
12. Al Lily, A.E., Ismail, A.F., Abunasser, F.M., Alqahtani, R.H.A.A.: Distance education as a response to pandemics: coronavirus and Arab culture. Technol. Soc. **63**, 101317 (2020)
13. Dahlstrom-Hakki, I., Alstad, Z., Banerjee, M.: Comparing synchronous and asynchronous online discussions for students with disabilities: the impact of social presence. Comput. Educ. **150**, 103842 (2020)
14. Gunawardena, C.N., Zittle, F.J.: Social presence as a predictor of satisfaction within a computer-mediated conferencing environment. Am. J. Distance Educ. **11**(3), 8–26 (1997)
15. Szeto, E.: Community of Inquiry as an instructional approach: what effects of teaching, social and cognitive presences are there in blended synchronous learning and teaching? Comput. Educ. **81**, 191–201 (2015)
16. Law, K.M.Y., Geng, S., Li, T.: Student enrollment, motivation and learning performance in a blended learning environment: the mediating effects of social, teaching, and cognitive presence. Comput. Educ. **136**, 1–2 (2019)
17. Molinillo, S., Aguilar-Illescas, R., Anaya-Sánchez, R., Vallespín-Arán, M.: Exploring the impacts of interactions, social presence and emotional engagement on active collaborative learning in a social web-based environment. Comput. Educ. **123**, 41–52 (2018)
18. Andel, S.A., de Vreede, T., Spector, P.E., Padmanabhan, B., Singh, V.K., de Vreede, G.J.: Do social features help in video-centric online learning platforms? A social presence perspective. Comput. Hum. Behav. **113**, 106505 (2020)
19. McCreery, M.P., Vallett, D.B., Clark, C.: Social interaction in a virtual environment: examining socio-spatial interactivity and social presence using behavioral analytics. Comput. Hum. Behav. **51**(A), 203–206 (2015)
20. Weidlich, J., Bastiaens, T.J.: Designing sociable online learning environments and enhancing social presence: an affordance enrichment approach. Comput. Educ. **142**, 103622 (2019)
21. Nadeem, W., Khani, A.H., Schultz, C.D., Adam, N.A., Attar, R.W., Hajli, N.: How social presence drives commitment and loyalty with online brand communities? The role of social commerce trust. J. Retail. Consum. Serv. **55**, 102136 (2020)
22. Lowden, R.J., Hostetter, C.: Access, utility, imperfection: the impact of videoconferencing on perceptions of social presence. Comput. Hum. Behav. **28**(2), 377–383 (2012)

23. Kreijns, K., Kirschner, P.A., Vermeulen, M.: Social aspects of CSCL environments: a research framework. Educ. Psychol. **48**(4), 229–242 (2013)
24. Kear, K., Chetwynd, F., Jefferis, H.: Social presence in online learning communities: the role of personal profiles. Res. Learn. Technol. **22**, 1–5 (2014)
25. Raisolsadat, M., Sanjar Moussavi, N., Farajpour, A., Meshkinyazd, A.: Investigating the effects of problem-based learning in a virtual group on collaborative learning, social presence and student satisfaction in surgery department. Interdiscip. J. Virtual Learn. Med. Sci. **11**(2), 102–111 (2020)
26. De Greef, P., Ijsselsteijn, W.A.: Social presence in a home tele-application. Cyberpsychol. Behav. **4**(2), 307–315 (2001)
27. Kim, J.: Developing an instrument to measure social presence in distance higher education. Br. J. Educ. Technol. **42**, 763–777 (2011)
28. Richardson, J.C., Swan, K.: Examining social presence in online courses in relation to students' perceived learning and satisfaction. J. Asynchronous Learn. Netw. **7**(1), 68–88 (2003)

E-assessment and Academic Integrity: A Literature Review

Theologos Tsigaros(✉) and George Fesakis

University of the Aegean, Rhodes, Greece
{tsigaros,gfesakis}@aegean.gr

Abstract. A literature review was conducted in order to study academic integrity in e-assessment. The research questions relate firstly to the prevalence of incidents that violate academic integrity and secondly to the countermeasures for addressing the challenges. In regard to prevalence, we found that e-cheating may not be as common as believed. In regard to countermeasures, we found that there are a lot of technical means to address the violations, but since technical countermeasures cannot fully ensure academic integrity, a long-term strategy should aim to redesign the learning process and to use alternative assessment methods.

Keywords: E-cheating · E-assessment · Academic integrity

1 Introduction

Emergency circumstances caused by the Covid-19 pandemic, forced the transition from the conventional, face to face education to the Emergency Urgent Online Education. Educational institutions, in order to continue providing educational services, utilized e-learning environments and adopted e-assessment practices, i.e. the use of computer systems to support assessment-related processes [13]. Since, the use of e-learning environments seems to expand steadily, regardless of emergencies, e-assessment will be increasingly utilized, both in purely online and in blended educational environments and accordingly there will be a strong need to ensure academic integrity in e-assessment. Ensuring academic integrity in e-assessment is essential, in order not to question the validity of diplomas and educational credit units awarded by educational institutions both for conventional curricula and for Massive Online Open Courses (MOOCs), where there is a constantly growing trend to award not only certificates of attendance, but also diplomas equivalent to those of accredited educational institutions [11].

Challenges related to academic integrity are seen as a key deterrent to the widespread use of e-assessment [15]. They are related to attempts to impersonate, to obtain assistance from a third party or from an unauthorized source of information, to plagiarize [9]. That is, with attempts to cheat electronically ("e-cheating"), where a student attempts to violate the rules of e-assessment and gain an unfair advantage over others.

These challenges are not new phenomena, since they do not only threaten e-assessment [12]. Similar forms of violations threaten the academic integrity of conventional assessments too. However, the use of Information and Communication Technologies (ICT) raises more concerns about increased risk level, although it is acknowledged

A. Reis et al. (Eds.): TECH-EDU 2020, CCIS 1384, pp. 313–319, 2021.
https://doi.org/10.1007/978-3-030-73988-1_24

that ICT offer means to confront the challenges [15]. According to Arnold [2], the degree of instructors' concern about the issue is inversely proportional to the degree of experience in e-learning environments. In particular, the more experienced the instructors are in e-learning environments, the less they express concerns about the issue, considering that violations are not more common than in conventional assessments.

The academic community, recognizing the importance of the issue, seeks strategies to address it, but, as Oosterhof, Conrad & Ely [17] observe, the intended degree of safeguarding e-assessment should not be greater than the degree of safeguarding conventional assessment. For, the financial and administrative costs paid to achieve a higher degree of safeguarding may be disproportionate and may limit, or even cancel out, the significant pedagogical and administrative advantages of e-assessment.

Following the instructions of state authorities for dealing with the Covid-19 pandemic, the Department of Preschool Education and Educational Design of the University of the Aegean, in Greece, implemented all the courses of Spring Semester 2019–2020 remotely (via internet). It then conducted remotely (via internet) the semester summative exams in June and in September 2020. During the planning and implementation of the exams, there was intense concern about ensuring the academic integrity of the assessment process. We felt that it would be useful to conduct a literature review, which would record the relevant findings of the literature in terms of ensuring academic integrity and highlight ways to manage relevant challenges in real conditions. The main results of the literature review are presented in this paper.

2 Methodology

We sought answers that would respond to the most common concerns of our Department's teaching staff. Instructors are primarily concerned with i) how often academic integrity is violated in e-assessment and ii) what countermeasures could be applied to shield the assessment process. Thus, we formulate the following research questions: RQ1. How common are the violations of academic integrity in e-assessment? RQ2. What are the countermeasures usually used to address these challenges? We searched for relevant literature sources on the Internet using the Google Scholar search engine. The search keywords we used, were: i) "e-assessment" combined with the terms "academic integrity", "academic dishonesty", "plagiarism" and ii) "e-cheating". The time period we conducted the search was April 2020. We narrowed our search to relatively recent (less than ten years) articles. Few, older interesting literature sources emerged during later stages of our study and added to our list. The initial set of articles which we collected, was further expanded with articles that we found in the reference lists of both the initial articles and the articles that were added in the set while the literature research was continued (backward snowballing) [21]. Due to the emergency and urgent circumstances of Covid-19 pandemic and to the limited time available to us, our review is unavoidably selective, including only few of the thousands of articles referring to the topic. We focused on articles that offer a general perspective on our research questions, and eventually we came up with the set of articles which are included in the reference list of the present paper.

3 Research Results

3.1 E-cheating Prevalence

As far as the research question *RQ1. E-cheating prevalence* is concerned, the literature review findings are equivocal as to whether academic dishonesty incidents are more frequent and more serious in e-assessment comparing to conventional assessment [11]. Watson and Sottile [20] found no evidence that cheating is more common in e-assessment. Arnold [2] states that according to a widespread belief, academic integrity violations are more common in e-assessment, as a result of the ineffective (due to the distance) invigilation. However, Arnold [2] adds that, the increased opportunities to cheat in unproctored e-assessment, does not automatically imply that students actually choose to take advantage of these opportunities. Lang [14] argues that, although e-learning environments are more vulnerable to cheating, the incidents' frequency is about the same as in the conventional learning environments. He assumes that this happens because of the fact that e-learning environments are used more by older students, who are less prone to cheating practices. Lang [14] also states, that in the future, as the use of e-learning environments will become popular for younger students too, the cheating incidents are likely to increase. However, at present, there is no clear evidence that cheating in e-learning environments is more common. Stuber-McEwen, Wiseley, & Hoggatt [18] express the view that cheating in e-assessment may not be as prevalent as believed. However, they consider that it is possible to increase, as the use of e-assessment increases. Arnold [2] states that the frequency of cheating incidents is inversely proportional to the maturity and to the diligence of students. Postgraduate students in particular are less prone to deceptive practices due to their motivation to master a knowledge domain and their commitment to learning. In addition, the academic integrity violations mainly concern the highly critical summative e-assessments, not the formative e-assessments. The students who cheat on formative e-assessments do not gain any long-term advantage, because they forsake learning opportunities that formative e-assessments may offer. On the contrary, if they choose to cheat on formative e-assessments, then their performance during the summative e-assessment will be probably lower compared to those who do not cheat [2]. Gikandi et al. [9] report that the incidents of academic integrity violation are less common in authentic formative assessment activities where students' commitment is increased.

3.2 Countermeasures

The findings in relation to the research question *RQ2: Countermeasures* are analyzed in this section. Most cheating attempts exploit the fact that e-assessment is offered mainly online. Students are assessed remotely using their own electronic devices, so the educational institutions cannot effectively check either their identity or their activity.

In regard to impersonation, basic methods (such as submitting a username and a password or accessing the network through a certified internet address) are used to assure user authentication. Since these methods cannot be considered sufficient, more sophisticated practices are utilized, which check the biometric characteristics of the student (e.g. iris recognition, facial recognition, voice recognition, typing rate check) [6].

Examples of such systems are proposed by Clarke, Dowland, & Furnell [5] and Ahlawat, Pareek, & Singh [1]. These systems continuously confirm the identity of the student, based on biometric characteristics, without requiring the installation of complex electronic devices on the student's computer. However, it is not uncommon for educational institutions, especially in highly critical summative assessments, to require students to attend assessment centers in person. There, students are physically authenticated and invigilated, while assessed using ICT. Obviously, this practice not only entails high financial and administrative costs for educational institutions, but also deprives students of the flexibility in terms of space and time, which is a key advantage of e-assessment. In general, the difficulties in invigilation are of great concern to educational institutions preventing them to adopt e-assessment practices, especially in the cases of highly critical summative assessments.

In regard to assistance from a third party or using unauthorized source of information, various cheating practices are documented. The most common and easy (due to the ineffective invigilation) cheating practice is searching the Internet for the right answers, a practice that according to Boitshwarelo, Reedy, & Billny [4] many students find acceptable. More serious cheating practices are those where students get assistance from a third party or form groups to jointly solve the quiz. In a similar cheating practice, many students simultaneously log on to the system, using the same user account, in order to co-solve the quiz [4]. To prevent mutual assistance between students in multiple choice tests, various countermeasures are applied, such as asking students different questions, changing the order of the answers and producing multiple variations of questions that differ in their numerical values [8, 10]. The implementation of such countermeasures has been simplified through the use of Learning Management Systems (LMS) that facilitate the construction and delivering of online quizzes and the use of question banks.

Question banks are digital repositories or databases where questions are not only stored, but also classified into categories, according to the subject, level of knowledge, type, level of difficulty, assessed skills or knowledge [3]. Question banks may be used to prevent academic integrity violations, such as the students' mutual assistance. They facilitate the construction of quizzes that are completely or partially different. The LMS, draws questions from the question bank and produces many different versions of the quiz, ensuring that the questions in every version are of the same difficulty level and assess same skills and knowledge. This way, it prevents injustices that might arise if the questions were chosen in a random but unequal way. If the quiz versions are not completely different for each student, that is, if a few or many questions are common, then the LMS can place the common questions in a random (different for each student) order, or randomly shuffle the answers in the questions.

Additionally, it is possible to populate the question bank with many variations of the same question. Many question variations could be automatically produced by the LMS, once free variables take the place of constant numerical values. Particularly, the question is typed into the LMS, as a "calculated question" [8, 10] such as the following example: «How long would it take for a bicycle to travel a distance of X km at a constant speed of Y km/h?». In the example, free variables (X and Y) replace the constant numerical values. The free variables (X and Y) derive numerical values from a predefined set of permitted values, e.g. $X \in \{20, 40, 60, \ldots, 1000\}$ and $Y \in \{2, 4, 6, \ldots, 100\}$. With this method (which is obviously easier to implement in cognitive domains that require mathematical calculations), it is possible to automatically produce as many different question variations as the set's range permits.

In regard to plagiarism, Davies and Howard [7] report that there is no empirical research which substantiates the popular conception that the Internet facilitates and enhances plagiarism. Plagiarism is indeed a great challenge for e-assessment, but technology has developed tools that offer effective countermeasures. In particular, quite common is the use of anti-plagiarism software that detects similarities between students' assignments and texts posted on the Internet (e.g. texts contained in websites, books, journals, research papers, dissertations, etc.). Anti-plagiarism software is based on powerful search engines that scan the Internet, analyze huge number of text bodies and detects signs of plagiarism with accuracy and speed that is impossible to be achieved by a person. However, it should be noted that anti-plagiarism software is not problem-free. Similarity reports are not always easy to understand. Correctly referenced text may be marked as plagiarism. Plagiarized text may not be detected as such. Different systems, while they analyze the same text, produce different reports [15]. Lang [14] praises the usefulness of anti-plagiarism technology, but he notes that it just highlights matching text and it does not prove plagiarism. It is a teacher's task to judge whether the highlighted matching suggests plagiarism or not. Lang [14] also suggests that the similarity reports produced by anti-plagiarism software may be used to teach students the proper way to incorporate bibliographic sources into their work.

There are many references that emphasize the need for broader prevention strategies, in addition to technical countermeasures. Oosterhof, Conrad & Ely [17] argue that the most effective strategy is to limit the use of specific e-assessment types, such as multiple-choice questions and essays. They believe that "performance assessments", where the student completes a task, plays a role, solves a problem, demonstrates and applies skills, are best shielded against academic integrity violations. However, they do not fail to mention that the use of performance assessments has disadvantages such as reduced efficiency, subjective scoring, difficulty to generalize [17]. Lang [14] also argues that technical countermeasures cannot fully ensure academic integrity. A good prevention strategy should aim to redesign the learning process providing opportunities for deep learning and encouraging active student participation. Talbert [19] opposes the use of technical countermeasures, such as network surveillance systems, which he considers as ineffective and as threat to privacy. He advocates the replacement of conventional points-based grading (which he considers favoring the accumulation of points, "through whatever means necessary"), with alternate methods such as "specifications grading" [16].

4 Conclusion

E-assessment is expanding in parallel with e-learning and will be a common practice in the future. Therefore, shielding e-assessment against academic integrity violations is a crucial issue that will retain its importance even after the emergency caused by the Covid-19 pandemic is lifted. Conducting a literature review, we searched for answers to questions concerning a) e-cheating prevalence and b) the countermeasures that address the relevant challenges. The research showed that cheating in e-assessment does not seem to be more common than in conventional assessment, although e-learning environments offer more opportunities for academic integrity violations. The countermeasures that are mainly applied concern electronic invigilation, different variants of quizzes per student and utilization of anti-plagiarism software that identifies similarities between student assignments and online resources. Additionally, since technical countermeasures cannot fully ensure academic integrity, a good prevention strategy should include the redesign of the learning process and the use of alternative assessment methods.

Our findings may support our Department's instructors, as well as the wider academic community to adapt to the new emergency conditions and extend the use of e-assessment, while shielding academic integrity.

As the use of e-assessment is constantly expanding, instructors must accept and be prepared for a moderate level of risk for academic integrity violations. After all, even in conventional assessments, academic integrity is not fully guaranteed. Hesitations to adopt forms of e-assessment should be less in the non-critical formative assessments, where the stakes are low and in postgraduate programs, where, due to the maturity and commitment of students, attempted violations are less common. The training of instructors is considered necessary in order to understand the challenges and to adopt countermeasures which are available and easily implemented. Instructors need to take advantage of the available educational technology tools such as LMS to form and deliver randomized online tests and antiplagiarism software to detect plagiarism attempts.

Finally, since technical countermeasures cannot alone guarantee complete shielding against violations, which they will be constantly intensified and upgraded, academic community may consider to adopt alternative, less vulnerable forms of assessment, to cultivate academic ethic that devalues deception and, more generally, to redesign the learning process in order to promote students' motive to learning.

References

1. Ahlawat, V., Pareek, A., Singh, S.: Online invigilation: a holistic approach. Int. J. Comput. Appl. **90**(17), 31–35 (2014)
2. Arnold, I.J.: Cheating at online formative tests: Does it pay off? Internet High. Educ. **29**, 98–106 (2016)
3. Azevedo, J., Oliveira, E.P., Beites, P.D.: E-assessment and multiple-choice questions: a literature review. In: Handbook of Research on E-Assessment in Higher Education, pp. 1–27. IGI Global (2019)
4. Boitshwarelo, B., Reedy, A.K., Billany, T.: Envisioning the use of online tests in assessing twenty-first century learning: a literature review. Res. Pract. Technol. Enhanc. Learn. **12**(1), 1–16 (2017). https://doi.org/10.1186/s41039-017-0055-7
5. Clarke, N.L., Dowland, P., Furnell, S.M.: e-Invigilator: a biometric-based supervision system for e-Assessments. In: International Conference on Information Society (i-Society 2013), pp. 238–242. IEEE (2013)
6. Crisp, G.: Teacher's Handbook on e-Assessment. An ALTC Fellowship Activity, 18 (2011)
7. Davies, L.J., Howard, R.M.: Plagiarism and the internet: fears, facts, and pedagogies. In: Handbook of Academic Integrity, p. 591 (2016)
8. de Sande, J.C.: Calculated questions and e-cheating: a case study. In: Carmo, M. (ed.) Education Applications & Developments, pp. 91–99. inScience Press, Lisboa (2015)

9. Gikandi, J.W., Morrow, D., Davis, N.E.: Online formative assessment in higher education: a review of the literature. Comput. Educ. **57**(4), 2333–2351 (2011)
10. Heyde, V.V., Siebrits, A.: Higher-order e-assessment for physics in the digital age using Sakai. Phys. Teach. **57**(1), 32–34 (2019)
11. James, R.: Tertiary student attitudes to invigilated, online summative examinations. Int. J. Educ. Technol. High. Educ. **13**(1), 1–13 (2016). https://doi.org/10.1186/s41239-016-0015-0
12. JISC: Effective Practice with e-Assessment (2007). https://www.webarchive.org.uk/wayback/en/archive/20130414000900mp_/http://www.jisc.ac.uk/media/documents/themes/elearning/effpraceassess.pdf. Accessed 16 Apr 2020
13. Jordan, S.: E-assessment: past, present and future. New Direct. Teach. Phys. Sci. **9**, 87–106 (2013)
14. Lang, J.M.: Cheating Lessons: Learning from Academic Dishonesty. Harvard University Press, Cambridge (2013)
15. Mellar, H., Peytcheva-Forsyth, R., Kocdar, S., Karadeniz, A., Yovkova, B.: Addressing cheating in e-assessment using student authentication and authorship checking systems: teachers' perspectives. Int. J. Educ. Integr. **14**(1), 1–21 (2018). https://doi.org/10.1007/s40979-018-0025-x
16. Nilson, L.: Specifications Grading: Restoring Rigor, Motivating Students, and Saving Faculty Time. Stylus Publishing LLC, Sterling (2015)
17. Oosterhof, A., Conrad, R.-M., Ely, D.P.: Assessing Learners Online. Pearson Merill Prentice-Hall, Upper Saddle River (2008)
18. Stuber-McEwen, D., Wiseley, P., Hoggatt, S.: Point, click, and cheat: frequency and type of academic dishonesty in the virtual classroom. Online J. Distance Learn. Adm. **12**(3) (2009). https://www2.westga.edu/~distance/ojdla/fall123/stuber123.html. Accessed 20 Apr 2020
19. Talbert, R.: Mastery grading and academic honesty, 20 July 2020. https://rtalbert.org/mastery-grading-and-academic-honesty. Accessed 27 Aug 2020
20. Watson, G., Sottile, J.: Do students cheat more in on-line courses? Online J. Distance Learn. Adm. **13**(1) (2010). https://mds.marshall.edu/eft_faculty/1. Accessed 16 Apr 2020
21. Wohlin, C.: Guidelines for snowballing in systematic literature studies and a replication in software engineering. In: Proceedings of the 18th International Conference on Evaluation and Assessment in Software Engineering, p. 10 (2014)

Shifting to Emergency Remote Teaching Due to the COVID-19 Pandemic: An Investigation of Greek Teachers' Beliefs and Experiences

Athanassios Jimoyiannis(✉), Nikolaos Koukis, and Panagiotis Tsiotakis

University of Peloponnese, Korinthos, Greece
{ajimoyia,nkoukis,ptsiotakis}@uop.gr

Abstract. During schools' closure, due to the pandemic of COVID-19, teachers around the globe were forced to transfer their instruction on-line. They were facing a range of barriers and difficulties to plan and provide online remote teaching to their students. This paper reports on a study exploring Greek primary and secondary education teachers' views about emergency remote teaching and e-learning. The survey conducted in May 2020, just after schools' reopening in Greece. A total of 694 K-12 teachers responded to an online questionnaire. The preliminary findings of data analysis showed that the majority of the participants perceived the pandemic as a turning point with regards to the role of digital technologies and e-learning in the schools. On the other hand, we identified teachers' needs for professional development and support, in terms of learning design abilities necessary to integrate synchronous and asynchronous learning in both, online and physical, classrooms.

Keywords: Emergency remote teaching · E-learning · Teacher beliefs · COVID-19 pandemic

1 Introduction

The COVID-19 pandemic had worldwide a disruptive effect on people's lives, since many of our personal, work and social activities were interrupted. In particular, the education sector faced an unexpected impact; universities and K-12 schools were forced to rapidly transfer their programs online by using remote teaching and e-learning modes. The transition of teachers and students to online learning environments was a disruption of the educational normality and school practices.

Teachers needed to design this transition to online teaching and to develop, very quickly, new competencies related to the use of learning technologies in their online classrooms. As they swiftly transferred their teaching online, they were facing new type of difficulties; for example, to familiarise with video-conferencing tools, to guide their students' participation, to create new educational plans with synchronous and asynchronous environments etc. In addition, they had to offer new type of support to their students due to school live interruption (i.e., emotional, social and psychological), to apply new assessment procedures, to communicate with parents etc.

A. Reis et al. (Eds.): TECH-EDU 2020, CCIS 1384, pp. 320–329, 2021.
https://doi.org/10.1007/978-3-030-73988-1_25

In this context, teachers' views and experiences of online remote teaching during the COVID-19 pandemic has been emerged as a new important research problem. Recent studies explored teachers' barriers, difficulties and professional development needs [1], students' response to remote online teaching [2], openness in terms of technologies, educational resources and educational practices used [3], parents' new roles and difficulties in educational involvement, teachers' psychological pressure and outcomes [4], new perspectives about educational inequities and student inclusion [5].

In this article, we present initial results and insights from a study reporting on Greek teachers' perceptions and beliefs about remote online teaching during the COVID-19 crisis. The survey conducted after schools restarting in Greece, in the middle of May 2020. The analysis of quantitative and qualitative results indicated that the majority of the participants were willing to adopt online learning tools and practices in their instruction, and to use them during and after the pandemic. They also reported the need for training and enhancing their pedagogical skills and learning design abilities. The paper concludes by providing recommendations for teacher preparation and support towards integrating online tools and e-learning practices in their classrooms, during and after the pandemic.

2 Emergency Remote Teaching

During the pandemic concepts such as *distance education* in the schools, *online teaching/learning* and *emergency remote teaching* were interchangeably used in both, educational and public discourse. These terms, particularly when they are seen in K-12 school contexts, need to be clarified. Accurate description and understanding of the concepts above, as well as the educational framework of implementation, is expected to help teachers to avoid misunderstandings as well as to design instructional practices suitable to respond to the needs of K-12 education during the pandemic of COVID-19.

Distance education is an established mode, with a long educational history. By definition, distance education is characterized by the distance, in time and space, of the interactions among the tutor, the learners and the educational content and resources [6]. According to Moore *"distance education is not simply a geographic separation of learners and teachers, but, more importantly, is a pedagogical concept"*. In this perspective, distance learning programs are properly designed to be offered from distance, in terms of learning objectives, appropriate pedagogical models, specifically designed educational material, student learning activities, learning tools and technologies, tutor's role, assessment procedures regarding learning outcomes etc.

The second related notion is *online learning*, since online technologies and e-learning platforms are used to support remote teaching. Online learning models place emphasis on interactions between different parties of learning (students-content-tutor) and through different forms of student engagement (i.e., individual and collaborative) in the learning process [7]. While online teaching has a long history in higher education contexts, recent research has explored its potential to support and extend students' learning within K-12 school settings [8].

The new notion, when discussing about education in the midst of the pandemic, is *emergency remote teaching*, which proposed by Hodges et al. [9] to describe this temporary shift of providing education by using alternative ways, due to crisis circumstances.

As Milman stated [10], a new pedagogy, so called it the *'pandemic pedagogy'*, was emerging in the schools and addressed teachers' decisions and students' participation in new form of online educational practices.

Therefore, the three educational modes have two features in common: a) they refer to the spatial distance between students and educators, and b) they use online technologies to provide education. On the other hand, they are fundamentally different. In the case of emergency remote teaching, the main objective is to set up, very quickly, a new educational model due to the crisis.

Nevertheless, remote teaching is not a new idea. Existing research findings indicated that online remote teaching has been reported for equal and inclusive education in rural areas in various countries [11–13]. A second mode of remote teaching was also applied when schools are closed or inaccessible due to a natural disaster [14, 15] or other emergency, for example the war crisis in Syria [16].

Therefore, emergency remote teaching should be considered as a temporary, rapid response to the school closure problem, due to the pandemic of COVID-19. The first studies that appeared worldwide have shown that teachers were facing barriers and difficulties in adapting their instruction to this unpredictable situation and provide online remote teaching to their students [17, 18]. The aim of the present study was to explore Greek teachers' perceptions and beliefs about remote online teaching during the COVID-19 crisis, as well as their abilities, concerns and difficulties to design and support e-learning interventions, both remotely and in physical classroom settings.

3 Research Method

3.1 Context and Procedure

On 11th of March 2020, the Greek government decided to temporarily close every educational institution with the aim to restrict and control the spread of the COVID-19 pandemic. School educators suddenly were forced to use online technologies, mainly videoconference technologies, as the only means to continue their teaching. However, they were not prepared and did not receive any training during schools' closure about online remote instruction. Schools' reopening started two months later, in the midst of May 2020, with low numbers of students present in the classrooms.

Data collection started just after school re-opening and lasted for 3 weeks. We thus expected to reveal critical information regarding teachers' experiences and readiness to provide remote online instruction during the global pandemic. We used an online questionnaire, provided through the LimeSurvey platform installation at the University of Peloponnese.

3.2 Instrument

The instrument was a five-point Likert-type scale (1 = strongly disagree, 5 = strongly agree) which included 23 statements that represent teachers' views and perceptions addressed along three dimensions: a) individual skills and competencies to apply online technologies in their instructional work; b) experiences in applying remote teaching as well as their difficulties and concerns about e-learning in school education, and c) perceptions about their professional development needs to apply e-learning in the schools during and after the pandemic. In addition, the questionnaire included three open questions which were also used in qualitative analysis.

The development of the questionnaire was relied on existing literature as well as on the authors extended experience with the design and implementation of teacher professional development programs regarding e-learning and digital technologies in primary and secondary schools [19, 20].

3.3 The Sample

Completely responded questionnaires for analysis received from 694 teachers coming from various district areas across the country; 153 (22.1%) were males and 538 (77.5%) females, while 3 teachers provided no gender information. Most participants were serving in public primary and secondary schools; 439 (63.3%) teachers were teaching in secondary schools, 188 (27.1%) in primary schools, 21 (3.0%) in kindergartens, and 36 (6.6%) in vocational and life-long learning institutions or in administration positions.

The majority of the participants reported their experience in using digital technologies for personal and educational purposes. 8 out of 10 teachers rated their ability to use digital technologies for educational purposes in the range good-excellent. The teachers reported that, prior to COVID-19 schools' closure, they had no experience of remote teaching. However, more than two-thirds of the participants had some experience of using asynchronous online tools in their instruction (i.e., LMS, blogs, Google Docs, wikis, etc.). Videoconferencing applications (77.2%) and learning management systems (69.6%), like eClass, Moodle, Edmodo, and e-me, were the prominent tools among teachers and used to support remote instruction during the pandemic.

4 Results

4.1 Descriptive Statistics

The findings regarding teachers' abilities to design and deliver online remote instruction are shown in Table 1. It is quite clear that the participants were positive and confident to use e-learning in their instruction. The vast majority of teachers believe that the experience of remote teaching, during the pandemic, strengthened their skills to integrate e-learning into instruction. The findings also revealed that many teachers faced difficulties to promote students' active participation in videoconferencing sessions. The participants appeared confident to design asynchronous learning activities with Web 2.0 tools (mean value $M = 3.53$) and activities that require students to explore online resources ($M = 3.63$). On the other hand, they rated lower their ability to design suitable synchronous online activities guiding students' homework and discussions in the virtual classroom ($M = 3.26$), asynchronous online discussions in the course platform ($M = 3.18$), and collaborative activities that promote students' active engagement in remote learning ($M = 3.38$).

Table 1. Teachers' beliefs of their abilities for online remote instruction (N = 694)

Item	Mean	SD
I faced difficulties to promote students' active participation in my instruction via videoconferencing	3.22	1.095
I know how to remotely guide students' homework and discussions in the virtual classroom (i.e. via videoconferencing)	3.26	1.022
I am able to design suitable asynchronous online discussions for my students in the forum of the course platform (i.e. LMS)	3.18	1.135
I can design asynchronous learning activities that require students' exploration of online resources to study a specific topic	3.63	0.979
I can design and integrate into my teaching collaborative activities that engage my students from home	3.38	1.029
I can design and integrate into my teaching learning activities with Web 2.0 tools (e.g. Google Docs, blogs, wikis)	3.53	1.033
I believe that, after the experience of remote teaching during the pandemic of COVID-19, I have strengthened my skills to integrate e-learning methods into my instruction	4.01	0.770

Table 2 presents teachers' beliefs and perceptions about online learning after their recent experience of remote teaching, due to the pandemic closure. The vast majority of the teachers considered that, after the COVID-19 pandemic, they have enhanced interest about digital technologies in education (M = 4.19). Despite their beliefs that online teaching cannot replace in-person instruction (M = 4.32), the participants were positive that e-learning technologies can enhance students' learning in face to face instruction as well (M = 4.16).

The teachers in the sample appeared divided with regards to the perspective of returning to the traditional teacher-centred model of instruction, after the pandemic. However, they are expecting changes in future educational practices, due to the enhanced role of digital technologies (M = 3.87) and the adoption of e-learning modes in the schools (M = 3.73). It is quite interesting that the majority of K-12 teachers in the sample believe that e-learning can support student-centred approaches (M = 3.82). On the other hand, they rated lower students' readiness to effectively participate in e-learning environments (M = 3.27).

Table 3 presents the results that represent teachers' beliefs about their professional development needs in order to effectively integrate online tools and learning practices in their instruction, regardless of the pandemic. Despite that 9 out of 10 participants reported a good level and confidence of using online tools in their work (LMS, Google Docs, and Web 2.0 applications), the teachers in the sample considered that they need to enhance their knowledge and skills in terms of pedagogy (M = 3.93), learning design (M = 4.19) and effective practices of using online technologies in their instruction (M = 4.12). In addition, interacting and collaborating with colleagues (e.g., interchanging

Table 2. Teachers' beliefs about online learning (N = 694)

Item	Mean	SD
Online distance learning cannot replace in-person instruction in the classroom	4.32	0.912
Online instruction is a trend that cannot really contribute to students' learning	2.42	0.993
I believe that e-learning technologies can enhance students' learning in face to face classrooms	4.16	0.735
I believe that the pandemic of COVID-19 has widely reinforced the interest about digital technologies in education	4.19	0.692
I believe that, after the pandemic, we will return to the traditional teacher-centered teaching model	2.92	0.869
I believe that, after the pandemic of COVID-19, a new situation is emerging in education due to the enhanced role of digital technologies	3.87	0.716
I believe that, after the COVID-19 pandemic, the traditional educational practices will be changed by adopting e-learning methods	3.73	0.771
I believe that the students are ready to respond to e-learning methods and environments	3.27	0.986
I believe that e-learning technologies enhance students' active participation	3.40	0.920
I believe that e-learning technologies can support student-centered instructional methods	3.82	0.829

Table 3. Teachers' beliefs about their professional development needs (N = 694)

Item	Mean	SD
Regardless of the pandemic, I need to be trained in online learning methods	4.51	0.644
I think that I was ready to shift my instruction to emergency remote teaching	3.24	1.138
I need to learn more about effective ways of using online platforms (e.g. LMS) in my lessons	4.12	0.805
I need to learn more about how to design my instruction by using online learning methods	4.19	0.721
I need to strengthen my pedagogical skills in order to effectively use online learning technologies in my work	3.93	0.935
I need interaction (exchanging ideas) with colleagues in order to effectively use e-learning technologies in my work	4.23	0.708

experiences and ideas) was considered necessary to integrate e-learning tools in their educational practices by the vast majority of the participants (M = 4.23).

4.2 Qualitative Analysis

In addition to quantitative data analysis, several issues have been also revealed through the open questions in the questionnaire. The analysis of extensive transcripts, extracted from teachers' written comments, revealed a range of critical parameters which determine their difficulties and concerns with regards to remote online teaching as well as the integration of online tools and e-learning practices in both, online and face-to-face instruction (during and after the pandemic). The key factors identified are classified into five main categories:

1. Difficulties to design/provide online learning
The majority of the teachers in the sample reported is that they lack the digital skills necessary to effectively use online tools in their instruction. More than half of the teachers provided comments like:

T125: I had difficulties in using the LMS platform (e.g. eClass).

T152: The main problem for me was that I lack a good level of digital knowledge and skills.

In addition, teachers need new pedagogical knowledge and skills to design and conduct different teaching practices and learning scenarios with online tools:

T5: I am not familiar with the pedagogical theories and the design principles of online education.

T109: I received some training but not in the extent needed to provide remote online teaching.

2. Student barriers to participate in online learning
The teachers reported that many students lacked suitable digital equipment and connectivity to the Internet, necessary to effectively participate in online learning. For example:

T107: It was difficult for some students to participate because they lack the necessary digital equipment.

T161: Some students do not have access to the Internet and/or suitable devices to participate in remote instruction.

3. Lack of time and personal barriers during the pandemic
The majority of the teachers focused on their lack of time and their beliefs that online learning requires more efforts compared in-person education. The following quotes are representative of teachers' perceptions:

T97: I needed too much time to prepare my remote lessons/instruction.

T121: Online instruction requires too much time for lesson preparation.

In addition, teachers' needed to solve new problems during the pandemic (i.e., parental duties and family needs); as a result they had limited time available for designing online activities for their students. For example:

T430: The time available to prepare online instruction was limited; especially, considering the additional family obligations.

4. Teachers' training and support
Many teachers expected more training programs and supportive actions during the pandemic from the Ministry of Education and other educational authorities. Many similar

statements like the following quotes are representative of their expectations regarding professional support during the pandemic:

T41: I was expecting from the Ministry of Education to provide more training opportunities to the teachers [in online education] … to enhance teachers' motivation without forcing and pressure.

T54: There was no systematic, well-organized and responsible support of the educational community by the educational leadership authorities.

5. Personal data protection

Finally, some teachers paid more attention on the issue of personal data protection for both, students and teachers.

T44: Protecting and securing personal data is a big issue in online instruction.

T117: I believe that synchronous online teaching exceeds the bounds of legality; the personal rights are violated as both, the teacher and the students, are not protected.

5 Conclusions

The results, presented in this paper, have shown that the teachers in the sample exhibited positive attitudes towards e-learning in the schools and appeared willing to adopt online tools in their instructional practices, during and after the pandemic. Despite that teachers in the sample lack experience with online teaching, our findings indicated a good level of ability to design/implement remote online teaching practices; however, they need further training and continuous support to enhance their pedagogical skills, necessary to design online teaching scenarios and engage their students in suitable learning activities.

The preliminary analysis of the qualitative data raised also a number of possibly generalizable factors related to teachers' difficulties and concerns regarding this shift to online instruction. Among others, new roles for teachers, students and parents, new pedagogical skills to overcome distance restrictions of communication/interaction with students, continuous teacher training and support, interaction-collaboration with colleagues, enhanced efforts and workload, lack of time, as well as the issues regarding personal data protection and students' inclusion (in particular for those students coming from lower socio-economic levels).

The findings provided also clear evidence that the transition of K-12 schools to online learning is not necessarily a new concept, in terms of digital technologies, pedagogy and learning design, as well as teachers' readiness and difficulties. Moving forward and thinking about a sustainable long-term impact into the schools (i.e., beyond emergency conditions), the present study confirmed recent findings that professional development programs need to support teachers in developing the pedagogical knowledge/dimension of the online scenarios they use in practice [17]. The difference in the midst of the COVID-19 pandemic is the urgency and the rapidness to achieve those outcomes in teachers' abilities to transform their instruction and harness the potential of online technologies.

A possible response to the educational needs, due to the COVID-19 crisis, is to create very quickly an open, flexible system providing to the teachers constant support and professional development. In this perspective and combining previous findings of our research group, this study suggests alternative/open modes for teacher professional development which appeared to be effective; for example, MOOCs [19], e-mentoring programs [21], teacher communities [22] and school networks. We expect thus to provide new forms of teachers' engagement, mutual interaction, support and professional development.

References

1. Trust, T., Whalen, J.: Should teachers be trained in Emergency Remote Teaching? Lessons learned from the COVID-19 pandemic. J. Technol. Teach. Educ. **28**(2), 189–199 (2020)
2. Jeffery, K.A., Bauer, C.F.: Students' responses to Emergency Remote Online Teaching reveal critical factors for all teaching. J. Chem. Educ. **97**, 2472–2485 (2020)
3. Van Allen, J., Katz, S.: Teaching with OER during pandemics and beyond. J. Multicult. Educ. **3**(4), 209–218 (2020)
4. Roman, T.A.: Supporting the mental health of teachers in COVID-19 through trauma-informed educational practices and adaptive formative assessment tools. J. Technol. Teach. Educ. **28**(2), 473–481 (2020)
5. Whittle, C., Tiwari, S., Yan, S., Williams, J.: Emergency remote teaching environment: a conceptual framework for responsive online teaching in crises. Inf. Learn. Sci. **121**(5/6), 311–319 (2020)
6. Moore, M.: Theory of transactional distance. In: Keegan, D. (ed.) Theoretical Principles of Distance Education, pp. 22–38. Routledge, London (1993)
7. Salmon, G.: E-Moderating: The Key to Teaching and Learning Online. Routledge, London (2003)
8. Pulham, E.B., Graham, C.R.: Comparing K-12 online and blended teaching competencies: a literature review. Distance Educ. **39**(3), 411–432 (2018)
9. Hodges, C., Moore, S., Lockee, B., Trust, T., Bond, A.: The difference between Emergency Remote Teaching and Online Learning. EDUCAUSE Rev. (2020). https://er.educause.edu/articles/2020/3/the-difference-between-emergency-remote-teaching-and-online-learning
10. Milman, N.B.: Pandemic pedagogy. Phi Delta Kappan (2020). https://kappanonline.org/pandemic-pedagogy-covid-19-online-milman
11. Hilli, C.: Distance teaching in small rural primary schools: a participatory action research project. Educ. Act. Res. **28**(1), 38–52 (2020)
12. Stenman, S., Pettersson, F.: Remote teaching for equal and inclusive education in rural areas? An analysis of teachers' perspectives on remote teaching. Int. J. Inf. Learn. Technol. **37**(3), 87–98 (2020)
13. Liu, R.-L., Li, Y.-C.: Action research to enrich learning in e-tutoring for remote schools. Syst. Pract. Act. Res. **33**(1), 95–110 (2020). https://doi.org/10.1007/s11213-019-09517-5
14. Joshi, R., Kong, J., Nykamp, H., Fynewever, H.: Universities shaken by earthquakes: a comparison of faculty and student experiences in Nepal and New Zealand. Int. J. High. Educ. **7**(4), 177–186 (2018)
15. Rush, S.C., Partridge, A., Wheeler, J.: Implementing emergency online schools on the fly as a means of responding to school closures after disaster strikes. J. Educ. Technol. Syst. **45**(2), 188–201 (2016)
16. Ramadan, R.: Unravelling Facebook: a pedagogical tool during the Syrian crisis. Open Learn.: J. Open Distance e-Learn. **32**(3), 196–213 (2017)
17. Gudmundsdottir, G.B., Hathaway, D.M.: "We always make it work": teachers' agency in the time of crisis. J. Technol. Teach. Educ. **28**(2), 239–250 (2020)
18. Schultz, R.B., DeMers, M.N.: Transitioning from emergency remote learning to deep online learning experiences in geography education. J. Geogr. **119**(5), 142–146 (2020)

19. Koukis, N., Jimoyiannis, A.: MOOCS for teacher professional development: exploring teachers' perceptions and achievements. Interact. Technol. Smart Educ. **16**(1), 74–91 (2019)
20. Roussinos, D., Jimoyiannis, A.: Examining primary education teachers' perceptions of TPACK and the related educational context factors. J. Res. Technol. Educ. **51**(4), 377–397 (2019)
21. Spanorriga, C., Tsiotakis, P., Jimoyiannis, A.: E-mentoring and novice teachers' professional development: program design and critical success factors. In: Proceedings of EdMedia: World Conference on Educational Media and Technology, pp. 1315–1324. AACE, Amsterdam, Netherlands (2018)
22. Tsiotakis, P., Jimoyiannis, A.: Critical factors towards analysing teachers' presence in online learning communities. Internet High. Educ. **28**, 45–58 (2016)

Rapid Design and Implementation of a Teacher Development MOOC About Emergency Remote Teaching During the Pandemic

Athanassios Jimoyiannis(✉), Nikolaos Koukis, and Panagiotis Tsiotakis

University of Peloponnese, Korinthos, Greece
{ajimoyia,nkoukis,ptsiotakis}@uop.gr

Abstract. The pandemic of COVID-19 forced K-12 schools worldwide to transfer their educational programs from in-person instruction to remote online teaching. Teachers faced a range of difficulties towards providing remote teaching and integrating e-learning tools in their practices. This paper reports on a study concerning the rapid design and implementation of a MOOC to support primary and secondary education teachers in Greece towards using online tools in their remote instruction during the pandemic of COVID-19. The design framework and the implementation procedure of this particular MOOC are presented. The preliminary findings of a survey concerning 171 teachers who responded to an online questionnaire after completing this MOOC, are also presented. The results revealed teachers' satisfaction with regards to their personal outcomes and achievements, in terms of abilities to apply online instructional practices in their remote classrooms. The majority of the participants considered that this MOOC was an efficient environment to enhance their pedagogical knowledge and e-learning design skills necessary to provide remote instruction during the pandemic.

Keywords: Emergency remote teaching · E-learning · MOOCs · COVID-19 pandemic

1 Introduction

Nowadays, the education sector around the globe is facing a disruptive impact, as a result of the COVID-19 pandemic. Universities and K-12 schools are forced to transfer their programs online by using e-learning and/or blended learning modes. Academics and school teachers are facing major difficulties, since they have to adapt to emergency changes, in terms of adopting new instructional ways, using open educational resources (OER), digital tools and online platforms, applying novel pedagogical approaches and assessment procedures etc. This new situation has generated major challenges for universities and K-12 schools in order to keep their educational programs alive. In addition, it revealed the need of both, Higher Education (HE) tutors and school teachers, to develop their learning design abilities necessary to provide online remote instruction to their students.

A. Reis et al. (Eds.): TECH-EDU 2020, CCIS 1384, pp. 330–339, 2021.
https://doi.org/10.1007/978-3-030-73988-1_26

As stated by Hodges et al., Emergency Remote Teaching (ERT) is a temporary shift of instructional delivery to an alternate mode due to crisis circumstances [1]. Milman argued that a new pedagogy was emerging, the pandemic pedagogy, which addressed teachers' decisions and students' participation in new type of educational practices that appeared online during the pandemic [2]. Existing research findings indicate that online remote teaching has been reported in the past because of two main reasons: a) to provide equal and inclusive education in rural areas [3, 4] and b) when schools are closed or inaccessible due to a natural disaster [5, 6] or another emergency, for example war crisis [7].

Undoubtedly, remote teaching is based on online tools and learning platforms that are also used a) to extend face-to-face instruction and learning practices and b) to support blended or fully online courses. On the other hand, the online programs offered worldwide by HE and life-long learning institutions are properly designed, from the beginning; i.e., they are using appropriate pedagogical and well-documented e-learning models. However, in the case of ERT the main objective is to set up a new educational model very quickly. In this perspective, existing e-learning models, specific online tools (both synchronous and asynchronous), pedagogical approaches and effective educational practices as well, can outline a valuable framework for rapid design of instruction, learning material, curriculum modifications as well as initiatives for teacher support during the COVID-19 crisis.

In the last two decades, teacher professional development in terms of the competencies they need to integrate digital technologies in classroom practices, is a big issue for education worldwide. Literature review revealed a wide range of research findings, in different educational contexts, which show that teachers need to integrate their educational design knowledge and skills in order to integrate digital technologies in their instruction, i.e. to facilitate and enhance students' learning in both, physical and online, classrooms (for example [8–10]. Additionally, in their literature review Pulham & Graham addressed similarities and differences in digital technology integration, blended learning and fully online teaching, as well as teaches' abilities necessary for these different education modes [11].

During the last decade MOOCs have been rapidly evolved as an alternative online education mode that can effectively respond to the educational needs of great numbers of participants with diverse backgrounds. MOOCs have been also recognized as a new form to offer Teacher Professional Development (TPD) programs. Existing research findings indicate that they provide enhanced opportunities to the teachers for self-directed and collaborative learning within communities of peers [12–14]. Hence, the assumption, upon which the present study was designed, is that MOOCs can be an efficient alternative mode to provide teacher professional development programs, particularly in emergency situations like the crisis of COVID-19.

2 Design Framework of TPD-MOOC About ERT

2.1 Pedagogical Design Principles

The TPD-MOOC presented in this study was rapidly designed during the pandemic with the objective to support K-12 teachers towards developing and enhancing their abilities to design and provide online learning in their remote classrooms. The starting point was the hypothesis that, once the pandemic is over, online tools and e-learning practices are expected to be an integral part of the future classrooms in both, physical and virtual, modes. Therefore, we did not consider only teachers' current needs towards providing emergency remote teaching; for example, to familiarize them with the basic features of synchronous and asynchronous systems, learning management systems (LMS) and other online tools.

Secondly, we have adopted a common pedagogical context of understanding learning and online learning. The key idea is that learning does not only happen when students and teachers are together in a physical classroom or in an online space (e.g. via Zoom). Learning is considered as the outcome of students' active participation in properly designed activities implemented in the physical classroom and/or in the online classroom, and supported by both, synchronous and asynchronous tools [15, 16].

The third principle determining the design framework of this MOOC, was that learning is considered as both, an individual and a collaborative process [13]. In this perspective we adopted current ideas and schemata of online learning that emphasize on active, self-directed and collaborative learning [17].

Based on previous research findings and our experience of providing TPD-MOOCs [12, 13, 18], we used an on-going design procedure by estimating in combination a) the MOOC objectives initially set, and b) teachers' needs, personal expectations, and teaching experiences during the pandemic, which dynamically emerged and discussed in the MOOC forum. Under this process, we were able to determine the course topics, to produce learning materials specifically for this purpose, to choose relevant OERs, to assign discussion topics, to organise online conference sessions etc.

2.2 MOOC Structure and Timeline

This MOOC was structured on weekly basis, thus adopting the xMOOC mode in terms of content organisation and teachers' learning activities. On the other hand, the course was not focused upon delivering learning content to the participants as well as supportive material about specific online tools used in remote teaching. Teachers' active participation was addressed by adopting ideas of the cMOOC mode [13, 19]. Thus, we expected to create a community of peers who share common interests, challenges and concerns regarding online tools and methods that can be used in remote teaching practices during the pandemic.

The course was delivered through the Open eClass learning management system. Our choice was justified since this system a) is an open source LMS with a large installation basis and adequate technical support by the Greek School Network, and b) was already used in Greek schools before and during the pandemic. Therefore, we expected that many teachers were familiar with Open eClass and, therefore, they will be motivated to actively participate in the planned activities.

Table 1 shows the organisation of the weekly topics and the timeline of teachers' activities. The first week started with an introduction to remote online instruction and a brief presentation of the common aspects and the key differences with regular e-learning programs. Then teachers were guided toward exploring various aspects of synchronous and asynchronous online learning, identifying pedagogical frameworks for e-learning, discussing about challenges and difficulties across content areas, and sharing good ideas and practices that could be applied in their classrooms.

Table 1. MOOC topics and weekly units

Week	Course topics
1	Familiarisation with the MOOC platform Emergency Remote Teaching and online instruction/learning
2	Principles of e-learning
3	Design factors for e-learning and distance learning
4	Design and management of e-courses
5	Design of synchronous learning activities (online videoconference based)
6	Design of asynchronous learning activities (e-tivities)
7	Flipped classroom and flipped learning
8	Critical reflection and discussions Course outcomes and conclusion

2.3 Implementation and Participants

This MOOC was designed and offered by the eLearning Research Group of the University of Peloponnese, in Greece. The course activities started in the middle of May 2020 and lasted for 8 weeks. After an open call, a total of 694 primary and secondary education teachers expressed their interest; they were coming from various district areas across Greece. Finally, 578 teachers were enrolled and completed the course. One tutor and two assistants were the moderators-facilitators of teachers' online learning activities.

The learning material of the MOOC was designed, developed and properly organised by the authors. It was available through the course platform in the form of presentations and short notes, short tutorials and video-lessons, open educational resources, educational portals and websites, etc.

An emerging way of MOOC design and implementation was adopted. The course units, the learning material provided as well as the learning activities were dynamically shaped and adapted over time, according to the specific needs of the participants. For example, a) an online discussion among two university professors about emergency remote teaching was organized and shared, b) three 2 h video-conference sessions were also organised using Zoom in the 2nd, 4th and 7th course week, c) additional online material and educational resources were also provided etc.

The objective of the synchronous online sessions in this MOOC was not to provide typical, tutor-centred lectures but to encourage teachers' active participation in open discussions by presenting their beliefs, pedagogical ideas and difficulties regarding remote online teaching during the pandemic. The online sessions achieved a mean number of 70–80 active participants. In addition, they were recorded and uploaded on YouTube, so everyone could watch them off-line.

Discussion forum was an integral part for every course unit. The participants were asked to participate, in a regular manner, in detailed forum discussions about week topics, related pedagogical issues, technical difficulties, student engagement etc. Therefore, they were able to communicate and interact with peers, to share ideas about specific e-learning tools and approaches, and provide mutual support.

Every MOOC unit included also an optional assignment. The teachers had the opportunity to work, both individually and with peers, in order to apply new knowledge and skills concerning design principles of e-learning and remote online instruction (e.g., to design synchronous and asynchronous learning activities for their students, to share flipped learning ideas and plan flipped learning scenarios that could be applied in their virtual classrooms during the pandemic etc.).

3 Research Method

3.1 Instrument and Procedure

The survey presented in this paper was administered with the aim to record teachers' beliefs, views and estimations regarding the impact of this teacher professional development MOOC and their personal achievements. The participants responded anonymously to an online questionnaire provided through the LimeSurvey installation in the University of Peloponnese, one week after completing this MOOC. Data were analysed using SPSS ver. 23.0.

The scale included 40 items (in the form of 5-point Likert-type statements) presenting teachers' perceptions and beliefs regarding their participation in this particular MOOC. The questions were in line with the current context of online remote teaching, the design framework of the MOOC, the extended literature of online learning and the research experience of the researchers about TPD-MOOCs [13, 19]. Harnessing findings from our previous studies the scale was suitably adapted in response to the needs of this particular research [18].

In addition, the questionnaire included five open questions which were also used in qualitative analysis. Due to limitations in manuscript length, in this paper we present the preliminary findings of our analysis concerning 17 items representing teachers' perceptions of the impact of this MOOC in relation to their

- current professional development needs about ERT during the pandemic
- abilities to design e-learning activities and integrate them in their online remote classrooms.

3.2 The Sample

Completely responded questionnaires provided by 171 teachers (32 males and 138 females). They were teaching in secondary schools (71.4%), primary schools (17.5) and kindergarten (2.9%). In addition, 8.2% of the teachers in the sample were serving in various educational and lifelong learning institutions or in administration positions. The majority of the participants reported that they had a masters' degree (50.9%) while 9.9% had a PhD.

All participants reported experience of using digital technologies for both, personal and educational purposes. They were attending the official teachers' training program about ICT in education, provided by the Greek Ministry of Education. Among them, 26.3% attended the basic digital skills program (A' level) and 67.8% the advanced one (B' level). In addition, 10 teachers reported a good level of digital skills through training programs offered by other institutions. The majority of the teachers (81.3%) had previous e-learning experiences in the form of fully online programs from distance, MOOCs or blended learning.

4 Results

4.1 Descriptive Statistics

Table 2 presents the results of the descriptive statistics concerning ten items that represent the impact of this particular MOOC on teachers' pedagogical thinking and their abilities to use e-learning technologies in their instruction. The overall mean value of the items in this research dimension is equal 3.94. This means that the vast majority of the participants were positive about their professional development outcomes in this MOOC, in terms of knowledge, skills and attitudes for online learning and remote instruction. In addition, the teachers considered that this MOOC offered opportunities to them to deepen their pedagogical knowledge about online learning (mean = 4.11). Mann-Whitney and Kruskal-Wallis parametric tests were also conducted and showed no statistic difference in teachers' scores with regards to their gender and the level of school they are teaching.

Table 3 presents the results of the descriptive statistics concerning teachers' achievements with regards to their abilities to design and implement online instruction. Overall, the mean value of this dimension is also high (4.03), thus indicating that the participants were able and confident to integrate e-learning tools in their classroom practices. In particular, the findings demonstrated that the participants consider their competencies high towards designing synchronous and asynchronous activities and applying the flipped learning approach.

Table 2. Teachers' believes about their professional development (N = 171)

Item	Mean	SD
I believe that this MOOC enhanced my confidence to systematically use online learning technologies in my instruction	4.01	0.763
I believe that this MOOC enhanced my abilities to design learning activities for my students using specific online tools	4.04	0.702
I believe that this MOOC enhanced my motivation to integrate e-learning activities in my instruction	4.06	0.692
I feel more confident to use e-learning technologies in my instruction	3.88	0.906
I believe that this MOOC provided new perspectives (that I was not aware about) for my educational work after the pandemic	3.94	0.741
I believe that I deepened my pedagogical knowledge regarding the design of e-learning activities for my remote instruction	4.11	0.598
I believe that exchanging of ideas with peers in this specific MOOC did strengthen my self-confidence as a teacher	3.84	0.866
This MOOC offered opportunities to enhance my competencies to integrate e-learning technologies into remote instruction	4.06	0.729
This MOOC helped me to revise the way of thinking about e-learning in primary/secondary education	3.62	0.977
This MOOC covered my current needs as a teacher in the midst of the pandemic	3.81	0.946

Table 3. Teachers' achievements in terms of e-learning abilities (N = 171)

Item	Mean	SD
I am able to design appropriate learning activities, based on synchronous technologies, so that my students can achieve specific learning outcomes	4.07	0.619
I am able to design inquiry learning activities, based on asynchronous technologies, so that my students can achieve specific learning outcomes	4.03	0.618
I am able to design collaborative learning activities, based on asynchronous technologies, so that my students can achieve specific learning outcomes	3.94	0.712
I am able to design and manage my own online courses in a LMS (e.g. e-Class, e-me, Moodle)	4.16	0.581
I am able to design and manage students' online meetings based on video-conferencing tools (e.g. Webex, Zoom, SfB)	4.15	0.591
I am able to effectively integrate into my courses asynchronous activities using online tools (e.g. discussion forums, blogs, wikis, etc.)	3.92	0.739
I am able to design appropriate educational scenarios for my students using the flipped classroom approach	3.92	0.775

4.2 Qualitative Analysis of Teachers' Receptions About TPD-MOOC

Teachers provided also detailed comments in the open questions regarding how this MOOC has influenced them (or may influence them in the future) in terms of designing and providing their instruction. Following we present indicative quotes extracted from responses concerning teachers' overall evaluation of this MOOC and their perceptions about the role of online learning after the pandemic:

E14: "This MOOC helped me to find answers in many questions about my work during the pandemic… It helped me to organize and implement my instruction, and to inspire my students in distance learning."

E54: "Attending this MOOC had a positive impact to me; …it enhanced my self-confidence, because I realized that I have common concerns and difficulties with other peers in this MOOC."

E71: "This particular MOOC strengthened my determination to try/apply innovative teaching methods such as the flipped classroom."

E86: "I feel able to create my own online lessons in a LMS (Open eClass)… To decide about the course structure, to properly organize the course sections according to specific learning objectives, to assign various learning activities, e.g. forum discussions, individual and group activities."

E101: "My teaching methods could be further enhanced in the future by using online tools, like Open eClass and Webex…"

E106: "I am able to create online worksheets for my students, to produce/edit my videos and to develop self-assessment exercises in the Open eClass platform…"

The transcripts above are representative of many similar statements that reflect teachers' perceptions regarding their professional development achievements in this MOOC.

5 Conclusions

This paper reported upon the rapid design of a teacher professional development MOOC, which delivered during the COVID-19 pandemic as an online program aiming to support Greek K-12 educators to improve their online remote teaching. Detailed descriptions of the on-going design procedure, the MOOC structure as well as teachers' engagement and mutual interaction were also presented. The preliminary findings, based on the analysis of data from teachers' responses to an online questionnaire, clearly confirmed the assumption that MOOCs can be an efficient mode to provide teacher professional development very quickly and, particularly, in the emergency situations like the pandemic school closure.

Confirming existing research [12–14], our findings provided also supportive evidence that the open, self-regulated and collaborative features of this MOOC were effective towards enhancing teachers' abilities to design online lessons and support their remote classrooms. The majority of the participants reported that this MOOC was efficient towards enhancing their learning design skills and their pedagogical knowledge in order to provide online remote instruction during the pandemic. In terms of MOOC design, the findings confirm that the balance between course structure (xMOOC features) and openness-flexibility (cMOOC features) was effective and influenced teachers' achievements [18–20].

Our findings provided supportive evidence that the transition to online learning in K-12 schools is not necessarily a new concept, in terms of digital technologies and pedagogy, as well as teachers' readiness and difficulties to integrate online tools in their classrooms, both remote and physical (i.e. after the COVID-19 pandemic). However, the difference in this uncertain situation we are currently living, in the midst of the pandemic, is that the educational system needs a rapid, urgent and effective response for the benefit of our students.

Despite that this study could be limited by the specific sample (for example, the majority of the participants held a Master's degree or a PhD) and the particular conditions of implementation under the emergency context of the pandemic, the findings could be internationally valuable for the designers and the researchers in both these fields, TPD-MOOC and online programs for teacher professional development. The next step of our investigation will be directed to a comparative analysis of qualitative data extracted from teachers' interviews. We thus expect to shed light into the different ways of remote teaching practices applied in the Greek K-12 schools during the second phase of the COVID-19 pandemic.

References

1. Hodges, C., Moore, S., Lockee, B., Trust, T., Bond, A.: The difference between emergency remote teaching and online learning. EDUCAUSE Rev. (2020). https://er.educause.edu/articles/2020/3/the-difference-between-emergency-remote-teaching-and-online-learning
2. Milman, N.B.: Pandemic pedagogy. Phi Delta Kappan (2020). https://kappanonline.org/pandemic-pedagogy-covid-19-online-milman
3. Stenman, S., Pettersson, F.: Remote teaching for equal and inclusive education in rural areas? An analysis of teachers' perspectives on remote teaching. Int. J. Inf. Learn. Technol. **37**(3), 87–98 (2020)
4. Liu, R.-L., Li, Y.-C.: Action research to enrich learning in e-tutoring for remote schools. Syst. Pract. Act. Res. **33**(1), 95–110 (2020). https://doi.org/10.1007/s11213-019-09517-5
5. Joshi, R., Kong, J., Nykamp, H., Fynewever, H.: Universities shaken by earthquakes: a comparison of faculty and student experiences in Nepal and New Zealand. Int. J. High. Educ. **7**(4), 177–186 (2018)
6. Rush, S.C., Partridge, A., Wheeler, J.: Implementing emergency online schools on the fly as a means of responding to school closures after disaster strikes. J. Educ. Technol. Syst. **45**(2), 188–201 (2016)
7. Ramadan, R.: Unravelling Facebook: a pedagogical tool during the Syrian crisis. Open Learn.: J. Open Distance e-Learn. **32**(3), 196–213 (2017)
8. Ottenbreit-Leftwich, A., Liao, J.Y.-C., Sadik, O., Ertmer, P.: Evolution of teachers' technology integration knowledge, beliefs, and practices: how can we support beginning teachers use of technology? J. Res. Technol. Educ. **50**(4), 282–304 (2018)
9. Roussinos, D., Jimoyiannis, A.: Examining primary education teachers' perceptions of TPACK and the related educational context factors. J. Res. Technol. Educ. **51**(4), 377–397 (2019)
10. Tsai, C.-C., Chai, C.S.: The "third"-order barrier for technology integration instruction: implications for teacher education. Australas. J. Educ. Technol. **28**(6), 1057–1060 (2013)

11. Pulham, E.B., Graham, C.R.: Comparing K-12 online and blended teaching competencies: a literature review. Distance Educ. **39**(3), 411–432 (2018)
12. Koutsodimou, K., Jimoyiannis, A.: MOOCs for teacher professional development: investigating views and perceptions of the participants. In: Proceedings of the 8th International Conference of Education, Research and Innovation – ICERI 2015, pp. 6968–6977. IATED, Seville (2015)
13. Koukis, N., Jimoyiannis, A.: Designing MOOCs for teacher professional development: analysis of participants' engagement and perceptions. In: Mesquita, A., Peres, P. (eds.) Proceedings of the 16th European Conference on e-Learning-ECEL 2017, pp. 271–280. Academic Conferences and Publishing International, Porto (2017)
14. Laurillard, D.: The educational problem that MOOCs could solve: professional development for teachers of disadvantaged students. Res. Learn. Technol. **24**(1), 29369 (2016). https://doi.org/10.3402/rlt.v24.29369
15. McLoughlin, C., Lee, M. J. W.: Personalised and self-regulated learning in the Web 2.0 era: international exemplars of innovative pedagogy using social software. Australas. J. Educ. Technol. **26**(1), 28–43 (2010)
16. Jimoyiannis, A., Tsiotakis, P., Roussinos, D., Siorenta, A.: Preparing teachers to integrate Web 2.0 in school practice: toward a framework for Pedagogy 2.0. Australas. J. Educ. Technol. **29**(2), 248–267 (2013)
17. Shea, P., Bidjerano, T.: Learning presence: towards a theory of self-efficacy, self-regulation, and the development of a communities of inquiry in online and blended learning environments. Comput. Educ. **55**, 1721–1731 (2010)
18. Koukis, N., Jimoyiannis, A.: MOOCS for teacher professional development: exploring teachers' perceptions and achievements. Interact. Technol. Smart Educ. **16**(1), 74–91 (2019a)
19. Koukis, N., Jimoyiannis, A.: Investigating participants' collaborative patterns in a MOOC for teacher professional development. In: Ørngreen, R., Buhl, M., Meyer, B. (eds.) Proceedings of the 16th European Conference on e-Learning-ECEL 2019, pp. 303–312. Aalborg University, Copenhagen. Academic Conferences and Publishing International (2019b)
20. Koukis, N., Jimoyiannis, A.: Towards a design framework of MOOCs for teacher development: theoretical issues and analysis of teachers' achievements about Web 2.0 in language instruction. Themes e-Learn. **13**, 69–86 (2020)

SciLOET: A Framework for Assessing Digital Learning Objects for Science Education

Tassos A. Mikropoulos(✉) and Nikiforos M. Papachristos

The Educational Approaches to Virtual Reality Lab, University of Ioannina, 45500 Ioannina, Greece
amikrop@uoi.gr

Abstract. There is a growing interest in Open Educational Resources building up in the last decade. Among them Digital Learning Objects (DLOs) attract the interest of educational research and practice as there is evidence that they have a positive effect on learning. Especially in Science Education, DLOs are considered as important tools to support achieving high-level learning outcomes. Evaluation of DLOs is critical. A handful of tools are available, but they are too generic. There seems to be a lack of evaluation methods and tools specifically for Science Education DLOs. This work presents the SciLOET (Science Learning Objects Evaluation Tool), a DLOs' evaluation tool specialized in Science Education. The tool is meant mainly to be used by teachers who are in the process of evaluating, selecting, and using DLOs in their teaching. It could also prove useful for education researchers who design empirical studies and instructional interventions with DLOs. The SciLOET evaluates four dimensions of DLOs, namely content quality, teaching effectiveness, design, and documentation. Each one of these dimensions, consists of a series of questions.

Keywords: Digital Learning Object (DLO) · Evaluation · Science Education

1 Introduction

In the last decade, intense interest has developed in the creation and sharing of high-end Open Educational Resources (OERs). The need for available K-12 education OERs has been urged and many national and international projects are underway to create and distribute open OERs.

The term "Open Educational Resources" (OERs) is used to describe educational material of any kind, which is freely available, as "public domain", without any restriction of intellectual property, or with any open license that allows free use, adaptation and redistribution [1]. Open Learning Resources include a wide range of resources, from micro-activities to integrated open digital applications to Digital Learning Objects (DLOs), which seem to have a positive effect on the learning process and learning outcomes [2–4]. DLOs, as web-based learning tools, seem to play important role in distance learning, especially in situations like the emergency on-line teaching we experience due to COVID-19 pandemic.

A. Reis et al. (Eds.): TECH-EDU 2020, CCIS 1384, pp. 340–348, 2021.
https://doi.org/10.1007/978-3-030-73988-1_27

Digital Learning Objects - a subclass of OERs, with unique characteristics - are small units of digital content that can be (re)used to support the learning process. They are designed as small, autonomous entities to maximize the learning situations in which they can be utilized. There does not seem to be a clear and widely accepted definition for the DLOs in the literature. Many authors focus on the characteristics that a DLO should have or on its reusability and autonomy, while others focus on their pedagogical value or ability to be accessible through the World Wide Web. However, there seems to be a common perception that a DLO should be reusable, analytical, discoverable, accessible, interoperable, adaptable, resilient, generative and manageable [5].

In the context of this work, regarding the definition of DLOs, the approach followed by the Learnativity content aggregation model is adopted [6]. A DLO is defined as a "small, autonomous, reusable and pedagogically integrated learning content structure". DLO consists of content elements (e.g., multimedia elements) and information objects (e.g., concepts) and is a building block of a learning environment. The term "small" refers on the one hand to the academic time required for its educational utilization and on the other hand to the fact that it is of a suitable size to be used through the world wide web. The term "reusable" implies that it can be utilized in a variety of technological environments and educational approaches and situations. Finally, the term "pedagogically integrated" means that the creator of the DLO has designed it following a clear pedagogical approach, without restricting the teacher or student in terms of its use. In addition, it can contribute to the realization of learning objectives as an autonomous digital entity [7].

It is important to have in mind the position of a DLO within a content aggregation model, which classifies and describes the process of combining a set of functional content resources [8]. The most common aggregation models are SCORM (Sharable Content Object Reference Model), ALOCOM (Abstract Learning Object Content Model), IEEE LOM (Learning Object Metadata) and the Learnativity Aggregation Model. In the context of this work, the latter is followed, as it seems to be more detailed and clearer in terms of the categorization of educational resources. According to the Learnativity Aggregation Model, there are five levels of resolution from the simplest and smallest to the widest and largest. A DLO is placed in the third aggregation level of the model, with content element (multimedia element) in the first and information objects as a concept in the second. A learning component such as an educational scenario, would be in the fourth level and a whole learning environment in the fifth level [6].

1.1 Digital Learning Objects in Science Education

Particularly in Science Education, DLOs have been acknowledged as invaluable tools to support the achievement of high-level learning outcomes. Simulations, dynamic visual representations and visualizations of natural phenomena and quantities, among other types of DLOs, play in important role in learning processes and learning achievements [9–15].

The ever-increasing availability of DLOs due to technological advances in computing power, internet speed but also due to the involvement of teachers from all over the world in their development, inevitably raises issues of evaluation and assessment of these educational resources [16]. A consistent approach to the assessment of learning objects should include all the relevant factors considering, at the same time, the pedagogical and technological dimensions of the issue [17, 18].

Over the last years, several efforts have been made to develop methods, frameworks and tools for assessing DLOs. After a thorough review of the relevant literature searching for scientifically substantiated and comprehensive models for evaluating DLOs, SREB-SCORE (Southern Regional Education Board) [19], LORI (Learning Object Review Instrument) [20], LOEM (Learning Object Evaluation Metric) [15], LOES-T (Learning Object Scale for Teachers) [21], LOES-S (Learning Object Scale for Students) [22], and MERLOT (Multimedia Educational Resource for Learning and Online Teaching) [23], are among the well documented and most widely used tools for the evaluation of educational resources and especially Learning Objects.

The SREB-SCORE "is designed to assist schools and colleges in determining the quality and effectiveness of learning objects" [19]. It is a two-points checklist and comments on the evaluator's check. The LORI can be used by teachers and instructional designers and consists of a five-level scale accompanied by comments [20]. The LOEM addresses to students and teachers and consists of three-level components that are thoroughly described. LOES-T and LOES-S have developed by the same authors with LOEM and are addresses to teachers and students respectively. LOES-T items are rated on a seven-point Likert scale, while LOES-S uses a five-point scale. All the above evaluation metrics are general purpose tools, namely refer to all disciplines and educational levels. The MERLOT peer review process offers different versions for different disciplines. Among these disciplines refers to Science and especially Physics and involves any type of open educational resource and learning material. The ratings in the MERLOT questions are in a 1–5 scale. The above six tools are configured by items that consist of three (MERLOT) to 10 (SREB-SCORE) sections. They all involve three common sections, namely content quality, learning goals, and usability. These are the core factors that designate knowledge acquisition or even better knowledge construction, since learning objects are or have to be used in student—centered constructive approaches. The SREB-SCORE, LOES, LOEM, and LORI have distinct sections for motivation, feedback, and presentation of the DLOs. These parameters are also involved in various sections of the rest of the tools. For example, feedback is among the four criteria in the section "ease of use" of the MERLOT tool. The same holds for the presentation design, which is the second part of the MERLOT's quality of content section. The SREB-SCORE and LORI refer to three of the features that characterize the DLOs that is reusability, accessibility, and standards. Copyright is reported only in the SREB-SCORE checklist.

The need for a tool that refers to one certain discipline such as it is with MERLOT, seems to be a necessity in the field of Science Education. Science Education mainly aims at the understanding of the natural world. It deals with magnitudes and phenomena often without everyday experience as well as with abstract concepts. Science Education involves "information and knowledge organization and processing, attentional demands, understanding of abstract concepts and models, problem solving, spatial perception and orientation, visual perception, selection of features and objects, reflection of emotional and cognitive processes, metacognitive abilities, different cognitive styles" [24]. The standards for Science Education incorporate organization, classification and relationships; cause and effect; space and time scales; systems and models; energy and matter;

structure and function; stability and change [25]. In Science Education it seems that visual representations play an important role for the communication of scientific ideas and concepts [26]. Because of the above characteristics and standards, "Science Education constitutes a privileged subject matter when considering ICT integration and the related issues to enhance teachers' instructional potentialities and students' active engagement and learning opportunities [27]. This is mainly because of digital technology's affordances to represent information in multimodal, dynamic, and interactive ways as well as to support communication [28].

This work presents the "Science Learning Objects Evaluation Tool – SciLOET", an evaluation tool for DLOs devoted to Science Education. The tool addresses mainly to teachers who want to choose a DLO for their teaching process. It also addresses to education researchers who design empirical studies and instructional interventions with DLOs.

2 Methodology

The methodology in this work is similar to the one followed by Akhavan and Arefi who have presented a framework for the evaluation of e-content [23]. Their framework has come as a result of a critical review followed by a two rounds Delphi study.

The methodology followed in the present work consists of three steps.

The first step involves the formation of the first edition of the DLOs' evaluation tool. It is based on the study of general purpose [16, 19–22] and discipline based [23] evaluation tools as well as on their relevant empirical studies.

A pilot empirical study followed with the first version of the tool. Ten special users used the tool to evaluate three DLOs concerning Physics, Chemistry and Biology teaching. They all were postgraduate students attending a M.Sc. Program in Science Education and Learning Technologies. Five of the participants were secondary education science teachers with 10–20 years of experience. The rest of the participants were primary education teachers with 2–10 years of experience Because of the small number of the participants, the study was qualitative. The teachers used the SciLOET, recorded notes on the questions of the tool, interviews and a plenary session discussion followed.

The second version of the SciLOET came from the results of the pilot study.

A two round Delphi study consisted the third step. Fifteen experts on educational technology and DLOs were invited to participate in the study, but only seven completed its two rounds. The seven experts studied the second version of the SciLOET. The first round transformed the experts' opinions into group consensus as far as it regards the criteria and dimensions of the tool. The second round of the Delphi study gave the stability of the exports' judgments and resulted in the final version of the evaluation tool.

3 Results

The first version of the SciLOET consists of four dimensions. They refer to the content of the DLOs, their use in the teaching and learning process, the design, and their documentation. The evaluation tool is oriented in the instructional design and the teaching process.

Table 1. The first version of the SciLOET.

Content quality
1. Does the content follow the scientific symbols?
2. For quantitative data, are the results correct and in agreement with graphs?
3. For qualitative data, do the numerical data of the magnitudes match their representations?
4. Does the text present ideas and concepts in a complete way?
Comments
Teaching effectiveness
5. Is the LO attractive for the student?
6. Does the interactivity of the LO promote the student's active engagement?
7. Does the LO improve the content of the textbook?
8. Does the LO allow the student to make predictions?
9. Does the LO imply teaching and learning goals?
10. Does the LO promote the design of learning activities?
11. Does the LO uses multiple representations for the concepts, magnitudes, and phenomena?
12. Does the LO promote discovery or inquiry learning?
13. Does the LO advance reflection?
14. Does the LO contribute to critical thinking?
15. May the LO be used in more than one situation (e.g., different goals, other discipline)?
Comments
Content presentation and ease of use
16. Is the design attractive for the students' age?
17. Do multimedia elements attribute effectively the magnitudes and phenomena?
18. Do the interactive elements (buttons, sliders, etc.) operate in an understandable manner?
19. Is the LO easy to use?
Comments
Documentation
20. Are the instructions easy to understand?
21. Do the instructions include proposals for instructional interventions?
Comments

Thus, it does not involve items referring to the features of the DLOs, as some other tools do (e.g., granularity, durability, manageability). This was also pointed out by the participants of the empirical study. The evaluation tool uses a 4-point Likert scale. This forced scale is chosen in order the evaluator to give a specific response to each one of the questions. Table 1 shows the items of the first version of the evaluation tool.

Table 2. The dimensions and items of the SciLOET after the first round of the Delphi study.

Content quality
1. The topic under study is compatible with the curriculum
2. The LO refers to a topic for which students have difficulties or misconceptions
3. The LO refers to a topic that is difficult to be taught without the support of the digital technology
4. The LO adds pedagogical value to the topic under study
5. The content of the LO follows the scientific symbols
6. The text presents ideas and concepts in a clear way
Comments
Teaching effectiveness
7. The LO involves feedback that promotes knowledge construction
8. The LO improves the content of the textbook
9. The LO implies the design of learning activities
10. The LO uses multiple representations for the concepts, magnitudes, and phenomena
11. The LO promotes discovery or inquiry learning (e.g., inductive reasoning, hypothesis testing, problem solving, metacognitive skills acquisition)
12. The LO advances reflection (e.g., connection of existing knowledge with new information for problem solving)
13. The LO contributes to critical thinking (e.g., analysis and synthesis, metacognitive process, creation)
14. The LO can be used in more than one situation (e.g., different goals, other discipline)
Comments
Design
15. Graphics are suitable for the age of the students
16. Multimedia elements attribute effectively the magnitudes and phenomena
17. The LO is easy to use
18. The time needed for an activity with the LO is short enough
19. During its use, the LO records the student's actions
20. The LO supports game-based learning
21. The LO works in mobile devices
Comments
Documentation
22. There are user's instructions
23. There are proposals for instructional interventions
Comments

The first round of the Delphi study maintained the four dimensions, proposing the modification of "content presentation and ease of use" to "design". Table 2 presents the SciLOET, as a result of the first round of the Delphi study. The experts modified the items regarding content quality and focused at the pedagogical added value the DLO could offer. The items in the teaching effectiveness dimension concerning instructional models filled with explanations in order to guide the teacher who evaluates the DLO. The dimension of design was extended by adding three more items. The second round of the Delphi study begun with the SciLOET as presented in Table 2, looking for the experts' consensus. The final version of the SciLOET came as a result of more than 85% consensus among the experts for each one of its items. Table 3 presents the SciLOET after the second round of the Delphi study. It consists of 12 items in a 4-point Likert scale. The content dimension remained only with three items, which refer to the pedagogical added value of the DLO. The experts agreed to leave only two items in the design dimension and one in the documentation.

Table 3. The final version of the SciLOET after the second round of the Delphi study.

Content quality
1. The LO refers to a topic for which students have difficulties or misconceptions
2. The LO refers to a topic that is difficult to be taught without the support of the digital technology
3. The LO adds pedagogical value to the topic under study
Comments
Teaching effectiveness
4. The LO involves feedback that promotes knowledge construction
5. The LO implies the design of learning activities
6. The LO uses multiple representations for the concepts, magnitudes, and phenomena
7. The LO promotes discovery or inquiry learning (e.g., inductive reasoning, hypothesis testing, problem solving, metacognitive skills acquisition)
8. The LO advances reflection (e.g., connection of existing knowledge with new information for problem solving)
9. The LO can be used in more than one situation (e.g., different goals, other discipline)
Comments
Design
10. Graphics are suitable for the age of the students
11. Multimedia elements attribute effectively the magnitudes and phenomena
Comments
Documentation
12. There are proposals for instructional interventions
Comments

4 Discussion

This work presented the SciLOET (Science Learning Objects Evaluation Tool), an evaluation tool for digital learning objects for Science Education. While Merlot seems to be a valued tool for DLO evaluation, it is not specifically made for Science Education and is too generic for the needs of Science Education teachers and practitioners.

Given the particular characteristics of Science Education and the concepts it deals with, DLOs with specific characteristics and affordances are needed and, in the framework of this paper, this leads to the need of an evaluation tool made specifically for Science Education DLOs. SciLOET emerged as a result of the study of the relevant literature and a Delphi study. The SciLOET addresses mainly to teachers, so it does not involve items others than those referred directly to the teaching and learning processes. Our approach is similar to de Jong's and his colleagues who have presented the "Science Created by You" learning environments and gave emphasis on instructional design [29].

An empirical study with SciLOET followed, in order to validate the tool (under preparation). It was conducted with 104 primary school teachers. The only dimension the validation process exempted was the documentation dimension. A second validation study is prepared with secondary school science teachers.

References

1. UNESCO, What are Open Educational Resources (OERs)? https://www.unesco.org/new/en/communication-and-information/access-to-knowledge/open-educational-resources/what-are-open-educational-resources-oers/. Accessed 13 July 2018
2. Kay, R.H.: Examining factors that influence the effectiveness of learning objects in mathematics classrooms. Can. J. Sci. Math. Technol. Educ. **12**(4), 350–366 (2012). https://doi.org/10.1080/14926156.2012.732189
3. Shank, J.D.: The emergence of learning objects: the reference librarian's role. Res. Strateg. **19**(3), 193–203 (2003). https://doi.org/10.1016/j.resstr.2005.01.002
4. Weller, M.: Learning objects, learning design, and adoption through succession. J. Comput. High. Educ. **19**(1), 26–47 (2007). https://doi.org/10.1007/BF03033418
5. Gürer, M.D.: Utilization of learning objects in social studies lesson: achievement, attitude and engagement. Doctoral dissertation, Middle East Technical University (2013)
6. Reusable Learning, Granularity. https://www.reusablelearning.org/about/Granularity.html. Accessed 08 Nov 2014
7. Topali, P., Mikropoulos, T.A.: Digital learning objects for teaching computer programming in primary education. In: Proceedings of TECH-EDU 2018 – Technology and Innovation in Learning, Teaching and Education, 20–22 June 2018. Aristotle University of Thessaloniki (2018)
8. ADL, SCORM 2004 4th Edition Version 1.0. https://www.adlnet.gov/Technologies/scorm/SCORMSDocuments/2004%204th%20Edition/Overview.aspx. Accessed 01 Nov 2014
9. Gilbert, J.K. (ed.): Visualization in Science Education. Springer, Dordrecht (2005). https://doi.org/10.1007/1-4020-3613-2
10. Lin, H., Dwyer, F.M.: The effect of static and animated visualization: a perspective of instructional effectiveness and efficiency. J. Educ. Technol. Res. Dev. **58**, 155–174 (2010)
11. Yarden, H., Yarden, A.: Learning using dynamic and static visualizations: students' comprehension, prior knowledge and conceptual status of a biotechnological method. Res. Sci. Educ. **40**(3), 375–402 (2010). https://doi.org/10.1007/s11165-009-9126-0

12. Barak, M., Dori, Y.J.: Science education in primary schools: is an animation worth a thousand pictures? J. Sci. Educ. Technol. **20**, 608–620 (2011)
13. Nguyen, N., Nelson, A.J., Wilson, T.D.: Computer visualizations: factors that influence spatial anatomy comprehension. Anat. Sci. Educ. **5**(2), 98–108 (2012)
14. Hsin-Kai, W., Lin, Y.-F., Hsu, Y.-S.: Effects of representation sequences and spatial ability on students' scientific understandings about the mechanism of breathing. Instr. Sci. **41**(3), 555–573 (2013). https://doi.org/10.1007/s11251-012-9244-3
15. Sudatha, G.W.I., Degeng, N.S.I., Kamdi, W.: The effect of visualization type and student spatial abilities on learning achievement. J. Baltic Sci. Educ. **17**(4), 551 (2018)
16. Kay, R.H., Knaack, L.: A multi-component model for assessing learning objects: the learning object evaluation metric (LOEM). Australas. J. Educ. Technol. **24**(5), 574–591 (2008)
17. Sinclair, J., Joy, M., Yau, J.Y.K., Hagan, S.: A practice-oriented review of learning objects. IEEE Trans. Learn. Technol. **6**(2), 177–192 (2013)
18. Clements, K., Pawlowski, J., Manouselis, N.: Open educational resources repositories literature review–towards a comprehensive quality approaches framework. Comput. Hum. Behav. **51**, 1098–1106 (2015)
19. SREB-SCORE: Checklist for evaluating SREB-SCORE Learning objects, educational Technology Cooperative (2007)
20. Leacock, T.L., Nesbit, J.C.: Framework for evaluating the quality of multimedia learning resources. Educ. Technol. Soc. **10**(2), 44–59 (2007)
21. Kay, R., Knaack, L., Petrarca, D.: Exploring teachers perceptions of web-based learning tools. Interdisc. J. E-Learn. Learn. Objects **5**(1), 27–50 (2009)
22. Cafolla, R.: Project merlot: bringing peer review to web-based educational resources. In: Willis, D., Price, J., Davis, N. (eds.) Proceedings of SITE 2002–Society for Information Technology & Teacher Education International Conference, pp. 614–618. Association for the Advancement of Computing in Education (AACE), Nashville (2002)
23. Akhavan, P., Arefi, M.F.: Developing a conceptual framework for evaluation of e-content of virtual courses: e-learning center of an Iranian university case study. Interdisc. J. E-Learn. Learn. Objects **10**, 53–73 (2014)
24. Mikropoulos, T.A.: Brain research in science education research. In: Psillos, D., Kariotoglou, P., Tselfes, V., Hatzikraniotis, E., Fassoulopoulos, G., Kallery, M. (eds.) Science Education Research in the Knowledge – Based Society, pp. 353–360. Kluwer Academic Publishers, The Netherlands (2006)
25. Osborne, J., Rafanelli, S., Kind, P.: Toward a more coherent model for science education than the crosscutting concepts of the next generation science standards: the affordances of styles of reasoning. J. Res. Sci. Teach. **55**, 962–981 (2018)
26. Cook, M.P.: Visual representations in science education: the influence of prior knowledge and cognitive load theory on instructional design principles. Sci. Educ. **90**, 1073–1091 (2006)
27. Jimoyiannis, A.: Designing and implementing an integrated technological pedagogical science knowledge framework for science teachers professional development. Comput. Educ. **55**, 1259–1269 (2010)
28. Mikropoulos, T.A.: Research on e-Learning and ICT in Education: Technological, Pedagogical and Instructional Perspectives. Springer, Switzerland (2018). https://doi.org/10.1007/978-3-319-34127-9
29. De Jong, T., et al.: Using scenarios to design complex technology-enhanced learning environments. Educ. Technol. Res. Dev. **60**, 883–901 (2012)

Transforming Teaching and Learning Through Technology

The Potential of Audiovisual Online Collaborative Platforms as a Teaching/Learning Aid of ESP – Testing and Validating a Prototype

Tiago da Silva Carvalho(✉)

Faculty of Arts, University of Helsinki, Helsinki, Finland
tiago.dasilvacarvalho@helsinki.fi

Abstract. The rise of enthusiasts in Mobile Assisted Language Learning (MALL), benefiting from well-established benefits of consuming audiovisual content for autonomous learning, has risen during the last decade. Simultaneously, there is constant debate about how would an Online Collaborative Platform (OCP) has the potential to respond to the needs of teachers and learners, as well as change their audiovisual consumption habits when the latter is intended to improve their foreign language teaching and learning proficiency. Bearing this in mind, this chapter focuses on the content analysis of a Research-Development doctoral project, where a prototype of an OCP was developed and tested with teachers of English as Foreign Language (via a Think-a-loud Protocol) and learners of English for Specific Purposes. The oral and written feedback of the trials' participants identified threats, and proposed improvements to the prototype's conceptual nature and suggestions that the teachers believe will be useful for the operationalization of the platform. The feedback also shows that teachers would be interested in this platform, as they consider it fulfills a purpose for both teachers and learners, and it has value to add to the English for Specific Purposes/Business English teaching/learning community.

Keywords: EFL teaching/learning · ESP · Audiovisual consumption · Online Collaborative Platforms

1 Introduction

Online Collaborative Platforms (OCP) that function as a repository or as an aggregator for Audiovisual Content (AVC), like YouTube [1], have seen a constant growth of users, to a solid number of 1.5 million visitors a month (Think with Google, 2017a) [2]. According to Shalavi (2020) [3], YouTube is now a platform that is occupying more and more time on TV sets, with a 180% increase of consumption time on current TV sets in 2020. Regarding the viewing of AVC for educational purposes, YouTube stated that it amounts to "*1 billion views of learning-related content (…) every day*", and that "1*M learning videos are shared everyday on Youtube*" (Thinkwithgooglecom, 2017) [4]. This report validates that educational AVC, like the ones produced by Khan Academy [5], BBC [6], or renowned universities (like MIT [7], or Cambridge [8], is distributed, appreciated,

A. Reis et al. (Eds.): TECH-EDU 2020, CCIS 1384, pp. 351–369, 2021.
https://doi.org/10.1007/978-3-030-73988-1_28

and shared by users. According to Twinwordcom (c2018) [9], the amount of learning related AVC on YouTube in 2018 was about 5%. Google Data U.S. also informed that the watch time of "study skills" videos on YouTube has increased more than three times, when comparing 2018 to 2017 (Thinkwithgooglecom, 2018) [10].

The previous numbers can be complemented with statistics provided by Nielsencom (2018 [11], c2019 [12]), Statistacom (2017 [13], 2018 [14], 2019 [15]), Twinwordcom (c2018) [9], and Ericson Consumer Lab (2016) [16] which confirmed a massive consumption of AVC on a global scale in all demographics, with a balanced number of female and male consumers. Moreover, younger generations are keener on using mobile devices to satisfy their viewing needs, whereas older generations are staying loyal to the television. Moreover, Nielsoncom (2018 [11], c2019 [12]) report increasing numbers of consumption of User-Generated Content (UGC), TV series, Movies, TV Programs, Sports, and News. These reports analyzed the hours users dedicated to the consumption of AVC, the various types of devices users used, the video-on-demand habits, and the most-watched content, which led Carvalho (2020) [17] to conclude that:

i. the time spend interacting with AVC has a propensity to be constant;
ii. TV sets remains the primary device for interaction with the content, but mobile consumption is proliferating;
iii. viewers adapt to modern functions of broadcasters, such as the video-on-demand and streaming-on-demand, thus altering their choices to more self-relevant AVC and consumption patterns matching time and mood;
iv. users consume AVC in various periods of a day, and these periods impact their selection of consumption;
v. users accessing AVC while commuting is increasing;
vi. mobile devices are frequently for short-duration videos, while TV is for longer-duration videos;
vii. UGC is the most uploaded sort of video creation; and
viii. UGC, TV series, and movies represent the most searched typology of content.

With this perspective, it is no surprise that English as Foreign Language (EFL) learning videos flourish, with users and institutions devoting whole channels to EFL – like BBC [6] or British Council [18]. It is essential to highlight that English – for economic, political, and social reasons – is the lingua franca of the world (Crystal, 2005) [19]. Moreover, AVC created for entertainment purposes also provides EFL learners with informal educational chances, considering they receive input in the target language, as stated by the theoretical framework sustaining the work of Carvalho and Almeida (2015) [20]. Another example of how vital AVC became a useful strategy in Computer Assisted Language Learning (CALL) for EFL is its usage in Massive Online Open Courses (MOOC) platforms (Martín-Monje et al., 2018 [21]; Bárcena et al., 2014 [22]).

Finally, for an overview of AVC repositories and aggregators directed at EFL learning, which according to Jin (2017:200) [23], are "*too numerous to mention*", one can divide them into three main groups:

I.general repositories like YouTube, Vimeo [24], or Dailymotion [25];

II.mobile and web-based aggregators of AVC like English Central [26], VoiceTube [27] or FluentU [28];
III.repositories of AVC specially produced for English learners by players like BBC Learning English [6], or British Council Learn English Great Videos [29].

According to Carvalho (2020) [17], these online platforms based on AVC are able to provide autonomous language learners with

i. a high number of miscellaneous AVC;
ii. a tag system for difficulty, view count and accent;
iii. autonomous work possibilities (games, quizzes, explanations);
iv. progress/activities trackers to accompany users' proficiency evolution;
v. the possibility, in some platforms, to interact with a tutor; and
vi. functions of the player (subtitles, dictionary, play speed).

On the other hand, the finite number of AVC, the lack of variety of genres, the lack of flexibility to watch AVC freely, the poor amount of tags for an AVC, the lack of gamification features to promote consumption of AVC, and lack of a user validation system to comment and rate the AVC can be seen as relevant shortcomings (these shortcomings are especially pertinent in Group II repositories).

In fact, the consumption of AVC, its educational use in EFL, and how OCP were influencing new educational contexts were the focuses of a doctoral project in Multimedia in Education (Carvalho, 2020) [17], which viewed the use of AVC, stored in OCP as an efficient aid towards English as Foreign Language (EFL) learning.

One of the goals of the doctoral project from which this paper stemmed from was the development and testing of a prototype embodying a validated Matrix (Carvalho et al., 2018) [30] of a mobile application aimed at EFL teachers, and at the particular case of English for Specific Purposes/ Business English (ESP/BE) learners. It was a prototype of an OCP that allowed the sharing and mapping of audiovisual content. This mapping also allowed for the search of content on the same platform. The idea was that teachers would look for AVC to use in their sessions, or to recommend as extra language input to their learners (or to their peers), whereas learners would search for AVC to complement their language training in informal contexts.

The project consisted of the following tasks:

i. the identification of the variables to be included in a Matrix, which would support content (AVC) mapping, and assist on the searching operations,
ii. the embodiment of this Matrix into a Form, to be tested by an expert panel,
iii. the selection of the tools used to build the high-fidelity prototype, and
iv. testing and evaluation of the prototype by a sample of both groups of target-users.

Regarding the methodology, this project was a development-research work, in which four different phases were outlined:

i. the construction of a Matrix – through an exploratory study of literature, learning platforms and software, and AVC repositories/aggregators;

ii. the validation of the Matrix by an experts' panel;
iii. the incorporation of the Matrix into a prototype – using prototyping freeware online tools;
iv. the experimental use of the prototype by target-users.

As for the definition of target-users, the targeted ones were EFL teachers and BE/ESP learners. The teachers were targeted because their academic background and training asserts them with clearer notions when it comes to map content, evaluate the didactic/communicative purpose of content, or to take the time to map a content completely. As for learners, their presence is essentials because it is predicted that the OCP would be used in larger numbers by learners searching for AVC, so one has to verify the elements that would guarantee learners' participation (like gamification features, adequacy of the content to their reality/proficiency, or availability to map content).

With the data gathered in Phase IV, the potential of implementing such a platform was evaluated. Thus, this paper will focus on the latter, the experimental phase, in order to share the target-users' oral and written feedback concerning the features of the prototype, its navigation and interaction environment, a global validation of the concept of the prototype, and threats, corrections, and suggestions to operationalize the prototype.

2 Methodology

The methodology adopted in this experimental phase was divided in two stages. Stage 1 comprised experimental tasks executed by EFL teachers, observation tasks by the researcher and participants' feedback. Stage 2 comprises experimental tasks executed by BE/ESP learners, and their feedback when gathered in a focus group.

The controlled testing's purpose was to:

i. test the prototype's usability and functions;
ii. collect feedback about interaction of teachers with the prototype, and;
iii. collect opinions on the experience of using such a platform, and perspectives for future use from the teachers and ESP/BE learners.

Participants in this Phase were the intended target-users of the OCP, i.e., the EFL teachers and the ESP/BE learners, following the orientations provided by Ferraz and Almeida (2013) [31]. As for the selection of four videos to be viewed during the experimental sessions, the criteria was: i. videos that exhibited a BE communicative skill; ii. Videos available on YouTube; iii. Videos 5 to 10 min long; iv. Videos that cover UGC, TV Shows, and Films. Figures 1 and 2 summarize how the experimental phase was structured and how the data was collected:

This paper will focus on oral and written feedback of the trial participants, therefore the procedures concerning the comments of the Teachers consisted in the transcriptions of the oral comments, the preparation of the data, and the analysis of the textual artifacts via content analysis. A second task of qualitative analysis intended to draw conclusions from the open questions asked by the Google Form questionnaire appearing after the trial. The subcategories of this content analysis were defined in vivo. The next section will present the results of the content analysis.

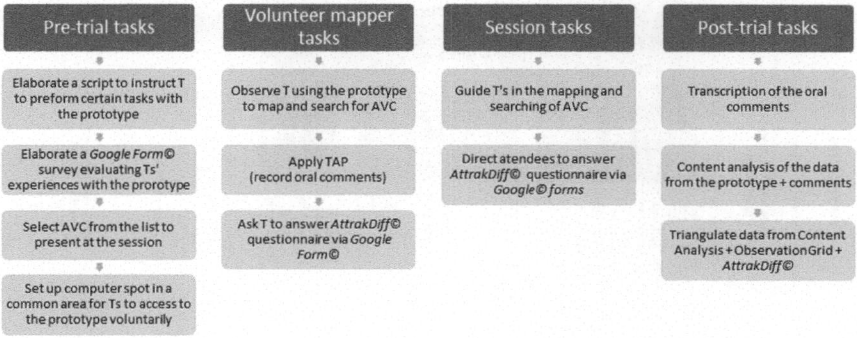

Fig. 1. Outlined tasks for the conference's experimental sessions

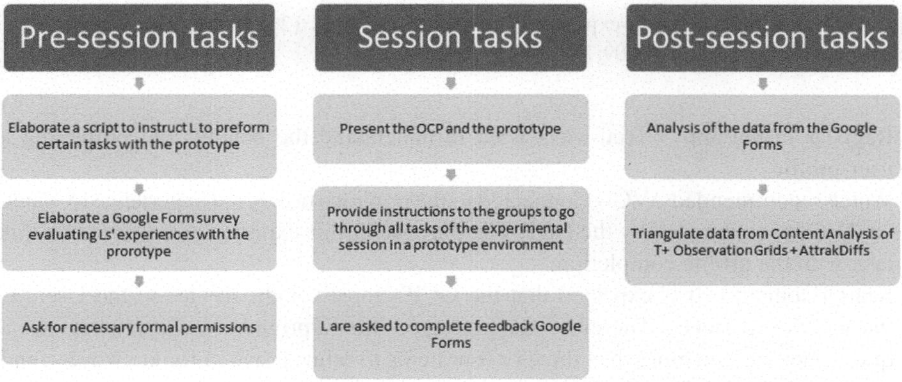

Fig. 2. Outlined tasks for the experimental sessions with Learners

3 The Prototype

Using a prototype in the experimental phase of the project was because it is "an original model, form or an instance that serves as a basis for other processes. In software technology, the term prototype is a working example through which a new model (…) can be derived" (Techopedia, c2018) [32]. This implied that trial users could work with an interactive and designed tool; they could also understand what the research project was proposing, as the prototype form reduced misunderstandings of what the future OCP is supposed to be. The development of the prototype was based on James (2002) [33] elements of the user-experience (Fig. 3). James (2002) [33] proposal consists of five dependent layers, in which each is sustained by the previous one, and they start from abstract towards more concrete layers.

The development of the prototype also required predicting the user-experiences this research project needs its trial-users to execute, in order to provide valuable feedback. Thus, the pinpointed experiences for the trial-users were the following:

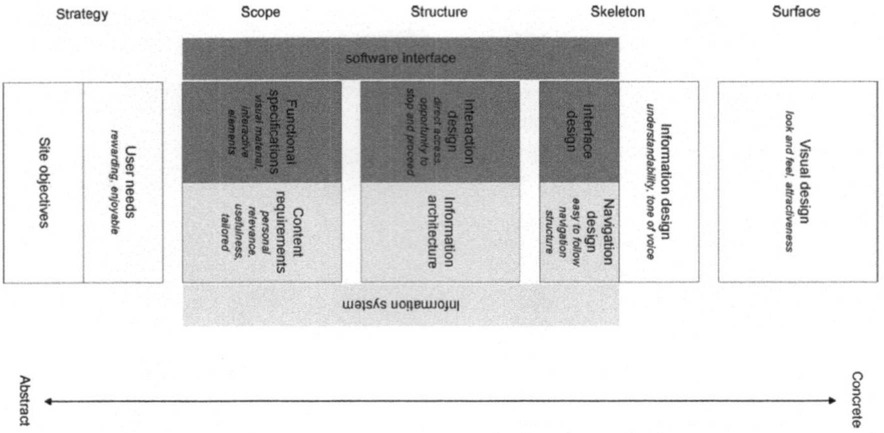

Fig. 3. The elements of user-experience according to James (2002), as quoted and further developed in Crutzen et al. (2009:79) [34].

- Register in the app – Trial-users need to understand the benefits of completing a user-profile.
- Watch recommended AVC – Connected to the previous task is the experience to watch an AVC recommended by the OCP. The purpose of this experience is to connect this task with the profile completion.
- Search content – It is expected that the OCP's most sought service to the Users is the search experience. Therefore, the prototype should provide two search options, a quick one (with no more than three or four items to refine a search for keywords), and an advanced one where the Users can select several specific details.
- Share an AVC – Taking into account the collaborative aspect of the OCP, a trial-user needs to understand the importance of sharing and cataloguing AVC. Hence, a trial of this nature needs to lead trial-users to a task of sharing and cataloguing AVC.
- Post-viewing mapping – In the editing page, trial-users can attribute ratings, share opinions or edit some pieces of information about an AVC after viewing it (being either from a recommended viewing or from a search experience).
- Gamification – The gamification features of the OCP should be presented after all viewings/shares. The trial-users need to understand how the points and badges are attributed and how achievements can be consulted.

Taking all of the above in consideration, the researcher used the software Marvelapp, and below are some of the screens presented to the trial users (6 out of 117 – Fig. 4, 5, 6, 7, 8 and 9).

In conclusion, this prototype was a guarantee that the trial would be executed with an interactable tool for hands-on use. The next subsection will focus on the oral and written feedback from the subjects who experimented with the prototype.

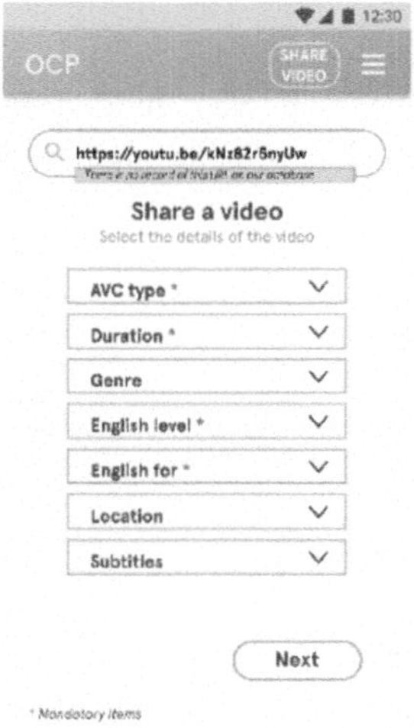

Fig. 4. Share video page

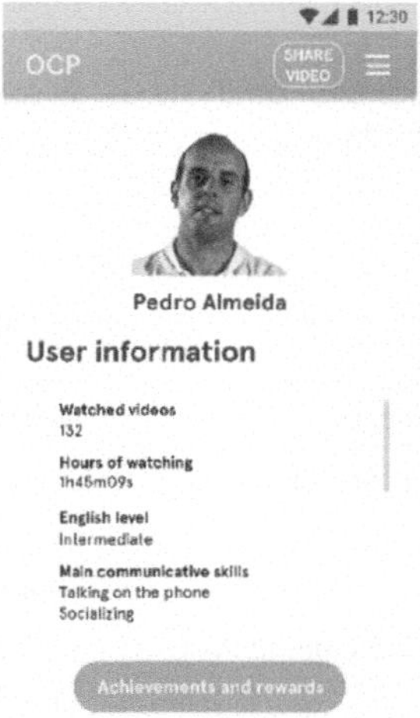

Fig. 5. Profile

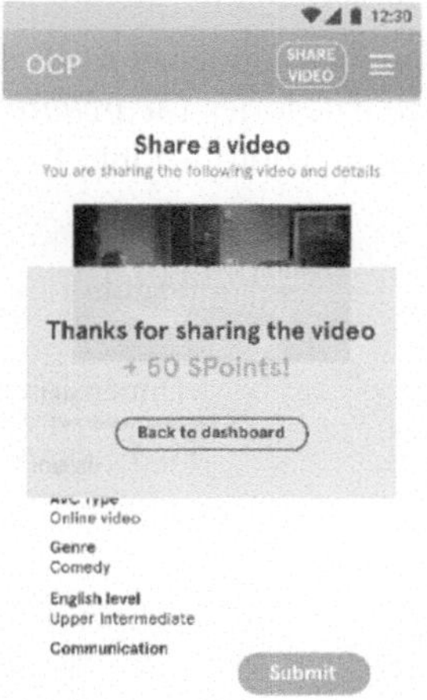

Fig. 6. Gamification notification

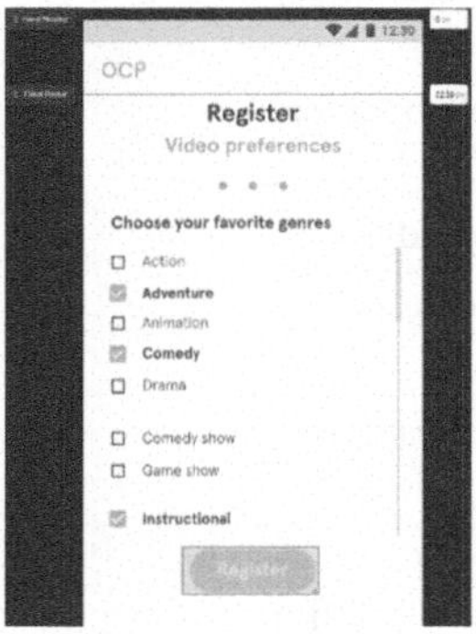

Fig. 7. New User-registration

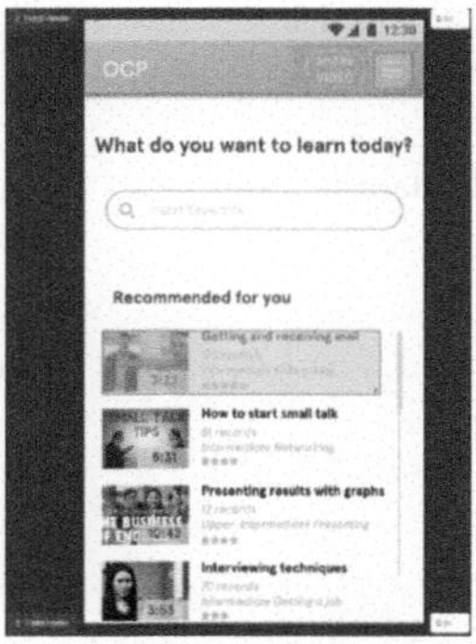

Fig. 8. Dashboard

Fig. 9. Video details

4 Teachers and Learners' Oral and Written Feedback

To gather the teachers' views during the trial with the prototype these were encouraged to verbalize their thoughts. The goal of the TAP was to get opinions from teachers concerning three dimensions: Features; Navigation and Interaction, and; Global Validation of the OCP. In addition, participants were also asked to identify operationalization threats and propose suggestions for a future evolution of the prototype. Below, each subsection focuses on a dimension that branches out into a category structure underlying the content analysis, where one can envision the distribution of the most relevant subcategories identified *in vivo*. The threats and suggestions are listed separately, as these were also aspects pinpointed *in vivo*. While presenting the views of the teachers and learners some possible suggestions for the improvement of the prototype may also be highlighted.

4.1 Features

The first dimension of the content analysis is *Features*, which was divided into five categories (*Searching AVC*; Mapping AVC; Creating playlists; Social interaction; Gamification) – Table 1.

Table 1. Content analysis structure for **Features** dimension

Dimension	Category	Subcategory
1. Features	1.1. Searching AVC	1.1.1. Search
		1.1.2. Advanced search
	1.2. Mapping AVC	1.2.1. Review
		1.2.2. Catalogue
	1.3. Creating Playlists	
	1.4. Social interaction	1.4.1. Comments
		1.4.2. Flagged/dead links
		1.4.3. Collaboration
	1.5. Gamification	1.5.1. Rewards/Badges
		1.5.2. Feedback pop-ups
		1.5.3. Motivation

Focusing on the Category 1.1., *Searching AVC*, it gathers validation from trial users concerning the experience to search for content. It subdivides into subcategories related to *Search* and *Advanced search.* Concerning *Search,* S02, S16 and S17 were unsure about the options of the *Choice of AVC* question (*Film*, *TV Show* and *Online video*). A possible improvement would be renaming "*Online video*" to "*Other type*" or to "*User Generated Content*". Another possibility would be deleting the *Online video* option and highlight to the *Duration* options.

Nevertheless, teachers voiced positive opinions about how much faster it would be to search for content (S01), and also how "*It would be easier (…) to search for things (…) to try in class*" (S19). One can also assume that other participants validated this feature, as no opinions were skeptical about the conceptual nature of the *Search* function. S12, for instance, was even astonished not to have seen that the result list was shifting while using the *refine elements* functions (S12: "*Is it already filtered?*") – a sign of how natural that chore was for S12.

Focusing on subcategory 1.1.2., *Advanced Search*, S03 and S08 were uncertain about the difference between some of the meso-categorization options. These uncertainties disappeared when informed that the categorization was based on a study of BE manuals.

More reactions about CS came from S12, S13, and S18, who agreed that choosing only one macro-category showed inflexibility of the platform, and that the OCP should arrange for multiple selections. Therefore, a possible improvement would be to provide multiple selection options for the CS on the *Advanced search page* (and extend them to the *Share video page* for consistency purposes).

Concerning the concept of selecting and disputing CS' information, all participants concurred that the user-opinion about the CS shown in the content information was paramount.

Category 1.2. concerns Mapping AVC, i.e. an assemblage of comments and endorsements of the mapping tasks and it offshoots into two subcategories (*Review* and *Catalogue*). Regarding the latter, S16 mentioned that "*One thing that I would like to have is a box for notes that I would keep attaching to a video I like*". A possible improvement would be the inclusion of a field for tracking notes that would only be seen by the user in the *Video details page.*

The *Catalogue* subcategory's feedback can be organized into two levels: the proficiency calculator and the validation of a Hidden CS question that would make the questionnaire complete, but not cumbersome. Concerning the former, teachers validated and there were no objections (S02, S03, S15, and S19 to name a few) to the notion that the proficiency level to be credited to the AVC should be an average of the users' mapping.

Regarding the sharing and mapping an AVC functions, the feedback was very positive toward the manner the mapping questionnaire was presented to the participants (which allows to infer that this type of cataloging would be well accepted in a future real OCP). A confirmation of this assumption came from S02, who verbalized all steps of the mapping experience indicating a clear comprehension of all that the prototype was requiring. S11 also validated the choice of CS (Meso-categories) originating from previous selections (S11: "*OK, good!*").

Improvements to the mapping experience were also shared by a learner, who would like more clarification of how the AVC could relate to different purposes, areas of interest, and academic fields and achievements: "*Purpose, area of interest, academics*".

Therefore, the overall sensation was that both mapping tasks are well constructed and grounded (S11), the tasks are "*intuitive and unproblematic*" (S13), and "*really useful*" (S18) for EFL teachers.

Category 1.3., Creating playlists, address the option to add an AVC to a previously created playlist. As no subjects presented doubts about this specific function, it was considered validated. Only S03 suggested an extra function, namely the option to share playlists with other users.

Considering the Category 1.4., *Social interaction*, it gathers support from participants regarding social interaction features. It is branched into 3 subcategories: *Comments, Flagged/dead links* and *Collaboration.*

As to 1.4.1., S08, for example, had doubts about the *Title* field ("*This is not a title to me. How do you describe this video, or what does this video exemplify?*"). Another instance provided by the TAP is related to S19, who was asked to provide a distinct title to Video 4 (S19: "*In my opinion, I [would be] sharing this because I believe this could be a good way to show my students how things can go wrong while they are in a phone conversation*". This confirmed an understanding by S19 of the intent of *Title* as a mapping element, thus validating this item.

1.4.2. addressed the necessity to flag improper AVC and the topic of dead links to the videos. These concerns arose when S17 asked *"Do you have any protocol or procedure in the event of there not being a video anymore. What if the video is not there at all?"*. S16 and S17's attention was then turned to the "*dead link*" function on the *Rating/comments page* and was asked if it would be enough as a warning tool. Participants presented no objections.

The last subcategory addresses *Collaboration* fostered by the OCP's social interaction functions to guarantee the collaborative component of the OCP. The confirmation of this subcategory can be structured on three levels. On the first, participants were evaluating how the OCP would attract teachers to share more AVC with their peers. S18 and S19 were more unequivocal about this element, with a consensus opinion that teachers "*should share more*" (S19) and this platform has the proper features for this. Thus, it can be assumed that the development of a tool like the OCP, which gives teachers the chance to share validated content among them, is valid.

The second level concerns collaboration between teachers and learners being fostered via OCP. An example is stated by S18 and it addresses the use of the OCP, either to map or to search for/consume AVC as a homework task ("*You ask them to watch it the day before (…), develop it and get more from it*"). Moreover, S08 was sympathetic of both teachers and learners opinionating on the English level. Finally, S18 also asked whether the OCP will permit the creation of work groups so that "*learners could work together*". A possible improvement would be the function to create work groups to connect all users (learner – learner; learner – teacher; teacher – teacher). This seems to be a valid and a logical upgrade to be included in the development of the OCP.

The third level of this subcategory summarizes generalized praise by the participants, like S19 "this is one of the things I look for when I search. Because I know that, so people have used them, so it is probably a good thing to use as well".

Category 1.5. of this dimension is Gamification. This category divides into three subcategories: *Rewards/Badges*; *Feedback pop-ups*; *Motivation.* As to *Rewards*, S03 responded very eagerly to the idea of getting "prizes", and S08, S16 and S17 highlighted the possibility of the OCP branching out externally to seek of partnerships to collect appropriate rewards for both types of target-users.

Another gamification characteristic tackled by the participants was concerning the accumulation of V-Points and S-Points. There were doubts in the instructions shown in gamification screens. For example, S16 was unsure about users comprehending what S-points and V-points are, and how they link to the gamification features. During this TAP with S16 and S17, the researcher needed to explain all features of the gamification features (S-Points, V-Points, badges, and rewards), and doubts faded. However, both participants consented that the point was the lack of clear-cut information about the rewards during the tasks. This led to the realization that users will not instinctively understand the rewards. Furthermore, S17 questioned the badges naming, in particular, the *Rookie* badge, which is not very suitable to teachers. Several recommendations were thus verbalized:

a. The OCP should feature help icons in all pages and pop-up messages explaining the gamification features, namely, the *Achievements and rewards* page;
b. The Help icons are to be present for all the functions of the platform and not just for Gamification features;
c. The naming given to the badges must be revised – one can conduct a simple survey with several proposals of badges for teachers to choose some.

Regarding *Motivation*, i.e., whether the gamification features would motivate users to contribute, S01 was the only not clinging to this concept: "*I can see it being motivating for* others, *but it is not for me*". (S01). However, S12 thinks "*it is a very good idea to actually involve the teacher and the user in general*", S11 also reacted very positively to point accumulation (regular nodding and optimistic interjections), and S02 valued the concept of level ladder, accumulating badges and graduating to upper levels.

4.2 Navigation and Interaction

The second dimension of the content analysis is *Navigation and Interaction*, which was divided into two categories (*Layout*; *Icons*) – Table 2.

Table 2. Content analysis structure for the Navigation and interaction dimension

Dimension	Category	Subcategory
2. Navigation and interaction	2.1. Layout	2.1.1. Redundancies
		2.1.2. Instructions
		2.1.3. Messages
	2.2. Icons	2.2.1. Advanced search
		2.2.2. Heart
		2.2.3. Share video
		2.2.4. Checkboxes
		2.2.5. Dashboard

Considering the **Category 2.1.**, *Layout*, it branches into subcategories entitled *Redundancies*, *Instructions*, and *Messages.* Regarding *Redundancies*, S17 pinpointed the redundant clicking. Further opinions were shared regarding the *Redundancies* subcategory during a task to edit details of AVC based on the choices made in the *Search results page.* S16 and S17 believe that these restrictions are unnecessary. Moreover, S16 and S17 considered again that the clicking could be reduced while working on the *Advanced search page.* A final issue concerning this subcategory was raised by several participants who did not understand why the "S-" and "V-Points" were hidden in the *Achievements and rewards page* (Fig. 10). Not only was it "*Not so clear to see*" (S03), but it was also forcing to search and click unnecessarily – similar opinions were shared by S02, S08.

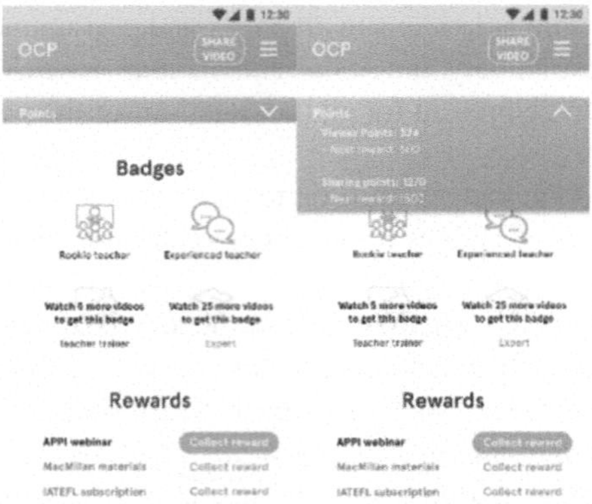

Fig. 10. Achievements and rewards screen (without and with displayed points)

Possible improvements can be:

a. Eliminate unnecessary clicking by developing the following interaction: 1. Watch a content - > 2. Rate and comment it - > 3. Receive a gamification message that would fade - > 4. Go to the *Edit details page*, and 5 - > Edit details. S17 expressed more enthusiasm and endorsed this improvement (S17: "*Absolutely!*"). This recommendation should be taken into account for other experiences in the OCP.
b. Eliminate barriers to detail editing. Both S16 and S17 support that the *Edit details page* does not need constraints. Users should edit the video details they see fit, either after watching a suggested AVC or subsequently to a search.
c. Include a *check/uncheck all* function to both the *Advanced search page* and the *Share video page.*
d. Get the platform to 'remember' previous choices in multiple-choice sections, and the most written keywords, while searching for AVC. This can be done using *cookies* which will individualize the experience with the OCP or by counting on the user-profile to narrow down the video selection possibilities.
e. Exhibit points evidently on the *Achievements and rewards page.*

Regarding the subcategory *Instructions*, participants detected dubious instructions both on the *Dashboard* (Fig. 11) and on the *Refine Search Screen* (Fig. 12). The former had the instruction "*What do you want to learn today?*" on the teachers' profile, hence, an inadequate instruction. The latter required a written/explicit directive for users to refine their search. S19 identified a third dubious instruction on the "*Subtitles*" question (Fig. 13). This subject believed that learners may think the subtitles are presented in their native language (and not in English).

Possible improvements for these issues can be:

a. (Figure 11) Alter the inadequate instruction on the teacher's profile to "What are you looking for?".

b. (Figure 12) Include the instruction "Filter results" bellow the search box – a web designer should certify this recommendation.
c. (Figure 13) Alter the heading of the drop-down menu to "English subtitles"

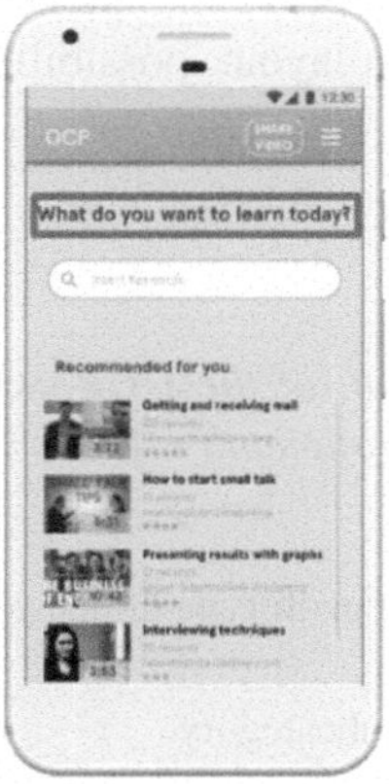

Fig. 11. Dashboard: inadequate instruction

Fig. 12. Missing instruction

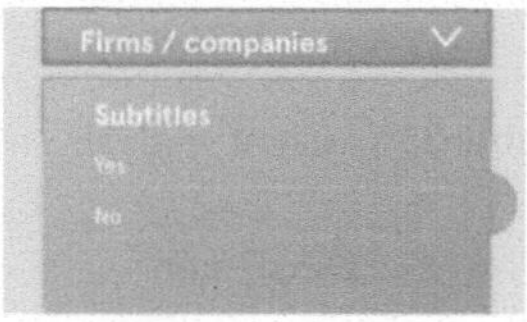

Fig. 13. Subtitles question

Shifting to the *Messages* subcategory, S01, S03, and S06 did not distinguish immediately which message was the most recent (Task 7, Appendix II). S02 even added "*I am missing something. Select the message about viewing scores*". S17 hinted that a reason for the Inbox not to be so clear might be the lack of "*dates or hours of the messages*". Hence, the future OCP's Inbox this information to the *Messages page.* A web designer should be consulted for this improvement.

As to the Category *2.2.*, *Icons*, it branches into the *Advanced search, Heart, Share video, Checkboxes,* and *Dashboard* subcategories. As mentioned, *Advanced search* was one of the prototype's instructions that raised doubts. From the users' viewpoint, it did not have enough visibility on the screen. This led to some uncertainty by, for instance, S01, S09, and S19. A possible improvement would be to heighten visibility and outline of the "*Advanced Search*" icon.

Subcategory 2.2.2., i.e. *Heart*, focuses on the button. S03, S08, S13, and S17 suggested an outlined "*heart*" button and a colored-in button after clicking on it: "*I don't think the heart should be colored in. It should outline, and when I click on it, it would be solid*". (S08). The developers should follow the participants' correction, and place an outlined heart ( ), when unclicked, and a full heart ( ), when clicked.

Regarding the subcategory *Share video* participants complained that ( ) was not perceptible, so developers have to improve visibility and outline of this command.

Another subcategory (*Checkboxes*) addresses the checkboxes, which, according to S01, S03 and S13, were small. S13 also found frustrating that a user needs to press a very small area on the screen (;). To improve, developers should devise a clickable area which is the combination of checkbox + choice ( ), which is the standard for checkboxes in mobile operating systems.

Finally, S03, S06, S13, S14, S15, and S16 addressed the subcategory Dashboard. Participants did not realize that the logo OCP was a connection to the *Dashboard*. A simple improvement for this limitation is to substitute the logo with a *Homepage* icon (S06) and add the same command on the *User-menu* (S13).

The written feedback of learners also referred the need to improve the interaction functions: "more interactive and simple feed, better presentation layout, possibility to link to other platforms [YouTube, Moodle]".

4.3 Global Validation Of The Prototype

The third dimension of the content analysis is *Global validation of the OCP*, which branched into three categories (*Concept; Structure; Mobile environment*) – Table 3.

Table 3. Content analysis structure for the **Global validation of the prototype** dimension

Dimension	Category	Subcategory
3. Global Validation of OCP	3.1. Concept	
	3.2. Structure	
	3.3. Mobile environment	

Concerning Category 3.1., i.e. participants' views about the *Concept* of the platform, it is relevant to mention endorsements to the purpose of developing such a tool: "*The whole experience was really interesting. This could be a very helpful too indeed. A sort of curated YT for BE/ESP purposes*" (S20).

Written feedback from learners and teachers was also encouraging, as they conceptually validated the platform, as well as the informal education potential:

- "This application has a lot of potential by filtering the various YouTube videos into categories and degrees of difficulty allied to a reward system similar to that of computer games… Great";
- "This platform can be a good medium for people with language difficulties since we can choose different levels of English".
- "I like the idea of a dedicated platform/repository to search for AVC content for classes, and especially one where the content can be vetted/rated/categorized by our peers, which I believe is the great strength of this app".
- "Quite an intuitive and potentially useful resource for both students and teachers"
- "it would be better for personal use"

In Category 3.2., trial-users shared positive testimonials of the prototype's user-experience, namely: "It is quite easy in the sense that it is clear. I can see the details, and I can see who it is for through the video, as well. I think it is important to know what I am doing. So far, it's been quite clear what needs to be done and how it works. (…) I really like the layout. It is straightforward". (S10);

Concerning Category 3.3., only S18 opinionated positively about the OCP's "*Mobile environment*", however, none of the remaining participants expressed doubts about the embodiment of the prototype in a mobile environment. Hence, one can infer that the participants validated the mobile nature of the OCP.

4.4 Threats and Suggestions

What appeared to be the earnest threat to an OCP of this nature was the danger of users with a low-level of English proficiency providing inaccurate mapping. This issue was raised by S09 and S17: "*What if there is a bunch of rogue users who do the nasty thing so… maybe not on purpose, but just because they are not competent enough*" (S17).

The latter threat (S17) refers to the possibility of low-linguistic quality AVC being uploaded to the OCP by the low-level users. Firstly, these may not be competent enough to recognize mistakes in the AVC, due to their limited language level (S09). Secondly, the fact that low-level users tend to upload "*too much of what they like, rather than what they need or benefit from. Because with massive input influences the results quality*" (S09). The combination of these two behaviors may pose a threat to the AVC quality provided by the OCP. Low-level users may even be attracted by ACV that is "*made with good digital cover/look; but the language is really bad, bad pronunciation, mispronunciation, (…)" (S09).*

Possible solutions can be:

a. The implementation of a validation system where high-level users will be invited to confirm the mapping of low-level users, in exchange for rewards. S17 proposes that "It may also be an idea to incorporate/embrace/accept the modifications more willingly when they come from experienced teachers [the badge], or those who are ranking high in the badge scale. Because they are experienced, they probably know what they are doing".
b. The trust in the collaborative element of the OCP, which (as Ed1 had put it) will marginalize inaccurate mapping (S17 agreed with this view). This improvement also includes the "flag" system mentioned above, which raised doubts to S09 ("I don't see how you would be able to control that. If you have open access to anything (…) if you create a flag system, then that would mean some administrator would have to control and delete it often. That would be a lot of work because you'd have to see it every day").
c. The platform can avoid overloading high-level users with mapping requests by immediately allowing content from trustworthy platforms ("If you use BBC English or stuff from the British Council [or.org websites] … that stuff is always being screened. The language level may be too difficult, but the language in itself is correct". [S09]).

One can also infer from the previous subsections that minor threats are related to the misunderstandings of how the Gamification features work, and the uncertainty of how to map CS. It is believed that the proposed improvements would diminish these threats.

Naturally, due to the nature of the TAP, as participants were conducting the trial, some operationalization suggestions to the threats were shared. These suggestions/improvements can be organized into three dimensions:

1. Improve the teacher experience in the OCP
   a. Give information about how many teachers and learners have already mapped an AVC;
   b. Integrate the user accounts and *cookies* to improve the personalization and content retrieval from previous sessions.;
   c. Add a "*My shared videos*" page;
   d. Assure private social-interaction tools;
   e. Build a content base before launching the OCP.
2. Guarantee quality AVC in the OCP
   a. Ask High-level users to validate the mapping of AVC shared by low-level users;
   b. Automatically allow AVC from trustworthy repositories and when a content from an untrustworthy repository is uploaded, send it for high-level users to validate the mapping before appearing on search results;
   c. Improve the rating system of the teachers' experience.
3. Use the OCP for teaching purposes
   a. Provide a lesson plan template which teachers can complete after sharing new AVC;
   b. Insert a field for private tracking notes about the AVC;
   c. Give teachers the possibility to define new search/ catalogue criteria;
   d. Allow for the construction of teacher and learner Groups;
   e. Develop a similar research project to branch out to GE.

5 Conclusion

In conclusion, the TAP focused on three dimensions: *Features, Navigation and Interaction* and *Global validation of the OCP*. From these dimensions, it was feasible to identify threats and suggest enhancements to the OCP's conceptual nature, as well as useful suggestions for the operationalization of the platform.

The TAP with teachers was a methodological step to i. Test the prototype in what concerns usability and functions; ii. Collect feedback concerning the interaction of the target-users with the prototype; and iii. Collect comments on the experience of using such a platform in the future. By supporting the prototype and specifically its features, teachers were confirming the core concept of the OCP and the importance it would have in the EFL community. By supporting the prototype's navigation and interaction functions, trial-users were validating the development of a usable tool, thus confirming that the future OCP would be user-friendly and able to be used by the target users.

It was also clear that teachers understood all the functions and features of the prototype and how they would be advantageous to the purpose of the OCP. The gathered data allowed identifying corrections to be made in the operationalization of the OCP, which can be to 1. Improve to the user experience – like making buttons and clicking easier, highlight certain functions, or remove redundant screens – and; 2. Correct and revise instructions, badges' names, or the aspect of the inbox.

As for the learners, their written comments stressed the informal education potential, and necessary improvements to the mapping and user-interaction functions. However, given the rich qualitative data gathered from the TAP with the teachers, the fact that there was no time to execute a similar task with learners is clearly one of this project's shortcomings.

For future work, it would be interesting to execute a TAP in the same framework with the learners in order to get more feedback about the three dimensions, as well as more threats and operationalization strategies from learners. Another development for future work is the embodiment of a digital formative assessment mechanism to the OCP, as suggested by Carvalho et al. (2020) [35]. This mechanism would provide learners with the opportunity to select a Learning Path in the OCP, in order to be exposed to a massive amount of AVC focused on a given communicative skill.

To clarify the abstract idea of this Learning Path, Fig. 14 shows the three steps to follow in this hypothetical addition: Step 1 – Choosing a path for assessing a communicative skill; Step 2 – Watching and mapping videos from a pre-set playlist; and Step 3 – Production, upload, and mapping of learners' own content.

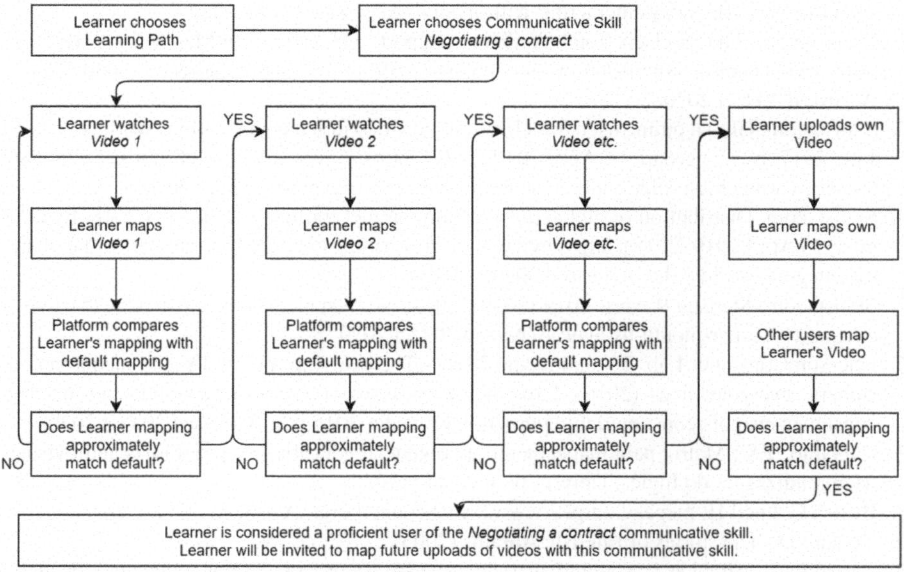

Fig. 14. Flowchart of the learning path summarizing steps 1, 2, and 3 (Carvalho et al., 2020) [35]

This development intends to increase the motivation of learners to use the OCP, and must therefore be sustained in an effective reward system – being the maximum reward a certification of high language proficiency in certain communicative skills. The Learning Path would assure more learners to participate in mapping of content, and hence guarantee the collaborative element.

References

1. YouTube Homepage. https://www.youtube.com. Accessed 30 Oct 2020
2. Think with Google. YouTube Internal Data, Global. Google, May 2017
3. Shalavi, G.: More people are streaming YouTube on their TV screens. Here's what they're watching, September 2020. https://www.thinkwithgoogle.com/intl/en-cee/consumer-insights/consumer-trends/watch-youtube-on-tv/. Accessed 30 Oct 2020
4. Thinkwithgooglecom. Learning-video shares statistics, 18 April 2019 (2017b). https://www.thinkwithgoogle.com/data/learning-video-shares-statistics/. Accessed 30 Oct 2020
5. Kahn Academy Homepage. www.kahnacademy.com. Accessed 30 Jan 2020
6. BBC Learn English Homepage. https://www.bbc.co.uk/learningenglish. Accessed 30 Oct 2020
7. MIT Homepage. https://www.mit.edu/. Accessed 30 Oct 2020
8. Cambridge Homepage. https://www.cambridgeenglish.org/. Accessed 30 Oct 2020
9. Twinwordcom. 6 Common Features of Top 250 YouTube Channels (c2018). https://www.twinword.com/blog/features-of-top-250-youtube-channels/. Accessed 5 February 2019
10. Thinkwithgoogle. Google Data, U.S. Think with Google, March 2018. https://www.thinkwithgoogle.com/marketing-strategies/video/study-skills-video-watch-time-statistics/. Accessed 30 Oct 2020
11. Nielsencom. Time flies: us adults now spend nearly half a day interacting with media, 24 July 2019 (2018). https://www.nielsen.com/us/en/insights/article/2018/time-flies-us-adults-now-spend-nearly-half-a-day-interacting-with-media/. Accessed 30 Oct 2020
12. Nielsencom. The Nielsen Total Audience Report: Q3 2018, 19 March 2019 (c2019). https://www.nielsen.com/us/en/insights/reports/2019/q3-2018-total-audience-report.html. Accessed 30 Oct 2020
13. Statistacom. Global online users watching online video in selected locations worldwide as of June 2017, by age group, 16 April 2019 (2017). https://www.statista.com/statistics/785586/locations-watching-online-videos-by-age-worldwide/. Accessed 30 Oct 2020
14. Statistacom. Distribution of global downstream internet traffic as of October 2018, by category, 15 April 2019 (2018). https://www.statista.com/statistics/271735/internet-traffic-share-by-category-worldwide/. Accessed 30 Oct 2020
15. Statistacom. Statista, 9 April 2019 (2019). https://www.statista.com/statistics/807510/visit-cinema-twice-per-month-us-age/. Accessed 30 Oct 2020
16. Ericsson Consumer Lab. TV and media 2016 – The evolving role of TV and media in consumers' everyday lives (2016). https://www.ericsson.com/assets/local/trends-and-insights/consumer-insights/consumerlab/reports/tv-and-media-2016.pdf. Accessed 30 Oct 2020
17. Carvalho, T.S.: Matriz para mapeamento do potencial educativo de programas audiovisuais na aprendizagem do Inglês. University of Aveiro (2020)
18. British Council Homepage. https://www.britishcouncil.org/. Accessed 30 Oct 2020
19. Crystal, D.: The stories of English. Abrams (2005)
20. Carvalho, T., Almeida, P.: Caraterísticas de conteúdo AV procuradas por aprendentes de inglês língua estrangeira. In: COIED Proceedings (Not published) (2015). https://drive.google.com/file/d/1c2O8inzCcWDYm3qV2n7OxVn_kfxXWXy-/view?usp=sharing. Accessed 30 Oct 2020
21. Martín-Monje, E., Castrillo, M.D., Mañana-Rodríguez, J.: Understanding online interaction in language MOOCs through learning analytics. Comput. Assist. Lang. Learn. **31**(3), 251–272 (2018)
22. Bárcena, E., Read, T., Martín-Monje, E., Castrillo, M.D.: Analysing student participation in Foreign Language MOOCs: a case study. In: EMOOCs 2014: European MOOCs Stakeholders Summit, pp. 11–17 (2014)

23. Jin, H.: VoiceTube [Review]. In: O'Brien, M., Levis, J. (eds.) Proceedings of the 8th Pronunciation in Second Language Learning and Teaching Conference. Iowa State University, Ames (2017)
24. Vimeo Homepage. https://vimeo.com. Accessed 30 Oct 2020
25. Dailymotion Homepage. https://www.dailymotion.com. Accessed 30 Oct 2020
26. English Central Homepage. https://www.englishcentral.com. Accessed 30 Oct 2020
27. VoiceTube Homepage. https://www.voicetube.com/. Accessed 30 Oct 2020
28. FluentU Homepage. https://www.fluentu.com. Accessed 30 Oct 2020
29. British Council Learn English Great Videos Homepage. https://learnenglish.britishcouncil.org/apps/learnenglish-great-videos. Accessed 30 Oct 2020
30. Carvalho, T., Almeida, P., Balula, A.: Audiovisual content as a learning aid for Business English learners: developing and validating a Matrix. In: 4th International Conference on Higher Education Advances (HEAD 2018), pp. 1429–1437. Editorial Universitat Politècnica de València, July 2018
31. Ferraz, J., Almeida, P.: Avaliação de protótipos iTV e mobile. Apresentação na disciplina de Seminário do MCMM. Universidade de Aveiro (2013)
32. What is a prototype, 9 June 2017. https://www.Techopedia.Com/, https://www.techopedia.com/definition/678/prototype. Accessed 30 Oct 2020
33. James, G.J.: The Elements of User Experience: User-Centered Design for the Web and Beyond (2002)
34. Crutzen, R., de Nooijer, J., Brouwer, W., Oenema, A., Brug, J., de Vries, N.K.: A conceptual framework for understanding and improving adolescents' exposure to Internet-delivered interventions. Health Promot. Int. **24**(3), 277–284 (2009)
35. Carvalho, T.S.: Chapter 7: Reliability of digital formative assessment practices and instruments: theoretical review towards an assessment proposal. In: Handbook of Research on Determining the Reliability of Online Assessment and Distance Learning, 1st edn., p. To be disclosed. IGI Global (2020a, to be published in December)

Bring the Social Media to the Classroom of Portuguese as a Foreign Language in China: Possibilities and Challenges

Yuxiong Zhang(✉) and António Moreira

University of Aveiro, Aveiro, Portugal
{yuxiongzhang,moreira}@ua.pt

Abstract. Although introducing social media in a Foreign Language classroom is nothing new in the academic world, studies regarding Portuguese as a Foreign Language (PFL) in fact has been insufficiently studied, particularly in the case of Chinese learners. We implemented two interventions with a duration of 14 weeks and the participation of 10 Chinese students in total by using a Chinese microblogging platform, Weibo. Although obtained some evident positive results from a test performed after the activities, the participants revealed in the interview some differences brought by this tool during the learning process might not even correspond effectively to their learning expectation due to the learning strategy usually applied in daily routine, which indicates some challenges existing in PFL teaching model reform in China and in the integration of these technologies in actual didactic practice based mainly on the passive memorization by students. Therefore, before applying social media in PFL classroom, it's urgently necessary to help students to build awareness about a full-scale learning system of Portuguese language, which does not be confined solely to the memorization of vocabulary and grammar rules, and emphasize the importance of the social nature and communicative practicability of languages in real-life occasions.

Keywords: Foreign language learning · Portuguese as a Foreign Language · Social media · Microblogging · M-learning

1 Introduction

Due to the wide popularity of social media, which are completely deep-rooted in our daily life, and its significant potential nowadays, a creasing number of educators and researchers cast their eyes on these tools and investigate the possibilities they bring to the didactic practice. In their study, Hwang e Fu [1] analyzed 96 studies with regard to mobile technology-assisted language learning published from 2007 to 2016 and reached the conclusion that the number of researches in such area was stably increasing. Several authors have already revealed some relevant advantages of using social media in language teaching practice, which can enhance the students' knowledge of grammar and vocabulary, promote language awareness and self-expression, and develop communicative competence, for example [2–5]. It is believed that the introduction of social media

A. Reis et al. (Eds.): TECH-EDU 2020, CCIS 1384, pp. 370–379, 2021.
https://doi.org/10.1007/978-3-030-73988-1_29

makes language learning more authentic and applicable, connecting the learners to the real world. In the words of Lantz-Andersson, these tools provide opportunities for them to practice and prepare for daily communication in a foreign language [6]. However, the usage of social media tools in Portuguese learning is so far barely discussed, especially concerning Chinese learners' Portuguese as a Foreign Language (PFL) learning.

Under the circumstance of globalization, as a strong potential with remarkably increasing economic strength on the global stage, China has demonstrated a close collaboration with Portuguese-speaking countries in recent years, especially with Brazil, within the framework of cooperation of BRICS, and Angola, due to the post-war reconstruction support. The demand for talents who master Portuguese language has been enhanced in the Chinese labor market. Therefore, it can be said that PFL is currently receiving a lot of attention in this Far East country, and in 2018, there were 17 universities and colleges that set up courses related to Portuguese language and studies [7]. However, most of the time, Portuguese language didactic strategy relies on a traditional approach depending on the lecture's unidirectional transmission which was defined by Água-Mel [8] as a very "devalued" and "indeed abandoned" method in the West. In the meantime, the limited opportunity to contact and use Portuguese language outside the classroom was also considered as one of the most important influencing factors during its learning process [8]. Thus, we decided to introduce the Chinese microblogging platform, Weibo, due to its accessibility in mainland China and possibility to foster a sense of community inside and outside the classroom [9] and a situated learning environment motivated by curiosity, creativity or practical factors [10], to Chinese students PFL learning with the purpose of investigating the possible influence it can bring on their Portuguese written skills, which is solely studied as yet.

2 Methodology

In order to simulate the daily usage of Weibo, we prepared a set of topics including a great range of occasions which allowed a daily use of Portuguese and recruited five Chinese sophomores of Portuguese Studies major and five Portuguese juniors who attended Mandarin lessons at university in the academic year 2018/2019. All the participants were solicited to make posts and interact with these topics with the target language twice a week for 14 weeks. In the following academic year, other five sophomores of the same major and a native Portuguese lecture participated in the activity and the duration and frequency were remained. All the participants took part voluntarily.

All the second-year students of Portuguese Studies major in the academic years 2018/2019 and 2019/2020 wrote two articles in accordance with identical writing exercises respectively before and after the activities with the purpose of drawing a comparison of Portuguese written skills between participants and the other students who did not participate in the activities developed on Weibo. These two writing exercises were retrieved from a PFL standard test of the book <Exames de Português CAPLE-UL> [11]. We analyzed all the articles and focused on Chinese students' common difficulties in PFL learning – inflection. As a grammatical phenomenon which does not exist in Chinese language system, the command of the nominal agreement is considered as one of Chinese learners' constant difficulties since there is no parameter corresponding to the plural agreement in such an analytic language [12, 13]. According to Ma [14], making errors in the verbal agreement is also a very usual factor in PFL learning for Chinese students no matter where they learn Portuguese. Thus, we focused our attention mainly on analyzing the students' mistakes related to nominal number agreement, nominal gender agreement, verbal agreement, and usage of tense and grammatical modes of Portuguese. Nevertheless, during the analysis of the articles, we also found the correct spelling of Portuguese words as a common difficulty among the learners in their writing and, for this reason, we also compared Portuguese spelling situation between the two groups of students. Considering the difference between the number of words used by different students in different articles, the results were presented by error rate differential between the same writing exercise accomplished in different periods regarding the five aspects we concerned. And the error rate was calculated by dividing the number of errors in a certain aspect by its corresponding part of speech or the total number of words used as the formula below shows.

$$\begin{aligned}&\text{Error rate differential} = ((\text{number of errors in X aspect of a writing exercise in the}\\&\text{first test})/(\text{number of its corresponding part of speech or total number of words})-\\&(\text{number of errors in X aspect of the same writing exercise in the second}\\&\text{test})/(\text{number of its corresponding part of speech or total number of words})) \times 100\%\end{aligned} \quad (1)$$

After the completion of the activities, all the ten Chinese participants were also interviewed and asked eight questions in order to compare the differences between the usage of Weibo to practice Portuguese language and their usual study strategies, get to know their attitude about the usage of social media to learn PFL and understand the advantages and disadvantages of using Weibo in learning PFL from their points of view which the writing exercise tests might not demonstrate. Those questions were:

1. Normally, how are you used to studying Portuguese? What kind of strategies do you use more?
2. What are the biggest difficulties in your Portuguese learning?
3. What is your opinion about using social media to practice Portuguese? Do you think it is possible to learn Portuguese on social media? In what way?
4. What is the most evident difference between practicing Portuguese on Weibo and the strategies you usually use? Which one do you prefer? Why?
5. For your consideration, what are the advantages and disadvantages of using social media in learning Portuguese?
6. Do you think that you have learned anything in the activities? In what aspects for example?

3 Positive Learning Outcomes and Its Possibility

As a matter of fact, the two writing exercises reveal two completely different writing styles, and the related vocabulary, tense and grammatical moods usage may also vary. Therefore, the results can differ in distinct articles. According to the results we obtained, tenses and grammatical moods usage demonstrated an overall progress between the two testes in the academic year 2018/2019; the students who did not take part in the activities on Weibo presented greater progress in the first exercise while the five participants in the first intervention improved more in the second article writing. As for the second-year students in the forthcoming academic year, even though the general situation was positive, the two groups of students showed drastic differences in different writing exercises. When one group revealed progress, another fell behind. Thus, there was no clear proof of disparity between the two groups in such aspect. Nevertheless, the ten participants of the two interventions represented a noteworthy improvement in verbal agreement in all writing exercises, showing a better command, and, in the meantime, other students regressed in this part. Regarding the nominal agreement, the participants in the academic year 2019/2020 obtained an overall progress, widen a significant gap between the two groups of students, though the students who did not participate in the activities also demonstrated relatively slighter progress. However, in the previous academic year, the five participants revealed a better proficiency in neither number agreement nor gender agreement, on the whole, representing irregular variances (Table 1).

With respect to the issue of correct spelling, due to the relatively negative completeness of the first writing exercise and the limited number of words used in the second exercise in the test before the activities on Weibo in the academic year 2018/2019, we could not perceive the actual situation of students' level. But the participants indeed committed far fewer mistakes in word spelling in both writing exercises of the second test. As for the succeeding academic year, although the five participants revealed a worse command in such aspect in all writing exercises than the other students without participating in the activities, their error rate differentials were remarkable; the participants' group enhanced Portuguese words spelling in the first exercise of the second test while the other group made even more mistakes. And participants' error rate differential with respect to spelling in the second exercise was more than six times greater than the other students (Table 2).

Furthermore, the ten participants also expressed their positive attitudes toward the usage of social media in Portuguese learning in the interview carried out after the activities. For them, Weibo provided a nice learning method (two participants), which is useful (two participants) and convenient (one participant). And in their opinion, it also created new expectations (one participant) and possibilities (six participants). According to a participant, when pretended to express their thoughts on Weibo, they spontaneously turned to a dictionary and tried to transmit their ideas to Portuguese, by this way, they acquired new vocabulary. It was also possible to learn other uses of words and expressions by observing what others wrote in the target language since the input was always related to Portuguese usage. Thus, the participants got more acquainted with the target language (two participants).

In accordance with the participants, the introduction of Weibo was easily accepted by them and all of them affirmed feeling the improvement in writing Portuguese. It allowed them to practice what they have learned in the classroom in a real linguistic environment and meanwhile helped to expose their shortcomings in PFL learning. Three of the ten participants regarded the accomplishment of the activities as a review process and during the activities, they could maximize in practice the use of the knowledge they learned in a synthetic way (four participants). Through the interaction with the native speakers, they

Table 1. Error rate differentials of inflection concerns

		First exercise			Second exercise		
		Overall	Participants	Others	Overall	Participants	Others
The academic year 2018/2019	Wrong usage of tenses and grammatical moods (%)	3.46	2.69	4.15	2.69	3.36	2.55
	Verbal disagreement (%)	−1.26	0.49	−2.37	−2.75	2.05	−4.6
	Nominal number disagreement (%)	−1.74	−0.74	−2.1	0.73	−1.18	1.49
	Nominal gender disagreement (%)	−1.51	−2.12	−1.63	−3.4	2.42	−5.74
The academic year 2019/2020	Wrong usage of tenses and grammatical moods (%)	0.53	5.46	−1.59	1.02	−4.37	3.03
	Verbal disagreement (%)	0.28	2.78	−0.81	0.53	3.81	−0.65
	Nominal number disagreement (%)	0.51	1.07	0.22	1.99	6.87	0.15
	Nominal gender disagreement (%)	1.13	1.66	0.81	2.06	4.08	1.24

also learned some new authentic expressions which their textbook did not contain (three participants), extending the scope of knowledge in Portuguese (one participant). In the words of a participant of the academic year 2018/2019, there were more opportunities for her to think and organize phrases with Portuguese expression logic when she was doing the activities on Weibo. The participants could also become more careful with the usage of Portuguese. For example, another participant, who also participated in the activities in the same academic year, said the interaction with Portuguese participants helped her realize that existed Chinese linguistic logic in her Portuguese expression. Nevertheless, a participant also mentioned in the interview that she started to pay more

Table 2. Words spelling situation

	First exercise			Second exercise		
	Overall	Participants	Others	Overall	Participants	Others
Second test in the academic year 18/19	1,53	0,82	1,79	1,28	0,31	1,63
First test in the academic year 19/20	1,75	2,40	1,48	1,99	4,79	1,76
Second test in the academic year 19/20	2,02	2,13	1,98	1,38	1,76	1,26

attention to the nominal agreement after producing some texts for the activities and this participant indeed demonstrated an evident improvement in such aspect during the activities. In addition, three of them felt at ease in writing Portuguese after participating in the activities and six participants affirmed that they have learned more vocabularies in the target language. And according to a participant, the vocabulary expansion was reflected in spending less time reading long Portuguese articles for example.

4 Limitations and Challenges in Practice

Nevertheless, although as a popular Chinese social network platform, Weibo was accepted by the ten participants without difficulty and, in the meantime, provided a seamless virtual environment for the Chinese participants to interact with native Portuguese speakers, when were asked their preference between the usage of Weibo and learning strategies they were used to, solely three of them preferred applying the microblogging platform in their PFL learning. Some of them could be more accustomed to passively receiving the information previously selected and uniformly taught due to the fixed pattern in their learning. In accordance with Jin and Cortazzi [8], considering its complex isolating language system, the production of Chinese language is a task that can merely be achieved by memorization. On the other hand, the assessment system based on written tests, which is deep-rooted in the Chinese education process, determined memorization as a fundamental part of students' study [8]. The didactic strategy and study habits based on this pattern impact unavoidably their PFL learning. Many students treat language learning as a process of memorizing vocabulary and grammatical rules and do not place a very high value on language usage in an authentic context. Therefore, they can be very familiar with theoretical knowledge but have difficulties in using language to communicate. For example, in the interview, one of the participants of the academic year 2019/2020 gave an unusual answer who wished to combine the two approaches. As for the daily study, she chose to use her own learning strategies developed during their high school; for instance, taking notes, reading textbooks, and memorizing repetitively the knowledge points. However, her choice for practicing Portuguese communication and writing skills was Weibo, where she acquired new vocabulary by using the target language and the participation of her peers also stimulated interest in making inputs. Many participants were also aware of the distinction between Portuguese training activities on Weibo; their study generally emphasizes the theoretical part while the use of Weibo boosts written production, use of vocabulary, and capacity of expression. As a participant well summarized, the difference lies in the input and output, since they rarely used in practice what they have learned in the classroom. In fact, without practically using the knowledge, the students can not actually verify if they truly acquire it, and even they memorized the vocabulary and grammatical rules, still may not know how to correctly express their thoughts in Portuguese.

Although Weibo provided a virtual Portuguese learning environment, the learning effect actually depended on the learners themselves, which is completely different from the traditional classroom where the knowledge is systematically presented in textbooks with uniform explanations or previously chosen and introduced by lectures. In this way, three participants claimed the learning on Weibo was not sufficiently systematic and the knowledge they learned was piecemeal. At the same time, two participants mentioned in the interview their needs to know the correctness of the expressions they made due to the lack of correction during the activities, however, there was no reasonable way to urge the Portuguese participants to provide constantly timely feedbacks, which could be considered as an inherent drawback for their PFL learning. Since they are accustomed to written tests, Chinese learners may purse the perfect accuracy of their expression in learning a foreign language, precisely as the answer of a participant of the academic year 2018/2019 when was asked her biggest difficulty in learning Portuguese – "be able to say a phrase without grammatical errors". But it is also necessary to stay aware of the basic function of language as a communication tool for the human being [15], thus the capacity of communication is somehow more important than memorizing and repeating the rules printed on the grammars.

Another disadvantage of applying Weibo in their PFL learning practice mentioned by the participants was the absence of "obligation". Some other information on the cell phone could be an influencing factor and directly affect their concentration, revealing by any means the passivity and poor self-control of some participants. As a matter of fact, any task carried out at the same time parallelly with learning activities can bring the same influence [16] and there is no inherent power in technologies themselves. The introduction of Weibo merely provided a virtual environment with possibilities to use what they have learned but depends on their own effort and autonomy after all. On the other hand, it could also stem from the difference between the usual didactic approach and learning strategies they were used to. According to their responses of the interview, the main approach for overwhelming majority of them (9 participants) was the material given by the teachers in the class. Seven participants affirmed they usually memorized vocabulary, articles, and knowledge after the class. Moreover, they also mentioned strategies such as taking or arranging notes (2 participants), accomplishing homework (2 participants) and exercises (2 participants) and reading grammars (3 participants), news (1 participant), or articles (1 participant) in Portuguese. As for oral comprehension, listening to the audios (2 participants), news (1 participant), podcasts (1 participant), and music (1 participant) were the methods they were used to applying. Nevertheless, although some of them talked about the interaction with their classmates to practice the target language, peer learning was not a strategy they took into account. Many of them even were not aware that peer learning could be an efficient way to their study. And in fact, all the strategies they applied in their PFL learning were based on a one-side input except doing homework and exercises which did not in fact revive the authentic usage of the authentic language. Therefore, subconsciously they might not associate the use of cell phones or Weibo with PFL learning since the activities were developed in a completely different way from their usual study habits. The participants could also feel that they did not meet their learning expectations by participating in the activities on Weibo even though their Portuguese language ability was indeed improved in accordance with the tests' results.

5 Final Considerations

By introducing Weibo in Chinese students' PLE learning, their command of inflection in Portuguese was enhanced, especially with regards to the verbal agreement which the traditional didactic approaches may not reach. The microblogging platform undoubtedly allowed an easy contact with the target language in occasions of daily use and built a seamless authentic linguistic environment, improving their acquaintance of Portuguese. And one of the practical results was the progress in word spelling as the tests revealed. Therefore, it can be said that Weibo can indeed bring some new possibilities for PLE learning as a brand-new approach for the learners. However, exactly due to its noticeable difference from their usual learning strategies, students can be not satisfied with the learning effects on Weibo, which does not simulate Portuguese written test exercises nor help their vocabulary memorization. However, it is also important to consider if such approach is truly beneficial for their learning which draws special emphasis on accumulating theoretical knowledge and ignores the creation of practical language communication skills. It is urgently necessary to reconsider and rectify their learning expectations since their purpose of learning Portuguese is not just to pass the exams anymore but enhance Portuguese abilities to be capable of using it in reality. Clearly expressing the thoughts with a correct target language logic is somehow more crucial than making a sentence without grammatical errors.

Also, as a social interaction platform itself, Weibo merely provides a virtual environment for the learners to use the target language and the results depend a lot on their learning autonomy and initiative. For the Chinese students who are used to a relatively passive learning mode, using such social media in PLE learning may be challenging and not be in line with their usual habits. Therefore, cultivating autonomous learning awareness is a decisive step towards the application of social media in PFL learning since the learning resources are not solely limited to the vocabulary list and grammar rules, particularly when the learners are exposed to a natural linguistic environment with the participation of native speakers. In the meanwhile, teachers should also pay particular attention to the part of organizing and designing learning activities to filter information and avoid the information overload and involvement of inappropriate information which requires quite an investment of time and energy.

In conclusion, although Weibo enables an innovative approach to PFL learning, its implementation in practice actually requires a basis of a correct awareness of a full-scale learning system. As a social platform, Weibo can revive the social character of language, whose learning effects depend on learners' active participation and their usage of the target language, exposing shortcomings in PFL learning and acquiring new authentic use of the target language. Thus, it is extremely important to define the teaching objectives and build up a global learning awareness prior to introduce social media in the language classroom.

References

1. Hwang, G., Fu, Q.: Trends in the research design and application of mobile language learning: a review of 2007–2016 publications in selected SSCI journals. Interact. Learn. Environ. **27**(4) (2019). https://doi.org/10.1080/10494820.2018.1486861
2. Wu, H., Wu, P.: Learners' perceptions on the use of blogs for EFL learning. US-China Educ. Rev. A **3**, 323–330 (2011)
3. Pimmer, C., Chipps, J., Brysiewicz, P., Walters, F., Linxen, S., Gröhbiel, U.: Facebook for supervision? Research education shaped by the structural properties of a social media space. Technol. Pedagogy Educ. **26**(5) (2017). https://doi.org/10.1080/1475939X.2016.1262788
4. Manca, S.: Snapping, pinning, liking or texting: investigating social media in higher education beyond Facebook. Internet High. Educ. **44** (2020). https://doi.org/10.1016/j.iheduc.2019.100707
5. Gonulal, T.: The use of Instagram as a mobile-assisted language learning tool. Contemp. Educ. Technol. **10**(3) (2019). https://doi.org/10.30935/cet.590108
6. Lantz-Andersson, A.: Language play in a second language: social media as contexts for emerging sociopragmatic competence. Educ. Inf. Technol. **23**(2), 705–724 (2017). https://doi.org/10.1007/s10639-017-9631-0
7. Information Technologies. https://doi.org/10.1007/s10639-017-9631-0 Jornal de Notícias. https://www.jn.pt/nacional/especial/xi-jinping-uma-amizade-que-transcende-o-tempo-e-o-espaco-uma-parceria-voltada-para-o-futuro-10268084.html. Accessed 19 Oct 2020
8. Água-Mel, C.: O ensino do Português em Macau: Por que razão aprender só a escrever não chega? In: Grosso, M.J., Godinho, A.P.C. (eds.) O Português na China. Lidel, Lisboa (2014)
9. Lomicka, L., Lord, G.: A tale of tweets: analyzing microblogging among language learners. System **40** (2012). https://doi.org/10.1016/j.system.2011.11.001
10. Cacchione, A.: Creative use of Twitter for dynamic assessment in language learning classroom at the university. Interact. Des. Architect. J. **24** (2015)
11. Pascoal, J.L., Oliveira, T.B.: Exames de Português CAPLE-UL. Lidel, Liboa (2013)
12. Godinho, A.P.: A aquisição da concordância de número e a sua relação com a aquisição da concordância de género: Um estudo realizado com aprendentes chineses de Português L2. In: Marçalo, M.J., Lima-Hernandes, M.C., Esteves, E., Fonseca, M.C., Gonçalves, O., Vilela, A.L., Silva, A.A. (eds.) Língua portuguesa: Ultrapassar fronteiras, juntar culturas. Universidade de Évora, Évora (2010)
13. Godinho, A.P.: Aquisição da concordância em género e número no contexto de ensino/aprendizagem de Português Língua Estrangeira em Macau. In: Grosso, M.J., Godinho, A.P.C. (eds.) O Português na China. Lidel, Lisboa (2014)
14. Ma, X.: Concordância verbal na língua portuguesa: Principais problemas para alunos chineses e portugueses. Master dissertation. University of Aveiro (2015)

15. Borau, K., Ullrich, C., Feng, J., Shen, R.: Microblogging for language learning: using Twitter to train communicative and cultural competence. In: Spaniol, M., Li, Q., Klamma, R., Lau, R.W.H. (eds.) ICWL 2009. LNCS, vol. 5686, pp. 78–87. Springer, Heidelberg (2009). https://doi.org/10.1007/978-3-642-03426-8_10
16. Kirschner, P.A., Karpinski, A.C.: Facebook and academic performance. Comput. Hum. Behav. **26** (2010). https://doi.org/10.1016/j.chb.2010.03.024

Creating Collaborative Research Opportunities at a Distance: From Porto to Cluj-Napoca

Carla Melo[1,2,3](✉), Sandra Vasconcelos[1,4,5], Dália Liberato[1,2], Cândida Silva[1,2], Paula Amaral[1], Adina Letiția Negrușa[6], Smaranda Adina Cosma[6], and Cristina Fleșeriu[6]

[1] School of Hospitality and Tourism, Polytechnic Institute of Porto, R. Dom Sancho I, 4480-876 Vila do Conde, Portugal
carlamelo@esht.ipp.pt

[2] CiTUR: Tourism, Innovation and Development Research Centre, Madeira, Portugal

[3] VALORIZA: Research Centre for the Enhancement of Endogenous Resources, Portalegre, Portugal

[4] CIDTFF - Research Centre On Didactics and Technology in the Education of Trainers, University of Aveiro, Aveiro, Portugal

[5] ESTGA – Águeda Superior School of Technology and Management, University of Aveiro, Aveiro, Portugal

[6] Department of Hospitality Services, Faculty of Business, Babeş-Bolyai University, Horea 7, 400174 Cluj-Napoca, Romania

Abstract. Focusing on an Interdisciplinary Project (IP) involving Higher Education Institutions from Portugal (School of Hospitality and Tourism – Polytechnic Institute of Porto) and Romania (Faculty of Business – Babeş-Bolyai University), this short paper describes a joint project developed by tourism students attending tourism courses at both institutions. This project, which concentrated on the cities of Porto (Portugal) and Cluj-Napoca (Romania), involved different courses and set out to identify motivations, attitudes and perceptions of generation Z tourists, by collaboratively designing, applying and analyzing a joint questionnaire for each destination.

Relying heavily on a technology-mediated, innovative approach that focuses on problem-solving, collaboration and communication skills, this paper draws on literature, field observation and informal feedback to give a general overview of the teaching and learning strategies used throughout the project and describe its implementation. Based on these premises, and taking into account the challenges currently being faced by HEI and the need to further enhance students' learning experience and promote an articulated development of skills that meet the needs of an increasingly digital workplace, this project provides a practical framework for other initiatives within this scope, thus making a viable and constructive contribution towards educational innovation, particularly in the field of tourism education.

Keywords: Collaboration · Cross-cultural communication · Interdisciplinary · Tourism education · Young tourists

A. Reis et al. (Eds.): TECH-EDU 2020, CCIS 1384, pp. 380–388, 2021.
https://doi.org/10.1007/978-3-030-73988-1_30

1 Introduction

In today's increasingly globalized and digitalized word, the tourism industry is faced with a wide range of new and complex challenges, including the persistent want of well-prepared, highly skilled professionals, who are able to keep up with the industry's demands. Much like in other areas, this pressing need has prompted stakeholders and Higher Education Institutions (HEI) to redefine their tourism and hospitality programs, gradually shifting from its once utilitarian, industry-driven nature, whose primary focus was to fill existing skill shortages [1, 2] towards a "science-based management model" [3]. Leveraged by innovative pedagogical approaches and technology, these changes are transforming the face of tourism education and paving the way for new trends and research within the scope, namely in what concerns active and experiential learning, online education, internationalization and cultural competencies [4].

Framed by these recent trends and aiming to further contribute towards the reflection surrounding tourism education in a digital age, this short paper sets out to describe a collaborative online international project that involved students and faculty from the Superior School of Hospitality in Tourism (ESHT – Portugal) and Faculty of Business FB – Romania). Resulting from an ERASMUS+ Teaching Mobility (2019) which involved researchers from both countries, the project originally aimed to design shared activities that would allow students to compare the cities of Porto and Cluj-Napoca in what concerns young tourists and their motivations, attitudes and perceptions. This initial premise was discussed and negotiated with the students and other faculty members, as to establish an interdisciplinary foundation for the project and its implementation, within a framework of skill articulation and project-based learning. In addition to focusing on management and marketing, the project involved ICT, intercultural behavior and English for Specific Purposes (ESP) courses, whose faculty actively contributed towards its outcomes, namely by helping students design, apply and analyze a questionnaire that was discussed and presented in different joint virtual sessions, all of which will be described in the following sections.

Hence, after establishing a theoretical rationale, based on the concepts of mobility, collaborative online international learning (COIL) and interdisciplinarity, the authors mostly focus on the pedagogical strategies used throughout the project. In addition to drawing a general outline, providing an insight on the project's different stages, materials, activities and outputs, they will also describe how these were put into effect, putting forward a reflection on their affordances and limitations. Given the particularly challenging period in which the project took place, namely the ongoing COVID19 pandemic and ensuing contingency plans that drove most HEI to seek out digital and online alternatives, special emphasis is also given to the collaborative platforms used by faculty and students.

Based on these premises, and taking into account the challenges currently being faced by HEI and the need to further enhance students' learning experience and promote an articulated development of skills that meet the needs of an increasingly digital workplace, this project provides a practical framework for other initiatives within this scope, thus making a viable and constructive contribution towards educational innovation, particularly in the field of tourism education.

2 Background

Regarded as interdisciplinary research areas by definition [5], as they entail the "creation or delivery of new knowledge that is not reducible to established disciplines due to profound integration of disciplinary concepts and/or methodology" [6], tourism and tourism research are still at an early stage of understanding the real potential of collaboration [5]. This "challenging endeavour" [6] ultimately translates in an "identifiable gap in inter-disciplinary collaboration" [5], one that can only be overcome through the use of context-driven, sustainable, interdisciplinary and participatory approaches, that take into account the diverse interests and requirements from different fields and stakeholders [7].

In addition to promoting interdisciplinarity, over the last decades, HEI have also been increasingly challenged to further internationalize their curricula. Considered to be crucial [8, 9], this internationalization includes not only student and faculty mobility, but also "institutional incorporation of global perspectives into undergraduate and graduate research and teaching at the home campus" [10], which has prompted institutions to look for alternative ways to foster academic collaboration in international settings, namely through the use of digital platforms. Also referred to as globally networked learning and cyber-pedagogy [10–12], these virtual exchanges rely on new pedagogical approaches and remote collaboration, paving the way for innovative experiences based on shared teaching and learning spaces.

Stemming from the concept of collaborative learning, a student-centered educational approach based on group projects and cooperation [13, 14], collaborative online international learning (COIL) is an augmented and enhanced instructional method that makes use of technology to connect classrooms and promote collaboration between students in geographically distant locations [11]. Traditionally associated with eLearning and massive open online courses (MOOCs) [12] the acronym has come to include activities such as "virtual exchange, virtual mobilities, globally networked learning, telecollaboration, and online intercultural exchange" [11], i.e., activities that engage "students in global learning, facilitates access to co-construction of discipline-specific knowledge, and encourages exposure to different worldviews by engaging in cross-cultural interactions" [15]. Hence, besides being perceived as cost effective and innovative [11], COIL projects promote collaboration and exchanges "between university-level teachers and students with geographically, culturally and linguistically distant peers" [15], thus supporting the articulated development of a wide range of skills.

Despite receiving limited attention, joint inter-institutional online collaboration is gradually emerging as a research trend, particularly after the ongoing health crisis limited traditional mobility programs and onsite collaboration, thus presenting itself as a relevant opportunity for innovation in the teaching-learning process [12, 16]. As a result, there is an increasing number of studies focusing on the topic, namely in tourism [9, 17, 18], all converging on the need to further explore the topic and ultimately support the enhancement and prevalence of curricula.

3 Interdisciplinary Project

3.1 Project Overview

In 2019, as part of an ERASMUS+ Teaching Mobility program, professors from the Faculty of Business (FB – Romania) had the opportunity to visit the Superior School of Hospitality and Tourism (ESHT – Vila do Conde, Portugal), where they were able to meet with faculty and students to discuss potential joint projects, namely within the scope of urban destinations and smart tourism. Having found common interests, namely in what concerns the characteristics of the regions in which both institutions are based, and the profile of students attending their tourism programs, this initial onsite discussion, was followed by several online meetings and networking sessions, that ultimately resulted in a joint project to be implemented in the summer semester (2020).

In order to define the scope, goals and outputs of the project, team members started out by defining a common theme, that would not only be topical and relevant, but could also easily fit in with their respective programs and syllabi. Having previously established what courses would be involved in the project, namely Destination Marketing, Customer Relationship Management, Intercultural Behavior and Lodging Operations (Romania) and Destination Management, English, and ICT II (Portugal), this theme should reflect the interdisciplinary nature of this collaboration and incorporate content and skills from the different disciplinary fields.

Based on these premises, partners agreed on tackling the topic of "motivations, attitudes and behavior of young tourists (Generation Z: 18 to 25 years) in urban destinations". This choice was supported by the fact that understanding and attracting young tourists is a challenge currently faced by the management of urban destinations in their efforts to increase attractiveness and competitiveness by creating a brand/image. Moreover, this particular segment relies heavily on the use of ICT and is particularly aware of environmentally related issues and sustainability, something that impacts the different stages of the tourist experience and the way tourists perceive different destinations. On the other hand, even though youth tourism is not a new phenomenon, research on the role it currently plays within the industry and how it converges with key concepts such as authenticity and identity, is still lacking, particularly within the scope of tourism education and training.

Following this decision, partners then designed a joint strategy that encompassed a series of tasks that were carefully thought out as to foster students critical thinking, collaboration and communication skills. In addition to the project's goals, these joint guidelines provided a detailed outline for the tasks to be carried out, as well as an implementation schedule, a template for the final report and common assessment criteria, which were then adapted to each course's and HEI's rules and specificities.

3.2 Implementation

Given the complexity of the theme, how it correlated with the different syllabi, and the decision of having international work groups with students from the two different HEI (i.e. the need for students to interact and write in English), the project was pitched to 3rd year Tourist Activities Management students (ESHT) and to students attending the

Bachelor degree in Business Administration in Hospitality Services (FB). In addition to these students, four students from the Master Program of International Business Administration in Tourism and Hospitality (FB), were also given the opportunity to take part in the project. Considering these students had already completed some of the project's module courses, they were distributed among the different groups. This was considered a more productive mix, as it was assumed they could assist their colleagues with the transfer of specific concepts, information and theoretical background, and finally, the complementarity of knowledge and perspectives needed to complete the project.

Taking into account these premises and the number of students taking part in the Project (77 students - 49 Portuguese and 28 Romanian), partners reviewed the project's timeline and general organizational aspects regarding the work groups, assessment and joint online sessions (see Table 1).

Table 1. Project timeline and operationalization plan

Schedule	Tasks
Week 1	Introductory session (onsite – national level): project presentation and work group formation
Week 2	Project launch (online – live joint session): organization of the international teams
Weeks 3 and 4	Task 1 – Project background/literature review (group work – autonomous)
Weeks 5, 6 and 7	Task 2 – Questionnaire design (group work – autonomous)
Week 8	Task 2 – Presentation, discussion and validation of the questionnaire (online – live joint session)
Weeks 9 and 10	Task 2 – Questionnaire application (group work – autonomous)
Week 11	Tasks 2 – Data analysis (group work – autonomous)
Week 12	Task 4 – Final report (conclusion)
Week 13	Task 5 – Final project presentation (online – live joint session)

This plan was adapted taking into account the HEI's specificities (e.g. the different calendars) and the events resulting from the unforeseen COVID-19 pandemic and ensuing school closure and transition to online learning. All these changes were discussed and agreed on by partners and negotiated with students.

To facilitate group formation and first contacts, partners used the collaborative platform Microsoft Teams to create a common area where students and facilitators could access the project's guidelines and other information, as well as interact and work together in different groups. This platform was chosen due to its practicality and accessibility, particularly for students attending ESHT, as it is included in students' office 365 suite and associated to their school accounts. However, even though this was the project's official platform, students were free to use other tools/channels to collaborate and communicate with each other, as they were expected to work autonomously and come up with solutions for the challenges at hand, with teachers acting as facilitators, overseeing rather than directing task completion. In addition to the different joint-sessions, in which they were expected to discuss their progress and results, students were required to hand in a final report (Task 4 –1 per group), that should incorporate the work carried out within the Tasks 1, 2 (see Table 1), as described below.

Task 1

Working in groups of 6 (in which 4 members were students from ESHT and 2 from FB, students were asked to provide background information regarding the theme, based on a previously provided list of references, which included papers, book chapters and reports. These references allowed students to contextualize the current challenges to tourism planning and development and help them identify the main dynamics of tourist destination marketing and management and urban tourism, as well as characterise the young tourism market segment, in particular, generation Z (18–25 years old), with regard to its preferences, motivations and travel/tourism behaviour. This preparatory work would help frame task 2: designing a questionnaire.

Task 2

This task involved designing a questionnaire to be applied to young tourists visiting the cities of Porto and Cluj-Napoca, in order to identify their motivations, attitudes and perceptions towards these cities. To carry out this task, each group was responsible for preparing a section of the questionnaire, covering the following dimensions: 1) sociodemographic profile; 2) characteristics of the trip; 3) use of technology (in general terms) - connectivity in tourism; 4) use of technology in the pre-travel phase; 5) use of technology - during the trip/stay; 6) motivations; 7) characteristics of the destination; 8) resources and attractions of the destination; 9) sustainability of the destination; 10) sustainable behavior of tourists; and 11) overall satisfaction and recommendation.

In class, students had the opportunity to analyse and discuss examples of questionnaires that had been validated and used by national and international organizations and enterprises. Following this analysis and ensuing discussion, each group was expected to collaborate and design a section of the questionnaire. The questions designed by the groups were then put forward in a joint online session and edited as to produce a complete questionnaire to be disseminated among young tourist both in Porto and Cluj-Napoca. Taking into account each destinations' specific characteristics, as well as their resources and attractions, two different versions were circulated. However, despite this customization (namely in Sects. 7 and 8), a common matrix was used as to ensure data validity and comparability. Due to the restraints resulting from COVID-19 pandemics, the questionnaire was circulated online, having garnered 171 valid responses, which were then quantitively analyzed by each group.

Tasks 4 and 5

Following data collection and analysis, students were asked to hand in a report in which they included the outcomes of Task 1 (Background) and 2 (Questionnaire Design and Application and Data Analysis), as well as a brief reflection on the results and how they could impact each destination regarding the theme of the project. This report was then presented and publicly discussed in a final online joint session, via teleconference.

Task 3

In addition to the tasks featured in Table 1, students attending the ICT II course (ESHT) also developed dissemination websites within the scope of the project. In addition to helping support the different activities, the websites (website development and multimedia production/edition are part of the course's syllabus) focused on the two cities central to the project: Porto and Cluj-Napoca, thus contributing to their promotion, namely among young tourists. Due to the specificity of the subject matter, this particular task was only carried out by the Portuguese students.

3.3 Interdisciplinarity in Context

Currently, there is a widespread recognition of the current need to think globally, both from an individual and a societal perspective, something that is particularly important in the case of young people who represent the future society. Thus, several studies have demonstrated the impact of educational programs on student learning outcomes, particularly in areas of intercultural awareness and understanding, something that is covered in the courses of Intercultural Behavior in the Hospitality Industry (FB) and English Applied to Tourism (ESHT). On the one hand, in terms of content, the project worked on the premise that the degree of importance of young tourists' motivations and needs would be influenced by national culture. As a result, their behavior was analyzed not only from a managerial and marketing perspectives (within the scope of the Destination Marketing, Customer Relationship Management and Destination Management courses) but also from a cross-cultural perspective. This approach created the ideal context for the students to recognize the impact of national culture on people's attitude towards travelling to the same destination, as well as their motivations and preferences, and the role played by travel information sources and ICT for tourism purposes.

On the other hand, their involvement in international teamwork and the use of digital platforms has helped students gain and develop global competences. Throughout this educational experience, students had the opportunity to experience deep cultural immersion, by being exposed to values and beliefs different from what they known, which made it possible to develop a set of critical skills.

4 Challenges and Constraints

Working in multidisciplinary, international teams, albeit rewarding, can be very challenging, particularly in a time of crisis. In this project, in addition to different time zones, schedules and calendars, faculty and students had to tackle the additional challenge of working remotely, not only when working with partners from other countries, but also at home. This added a new layer of complexity to the project, as collaboration between all group members was made more difficult and required a higher degree of adaptation and flexibility. Adding to these methodological and technological constraints (as all communication had to be digitally mediated), there was also a language barrier, as students had to communicate in a foreign language (English), despite the different levels of fluency within the groups. Moreover, cultural differences pertaining to way academic work and assessment are perceived in both HEI also led to some confusion, particularly at an early stage of the project.

However, though time consuming, all these mishaps were manageable and did not have a direct impact on the project's outcomes. The fact there were clear guidelines and templates was advantageous and undermined further misunderstandings, thus highlighting the importance of planning.

5 Final Considerations and Future Work

Having a deeply rooted affinity and interdependence with a wide range of sectors and industries, tourism is, by nature, an interdisciplinary field. However, despite this realization, in regards to tourism education there are often barriers to the development of interdisciplinary research and active collaborative projects involving different disciplines, particularly in what international collaboration is concerned.

Aiming to overcome these barriers, the project described in this paper harnessed the potential of COIL as a way of promoting innovative teaching and learning strategies and activities in multimodal international settings, giving students the opportunity to collaborate in practical, context-driven and market-oriented activities. Grounded on didactical principles, collaboration and technology, this approach made it possible to address key issues within the scope of destination management and marketing, and ultimately support the development of a comprehensive and diverse range of skills.

Based on a relevant and current theme and the completion of interconnecting progressive tasks, the project succeeded in raising the awareness of diverse cultural values, beliefs, norms and behaviour, and support the ability to communicate across cultural boundaries effectively and efficiently, namely in international settings.

Drawing from observational research and their hand-on experience and accounts, facilitators have agreed that this type of joint initiatives, though challenging, can support integrated learning, ultimately benefiting students, by providing them augmented work and learning experiences. At a time internationalization is often assigned and limited to international offices and individuals, this sort of initiative can, therefore, play a relevant role in enhancing participants' educational experiences.

References

1. Xiao, C., Qiu, H., Cheng, S.M.: Challenges and opportunities for effective assessments within a quality assurance framework for MOOCs. J. Hosp. Leis. Sport Tour. Educ. **24**, 1–16 (2019)
2. Edelheim, J.: How should tourism education values be transformed after 2020? Tour. Geogr., 1–8 (2020)
3. Catrett, J.B.: Hospitality education: a third paradigm. In: Oskam, J.A., Dekker, D.M., Wiegerink, K. (eds.) Innovation in Hospitality Education. ICPE, vol. 14, pp. 15–32. Springer, Cham (2018). https://doi.org/10.1007/978-3-319-61379-6_2
4. Kim, H.J., Jeong, M.: Research on hospitality and tourism education: now and future. Tour. Manag. Perspect. **25**, 119–122 (2018)
5. Oviedo-García, M.Á.: Tourism research quality: reviewing and assessing interdisciplinarity. Tour. Manag. **52**, 586–592 (2016)
6. Volgger, M., Pechlaner, H.: Interdisciplinarity, transdisciplinarity and postdisciplinarity in tourism and hospitality education. In: The Routledge Handbook of Tourism and Hospitality Education, pp. 117–134. Routledge (2014)
7. Jamal, T., Taillon, J., Dredge, D.: Sustainable tourism pedagogy and academic-community collaboration: a progressive service-learning approach. Tour. Hosp. Res. **11**, 133–147 (2011)
8. Leask, B., Bridge, C.: Comparing internationalisation of the curriculum in action across disciplines: theoretical and practical perspectives. Compare J. Comp. Int. Educ. **43**, 79–101 (2013)

9. Qiu, L., Qi, L.: E-learning assessment for tourism education LISREL assisted intercultural tourism perception and data integrated satisfaction perspectives. J. Comput. High. Educ. **32**(1), 89–108 (2019). https://doi.org/10.1007/s12528-019-09223-0
10. Duffy, L.N., Stone, G.A., Townsend, J., Cathey, J.: Rethinking curriculum internationalization: virtual exchange as a means to attaining global competencies, developing critical thinking, and experiencing transformative learning. SCHOLE J. Leis. Stud. Recreat. Educ., 1–15 (2020)
11. Esche, M.: Incorporating collaborative online international learning (COIL) into study abroad courses: a training design (2018)
12. de Wit, H.: Collaborative online international learning in higher education. Encycl. Int. High. Educ. Syst. Inst. 1–3 (2018)
13. Johnson, D.W., Johnson, R.T., Holubec, E.J.: Cooperation in the Classroom Revised. Interaction Book Co., Edina (1993)
14. Gunawardena, C.N., Layne, L.C., Frechette, C.: Designing wise communities that engage in creative problem solving: an analysis of an online design model. In: 62nd Annual Conference of the International Council of Education Media, pp. 369–379 (2012)
15. Vahed, A., Rodriguez, K.: Enriching students' engaged learning experiences through the collaborative online international learning project. Innov. Educ. Teach. Int. 1–10 (2020)
16. Swartz, S., Barbosa, B., Crawford, I., Luck, S.: Professional learning through collaborative online international learning (2020)
17. Goh, E., King, B.: Four decades (1980–2020) of hospitality and tourism higher education in Australia: developments and future prospects. J. Hosp. Tour. Educ. 1–7 (2019)
18. Munar, A.M., Bødker, M.: Information technologies and tourism: the critical turn in curriculum development. In: The Routledge Handbook of Tourism and Hospitality Education, pp. 105–117. Routledge (2014)

Technology-Supported Collaborative Learning in Language Teaching

Giedrė Valūnaitė-Oleškevičienė(✉), Liudmila Mockienė, and Viktorija Mažeikienė

Mykolas Romeris University, Ateities street 20, 08303 Vilnius, Lithuania
{gvalunaite,liudmila,vmazeikiene}@mruni.eu

Abstract. Teaching English at the university level often focuses on the professional areas, i.e. English for Specific Purposes (ESP). The focal point of ESP is the language that is specific to a particular domain and is full of context-bound lexical units used in the classroom environment to operate certain curricular concepts. Nevertheless, based on numerous evidence scholars have come to a conclusion that receptive skills (listening and reading) and productive skills (writing and speaking) are mastered unevenly in ESP courses. Occasionally students cannot be provided with enough opportunities to start a conversation in the classroom environment. Collaborative learning supported by technology may seem like a solution that improves communication and interaction among students. Classroom interaction has impact on the social, academic and cognitive development of students. Engagement in group activities allows students to practice content-specific language in a meaningful context. Through deliberations and discussions, students have the opportunity to express the key concepts in different words that they all understand thus making their study process easier. Learners also link the newly received linguistic knowledge with the knowledge they have already acquired. Group work that involves discussions improve cognitive processes through challenging and thought-provoking exchange of thoughts and ideas. Learners need to respond immediately, formulate their thoughts and ideas. Moreover, group discussions contribute to greater motivation due to similarity to real life situations in which opinions are formed and shared. In terms of group dynamics, learners concentrate on interaction with their peers, develop social skills (such as expressing opinions, active listening, encouraging, etc.) that also has positive effect on their interaction with the teacher. In summary, teachers can greatly enhance learners' competencies in the ESP classroom by applying Technology-Supported Collaborative Learning (TSCL).

Keywords: Languages for specific purposes (LSP) · Technology-supported collaborative learning (TSCL) · Social skills · Group dynamics · Language skills

1 Introduction

Numerous communities of language educators have focused recently on the technology-supported collaborative learning (TSCL) approach, which is believed to be particularly

A. Reis et al. (Eds.): TECH-EDU 2020, CCIS 1384, pp. 389–397, 2021.
https://doi.org/10.1007/978-3-030-73988-1_31

effective in learning a language for specific purposes (LSP). There is a growing area of research to support the view that TSCL develops not only receptive (listening and reading) and cognitive skills, but also communicative skills and the quality of interactions with other actors in the learning process. This approach enables students to better and more comprehensively understand the subject or area of study, learn to express their thoughts and opinions in a foreign language, develop effective and ethical argumentation skills and, most importantly, it promotes growth of a comprehensive personality. This article analyses the most prominent studies on the TSCL method, describes the research conducted by the authors of the article and the experience of teaching LSP via the TSCL method, and provides recommendations that may be useful in application of the TSCL method in teaching LSP. The object of this research is the interaction of TSCL and linguistic and social competences. The problem of the research lies in the question of how TSCL is connected to the development of linguistic and social competences, and the aim of the research is to disclose the connection and expression of TSCL and linguistic and social competences. The research methods of the current study are the analysis of scientific literature and interpretation of the research data.

2 Theoretical Background

While presenting the approach of TSCL it is necessary to look briefly into the development of the concept. In a broad sense, looking at the origins of the concept of collaborative learning (or cooperative learning) (CL) can be defined as an area that explores the efficiency of collaborative learning. A more specific and quite widespread definition is proposed by Kagan [15], who states that CL is a teaching method suitable for not numerous groups of learners with different abilities and needs, whose members work/study together to achieve one collective goal. Learners study in a group, and at the same time they clearly perceive their individual responsibility as a crucial contribution to the achieved group and individual results. Olsen and Kagan [21] observe that the CL method offers possibilities to organize group work in such a way that considerably improves learning outcomes and academic achievement. Consistently applied CL enhances students' sense of confidence, improves task comprehension and better understanding of each other. In addition, CL is especially effective in developing learner-friendly social interaction and group collaboration, as CL helps to quickly overcome the fear of speaking in front of an audience [12, 14]. In addition to theoretical research, many studies focus on the CL method and analyzed cases of its successful practice in foreign language teaching. Casal [3, 4] introduces an explicit description of the development of studies on the application of CL in language teaching. Other famous works include Bejarano [1], Coelho [7], High [10], Crandall [8], and McCafferty et al. [18]. A detailed comparative analysis of CL and other methods is presented by Johnson and Johnson [13].

Looking at the origins, the evolution of the CL methodology and method and its modern conception were influenced mainly by such theoretical approaches and research fields as theory of group dynamics, humanistic psychology, constructivism, and sociocultural theory by Vygotsky. At the heart of humanistic psychology is creation of the group climate that reduces anxiety and removes learner fears. In the CL environment, students first discuss the issues in groups, search for the appropriate answer together and only then talk to the entire group or the teacher, whereas less eloquent students usually have the possibility to make a contribution to the overall results of the group without immediate pressure or open demand to do so. Reduction in tension yields results such as respect for different opinions, tolerance for those who think differently. What is more, the role of learner autonomy, which is a very important concept in humanistic psychology, is also more salient. Autonomy strengthens the learner's understanding of responsibility for the learning outcomes. From the point of view of constructivism, CL-based teaching encourages students to find out unclear aspects, find the missing words and choose the necessary grammatical structures while learning a language, thus exploring the meanings and functions of language units, which helps them master linguistic subjects and become more fluent. The principles of constructivism are very closely connected to the theory of group dynamics which stresses student communication. While using a variety of CL techniques, students develop social skills (e.g., speaker sequence rules, active listening and etiquette, support, expression of opinion, and argumentation) that consequently relate to the ability to maintain attention and establish constructive relationships. Vygotsky's socio-cultural theory seems to summarize the theoretical foundations of CL, allowing us to state that the teaching/learning process should be viewed as a social process. This theory is apparent in the CL environment when students are given the opportunity to communicate in their own group and listen to other speakers in a foreign language; this reduces the teacher speaking time and focuses on content and fluency rather than correction of errors. The four approaches discussed above, although emerging at different times and based on different aspects, are indeed closely connected because, in general, all of these theoretical approaches stress the importance of learner personality growth as an outcome.

Another comprehensive and well-reasoned study by Casal [5] should be mentioned here. The study perfectly reveals and substantiates the connection between language learning and overall personality development. According to Casal [5], the CL methodology and its techniques in particular allow to achieve the desired results in language teaching. Casal [5] relies on the way to organize work, as proposed by Coelho [7], by presenting/allocating tasks in the classroom: (i) tasks that are performed by all members working with the same material and using the same information; (ii) tasks where each member receives different information on a topic common to the whole group, and (iii) tasks where each member works on a different topic in the classroom. In addition, Casal [5] draws on the popular and detailed structural methodology of Kagan [14] and classifies the methods of structural methodology as the so-called "task specialization methods". The most important question here is how particular tasks are structured (organized) according to these techniques and how information is allocated among the group members. Tasks/information can be divided into as many parts as there are members in the group. In addition, a particular task may focus on conducting the research and presenting the results obtained (e.g., in the form of a report to the audience). In this particular case, the task is organized into three components: research (analysis of the problem in certain aspects); interaction and communication of members in search for information (skills and various activities); and interpretation (presentation of the results to the entire class) [24]. To sum up the most important studies on CL, it can be concluded that CL is most often mentioned by researchers as a way to address the lack of time learners have to improve their language skills. Although the idea of group work is no longer new, CL is in any case useful by its emphasis on the aspects such as a favorable environment for communication and collaboration, personal responsibility and contribution, participation and involvement of all group members in the teaching/learning process, and continuous communication and interaction. The quality of interaction between students who work in a group gets better when they need to exchange/share the available information. The need for sharing encourages them to get involved in group activities, overcome feelings of restraint or discouragement, and take the opportunity to improve speaking skills. In addition, by engaging in immediate communication with their group members in the process of learning, students tend to use and begin to use the foreign language they are studying in a much more creative way than speaking in front of the entire class. CL and group work provide a supportive environment and facilitate combination of listening, reading, writing, and speaking through communication and interaction while working in the classroom and, most importantly, engagement of students in communication outside classroom [18]. Although structural methodology is one of the many methods which are great for teaching LSP, its techniques and methods are particularly advantageous in that they are based on structures that can be readily packed with content and are particularly effective when combining the content of a certain subject with teaching of a foreign language.

The rapid integration and spread of modern technologies, which have brought interactivity and virtuality into the educational world, have substantially changed knowledge acquisition modes but the essence of the process of collaboration in learning and the aims of collaborations has not changed. Technologies are seen as acting "in support" of collaborative learning by a number of researchers [9, 19, 22, 23]. Collaboration in technology-mediated classroom is a very complex process that has configured learning processes in all levels of education starting with elementary levels and ending with higher education [2, 6, 20, 25] and in all fields. As regards language learning, there is ample research focusing on the integration of technologies in collaborative language learning processes [2, 11, 17, 27] and research into how they contribute to development of different linguistic skills [16, 26].

3 Research Methodology

While teaching LSP, we have noticed that students' speaking skills are less well developed than reading and listening skills. Often, especially if an individual self-autonomous approach is used, then students do not have enough possibilities to initiate discussion during the session. We have also noticed that the TSCL method provides more opportunities for communication, discussion and expression of opinions which is observed by Kukulska and Viberg [17] stressing the "authentic communication and the integration of language skills" promoted by the technology-supported collaborative learning. In turn, Belda-Medina [2] also observed that communication during ESP classes promotes not only academic, but also cognitive and social development of students, thus students are able to learn from their peers. Participating in group discussions allows students to practice the language in a purposeful context. Discussions and negotiations provide an opportunity to paraphrase and interpret meaningful concepts, which helps to master the material. Group discussions encourage the cognitive process, generation of new ideas and exchange of views. Students need to react immediately, forming and expressing their thoughts during the process of cognition. In addition, group work increases motivation and creates real-life situations in which ideas are shared. Group dynamics provides for student communication and development of social skills (active listening, giving opinions, encouragement, etc.) and at the same time, this changes students' communication with the teacher. Communication with the teacher becomes direct and collegial, creating an atmosphere of mutual trust and cooperation.

Based on the theoretical assumptions discussed above and personal insight, the following research questions were formulated:

- How are language skills developed when learning via the TSCL method?
- How does TSCL promote social interaction?
- What new skills do students acquire through the TSCL method?

In order to find out the answers to the research questions, a questionnaire was developed, which included open-ended and closed-ended questions to collect qualitative and quantitative data. The participants of the study were Mykolas Romeris University second semester students. The questionnaire was provided to second semester students because they already had almost one year of experience of studying English for Specific Purposes at the university and the TSCL approach was applied in these groups. The questionnaire was submitted to 90 respondents and they were informed that it aimed to describe and generalize their authentic experiences in the language learning process and understand what they think about TSCL, as well as use their insights to improve the learning process in the future.

4 Research Results

According to the results of the student survey, as many as 100% of the research participants answered that TSCL and involvement in group discussions create preconditions for a favorable learning environment. According to one of the respondents: 'TSCL ensures a good atmosphere, you can learn from others', another comment: 'TSCL creates a favorable atmosphere for learning, because in a group you learn to collaborate with others, to work in a team' which relates to the insights provided by Belda-Medina [2].

Moreover, 95% of the respondents answered the question whether TSCL improves the relationship between group members and the relationship with the teacher in the affirmative way, stating in the comments that students interact more with each other and with the teacher, and only 5% thought that this is not always the case because sometimes disputes can arise, especially when opinions differ widely. Despite possible differences in opinions, 95% of the respondents said that TSCL and group work help learners to get to know and understand other people better. One of the comments stated that 'while working in a group in chat rooms, you do tasks with different people, try to communicate, listen, and understand others'.

Regarding the development of language skills through TSCL, 89% of the respondents indicated that they developed language skills more efficiently, 74% also mentioned listening skills and only 16% thought that they also developed reading skills, while only 11% mentioned writing skills (Table 1). Respondents also mentioned other communicative skills such as the ability to discuss, the ability to negotiate, and tolerance which relates to the observations by Kukulska and Viberg [17].

Table 1. Skills developed by TSCL

Skills developed	Respondents (percentage)
Listening	74%
Writing	11%
Reading	16%
Speaking	89%

For comparison, we asked a question about the skills that students develop when performing tasks individually. The majority, i.e. 79%, of the respondents indicated reading, 30% of the respondents mentioned listening, 23% of the respondents mentioned writing and only 13% mentioned speaking (Table 2). In addition, none of the respondents indicated any additional skills.

Table 2. Skills developed during individual work

Skills developed	Respondents (percentage)
Listening	30%
Writing	23%
Reading	74%
Speaking	13%

Comparison of the results of the responses to these two questions shows that TSCL significantly develops speaking skills, thus the TSCL and group work approach should be used more often. This means teachers should practice arranging student collaborative work in chat rooms.

Students were also asked about social skills that the developed through the TSCL approach. 100% of the respondents indicated that they learnt how to express their opinion. 89% of the respondents said they were able to agree or disagree with a colleague. 79% of the respondents indicated the ability to listen to a colleague, 25% of the respondents learnt how to praise and encourage, and 17% of the respondents indicated the ability to enter / intervene the discussion (Table 3).

Table 3. Social skills developed during TSCL tasks/ activities

Skills developed	Respondents (percentage)
The ability to express their opinion	100%
The ability to agree or disagree with a colleague	89%
The ability to intervene	17%
The ability to listen	79%
The ability to praise and encourage	25%

When asked what they like about the TSCL method, the respondents mentioned such factors as listening, communication, expressing personal opinions, new ideas expressed by the other students, help, and cognition of their peers as personalities.

When asked what disadvantages the TSCL method might have, the majority of the respondents, i.e. 94%, said that they liked learning in this way very much and only a few indicated that there could be disputes, interruptions and lack of attention. Finally, when asked what activities they would like during the seminars, the majority of the respondents, i.e. 89%, answered that they would like to learn in TSCL way.

To sum up the results of the survey, we can state that they demonstrate that the TSCL method significantly improves the development of speaking skills, as well as learners' social skills such as being able to convey one's opinion, agree or disagree with colleagues, intervene, listen, praise or encourage; it helps to create a learner-friendly atmosphere, improves interpersonal relationships in the group and is attractive to learners, as most respondents indicated that they would like to learn in a this way.

5 Conclusions

The analysis of the results of the survey reveals that the TSCL enabling students working in groups is excellent for the development of speaking skills and is very attractive to learners. Comparison of the indicators of individual work and the TSCL method as revealed by the results of the survey shows that the TSCL method is much better for developing speaking skills in learning LSP. In addition, the TSCL approach helps to create a learner-friendly atmosphere during seminars. It also helps to develop learners' social skills, such as active listening to a colleague, expressing one's opinion, encouraging or correcting a colleague. Such skills are very useful in learners' further professional activities, as learners learn language skills together with teamwork, participation in discussions and reasoning their opinions. Another positive outcome is that the TSCL approach helps to improve interpersonal relationships in the group as learners become familiar with each other better and acquire knowledge or learn from each other. Finally, for the future research it would be advantageous to research further how TSCL could apply in different contexts.

References

1. Bejarano, Y.: A cooperative small-group methodology in the language classroom. TESOL Q. **21**(3), 483–503 (1987)
2. Belda-Medina, J.: El Aprendizaje Del Inglés (L2) Mediante Herramientas Digitales (Tic) Por Estudiantes Mayores Desde Un Modelo Andragógico Y Heutagógico. Tonos Digital **38**, 1–24 (2020)
3. Casal, S.: Enseñanza del inglés. Aplicaciones del aprendizaje cooperativo. Abecedario, Badajoz (2005)
4. Casal, S.: Essential glossary for the teacher: cooperative learning. Greta J. **14**(1, 2), 80–84 (2006)
5. Casal, S.: Cooperative Learning in CLIL Contexts: Ways to improve Students' Competences in the foreign Language Classroom. Universidad Pablo de Olavide, Sevilla-Spain (2008)
6. Cerratto Pargman, T., Nouri, J., Milrad, M.: Taking an instrumental genesis lens: new insights into collaborative mobile learning. Br. J. Edu. Technol. **49**(2), 219–234 (2018)
7. Coelho, E.J.: Integrating language and content. In: Kessler, C. (ed.) Cooperative Language Learning. A Teacher's Resource Book. Prentice Hall, Englewood Cliffs (1992)
8. Crandall, J.: Cooperative language learning and affective factors. In: Arnold, J. (ed.) Affect in Language Learning. Cambridge University Press, Cambridge (1999)
9. Ferdig, R.E.: Assessing technologies for teaching and learning: understanding the importance of technological pedagogical content knowledge. Br. J. Edu. Technol. **37**(5), 749–760 (2006)
10. High, J.: Second Language Learning Through Cooperative Learning. Kagan Cooperative Learning, California (1993)
11. Hsieh, Y.C.: A case study of the dynamics of scaffolding among ESL learners and online resources in collaborative learning. Comput. Assist. Lang. Learn. **30**(1/2), 115–132 (2017)
12. Johnson, D.W., Maruyama, G., Johnson, R., Nelson, D., Skon, L.: Effects of cooperative and individualistic goal structures on achievement: a meta-analysis. Psychol. Bull. **89**(1), 47–62 (1981)
13. Johnson, D.W., Johnson, R.: Learning Together and Alone: Cooperative, Competitive, and Individualistic Learning, 5th edn. Allyn and Bacon, Boston (1999)
14. Kagan, S.: The structural approach to cooperative learning. Educ. Leardership **47**, 12–15 (1989)
15. Kagan, S., Kagan, M.: The structural approach: six keys to cooperative Learning. In: Sharan, S. (ed.) Handbook of Cooperative Learning Methods. Greenwood Press, Westport (1994)
16. Knight, J., Barbera, E., Appel, C.: Framework for learner agency in online spoken interaction tasks. ReCALL **29**(3), 276–293 (2017)
17. Kukulska, H.A., Viberg, O.: Mobile collaborative language learning: state of the art. Br. J. Edu. Technol. **49**(2), 207–218 (2018)
18. McCafferty, S.G., Jacobs, G.M., DaSilva Iddings, A.C.: Cooperative Learning and Second Language Teaching. Cambridge University Press, Cambridge (2006)
19. Naujokaitienė, J.: Informacinių komunikacinių technologijų naudojimas mokymesi bendradarbiaujant. Bendrojo ugdymo mokytojo perspektyva: Using information and communication technologies in collaborative learning. General education teachers' perspective: daktaro disertacija. Vytauto Didžiojo universitetas (2019)
20. O'Dowd, R.: Innovations and challenges in using online communication technologies in CLIL. Theory Pract. **57**(3), 232–240 (2018)
21. Olsen, R.E.W-B., Kagan, S.: About cooperative learning. In: Kessler, C. (ed.) Cooperative Language Learning. A Teacher's Resource Book. Prentice Hall, Englewood Cliffs (1992)
22. Pragnell, M.V., Roselli, T., Rossano, V.: Can a Hypermedia cooperative e-learning environment stimulate constructive collaboration? J. Educ. Technol. Soc. **9**(2), 119–132 (2006)

23. Resta, P., Laferrière, T.: Technology in support of collaborative learning. Educ. Psychol. Rev. **19**, 65–83 (2007)
24. Sharan, S. (ed.): Handbook of Cooperative Learning Methods. Greenwood Press, Westport (1994)
25. Sun, Z., Lin, C., Wu, M., Zhou, J., Luo, L.: A tale of two communication tools: discussion forum and mobile instant messaging apps in collaborative learning. Br. J. Edu. Technol. **49**(2), 248–261 (2018)
26. Wang, Y.-C.: Promoting collaborative writing through wikis: a new approach for advancing innovative and active learning in an ESP context. Comput. Assist. Lang. Learn. **28**(6), 499–512 (2015)
27. Yasushige, I., Smith, C., Masayuki M., Maher, K., Wada, N.: Flipped learning in a university EFL course: the merits of a collaborative learning approach. In: International Conference E-Society, pp. 35–42 (2015)

Digital Platforms in the Age of Mobility: A Contribution Towards Language Teaching and Learning

Ana Balula[1,2], Sandra Vasconcelos[1,2,3](✉), and António Moreira[2,4]

[1] ESTGA- University of Aveiro, R. Cmte. Pinho e Freitas 5, 3750-127 Águeda, Portugal
balula@ua.pt

[2] CIDTFF - Research Centre on Didactics and Technology in the Education of Trainers, University of Aveiro, Aveiro, Portugal
moreira@ua.pt

[3] School of Hospitality and Tourism, Polytechnic Institute of Porto, R. Dom Sancho I, 4480-876 Vila do Conde, Portugal
s.vasconcelos@esht.ipp.pt

[4] University of Aveiro, Campus Universitário de Santiago, 3810-193 Aveiro, Portugal

Abstract. As the continuous development of digital technologies continues to have a profound impact on educational contexts (including teacher education settings), it has become paramount to not only understand whether and how teacher education and training is keeping pace with the ubiquitous nature of digital technology, but also to contribute to the continuous development of competences and initiatives within this scope.

Focusing on language teaching and learning, this paper aims to support teachers and teacher educators working in technology-laden environments by putting together a broad ranging annotated list of digital platforms and tools that can be used to augment and support online activities and collaboration and promote articulated, technology-enhanced teaching and learning activities. Emphasizing the role played by Mobile Assisted Language Learning (MALL) and drawing from recent trends and an extensive review resulting from a collaboration that involved teacher educators, researchers and practitioners, these tools are described taking into account current approaches to language learning and assessment, as well as their perceived applicability, effectiveness and shortcomings. Highlighting the importance of collaboration, this work is effective in providing practical examples and best practices, whose potential can be harnessed and ultimately replicated by other practitioners and teachers in training, thus contributing the ongoing momentum of practice-driven innovation, that could ultimately inform language learning and teaching policies.

Keywords: MALL · Mobility · Language teaching and learning

1 Introduction

As evidenced by the development of several European guidelines, e.g. DigComp 2.1: The Digital Competence Framework for Citizens (DigComp), The Digital Competence

A. Reis et al. (Eds.): TECH-EDU 2020, CCIS 1384, pp. 398–407, 2021.
https://doi.org/10.1007/978-3-030-73988-1_32

Frameworks for Educators (DigCompEdu), and The European Framework for Digitally Competent Educational Organisations (DigCompOrg), as well as other studies and reports, e.g. The EDUCAUSE Horizon Reports, which aim to encourage the development of digital competences and document recent trends and emerging technologies, this subject has been greatly impacting educational contexts (including teacher education settings). This increased awareness from stakeholders and practitioners regarding the affordances and challenges of technology-enhanced teaching and learning, has resulted in a growing need for research that further complement these frameworks by providing practical examples and guidelines that support the implementation of digital initiatives in teaching and learning contexts.

When it comes to language learning, there are several works that focus on characterising technology-enhanced language learning, e.g. Ghanizadeh, Razavi and Jahedizadeh [1], Duman, Orhon and Gedik [2], Shadiev, Hwang and Huang [3], Shadiev and Yang [4]. In addition to research focusing on the use of mobile devices [5–9], most studies highlight the implications of using digital technology in language learning, specifically the fact it can promote learner engagement and improve "quality of input, making communication authentic, and providing timely and relevant feedback" [4]. In order to enhance it, and given the continuous evolution of the applications' functionalities, there seems to be a need to take a closer look into the uses of technology in earlier and present language learning practices to rethink and better foresee how to use them in the future.

In addition to these issues, learning analytics is also garnering more attention, as it is increasingly perceived as beneficial for language learning, namely as far as progress assessment and evaluation is concerned. Besides being used for purposes of retroaction on the part of teachers, course designers and the students themselves, analytics can also facilitate classroom management and routine tasks, as platforms will keep records of logs, completed assignments, automatic marks, archiving, as well as of all system interactions (what, when, with whom and how). As a result, analytics can potentially benefit all stakeholders involved in the teaching and learning process, from students and teachers to syllabus directors, heads of department/faculty, up to accrediting agencies appointed by the ministries in charge at a national level, going beyond the scope of administrative efficiency. In fact, analytics can improve student and teacher involvement and motivation, by providing a wealth of information that can be gathered from the data generated throughout a course [10, 11]. This information can actually be fed back to the students, either for their own self-perception of progress or to compare their outcomes with that of other peers, allowing them to learn from it, and ultimately help them improve their performance.

Based on all these premises, and resulting from a collaboration that involved teacher educators, researchers and practitioners, this paper outlines current approaches to language learning and assessment, putting together a list of digital tools that can be used to promote articulated, technology-enhanced teaching and learning activities. Focusing on mobile learning, the authors explore different possibilities within the scope of digital language learning, including evidencing and language learning analytics, as a way of fostering the concerted and synergetic development of skills, putting forward a final reflection that aims to inform and complement current language learning and teaching policies, thus contributing to their enhancement and topicality.

2 MALL and Technology Enhanced Language Learning

Perceived as an emergent and advantageous trend in education, the use of mobile devices, has been described as a "vital part of the entire learning experience" [12]. However, when considering teacher education scenarios and research, the use of mobile learning appears to be theoretically and conceptually fragile. In addition to different perceptions and use patterns of both teachers and learners, the urgency in adopting mobile technologies is not always accompanied by adequate, hands-on, training [13]; thus, due to "both the pressure to provide teachers with effective technology integration skills and the rapid growth of mobile technologies as learning devices, teacher education programs need to implement theoretically and pedagogically sound mobile learning initiatives" [13].

Having been converted into teaching and learning tools, mobile devices are having and increasingly relevant and widespread impact in different areas of knowledge, including language learning, which has ultimately resulted in the emergence of MALL (Mobile-Assisted Language Learning). In the context of language learning and teaching, MALL, also referred to as 'mobile technology-supported language learning' makes it possible for teaching and learning to take place in authentic, situated communication environments [9, 14, 15]. Globally, according to recent research, the integration of MALL with task-based and problem-solving approaches seems to favour communicative outputs, potentiating the combination of the learners' individual and collaborative language learning experiences. As Kukulska-Hulme and Viberg [14] point out, "the communicative approach is often applied along with game-based learning design to promote students' communication in the target language and to increase their motivation".

As to recent trends in the use of MALL, several authors [7, 9, 14, 15] stress its effectiveness in the development and integration of language skills, particularly speaking and writing, having established its potential in improving pronunciation, as well as vocabulary expansion and consolidation [9, 16]. Even though there are studies that target other skills, it seems that "more evidence is needed to further confirm its impacts on listening, reading, grammar, and integrated/whole language learning" [9]. On the other hand, MALL is also important for the development of plurilingual competences, intercultural awareness and communication skills, as it facilitates the fruitful and meaningful interaction between learners, teachers and contexts. MALL incorporates a myriad of possibilities, namely through the (co-)presence of manifold stimuli, such as multimodal sensory touch screens, digital simulations, and game elements, which paves the way for augmented experiences in which "enjoyment and fun" to go hand in hand with "collaborative mobile language learning" [13]. Therefore, it constitutes an effective means to promote teacher-facilitated learner agency and self-direction, which, in turn, can generate a loop dynamic by increasingly triggering motivation, thus augmenting teaching and learning experiences.

However, despite this mostly positive outlook on MALL and its pedagogical affordances, Kukulska-Hulme and Viberg [14] highlight the fact that, although "affective aspects include increases in motivation, engagement and enjoyment, mutual encouragement, reduction in nervousness and embarrassment (…) [, there are also] a few negative reports of risk of distraction, safety concerns, feelings of uncertainty and technical problems", which participants in the teaching and learning processes have to be aware of. As a result, while studies suggest that MALL will continue to evolve and have an important role within educational setting (with recent trends including virtual and augmented reality and wearable tech devices), educators must be able to quickly and critically assess its application and find ways of harnessing this potential, particularly for promoting student engagement and meaningful learning experiences. Considering the increasingly wide suite of tools and platforms available today, this collective effort will imply a deeper understanding of current approaches to language learning and assessment, as well as of the many possibilities opened up by digital language learning.

3 Methodology

In what concerns the methodology used, this study is of exploratory nature aiming at providing an overview over the digital platforms and tools that can be used to augment and support online language learning and teaching activities, in particular in the scope of MALL. Therefore, and drawing from recent trends on language teaching and learning, the option was to produce an annotated list of the digital platforms and tools focussing on practical examples and best practices, also highlighting e-assessment possibilities, thus contributing for the ongoing momentum of practice-driven innovation, which practitioners and teachers in training are urged to embrace.

4 Approaches to Language Learning/Assessment

Since assessment strongly impacts the way learners develop their learning, there are clear advantages in having a paradigm shift – from 'assessing learning' (i.e. testing) to 'assessing as learning', which refers to the full embedment of assessment in the learning process. In other words, assessment merges into learning activities, thus reflecting the learning processes and products. Chapelle and Voss [17] also underline that the "assessment of learners' language ability is an important part of language education, which has been affected by computer technology at least as significantly as language learning has". In this scenario, the use of digital technology may be seen as a means to add different layers to educational processes and may also open up opportunities to the design of innovative learning/assessment solutions. On the other hand, technology has also facilitated "fine-grained data collection and analysis" [18], which can be particularly useful increasingly mediatized and multimodal learning environments. As assessment and feedback have become even more challenging [18, 19], the use of learning analytics made available by the platforms used for teaching and learning gives educators information that can help optimize and continuously improve these experiences.

When it comes to the learning/assessment process, one of the most widely used type of digital tools are Electronic Classroom Response Systems (CRSs), which enable teachers to launch questions and to provide student feedback (as well as automatic grading). Their popularity is grounded in the possibility to launch questions and gather student answers in real-time. Even though these platforms somehow differ in terms of functionalities, most include game-based features, which may enhance student engagement through BYOD teaching and learning initiatives. Some examples are: Kahoot! (https://kahoot.it/v2/), Quizizz (https://quizizz.com/), PollEverywhere (https://www.polleverywhere.com/), Socrative (https://www.socrative.com/), Top Hat (https://tophat.com/).

The use of digital technology can also be an important asset to promote critical thinking and creativity. In this respect, there are two recurrent teaching and learning approaches in the literature, namely: digital storytelling (e.g. Mohamed and Lamia [20]; Ahmad and Yamat [21]) and game-based approaches (e.g. Sriharee [22]). Regarding digital storytelling, it is used not only to develop listening but also writing, reading and speaking skills. In fact, it is a learning approach that often relies on reading and writing in a first stage; nevertheless, through the use of digital tools it tends to evolve to dynamic, collaborative presentations, bringing stories to life. Several tools can assist in the creation of a digital support for storytelling, for example to create interactive timelines for the stories, with multi-format information (https://www.timetoast.com/), to create digital comics (https://www.pixton.com/), to develop multi-format stories collaboratively (https://www.utellstory.com/).

From the teachers' perspective, other tools can also be found on the web, namely: sutori (https://www.sutori.com), "a highly versatile web tool to create interactive timelines to share content and stories"[1], with the added value of including assessment tools and room for comments, etc., and an extra bonus: embedded learning analytics.

Not less frequently, game-based approaches are also used for boosting the learners' engagement and motivation. In fact. Several studies point out that learning effectiveness increases with the use of game-based learning strategies [23, 24]. In this context, it poses as a relevant means for real-life-like communication [14], since they seem to potentiate more vivid learning processes by crosscutting in-class and out of the class settings and interlocutors, as well as complying with the learners' pace in terms of time and space [14, 16].

Authors as Hwang et al. [25], Calvo-Ferrer [26], as well as Chen, Liu and Huang [27], have found evidence that game-based language learning allows for the development of most language skills, particularly in the scope of vocabulary, pronunciation, listening and speaking skills. As games take part of the daily routine of young adults, they pose as an important means to develop learning, as they can more easily attract learners' attention, as well as promote greater involvement and collaboration within learning.

Finally, as to participants, several authors consider that there are advantages in diversifying interaction dynamics in the learning process. Thus, in terms of assessment elements, these contributions (from different agents in various moments) should be balanced, resorting, for instance, to self-assessment, peer-assessment, etc. In this case, assessment rubrics may be included as important tools to manage the participation of different agents, which can be co-constructed by the teacher and the learners, thus holding them not only accountable for their learning outcomes, but also self-aware of their stance in the learning process towards the "negotiated" outcomes. Ghaffar, Khairallah and Salloum [28] define assessment rubrics as (qualitative or quantitative) rating scales, in which the criteria and the different levels of the quality of work can be outlined. There are many user-friendly possibilities to create this type of assessment tool, such as those listed by the Canadian Lakehead University Teaching commons (see https://teachingcommons.lakeheadu.ca/creating-rubrics-online-resources).

In the section below, some examples are presented to illustrate activities and digital tools that can be articulated in learning for the development of various language skills;

[1] See https://www.sutori.com/story/what-is-sutori--BxqPMmCCiF65i3TaSRVPsTHr.

nevertheless, other can suit identical purposes. The examples given should be seen as a starting point for an in-depth reflection on how language education can be transformed by integrating learning/assessment activities to fully meet ambitious pedagogical goals in innovative ways.

4.1 Digital Language Learning: Exploring Possibilities

As aforementioned, the richness of the teaching/learning/assessment processes lies on the articulation of several activities that serve different learning purposes. Furthermore, given that teachers and learners have their individual profiles, it is not possible to rely on "one size fits all" solutions; consequently, this section further complements the approaches and tools described above, putting forward a set of different activities and technological tools that can be equated by teachers in the design of their own personal teaching/learning strategies, according to the defined educational goals.

Starting with warm-up activities, several online resources can be used, not only to elicit vocabulary, but also to introduce the topic more visually and using, for instance, oral prompts, stemming from vocabulary already being worked upon, specific grammatical structures, as well as speaking and listening skills. As far as images are concerned, teachers can use Google Images (especially those labelled for reuse in terms of copyright); besides, there are also other possible sources to search for, such as freeware images and pictures, e.g. Unsplash – https://unsplash.com/, Flickr – https://www.flickr.com/photos/eltpics/ or Pixabay – https://pixabay.com/. Alternatively, or in combination, quotes (by topic or by author) can also be found on webpages such as BrainyQuote – https://www.brainyquote.com/ or Cool Funny Quotes – https://www.coolfunnyquotes.com/.

Warm-up activities can be articulated with a flipped classroom strategy, for instance, in which you ask the learners to do something beforehand (as a pre-activity, at home), e.g. to identify relevant vocabulary. For this purpose, we can use ESL Video (https://www.eslvideo.com/), in which you can create different classes and use pre-established activities, or Film English (https://film-english.com/) to follow the proposed video-based lesson plans. Another interesting tool that works with video is LyricsTraining (https://lyricstraining.com/), which allows teachers to upload short Youtube videos (music, trailers, TV shows, etc.) and use them to design gap-filling listening exercises (mimicking a Karaoke style). In addition, teachers can also promote other skills by asking learners to interact with several dictionaries, glossaries, thesauruses, which can be text-based and multilingual (e.g. DeepL – https://www.deepl.com/translator) or even multi-format (e.g. Visual dictionary online – https://www.visualdictionaryonline.com/).

Regarding speaking skills, as an alternative to the more traditional description of real pictures, teachers can also create/explore infographics, using, for instance, Infographics – https://infogram.com/, easel.y – https://www.easel.ly/, or Piktochart – https://piktochart.com/). These are particularly useful for fact finding/ checking, process description, true or false questions, etc. and can not only be used for stand-alone spoken presentations, but also be combined with a follow-up activity focussed on the development of writing skills. Another tool for creating multi-format visual aids for spoken presentations (as well as learning materials, e.g. virtual tours with interactive 360° images and videos) is thinglink (https://www.thinglink.com/), especially useful for students to verbalise (describe) what they see and feel – factual and emotional components of language production.

When it comes to reading skills, there are two main approaches that can be followed – on the one hand, gist reading, skimming and scanning, and, on the other, in-depth reading. The former usually targets vocabulary enrichment and understanding of the main topics. To develop this skill, learners can use CuePrompter (https://cueprompter.com/), which offers a teleprompter service, with adjustable speed and forward, stop and reverse scrolling functionalities. This tool can be used for individual and group challenges based on timing and accuracy of the selected pieces of information, or used to create gap-filling exercises that learners are asked to complete afterwards, using, for instance, l.georges (https://l.georges.online.fr/tools/cloze.html), which allows for focussing on specific language elements (i.e. prepositions, quantifiers, linking words, etc.). For in-depth reading, it may be interesting to use other tools, such as scribble (https://www.scrible.com/), which is used to manage, comment on and share annotated documents on the web.

As to the development of writing skills, online collaborative real-time writing and editing has been used for a long time, especially to develop webpages (e.g. WordPress – https://wordpress.com/ and eLink – https://elink.io/), wikis and blogs (e.g. Wikipage creator – https://wikipagecreator.net/, Plexie – https://plexie.com/), or simply to develop texts collaboratively (e.g. Dropbox Paper – https://www.dropbox.com/paper and GoogleDocs – https://www.google.com/docs/about/). Besides, there are also several tools that can be used for more vivid, communicative purposes, i.e. to practice dialogues in writing, using scenes and plots to create short films (e.g. Dfilm – https://dfilm.com/build).

As to short video production, Shadiev and Yang [4:5] underline that this type of activity cultivates "students' multiliteracies to different degrees and expand[s] their comprehension of the interplay between different symbolic resource modes of meaning construction". This opportunity can add extra layers to more traditional role-play activities, since it offers the possibility of bringing authenticity through context and fosters the development of the learners' creativity and collaboration skills. For this purpose, learners can simply use their smartphones or, alternatively, videoconferencing tools (e.g. Skype – https://www.skype.com/, Zoom – https://zoom.us/, WebEx – https://www.webex.com/), Teams – https://teams.microsoft.com/ and/or other specialised tools to edit their videos (e.g. Vimeo – https://vimeo.com/, OpenShot – https://www.openshot.org/, Blender – https://www.blender.org/).

5 Conclusion

Research on language teaching and learning acknowledge the potential of technology within this scope and the benefits of learners' and teachers' digitally mediated interaction in educational settings, being them face-to-face, online or a mix of both. When addressing the issue of the usage of digital tools in language learning processes, assessment for online learning, which includes feedback and learning analytics, MALL is often perceived as an effective approach, in particular because it allows for teaching and learning to take place in real communication contexts.

Even though some of the approaches to mobile learning sometimes appear to be theoretically and conceptually fragile, particularly when it comes in teacher education, research, MALL integration with task-based and problem-solving approaches seems to open more room for communicative output, potentiating the combination of the learners' individual and collaborative language learning experiences. Nevertheless, its affordances in other areas of foreign language learning, it seems that we are far from having strong evidence of MALL's impact on several language skills, although recent tendencies in the use of MALL stress its effectiveness for their development and integration, a common paradox in research.

As to digital language learning, some examples were presented to illustrate activities and digital tools that can be articulated in learning for the development of various language skills and other that can suit identical purposes. In the literature, we found several studies that focus on characterising technology-enhanced language learning, and most highlight the use of digital technology as a promoter of learner engagement and language acquisition. Assessment rubrics were found to be important tools to manage the participation of different agents, which can be co-constructed by teachers and learners. From the teachers' perspective, several useful tools can be found on the web for language learning (individual and group challenges, gap-filling exercises, in-depth reading, etc.), which can pose as means to develop assessment/learning activities. In fact, the web is a haven of tools, suggestions and information that can be used, adapted, replicated, in all sorts of formats and licence types, for manifold needs of both teachers and students: from warm-up to consolidation activities, it is all available to those who have the will.

When complemented by learning analytics, these activities can have a positive impact, both in terms of efficiency and of student and teacher involvement and motivation. This, in turn, generates information that can be fed back to the students, improving their performance. Routinized work can be removed from the teachers' functional descriptions, allowing them precious time to other tasks. Learning Analytics is therefore a promising field of research, language teaching, progress assessment and evaluation, feedback, and course design and repurpose, predicting learner performance and allowing informed decision to be taken, benefitting all involved. As put forth in this text, the importance of learning analytics offerings is paramount for understanding particular aspects of language being that influence/are influenced by learning or teaching style/materials. This surely would be an aspect that could inform language learning and teaching policies, as well as future research.

References

1. Ghanizadeh, A., Razavi, A., Jahedizadeh, S.: Technology-enhanced language learning (TELL): a review of resources and upshots. Int. Lett. Chem. Phys. Astron. **54**, 73 (2015)
2. Duman, G., Orhon, G., Gedik, N.: Research trends in mobile assisted language learning from 2000 to 2012. ReCALL J. EUROCALL **27**, 197 (2015)
3. Shadiev, R., Hwang, W.-Y., Huang, Y.-M.: Review of research on mobile language learning in authentic environments. Comput. Assist. Lang. Learn. **30**, 284–303 (2017)
4. Shadiev, R., Yang, M.: Review of studies on technology-enhanced language learning and teaching. Sustainability **12**, 524 (2020)
5. Godwin-Jones, R.: Emerging technologies mobile apps for language learning. Lang. Learn. Technol. **15**, 2–11 (2011)
6. Kukulska-Hulme, A.: Will mobile learning change language learning? ReCALL **21**, 157–165 (2009)

7. Kukulska-Hulme, A., Lee, H., Norris, L.: Mobile learning revolution: implications for language pedagogy (Chap. 15). In: Handbook of Technology and Second Language Teaching and Learning, p. 217 (2017)
8. Vasconcelos, S.V., Balula, A.: Socrative: using mobile devices to promote language learning. In: Empowering Learners with Mobile Open-Access Learning Initiatives, p. 242 (2017)
9. Hwang, G.-J., Fu, Q.-K.: Trends in the research design and application of mobile language learning: a review of 2007–2016 publications in selected SSCI journals. Interact. Learn. Environ. **27**, 567–581 (2019)
10. Reinders, H.: Learning analytics for language learning and teaching. JALT CALL J. **14**, 77–86 (2018)
11. Reinders, H.: Backchannelling in the language classroom: improving student attention and retention with feedback technologies. J. Lang. Learn. Teach. **4**, 84–91 (2014)
12. Alexander, B. et al.: EDUCAUSE Horizon Report: 2019 Higher Education Edition. EDUCAUSE (2019)
13. Baran, E.: A review of research on mobile learning in teacher education. J. Educ. Technol. Soc. **17**, 17–32 (2014)
14. Kukulska-Hulme, A., Viberg, O.: Mobile collaborative language learning: state of the art. Br. J. Educ. Technol. **49**, 207–218 (2018)
15. Viberg, O., Grönlund, Å.: Mobile assisted language learning: a literature review. In: 11th World Conference on Mobile and Contextual Learning, pp. 1–8 (2012)
16. Tu, Y.-F., Hwang, G.-J.: Trends and research issues of mobile learning studies in hospitality, leisure, sport and tourism education: a review of academic publications from 2002 to 2017. Interact. Learn. Environ. 1–19 (2018)
17. Chapelle, C.A., Voss, E.: 20 years of technology and language assessment in language learning & technology. Lang. Learn. Technol. **20**, 116–128 (2016)
18. Blikstein, P.: Multimodal learning analytics. In: Proceedings of the Third International Conference on Learning Analytics and Knowledge, pp. 102–106 (2013)
19. Maseleno, A., et al.: Demystifying learning analytics in personalised learning. Int. J. Eng. Technol. **7**, 1124–1129 (2018)
20. Mohamed, H., Lamia, M.: Efficacy of the flipped classroom to teach the digital storytelling process. In: Developing Technology Mediation in Learning Environments, pp. 57–77. IGI Global (2020)
21. Ahmad, W.I.W., Yamat, H.: Students' perception on learning English language through conventional and digital storytelling. Int. J. Acad. Res. Bus. Soc. Sci. **10**, 484–504 (2020)
22. Sriharee, G.: the design patterns for language learning and the assessment on game-based learning. Int. J. Inf. Educ. Technol. **10**, 95–103 (2020)
23. Sandberg, J., Maris, M., Hoogendoorn, P.: The added value of a gaming context and intelligent adaptation for a mobile learning application for vocabulary learning. Comput. Educ. **76**, 119–130 (2014)
24. Usai, F., O'Neil, K.G.R., Newman, A.J.: Design and empirical validation of effectiveness of LANGA, an online game-based platform for second language learning. IEEE Trans. Learn. Technol. **11**, 107–114 (2017)
25. Hwang, W.-Y., Shih, T.K., Ma, Z.-H., Shadiev, R., Chen, S.-Y.: Evaluating listening and speaking skills in a mobile game-based learning environment with situational contexts. Comput. Assist. Lang. Learn. **29**, 639–657 (2016)
26. Calvo-Ferrer, J.R.: Educational games as stand-alone learning tools and their motivational effect on L 2 vocabulary acquisition and perceived learning gains. Br. J. Educ. Technol. **48**, 264–278 (2017)

27. Yen, L., Chen, C.-M., Huang, H.-B.: Effects of mobile game-based English vocabulary learning APP on learners' perceptions and learning performance: a case study of Taiwanese EFL learners. In: International Conference on e-Learning, p. 255 (2016)
28. Ghaffar, M.A., Khairallah, M., Salloum, S.: Co-constructed rubrics and assessment for learning: the impact on middle school students' attitudes and writing skills. Assess. Writ. **45**, 100468 (2020)

The Effect of Agency on Cognitive Load in Dyads Learning Physics with a Serious Computer Game

Julien Mercier(✉), Ariane Paradis, Ivan Luciano Avaca, and Kathleen Whissell-Turner

NeuroLab, University of Quebec in Montreal, 1205, rue Saint-Denis, Montréal H2X3R9, Canada
mercier.julien@uqam.ca

Abstract. This paper articulates an innovative systems dynamics model of learning based on a predictive cognitive architecture by interrelating six modules: knowledge, affect, cognition, performance, external agents, and context. To test aspects of this model, this paper focuses on cognitive load theory predicting that a manipulation of the learning task can affect at least one of the three types of load (intrinsic, germane and extraneous). More precisely, agency is hypothesized to affect either the intrinsic or extraneous load. Therefore, the goal of this paper is to explore the effect of agency on cognitive load. Thirty-six dyads (1 player and 1 watcher) played a serious game for learning physics for 120 min while dual-EEG was recorded for all participants. Results of time series analysis show that agency (being a player or a watcher) as no effect on the overall cognitive load when the comparison is made either by group (all players versus all watchers), or within a single dyad. Moreover, nor did agency affect instantaneous cognitive load for a vast majority of dyads. Indeed, only four dyads exhibited one or two significant cross-correlations. However, those exceptional cases cannot be generalized. Finer-grained analyses are proposed in the discussion to better explore the role of agency on cognitive load in further research.

Keywords: Educational neuroscience · Cognitive load · Agency

1 Introduction

The transdisciplinary field called online measures of learning has been attracting a lot of attention and gaining momentum in recent years. However, the biggest challenge facing this field at the moment is to establish analytic procedures oriented on firm theoretical grounds from a variety of domains in cognitive science. These domains include psychology, neuroscience, and educational psychology, which explain learning at various levels of analysis. Moreover, the focus on temporally fine-grained observations has been found in our previous work to be largely intractable by conventional statistics aimed at comparing group means for two reasons: individual variability when averaging over too lengthy episodes and the difficulty of generalizing results in different contexts. Systems dynamics models may help to overcome these shortcomings by shedding light

A. Reis et al. (Eds.): TECH-EDU 2020, CCIS 1384, pp. 408–420, 2021.
https://doi.org/10.1007/978-3-030-73988-1_33

on causality in the form of positive and negative feedback attributable to variations of the variables in the model. To the best of our knowledge of the learning sciences, this paper presents the first complex systems model of human learning bridging behavioral and psychophysiological data across time scales. This model is too ambitious to be tested as a whole at the present time, especially since each of the variables included require in-depth definitions and operationalizations. Thus, the model is presented next as a whole to understand how specific issues regarding cognitive load can be studied as a specific case within the model as presented in this paper.

Developed by Jay Forrester in the 1950s, a systems dynamics model contains stocks, flows and rates which must be conceptualized and eventually parametrized empirically (Forrester 1971). The specification of the variables involved is based on extent theory. The empirical test of a systems dynamics model is achieved through a range of approaches, including time-series analysis.

For the sake of clarity, the presentation of the model is structured according to (Kortelainen et al. 2008).

2 Theoretical Framework

2.1 Background and Structure of the Systems Dynamics Models

Conceptual Background. The systems dynamics model hinges on an integrative framework and cognitive architecture for learning in order to set important high-level a priori constraints in the model: The framework has to be amenable to computational modeling, biologically plausible and applicable to multi-individual joint functioning. The framework constrains the constructs included in the SDM and points to how the main components of a SDM (stocks, flows and rates) apply to human learning.

In cognitive science, the brain is pervasively viewed as an engine of probabilistic prediction (Lupyan and Clark 2015). Clark's prediction-action framework (2013a) is biologically plausible and applicable to individual functioning as well as multi-individual joint functioning. It is based on the mechanism of predictive processing: mental representations—from the perceptual to the cognitive—reflect an interplay between downward-flowing predictions and upward-flowing sensory signals. This series of hierarchical layers constitutes an organized system in which a given layer predicts the activity at the level immediately below. As a consequence, this system produces representations at multiple levels of abstraction, and those representations incorporate any knowledge that reduces prediction error. The higher-level (more abstract) representations are stored in memory to enable better predictions in the future. "Prediction-driven learning, when implemented using hierarchical (hence multi-level) machinery automatically uncovers structure at multiple scales of space and time" (Clark 2018, p. 522). Conversely, data from various levels in the hierarchy can also lead in principle to explanations of learning at various time scales.

At the inter-individual level, (Sun 2018) illustrated the value of computational modeling in understanding social-cognitive issues by examining both individual and social processes and their interaction. Computational modeling is a suitable basis to elaborate and test detailed theories that go beyond verbal–conceptual theories. He insisted especially on using computational social simulation with realistic cognitive models in conjunction with cognitive architectures. At the individual level, cognitive architectures specify, often in considerable computational detail, the mechanisms and processes underlying cognition (Sun 2018). Although computational modeling is often applied to a particular level at a time (e.g., the social, the cognitive-psychological, etc.), this is not an intrinsic limitation. Cross-level and multilevel analysis and modeling could be enlightening, and even essential (Sun 2018).

Assumptions in the Model. Based on what humans do in leaning settings, the model assumes that chance has a role in correctly performing a learning task, through trial and error. Any moment in doing a learning task has an impact on something within the learner. The model assumes the cumulative nature of learning and emphasizes the time scale related to specific levels in the hierarchy: lower levels changing more rapidly than higher levels and readiness to learn based on the quantity of change needed at underlying levels.

Desiderata in the Model. There is a gap between the previous integrative framework and the need to specify variables in the SDM which could represent the main ingredients of learning. Despite obvious limitations, the choice was made to operationalize constructs from, or pertinent to, educational research compatible with the integrative framework and analyze them using the most conventional data analyses instead of applying machine-learning techniques on raw data. This way, the explanatory power and potential for applications of the model in educational settings can be secured more easily by the possibility to link hypotheses and results with extent theory. Thus, the modeling of agency in cooperative learning has to include affective and cognitive aspects, since they are of prime importance for learning (Immordino-Yang 2011; Patten 2011). Affect and cognition are also intertwined in prediction-action processes. Affect can even subsume cognition in certain circumstances (Patten 2011).

Structure of the Model. Figure 1 is an illustrative representation of a systems dynamics model of learning. The different modules in the model are based on educational literature from the perspective of cognitive science. The modules are driven by the prediction-action architecture. Six modules are included: knowledge, affect, cognition, performance, external agents, and context. The modules are intended to be generic, applicable to any learning context. External agents can be optional, depending on the learning context.

The variables specified within a module are those that are sufficiently operationalized in extent research to be obtained in current experiments focusing on online, fine-grained measures, which are necessary conditions so that they can be translated in a SDM in terms of stocks, flows and rates. The model is centered around action, in the sense of decision-making and motor actions (Kotseruba and Tsotsos 2020). As such, modules are specified to deploy a prediction-action framework. They are also in line with prevalent biologically and psychologically plausible architectures (LEABRA and CLARION respectively). They delineate complementary bodies of research that jointly describe the necessary ingredients for learning.

In the systems dynamics model of learning, each of the six modules contains various variables. The role of the *knowledge module* is to store knowledge, in the form of

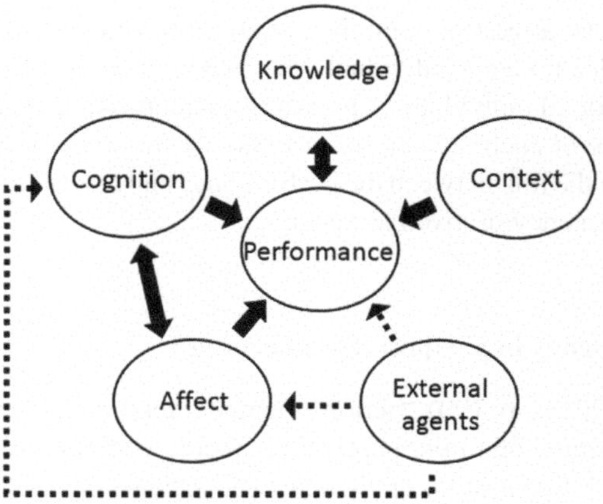

Fig. 1. A systems dynamics model of learning.

representations at multiple levels of abstraction, flexibly incorporating whatever sources of knowledge help to reduce the overall prediction error (Lupyan and Clark 2015). The brain thus uses the prediction task to bootstrap its way to the structured world-knowledge that is later used to generate better (and better) predictions (Clark 2018). This module also includes prior knowledge on the target learning subject. The role of the *affect module* is to provide and manage the affective resources involved in learning. Affective resources during learning are available with arousal (EDA; Electrodermal activity) and valence (FAA; Frontal Alpha Asymmetry) measures. As the affect module, the *cognition module* is inherent to the learner, providing and managing the cognitive resources involved in learning. To do so, measures of cognitive load, cognitive engagement, and visual attention can be extracted for psychophysiological online measures of learning. In learning efforts, the learner performs multiple behavioral actions, which represent the *performance module.* Also, for every learning task, the *context* is essential. This module considers all inert non-interactive resources that are either prerequisite or present during a learning effort like the time of the task of the tools needed to succeed. The final module is often present in learning, but still facultative among some learning contexts. *External agents module* refers to the learner's extraneous concepts such as the presence of a feedback giver of the use of an interactive tool.

Causalities in the Model. At the top level, causalities between two modules indicate that at least one variable in one of the modules will have a causal impact on at least one variable in the other module. A bidirectional relation between two modules indicates that at least one variable in one of the modules will have a causal impact on at least one variable in the other module and that at least one variable in one of the other modules will have a causal impact on at least one variable in the first module. At the lower level, causalities are by definition unidirectional and involve variables within or between modules.

Extending the Model to Multi-Individual Joint Functioning. When considering more than one learner in joint functioning during learning (doing something at the same time and the actions of at least one affecting at least one other individual), the model takes the following form. An affective, cognitive, knowledge and performance module (and their relations) is added for each individual. The context module affects the performance in the same manner for all individuals. The external agent(s) module affects the affective and cognitive module of each learner, not necessarily in the same manner. Finally, the existence or nature of the link between the performance and external agents is determined by the possibility of agency of given learners.

2.2 The Role of Agency in Cooperative Learning

According to (Clark 2013a, p. 190), "action-oriented (hierarchical) predictive processing models promise to bring cognition, perception, action, and attention together within a common framework". Because these elements can articulate agency at multiple levels within and between individuals, in a manner amenable to empirical investigation using trace methodologies with behavioral and psychophysiological data, this view can provide new insights concerning cooperative learning settings. This is especially the case since it can be argued that net benefits of collaboration, if any, have to be leveraged by some kind of active co-optimization by the learners (Caballé et al. 2011; Chan 2012), which must include the level of inter-individual functioning (Stahl 2013), and even the group level (Järvelä and Hadwin 2013; Lajoie and Lu 2012) in addition to the individual level. Referring specifically to learning, (Clark 2013a, p. 190) adds: "This framework suggests probability-density distributions induced by hierarchical generative models as our basic means of representing the world, and prediction-error minimization as the driving force behind learning".

According to (Clark's 2013a) prediction-action cognitive architecture, teaching and fostering learning involves providing input that will ultimately lead a learner to formulate predictions adequately representing the state of the world. For one thing, that can mean not relying on prior knowledge, when no interfering knowledge is present in the learner. When such interfering knowledge is likely to have been acquired, it is the basis for formulating predictions and as such must be the unavoidable basis for learning, as research on conceptual change has shown.

In this view, agency is the ability to act on the environment, notably using tools, to structure information. This view is critical in examining the moment-by-moment, complex and dynamic interplay between psychophysiological and behavioral functioning of learners in dyads and how inferences about cognition and affective functioning drawn from these data can be used to identify the main determinants of students' learning. At each moment and at different temporal grain sizes, this view postulates a state of each individual, represented on multiple dimensions classified in the systems dynamics model and derived from psychophysiological and behavioral measurement. These dimensions interact within a level and between levels (such as intra-individual and inter-individual). Such states combined at the individual level can characterize the team level, and emergent group-level properties can be conceptualized if they are related to bottom-up constraints. Empirical studies in this perspective can provide answers to questions such as: Is doing better than watching? Is it possible for a bystander to learn misconceptions from the generation of a simulation model in the game based on misconceptions by the active player?

Incidentally, (Clark 2013a, p. 195) asked a cornerstone question for educational neuroscience: "What are the potential effects of such stacked and transmissible designer environments upon prediction-driven learning in cortical hierarchies?" This question is in principle amenable to empirical investigation: "Such learning routines make human minds permeable, at multiple spatial and temporal scales, to the statistical structure of the world as reflected in the training signals." (Clark 2013a, p. 195). Thus, learning is a gradual process in which the likelihood of predictions changes cumulatively over time (Anderson 2002).

Learner agency seems therefore to be favorable to learning, since it enables a learner to select the predictions to be tested, presumably considering pertinent prior knowledge, and not just be a witness of tested predictions that do not correspond at least to some extent to predictions that have to be tested to produce change in a learner's knowledge. From this understanding of the human cognitive architecture, this generation and test of predictions appear to be the main process for learning, seen as change in the architecture, including at the knowledge level. This change in the architecture also applies to multi-agent functioning, in which needs for coordination between agents will be contingent on the predictions concurrently held by the agents.

Learner agency in a learning task would imply that "The successful student [given a possibility for agency] would have to command a 'generative model', enabling her to construct various predictions within a learning domain which hold true when tested" (Clark 2013b, p. 475).

2.3 Cognitive Load and Agency

Cognitive load is currently seen as a major factor in learning that is amenable to manipulation through pedagogical design. It is related to the functioning of the working memory and represents the number of elements held in working memory in order to be manipulated through cognitive processes. This number of elements is limited. Since learning involves processing information, cognitive load is necessary for learning. However, the learning context may solicit cognitive load in such ways that the number of elements needed performing the learning task (intrinsic load) and for learning from it (germane load)—for example by performing new operations towards their automatization—are not available due to extraneous demands from the learning situation (extraneous load).

Notwithstanding the previous distinction emanating from the learning context, it should be noted that cognitive load is operationalized psychologically and psychophysiologically as a unidimensional construct with a threshold: the number of elements held concurrently in a limited-capacity working memory. The three types of cognitive load cannot be measured directly but rather inferred from a characterization of the learning context and its eventual manipulation. The nature of the cognitive load involved in manipulating the simulation in a learning situation in which manipulating the simulation is not the object of learning but rather part of the task (intrinsic load) or even detrimental to learning (extraneous load) is an open question to be resolved empirically. Since the present study involves a well-controlled manipulation of agency, it examines the effect of agency on cognitive load and if any, whether agency represents mostly intrinsic or extraneous cognitive load. Cognitive load theory can classify the load attributed to agency as intrinsic if using the simulation fosters the generation or test of hypotheses. Cognitive load theory can classify the load attributed to agency as extraneous if using the simulation is an additional burden that does not foster the generation or test of hypotheses.

2.4 Research Questions

Grounded in the systems dynamics model for learning, the research questions focus on one aspect of the SDM and address group differences in individual stocks in cognitive load, as well as inter-individual relationships in cognitive load in the context of an asymmetrical agency. The research questions are: (1) what is the effect of agency on cognitive load? (2) what is the relationship between the total cognitive load of the two learners in a dyad when one is an active player and the other is a passive watcher? (3) what is the relationship between the instantaneous cognitive load of the two learners in a dyad when one is an active player and the other is a passive watcher? These questions seem important in themselves as cognitive load is an important topic of research in the learning sciences. Also, separate examinations of aspects of the SDM seems warranted before tackling the complexity of the overall model.

3 Methodology

3.1 Participants

This paper is part of a multidimensional project where 82 undergraduates' volunteers from a Canadian university were recruited. Based on their mutual availability, participants were paired by the research coordinator (except for participants who already demonstrated their interest in pairs). Participants were 47 females (mean age: 26 years old). All participants had a novice background in physics, namely a maximum of 11th grade equivalent in physic. Only one participant attended a physic's class in college. Prior to their participation, all participants were asked to read and sign the consent form preapproved by the University ethics committee. Also, participants were paid for their participation in this study. Because of bad electroencephalography (EEG) data contaminated by large artifacts, 5 dyads were removed from the present analyses. Therefore, the data from 36 dyads were subjected to analysis.

3.2 Experimental Task and Setting

Although this research should contribute applied insights regarding collaborative learning, it was decided to begin with the simplest contrast; one person in the dyad would be active and the other would not. Randomly, participants were assigned to one or the other role. One participant played *Mecanika* for two hours, while the other was watching a real-time duplication of the player's gameplay on a separate screen. Teammates were seated in the experimental room side by side, each in front of a computer, and they were instructed not to communicate. A 20 min stop rule was established for every level to avoid discouragement caused by repetitive failure.

Mecanika (Boucher-Genesse et al. 2011) is a serious computer game comprised of 50 levels where the player needs to use scientific conceptions in order to figure out the movement behavior of physical objects when multiple forces are applied. Every level is built on the same format. A specific path is defined by stars. The player needs to apply various forces on an object to follow precisely the path. On his way, the object illuminates the stars as an instant feedback. The level is solved when all the stars are light up simultaneously, a sign that the object driven by the various forces is perfectly following the path.

3.3 Measures

Participants were installed side by side in a dual-EEG setup (64 channels per head plus reference and ground), using the 10–20 electrodes placement system of (Chatrian et al. 1985) and (Chatrian et al. 1988). As part of the larger study, eye-tracking, electrodermal activity (EDA) and blood pulse were also measured, but the results are not reported in the present paper, as well as the *Force Concept Inventory* questionnaire (Hestenes et al. 1992) filled pre and posttest by the participants as a measure of their physic's knowledge. All 132 channels of the dual head montage were recorded in a single file to ensure perfect synchrony of the signals. The recordings lasted for the entire experiment.

3.4 Data Preparation

The recordings were first divided to isolate the Player's data from the Watcher's data and permit individualized artifact rejection. To remove eye movement artifacts such as blink and lateral movement, an independent component analysis was performed prior to computing the metric of interest, in this case, cognitive load. Following the right mastoid (TP10) as a reference, the electrodes Fz and Pz were then used in order to extract the cognitive load metric from the EEG recording. After performing an FFT the theta signal (4–8Hz) from Fz and the alpha signal (8–12Hz) from Pz were extracted. Each data point of the theta signal was then divided by the corresponding alpha data point to obtain the CL metric, following (Holm et al. 2009).

For analyses involving the area under the curve, and because cognitive load cannot be a negative quantity, 3 standard deviations (SD) were added to every data point so that the value of −3 SD becomes the absolute zero. Since 99.5% of normally distributed data points fall between −3 and 3 SD, the few data points (less than 10 for a dyad) were replaced with a value of −3 or 3 respectively.

From these data, instantaneous load and total load (the area under the curve) were used in the analyses.

4 Results

This first step in time-series analysis is the identification and diagnosis of the ARIMA model: autocorrelation functions (ACFs) and partial autocorrelation functions (PACFs) are examined to see which of the three potential patterns (auto-regression, trend and seasonal effect) are present in the data. This preliminary step was performed with SPSS using a dyad randomly selected from the sample, under the assumption that the results from one dyad would apply to all dyads.

Results presented in Table 1 suggest an ARIMA (1, 1, 0) model for player 38 and an ARIMA (1, 1, 0) model for watcher 38. With this model, there is both auto-regression in the model (cognitive load at one point depends on the cognitive load in the preceding data point), trend (the quality and variability of cognitive load is generally increasing over 120 min), but no seasonal effects (there are no cycles of variations of cognitive load in time).

Table 1. Identification and diagnosis of the Arima (1, 1, 0) model for dyad 38.

Model	Auto-regression Fit Statistics			Ljung-Box Q (18)		
	t	p	Stationary R^2	Statistics	DF	Sig
Player	−19.32	.00	.25	202.65	17	.00
Watcher	−21.54	.00	.26	209.2	17	.00

Because of the trend (the second number) in the ARIMA (1, 1, 0), the cross-correlation analysis is based on the difference between the value of one point and the value from the preceding point for each individual series. The results are presented according to the research questions.

4.1 Question 1: What is the Effect of Agency on Cognitive Load?

When all dyads are observed within the same analysis, results of the between-group comparison between players and watchers indicate that agency has no effect on the overall quantity of cognitive load ($t_{71} = -.536, p > 0.05$).

4.2 Question 2: What is the Relationship Between the Total Cognitive Load of the Two Learners in a Dyad When One is the Active Player and the Other is a Passive Watcher?

When the dyad is the unit of analysis, the overall quantity of cognitive load between the player and watcher across all 36 respective dyads is completely uncorrelated ($r = -0.037, p > 0.05$).

4.3 Question 3: What is the Relationship Between the Instantaneous Cognitive Load of the Two Learners in a Dyad When One is the Active Player and the Other is a Passive Watcher?

Figure 2 presents the cross-correlations between the instantaneous cognitive load of the player and the watcher. Non-significant correlations do not appear in the graph. As shown in the figure, most of the dyads don't present a significant interrelationship regarding instantaneous cognitive load. Only 4 dyads display at least one significative cross-correlation, which are dyads 8, 14, 32 and 38. All of these four dyads show only one statistically significant correlation, except for dyad 32 which has two. The highest correlation between the instantaneous cognitive load of the player and watcher of a dyad is .213, and occurs at lag 3 (meaning that the watcher's cognitive load has a 3-s offset on the player's cognitive load).

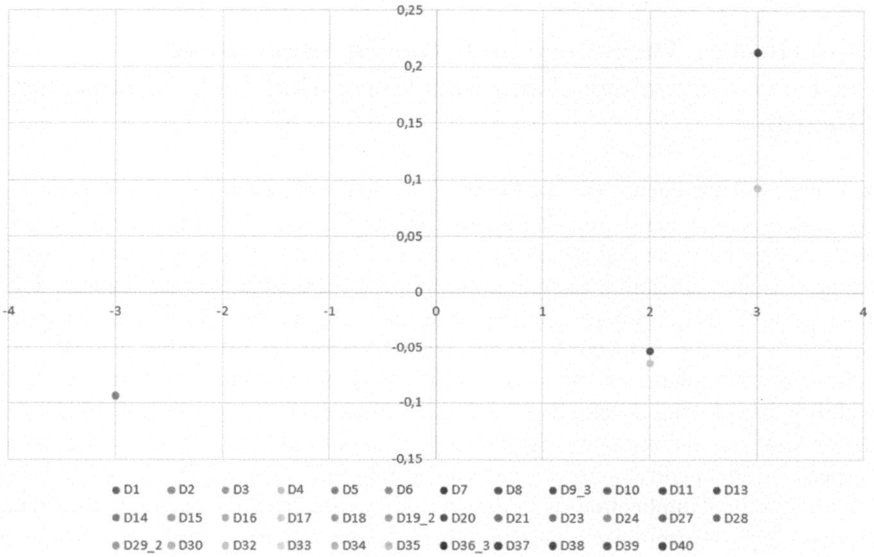

Fig. 2. Cross-correlations for all dyads.

5 Discussion

The results for question 1 indicate that agency (the fact of being an active player or a passive watcher) has no effect on the overall quantity of cognitive load. Moreover, question 2 indicates that agency creates an unsystematic discrepancy in total cognitive load between players and watchers, in the sense that the player is sometimes higher sometimes lower total cognitive load as compared to its counterpart watcher. It can be concluded regardless of the unit of analysis (participants grouped as players or watchers or as dyads) that agency does not systematically induce more, or less, cognitive load. This suggests that other factors, possibly identified in the model postulated, are responsible for variations in the overall quantity of cognitive load.

The results for question 3 indicate that the instantaneous cognitive load of the player and watcher of a dyad is uncorrelated. In very exceptional cases, significant correlations involve a lag of 2 or 3 data points (8 or 12 s). This absence of correlations, especially at lag 0 (which was found to be the highest in our analysis of an affective dimension, see [Mercier, Avaca, Whissell-Turner and Paradis in press]), suggests, on the one hand, that these correlations are spurious and, on the other hand, that the synchronous display of information from the game gets processed cognitively differently by the two teammates.

Another aspect to be further elucidated relates to the computation of the cognitive load metric, which provides a data point every 4 s. While it may be adequate to compute the overall quantity of cognitive load over entire learning activities or some reasonably long episodes within them, this grain size may not be adequate for analyzing time series of instantaneous cognitive load.

6 Conclusion: Theoretical and Applied Implications of Psychophysiological and Behavioral Modeling of Cooperative Learning

It was observed that agency (the fact of being an active player or a passive watcher) has no systematic effect on the overall quantity of cognitive load. For the systems dynamics model, that would mean that the total as well as instantaneous cognitive load in a given learning episode, although it fluctuates differently over time among the learners within a dyad, accumulates evenly irrespective of agency. That is, the stocks of cognitive load (and resulting fatigue) induced in the system are distributed at 50% between the learners.

Since the instantaneous cognitive load is rarely at maximum level, ruling out the possibility that playing is actually a source of germane or extraneous load, this can be interpreted as the playing being negligible in terms of required cognitive load. If true, this speaks of the quality of *Mecanika* as a learning tool.

The theoretical implications regarding question 3 are that if the learning environment doesn't produce even minimal correlations in cognitive load in two participants seeing the exact same thing, then the top-down individual differences may have a stronger impact on learning than bottom-up effects of the learning context. For the systems dynamics model, the apparent disconnection between the cognitive modules of members of a dyad needs to be further investigated using the other variables available such as cognitive engagement, and attention (Frontal Midline Theta).

If levels of instantaneous or total cognitive load are unrelated generally, are there some circumstances in which they are, such as specific game levels for which both participants have the same prior knowledge or misconceptions? Another question is: do the salient visual features of the simulation drive the gaze so that both participants generally look at the same thing within the screen? (Mercieret al. in press). Another factor might be differences among teammates in prior knowledge of the learning domain. It has been reported elsewhere that 16% of answers were already correct at pretest on the Force Concept Inventory (Mercier et al. 2020). Many questions remain to be explored such as: is it possible for a bystander to learn misconceptions from the generation of misconceptions by the active player?

The analysis presented in this study only includes a very limited portion of the original data collected. Other metrics extracted from the EEG as well as eye-tracking data and electrodermal activity will provide additional explorations of the use of the SDM in the study of learning as a cumulative multi-faceted and multi-layered process. Although fragmentary, these isolated vignettes are necessary because of the complexity of the data coupled with a relative scarcity of theory, which command a lot of interdisciplinary attention and precaution in the operationalization and interpretation of focused comparisons. Subsequently, they will have to be complemented with analyses involving all variables in order to disentangle their respective effects on learning. If successful, this last phase of analysis should point to complementary contexts for data collection to add potential comparisons to the current dataset, for example using the same serious computer game but with more interaction within the dyad, to be more representative of an authentic collaborative learning setting. This work may contribute insights in the design of computer tools, especially simulations and virtual reality involving cooperation, by providing insights about how learners cooperate in such contexts.

Acknowledgements. The study was conducted with the support of the Social Sciences and Humanities Research Council of Canada and the Canada Foundation for Innovation.

References

Anderson, J.R.: Spanning seven orders of magnitude: a challenge for cognitive modeling. Cogn. Sci. **26**, 85–112 (2002)

Boucher-Genesse, F., Riopel, M., Potvin, P.: Research results for Mecanika, a game to learn Newtonian concepts. In: Games, Learning and Society Conference proceedings, Wisconsin, pp. 31–38 (2011)

Caballé, S., Daradoumis, T., Xhafa, F., Juan, A.: Providing effective feedback, monitoring and evaluation to on-line collaborative learning discussions. Comput. Hum. Behav. **27**, 1372–1381 (2011)

Chan, C.K.K.: Co-regulation of learning in computer-supported collaborative learning environments: a discussion. Metacogn. Learn. **7**, 63–73 (2012). https://doi.org/10.1007/s11409-012-9086-z

Chatrian, G.E., Lettich, E., Nelson, P.L.: Ten percent electrode system for topographic studies of spontaneous and evoked EEG activity. Am. J. EEG Technol. **25**, 83–92 (1985)

Chatrian, G.E., Lettich, E., Nelson, P.L.: Modified nomenclature for the "10%" electrode system. J. Clin. Neurophysiol. **5**, 183–186 (1988)

Clark, A.: Whatever next? Predictive brains, situated agents, and the future of cognitive science. Behav. Brain Sci. **36**, 181–253 (2013a)

Clark, A.: Expecting the world: perception, prediction, and the origins of human knowledge. J. Philos. **110**(9), 469–496 (2013b)

Clark, A.: Surfing Uncertainty: Prediction, Action, and the Embodied Mind. Oxford University Press, New York (2018)

Forrester, J.: Counterintuitive behavior of social systems. Technol. Rev. **73**(3), 52–68 (1971)

Järvelä, S., Hadwin, A.F.: New frontiers: regulating learning in CSCL. Educ. Psychol. **48**(1), 25–39 (2013)

Hestenes, D., Wells, M., Swackhamer, G.: Force concept inventory. Phys. Teach. **30**, 141–158 (1992)

Holm, A., Lukander, K., Korpela, J., Sallinen, M., Müller, K.M.I.: Estimating brain load from the EEG. Sci. World J. **9**, 639–665 (2009)

Immordino-Yang, M.H.: Implications of affective and social neuroscience for educational theory. Educ. Philos. Theory **43**(1), 98–103 (2011)

Kortelainen, S., Piirainen, K., Tuominen, M.: A system dynamic model of learning and innovation process profitability. In: Proceedings of the 26th International Conference of the System Dynamics Society, Athens, Greece (2008)

Kotseruba, I., Tsotsos, J.K.: 40 years of cognitive architectures: core cognitive abilities and practical applications. Artif. Intell. Rev. **53**(1), 17–94 (2020). https://doi.org/10.1007/s10462-018-9646-y

Lajoie, S.P., Lu, J.: Supporting collaboration with technology: does shared cognition lead to co-regulation in medicine? Metacogn. Learn. **7**, 45–62 (2012). https://doi.org/10.1007/s11409-011-9077-5

Lupyan, G., Clark, A.: Words and the world: predictive coding and the language-perception-cognition interface. Curr. Dir. Psychol. Sci. **24**(4), 279–284 (2015)

Mercier, J., Avaca, I.L., Whissell-Turner, K., Paradis, A.: Towards modeling the psychophysiology of learning interactions: the effect of agency on arousal in dyads learning physics with a serious computer game. In: Proceedings of the 2020 International Conference on Technology and Innovation in Learning, Teaching and Education (in press)

Mercier, J., Whissell-Turner, K., Paradis, A., Avaca, I.L., Riopel, M., Bédard, M.: Do individual differences modulate the effect of agency on learning outcomes with a serious game? In: Zaphiris, P., Ioannou, A. (eds.) HCII 2020. LNCS, vol. 12206, pp. 254–266. Springer, Cham (2020). https://doi.org/10.1007/978-3-030-50506-6_19

Patten, K.E.: The somatic appraisal model of affect: paradigm for educational neuroscience and neuropedagogy. Educ. Philos. Theory **43**(1), 87–97 (2011)

Stahl, G.: Learning across levels . Comput.-Support. Collaborative Learn. **8**, 1–2 (2013). https://doi.org/10.1007/s11412-013-9169-0

Sun, R.: Cognitive social simulation for policy making. Policy Insights Behav. Brain Sci. **5**(2), 240–246 (2018)

Towards Modeling the Psychophysiology of Learning Interactions: The Effect of Agency on Arousal in Dyads Learning Physics with a Serious Computer Game

Julien Mercier(✉), Ivan Luciano Avaca, Kathleen Whissell-Turner, and Ariane Paradis

NeuroLab, University of Quebec in Montreal, 1205, rue Saint-Denis, Montréal H2X3R9, Canada
mercier.julien@uqam.ca

Abstract. It is generally assumed that making the learner active leads to better learning although this improvement has not be firmly quantified experimentally. The goal of this paper is to test the effect of agency in cooperative learning and to explore methodological strategies as well as theoretical and applied implications of agency in the study of cooperative learning, in this case with data on arousal. Results from 27 dyads (1 player and 1 watcher) who played a serious game for learning physics for 120 min show that agency has no effect on the overall quantity of arousal, but that the arousal of a watcher and player is synchronized. A watcher's arousal may precede or be delayed from the player's. The results point to refinements for the use of multimodal data in process-oriented studies of cooperative learning.

Keywords: Educational neuroscience · Cooperative learning · Agency

1 Introduction

In studying the role of agency in learning, we seek and consider theories and methods that can inform about how affective and cognitive states jointly contribute to learning processes and outcomes when the possibility to act during a learning activity is manipulated to extremes, and how learners individually and eventually in cooperative settings can act productively upon these states within themselves or in teammates.

According to (Castelfranchi 2014), a complete model of cognition has to specify the cognitive mechanisms producing and controlling behavior as well as their neural and body implementation. It should be known how and why brain structures are associated with brain micro-mechanisms and emergent cognitive processes, including inter-individual functioning. While cognitive psychology has been fertile in suggesting models of cognition, cognitive neuroscience cannot at this time provide complete interfacing mechanism(s) between psychophysiological functioning and cognition as observed and explained in behavioral terms, and this scarcity of theory is exacerbated in the study of social interactions (Konvalinka et al. 2014). Such theoretical developments

A. Reis et al. (Eds.): TECH-EDU 2020, CCIS 1384, pp. 421–431, 2021.
https://doi.org/10.1007/978-3-030-73988-1_34

are needed to ground an educational neuroscience perspective towards possible contributions to educational research and applications, especially in light of the importance of social interactions in learning contexts. The translational research implied in educational neuroscience involves bidirectional relations bridging three disciplines respectively representing the psychophysiological implementation, the target phenomenon (learning), and a field of application (education): cognitive neuroscience, cognitive psychology, and educational psychology (Hruby 2012). (Newell 1990)'s classic demonstration of the plausibility of unified theories of cognition indicates that, in principle, these multiple layers of explanations can be related notably by means of the notion of cognitive architecture, at least those plausible biologically.

The goal of this paper is to articulate a model of cooperative learning based on a predictive cognitive architecture and to explore methodological strategies as well as theoretical and applied implications of agency for the study of cooperative learning. These broad issues are explored in this specific case with data on arousal within an experimental manipulation of the possibility to act during a learning activity which is maximally and artificially contrasted as a prototype for additional developments using other measures of the same nature. The present work offers a glimpse into the study of more authentic collaborative learning, construed as switches of the possibility to act among participants during a learning situation.

2 Theoretical Framework

2.1 Integrating Affect, Cognition, Action, and Knowledge Within and Between Individuals Across Levels of Explanation and Timescales

(Clark 2013a)'s prediction-action framework is the theory underlying the present model of cooperative learning. It is very useful in explaining how a multi-layered conception of the mind – taking into account physiological, sub-symbolic, symbolic and inter-individual levels – may be extended to inter-individual interactions. Science learning is frequently described as conceptual change, in which misconceptions can interact with scientific conceptions (Potvin 2013). According to (Clark 2013a), learning occurs when prediction errors drive change in memory structures in the brain. In learning scientific conceptions, misconceptions predict phenomena in a manner incongruent with scientific knowledge (Potvin 2013). Clark's model implies that these misconceptions must be overcome by input that makes prediction errors apparent. When there is a discrepancy between sensory input and prediction, this discrepancy must be resolved by either change in memory structures or change in the source of sensory input.

2.2 The Role of Agency

Agency comes into play in this possibility of change in the source of sensory input, which depends on the possibility to act upon stimuli by modifying the environment. In other words, agency can be seen as the potential to use a generative model to test predictions about the world by acting upon it. "Perception and action, if these unifying models are correct, are intimately related and work together to reduce the prediction error by sculpting and selecting sensory inputs." (Clark 2013a, p. 183). Generative models, which are held in long-term memory, reduce prediction errors at each level in the architecture in a top-down manner. "... the neuronal responses that follow an input (the "evoked responses") may be expected to change quite profoundly according to the contextualizing information provided by a current winning top-down prediction" (Clark 2013a, p. 189). A learner can develop knowledge, in the sense of modifying knowledge structures, through taking actions and reasoning about the outcome of those actions (Lindgren and McDaniel 2014). (Damşa et al. 2010) posited that both customary and innovative, creative actions can account for agentic behavior in terms of greater imagination, choice, and conscious purpose. For them, agency emerges in problematic situations through the enactment of new actions. Overall, learning with open-interface serious games is enhanced when students actively control their interaction pattern based on their own choices (Snow et al. 2015).

2.3 A Systems Dynamics Model of Cooperative Learning

A systems dynamics model specifies key parts (quantities) and the relationships between them, in the form of positive and negative feedback loops. The modules specified are unified by the prediction-action framework. Six modules are included: knowledge, affective, cognitive, performance, external agents, and context. The modules are intended to be generic, applicable to any learning context. However, external agents can be optional because they may not always be part of a learning context. The modules are also intended to represent a tenable view of cognitive science, while the variables within those modules (in parentheses) are currently underspecified and likely to benefit from theoretical developments and operationalizations. Also, the details about causal correlations (positive and negative feedback loops) are left unspecified because they largely remain to be established through empirical work.

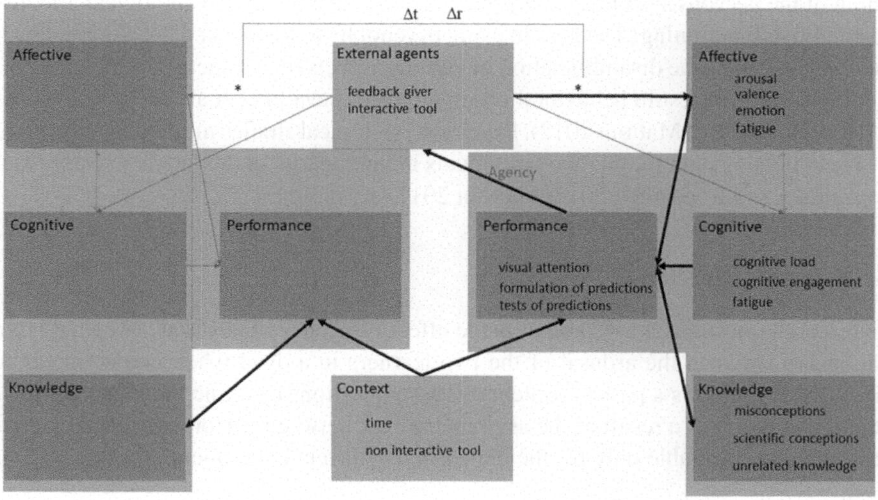

Fig. 1. A systems dynamics model of cooperative learning

A learner is modeled through four modules. The affective and the cognitive modules contain respectively the affective (arousal, valence) and cognitive (cognitive load, cognitive engagement) resources of the learner. The knowledge module contains the extent knowledge of the learner (scientific conceptions, misconceptions, unrelated knowledge). The performance module selects and performs actions in relation to the learning task (selection of prediction, test of prediction, visual attention). If a learning situation involves two or more learners involved in joint activity, these four modules and the links between them can be replicated (as shown in Fig. 1). It should be noted that the links with external agents and context may be modulated depending on the situation. The external agent(s) module contains any interactive element within the situation (feedback giver, interactive tool), while the context module contains inert resources (such as time on task and non-interactive tools).

Learner agency seems therefore to be favorable to learning, since it enables a learner to select the predictions to be tested, presumably considering pertinent prior knowledge, and not just be a witness of tested predictions that do not correspond at least to some extent to predictions that have to be tested to produce change in a learner's knowledge.

2.4 Methodological Considerations in Modeling Agency Using Psychophysiological and Behavioral Data

The present work is grounded in trace methodology involving the coupling of psychophysiological and behavioral channels of data over extended periods of time corresponding to significant learning episodes. Behavioral data regarding individual and joint affective and cognitive processes include spoken and written discourse, facial configurations representing emotions, gesture, performance (which may include the use of tools such as computers and learning software). Behavioral data is subjected to analysis using conventional methods, which may include qualitative and quantitative strategies. Behavioral data is complemented by psychophysiological data, referring to the functioning of the nervous system as interpreted in relationship with psychological affective and cognitive functioning. The gain in using psychophysiological and behavioral data in modeling agency is the disambiguation of various aspects of joint action, which may not be completely manifest in behavioral observations (Konvalinka et al. 2014; Konvalinka and Roepstorff 2012; Mattout 2012). Psychophysiological studies hinging on this model involve collecting data for the two individuals in interaction, in the interactive approach (Konvalinka and Roepstorff 2012; Mattout 2012).

2.5 Research Questions

The research questions are: (1) what is the effect of agency on arousal? (2) what is the relationship between the arousal of the two learners in a dyad when one is the active player and the other is a passive watcher? These questions examine the links identified with an * in Fig. 1 as a result of the asymmetric link between performance and external agent, which is available only for the player in the current experiment.

3 Methodology

3.1 Participants

Twenty-seven dyads of undergraduate students with novice background in physics played through a maximum of 50 levels of a serious game for learning physics for two hours. Only two dyads reached the last level. Participants volunteering in pairs formed a dyad for the experimentations, while individual volunteers were matched based on lab schedule and their respective availability. The ethics approval for this study was granted by the university of the authors and participants were paid for their participation.

3.2 Experimental Task and Setting

Although this research should contribute applied insights regarding collaborative learning, it was decided to begin with the simplest contrast; one person in the dyad would be active and the other would not. One participant played *Mecanika*, while the other was watching on a separate screen. Thus, agency is manipulated in terms of the possibility of taking actions, whereas both members of the dyad are reasoning about the outcome of those actions (Lindgren and McDaniel 2014). These roles were assigned randomly prior to the participants' arrival at the lab. Teammates were seated in the experimental room side by side, each with a computer, and were asked not to communicate.

Mecanika is a serious computer game addressing 58 widespread misconceptions in Newtonian physics (see Hestenes et al. 1992) at a conceptual level through simulation – no calculations are involved (Boucher-Genesse et al. 2011). Each of the 50 levels in the game systematically addresses one (and sometimes two) of these 58 misconceptions by fostering a cognitive conflict (Dreyfus et al. 1990) to stimulate conceptual change (Potvin 2013).

Participants solve levels by applying different types of force to objects to make them move according to a target path. This involves choosing the type(s) of force, the quantity of sources, and their positioning. When the player is convinced that s/he configured the forces to make the object follow the prescribed trajectory, a click on a button will trigger an animation. Stars placed on the target trajectory will illuminate if the object has followed the target trajectory and a line representing the actual trajectory of the object will be displayed. A level is successfully performed when all stars are lit during a single trial. Superficial trial and error are discouraged by putting a premium on lower number of trials and forces used to complete a level. In the view presented earlier, *Mecanika* is a tool to command a generative model of Newtonian mechanics and to test predictions about how physical objects behave.

3.3 Measures

Participants were installed with non-invasive eye-tracking devices, high-density electroencephalography, blood pulse sensors, and electrodermal activity (EDA) sensors, but only the EDA data is used in the present study. The two electrodes were positioned on the index and middle finger of the left hand. This hand was also stuck to the table with medical tape to minimize data contamination due to movement. The EDA was recorded at 1000 Hz. Performance data was recorded concomitantly and synchronized to the millisecond with the use of TTL triggers. For the present study, these data were used only to determine the beginning and end of the 120-min episode of play for each dyad. Participants' knowledge of Newtonian physics was assessed pre- and posttest with the *Force Concept Inventory* (Hestenes et al. 1992).

3.4 Data Preparation

The EDA for each participant was first z-scored using a two-minute neutral episode before the gameplay. The total amount of arousal was computed using the area under the curve of the absolute value of the EDA. For the time-series analysis, the data was downsampled to 1 Hz (one data point per second) so that significant variation could be captured in a few lags.

3.5 Plan of Analysis

For question 1, the total amount of arousal (the area under the curve) was subjected to a paired-sample *t* test (player-watcher). For question 2, the total amount of arousal (the area under the curve) nested over dyad was subjected to a correlation analysis also, the instantaneous arousal (normalized arousal over time) nested over dyad was subjected to a time-series analysis.

This first step in time-series analysis is the identification and diagnosis of the ARIMA model: autocorrelation functions (ACFs) and partial autocorrelation functions (PACFs) are examined to see which of the three potential patterns (auto-regression, trend and seasonal effect) are present in the data. This preliminary step was performed using a dyad randomly selected from the sample, under the assumption that the results from one dyad would apply to all dyads.

Results presented in Table 1 suggest an ARIMA (1, 1, 1) model for player 15 and an ARIMA (1, 1, 1) model for watcher 15. With this model, there is both auto-regression in the model (arousal at one point depends on the arousal in the preceding second), trend (the quality and variability of arousal are generally increasing over 120 min), and seasonal effects (there are cycles of variations of arousal in time).

Table 1. Identification and diagnosis of the ARIMA model for dyad 15

Model	Model Fit Statistics			Ljung-Box Q(18)		
	Stationary R^2	R^2	RMSE	Statistics	DF	Sig
Player	.44	.99	.05	99.69	16	.00
Watcher	.62	.99	.05	286.39	16	.00

Because of the trend (the second number) in the ARIMA (1, 1, 1), the cross-correlation analysis is based on the difference between the value of one point and the value from the preceding point for each individual series.

The analysis involves lags −20 to 20, that is 20 points before and after a given point. Because the data is sampled at 1 Hz, a lag corresponds to 1 s.

Since recent books on time-series analysis (Box et al. 2016) do not provide equations for testing hypotheses with time series nested by dyads, the sample data are aggregated in the form of a graph (see Fig. 2).

4 Results

The results are presented according to the two research questions. In terms of learning gains, a 12.04% increase in good answers was observed, in addition to the 16.44% of answers already correct at pretest. In addition, watchers were systematically found to learn more than players (Mercier et al. 2020). In a previous study about the effectiveness of the game, involving the same population used in this study (Charland et al. 2015), the 50 levels in the game were associated with a 30% gain in good answers on corresponding items of the *Force Concept Inventory*.

4.1 Question 1: What is the Effect of Agency on Arousal?

Results of the between-group comparison between players and watchers show that agency has no effect on the overall quantity of arousal ($t24 = -.306$, $p > 0.05$).

4.2 Question 2: What is the Relationship Between the Arousal of the Two Learners in a Dyad When One is the Active Player and the Other is a Passive Watcher?

Likewise, when the dyad is the unit of analysis, the overall quantity of arousal between the player and watcher across all 27 dyads is completely uncorrelated ($r = -0.08$, $p > 0.05$).

Results from the time series analysis for all dyads are presented in Fig. 2. Non-significant correlations, established in the context of time-series analysis, do not appear in the graph. The highest correlation between the instantaneous arousal of the player and watcher of a dyad is .22, and occurs at lag 0 (that is, at the same moment).

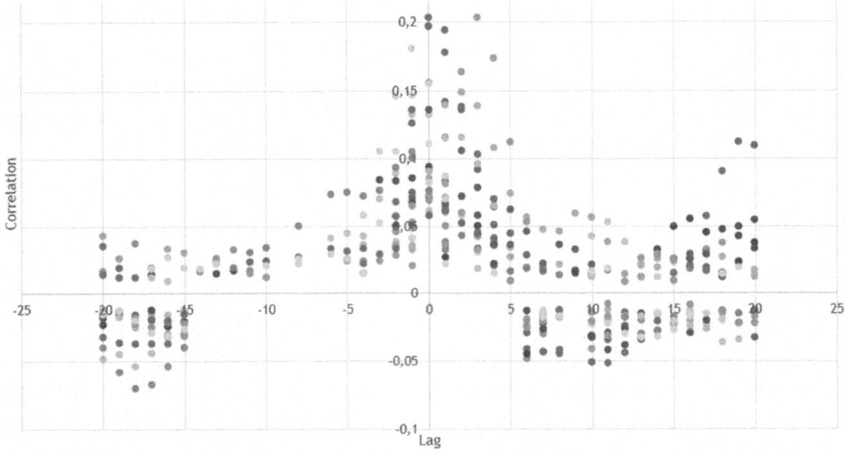

Fig. 2. Cross-correlations for all dyads

Figure 3 presents the same correlations as Fig. 2, but averaged across dyads. As can be seen from these sample averages, higher cross-correlations are concentrated from lag −3 to lag 5, with peaks at lag 0 (reaction at the same moment) and lag 2 (the reaction of the watcher occurs 2 s behind the reaction of the player).

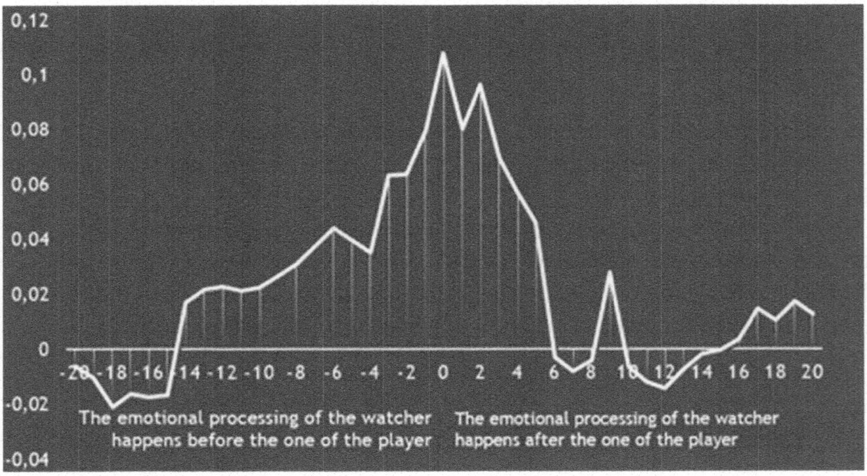

Fig. 3. Cross-correlations averaged across all dyads

As examples, Fig. 4 shows the cross-correlations patterns for two single dyads purposely chosen as intriguing cases, dyad 16 and 17. The left portion of Fig. 4 represents higher cross-correlations in the negative lags, which means that the watcher's variation in arousal preceded the player's. In contrast, the right portion of Fig. 4 shows a case where the arousal of the watcher varies after the player's, as seen with the higher cross-correlations at the positive lags.

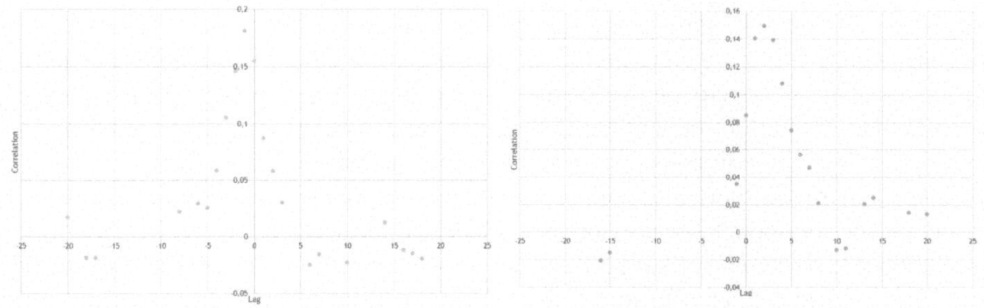

Fig. 4. Cross-correlations for dyad 16 and dyad 17

5 Discussion

The results for question 1 indicate that the players and watchers are not different in terms of overall quantity of arousal. Indeed, if an affective implication is needful for learning, it seems present equally for the watcher and the player.

The results for question 2 indicate that at every moment of 120 min of gameplay, the quantities of arousal in the affective module of a watcher and a player is for the most part synchronous. For some pairs, it can also be asynchronous: the data shows up to a 5-s reaction and a 3-s anticipation from the watcher. This anticipation can be interpreted as participation from the watcher (wishing for the player to perform an action) even if he has to "undergo" the player's performance without acting upon the situation. In light of this, it is tempting to postulate a relation to be further tested between the asynchrony of affectivity and the learning of the watcher. As reported previously, the watchers learn more. Can this anticipation/reaction be correlated with learning, possibly because a watcher who anticipates is more analytical of the current learning challenge? A key aspect to further examine to disambiguate this speculative finding is the prior knowledge of the members of a dyad as it is likely to be a major driver of the cognitive, affective and performance processes involved in solving a game level requiring this particular knowledge, as specified in our systems dynamics model. Furthermore, the cases in which the watcher anticipates and already possesses more sophisticated scientific knowledge to solve a given game level than the player should be explained in light of cognitive load (presumably lower than the player's) or visual attention to the feedback from the interactive game in a more general effort to disentangle how configurations of theses variables are more or less beneficial to learning. With respect to this interindividual synchronization/desynchronization, it would be interesting to see if the affectivity is more in synchrony when the two participants are more cognitively engaged in the task. In addition, does the watcher anticipate more when he is more engaged and the player is less engaged, and does he react when he is less engaged, and the player is more engaged?

The results also show data suggesting that the watcher reacts up to 20 s before and after the player. According to our ARIMA model (1, 1, 1) suggesting the presence of cycles of variation of the arousal in time, we hypothesize that cross-correlations at these extreme lags are rather part of another previous or next cycles, an explanation that needs to be verified by linking arousal with the actual performance of the game. Also, we do not know if this anticipation is the result of a new content learned while watching the game or an already known concept. As conceptualised in the model, this complex link between performance, vicarious learning, prior knowledge and knowledge acquired during the learning activity or an already known concept is now within empirical grasp. In particular, the bottom-up and top-down interplay between simulation data from the game and players' predictions is now amenable to analysis.

Is the anticipation here the result of a prediction where the performance experienced by the player contradicts the previous knowledge of the watcher or is it the result of a prediction where the player's performance seems wrong from the point of view of the watcher's knowledge of performance and not the scientific concept? Further analysis of the data collected with the physics knowledge test will inform us on this possible avenue.

Regarding the effect of agency on arousal, most theoretical models of affect usually use the arousal-valence couple. It would therefore be interesting to investigate the integration of a psychophysiological proxy to measure valence, which is actually considered using the frontal alpha asymmetry (FAA) from the EEG.

6 Conclusion: Theoretical and Applied Implications of Psychophysiological and Behavioral Modeling of Cooperative Learning

The test of this model, firstly in the form of partial examinations of specific links within it, can ultimately have applied implications for cooperative learning, as well as human and computer tutoring. This currently underdeveloped model nevertheless integrates and fosters the resolving and reuse of operational considerations necessary for the study of cooperative learning from a process-oriented point of view in which all time scales related to learning are jointly considered. These solutions, transferable to other datasets and contexts, appear highly needed within the emerging field of online measures of learning (Azevedo 2015). Considering the notion of "multi-agent flow in coordination", one overarching hypothesis is that psychophysiological and behavioral processes at various levels and time scales are synchronized, but not necessarily isomorph. Indeed, interpersonal interaction is reflected in synchrony – not necessarily similarity – of brain processes at the psychophysiological level (Konvalinka et al. 2014; Stevens et al. 2011). If synchronization occurs at the level of conversation between agents, there should be synchronization of lower levels, since behavior at one level can be seen as the cumulative effect of temporally faster, "inferior" events, in addition to effects within that level. If relationships with learning outcomes can be established, this can serve as a diagnostic of group functioning and as a grouping mechanism, and as a basis for teaching collaboration skills. It can inform the design of computer tools, especially simulations and virtual reality involving cooperation, by providing insights about how learners co-operate in such contexts.

Acknowledgements. The study was conducted with the support of the Social Sciences and Humanities Research Council of Canada and the Canada Foundation for Innovation.

References

Azevedo, R.: Defining and measuring engagement and learning in science: conceptual, theoretical, methodological, and analytical issues. Educ. Psychol. **50**(1), 84–94 (2015)

Boucher-Genesse, F., Riopel, M., Potvin, P.: Research results for Mecanika, a game to learn Newtonian concepts. In: Games, Learning and Society Conference Proceedings, Wisconsin, pp. 31–38 (2011)

Box, G.E.P., Jenkins, G.M., Reinsel, G.C., Ljung, G.M.: Time Series Analysis: Forecasting and Control, 5th edn. Wiley, Honoken (2016)

Castelfranchi, C.: For a science of layered mechanisms: beyond laws, statistics, and correlations. Front. Psychol. **5**, 1–2 (2014)

Charland, P., et al.: Assessing the multiple dimensions of engagement to characterize learning: a neurophysiological perspective. J. Vis. Exp. **101** (2015)

Clark, A.: Whatever next? Predictive brains, situated agents, and the future of cognitive science. Behav. Brain Sci. **36**, 181–253 (2013a)

Damşa, C.I., Kirschner, P.A., Andriessen, J.E.B., Erkens, G., Sins, P.H.M.: Shared epistemic agency: an empirical study of an emergent construct. J. Learn. Sci. **19**(2), 143–186 (2010)

Dreyfus, A., Jungwirth, E., Eliovitch, R.: Applying the "cognitive conflict" strategy for conceptual change – some implications, difficulties, and problems. Sci. Educ. **74**(5), 555–569 (1990)

Hestenes, D., Wells, M., Swackhamer, G.: Force concept inventory. Phys. Teach. **30**, 141–158 (1992)

Hruby, G.G.: Three requirements for justifying an educational neuroscience. Br. J. Educ. Psychol. **82**, 1–23 (2012)

Konvalinka, I., Bauer, M., Stahlhut, C., Hansen, L.K., Roepstorff, A., Frith, C.D.: Frontal alpha oscillations distinguish leaders from followers: multivariate decoding of mutually interacting brains. Neuroimage **94**, 79–88 (2014)

Konvalinka, I., Roepstorff, A.: The two-brain approach: how can mutually interacting brains teach us something about social interaction? Front. Hum. Neurosci. **6**, 1–10 (2012)

Lindgren, R., McDaniel, R.: Transforming online learning through narrative and student agency. Educ. Technol. Soc. **15**(4), 344–355 (2014)

Mattout, J.: Brain-computer interfaces: a neuroscience paradigm of social interaction? A matter of perspective. Front. Hum. Neurosci. **6**, 1–10 (2012)

Mercier, J., Whissell-Turner, K., Paradis, A., Avaca, I.L., Riopel, M., Bédard, M.: Do individual differences modulate the effect of agency on learning outcomes with a serious game? In: Zaphiris, P., Ioannou, A. (eds.) HCII 2020. LNCS, vol. 12206, pp. 254–266. Springer, Cham (2020). https://doi.org/10.1007/978-3-030-50506-6_19

Newell, A.: Unified Theories of Cognition. University Press, Harvard (1990)

Potvin, P.: Proposition for improving the classical models of conceptual change based on neuroeducational evidence: conceptual prevalence. Neuroeducation **2**(1), 16–43 (2013)

Snow, E.L., Allen, L.K., Jacovina, M.E., McNamara, D.S.: Does agency matter?: exploring the impact of controlled behaviors within a game-based environment. Comput. Educ. **82**, 378–392 (2015)

Stevens, R., Galloway, T., Wang, P., Berka, C.: Mapping neurophysiologic synchrony attractor states and entropy fluctuations during submarine piloting and navigation. In: Proceedings of the 2011 Annual Meeting on Human Factors and Ergonomics Society, vol. 55, no. 1, pp. 212–216 (2011)

Worker Support and Training Tools to Aid in Vehicle Quality Inspection for the Automotive Industry

Ana Teresa Campaniço(✉), Salik Khanal(✉), Hugo Paredes(✉), and Vitor Filipe(✉)

Universidade de Trás-os-Montes e Alto Douro, Vila Real, Portugal
{acampanico,salik,hparedes,vfilipe}@utad.pt

Abstract. In the competitive automotive market, where extremely high-quality standards must be ensured independently of the growing product and manufacturing complexity brought by customization, reliable and precise detection of any non-conformities before the vehicle leaves the assembly line is paramount. In this paper we propose a wearable solution to aid quality control workers in the detection, visualization and relay of any non-conformities, while also reducing known performance issues such as skill gaps and fatigue, and improving training methods. We also explore how the reliability, precision and validity tests of the visualization module of our framework were performed, guaranteeing a 0% chance occurrence of undesired non-conformities in the following usability tests and training simulator.

Keywords: Quality control · Information visualization · Automotive industry

1 Introduction

In order to remain competitive in the current market automotive companies must follow the trend of increasing customer customization, which leads to frequent addition and discontinuation of model variants on the assembly line [1]. This inevitably results in an increase of product complexity and a subsequent negative impact on manufacturing performance. However, the industry must maintain an extremely high-quality standard at all points of its production, as undetected faults, defects and other non-conformities would result in a severe impact on the brand's reputation [1, 2].

While this industry is characterized by its heavy investment on automation to help increase process efficiency, quality assurance still relies heavily on the highly tuned observational expertise provided by manual labor [3, 4]. But factors such as mental and ocular fatigue, the skill gap between seasoned and newly employed workers, etc. lead to human error [1, 5] which, thanks to the increase of computational power and the growing adoption of Industry 4.0 methodologies, such as Machine Learning [2], there have been technological attempts to reduce. However the automated detection and classification of defects and non-conformities in real time still struggle in many contexts that are trivial to a human observer, such as reflective surfaces [5, 6].

A. Reis et al. (Eds.): TECH-EDU 2020, CCIS 1384, pp. 432–441, 2021.
https://doi.org/10.1007/978-3-030-73988-1_35

This leads instead to a growing adoption of hybrid assembly lines, which combines the repetitive, fast and precise mechanical work performed by automation with the more highly adaptable and agile qualitative tasks humans can perform [1, 3, 4]. However in order to make production lines more flexible and responsive to the pressures imposed by the market the design of how effectively and efficiently, rather than just how functionally and reliably, information is transmitted and/or taught is also key to proper quality control [6, 7].

Our work focuses specifically on the last section of the assembly line, where a final quality inspection for non-conformities is performed before the vehicle is deemed fit to exit the factory floor. Our goal is to introduce a technically advanced, real-time mixed model approach that can aid workers and address their workstation's specific requirements and needs. In this paper we present the outline of our ongoing project and how it aims to combine a computer vision system and a head mounted display (HMD) to more efficiently deliver the detected non-conformities and other interactive visual information to the human operator, as well as serving as a training simulator.

In Sect. 2 we present the quality control status quo in vehicle production, its drawbacks and some of the approaches on its improvement. In Sect. 3 we outline how our main solution will function and focus how we ensure the reliability of its 3D visualization module. Section 4 discusses our findings and future works.

2 Status Quo in Vehicle Production Quality Control

Although rudimentary, the use of paper conformity lists (Fig. 1) is still a rather common occurrence in the automotive industry. These provide the workers with a description of all the components that compose the vehicle, so they can compare the assembled product with a previously memorized library of all possible variants each element can possess and verify if the text description correctly matches their visual inspection. A process that must be performed accurately and reliably on every quality assessment [1, 3, 7].

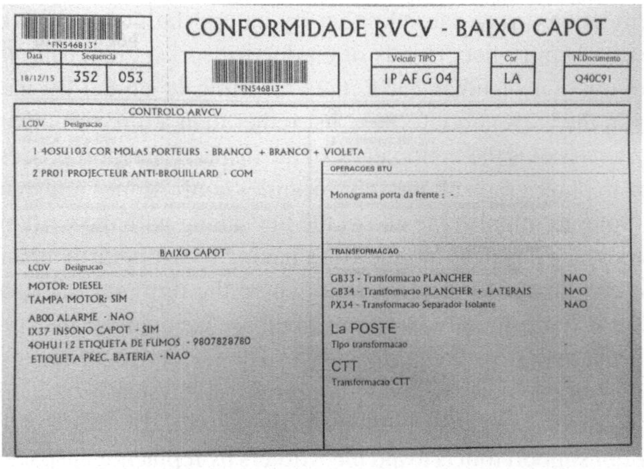
CONFORMIDADE RVCV - BAIXO CAPOT

FN546813

Data	Sequencia	
18/12/15	352	053

FN546813

Veiculo TIPO	Cor	N.Documento
IP AF G 04	LA	Q40C91

CONTROLO ARVCV

LCDV Designacao

1 4OSU103 COR MOLAS PORTEURS - BRANCO + BRANCO + VIOLETA

2 PRO1 PROJECTEUR ANTI-BROUILLARD - COM

OPERACOES BTU

Monograma porta da frente : -

BAIXO CAPOT

LCDV Designacao

MOTOR: DIESEL
TAMPA MOTOR: SIM
AB00 ALARME - NAO
IX37 INSONO CAPOT - SIM
4OHU112 ETIQUETA DE FUMOS - 9807828780
ETIQUETA PREC. BATERIA - NAO

TRANSFORMACAO

GB33 - Transfomacao PLANCHER NAO
GB34 - Transfomacao PLANCHER + LATERAIS NAO
PX34 - Transfomacao Separador Isolante NAO

La POSTE
Tipo transformacao -

CTT
Transformacao CTT -

Fig. 1. Paper conformity list.

While human flexible observation capabilities make this method tolerant to environmental and minor product variations, all workers must be regularly trained in order to keep them on-par with the constant model changes, often directly *in-situ*. A process that is particularly error prone in the initial stages of production line model updates, as the worker not only needs to increase their mental library with every update, but they also need to remember which components and combinations are now considered as discontinued. Outside of this mental toll, other important disadvantages tied to this solution are errors that result from fatigue, inattentiveness, variation in proficiency levels, etc. [1]. As for the efficiency of the paper information visualization itself, this is an inflexible method that is not individualized for the different workstations, does not provide feedback on previously detected non-conformities, be it on the current vehicle or common occurrences in that particular model configuration, nor can it exchange information with the factory's information system, among other drawbacks [3, 7].

Many automated solutions have been developed to combat these issues and improve the production quality control, such as component fault detection [8, 9], classification of surface defects [5, 10], or development of training, diagnostic and maintenance applications [3, 6, 11, 12]. Commercial technological solutions also exist in the form of companies, such as MobileDemand [13], Zebra [14] or Vuzix [15], that provide a wide collection of hardware, software and services that best fit the different needs of the different workers along the production line.

3 Methods

3.1 Design of the Quality Control Support Tool

Our work focuses on the very final workstation where, in our specific factory context, a walk-in quality inspection is performed on every vehicle solemnly by human workers, with the aid of the paper based information to detect any existing non-conformities on the vehicle's exterior and the engine labels. Outside of the already identified inefficiencies of this rather outdated method, one of the main problems with the current inspection process are verification errors caused either by natural fatigue or lack of proper consultation of the conformity list. This is often due to workers requiring the use of both hands in the completion of other tasks, thus resorting to on-the-fly memorization of the components in the current conformity list rather than a direct comparison. Another commonly reported issue is the inefficiency of the inspection report process itself, which requires workers to photograph all non-conformities conformities and manually transfer them at the computer terminal at the end of the line, along with the written report, which introduces unnecessary physical fatigue from having to temporarily abandon their post and walk to the end of the verification line, where the terminal is located. As for the training process it is done directly *in-situ* in a real scenario, under the supervision of an outside observer that monitors the performance. The factory regularly tests the workers by purposefully having vehicles with non-conformities physically built and measure the correct detection rates via the submitted inspection reports.

The goal for our support tool is to aid the workers by replacing the paper solution with a digital one that will not only free the use of their hands, but also increase their autonomy and greatly improve their performance. By providing them with a non-intrusive, interactive wearable device (e.g.: smart glasses), equipped with a camera, barcode reader, voice recognition, etc., that is wirelessly connected to the factory's network, the worker can be given access in real-time to just their section of the conformity list. This way they can directly compare the components with the assembled product, avoiding oversight errors, and send their inspection report without having to move away from their station. This not only represents an important economy of time and effort, but if the components are paired with a visual representation rather than just a text description, it removes the reliance on memorization and the errors that derive from it. This additional improvement of worker efficiency has the added benefit of reducing the skill gap between experienced and recent workers.

To further reduce human error, and bring the production line closer to the Industry 4.0 standards, we intend to take advantage of the power held by computer vision algorithms (CV) to perform the initial quality inspection of each vehicle and have it report its findings to the worker's device for final confirmation (Fig. 2). This hybrid approach guarantees the system has a higher degree of flexibility to change and eliminates any recognition errors performed by the automatic inspection system, especially during the initial learning phase of newly introduced model variants to the production line.

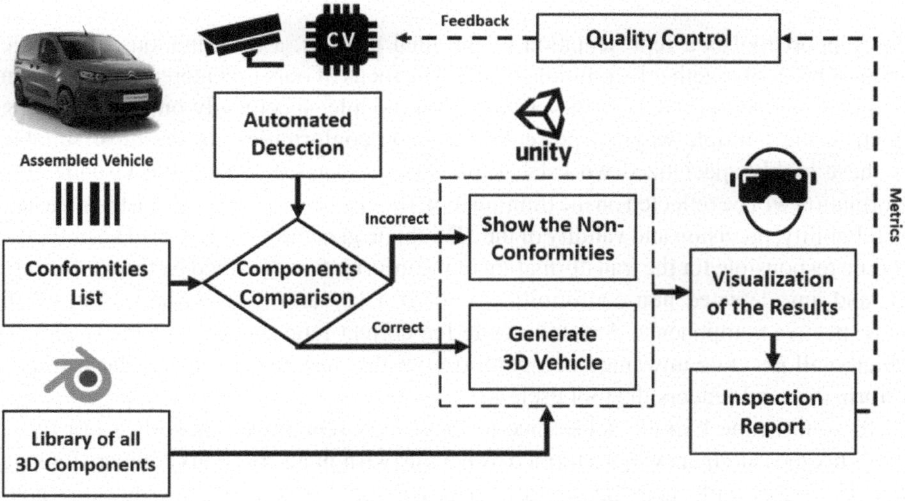

Fig. 2. Diagram of the quality control support tool.

As we can see, by reducing the former conformity list to its vehicle barcode and having its information wirelessly accessible through the factory's network, each workstation can access the database and only fetch the relevant information for their respective quality assessment. For ours we intend to have several mounted cameras set up at the entrance of the line and have the computer vision algorithm automatically detect a set of components [16, 17]. The classification results are then compared with those on the database to generate a 3D representation of the vehicle. The visualization module that performs this task uses the same database information to fetch the respective pre-modeled 3D components indicated by the barcode, with exception of any detected non-conformities, which are replaced by their own respective components. These results are then sent to the worker's wearable device for the final confirmation process, sending the inspection report to the administrative system for processing. Collected metrics, such as the detection's confidence values, correct detection rate, worker's response time, etc., are also relayed to a quality control evaluation system [3, 7], whose feedback can be used to refine the automated detection system and provide other important insights.

As for the training tool, our goal is to completely remove the cost costly and time consuming process of building real, non-conforming vehicles to test the worker's detection abilities. This is achieved by using the same visualization module of the support tool, but receiving a list of predetermined vehicle conformity lists and respective non-conforming components. This simulated environment not only allows to instantaneously generate multiple training vehicles in a short amount of time, compared to the current solution, but it can also provide immediate feedback on the worker's correct detection rate, speed, etc. and compare the results with their previously collected performance metrics or perhaps even with the ones of other workers if a gamification approach is taken to incentivize achieving better results.

3.2 Visualization Module's Reliability Test

This support tool is a representation of the final product, a combination of multiple modules brought together by multiple teams. The focus of ours is centered on the human computer interaction (HCI) of the visualization module, specifically on understanding which of the multiple ways of presenting the non-conformities are the most suitable for these highly specialized workers in this specific context. This same visualization information will be reflected on the training tool. But in order to do so we must first ensure the reliability, precision and validity of the 3D vehicle generator (codenamed kSim9), the module responsible for the transformation of the information provided by the conformity list, and any detected non-conformities, into an accurate, digital visualization of all the respective components. Any failures in the correct representation of the requested vehicle will generate unwanted non-conformities that negatively impacts the worker's performance and renders the tool useless.

To confirm the kSim9's adherence to these high reliability standards a test-retest variability measurement was performed by having two human observers compare footage of real vehicles with their 3D digital counterparts and note down any detected non-conformities. The results are crossed with the observations performed by the researcher, who can ensure the precision of the data by possessing enough insight to detect which of the mismatches resulted from the instrument itself and which are derived from human observation error (e.g.: mistaking dark grey paint for chrome). Given we are dealing with results based on qualitative observations, the Cohen's kappa was used to statistically measure the amount of agreement between one's own observations (intra-rater) and/or between different observers (inter-rater). Since it takes into account the probability of data imbalances introduced by chance, randomness or other sources or error, it serves as a robust reliability measurement index [18, 19].

3.3 Participants

The observers are two experts from the Laboratory of Observation in Sports from the University of Trás-os-Montes and Alto Douro who, although not trained in the automotive field, are highly qualified in the detection of patterns and in the use of observational instruments. They also possess an unbiased view on the components category system, as they have not been previously exposed to previous model variations, nor have had the prolonged exposure to develop the instant recognition of certain combinations.

The researcher is the leading expert on the kSim9's 3D models and software development, as well as its category system.

3.4 Development

From 3891 photos collected at the PSA Mangualde factory, of both Citroën and Peugeot commercial and family models, we identified 259 distinct components. A further investigation of the different personalization options and the mutual exclusivity between certain individual component selections and/or pack options led to the identification of 71 distinct combinations. This information was condensed into 5 categories (brand, model, version, color and customization option list), which kSim9 uses as its input to generate any given vehicle. The 3D models of all components were developed in Blender 2.80 [20] and then export into Unity3D 2019.2.11 [21], the cross-platform engine used for the software development.

Prior to the reliability test a manual category selection version of kSim9 was sent to the PSA Mangualde management to perform the face validation and confirm all possible combinations are in accordance with the product versions being assembled on their factory floor at the time of this study. The reliability test-retest was performed with a 2-week interval with a sample of 10 videos fully circling each vehicle, 5 Citroën and 5 Peugeot, with 2 commercial and 3 family models for each brand. Each represents a different vehicle combination to provide maximum observation variability, with a maximum 5% unobservability limit, as not all components can be easily inspected due to the videos' camera angles. In kSim9 each vehicle shares the same ID number as its matching video (Fig. 3), which is generated on-the-fly based on the previous and next buttons. The rest of the interface is composed by a text field that displays the current brand and model being observed and 4 rotation buttons, one for each location plane.

Fig. 3. Reliability test.

Both observers were provided an observation manual [18] of the 43 components out of the 259 that were identified as the variable, observable events (Table 1), with visual examples of their locations on the 5 different planes of the vehicle (front, back, right, left and top) and the multiple variants each can possess according to their brand (Citroen or Peugeot), model (commercial or family) and/or material the component is made of. As the goal of this test is to observe the number of non-conformities between the real and virtual vehicle, the observers were to signal each match or mismatch as 0 or 1 respectively for each individual event, which led to a total sample of 430 codes.

Table 1. Ad-hoc observable events.

Location Planes	Front	Back	Left/Right	Top
Components	Fog Lights	Top Light	Side Panels	Roof Bars
	Fog Light Embellishers	Window	Front Door Pillar	
	Grille Rim	Window Hinges	Mirror	
	Bumper Bar	Wiper	XTR Logo	
		Door Handle	Door Handles	
		Side Lights	Back Door	
		Brand Logo	Back Door Window	
		Family Logo	Curved Window Panel	
		Bumper	Back Window	
		Bumper Bar	Rail	
			Tire Covers	

The intra-rater results displayed in Table 2 are the Cohen's kappa average between the individual agreements each observer obtained, while the inter-rater results are the average agreements between the 3 possible observation pairs (observer 1 + observer 2, observer 1 + researcher, observer 2 + researcher). These results were calculated with the aid of SPSS 26.0 [22].

Table 2. Test-retest Cohen's kappa (k) results.

	k Intra-rater Mean	k Inter-rater Mean
1st Test	100%	100%
2nd Test	100%	100%

The intra-rater results achieving an agreement value of 100%, independently of the 2 weeks wait period between test-retest, means the reliability measurement of the observations was absolute, with 0% chances of non-conformities to be noted down by chance. The inter-rater results consolidate the precision of these values, as crossing multiple observations reduces the possibility of chance agreements taking place, especially when observations performed by experts on the instrument being tested are also included.

The lack of internal variability in the data means it is not necessary to apply the generalizability coefficient to measure how well these findings can be applied to a wider population. The external validity is automatically granted by these edge-case values [23].

4 Conclusions and Future Work

Considering our observers had no prior exposure to automotive observation, nor had time to form observation biases resulting from overexposure, and all vehicle combinations presented were unique, their full agreement level proves the kSim9 is a highly reliable simulator that does not introduce unknown non-conformities into its 3D models. This means we can safely progress to the next phase of the visualization study of our non-conformity quality control support tool.

Our intention is to perform a usability test, where workers will be presented with a series of different interfaces, all representing the same information from the paper conformity list specific to their workstation in a digital format, and asked to perform the same non-conformity identification tasks. However the observations will be performed first on kSim9 vehicles, to more easily collect the worker's performance metrics, shorten the testing time and reduce overall costs. The results will inform us which of the multiple interface possibilities are the most efficient prior to developing them directly on the wearable devices and perform the test *in-situ*. As the mounted camera system to collect the necessary training data is not installed, we will be using the Wizard of Oz method to simulate the results produced by the computer vision algorithm, while previously prepared QR codes will simulate the connection with the database and provide the description within the conformity list.

Outside of its integration in these two studies, the kSim9 being a fully autonomous module allows it to be applied in other teams' projects, such as generating virtual vehicle combinations to train a computer vision algorithm that attempts to identify real components based on virtual representations. It can also serve as a visual reference to mark the exact location of detected paint and other assembly or manufacturing flaws on.

Other potential uses include its integration on a pop-up visual aid in worker wearable devices, a more interactive vehicle configurator for the brands' websites, etc. As for the training simulator, its development can take place once the laboratorial and *in-situ* results are obtained.

Acknowledgements. This work was funded by Project "INDTECH 4.0 – New Technologies for smart manufacturing", n.º POCI- 01-0247-FEDER-026653, financed by the European Regional Development Fund (ERDF), through the COMPETE 2020 - Competitiveness and Internationalization Operational Program (POCI).

References

1. Piero, N., Schmitt, M.: Virtual commissioning of camera-based quality assurance systems for mixed model assembly lines. Procedia Manuf. **11**, 914–921 (2017). https://doi.org/10.1016/j.promfg.2017.07.195
2. Escobar, C.A., Morales-Menendez, R.: Machine learning techniques for quality control in high conformance manufacturing environment. Adv. Mech. Eng. **10**(2) (2018). https://doi.org/10.1177/1687814018755519
3. Gewohn, M., Beyerer, J., Usländer, T., Sutschet, G.: Smart information visualization for first-time quality within the automobile production assembly line. IFAC-PapersOnLine **51**(11), 423–428 (2018). https://doi.org/10.1016/j.ifacol.2018.08.333
4. Pfeiffer, S.: Robots, Industry 4.0 and humans, or why assembly work is more than routine work. Societies **6**(2), 16 (2016). https://doi.org/10.3390/soc6020016
5. Zhou, Q., Chen, R., Huang, B., Liu, C., Yu, J., Yu, X.: An automatic surface defect inspection system for automobiles using machine vision methods. Sensors **19**(3), 644 (2019). https://doi.org/10.3390/s19030644
6. Borisov, N., Weyers, B., Kluge, A.: Designing a human machine interface for quality assurance in car manufacturing: an attempt to address the "functionality versus user experience contradiction" in professional production environments. Adv. Hum.-Comput. Interact. **2018**, 9502692 (2018). https://doi.org/10.1155/2018/9502692
7. Gewohn, M., Beyerer, J., Usländer, T., Sutschet, G.: A quality visualization model for the evaluation and control of quality in vehicle assembly. In: 2018 7th International Conference on Industrial Technology and Management (ICITM), p. 10. IEEE, Oxford (2018). https://doi.org/10.1109/icitm.2018.8333910
8. Chauhan, V., Surgenor, B.: Fault detection and classification in automated assembly machines using machine vision. Int. J. Adv. Manuf. Technol. **90**(9–12), 2491–2512 (2016). https://doi.org/10.1007/s00170-016-9581-5
9. Pei, Z., Chen, L.: Welding component identification and solder joint inspection of automobile door panel based on machine vision. In: 2018 Chinese Control and Decision Conference (CCDC), pp. 6558–6563. IEEE, Shenyang (2018). https://doi.org/10.1109/CCDC.2018.8408283
10. Chang, F., Liu, M., Dong, M., Duan, Y.: A mobile vision inspection system for tiny defect detection on smooth car-body surfaces based on deep ensemble learning. Meas. Sci. Technol. **30**(12), 125905 (2019). https://doi.org/10.1088/1361-6501/ab1467
11. Halim, A.: Applications of augmented reality for inspection and maintenance process in automotive industry. J. Fundam. Appl. Sci. **10**(3S), 412–421 (2018)
12. Lima, J.P., et al.: Markerless tracking system for augmented reality in the automotive industry. Expert Syst. Appl. **82**, 100–114 (2017). https://doi.org/10.1016/j.eswa.2017.03.060
13. MobileDemand. https://www.ruggedtabletpc.com/industries. Accessed 27 Aug 2020
14. Zebra. https://www.zebra.com/us/en/solutions/industry.html. Accessed 27 Aug 2020
15. Vuzix. https://www.vuzix.com. Accessed 27 Aug 2020
16. Capela, S., Silva, R., Khanal, S.R., Campaniço, A.T., Barroso, J., Filipe, V.: Engine labels detection for vehicle quality verification in the assembly line: a machine vision approach. In: Gonçalves, J.A., Braz-César, M., Coelho, J.P. (eds.) CONTROLO 2020. LNEE, vol. 695, pp. 740–751. Springer, Cham (2021). https://doi.org/10.1007/978-3-030-58653-9_71
17. Khanal, S.R., Amorim, E.V., Filipe, V.: Classification of car parts using deep neural network. In: Gonçalves, J.A., Braz-César, M., Coelho, J.P. (eds.) CONTROLO 2020. LNEE, vol. 695, pp. 582–591. Springer, Cham (2021). https://doi.org/10.1007/978-3-030-58653-9_56
18. Losada, J.L., Manolov, R.: The process of basic training, applied training, maintaining the performance of an observer. Qual. Quant. **49**(1), 339–347 (2014). https://doi.org/10.1007/s11135-014-9989-7

19. Cohen, J.: A coefficient of agreement for nominal scales. Educ. Psychol. Measur. **20**(1), 37–46 (1960). https://doi.org/10.1177/001316446002000104
20. Blender. https://www.blender.org. Accessed 05 Sept 2020
21. Unity3D. https://unity.com. Accessed 05 Sept 2020
22. SPSS Software. https://www.ibm.com/analytics/spss-statistics-software. Accessed 05 Sept 2020
23. Shavelson, R.J., Webb, N.M.: Generalizability Theory: A Primer, 1st edn. Sage Publications, Inc., Thousand Oaks (1991)

Students Drop Out Trends: A University Study

Bruno Silva[1,2(✉)], E. J. Solteiro Pires[1,2], Arśenio Reis[1,2], Paulo B. de Moura Oliveira[1,2], and João Barroso[1,2]

[1] University of Trás-os-Montes and Alto Douro, Vila Real, Portugal
{epires,ars,oliveira,jbarroso}@utad.pt
[2] Vila Real, Portugal

Abstract. The dropout of university students has been a factor of concern for educational institutions, affecting various aspects such as the institution's reputation and funding and rankings. For this reason, it is essential to identify which students are at risk . In this study, algorithms based on decision trees and random forests are proposed to solve these problems using real data from 331 students from the University of Trásos-Montes and Alto Douro. In this work with these learning algorithms together with the training strategies , we managed to obtain an 89% forecast of students who may abandon their studies based on the evaluations of both semesters related to the first year and personal data.

1 Introduction

School failure and dropout have always been a primary concern for educational institutions. Detecting and predicting failure is a major social problem, and it has become imperative for education professionals to understand better why so many students fail to complete their studies. According to the survey carried out by the Portuguese Directorate-General for Education and Science Statistics (DGESS) between 2011 and 2015, the academic trajectory of all students enrolled in undergraduate courses (with a theoretical duration of 3 years) in the academic year of 2011/12 were analyzed, based on the results obtained, 29% of students had dropped out, and 14% were still enrolled after four years without having completed the course [1].

This research uses a dataset provided by the University of Trás-os-Montes and Alto Douro. It contains the personal and school data of students enrolled in the Computer Engineering plan study between 2011 and 2019. This work aims to create tree-based algorithms and random forests to predict, from the students dataset in the first year, school dropout. Ensemble algorithms (Random forests) were used because, according to Breiman [2], they are more precise and robust to noise than a single classifier. This research shows that, with sufficient data, it is possible to successfully predict school dropout, so that it is possible to take measures to combat failure.

The rest of this paper is organized as follows: Sect. 2 presents a literature review. Section 3 describes the methodology used in our experiments about applying data mining techniques on the educational data for prediction. Section 4 present and discusses the results obtained. Finally, in Sect. 5 the conclusion of this paper and propose future work are drawn.

A. Reis et al. (Eds.): TECH-EDU 2020, CCIS 1384, pp. 442–450, 2021.
https://doi.org/10.1007/978-3-030-73988-1_36

2 Literature Review

Nowadays, with the introduction of artificial intelligence and data science, together with a large volume of data available in educational databases, several tests have been carried out. J.-P Vandamme et al. [3], addressed the academic failure of first-year university students to classify it into three groups. This study was based on a questionnaire sent to 533 students in the first university year, using discriminant analyzes, neural networks, random forests, and decision trees designed to predict academic success. Vandamme says he can predict the success or failure of students with an accuracy of 80%. Another work carried out was that of Nghe et al. [4], used decision trees and Bayesian Network algorithms to predict students' performance in the 3rd year based on the data obtained in the 2nd year. Thus, like M. Azmi and I. Paris [5] with a work based on the same method. In another work, SB Kotsiantis [6], compared the prediction of six different methods, namely decision trees (DTs), support vector machines (SVM), naive bayes, artificial neural network (ANR), and with the K-NN algorithm to predict student dropout in the middle of the course. These data were based on the first assignments of 350 students. The results showed that the neural network and naive Bayes were able to predict about 80% of student dropouts. Plagge [7] studied the prediction of student retention at Columbus State University in the context of ANR. For this, he used a large amount of data from former students between 2005 and 2011. In this study, he concluded that the inclusion of the two semesters allowed to obtain significantly better results than when using only one semester, predicting a rate of 75% with more sophisticated algorithms and different training modes of the network. Dele [8] also trained a network using five years of data with various data mining techniques, both in individuals and in the data set, to understand the reasons for students academic failure. He was able to predict a retention rate of 80% for first-year students. He also produced a forecast model to identify students who are likely to drop out of the plan study before the second year. In this work, the prediction model that obtained the best results was that using the SVM. Additionally, he concluded that the data mining techniques that achieved the highest forecast rate were those that considered variables of an educational and financial nature.

Borgan et al. [9] used three years of students data of the first year of the university and compared the results of logistic regression, decision trees, ANR, and set models implemented using the SAS Enterprise Miner, and developed the final model using decision trees. However, the decision tree presents a clear disadvantage in some phases of this work. With a different approach, Márquez-Vera et al. [10], used a genetic programming algorithm with several data mining techniques to predict school failure, using real data from 670 high school students from Zacateras, Mexico. They selected the best attributes to solve with the best possible performance, paying particular attention to the students grades and applying different classification approaches to predict the student's final performance. According to Márquez-Vera, one of the most influential explanations for the cause of this problem is a model published in [11], this model suggests that the leading cause for an effective forecast is the integration of young people, social and academic in the institution, being the family history of the student, personal characteristics, and previous education a vital influence on their integration.

3 Methodologies

This section describes the prediction models used, the dataset cleaning and analyzing process. Moreover, we present our academic failure prediction model and the parameter adjustment of the prediction algorithms to improve these results.

3.1 Prediction Models

This section lists a brief explanation of Decision Trees (DT) and Random Forests (RF) algorithms.

Decision Tree. Decision trees are simple yet successful techniques for prediction and explaining the relationship between some measurements about an item and its target value. DTs are versatility for a wide variety of data mining tasks, such as classification, regression, clustering, and feature selection. However, DT can have a high predictive performance for a relative small computational.

A decision tree is a simple recursive structure for expressing a sequential classification process in which a case, described by a set of attributes, is assigned to one of a disjoint set of classes. Each leaf of the tree denotes a class. An interior node denotes a test on one or more of the attributes with a subsidiary decision tree for each possible outcome of the test. To classify a case, we start at the root of the tree. If this is a leaf, the case is assigned to the nominated class; if it is a test, the outcome for this case is determined, and the process continued with the subsidiary tree appropriate to that outcome [12].

Random Forest. A random forest (RF) is a classifier consisting of a collection of tree-structured classifiers $h(x, \theta k)$, $k = 1,\ldots, N$, where the θk are independent identically distributed random vectors and each tree casts a unit vote for the most popular class at input x [2].

The random forest classifier used for this study consists of using data selected at random to build decision trees. To classify a new dataset, each case of the datasets is passed down to each of the N trees. The forest chooses the class having the most out of N votes, for that case [13].

3.2 Train Test Split

The Sklearn model selection train test split function is handy when we only have one dataset. This function randomly divides the data into two, to use one for training and the other for testing.

3.3 Feature Importance Method

To identify the most important variables in this dataset, we use the ExtraTreesClassifier method. This method uses the entire dataset and draws random splits (decision trees) for each of the randomly selected features, and then the best division is chosen. For each tree, the importance is calculated from the impurity of the splits, obtaining a higher value where the characteristics are more important [14]. The separations are random to ensure that the model does not overfit the data.

ExtraTreesClassifier method contains a property "feature importances" that returns the weight of each variable. The importance of a feature is computed as the (normalized) total reduction of the criterion brought by that feature. It is also known as the Gini importance [15].

3.4 Grid Search

A grid search is a common approach to finding the best hyperparameters values. It is a well-known model in machine learning that finds the combination of hyperparameters values to provide the best accuracy.

3.5 Cross-Validation

In machine learning, when we work with data, we usually split the dataset into one training set and another for testing. The training data is used to train the model, and the test data is used to perform the final test, where has never seen these data. Usually, 80% of the data are used for training and 20% for the final test. In cross-validation (CV) we make some divisions in the training data. These splits are called folds, as illustrated in Fig. 1.

In k-fold cross-validation, the dataset is randomly split into k subsets (the folds) of approximately equal size.

3.6 Data Preparations

The initial dataset used in this study consists of personal data and grades from computer engineering students at the University of Trás-os-Montes and Alto Douro (UTAD) enrolled between the years 2011 and 2019.

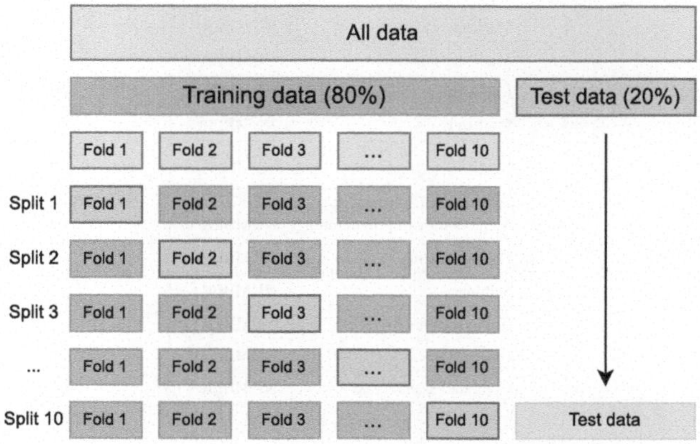

Fig. 1. Cross-validation and data splitting

3.7 Data Selection and Transformation

The original dataset is composed of a referred in Sect. 3.6 by the students' personal and academic data. Due to the lack of information on some student's personal data, these features were removed from the dataset. It was also excluded all students that have yet to finish their course and those who gave up after entering university.

Data from units of the first year study plan were extracted through the number that identifies each course unit. After this, we obtain the input variables presented in Table 1. A new binary variable was created to serve as an output of this research that corresponds to the student's dropout.

With the cleaning of the dataset, we have 331 students to be used in our study.

4 Results and Discussion

Initially, using the method referred to in Sect. 3.2, we split the dataset in two, 80% for training data where we will apply the cross-validation referred to in Sect. 3.4 with the respective forecasting algorithms for this research and another with 20% for the final test.

To get the best features, we use ExtraTreesClassifier method, as referred to in Sect. 3.3. We will use the six best features to analyze and compare with the results using all features. The results of this method are presented in Fig. 2.

In this study, cross-validation (Sect. 3.5) was used to predict and train the prediction models performance. The 10-fold approach was used because this is the ideal number, according to several kinds of researche [16]. However, for the CV to be performed with the best parameters, we use the Grid Search (Sect. 3.4) for both models.

Table 1. Data categories used for Decision Trees and Random Forest

Category	Data type
Age	NUMBER
Math analysis I	NUMBER
Math analysis II	NUMBER
Engineering introduction	NUMBER
English I	NUMBER
English II	NUMBER
Laboratory	NUMBER
Methodology of programming	NUMBER
Digital systems	NUMBER
Seminar	NUMBER
Computational logic	NUMBER
Linear algebra	NUMBER
Computer architecture	NUMBER

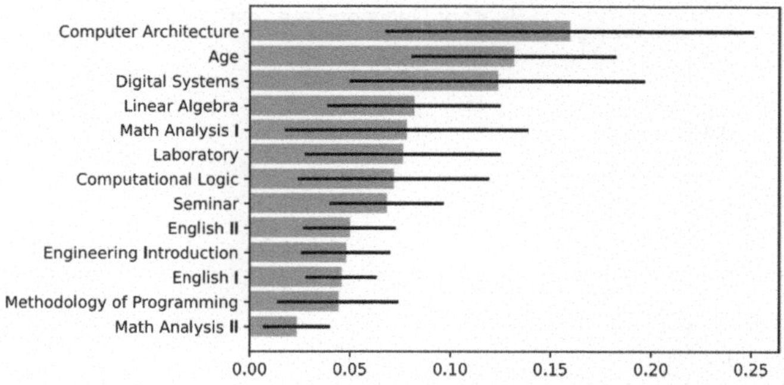

Fig. 2. Importance features obtained by ExtraTreesClassifier method

Table 2 shows the results achieved from models trained with 10-fold crossvalidation using training data. In DT, we obtained good results using the six best features, presenting an accuracy of 0.86 and a standard deviation of 0.05. In the RF, the results were even better. We obtained an accuracy of 0.89 and a standard deviation of 0.04 with the training model, which shows that these models can be accurate and consistent for the prediction of school dropout.

We compare the F1-Score (1) metric that is defined as the harmonic mean of the model's precision and recall.

Where precision is the fraction of the true positive examples among the examples that the model classified as positive and recall is the fraction of examples classified as positive, among the total number of positive examples (true positives plus false negatives).

$$F1\ Score = 2 \times \frac{Precision \times Recall}{Precision + Recall} \tag{1}$$

The results of the final test shown in Tables 3 and 4 are obtained using 20% of the initial dataset. We compared the results obtained with the six best features in Table 3 and with all the features in Table 4.

In Fig. 3 and 4 we represent the results of the metric AUROC (Area Under the Receiver Operating Characteristics) that were obtained in the final test using the six best features.

ROC is a probability curve and AUC represents the value of the area below the curve, the higher the AUC, the better the model will be in predicting dropouts as dropouts. The ROC curve is plotted with True Positive Rate (TPR) against the False Positive Rate (FPR), where TPR is on the y-axis, and FPR is on the x-axis.

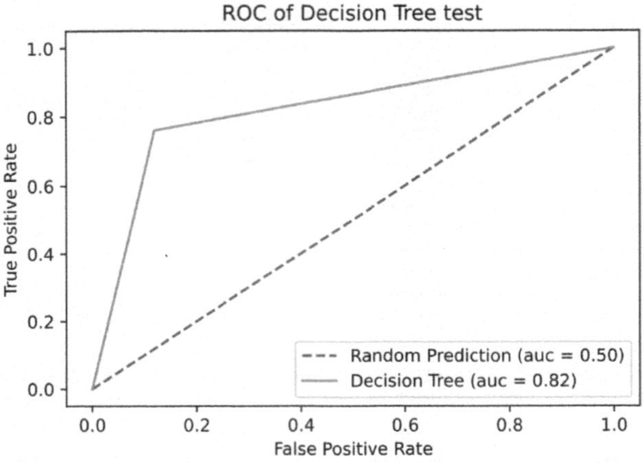

Fig. 3. ROC of Decision Tree test

Table 2. Comparison of model results using the 10-fold cross validation on training data (best six features)

	Accuracy		Precision		Recall		F1 Score		AUROC	
	Train	Test	Train	Test	Train	Test	Train	Test	Train	Test
Decision tree	0.92 ± 0.01	0.86 ± 0.05	0.91 ± 0.03	0.82 ± 0.09	0.87 ± 0.04	0.80 ± 0.09	0.89 ± 0.01	0.81 ± 0.07	0.98 ± 0.00	0.87 ± 0.08
Random forest	0.95 ± 0.01	0.89 ± 0.04	0.95 ± 0.01	0.89 ± 0.08	0.91 ± 0.02	0.83 ± 0.09	0.93 ± 0.01	0.85 ± 0.07	0.99 ± 0.00	0.94 ± 0.06

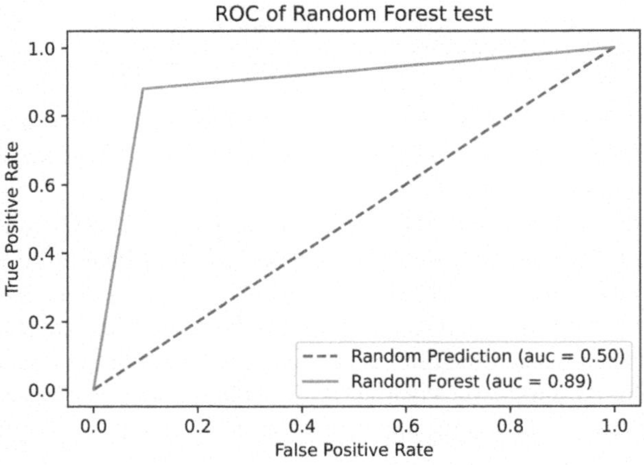

Fig. 4. ROC of Random Forest test

In this study, there were significantly better results in all metrics in the random forest model using only the six best features, with an accuracy of 0.89 in the final results, presented in Table 3.

Table 3. Comparison of model results on final test data (best six features)

	Accuracy	Precision	Recall	F1 Score	AURCOC
Decision Tree	0.83	0.79	0.76	0.77	0.82
Random Forest	0.89	0.84	0.88	0.86	0.89

Table 4. Comparison of model results on final test data (all features)

	Accuracy	Precision	Recall	F1 Score	AURCOC
Decision Tree	0.79	0.73	0.68	0.70	0.76
Random Forest	0.85	0.77	0.84	0.80	0.84

5 Conclusion and Future Work

This paper proposed a methodology to predict dropout students. This methodology aims to predict which students are at risk so that it is possible in advance to alert educational institutions so that they can correct the failing patterns. The need to eliminate these standards is global and has been a major concern for teachers and academic institutions. This methodology proposes to anticipate school drop outs in advance so that it is possible to correct students' standards at risk from their assessments of the university's first year. Algorithms based on decision trees and random forests were used to build this model. The best features among student's age and grades of the first year were used to train the model with the highest success rate. The results show that the methodology can successfully predict school dropouts, obtain better results using random forests, and with the six best features presented in this study.

As future work, more personal data of students should be considered, such as financial variables, which can have a significant impact on the prediction. These methods can also be tested with other courses, and different predictive algorithms can be used so that alternatives can be tested and compared with this study.

References

1. Engrá cia, P., Baptista, J: Percursos no ensino superior: situação após quatro anos dos alunos inscritos em licenciaturas de três anos. Lisboa: Direção-Geral de Estatísticas da Educação e Ciência (2018)
2. Breiman, L.: Random forests. Mach. Learn. **45**(1), 5–32 (2001)
3. Vandamme, J.-P., Meskens, N., Superby, J.-F.: Predicting academic performance by data mining methods. Educ. Econ. **15**(4), 405–419 (2007)

4. Thai Nghe, N., Janecek, P., Haddawy, P.: A comparative analysis oftechniques for predicting academic performance. In: 2007 37th Annual Frontiers in Education Conference-Global Engineering: Knowledge without Borders, Opportunities without Passports, pp. T2G–7. IEEE (2007)
5. Azmi, M.S.B.M., Paris, I.H.B.M.: Academic performance prediction based on voting technique. In: 2011 IEEE 3rd International Conference on Communication Software and Networks, pp. 24–27. IEEE (2011)
6. Kotsiantis, S.B., Pierrakeas, C.J., Pintelas, P.E.: Preventing student dropout in distance learning using machine learning techniques. In: Palade, V., Howlett, R.J., Jain, L. (eds.) Knowledge-Based Intelligent Information and Engineering Systems, pp. 267–274. Springer Berlin Heidelberg, Berlin, Heidelberg (2003). https://doi.org/10.1007/978-3-540-45226-3_37
7. Plagge, M.: Using artificial neural networks to predict first-year traditional students second year retention rates. In: Proceedings of the 51st ACM Southeast Conference, pp. 1–5 (2013)
8. Delen, D.: A comparative analysis of machine learning techniques for student retention management. Decis. Support Syst. **49**(4), 498–506 (2010)
9. Bogard, M., Helbig, T., Huff, G., James. C.: A comparison of empirical models for predicting student retention. White paper. Office of Institutional Research, Western Kentucky University (2011)
10. Márquez-Vera, C., Cano, A., Romero, C., Ventura, S.: Predicting student failure at school using genetic programming and different data mining approaches with high dimensional and imbalanced data. Appl. Intell. **38**(3), 315–330 (2013)
11. Tinto, V.: Dropout from higher education: a theoretical synthesis of recent research. Rev. Educ. Res. **45**(1), 89–125 (1975)
12. Quinlan, J.R.: Generating production rules from decision trees. In: ijcai, vol. 87, pp. 304–307. Citeseer (1987)
13. Pal, M.: Random forest classifier for remote sensing classification. Int. J. Remote Sens. **26**(1), 217–222 (2005)
14. Hassan, S.U., Akram, A., Haddawy, P.: Identifying important citations using contextual information from full text. In: 2017 ACM/IEEE Joint Conference on Digital Libraries (JCDL), pp. 1–8. IEEE (2017)
15. Pedregosa, F., et al.: Scikit-learn: machine learning in Python. J. Mach. Learn. Res. **12**, 2825–2830 (2011)
16. Kohavi, R., et al.: A study of cross-validation and bootstrap for accuracy estimationand model selection. In: Ijcai, Montreal, Canada, vol. 14, pp. 1137–1145 (1995)

Visualization of Scientific Phenomena for Education

Roman Rudenko[1(✉)], Arsénio Reis[1], José Sousa[2], and João Barroso[1]

[1] Universidade de Trás-os-Montes e Alto Douro & INESC TEC, Vila Real, Portugal
{ars,jbarroso}@utad.pt
[2] Universidade de Trás-os-Montes e Alto Douro, Vila Real, Portugal
jmsousa@utad.pt

Abstract. Visualization can be defined as a technique that allows us to obtain the perception of an object/event in a clear and consistent way. The use of visualization in education is a key factor to explain complex information in a clear way. Therefore, it is essential to have tools capable of visualizing various types of data. An example of a data type is the weather forecast data, which includes various atmospheric data for a given place, and allows the simulation of the atmospheric evolution. It is used for decision making in many areas, such as, agriculture, fishing, tourism, etc. Thus, it is beneficial to demonstrate the usefulness of this type of visualization to better understand the meteorological phenomena, as well as to teach scientific visualization techniques in order to enable access to information that otherwise can only be interpreted by qualified people. In this article it will be discussed the scientific visualization and its benefits to the area of meteorology, and it will be presented a case study of data visualization using the ParaView tools for meteorological data visualization and analysis. ParaView is a multiplatform tool based on the Visualization Toolkit (VTK) that provides features to process, analyze, and visualize various types of data. This study aims to present a tool for scientific visualization and to demonstrate its applications and usefulness for education.

Keywords: Visualization · Scientific visualization · Paraview · VTK toolkit

1 Introduction

Climate is the atmospheric variation over a period, in a defined geographic area [2]. According to the Intergovernmental Panel on Climate Change (IPCC), human activity has caused an increase in global warming of 1.0C above the pre-industrial estimates (before the industrial revolution period, year 1760). Considering an increase of 1.5 C between the years 2030 and 2052 [3], the impact of the increase in global warming will reflect in various living ecosystems and in the health of all living beings [2, 4], as well as in the increase of the frequency and severity of extreme atmospheric phenomena [5].

Visualization provides technology for presentation and simulation in the study areas of weather and atmosphere [6, 7]. Currently, hight quantities of data are available from multiple institutions and is used in simulations and presentations, in order to better

A. Reis et al. (Eds.): TECH-EDU 2020, CCIS 1384, pp. 451–459, 2021.
https://doi.org/10.1007/978-3-030-73988-1_37

understand the atmospheric and meteorological phenomena [7]. The usage of scientific visualization has succeeded due to the easiness of data processing by computer systems, namely, image and/or geographical presentations for information retrieval; understanding data, thus leading to new discoveries in several areas [8, 9].

Visualization is a key technology for science and its integration in the field of education is advantageous, as it provides a mean to present the information in a clear way, captivating the students' interest in an innovative area, as well as contributing to develop their computer skills. [10].

In this study, we intend to introduce ParaView as an effective visualization tool in the educational context, with a friendly user interface, which can be used to enable the presentation of information to the young population [11].

This article contains the following sections,

- **Background**, which introduces the area of scientific visualization and its application in education, as well as the tools capable of performing this type of visualization.
- **Ophelia 2017 case study**, which presents the Ophelia 2017 case study, including a methodology for the simulation of Hurricane Ophelia using Paraview, as well as the demonstration of the results obtained and its discussion.
- **Conclusion**, stating the final considerations regarding the study and perspectives for future work.

2 Background

Since the beginning of 1958, researchers tried to create models to better understand data [12], and later to better understand/predict future events based on data visualizations simulations [13, 14].

As the data usage grown, the data and the analysis became increasingly complex [15], which led to the necessity of specific software and hardware capable of processing such data. Thus, the concept of scientific visualization, information treatment and data analysis, emerged [16], with the objective to promote a new vision in the understanding and research of data, using aspects of several areas such as, computer graphics, user interface (UI) methodology, image processing, systems design and signal processing [17].

The complexity and the large amounts of data, such as climate data, requires new tools to discover, access, manipulate and visualize it. The biggest challenge is to integrate advanced visualization tools and to support workflows and high performance [18].

There are various software platforms capable of providing scientific visualization features, some of which are specific to some research areas, while others are generic. Next, there is a list of some applications (resumed in Table 1), currently used by researchers for scientific visualization, and their main characteristics:

- ParaView, it is a free software, based on the VTK architecture. It has a graphical user interface for processing large amounts of data from various sources. The meteorological data features is developed by Kitware, which provides a wide range of filters and personalized definitions [19], based on the VTK's C++ libraries [19]. It is a multi-platform tool available on popular platforms, e.g., PC, Python and WEB [20]. There is good documentation [21] available, as well as several tutorials [22] and a good support community.

- Open data Explorer (OpenDX), it is a free software, developed by IBM with the objective of graphically visualize large data sets. It requires the introduction of a visualization module to demonstrate the results in graphical formats [23]. It has documentation [23] and supports the main software platforms, e.g., Windows and Mac OS [24].
- Visualization and Analysis Platform for Ocean, Atmosphere, and Solar Researchers [25] is a software system that provides features to view large georeferenced datasets in multiple resolutions, with variations in space and time, using only the capabilities of the computer. It supports several data formats [26] and operating systems, including Windows, Mac OS and Linux [25]. Just like Paraview, it has good documentation with tutorials and an active community [27].
- Makai Voyager is a commercial software used to visualize large datasets using Level of Detail (LOD) methods in different dimensions with variations in space and time, allowing simultaneous visualization of several datasets, which can be geographic (terrain) or simulations of data entered [28]. Available on the three most popular platforms, e.g., Windows, Mac Os and Linux [29], the documentation for this system was not found.

Table 1. Overview of 4 system of scientific visualization.

Name	Platforms support	Documentation	Community
Paraview	10 platforms	Yes	Yes
OpenDX	2 platforms	Yes	No
Vapor	3 platforms	Yes	Yes
Makai Voyager	3 platforms	No	No

Of the systems previously described, the most relevant, in our opinion, is ParaView. Mainly due to its support for greater number of operating systems platforms, a more active community, and the availability of a large amount of related information.

3 The Ophelia 2017 Case Study

3.1 Introduction

The purpose of this case study is to simulate a representation of a structure in three dimensions (3D), like the one shown in Fig. 1. It is an image related to the HIRLAM model [30], representing the Hurricane Ophelia [31], a meteorological phenomenon that occurred in October 2017. This figure shows a 3d model of the Jetstream wind current, defined as winds with intensities greater than 130 km/h, that occurred in 10/16/2017.

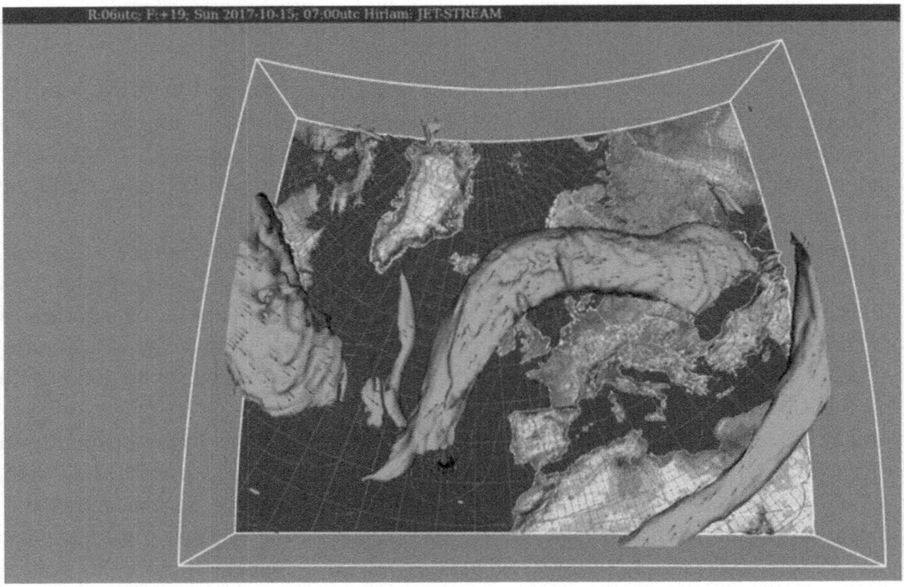

Fig. 1. HIRLAM model f the hurricane Ophelia (11 km resolution) in 3D (Weather3DeXplorer) [1].

The datasets used in the tests for this case study were obtained from the Copernicus Climate Changes Service (C3S) [32]. This service is part of the European Union's Corpernicus Program, and combines reliable climatic data, relating to the past, present and future forecasts of the world's climate [33]. The C3S platform provides access to data of various climate components in a simple way. For example, it provides information related to the time period and geographic location [34]. At the end of the access and download process, it is possible to obtain a file, in the Network Common Data Form (netCDF) format or GRIdded Binary or General Regularly-distributed Information in Binary (GRIB) format, with all the requested information, in a quickly and free of charge fashion.

3.2 Development Process

Figure 2 presents a simple flowchart that aims to facilitate and optimize the interpretation of the system, illustrating a full cycle of data visualization, from data reading, through processing and culminating in the presentation of the data to the user.

As already mentioned at the end of Sect. 3.1, obtaining the desired data from the C3S was possible by exporting the final file in netCDF forma with the representation of the previously selected meteorological data. In the next phase, there are several tasks to be performed: first, the usage of Paraview, which, when reading the file, allows us to choose a specific reader, from a set of readers, capable of interpreting it - in our specific case, we chose the "NetCDF Reader"; after the complete reading, the processing steps were followed, including the definition of the desired properties (the explanation of the properties can be found in the user manual available on the official paraview website).

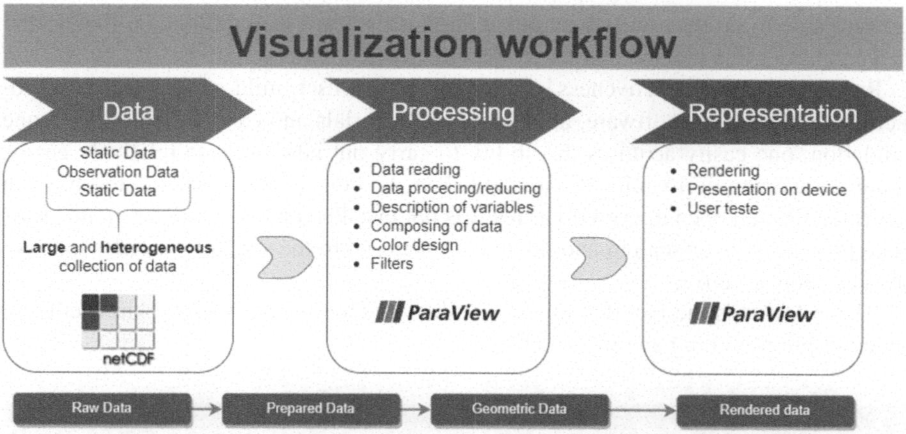

Fig. 2. Workflow for visualization of meteorological data (netCDF).

In these properties we can consider all imported variables, the amount of data and its structure. The final processing step is Filters - there is a vast number of filters that can be applied to a file. In general, in order to obtain the simulation shown in Fig. 1, it will be necessary to use four filters:

- the "C calculator" filter - in the case of wind speed, this is obtained by calculating the U and V components of the wind - in the case of most meteorological variables, calculations will not be necessary;
- the "Transform" filter to shape and scale our representation in a way more suitable for the user;
- the "Contour" filter, which allows us to represent the data by applying contour limits - in this case, wind speed, we can apply several limits in which each one is represented with a color, and the colors can be defined according to the scale desired colors (this can be imported directly into Paraview);
- the "Glyph" filter that allows the placement of arrows indicating the wind direction. The last two filters are the most important, as they are closely related to the visualization.

Finally, the great advantage of this visualization is its capacity of representation in various formats such as 2D, 3D and 4D, as well as the export the result in various types of files. We consider this system to be easy to use, allowing us to obtain very detailed simulations that can provide new knowledge in several areas.

3.3 Results

As it is possible to observe in Fig. 3 and Fig. 4, the results consists of a 3D model, from which the images were taken, very similar to Fig. 1. The data was retrieved from the C3S, which is a data source that can provide data for 37 vertical layers, spaced from 1 to 1000 hectopascal [35] and different variables. With this data, for that particular region, we were able to produce visualizations with greater detail then the one on Fig. 1, and so, we consider this method and the system as effective.

Regarding usage effectiveness, we are sure that a user, mild acquainted with productivity and graphics software, after observing tutorials and carrying out at least one simulation, one easily acquires the ability to carry out new projects relatively easily, taking an average of 15 min. When applied in the educational field, the teacher can export the file and open it, even if Paraview is not installed on his computer. In this way, it can present more appealing and interesting material to the students in order to make the class more creative.

Also relevant is the fact that this is possible to achieve even without knowledge of computer programming and free of charge.

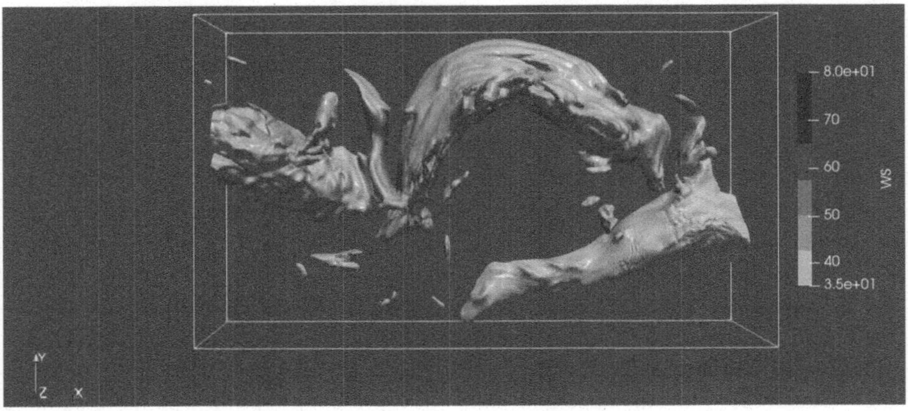

Fig. 3. Result of the simulation, view from top.

It is also possible to conclude that the usage Paraview applied to the area of education may be a tool with the potential to benefit teachers and students, since vision is one of the most important senses and, in this specific case, allows us to understand how a hurricane originates.

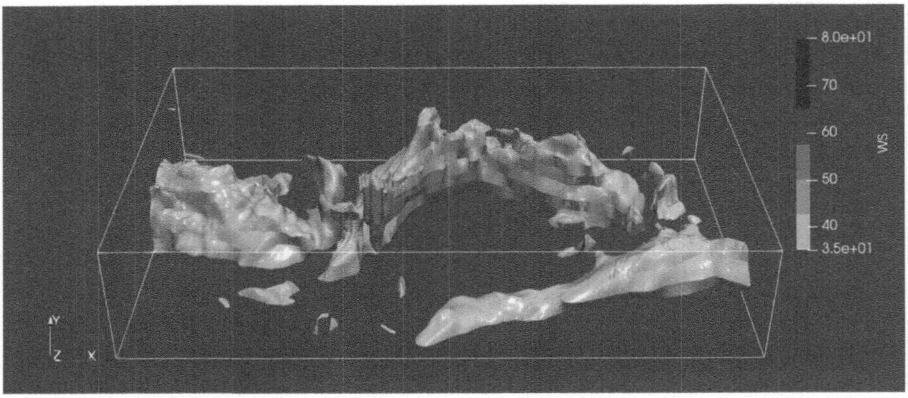

Fig. 4. Result of the simulation, seen with x-axis rotation of 60°.

4 Conclusion

In this article, the topic of visualization was approached in general terms and more specifically it was addressed the scientific visualization related to meteorological phenomena. Climate is a very important topic and its phenomena, changes and effects, e.g. hurricanes, will impact everyone's lives. The application of scientific visualization technologies aims to process and visualize large datasets, thus promoting a new way of viewing information that otherwise might be difficult to fully understand. Meteorological data, which is mostly comprised of large datasets, and scientific visualization allows us to interpret an atmospheric event and to grasp new perspectives in the area of meteorology.

The work demonstrates how the software tool a tool Paraview and the usage of some of its functionalities can be applied in several to build scientific visualization of large datasets. We evaluated Paraview's processing and visualization capabilities using the case study of Hurricane Ophelia that happened in the year 2017. For this purpose, we defined and tested a visualization workflow that can be replicated in order to achieve a scientific visualization of meteorological data stored in netCDF files. We believe that the application of innovative strategies in education allows their evolution, increasing the interest and consequent knowledge of the students.

In the future work, we consider that the next step will be to move towards virtual reality, integrating Paraview with a system capable of presenting the data in virtual reality. Such as. The Unity 3D, which is a platform for game development that provides feature for simulations in virtual and augmented reality.

Acknowledgements. This work was supported by the project "WEx-Atlantic - Weather Extremes in the Euro Atlantic Region: Assessment and Impacts" (PTDC/CTA-MET/29233/2017) funded by Fundação para a Ciência e a Tecnologia, Portugal (FCT) and Portugal Horizon2020.

References

1. KNMI: Weather3DeXplorer: Hurricane Ophelia 2017. https://projects.knmi.nl/w3dx/images/hurricane_ophelia_2017/. Accessed 08 2020
2. Shepherd, J., Shindell, D., O'Carroll, C.M.: What's the difference between weather and climate. NASA, vol. 6 (2016)
3. Change, P.C.: Global warming of 1.5 °C, World Meteorological Organization, Geneva, Switzerland (2018)
4. Pecl, G.T., Araújo, M.B., Bell, J.D., Blanchard, J., Bonebrake, T.C., Chen, I.-C., et al.: Biodiversity redistribution under climate change: impacts on ecosystems and human well-being. Science **355**(6332) (2017)
5. Schleussner, C.-F., Lissner, T.K., Fischer, E.M., Wohland, J., Perrette, M., Golly, A., et al.: Differential climate impacts for policy-relevant limits to global warming: the case of 1.5 C and 2 C. Earth Syst. Dyn. **7**, 327–351 (2016)
6. Nocke, T., Sterzel, T., Böttinger, M., Wrobel, M.: Visualization of climate and climate change data: An overview. Digit. Earth Summit Geoinform. 226–232 (2008)
7. Rautenhaus, M., Böttinger, M., Siemen, S., Hoffman, R., Kirby, R.M., Mirzargar, M., et al.: Visualization in meteorology—a survey of techniques and tools for data analysis tasks. IEEE Trans. Visual Comput. Graph. **24**(12), 3268–3296 (2017)

8. Nielson, G.: Scientific visualization. Institute of Electrical & Electronics Engineers (1997)
9. Sander, T., Freyss, J., von Korff, M., Rufener, C.: DataWarrior: an open-source program for chemistry aware data visualization and analysis. J. Chem. Inf. Model. **55**(2), 460–473 (2015)
10. Liu, Z.-J., Levina, V., Frolova, Y.: information visualization in the educational process: current trends. Int. J. Emerg. Technol. Learn. (iJET) **15**(13), 49–62 (2020)
11. Cedilnik, A., Geveci, B., Moreland, K., Ahrens, J.P., Favre, J.M.: Remote large data visualization in the paraview framework. In: EGPGV2006, pp. 163–170 (2006)
12. Bubenko, J.: From information algebra to enterprise modelling and ontologies—a historical perspective on modelling for information systems. In: Krogstie, J., Opdahl, A.L., Brinkkemper, S. (eds.) Conceptual Modelling in Information Systems Engineering, pp. 1–18. Springer Berlin Heidelberg, Berlin, Heidelberg (2007). https://doi.org/10.1007/978-3-540-72677-7_1
13. Schacter, D.L., Addis, D.R., Buckner, R.L.: Episodic simulation of future events: concepts, data, and applications. Annals of the New York Academy of Sciences (2008)
14. Sugimoto, S., Crook, N.A., Sun, J., Xiao, Q., Barker, D.M.: An examination of WRF 3DVAR radar data assimilation on its capability in retrieving unobserved variables and forecasting precipitation through observing system simulation experiments. Mon. Weather Rev. **137**(11), 4011–4029 (2009)
15. Papastefanatos, G., Stavrakas, Y., Galani, T.: Capturing the history and change structure of evolving data. Proc. DBKDA **2013**, 235–241 (2013)
16. Wald, I., Johnson, G.P., Amstutz, J., Brownlee, C., Knoll, A., Jeffers, J., et al.: Ospray-a cpu ray tracing framework for scientific visualization. IEEE Trans. Visual Comput. Graph. **23**(1), 931–940 (2016)
17. Brodlie, K.W., Carpenter, L.A., Earnshaw, R.A., Gallop, J.R., Hubbold, R.J., Mumford, A.M., et al.: Scientific visualization: techniques and applications. Springer (2012)
18. Li, W., Wang, S.: PolarGlobe: a web-wide virtual globe system for visualizing multidimensional, time-varying, big climate data. Int. J. Geograph. Inf. Sci. **31**(8), 1562–1582 (2017). https://doi.org/10.1080/13658816.2017.1306863
19. Ahrens, J., Geveci, B., Law, C.: Paraview: an end-user tool for large data visualization. In: The Visualization Handbook, vol. 717 (2005)
20. Paraview: Falvours. https://www.paraview.org/flavors/. Accessed 09 2020
21. Paraview: Documentation. https://www.paraview.org/documentation/. Accessed 09 2020
22. Paraview: The ParaView Tutorial. https://www.paraview.org/Wiki/The_ParaView_Tutorial. Accessed 09 2020
23. Thompson, D., Braun, J., Ford, R.: OpenDX: paths to visualization; materials used for learning OpenDX the open source derivative of IBM's visualization Data Explorer. Visualization and Imagery Solutions (2004)
24. Sale, J.: Visualization Tools. https://serc.carleton.edu/NAGTWorkshops/visualize04/tool_examples/opendx.html. Accessed 09 2020
25. Vapor: Downloads - Vapor 3.2.0.59c3322 documentation. https://www.docs.vapor.ucar.edu/downloads.html#installation-instructions. Accessed 09 2020
26. Huang, J., Lucash, M.S., Scheller, R.M., Klippel, A.: Visualizing ecological data in virtual reality. In: 2019 IEEE Conference on Virtual Reality and 3D User Interfaces (VR) 2019, pp. 1311–1312 (2019)
27. Vapor: Vapor 3 - Vapor 3.2.0.59c3322 documentation. https://www.docs.vapor.ucar.edu/index.html. Accessed 09 2020
28. Anderson, J.C., Andres, J.M., Davis, M., Fujiwara, K., Fang, T., Nedbal, M.: Voyager: an interactive software for visualizing large, geospatial data sets. Mar. Technol. Soc. J. **44**(4), 8–19 (2010)
29. Magazine, L.: Makai Voyager Released. https://lidarmag.com/2011/12/22/makai-voyager-released/. Accessed 09 2020

30. Lynch, P., Huang, X.-Y.: Initialization of the HIRLAM model using a digital filter. Mon. Weather Rev. **120**(6), 1019–1034 (1992)
31. Met Office Ex-Hurricane Ophelia 16 October 2017. Met Office. Met Office: Met Office, p. 11 (2018)
32. Store CCD: About C3S. https://cds.climate.copernicus.eu/about-c3s. Accessed 10 2020
33. Buchwitz, M., Reuter, M., Schneising, O., Bovensmann, H., Burrows, J.P., Boesch, H., et al.: Copernicus climate change service (C3S) global satellite observations of atmospheric carbon dioxide and methane. Adv. Astronaut. Sci. Technol. **1**(1), 57–60 (2018)
34. Buontempo, C., Hutjes, R., Beavis, P., Berckmans, J., Cagnazzo, C., Vamborg, F., et al.: Fostering the development of climate services through Copernicus climate change service (C3S) for agriculture applications. Weather Clim. Extremes **27**, 100226 (2020)
35. Wheeler, G., Deng, S., Toussaint, N., Pushparajah, K., Schnabel, J.A., Simpson, J.M., et al.: Virtual interaction and visualisation of 3D medical imaging data with VTK and unity. Healthc. Technol. Lett. **5**(5), 148–153 (2018)

Educational Proposals Using Technology to Foster Learning Competences

A Proposal for an Educational Game Platform for Teaching Programming to Primary School Students

Andreas Giannakoulas(✉), George Terzopoulos, Stelios Xinogalos, and Maya Satratzemi

University of Macedonia, 156 Egnatia Street, 546 36 Thessaloniki, Greece
{agiannakoulas,gterzopoulos,stelios,maya}@uom.edu.gr

Abstract. Programming is considered by many a core skill of the 21st century. Learning the fundamentals of coding or programming encourages children to acquire new skills, such as problem solving, logical thinking, critical thinking, and Computational Thinking (CT), and moreover to be active creators of tomorrow. There are various platforms for learning coding and programming, and in particular game-based ones, which, through the gamification process, focus on increasing learners' motivation and engagement. Most existing games are nowadays distributed through web platforms or mobile applications. Most suffer from major drawbacks, which make them difficult to use in a classroom environment, and there lack of an administrative platform does not allow the educator to assign tasks to students when at home. This paper proposes the design of an educational platform for teaching programming to primary school children. It has been designed and is to be developed on the CMX framework. The educational platform includes a web-based game for in classroom teaching, a mobile application game for outside of the classroom, and an administrative module for the teacher to organize the educational process and monitor pupils' performance. Through specific learning analytics the instructor will be able to draw conclusions on whether the students achieved the specific learning objectives, as well as understanding the educational impact that these types of games actually have on students.

Keywords: Programming · Computational thinking · Mobile learning · Primary education · Game-based learning · Educational games

1 Introduction

Computer programming is considered an essential ability for 21st century learners, and has already become a key component of many curriculums, even in primary schools. Recognizing the important role of programming, more and more actions are being carried out on a global scale by important IT personalities, in order to promote computer programming. Global events for schools, like the Hour of Code, give people the chance to see what computer science is all about. The Hour of Code is organized annually, and in 2019, more than 180 countries with millions of students participated in the 140,168

A. Reis et al. (Eds.): TECH-EDU 2020, CCIS 1384, pp. 463–475, 2021.
https://doi.org/10.1007/978-3-030-73988-1_38

events which had been registered [1]. All this suggests that programming should be an integral part of information literacy (Information and Communications Technology literacy), and recognized as a key skill for 21st century students.

Having said this, it appears that not as many students as one would have expected are interested in studying Computer Science or in learning computer programming. Code.org [2] states that a mere 11% of STEM graduates study Computer Science, and this is in spite of the fact that the situation in the work area presents an entirely different picture. According to the U.S. Bureau of Labor, projections from 2018 to 2028 show that computing occupations in the U.S will make up 67% of all new jobs in STEM fields [3].

Even so, learning programming for novice developers is considered to be difficult [4]. The difficulties that students often face in understanding the abstract concepts of programming and in composing programs which fulfill certain specifications using professional programming environments seem to be the main cause in their decreased interest and motivation [5]. With an aim to reversing this, as well as to soften students' difficulties in the learning of programming, various approaches have been proposed, such as: programming microworlds [6], educational robotics activities [7], and more recently, educational games [8].

The use of educational games in the teaching process has numerous benefits. They offer students a different kind of learning experience, allowing them to interact in an engaging learning environment that motivates them, at the same time, providing appropriate feedback, challenge and scaffolding [9, 10]. By the same token, when involved with primary school pupils, the use of educational games as a means of promoting Computational Thinking (CT) through programming becomes even more important. CT comprises a set of skills, techniques, methods, and attitudes which enable a wide range of problems to be addressed, and not only in the field of information technology [11]. When children develop CT skills, they are able to express a problem and think logically. It helps them to analyze issues and predict what might happen in the future. It also helps them explore cause and effect, and analyze how their actions or the actions of others affect a given situation. These skills can have a profound effect on children and the way they manage their relationships with those around them. Although CT can be applied to a number of other subjects, such as Mathematics or Biology [12], at present, research indicates that the most effective way to cultivate CT at an early age, is through programming activities [13]. Therefore, in recent years several educational games for learning programming have been developed. The rationale is that because games are engaging and motivational, students will be encouraged to learn programming constructs in an entertaining and potentially familiar environment [9].

Teachers' adoption of educational games plays a determining role in their becoming the main drivers of change. However, all too often they report that they do not have the necessary education (e.g. pedagogical approaches), and are, therefore, unsure as to how to incorporate educational games into their teaching. For teachers to be able to adopt games in their practices, they need to know information, such as how students play, and how they actually learn, which of the available games are better suited to their respective curricula, and the support tools that help teachers know what happens when educational games are used in the classroom. Knowing how students play, learn and improve their skills is a key factor in educational games being more widely adopted; it would make it easier for educators to accept them, allowing them to "sneak a look" into the learning process, which will facilitate their intervention when required [14].

This paper proposes an educational platform that aims to enhance teaching programming skills to primary school children starting from the age of 8, since according to a recent study [15], early intervention can have compounding effects later in life, influencing both personal and academic outcomes. The platform combines web and mobile technologies, and is a complete tool for the teacher, which can be used inside and outside the classroom.

The structure of this paper is as follows: In Sect. 2 an overview of related work is given, while in Sect. 3 the platform architecture and its components are described, along with the framework and the basic features of the games of the platform. Finally, in Sect. 4, the conclusions, as well as the future steps of this study are presented.

2 Related Work

In recent years, several educational games that aim to teach basic programming concepts and cultivate CT aspects to novice programmers have been developed [16, 17]. The most common way of distributing such games, nowadays, is mainly via web platforms or through mobile device applications. Usually, these games are classified as "puzzle games", the majority of which actually implement the same scenario, where the player must program the moves of the character on a path [9]. There are, of course, cases [18–20] where other types of programming activities are offered. As far as the educational content regarding programming is concerned, most games support sequences, loops, if statements and functions [21], while some support activities related to Object-oriented programming (OOP) [18, 22, 23]. Furthermore, most of these games support the cultivation of CT skills, such as algorithmic thinking, decomposition, pattern recognition and modularity, abstraction and generalization [16]. Regarding the programming environment, the games usually offer a programming editor where the player writes a program using blocks, like in Scratch, in this way, allowing students to practice programming without making syntax errors or having to memorize commands [8].

However, there are features missing from these games, which include: support for creating customized lesson plans, online classrooms, and monitoring students' progress through Learning Analytics [24] that can effectively assist instructors and students. There are two aspects concerning "traditional" learning analytics – the teacher/instructor side and the student side [14]. Regarding the latter, the main aim is to let students know how they are doing in the educational game. Self-assessment and motivation are important elements in the educational process, and an educational game should use data analysis techniques to let the students anticipate their potential outcomes by comparing their achievements with other students. Regarding the former, instructors need to trace the progress both in order to adjust the speed and the contents of their course through the educational game. These analyses may help instructors to identify those students who are experiencing difficulties, and perhaps even offer them specific remediation actions. Furthermore, the availability of tracking the educational process is one of the key elements which teachers consider when selecting applications to be used in their classrooms.

In Table 1 we summarize the learning analytics supported by seven games presented in a recent study [16], which reviews 22 educational games or platforms that aim to cultivate CT through teaching computer programming concepts to primary school students. Since the educational platform we propose in this paper focuses on primary school pupils, we selected only the games that support learning analytics. The games Kodetu [25], BOTS [26] and Pirate Plunder [27] collect learning analytics concerning various user interactions in logs, while CodeMonkey [23], Rapid Router [21] and Kodable [19], provide an online dashboard in order to make analytics available to the teacher. In 2018, Run Marco [28], provided a dashboard which allowed students' progress in the game to be monitored in real time, however, it should be noted that the game no longer supports this feature. Learning analytics can help teachers to effectively monitor students' progress, as well as investigate both user behavior and the ways in which these games facilitate learning [28], and more importantly, support teachers in evaluating students' gained knowledge [24]. The learning analytics that are available not only to the teacher but also to the student have been indicated with an asterisk.

Table 1. Games with learning analytics

Learning analytics	Games						
	Kodetu	BOTS	Pirate Plunder	CodeMonkey	Rapid Router	Runmarco	Kodable
Time needed to solve a challenge – level	√		√		√*	√	
Code length (number of blocks)	√						
Code depth (number of nests in control structures)	√						
Number of code changes in the workspace	√						
Number of attempts made for each participant and challenge (attempts per level)	√		√				√
Addition and removal of new code (blocks)		√	√				
Deletion and un-deletion of original code (the first buggy code given to the player to correct it)		√					
The last time that the player finished a level				√			
Number of stars (denotes the quality of the solution) player won (per level)				√*		√*	√
Exact time player finished the level							√

Finally, the educational programming games or tools that are available do not support adaptive learning and behave in the same way, without taking into account the particular characteristics of the user, such as their age, previous knowledge, or their progress in the game [29]. As a result, the learning experience is not attractive to some users.

At the same time, in recent years there has been a plethora of educational applications for tablets, with the aim of introducing children to programming. This is because children are more familiar with tablets than computers. Research shows that almost 97% of children have used mobile devices before they are one year old [30]. Compared to computers, tablets are relatively inexpensive devices, easy to use, and thus, have now become common tools in everyday life. Furthermore, their processing power, as well as their wireless capabilities have increased significantly over the years. Portability is a key feature of tablets, allowing them to be used indoors and outdoors. Studies show that mobile devices can enhance educational impact when used in the classroom, since the overall result of using mobile devices is better than when using desktop computers or nothing at all [31, 32].

Interestingly enough findings have come from a study [17], where the authors explored whether mobile applications have a proven educational effectiveness based on related scientific research. The study concludes that most mobile applications have never been evaluated, thus, their educational value cannot be confirmed. Furthermore, most mobile applications support only sequential discovery of knowledge, meaning that students will have to complete one level and then move on to the next, hence there is no personalized learning and all students have access to the same information in the same order. The study also found that there was a complete lack of learning analytics.

At present, only a few games, such as CodeCombat, CodeMonkey, Kodable and Rapid Router are embedded into a broader learning platform, providing extensive support through a series of ready-made lesson plans that include activities based on game philosophy [16]. It must be noted that online platforms that host educational content, students' and instructors' profiles, communication logs, as well as other personal information, must be carefully reviewed by schools in order to ensure that privacy and security policies apply.

Since web and mobile applications for programming suffer from significant drawbacks, this study proposes the development of an educational platform, which aims to strengthen the teaching of computer programming, and its integration into the school curriculum. Compared to other solutions, the proposed platform combines a Web Game to be used inside the classroom environment, a Mobile Game to be played by each student at home, and an Instructor's Dashboard to manage the educational process. For adaptation to be incorporated into the game, various user's behavior statistics will be recorded in a database. For example, the amount of time a player spends solving an activity and its' deviation from the average time of other players; or the number of changes to the workspace and the number of blocks moved, which could indicate whether the player is having difficulties and needs help with the activity, so that the next mission is adjusted accordingly [25]. Our intention is that it will be easy for schools to install and implement the platform, and that it is available free of charge.

Various challenges need to be addressed in order for games to be accepted as reliable and powerful educational tools. Some of these include filling the gap caused by the lack of educational material, i.e., games should be accompanied by lesson plans, evaluation sheets, etc.; inadequate knowledge of how students interact while playing an educational game, and generally tools are needed which will improve our understanding of the educational impact that games actually have on students. These challenges must be overcome if we are to make full use of the potential of games as learning tools [14]. In the proposed platform, an attempt is made to meet the aforementioned challenges by providing educational material and guidance to teachers regarding the game's usage in class and at home, as well as evidence on the effectiveness of the game in achieving the articulated educational goals through the incorporated learning analytics.

3 Design of the Educational Game Platform

3.1 Platform Architecture

The aim of the platform is to provide a tool which the instructor can use free of charge, inside and outside the classroom. The platform provides support for distance learning by allowing the teacher to assign tasks to students, who for various reasons cannot be physically present at school. In today's society, this is an important feature, since as a result of the Covid-19 pandemic, some 1.6 billion learners (91.3% of total learners), who were enrolled at the pre-primary, primary, lower-secondary, and upper-secondary levels of education, as well as at tertiary education levels, were thus affected [33].

Our proposed platform incorporates three different modules. The first module is the Web Game (Module 1) to be used inside the classroom setting. In the Web Game, the player guides a character through maze-like puzzles, designed on a grid-based environment with the intention of reaching a particular destination. To do this, the player joins visual code blocks that represent specific commands, affecting the main character's behavior. The game's levels are to be organized into sections, which will cover the teaching of specific programming concepts. Depending on the programming concepts the instructor has scheduled to teach, certain levels of the game will be used. To complete the mission at each level, the player must use specific command blocks corresponding to specific programming structures, such as "sequence commands", "loops", "if-statements" etc., in an authentic real-life situation (for example, escape from a maze) that implements the game's scenario. As the player moves to the next levels of the game, more complex commands are unlocked, gradually introducing them to new programming concepts. At the beginning of each lesson, the instructor introduces students to a specific programming concept by presenting an example which requires familiar behavior, such as a situation where a series of steps have to be followed, or repeated or some decisions made. Students will then be asked to play the game at specific levels in order to understand the particular programming concept. The role of the instructor in this phase will be ancillary, offering help to those students who might be having difficulties at a level. At the end of each section there will be a debriefing session, in which the instructor will help students understand the implicit knowledge they used to solve the activities of the game. The Web Game will use Blockly [34], a visual programming language developed by Google, in conjunction with Phaser [35], a desktop and mobile HTML5 open source game framework. Blockly is a JavaScript library that adds a visual code editor to web and mobile apps. The Blockly editor uses interlocking, graphical blocks to represent code concepts like variables, logical expressions and loops. It allows users to apply programming principles without having to worry about syntax [34]. Blockly can also export blocks to many programming languages, including JavaScript, Python, PHP, Lua and Dart. The library is compatible with all major browsers: Chrome, Firefox, Safari, Opera, and IE and has been translated into over 40 languages. Additionally, Blockly comes with a large number of predefined blocks and supports the creation of new custom blocks. Another major advantage of Blockly is that there are no 3rd party dependencies in its code, and everything is open source. The combination of Blockly and Phaser has also been used in BattleBot [36], a visual programming game that is expected, according to the authors, to help provide a simplification method in understanding the basic logic of programming.

Since most computer labs in schools are equipped with desktops or laptops with various operating systems, the Web Game should be able to run through browsers regardless of the operating system used. It should be noted that the purpose of the Web Game is to assist the instructor in the teaching process, and in most cases, small groups of students tend to share the same computer.

The second module of the platform is the Mobile Game (Module 2) to be played by each student at home. It is the means whereby students practice and familiarize themselves with the programming concepts taught during their computer lab lesson at school. The Mobile Game has the same scenario as the Web Game, with a variety of additional levels and activities, which are expected to support students in understanding the programming concepts and acquiring CT skills. All the extra material of the Mobile Game will be organized by the teacher, who will have the ability to assign personalized levels depending on the educational needs of each student. The Mobile Game will be developed as a tablet application, since a growing number of pupils now possess such a device and are fully familiar with it. Needless to say, using a mobile application, these young students will not only complete their homework but also be learning by playing and having fun. The Mobile Game will also be implemented using Google Blockly and Phaser, since both of these support the development of applications which can be run in a Web environment, such as a Web browser, as well as in a Mobile environment.

The third module of the platform is the Instructor's Dashboard (Module 3). Through a web environment, the instructor is able to fully manage the educational process and design the levels of the game for each lesson on the basis of the material and concepts needed to be taught in the class. Additionally, the instructor creates material and activities as levels of the game, to be assigned as students' homework. The content will be adapted to the student's progress as they play the game. The dashboard includes a level editor, through which the instructor is be able to design a custom game level and choose the available programming blocks needed to successfully complete each level. Custom game levels can cover individual student's educational needs.

Furthermore, the Instructor's Dashboard presents meaningful statistics on students and their progress, including information on difficulties students face in solving each level (showing the attempts a student needed in order to correctly complete each level). The Instructor's Dashboard will be hosted on the school server, thus, students' personal data will not be available to third parties as it will be managed by the classroom teacher. The dashboard will use PHP and CSS to create the environment, and all information will be stored on a MySQL database. As shown in Table 1, there are only a few games offering a set of -albeit limited– learning analytics, which in their majority are geared to teachers, enabling them to draw conclusions about students' progress; but they are not also available to students. Learning analytics are usually available through the logs, while some games, such as CodeMonkey, Kodable and Rapid Router, give teachers access to a dashboard. In our proposed model, we intend to take into account the knowledge gathered thus far from related work with the intention to offer a more effective Dashboard for instructors, while at the same time provide valuable information to students. Figure 1 shows the platform architecture.

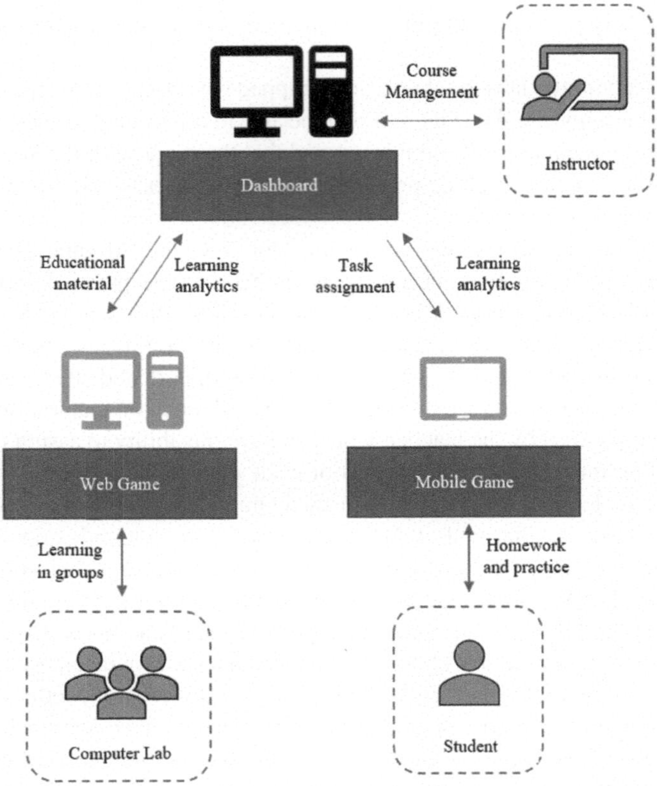

Fig. 1. Platform architecture.

3.2 Main Features of the Game

The game's design, both the web and mobile versions, is based on the CMX Design framework, proposed for the development of educational games for the teaching and learning of programming [37]. The CMX Design framework includes concepts that should be included by designers of any educational game whose objective is to teach computer programming concepts. It offers a substantial amount of detail forming a good basis for the design of programming games, while avoiding arbitraries [38]. In accordance with CMX, the most notable concepts that define the game's design are presented below.

Infrastructure. Infrastructure is an essential part of game design, and refers to the architecture and technical requirements which need to be taken into consideration to ensure proper game performance. The characteristics of the proposed educational platform related to this parameter of CMX have been analyzed in Sect. 3.1.

Learning Objectives. The proposed educational platform aims to teach basic programming concepts, as well as developing CT skills in primary school pupils from the age of 8. As mentioned in Subsect. 3.1, the player is introduced to specific programming concepts using code blocks that correspond to specific programming structures, such as "sequence commands", "loops", "if-statements" etc., in an authentic real-life situation. Furthermore, the activities which the pupils are called on to perform help them to develop CT skills. More specifically, they acquire "algorithmic thinking" as they need to formulate algorithms in order to complete the assigned tasks. "Pattern recognition" and "modularity" activities help pupils recognize the existence of patterns in a task and represent it using loops in order to reduce repetitive code. Moreover, through functions students are introduced to "abstraction and generalization", as well as "decomposition" through activities where the students have to break down an algorithm into smaller parts [16]. The learning objectives of the proposed educational platform are to be synchronized with those of the curriculum set by the Hellenic Ministry of Education for the subject of Informatics for primary education. By using the proposed platform, students should be able to:

- run ready-made programs that will be given to them;
- execute simple commands in a programming environment;
- analyze a problem in individual simpler sub-problems;
- recognize the operation of ready-made programs given to them;
- seek the optimal solution in a program;
- use variables, selection structure and iteration structure in the programs they develop;
- design, develop, and test a set of commands and procedures; and
- apply test and debug techniques to the programs they create.

Through specific learning analytics the instructor is able to see whether the students achieved the specific learning objectives or not. As the learning objectives have to do with computer programming, the proposed educational platform would also be able to cover curricula from other countries. Initially, the platform is to be available in Greek, but later on it will also be available in English.

Pedagogy. Students will initially engage in specific game activities that have been assigned by the teacher (Module 1), which help them to gain new knowledge regarding the programming concepts being taught. Following this, using the mobile application at home (Module 2), pupils will be engaged in activities set by the teacher (Module 3), leading them to better understand the taught programming concepts, as well as acquiring particular CT skills. The educational content is organized in specific educational units, with a substantially large number of levels for each unit; this is in contrast to most existing environments which provide only a limited number of levels. As the use of scaffolding features is considered one of the most effective ways to integrate constructivism into educational games [38], special emphasis is given to supporting students throughout their interaction with the game. This will be done through the use of various mechanisms, such as displaying explanatory messages, hints or visual and audio cues, or even offering levels that are actual tutorials. In this way, students will be supported throughout their interaction and will feel safer while becoming familiar with the new environment [24]. Furthermore, appropriate learning analytics that are collected during the gameplay, will allow the adaptation of game difficulty according to the level of the student's progress.

Learning Outcomes. Since the platform's target audience is primary school pupils, the programming concepts covered by the game are: *sequence commands, loops, if statements, procedures* or *functions* and *variables.* At present, only a few games, such as CodeCombat or Rapid Router cover all of these programming concepts [16]. As regards CT, the games support the cultivation of skills such as: *algorithmic thinking, decomposition, pattern recognition* and *modularity, abstraction* and *generalization* [7]. All these CT skills can be cultivated through the programming activities incorporated in the game, as described in the analysis of its learning objectives.

User. The system has two types of users: IT teacher and student. The proposed educational platform is intended to be used by primary school pupils from 8 years old onwards, and no prior computing knowledge is required.

Scenario. It is essential for children to first understand the logic of programming, before they attempt it. The game implements a scenario where the player guides a character to reach a destination through maze-like puzzles, which have been designed on a grid-based environment. We believe that the scenario of the game needs to have a connection to everyday activities so that children can relate to the game's activities. The scenario has been designed to recreate an attractive virtual world, consisting of an interesting character who has to successfully complete a clearly defined mission at each level. Since the scenario in the majority of programming games for young children usually involve the player having to program the movements of the hero on a path [16], the proposed educational platform offers the player a variety of missions. In this way, we believe the player has a more active interaction with the virtual world, thus not only increasing pupils' interest but also motivating them to carry out programming activities through play. Moreover, the choice of two or more available avatars, will increase the likelihood of the young player identifying with their main character in the game. In order to motivate pupils to play the game and to enhance the game's entertainment value, the player is called to defend themselves against enemies, or avoid them, as well as to either collect or avoid certain obstacles in their path.

Game Achievement: The students will be able to access their progress and achievements in the game through a mechanism which shows the relevant information. In this way, they can know to what extent they have been able to complete the goals of a particular educational unit. Data and analytics are to be collected during gameplay and transmitted to the school server which hosts the Instructor's Dashboard. Thus, through these valuable learning analytics on the Instructor's Dashboard, the teacher is able to monitor students' progress and their in-game behavior [14, 24], such as the completion time of each level, the number of retries etc.

Activities. The game includes a visual editor (programming area) based on Blockly, where the player solves a task, through writing a program by linking visual code blocks. The visual programming language of Blockly, as previously mentioned, gives students the chance to practice programming without having to worry about making syntax errors or having to memorize commands [8, 34].

4 Conclusions and Future Work

There is a plethora of applications that can assist the teaching of computer programming inside and outside the classroom. A few studies have evaluated these applications and concluded that not only can they help students to acquire programming skills, but also to enhance their computational thinking abilities, which nowadays is important as much in the field of informatics as in life generally. In this study, an educational game platform that can be used inside and outside the classroom by young students, from as early as eight years old, is presented. The platform combines three distinct modules: a management platform for the teacher to assign pupils tasks; a web-based game for use within the classroom; and a mobile application for pupils to play at home. The platform can also be used for distance learning, which is of growing importance nowadays.

The educational game has been designed and is to be developed on the CMX framework, and contain features not offered by existing applications. Furthermore, the platform can be installed on school servers and ensure that the students' and the teachers' data is not shared with third parties, thus ensuring both privacy and security.

The next step of the research is the implementation of the web-based game and the Instructor's Dashboard. These two modules will, then, be piloted and evaluated in a classroom setting by teachers and pupils in a number of primary schools. The evaluation findings will be used to make any necessary changes. In the following stage, the mobile application will be developed and the platform will again be piloted and evaluated by pupils and teachers. Overall, our intention is to make students, from their initial contact with the school environment, have a positive experience in learning programming through having fun while playing games.

References

1. Hour of Code Homepage. https://hourofcode.com/. Accessed 13 June 2020
2. Code.org, Why Computer Science? https://code.org/promote. Accessed 13 June 2020
3. U.S. Bureau of Labor Employment Statistics. https://www.bls.gov/emp/tables/emp-by-detailed-occupation.htm. Accessed 13 June 2020
4. Zaharija, G., Mladenović, S., Boljat, I.: Introducing basic programming concepts to primary school children. Proc.-Soc. Behav. Sci. **106**, 1576–1584 (2013)
5. Brusilovsky, P., Calabrese, E., Hvorecky, J., Kouchnirenko, A., Miller, P.: Mini-languages: a way to learn programming principles. Educ. Inf. Technol. **2**(1), 65–83 (1997)
6. Xinogalos, S., Satratzemi, M., Dagdilelis, V.: An introduction to object-oriented programming with a didactic microworld: objectKarel. Comput. Educ. **47**(2), 148–171 (2006)
7. Atmatzidou, S., Demetriadis, S.: Advancing students' computational thinking skills through educational robotics: a study on age and gender relevant differences. Robot. Auton. Syst. **75B**, 661–670 (2016)
8. Vahldick, A., Mendes, A.J., Marcelino, M.J.: A review of games designed to improve introductory computer programming competencies. In: Frontiers in Education Conference (FIE), pp. 1–7. IEEE, Madrid (2014)
9. Kazimoglu, C., Kiernan, M., Bacon, L., Mackinnon, L.: Learning programming at the computational thinking level via digital game-play. Proc. Comput. Sci. **9**, 522–531 (2012)
10. Laporte, L., Zaman, B.: Informing content-driven design of computer programming games: a problems analysis and a game review. In: Proceedings of the 9th Nordic Conference on Human Computer Interaction (NordiCHI 2016), p. 10, Article 61. ACM, New York (2016)

11. Wing, J.M.: Computational thinking. Commun. ACM **49**(3), 33–35 (2006)
12. Hsu, T., Chang, S., Hung, Y.: How to learn and how to teach computational thinking: suggestions based on a review of the literature. Comput. Educ. **126**, 296–310 (2018)
13. Moreno-León, J., Román-González, M., Robles, G.: On computational thinking as a universal skill: a review of the latest research on this ability. In: 2018 IEEE Global Engineering Education Conference EDUCON, pp. 1684–1689 (2018)
14. Freire, M., Serrano-Laguna, Á., Iglesias, B.M., Martínez-Ortiz, I., Moreno-Ger, P., Fernández-Manjón, B.: Game learning analytics: learning analytics for serious games. In: Spector, M., Lockee, B., Childress, M. (eds.) Learning, Design, and Technology, pp. 1–29. Springer, Cham (2016)
15. McCoy, D., et al.: Impacts of early childhood education on medium- and long-term educational outcomes. Educ. Res. **46**(8), 474–487 (2017)
16. Giannakoulas, A., Xinogalos, S.: A review of educational games for teaching programming to primary school students. In Kalogiannakis, M., Papadakis, S. (eds.) Handbook of Research on Tools for Teaching Computational Thinking in K-12 Education, pp. 1–30. IGI Global (2020)
17. Terzopoulos, G., Satratzemi, M., Tsompanoudi, D.: Educational mobile applications on computational thinking and programming for children under 8 years old. In: 13th International Conference on Interactive Mobile and Communication Technologies and Learning, Thessaloniki, Greece (2019)
18. Korpi, J.: Teaching programming to children through games (Master of Science Thesis), Tampere University of Technology (2014)
19. Kodable homepage. www.kodable.com. Accessed 26 June 2020
20. Lotfi, E., Mohammed, B.: Teaching object oriented programming concepts through a mobile serious game. In: Proceedings of the 3rd International Conference on Smart City Applications (SCA '18), pp. 1–6, Article 74. Association for Computing Machinery, New York (2018)
21. Rapid Router homepage. https://www.codeforlife.education/. Accessed 26 June 2020
22. CodeCombat homepage. https://codecombat.com/. Accessed 26 June 2020
23. CodeMonkey homepage. https://www.playcodemonkey.com. Accessed 26 June 2020
24. Malliarakis, C., Satratzemi, M., Xinogalos, S.: Integrating learning analytics in an educational MMORPG for computer programming. In: Proceedings of the 14th IEEE International Conference on Advanced Learning Technologies (IEEE ICALT), Athens, Greece, 7–9 July 2014, pp. 233–237. IEEE Computer Society Press (2014)
25. Eguíluz, A., Guenaga, M., Garaizar, P., Olivares-Rodríguez, C.: Exploring the progression of early programmers in a set of computational thinking challenges via clickstream analysis. IEEE Trans. Emerg. Top. Comput. **8**(1), 256-261 (2017)
26. Liu, Z., Zhi, R., Hicks, A., Barnes, T.: Understanding problem solving behavior of 6–8 graders in a debugging game. Comput. Sci. Educ. **27**(1), 1–29 (2017). https://doi.org/10.1080/08993408.2017.1308651
27. Rose, S.P., Habgood, J., Jay, T.: Pirate plunder: game-based computational thinking using scratch blocks. In: Proceedings of the 12th European Conference on Games Based Learning. Academic Conferences and Publishing International Limited, pp. 556–564 (2018)
28. Runmarco homepage. https://runmarco.allcancode.com/. Accessed 13 Sep 2020
29. Eguíluz, A., Garaizar, P., Guenaga, M.: An evaluation of open digital gaming platforms for developing computational thinking skills. In: Simulation and Gaming. InTech (2018)
30. Kabali, H.K., et al.: Exposure and use of mobile media devices by young children. Pediatrics **136**(6), 1044–1050 (2015)
31. Sung, Y.T., Chang, K.E., Liu, T.C.: The effects of integrating mobile devices with teaching and learning on students' learning performance: A meta-analysis and research synthesis. Comput. Educ. **94**, 252–275 (2016)

32. Papadakis, S., Kalogiannakis, M., Zaranis, N.: The effectiveness of computer and tablet assisted intervention in early childhood students' understanding of numbers. an empirical study conducted in Greece. Educ. Inf. Technol. **23**(5), 1849–1871 (2018). https://doi.org/10.1007/s10639-018-9693-7
33. UNESCO, School closures caused by Coronavirus (Covid-19). https://en.unesco.org/covid19/educationresponse. Accessed 13 June 2020
34. Blockly Homepage. https://developers.google.com/blockly. Accessed 13 June 2020
35. Phaser Homepage. https://phaser.io/. Accessed 13 June 2020
36. Noval, B.A., Safrodin, M., Hakkun, R.Y.: Battlebot: logic learning based on visual programming implementation in multiplayer game online. In: 2019 International Electronics Symposium (IES), Surabaya, Indonesia, pp. 138–142 (2019)
37. Malliarakis, C., Satratzemi, M., Xinogalos, S.: Designing educational games for computer programming: a holistic framework. Electron. J. e-Learn. **12**(3), 281–298 (2014)
38. Malliarakis, C., Satratzemi, M., Xinogalos, S.: CMX: the effects of an educational MMORPG on learning and teaching computer programming. IEEE Trans. Learn. Technol. **10**(2), 219–235 (2017)

Future Teachers Choose Ideal Characteristics for Robot Peer-Tutor in Real Class Environment

Anna-Maria Velentza[1,2(✉)], Sofia Pliasa[1,2], and Nikolaos Fachantidis[1,2]

[1] School of Educational and Social Policies, University of Macedonia, Thessaloniki, Greece
{spliasa,nfachantidis}@uom.edu.gr

[2] LIRES Robotics Lab, University of Macedonia, Thessaloniki, Greece

Abstract. In the coming years teachers are going to use robots as learning tools in education because of their beneficial outcome in children's practical and cognitive skills even in special education. Apart from using social educational robots as a tool, teachers are expected to collaborate with them in many ways, even as a peer teacher in the learning procedure and get involved into the robots' design process. Although those procedures are progressive, in many cases, teachers cannot provide very useful feedback because they do not have prior experience with robots operating within the target environment. Therefore, it is important to identify the best way to accurately identify the teachers' needs. In this paper, we introduce the idea of actively involve the future teachers in the design process by having them watching a robot performing the target task. Our target is to find the ideal robot-tutor characteristics from the teachers' perspective in order to collaborate with it and we compare the future teachers' opinions about the ideal characteristics (Appearance, Intelligence, Emotional Expression etc.), when they are actually taught by a social robot and when they are taught by a human tutor. Participants had statistically significant different opinions about the robot's characteristics after each class, such as their preference for machinery robots after the human-class which is non-existent after the robot-class. Our results clearly suggest that teachers as robots' future users should interact with a similar robot performing the target task, in order to be able to accurately select the target robot characteristics.

Keywords: Educational robots · Robot tutor · Pre-service teachers · Social robot design · Special education · Real class environment

1 Introduction

Educational robots are getting involved more and more in education as, for example, trainers and teachers. One of the main challenges of this new trend will be to match their social behaviour, style, appearance and interaction with the educational demands and the actual users' needs. Educational robots are also widely used in special education. The use of interactive social robots can improve children's behaviour while the robot- assisted treatment with imitation games encourage the response inhibition, cognitive flexibility and children's' joint attention [1]. Educational robots and robotic tools help special education students to practice and learn practical and cognitive skills, like collaboration and

A. Reis et al. (Eds.): TECH-EDU 2020, CCIS 1384, pp. 476–491, 2021.
https://doi.org/10.1007/978-3-030-73988-1_39

even gain self-confidence [2]. The use of Anthropomorphic Robot Intelligent ('AnRI') mobile robots have been proven successful in Special Education [3] and Kaspar robot can perform autonomous interactive tasks with children with special needs in a safe, useful and reliable way since 2005 [4].

Similarly, for students in typical education, social robots shown to achieve similar tutoring skills with human tutors on restricted tasks and are able to increase student's affective and cognitive outcomes [5]. Neumann believes that children inter-actions with social robots will enhance their language and communication skills [6].

In order to design efficient educational robots, there are still some answers about the users' perception regarding the ideal robots' characteristics that are certainly missing. Teachers are the first stakeholders who are going to use the robots as learning tools in education and thus their opinion about the educational robots' characteristics considered as important.

In the social-robot design procedure, there are four important factors that need to be taken under consideration· previous studies, the influence of robots in the target group's behaviour, the stakeholders' perceptions and finally their reaction on the final robot's appearance. In order to validate the efficiency of the robots when performing the target tasks there are several approaches including non-experimental ones, such as case studies and cross-sectionals and quasi- experimental ones such as pre- and post- tests [7]. Participatory design is also a widely used method when the stake-holders are involved in the whole design procedure, following rules such as 'making, enacting and telling [8]. A way of putting users and stakeholders directly into multiple scenarios of interacting with a robot is by utilizing Augmented Reality (AR) and Virtual Reality (VR) technologies [9]. Other interactive methods that enhance the participation of the stakeholders are by showing images of existing robots and, especially when referring to teenagers, there are drawing activities, where participants draw stories about the use of robots within the school [10]. Although there are very few experimental studies that utilize robots performing teaching tasks within a real educational environment, it is supported that it is crucial to have the potential stakeholders cooperate with robots within the targeted operational environment [11].

In our study, we conducted two experiments in a real university class, one with a human- lecturer and one with a robot-lecturer both teaching about intelligent systems. Our most important findings are that a) participants exposed to a robot tutor, statistically significantly changed their requirements about the ideal educational robot in comparison with their believes before the lecture and b) the changes in their requirements were significantly higher than those of the participants that were taught by a human. c) There is a correlation between the participants' believes about how a robot-tutor should look like, behave and act and their previous experience with robots. Since the participants in our experiments are pre-service teachers, they are important stakeholders in the educational environment. To the best of the authors' knowledge, there are no other studies actively involving the future educational stakeholders in the development process of robot-tutors, while their views, as expressed in our experiments, are by themselves, valuable contributions for the development of efficient educational robots.

2 Related Work

Typically, research on the design of education robots focuses on specific robot characteristics such as functionality and/or appearance since such characteristics affect significantly the human-robot collaboration and can increase or decrease the time humans spend with the robot [12]. Bartneck and Forlizzi mainly classified the characteristics of a robot interacting with humans into 5 main categories: form, modality, social norms, autonomy and interactivity [13]. It has also been proved that humans change their requirements about robot's appearance and personality traits depending on the activity the robot will perform; a cheerful personality robot is more attractive for joyful activities, while a serious personality is preferable for serious tasks such as performing gym exercises [14].

Reich-Stiebert [15] applied a user-centered design method and asked a group of 116 university students to select different robot features and robotic parts and put them together in a digital platform in order to create a prototype of the ideal educational robot. The characteristics taken into consideration by the students were the robot's Personality, Appearance, Emotion and Interaction. The results demonstrated that students preferred a machine-like robot but with humanoid characteristics and basic facial characteristics [16]. Those findings are also supported by Ray et his colleagues [17], who supported the idea that people generally prefer machinery- like robots and, especially for domestic use, they prefer small machines. Approximately 70% of the university students participated in the study in [15] argued that the ideal educational robot must be able to recognize emotion while half of the students indicated that robots should also be able to express their emotional state. University students also implied that an educational robot should be able to provide tailor-made support according to their learning needs [15, 18].

A 12-months longitudinal study with the Matilda robot in providing educational services to students with special needs revealed a 3-phase plan for special education robot applications: development, adoption and implementation. The peer- teacher's support is the key factor for the plan's success [19].

3 Present Study

Based on the research results described in the last section, it is very clear that it is important to investigate the impact of the pre-service teachers' opinions about the ideal characteristics that a robot-tutor should have so as to efficiently interact with students and collaborate with teachers. It is also important to identify those characteristics in a real university environment, as suggested by [20], and not only by approaching the stakeholders' believes theoretically or via VR and AR technologies.

Another important aspect when trying to identify the targeted robot's ideal characteristics, is the stakeholders previous experience with robots. Experiments with older adults suggested that their perception and acceptance regarding the humanoid Aldebaran NAO robot, increased statistically significantly after 30 to 60 min of interaction [21]. Despite the fact that younger adults are more familiar with robots than the previous generations, when a group of students instructed to draw a robot, the most frequent drawing stemmed from books' illustrations [22]. An online survey conducted by Hoeflich and El Bayed

[22] demonstrated that participants with earlier experience with robots had statistically significant higher scores in the questions regarding the evaluation of the trustworthiness, helpfulness, pleasance and entertainment skills of a robot.

The present study investigates whether there is any difference in the pre-service teachers' attitudes and ideas regarding the main characteristics of a robot in order to efficiently collaborate with it, before and after having a class with a robot-lecturer. The humanoid Aldebaran NAO robot served as the robot- lecturer based on previously successful use of this same robot in a similar environment [23]. In addition, we compared the future teachers' believes before and after having a class with a human lecturer about Intelligent systems. The current study, thus, explore how the requirements of teachers are formed based on their experience with robots, a) after having a university class on a relevant topic by a human professor and b) after having the same class conducted by a robot- lecturer. We, thus, compare the effect of a human lecturer with that of a robot lecturer on future teachers' preferences regarding, mainly, the robot's appearance (i.e. humanoid or machinery), ability to show positive or negative emotion, personalized experience, AI capabilities; our study utilizes a custom- made questionnaire, designed for educational robots stakeholders. Moreover, we are interested to find out how those requirements/categories correlate with each other after each class and how they correlate with the participants' general relationship with robots and technology.

3.1 Hypothesis

Our hypothesis is that the experience of a robot performing a teaching task will play a major role in teachers' opinions about the characteristics/behaviours that they want from a robot in order to efficiently collaborate with it. In closer detail, if our hypothesis is proved right, the educational stakeholders will have different responses in the questionnaire of the robot's characteristics when they have a class with a robot-tutor compared with their responses after a class with a human professor. We believe that future teachers will reconsider many of their, prior to the lecture, believes and they will also revise how important they consider specific robot's characteristics and/or traits. Thus, we expect to see different correlations between the different characteristics, in each experiment, since the different experiences (i.e. a robot tutor vs a human-tutor) will lead them to different conclusions, keeping in mind that experience is a key factor for accepting technology and robots [24].

4 Pilot Study/Pre-test

4.1 Participants

The total number of participants was 72, 70 Female and 2 Males, aged 17–30 years old. They were all first-year university students, studying to become special education teachers, in the University of Macedonia, School of Educational and Social Sciences. They all had normal or corrected to normal vision and hearing and their native language was the language of the questionnaires. The questionnaires were given to them on the first week of their classes. The participants had as much time as they wanted in order to fill the forms anonymously.

4.2 Procedure

The experiment took place in a real University classroom during the students' first day in the University campus. The professor entered the classroom and asked the students if they wanted to do a questionnaire relevant to the course before they start the lecture. The given questionnaire has been developed in the STIMEY Project [25] and it has been employed in the design of a robot that will be used in secondary and high schools. In particular, the STIMEY questionnaire (STQ) was designed by utilizing certain focus groups with the project's stakeholders and based on their replies, the project's partners designed, implemented and tested the personal assistant STIMEY robot [26]. There were 60 questions and the participants evaluated them in a Likert scale from "Strongly Disagree" to "Strongly Agree" (e.g. they replied with 1 to 5 if they wanted to collaborate with a robot which 'is able to remember personal information about me').

Additionally, we gave them another questionnaire in which a) we asked for the demographic characteristics of the participants (i.e. gender and age) and b) five Likert scale questions regarding the participant's relationship with robots and technology, firstly used by Velentza and her colleagues [27] (e.g. having questions like "Have you ever used a robot".

4.3 Data Analysis and Results

The scores of the STQ filled before any classes served as a control group regarding the initial students- future teachers' opinions. In order to process the results/scores we calculated a single number for each question by averaging the answers of all the participants for each question, and then we treated this average as the interval data; next we calculated the mean and standard deviation for the interval data. We followed the same procedure in order to end up with a single number/score for each participant. Those scores will be compared with the scores of the STQ filled after the class (human and robot condition), by applying a paired sample t-test. A multidisciplinary group of psychologists, special education teachers and engineers (one of them was among the designers of the questionnaire) split the questions into 10 general categories, each with certain sub-categories as follows: (in the parenthesis we have the number of questions in each sub-category).

1. Feedback, a) Positive feedback (6), b) Negative feedback (3),
2. Social Behaviour (3),
3. Physical Capabilities, a) Humanoid (5), b) Machinery (6),
4. Appearance (5),
5. Personalised Experience (11),
6. Personal Assistant (4),
7. Show Emotion, a) Understand-show emotion (2), b) Positive Emotion (3), c) Negative Emotion (3),
8. AI capabilities (3),
9. Learning Assistant (5) and.
10. Autonomy Capabilities (6).

Additionally, we performed a Cronbach's alpha reliability measure for measuring internal consistency in each category's items. Certain questions have been assigned in more than one category. The name of each category describes the content of the questions included in general terms. For example, the 'Appearance' category includes questions about how the future teachers want the robot to look like in order to collaborate with it. In Table 1 there is an indicative question per category. Finally, we performed a Pearson R correlation analysis, via SPSS 25 in order to find any correlations between the different categories. The correlations will help us understand if positive/negative attitudes about specific robot's characteristics affect student's attitudes about other characteristics and how those attitude relationships can alter after our manipulations. In general, knowing if the future teachers' attitudes about different technological variables are correlated and hence substitutable is useful for understanding variance structures in data which are the participants answers. Additionally, for building efficient predictive models, regarding technology integration in schools [28] we would ideally include variables (in our case characteristic categories) that uniquely explain some amount of variance in the outcome.

Analysing the participants' score in the STQ, the Mean Score (*MV*) per question was 3.3 with Standard Deviation (*SD*) 1.1 while the MV of the Sum of all the questions was 171.5. Extended results for each category are listed in Table 1.

The Pearson R analysis between the categories, in the STQ that were filled before any classes, indicated that the teachers' opinions about positive talking-feedback and negative talking-feedback, expressed by the robot were positively strongly correlated, r(215) = .333, p = .000[1]. Moreover, the participants' opinion about receiving positive feedback was strongly correlated with all the other categories, while their opinion about receiving negative feedback was strongly correlated with their opinion about "robot's social behaviour" (r(215) = .383, p = .000), "having a personalised experience" (r(215) = .261, p = .000), "personal assistant" (r(215) = .209, p = .002), "expressing positive emotion" (r (r(215) = .261, $p \leq .001$) and "expressing negative emotion" (r(215) = .247, $p \leq .001$). The teachers' opinions about a robot's social behaviour were also found to be moderately positively correlated with all the categories apart from the Appearance and Negative feedback ones. The Physical Capability (both Machinery and Humanoid) was positively correlated with all categories apart from the Negative feedback one. The Personalised Experience opinion was positively correlated with all categories apart from the general show of emotion, while the specific belief of "having a personalised experience" with the robot was corelated with all the other believes. The expression of negative emotion was strongly correlated with all the sub-categories, apart from the Social Behaviour and Learning Assistance ones. Furthermore, the Learning Assistance sub-category was not correlated with any negative expressions in terms of either talking feedback or emotion.

[1] R(degrees of freedom) = the r statistics, p = p value.

Table 1. Example Question for each category. In the parenthesis there is the Cronbach's alpha reliability measure for each category. Each cell shows the *MV* and *SD* per category, per condition. All questions start with 'I want to collaborate with a robot which' and then follows the questions on the cell 'Example question'.

Category	Example question	Before class	Human tutor	Robot tutor
Positive feedback (.78)	Tells me if it is happy with my behaviour	3.3, 1.27	3.33, 1.43	3.71, 1.26
Negative feedback (.80)	Tells me when my behaviour made it feel sad	2.93, 1.4	2.76, 1.56	3.08, 1.34
Social Behaviour (.87)	Interact with other people	3.06, 1.3	3.05, 1.51	3.59, 1.25
Humanoid Physical Capabilities (.84)	Make gestures	3.23, 1.27	3.09, 1.35	3.79, 1.2
Machinery Physical Capabilities (.75)	Speak like a robot	3.47, 1.27	3.42, 1.29	3.84, 1.15
Appearance (.88)	Could have lights	2.78, 1.41	2.62, 1.48	2.96, 1.51
Personalised Experience (.87)	Remembers personal information about me	3.3, 1.3	3.17, 1.48	3.68, 1.22
Personal Assistant (.81)	Reminds me of what I must do to achieve my goals	3.47, 1.33	3.43, 1.53	3.88, 1.16
Show Emotion (.92)	Understands my feelings	2.98, 1.44	2.93, 1.49	3.46, 1.37
Positive Emotion (.84)	Shows me that it feels grateful that we did an activity together	3.26, 1.25	3.2, 1.34	3.77, 1.69
Negative Emotion (.86)	Tell me it feels frustrated that I'm not trying hard enough	2.92, 1.4	2.76, 1.56	3.08, 1.34
AI capabilities (.83,5)	Gradually learn more	3.46, 1.19	3.6, 1.2	4.07, 1.07
Learning Assistant (.81)	Makes it easier for me to learn programming	3.98, 1.17	3.98, 1.23	4.19, 1.06
Autonomy Capabilities (.87)	Moves around autonomously	3.2, 1.31	3.06, 1.4	3.7, 1.17

5 Main Experiments-Experimental Design

5.1 Participants

The total number of participants was 138, 8 Males and 130 Females, aged 17–30 years old. They all had normal or corrected to normal vision and hearing and their native language was the language of the class and the questionnaires. They were all freshmen, pre- service teachers, in the University of Macedonia, School of Educational and Social Policies. They were randomly separated for administrative purposes into 2 groups. The first group participated in the first experiment with the human-lecturer (N = 66) and the second group in the class conducted by the robot-lecturer (N = 71); in order to avoid spoiling and/or developing hype from the robot lectures, we decided to conduct the experiment with the human tutor before the one with the robot. The experiments took place in two consecutive days, in the same hour and at the same classroom and this was the first lecture of the mandatory course 'Basic Principles of IoT'.

5.2 Design and Procedure

The experimental design was between-participants (i.e. in each experiment/condition we had different participants). During the first day, the course conducted by the course's professor (human- lecturer), who teaches the same as well as similar subjects for 20 years. During the second day, the course conducted by the Aldebaran Nao V3.3 (robot-lecturer) which was programmed to do similar body movements with the human-lecturer, since humans tend to trust more and feel more familiar when they are close to an agent/system that has similar characteristics with them [29]. There was also an assistant professor (different from the human-lecturer) who leaded the students into the classroom where the experiments conducted and two PhD Students who participated as undercover freshmen students; those two students, in both conditions, asked/answered the same pre-agreed questions in order to receive the same feedback and, in that way, demonstrate to the participants certain robot features which are relevant to those they had to evaluate. For example, the student answered a tutor's question and the tutor gave feedback, verbally rewarded the student and commented with a joke. The script (including the students-tutor interaction) was the same in both conditions. The lecturers, human and robot, stood in the middle of the class, as shown in Fig. 1, and taught about Intelligent Systems. The lesson included information about machine intelligence and autonomy in order students from both conditions to gain basic knowledge about Intelligent systems such as robots. Both lecturers used the exact same presentation and teaching style while the duration of both classes was 30 min. After the end of the class, the assistant professor gave to the students the STQ and the demographic and familiarity questionnaire. The participants had as much time as they wanted in order to fill the forms anonymously.

5.3 Data Analysis

For the analysis of the STQ, we used the same procedure as that described in the previous section for the Pilot Study. The scores in the questions of each category in the class conditions compared with the pre-class scores from the Pilot study with a paired sample t-test. In order to compare the results of all the experiments, we calculated Hedges' G [30], which provides a measure of the effect size weighted according to the relative size of each sample; this was essential since we have slightly different sample sizes in each experiment. For comparing the pre-test with the robot-lecturer condition we used the alternative Cohen's D analysis which is considered as the most appropriate for two groups that have similar standard deviations and same size [30].

Fig. 1. Classroom set up in the Robot Condition

We calculated a single number for each category as described in the Data Analysis sub-section of the Pilot-Study and then we compared all the numbers with the corresponding scores after the two classes, for all categories (e.g. the total score of all questions included in the 'Humanoid Physical Appearance' category in the robot condition compared with a t-test with the total score of all the questions included in the same category in the human condition); the results are demonstrated in Table 2. Furthermore, we performed a Pearson R correlation analysis, on the participants' familiarity and personal experience with their STQ scores. This analysis helped us understand more, how the self-reported experience of the participants affect their opinions about the ideal robot's characteristics. We also performed a Pearson R correlation analysis between the categories in the same condition to identify if the manipulations affected the correlations between the student's opinions. Finally, we investigated (through T-tests) if there were any significant differences between categories in the same condition (e.g. if there is any difference in the feedback preference -negative or positive- or the expression of emotion).

5.4 Results

Experiment1: Human Lecturer Condition

The *MV* for all the questions of the STQ was 3.54 and the *SD*, 1.14. The *MV* and the *SD* for each category is presented in Table 1.

Based on the MV of each category, the top priority of a future teacher in order to collaborate with a robot is the robot's ability to be a Learning Assistant and secondly, it's AI and personal assistant abilities. The ideal robotic characteristics would be a machinery appearance that gives positive feedback and shows positive emotion. After those preferences, it follows the robot's ability to offer a personalized experience (by adapting to the user's needs) and the robot's autonomous capabilities. On the contrary, future teachers are less interested about the robot's expression of social behavior, providing negative feedback and showing negative emotion.

Future teachers statistically significantly prefer Positive than Negative Feedback from the robot as t-test indicated, $t(197) = 4.41$, $p \leq .001$, $d = 0.57$). Moreover, future teachers prefer the Machinery-like appearance in a statistically significant manner, in comparison with the humanoid, t(329) = 7.82, $p \leq .001$, d = 0.34. By comparing the 3 aspects of emotional expression, positive emotional expressions were more preferable than both negative and general Show/Understand Emotions, but the difference is statistically significant only in favour of positive against negative emotion (t(197) = 2.99, p = 0.03, d = 0.44), as shown in Table 2.

By performing a thorough Pearson-R analysis we found some interesting correlations between the participants' answers. As identified also in the pre-test results, most of the student's opinions (categories) were positively correlated with the rest of their opinions in a statistically significant way. Although there were some exceptions. It is worth mentioned that in this human lecturer condition, the robot's AI capability was not correlated with a) any feedback (positive or negative) b) social behavior, c) Autonomous Capability. On the other hand, the participants' opinions regarding Negative Feedback and Social Behavior were significantly negatively correlated with the robot's appearance (r(197) = −.223, p = .002 and r(197) = −.043, p = .544 respectively) while robot's Appearance was not correlated with any of their opinions regarding Showing Emotion and Personal Assistant.

By analysing the technological and robotics familiarity questions, we found out that there was no correlation between the future teachers' opinions expressed in the STQ and their general knowledge about robots and technology. On the other hand, we found a strong negative correlation between the participants' familiarity and previous experience with a robot and their opinions about Getting Positive Feedback from the robot (r = −.297, p = 0.015), as well as several indicated characteristics of the robots namely Social Behaviour (r = −.346, p = .004), Show/Understand Emotion (r = −.287, p = .02), Negative Emotion (r = −.297, p = .015) and Learning Assistance (r = −.346, p = .004). Those results demonstrate that low scores in the familiarity with robots' questions lead to high scores in all those categories or, in other words, participants with minimal previous experience and familiarity with robots are interested in collaborating with a robot having the characteristics listed above.

Experiment2: Robot Lecturer Condition

The total MV for all the questions of the STQ was 3.67 and the SD, 1.05. The MV and SD for each category is presented in Table 1. After having a class with a robot- lecturer, the future teachers' priorities regarding the ideal robot's behavior and characteristics were the Learning Assistant, Personal Assistant and AI capabilities. On the other hand, they do not seem to have a clear preference on the robot's characteristics, since the MV of those who prefer to collaborate with a robot with Humanoid Physical Capabilities (MV = 3.79, SD 1.2), while the corresponding numbers for collaboration with Machinery characteristics was MV = 3.84, SD = 1.15 (t(359) = −0.6, p = .54, d = 0.05). Moreover, they statistically significantly (t(215) = 5.83, p = .000, d = 0.63) prefer a robot that gives positive Feedback (MV = 3.71, SD = 1.26) rather than Negative Feedback (MV = 3.08, SD = 1.34). Furthermore, they clearly prefer to collaborate with a robot that shows Positive Emotion (MV = 3.77, SD = 1.69) rather than Negative Emotion (MV = 3.08, SD = 1.34) and the difference is statistically significant as indicated by the t-test, t(215) = 5.65, $p \leq .001$, d = 0.69, as shown in Table 2. Those future teacher's preferences are followed by their opinions about the robot's Autonomous and Personalized Experience performance.

Moreover, based on the Pearson R correlations that performed between the Categories, the robot's Appearance is negatively correlated with the expression of Negative Feedback ($r = -.121$, p =,.076) and the Social Behavior characteristics of the robot, in a statistically significant manner, ($r = -.170$, $p = .013$) and positively significantly correlated with the following robot characteristics: a) Positive Feedback ($r = .225$, $p \leq .001$), b) Physical Capability, c) Humanoid appearance ($r = .220$, $p \leq .001$), d) Machinery appearance ($r = .227$, $p \leq .001$), e) AI Capabilities ($r = .175$, $p = .001$). Furthermore, the Learning Capability was not correlated with the Autonomous Capability, while it remains (just as in the pre-test) strongly correlated with the rest of the categories.

Apart from that, the future teachers' opinions about the robots' Autonomous Capability, after seeing the robot in action, are not correlated with Negative Feedback, Social Behavior, Personalized Experience and Personal Assistant characteristics. Finally, the Social Behavior was significantly correlated with almost all the categories apart from the Appearance, with which it is negatively correlated and the Machinery Physical Capability, Negative Emotion and Autonomous Capability categories with which it was not correlated at all.

Table 2. t-test comparison between the categories. Each cell includes the t value and p value. Bold are highlighted as being statistically significant, all in favour of the robot condition.

Category	Pre vs H	Pre vs R	H vs R
Positive feedback	−0.35, .73	−4.78, < **.001**	−4.04, < **.001**
Negative feedback	1.08, .279	−1.22, .221	−2.24, **.025**
Social Behaviour	0.069,.944	−4.32, < **.001**	−3.97, < **.001**
Humanoid Capability	1.3, .192	−6.04, < **.001**	7.09, < **.001**
Machinery Capability	0.53, .59	−4.44, < **.001**	4.89, < **.001**
Appearance	1.44, .148	−1.7, .088	−3.027, **.003**
Personalised Experience	2.097, .32	−7.91, < **.001**	−7.6, **.027**
Personal Assist	0.36, .72	−3.93, < **.001**	−3.92, < **.001**
Show Emotion	0.27, .79	−2.88, **.004**	−3.04, **.0025**
Positive Emotion	0.41, .68	−4.4, < **.001**	−4.57, < **.001**
Negative Emotion	1.08, .278	−1.23, .221	−2.24, **.025**
AI capabilities	−1.13, .259	−5.56, < **.001**	−4.22, < **.001**
Learning Assistant	−0.07, .943	−2.65, **.008**	−2.46, **.014**
Autonomy Capability	1.38, .166	−6.12, < **.001**	−7.22, < **.001**

By analysing the technological and robotics familiarity questions, we found that there was a positive correlation between the participants' general knowledge about technology and the Autonomous Capability ($r = .294$, $p = .012$) of the robots demonstrating that, after seeing a robot in action, the more they learn about robots and technology the more interested they become in collaborating with autonomous robots. Moreover, previous experience with robots was significantly positively correlated with the robot's Appearance, both Machinery ($r = .256$, $p = .03$) and Humanoid ($r = .314$, $p = .007$), as well as with the Show of Emotion ($r = .316$, $p = .007$) characteristic of the robot.

Comparison Between the Experiments

A visualized version of the *MV* scores of each category in each condition can be seen in Fig. 2. The measure of effect size between the robot and human- lecturer experiments proven to be important at Hedges' g = 0.4, but not important between the pre-test and the human-lecture condition (Hedges' g = (3.231–3.299)/1.155055 = 0.058872). On the other hand, the measure of effect size between the pre-test and the robot-lecture condition proved almost important at Cohen's d = (3.668–3.299)/1.074803 = 0.343319.

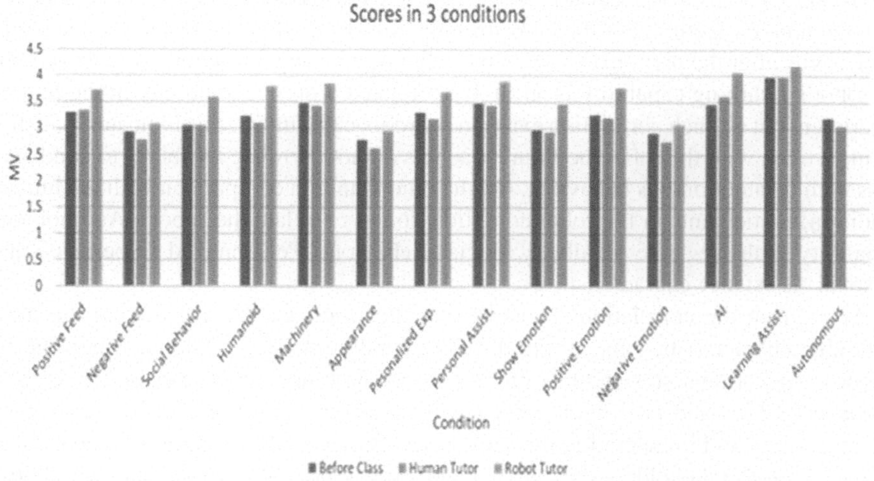

Fig. 2. Visualized MV scores of each Category in 3 conditions

Additionally, the t-test results demonstrated that there was no statistically significant change in the future teachers' opinions about the ideal characteristics that a robot should have in order to collaborate with, between the pre-test (before having any lecture) and after having the lecture with a human-lecturer, as demonstrated by the results in Table 2. In summary, 21.43% of the category scores remained the same between the two conditions, 7.14% increased and 71.42% decreased after the human-lecturer condition, in comparison with the pre-test, but none of those changes was statistically significant. On the other hand, between the pre-test and the robot-lecturer condition, we identified statistically significant changes in most of the future teachers' opinions (78,5%). Moreover, for all the categories, the scores after the lecture conducted by the robot was higher than their corresponding score in the pre-test. Finally, there was a big statistically significant difference in all the categories when comparing the future teachers' opinions after having the same lecture with a robot with those that have the conventional human-lecturer; in particular in all the categories the scores were higher in the robot condition comparing to the human one. This was another interesting result of our study, since it proves that the stakeholders' opinions changes radically after interacting with a robot.

6 Discussion and Conclusions

The different experimental conditions lead the underlined education stakeholders (future teachers) to very different opinions about the ideal robot-tutor's characteristics. The correlations in the experimental results help us understand the participants' perceptions about robots in education, by also considering their previous experience with robots. First of all, we find no correlation between the Learning aspect and the Negative feedback and negative emotion in the pre-test. This result gives us an indication on how future teachers perceive the learning process especially when it takes place by robots. Another interesting point from the identified correlations is the relationship of the robot's AI capabilities with its ability to give feedback and its social behaviour. Those aspects are not correlated after the human- lecture, but they are strongly correlated after the robot- lecture, or in other words after the participants show the robot performing a teaching task. Moreover, the robot's Learning capability is strongly correlated with its Autonomy in the human experiment but no such correlation exists in the robot experiment; this indicates that after having a class with the robot the future teachers do not correlate its ability to conduct a class with its autonomous behaviour. On the other hand, in comparison with the human condition, participants in the robot condition do not correlate the robot's Autonomous Capability with Negative Feedback, Social Behaviour, Personalized Experience and Personal Assistance characteristics.

Apart from the correlations between the categories, we identified what the most preferable characteristics are, in the different conditions. In the human condition the specified educational stakeholders prefer a robot with machinery capabilities as also indicated by [15] and [16] while after having a lecture with a humanoid robot, they like machinery and humanoid at the same level. Based on this finding we suggest that the educational stakeholders must first spend some time with a robot and then choose the ideal characteristics for a future teaching companion. After having a lecture with a human about intelligent systems, if the stakeholders have minimal previous experience with robots, they want to collaborate with robots that give positive feedback, express social behaviour, show and understand emotion and are used as learning assistants. On the contrary, the future teachers, after having a class with a robot, the more familiar they are with robots, the more they are interested in the robot's appearance and the robot's ability to show and understand emotion. Additionally, the existence of technological and general robotics knowledge, after having a lecture with a robot, is correlated with bigger interest in collaborating with autonomous robots. This is not the case when the participants have a human- lecturer.

Another interesting result of our study comes from the variation of the questionnaire scores after the experiments in comparison with the pre-test scores. After the robot lecture, all the scores (demonstrating how important the listed robot characteristics are considered) were increased (in a statistically significant manner) while after the human condition only 7.14% of the scores increased (none of the them in a statistically significant way) and the majority of them decreased. It seems that the future teachers have initially relatively high expectations from robots and their intelligence but after having a theoretical course on the subject, without seeing an actual robot, those expectations declined. On the other hand, after seeing an actual robot in action, they reconsider their believes and have more demands and suggestions for their use. Finally, it should be highlighted that most of the participants were female and thus we need further investigation in future studies about possible gender differences. One limitation of the study is that the future teachers may change their believes about their own needs after getting more practical experience into the teaching field.

Acknowledgments. This research funded in the context of the project "Mapping the characteristics of social robots in order to enhance cognitive functions and familiarity in humans" (MIS 5047258) under the call for proposals "Support for researchers with an emphasis on young researchers" (EDBM-103). The project is co-financed by Greece and the European Union (European Social Fund- ESF) by the Operational Programme Human Resources Development, Education and Lifelong Learning 2014–2020.

References

1. Amanatiadis, A., Kaburlasos, V.G., Dardani, Ch., Chatzichristofis, S.A.: Interactive social robots in special education. In: IEEE 7th International Conference on Consumer Electronics - Berlin (ICCE-Berlin), pp. 126–129 (2017)
2. Karna-Lin, E., Pihlainen-Bednarik, K., Sutinen, E., Virnes, M.: Can robots teach? Preliminary results on educational robotics in special education'. In: Sixth IEEE International Conference on Advanced Learning Technologies (ICALT 2006), pp. 319–321 (2006)
3. Zahariev, R., Valchkova, N., Wagatsuma H.H.: Service robots for special education of children with disabilities: robotized systems for social applications. In: Proceedings of the 21st International Conference on Computer Systems and Technologies 2020, New York, NY, USA, pp. 300–306 (2020)
4. Wood, L.J., Zaraki, A., Robins, B., Dautenhahn K.: Developing kaspar: a Humanoid robot for children with autism. Int. J. Soc. Robot. (2019). https://doi.org/10.1007/s12369-019-00563-6
5. Belpaeme, T., et al.: Social robots for education: a review'. Sci. Robot. **3**(21) (2018)
6. Neumann, M.M.: Social robots and young children's early language and literacy learning. Early Child. Educ. J. **48**(2), 157–170 (2020)
7. Toh, L.P.E., et al.: A review on the use of robots in education and young children'. J. Educ. Technol. Soc. **19**(2), 148–163 (2016)
8. Sanders, E.B.N., Brandt, E., Binder, T.: A framework for organizing the tools and techniques of participatory design. In: Proceedings of the 11th Biennial Participatory Design Conference, pp. 195–198 (2010)
9. Jalowski, M., Fritzsche, A., Möslein, K.M.: Applications for persuasive technologies in participatory design processes. In: Oinas-Kukkonen, H., Win, K.T., Karapanos, E., Karppinen, P., Kyza, E. (eds.) PERSUASIVE 2019. LNCS, vol. 11433, pp. 74–86. Springer, Cham (2019). https://doi.org/10.1007/978-3-030-17287-9_7
10. Rose, E.J., Björling, E.A.: Designing for engagement: using participatory design to develop a social robot to measure teen stress. In: Proceedings of the 35th ACM International Conference on the Design of Communication, Halifax, Nova Scotia, Canada, p. 10 (2017)
11. Salter, T., Werry, I., Michaud, F.: Going into the wild in child–robot interaction studies: issues in social robotic development. Intell. Serv. Robot. **1**(2), 93–108 (2008)

12. Faccio, M., Minto, R., Rosati, G., Bottin, M.: The influence of the product characteristics on human-robot collaboration: a model for the performance of collaborative robotic assembly. Int. J. Adv. Manuf. Technol. **106**(5–6), 2317–2331 (2019). https://doi.org/10.1007/s00170-019-04670-6
13. Bartneck C., Forlizzi, J.: A design-centred framework for social human-robot interaction. In: 13th IEEE International Workshop on Robot and Human Interactive Communication (IEEE Catalog No. 04TH8759), pp. 591–594 (2004)
14. Goetz, J., Kiesler, S., Powers, A.: Matching robot appearance and behavior to tasks to improve human-robot cooperation. In: 12th IEEE International Workshop on Robot and Human Interactive Communication, 2003. Proceedings. ROMAN 2003, pp. 55–60 (2003)
15. Reich-Stiebert, N., Eyssel, F., Hohnemann, C.: Exploring university students' preferences for educational robot design by means of a user-centered design approach. Int. J. Soc. Robot. (2019). https://doi.org/10.1007/s12369-019-00554-7
16. Mondada, F., et al.: Bringing robotics to formal education: the thymio open-source hardware robot. IEEE Robot. Autom. Mag. **24**(1), 77–85 (2017)
17. Mondada, F., et al.: The e-puck, a robot designed for education in engineering. In: Proceedings of the 9th Conference on Autonomous Robot Systems and Competitions (2009). https://infoscience.epfl.ch/record/135236. Accessed 13 Jan 2020
18. Reich-Stiebert, N., Eyssel, F.: Robots in the classroom: what teachers think about teaching and learning with education robots. In: Agah, A., Cabibihan, J.-J., Howard, A.M., Salichs, M.A., He, H. (eds.) ICSR 2016. LNCS (LNAI), vol. 9979, pp. 671–680. Springer, Cham (2016). https://doi.org/10.1007/978-3-319-47437-3_66
19. Khaksar, S.M.S., Slade, B., Wallace, J., Gurinder, K.: Critical success factors for application of social robots in special developmental schools: development, adoption and implementation. Int. J. Educ. Manag. **34**(4), 677–696 (2020)
20. Darriba Frederiks, A., Octavia, J.R., Vandevelde, C., Saldien, J.: Towards participatory design of social robots. In: Lamas, D., Loizides, F., Nacke, L., Petrie, H., Winckler, M., Zaphiris, P. (eds.) INTERACT 2019. LNCS, vol. 11747, pp. 527–535. Springer, Cham (2019). https://doi.org/10.1007/978-3-030-29384-0_32
21. Beuscher, L.M., et al.: Socially assistive robots: measuring older adults; perceptions. J. Gerontol. Nurs. **43**(12), 35–43 (2017)
22. Höflich, J.R., El Bayed, A.: Perception, acceptance, and the social construction of robots—exploratory studies. In: Vincent, J., Taipale, S., Sapio, B., Lugano, G., Fortunati, L. (eds.) Social Robots from a Human Perspective, pp. 39–51. Springer, Cham (2015). https://doi.org/10.1007/978-3-319-15672-9_4
23. Xu, J., Broekens, J., Hindriks, K., Neerincx, M.A.: Effects of bodily mood expression of a robotic teacher on students. In: IEEE/RSJ International Conference on Intelligent Robots and Systems, pp. 2614–2620 (2014)
24. Heerink, M.: Exploring the influence of age, gender, education and computer experience on robot acceptance by older adults. In: 6th ACM/IEEE International Conference on Human-Robot Interaction (HRI), pp. 147–148 (2011)
25. 'STIMEY'. https://www.stimey.eu/home.
26. Pnevmatikos, D., Christodoulou, P., Fachantidis, N.: Designing a socially assistive robot for education through a participatory design approach: guiding principles for the developers. Int. J. Soc. Robot.
27. Velentza, A.M., Heinke, D., Wyatt, J.: Human interaction and improving knowledge through collaborative tour guide robots. In: 28th IEEE International Conference on Robot and Human Interactive Communication (RO-MAN), pp. 1–7 (2019)
28. Anderson, S.E., Maninger, R.M.: Preservice teachers' abilities, beliefs, and intentions regarding technology integration. J. Educ. Comput. Res. **37**(2), 151–172 (2007)

29. Verberne, F.M., Ham, J., Midden, C.J.: Trusting a virtual driver that looks, acts, and thinks like you. Hum. Factors **57**(5), 895–909 (2015)
30. Ellis, P.D.: The Essential Guide to Effect Sizes: Statistical Power, Meta-Analysis, and the Interpretation of Research Results. Cambridge University Press (2010)

Creative Process for Designing a Hybrid Game for Nutrition Education

Pedro Reisinho(✉), Cátia Silva, Nelson Zagalo, Mário Vairinhos, and Ana Patrícia Oliveira

Digimedia, Department of Communication and Art, University of Aveiro, Aveiro, Portugal
{pedro.reisinho,csvs,nzagalo,mariov,apoliveira}@ua.pt

Abstract. In this paper we present and discuss the creative process behind a hybrid game, grounded in the research project "FlavourGame". The research project is developing a serious game for kids aged 10–12 years old to generate discussion and sense-making around nutrition, more specifically everyday choices of nourishment and food. The main aim is to develop a game design model for hybrid games, making use of digital and physical interactions with fictional worlds to create engaging experiences. In this paper we unravel the creation process of the game narrative, game board, cards and characters while enunciating the mechanics and rules needed to play the game. Additionally, we describe the implementation of the game, the used technological approach, and challenges faced by combining the digital and analog components.

Keywords: 3D · Augmented reality · Hybrid game · Game design · Nutrition education

1 Introduction

FlavourGame (FG) is developing a new model for the hybrid game design, working around the theme of nutrition, for kids aged 10–12 years and to be played at schools where the teacher acts as a game master. Nutrition is an important part of kids' growth and autonomy and has a high importance in their healthy and quality transition into adult life. FG intends to support the younger in autonomy and motivation for healthy food choices and to change eating habits by providing sensorial experiences through real food samples and spices [1–3] presented to the players throughout the game as challenges and by granting access to nutritional information and to recipes' cooking processes.

With FG development we intend to overcome the limitations of pure digital communication, typical of computer games or traditional apps. We want to combine digital functionalities with more powerful physical affordances to allow new uses and dynamics in game playing. The change of "painted bits" of GUIs (Graphical User Interfaces) to "tangible bits" [4] by giving physical form to digital information had a significant impact in entertainment industries, since it provides more engaging experiences to its users, with videogames as "Skylanders" [5] or "Disney Infinity" [6]. Now it is possible to design fully hybrid games with tangible characteristics in a shared traditional board

A. Reis et al. (Eds.): TECH-EDU 2020, CCIS 1384, pp. 492–505, 2021.
https://doi.org/10.1007/978-3-030-73988-1_40

game. This combination of components and strategies can contribute to a new experience of play, enhancing the player's immersion and interaction through the content, presentation, atmosphere, and game control [7].

The primary objective of this paper is to demonstrate the methods we used regarding creativity thinking inherent to the creation of a hybrid serious board game for nutrition. We go from the potentialities of hybrid games to the ones related with the incorporation of augmented reality and interactive narratives on a board game, as well as the actual implementation of the project. The second objective is to present the first draft of the FG functional design which includes a narrative and a low-fi prototype.

During the first stages of brainstorming, we started by establishing the game mechanics and some ground rules and how we could complement them with TUI and Augmented Reality technologies. With the backbone of the game becoming reliable, it was time to set the theme and begin to devise a story. Then, we began defining and sketching what was already idealized and redirected our attention to the selection of the game appearance, designing the characters and the game board.

After most context was defined and designed, to strengthen the link between healthy food and children, we analyzed and selected what types of challenges could be added to the game in order to motivate children.

In the following section of the paper, we present a brief state of the art about hybrid board games, along with the description of the creative phases of FG, namely the conceptualization of the narrative, an overview of the characters, world, and events of the story, as well as the game with the explanation of the mechanics, challenges, and goals. Afterwards, we introduce the concept of hybrid games and subsequently we describe the actual implementation of the prototype, its technological approach and the challenges faced by combining the digital and analog components. At last, we draw some conclusions and present the future work.

2 A Brief Review of Hybrid Games

To better understand the process from the validation of our idea to the decisions we made, it was necessary to conduct a research and analysis about hybrid board games available on the market that were related with the mechanics we wanted to implement. The purpose of this search was to comprehend what main mechanics hybrid games implement as well as the kind of technology used. Amid all of hybrid games we investigated, we considered "Queen Strike" [8] – due to its Pepper's Ghost technological approach –, "Chronicles of Crime" [9] – in order to interact with the story, the player must use the game's mobile application – and "Kitchen Rush" [10] – a restaurant game with a strong management component – to be the most relevant and the ones who contributed the most to help us define the concept of the FG.

"Queen Strike" [8] is a cooperative hybrid board game in which the main goal is to collect musical notes and defeat the Queen. To accomplish it, the players move their hero's pawns along the game board according to the number drawn by a six-sided die while facing the possibility to encounter the Queen's Guards and enter a fight based on the rock-paper-scissors mechanic. This combat is displayed in a holographic platform – utilizing the Pepper's Ghost Effect with the aid of the game's mobile application – that shows the gestures (rock, paper, or scissors). Besides the "holographic" effect, the platform also contains a detection feature where the player must lay down the cards with the gestures to face the guards. Initially, the Pepper's Ghost Effect, which recreates a hologram of the smartphone screen through the use of an acrylic sheet placed on a 45° angle, seemed quite promising as a contribution to the hybridism concept of the game, since holograms might easily captivate a child interest.

However, after deeply analyzing this approach, we realized that prototyping such technology would not be simple, since it was necessary to design and build a structure capable of supporting smartphones and tablets of different weights and sizes while, simultaneously, incorporate an acrylic sheet with an exact angle of 45°. Along with the possibility of creasing the sheet during the assembly and disassembly of the platform – thus ruining the experience of the game – it was necessary a strict control of the room's light to be able to see the hologram flawlessly. Therefore, although it deemed to be interesting, we chose to discard this approach.

"Chronicles of Crime" [9] is also a cooperative hybrid board game in which the objective is to investigate different murders and find its perpetrators. The game uses its own mobile application, which allows the user to choose which crime he/she wants to investigate and provides instructions of which places and characters he/she has to display on the game table. Moreover, the story develops within the mobile application – a feature we ended up implementing in the project – and, by using Quick Response (QR) codes, the player chooses the place he/she wants to investigate next and who to talk to in order to gather clues. In addition, to solve crimes and collect more information, the player has the possibility to use virtual reality and inspect the crime scene on a more detailed level. Although it is a complex game, the player must use logical thinking to get to the end of the story and find the culprit.

After analyzing the technological approach of this game, we compared the differences between using fiducials embedded on the design of the food cards and using QR codes and concluded that the first have the ability to be better integrated into the design because they are not conspicuous and provide a more harmonious pattern.

"Kitchen Rush" [10] is the one that is closer to the food theme, being a cooperative analog game with a strong management component and food confection. The game takes place at a restaurant where the players have to individually manage the time – turns of four minutes divided into eight actions of thirty seconds each – and the available resources – money to buy food and pay wages, employees to fulfill the tasks, available food and equipment – in order to cooperatively keep the restaurant running. During the game, the players strategically receive the customers – each one with a different order, requiring different food – guide them to an available table, serve them, receive the money, wash the dishes and restock the pantry. The orders made by clients are divided by difficulty, being the hardest ones also the most profitable but more time consuming in terms of preparation since it is necessary to use the stove more often – usually three times, leading the players to spend one and a half minute just to fully cook one meal.

Although we think the game has a strong management component, after a gameplay session between the FG researchers, we considered that the mechanics used as well as its rules were too complex to be used on a game classified as to be suited for children. It is also necessary to highlight the time we spent to start playing due to the several pieces and sections the game brings and the time it takes to dispose these pieces on the different sections, making this aspect a possible obstacle to captivate children of this age group. However, analyzing other components of Kitchen Rush was very enlightening as it allowed us to better understand the complexity of thinking about the structure of a game with resources – in our case, the food cards – and how to obtain and manage these same resources.

3 FlavourGame: Fundamentals and Description

3.1 Narrative

The inclusion of a narrative in a game brings added value due to its ability to focus [11] and engage the player in a way it would not be possible without it [12], leading them to more profound states of flow [13]. Flow corresponds to a full awareness state, intrinsically related with the immersion state [14] – a psychological illusion of being carried to another reality. This, for its part, is also related with Huizinga's "Magic Circle" [15]. So, since the theme of the game is informative and not problem-solving, we started developing the narrative, which is the way of organizing information that allows people to transmit and receive the referred information with emotional and memory effects [16].

The storyworld chosen for the game was grounded in escapism and fantasy, using the outer space and galaxies to arouse kids' imaginary. The characters followed fantasy with the impersonations of animals.

The designed narrative fits the branched type and takes advantage of the use of narrative choices [17] – the player is presented with multiple narrative choices and must choose one of them –, taking into account the idea that interactivity and the ability to make choices – agency – provides a bigger immersion to the player [11, 14]. Having decided about the structure, we decided to ground the storyworld in a fantastical and escapist genre, using the outer space and galaxies, to which we added characters made of animals' impersonations, all to instigate curiosity for the new and out of common elements.

Therefore the story takes place at a galaxy called Flavours – name given with the purpose to emphasize the importance of flavors in the project –, where its inhabitants – Flavourians – dedicate themselves to the registration and preservation of all cuisine techniques. The most famous and favorite event, it is the Flavour Tournament, a competition where all chefs aim to recreate autochthonous recipes belonging to each different planet and outperform the original recipe. In addition, while travelling through the galaxy, the chefs need to show their knowledge about food safety and hygiene on top of helping their friends. The first one to complete all challenges, gains the Galactic Chef title. In terms of the graphical approach for designing the game world (Flavour's Galaxy) and all its components, we used Voxel Art.

We also developed charismatic characters (Fig. 1) as a mean to amplify the bond between them and the players [18] and with the aim of creating a bigger engagement and an immersion experience. Hence, we devised four different characters – four chefs that excel amid the rest by being winners of previous editions – whom kids may identify with regarding its personality and life challenges: "Chico Verdinho", "Suco Lento", "Sá Fresquinha" and "Trinca Espinhas".

The first chef to be introduced is "Chico Verdinho", an Octopoda – octopus – that has 1741 Flavourian Years and lives in "Bio Peppin'o", a planet that specializes on vegan food. In terms of personality, he is shy and has social phobia. His main purpose is to overcome this last problem, thus become a more extroverted person. "Suco Lento", the second chef to be introduced, belongs to the order of Testudines – turtles – and is 2394 Flavourian Years old. He lives on "Carni Vohrós" planet – the main courses are constituted mostly by grilled meat – and inherited the most popular butchery on the planet from his father. His appearance is the principal motive of concern, thereby, he aims to either accept the way he is or to dramatically change his figure. "Sá Fresquinha" is the third and the youngest chef. She is an early-stage Lepidoptera – butterfly – at the age of 1247 Flavourian Years and lives on the planet whose specialty is soup – "Hortículus Agricola". Due to her age, she is dependent on her parents and is afraid of disappointing them. This situation causes her to be unable to progress with her chef career and embrace new challenges. Throughout the story, the player choices will influence whether she can cut the "umbilical cord", gain wings and fly to a promising chef career or if she will forever remain under the wings of her parents.

The fourth and last chef goes by the name of "Trinca Espinhas". She is a walrus, as it can be seen from her design, due to her brown color, back legs facing outside, tusks and the walruses' typical nose (Fig. 1), belongs to the genus Odobenus and has 1689 Flavourian Years. Besides these animal traits, in pursuance of giving her some human characteristics, we opted to replace her front legs with arms, give her a hat and a chef jacket as well as a chopping knife. Since she is a feminine character and to highlight her vanity, we added a flower on top of her head.

Fig. 1. "Trinca Espinhas", a character of the FlavourGame (Own Source).

Her hometown is called "Coralus Spumoso", a planet which seafood and fish make the delight of its locals. Being an early promise of the culinary world, rapidly gained fame and became obsessed with fishbook – an exclusive social network of her planet – being later diagnosed with Fear of Missing Out (FOMO) Syndrome. Between the nights spent with her friends and the continuous livestream on the social network, there was not much time left to help her brothers at the family restaurant. Due to her unrelenting behavior, the brothers end up firing her. When "Trinca Espinhas" realizes the nature of the argument between her and her siblings, she has to choose between one of sides – family or friends – or to conciliate the social part of her life and fame with the work at her family's restaurant.

It was our intention to link every planet of the Flavour's Galaxy to a different variety of food and then design the corresponding Space Station inspired by it. Besides the four planets introduced above, Flavour's Galaxy has seven more planets: "Pastallinni" – dedicated to pasta –, "Capsilava" – spicy food and vulcanos –, "Petitascus" – serves the all-time favorite snacks, commonly eaten at festivals and fairs –, "Beggitaliós" – related with vegetarian food –, "Clorosódius" – a planet that seasons salads with sodium chloride –, "Habitanti Stressó" – a planet where the residents are always in a rush and fast-food is served to ease the stress – and "Panteão dos Grandes Chefs" – located at the center of the galaxy, this planet manages all the other ones.

3.2 Game

Initially we were oriented to implement an RPG-style game where its main focus would be an interactive narrative and character progression and customization. However, this idea started to fade due to the time it would take per game session. Consequently, to maintain a maximum of two hours per session, we opted to keep the game simple and introduced a Dice Rolling mechanic [19] as a player's main way to move within the game board, akin to the Goose Game [20]. After determining this key mechanic, we started to match it with secondary ones, such as the Trading [21] – a system where players can trade cards (Fig. 4) among them or with a market-based structure –, Hand Management [22] – a game mechanic where a player is rewarded by playing cards in a certain order – and Race [23] – as the name implies, the winner is the first to reach the end of the track or to meet certain conditions –, and also improved the ground rules established before.

The game is being conceived to be played with three or four children at the same time. Each child choses one of the four characters highlighted above. After every character is chosen, the game's mobile application randomizes the turn order and before initiating the game each player draws six food cards and a functional cards kit.

The game begins with every player attending "Moura Gordito's" opening speech at "Panteão dos Grandes Chefs'" Space Station. Each turn, the player rolls a six-sided die that decides the number of hexagons he/she advances – Dice Rolling mechanic. The game board (Fig. 2) is composed by three types of hexagons: Markets, Community Gardens and Space Stations.

The first one, Market, is a place where a player can exchange one of its food cards with another available in the market. When the player lands on a Community Garden, one of the following four possible scenarios occur: Real Flavour – the player has the possibility to taste a food sample from the available food near the game board and must guess its name –; Real Scent – the player has the possibility to smell one of the spices available near the game board and must guess its name –; and Quiz – the player has the possibility to answer a multiple choice question related with food safety or hygiene– and Fortune Cookie – the player has the possibility to draw one of the following special cards. The first type enables him to go to a random Market hexagon and the second enables it to go to a random Space Station. The third type allows the player to travel to any hexagon and the last one makes possible to trade a random card with another player – Trading mechanic.

Space Stations are the main objective a player must conquer, and, therefore, have an increased difficulty. When one lands on such hexagon, the task is to guess the order whereby a randomized recipe related with the Space Station is cooked. This is achievable by combining the correct food cards – Hand Management mechanic. When such is accomplished, besides conquering the Space Station, the player also receives a random power up among five: Speed – the player can double the number rolled on the die –, Strength – when visiting a Market, the player can exchange three cards –, Resiliency – when a recipe cooking order is wrong, the player has a second attempt –, Intelligence – when taking part in a Quiz, the player removes two wrong answers – and Vision – when cooking a recipe, the order of two products are shown to the player. The power up disappears after its first use. To become a Galactic Chef, the player must be the first to arrive at "Panteão dos Grandes Chefs" Space Station with the following requirements: five challenges completed – between Real Flavour, Real Scent and Quiz– and three conquered Space Stations – Race mechanic.

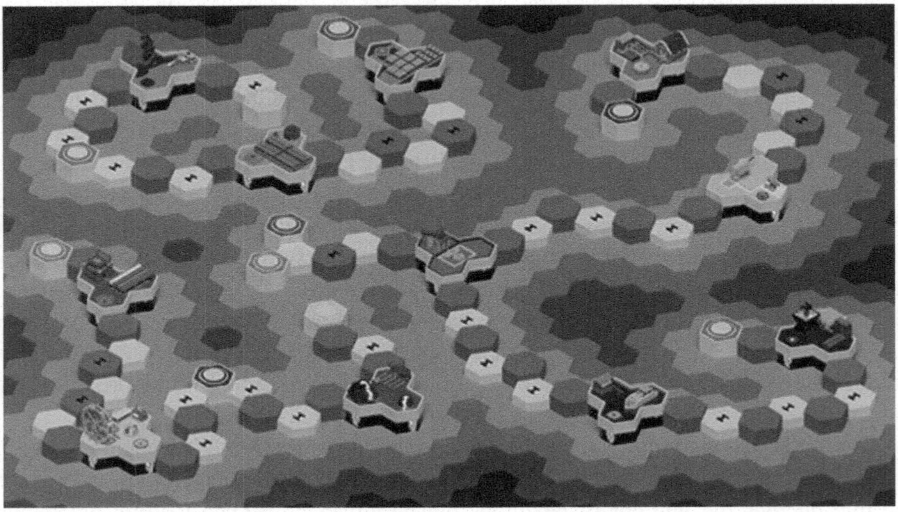

Fig. 2. Game board of the FlavourGame (Own Source).

4 Hybrid Gaming

Computers and videogames have known advantages compared to traditional board games, including complex simulations and rule based engines, evolving environments or the ability to save the state of the game [24], although some hobby board games due to analog design evolution are able to address this in clever new ways [25]. Also, the use of audiovisual components – animation, sound and music – mixed with real-time interaction, make videogames more attractive in the current century. We cannot forget that videogames are extending the experience of the 20th century most popular art form, the cinema, and with that are becoming the art form of this century. However, we tend to agree with Ishii [26] that interaction in videogames, with just pixels, seem to "impoverish the senses".

Hybrid games can combine the best from analog and digital games. They can profit from spatial socialization in a fun and learning way. Players like to maneuver the physical pieces and components, which help them to give meaning to the game world [27]. But hybrid games can also create digital solutions to help learning the rules and augment the simulation properties. The addition of the digital layer opens a realm of new multimedia solutions to make face to face playing in group even more immersive, using narration and sound effects—e.g. “Werewords” [28]—or augmented reality—e.g. “Chronicles of Crime” [9]. The computer calculation, the task and progress automatization can help in mitigating the need for drama or game managers—e.g. “Alchemists” [29]—freeing gamers to play and concentrate on the socialization. The simple task of sharing an electronic device like in “Chronicles of Crime” and “Alchemists” generate bonding and collaboration, even in competitive games like “Alchemists” and deepening the collaborative nature of “Chronicles of Crime”. In fact, the hybrid games create an additional game layer that is not only enhanced by digital, but also by the relationship that is established between players, which we believe can be researched and optimized in terms of user engagement [16].

FG follows the approach of maximization of interpersonal interactions. Very few hybrid games were conceived for social purpose, being within academy—e.g. “Pirates!” (2001) [30]; “False Prophets” (2002) [24]; “The TViews” (2008) [31]– or commercially – e.g. “Alchemists” (2014); “Werewords” (2017); “Chronicles of Crime” (2018).

4.1 Tangible Interaction and Augmented Reality

In accordance with cognitive psychology, namely in its behavioral approach, people develop during their lives the understanding of how to act in the physical world that surrounds them. So, the manipulation of tangible objects does not require, usually, a new type of learning [32]. The idea of a physical object as an interface for a digital system explores the conceptual advantages of the Tangible User Interfaces (TUIs) interaction paradigm.

TUIs add to the traditional board games the possibility of a more complex story, and the opportunity for players to change it during gameplay, while maintaining fiction and conversation alive. Something that can be even deeper with hobby games, mostly with the new hybrid genders that mix eurogame mechanics and American game narratives [33].

Alongside of TUIs, the rapid technologic evolution made possible a better symbiosis between virtual and physical object, aided by mixed realities (MR) [34]. This terminology is utilized since the various realities it comprises mix real and digital elements [35]. Based on the Virtuality Continuum model elaborated by Milgram and Kishino [36], inside MR there are two opposite sides: Augmented Virtuality (AV) and Augmented Reality (AR). Although AV is described as an enhancement of a virtual space with information sourced from the real world [37], AR represents the opposite, whereby digital objects are superimposed on the real world [38]. Whilst normally applied on Head Mounted Displays (HMD’s), Azuma [38] reckon that AR can be implemented on other technologies considering it provides real time interactivity and superimposes virtual elements on the real world three-dimensionally.

The utilization of AR on this project is correlated with its key advantage: almost every student has the necessary hardware. Due to this perk, the use of AR also implies a low implementation cost in comparison to a more permanent game-oriented technology [39]. With the integration of AR and with the recognition of the fiducials present on food cards, it is possible to implement the recipe cooking feature thus recreating an important piece of (re)discovering new flavors.

4.2 Graphics Approach

With Lowpoly and Voxel being the strongest options in graphics approach, our choice was the last one. Voxel graphics are commonly used on medicine, with the first model being a computed tomography scan of a female cadaver in 1984 [40]. However, in the last 10 years it is gaining popularity due to games such as "Minecraft" [41], a well-known videogame that promotes children creativity [42], and "Crossy Road" [43], where Voxel was chosen as the main art. Due to its increasingly popularity and the resemblance with the Mojang Studios game, we chose Voxel as the graphical approach for the characters (Fig. 1), game board (Fig. 2) and food cards (Fig. 4).

Regarding aesthetics and the strategical placement of Space Stations, we decided to use hexagons inspired by the Catan [44] board game. With this approach we could utilize the six-sided figures to build groups resembling constellations: one for the greens – vegetables, vegan and salads (Fig. 3) –, one for the festival/fair food – snacks, fast food and spicy food – and one for more traditional dishes – pasta, soup, seafood and meat.

Fig. 3. Detailed view of the Space Stations of the green's constellation – vegetables, vegan and salads (Own Source). (Color figure online)

While the Space Stations were being designed, we also began composing the recipes, always underlying our choices with both Flavour Bibles, the regular one [45] and its vegetarian variation [46]. As soon as the recipes were defined, the designing of food cards started.

The food cards (Fig. 4), an analog component, were divided in six distinct categories, each one with its own icon and color: red – dairy, meat and meat derived products; blue

– fish and seafood; turquoise – fruit; green – vegetables; orange – legumes; and purple – cereals. With the intent to improve the detection rating and to avoid the sensation of products floating, the cards were rendered with an isometric view of the product on top of a chopping board. These boards were positioned facing opposite directions or with different colors, easing the category customization.

To the lettering, we decided to use a pixelated font on behalf of making the card name easier to read. Additionally, we also placed the nutrition information of each food sample per 100g of product. We were prone to incorporate all nutrients, but with the objective to reduce communicational noise and to keep the food card design as minimalistic as possible, we opted by introducing the ones we considered the most significant: calories, carbohydrates and protein. Nevertheless, the nutritional information present on the cards is minimal so the mobile application will feature an exploration mode, allowing the player to analyze completely the nutritional information. Afterwards, to categorize the values by colors, we created a color system based on data collected from Frida Food Data database [47]. We used the database to search for each food sample and created a table with all nutrients. In relation to calories, since the least caloric food sample on our table – lettuce – has only 15 kcal and the most caloric – seitan – has 370 kcal, we determined that all values between 0 and 150 kcal are green, 150 and 300 kcal are yellow and above 300 are red. On carbohydrates, with the lowest – fish and meat – having 0g and the highest – white rice – having 77,8 g, we decided that green corresponds to all values between 0 and 10 g, yellow to 10 and 20 g and red to 20 g or above. We inverted this logic on the protein (last chosen nutrient), which means that all values between 0 and 10 g are red, 10 and 20 g are yellow and 20 g or above are green, since that the food sample with the most proteins – seitan – has 75,2 g and the least – lemon – has 0,5 g. With this color system, we anticipate that children will be able to understand which food is richer or poorer in terms of nutrients, by using the logic that having two green symbols on a card is better than having two yellow or two red.

Fig. 4. Example of food cards of the FlavourGame (Own Source). (Color figure online)

4.3 Implementation: Challenges of Hybridism

The introduction of a narrative in a hybrid game brings a range of variants to be considered during its conceptualization. Thus, in the process of creating the game, we were faced with several drawbacks regarding the integration of the narrative and how to conciliate it from an analog and digital point of view.

Usually, the story is prominently present in adventure, strategy and RPG games [48], not because of the genre, but because they are mostly single player games. However, it is also possible to find narrative in multiplayer games, where the players, sharing the same story, play simultaneously and together (cooperative games). Since FG is turn-based, the story cannot be shared amid all players, forcing each one to have his own individual story but linked to the same common narrative – the Flavour Tournament. The turns were conceived to be brief, in order to diminish any possible frustration that other players may have when waiting for their turns. For this reason, allied to the different types of players that exist, the story also cannot be extremely long, forcing our team to have a clear and a concise speech each time the player lands on a Space Station.

After we defined how the narrative could be embedded in the game, we were faced with how the digital and analog components could be conciliated and how the story of each character could be developed. This implicated thinking a whole mechanism that would allow us to identify the position of a player within the game board so that the story can be finished by the time the game ends. Initially, we had to define where we could strategically place sensors, so as to benefit from a narrative point of view as well as from an optimization of the game, preventing the production cost from becoming exaggeratedly high. Taking this into account, we decided to use sensors in the main objectives – conquering the restaurants. This means that whenever a player arrives at a Space Station, the respective sensor is triggered, and a small part of the story is unraveled on the mobile application. Besides the story elements shown at the Space Stations, there is also an introduction – presented at the beginning of the game – and a conclusion – this element will describe who won the game and it is exhibited when all players reach at "Panteão dos Grandes Chefs".

With the overcoming of the limitations described above, the hybridism boosts both components – analog and digital – making the experience of playing the game almost uninterruptible. The digital buttons were removed (except for buttons to navigate through the story) and sensors were implemented to replace them. The player's position is automatically detected when the pawn is placed at a Space Station and the system detects which restaurant the player is visiting and if it is the first, second or third time he/she visited a restaurant. This automatization, the recipe being chosen randomly and the story unfolding mechanism were conceived to make the player focus on the game board and to use the smartphone only when the task requires interactivity, such as inspecting the food cards (for discover information that cannot be seen in the cards) or to simulate a restaurant's kitchen (in order to cook the designated recipe).

5 Conclusion and Future Work

FG intends to become a game design model for platforms mixing real, fictional and digital worlds merged through physical and embodied interactions, and rich sensory experiences, unusual in videogames. In this perspective, the tangible dimension of FG, also grants an exciting feature to a game about nutrition: the possibility to add real food, with their flavors, aromas and textures, as elements in the gameplay, completely changing the regular gaming experience.

In relation to future work, we will implement the remaining components of what has already been idealized. Regarding the story and characters, we aim to develop "Trinca Espinhas" and her interactive narrative, providing agency to the player, allowing him to shape "Trinca Espinhas" personality and future – if she will be able to conciliate the social part of her life and fame with the work at her family's restaurant or if she will need to choose amid family and friends – Narrative Choice mechanic. In addition, to take the character development further, we considered designing special cards that complement the main story line without interfering directly with it. Afterwards, the story will be integrated on the mobile game application, which will be developed using the Unity Technologies game engine, Unity 3D.

In terms of technology and TUIs, we will be applying Radio Frequency Identification (RFID) readers into the Space Stations, so the mobile game application can detect the player's position and, that way, automatically generate a randomized recipe related with that Space Station. Concerning AR, through the fiducials printed onto the food cards, we will detect the order they are disposed to determine if the player has completed the challenge or not. Lastly, AR will also be used to show, relying on holograms, a detailed image of the food and its nutrition information.

Considering the educational dimension of the project, we intend to validate the model developed by conducting tests in a school with children of the age group of the project's target audience. These tests would serve to validate whether, through sensory experience with real food and spices, nutritional information and learning how to prepare recipes, children were able to retain the information.

Acknowledgments. The authors would like to acknowledge POCI-FEDER (Programa Operacional Competitividade e Internacionalização in its component Fundo Europeu de Desenvolvimento Regional) and FCT (Fundação para a Ciência e a Tecnologia) for funding this Project, under the Grant Agreement No. POCI-01–0145-FEDER-031024.

References

1. Tuorila, H., Meiselman, H.L., Bell, R., Cardello, A.V., Johnson, W.: Role of sensory and cognitive information in the enhancement of certainty and liking for novel and familiar foods. Appetite **23**, 231–246 (1994). https://doi.org/10.1006/appe.1994.1056
2. Mustonen, S., Tuorila, H.: Sensory education decreases food neophobia score and encourages trying unfamiliar foods in 8–12-year-old children. Food Qual. Prefer. **21**, 353–360 (2010). https://doi.org/10.1016/j.foodqual.2009.09.001
3. Reverdy, C., Schlich, P., Köster, E.P., Ginon, E., Lange, C.: Effect of sensory education on food preferences in children. Food Qual. Prefer. **21**, 794–804 (2010). https://doi.org/10.1016/J.FOODQUAL.2010.03.008
4. Ishii, H., Ullmer, B.: Tangible bits: towards seamless interfaces between people, bits and atoms. In: Proceedings of the ACM SIGCHI Conference on Human Factors in Computing Systems, pp. 234–241. Association for Computing Machinery, New York (1997). https://doi.org/10.1145/258549.258715

5. Editors, A.: Skylanders Video Game - Official Site. https://www.skylanders.com/. Accessed 15 Sep 2020
6. Editors, S.L.: Disney Infinity 3.0 Edition Game | PS4 – PlayStation. https://www.playstation.com/en-us/games/disney-infinity-30-edition-starter-pack-ps4/. Accessed 15 Sep 2020
7. Wehrum, T.: Evaluating the advantages of physical and digital elements in hybrid tabletop games (2014)
8. Editors, B.: Board Game Geek - Queen Strike. https://boardgamegeek.com/boardgame/204799/queen-strike. Accessed 10 Sep 2020
9. Cicurel, D.: Chronicles of Crime. Lucky Duck Games (2018)
10. Turczi, D., Bagiartakis, V.: Kitchen Rush. Artipia Games (2017)
11. Norman, D.A.: Emotional Design: Why We Love (or Hate) Everyday Things. Basic Books, United States (2003)
12. Adams, E.: Fundamentals of Game Design. New Riders, Berkley (2010)
13. Nakamura, J., Csikszentmihalyi, M.: Concept of flow. In: Flow and the foundations of positive psychology. pp. 89–105. Springer, Dordrecht (2014). https://doi.org/10.1007/978-94-017-9088-8_16
14. Murray, J.H.: Hamlet on the Holodeck: The Future of Narrative in Cyberspace. The Free Press, New York (1997)
15. Huizinga, J.: Homo Ludens. Editora Perspectiva S.A. (2000)
16. Zagalo, N.: Engagement Design : Designing for Interaction Motivations. Springer (2020). https://doi.org/10.1007/978-3-030-37085-5
17. BoardGameGeek, LLC: Narrative Choice (2020). https://boardgamegeek.com/boardgamemechanic/2851/narrative-choice-paragraph. Accessed 05 Aug 2020
18. Lebowitz, J., Klug, C.: Interactive Storytelling for Video Games: A Player-Centered Approach to Creating Memorable Characters and Stories. Focal Press, USA (2011)
19. BoardGameGeek, LLC: Dice Rolling (2020). https://boardgamegeek.com/boardgamemechanic/2072/dice-rolling. Accessed 05 Aug 2020
20. BoardGameGeek, LLC: Game of Goose (2020). https://www.boardgamegeek.com/boardgame/2785/game-goose. Accessed 10 Sep 2020
21. BoardGameGeek, LLC: Trading (2020). https://boardgamegeek.com/boardgamemechanic/2008/trading. Accessed 05 Aug 2020
22. BoardGameGeek, LLC: Hand Management (2020). https://boardgamegeek.com/boardgamemechanic/2040/hand-management. Accessed 05 Aug 2020
23. BoardGameGeek, LLC: Race (2020). https://boardgamegeek.com/boardgamemechanic/2876/race. Accessed 05 Aug 2020
24. Mandryk, R.L., Maranan, D.S.: False prophets: exploring hybrid board/video games. In: CHI 2002 Extended Abstracts on Human Factors in Computing Systems, pp. 640–641. ACM, New York (2002). https://doi.org/10.1145/506443.506523
25. Thrower, M.: Tabletop Gaming Manual: A Guide to the Diverse World of Modern Tabletop Games. Haynes Publishing, Sparkford (2018)
26. Ishii, H.: Tangible bits: designing the seamless interface between people, bits, and atoms. In: Proceedings of the 8th International Conference on Intelligent User Interfaces, p. 3. ACM, New York (2003). https://doi.org/10.1145/604045.604048.
27. Rogerson, M.J., Gibbs, M., Smith, W.: "I Love All the Bits": the materiality of boardgames. In: Proceedings of the 2016 CHI Conference on Human Factors in Computing Systems, pp. 3956–3969. Association for Computing Machinery, New York (2016). https://doi.org/10.1145/2858036.2858433.
28. Alspach, T.: Werewords. Bézier Games (2017)
29. Kotry, M.: Alchemists. Czech Games Edition (2014)

30. Björk, S., Falk, J., Hansson, R., Ljungstrand, P.: Pirates! using the physical world as a game board. In: Hirose, M. (ed.) Human-Computer Interaction INTERACT 2001: IFIP TC13 International Conference on Human-Computer Interaction, Tokyo, Japan, 9–13 July 2001, pp. 423–430. IOS Press (2001)
31. Mazalek, A., Basil, M., Elijah, O., Devender, D.: The TViews Table Role-Playing Game. JVRB - J. Virtual Real. Broadcast. **5**(8) (2008)
32. Gibson, J.J.: The Ecological Approach to Visual Perception. Houghton Mifflin, Boston (1979)
33. Sousa, M., Bernardo, E.: Back in the game. In: Zagalo, N., Veloso, A.I., Costa, L., Mealha, Ó. (eds.) VJ 2019. CCIS, vol. 1164, pp. 72–85. Springer, Cham (2019). https://doi.org/10.1007/978-3-030-37983-4_6
34. Flavián, C., Ibáñez-Sánchez, S., Orús, C.: The impact of virtual, augmented and mixed reality technologies on the customer experience (2019). https://doi.org/10.1016/j.jbusres.2018.10.050
35. Gutiérrez, M.A.A., Vexo, F., Thalmann, D.: Stepping into Virtual Reality. Springer, London (2008). https://doi.org/10.1007/978-1-84800-117-6
36. Milgram, P., Kishino, F.: Taxonomy of mixed reality visual displays. IEICE Trans. Inf. Syst. **12**, 1321–1329 (1994)
37. Gheorghiu, D., Ştefan, L.: Augmented Virtuality as an instrument for a better learning of history. In: International Conference on Virtual Learning, Romania (2018)
38. Azuma, R.T.: A survey of augmented reality. Virtual Augment. Real. **6**, 355–385 (1997). https://doi.org/10.1162/pres.1997.6.4.355
39. Craig, A.B.: Understanding Augmented Reality: Concepts and Applications. Morgan Kaufmann Publishers Inc., San Francisco (2013). https://doi.org/10.1016/C2011-0-07249-6
40. Gibbs, S.J., Pujol, A., Chen, T.S., Malcolm, A.W., James, A.E.: Patient risk from interproximal radiography. Oral Surg. Oral Med. Oral Pathol. **58**, 347–354 (1984). https://doi.org/10.1016/0030-4220(84)90066-5.
41. Mojang Synergies AB: Minecraft Official Site | Minecraft (2020). https://www.minecraft.net/en-us. Accessed 15 Sep 2020
42. Nguyen, J.: Minecraft and the building blocks of creative individuality. Configurations **24**, 471–500 (2016). https://doi.org/10.1353/con.2016.0030
43. Editors, H.W.: Crossy Road - Endless Arcade Hopper Game. https://www.crossyroad.com/. Accessed 15 Sep 2020
44. Editors, C.G.: Catan.com|The official website for the world of CATAN. https://www.catan.com/. Accessed 10 Sep 2020
45. Page, K., Dornenburg, A.: The Flavour Bible: The Essential Guide To Culinary Creativity, Based On The Wisdom Of America's Most Imaginative Chefs. Little, Brown and Company, New York (2008)
46. Page, K.: The Vegetarian Flavour Bible: The Essential Guide to Culinary Creativity with Vegetables, Fruits, Grains, Legumes, Nuts, Seeds, and More, Based on the Wisdom of Leading American Chefs. Little, Brown and Company, New York (2014)
47. Technical University of Denmark: Frida Food Data. https://frida.fooddata.dk/?lang=en. Accessed 05 Aug 2020
48. Lindley, C.: Game Taxonomies: A High Level Framework for Game Analysis and Design. https://www.gamasutra.com/view/feature/131205/game_taxonomies_a_high_level_.php. Accessed 10 Jan 2020

Motivating Students to Learn Computer Programming in Higher Education: The SimProgramming Approach

Ricardo Rodrigues Nunes[1(✉)], Gonçalo Cruz[2], Daniela Pedrosa[2], Ana Margarida Maia[3], Leonel Morgado[4], Hugo Paredes[5], José Cravino[6], and Paulo Martins[5]

[1] Brazilian Institute of Neuroscience and Neurotechnology (CEPID BRAINN FAPESP) & Faculdade de Ciências Médicas (UNICAMP), Campinas, São Paulo, Brazil
rnunes@unicamp.br

[2] CIDTFF - Universidade de Aveiro & Universidade de Trás-os-Montes e Alto Douro, Aveiro, Vila Real, Portugal
goncaloc@utad.pt, dpedrosa@ua.pt

[3] CIDTFF - Universidade de Aveiro, Aveiro, Portugal
margaridam@utad.pt

[4] Universidade Aberta & INESC TEC, Coimbra, Portugal
leonel.morgado@uab.pt

[5] Universidade de Trás-os-Montes e Alto Douro & INESC TEC, Vila Real, Portugal
{hparedes,pmartins}@utad.pt

[6] Universidade de Trás-os-Montes e Alto Douro & Research Centre Didactics and Technology in the Education of Trainers (CIDTFF), Aveiro, Vila Real, Portugal
jcravino@utad.pt

Abstract. This paper presents an action research study aiming to motivate undergraduate students to develop their computer programming learning skills, particularly within the transition from beginner to proficient level. The SimProgramming motivational approach is presented as a didactic proposal for this context. From the results of this iterative research process, we concluded that SimProgramming is a promising tool for teaching computer programming skills in intermediate classes, with potential to be used and/or applied in other educational contexts.

Keywords: Motivation to learn · SimProgramming · Computer programming · Computer science · Engineering education

1 Introduction

Motivation is a topic of great importance for computer programming teachers. It is quite common to hear them asking questions like "How can I motivate students to learn to code?", "What can I do to get students to actively participate in my programming classes?", or even "What can I do to engage students with educational programming activities?". These and other issues have been debated for many years in higher education, within the context of Engineering [1–3] and Computer Science courses [4–6].

A. Reis et al. (Eds.): TECH-EDU 2020, CCIS 1384, pp. 506–518, 2021.
https://doi.org/10.1007/978-3-030-73988-1_41

In intermediate level courses of two bachelor programmes at the University of the Trás-os-Montes e Alto Douro (UTAD), namely Informatics Engineering (IE) and Information and Communication Technologies (ICT), students typically create small programs by adapting and combining parts of pre-existing code. However, when challenged to develop other programs in advanced programming situations (e.g., when programmers need to write well-structured code leveraging pre-existing structures such as frameworks, libraries and/or APIs, Application Programming Interfaces) students do not seem to find the necessary motivation to learn, hampering their opportunities to realize the long-term benefits of organizing code in a more structured and manageable way. This is often a problem that will leave new graduates underprepared for the labour market, struggling in specific situations where these computer programming skills are fundamental.

Therefore, the main research objective of the study here presented is to tackle this problem, assuming the premise that students are not motivated and do not recognize the importance of better code organization due to their inexperience with team-based approaches to work in long-term software development settings. As an outcome, we present the SimProgramming motivational approach, arguing for the use of community-based learning environments to enable undergraduate students in becoming motivated and benefiting from contact with experienced (professional) programmers in order to succeed. In this approach, personal, behavioral, and environmental factors are dynamically related and strongly influence students' feelings about the needed skills to overcome possible challenges that arise during their learning process [7].

2 Motivation to Learn in Engineering Education

Much research has been conducted in Engineering Education on students' motivations to learn. Some of the most popular theories, adopted by different researchers are: achievement goal [8, 9], interest [10, 11], expectancy-value [12, 13], causal attributions [14, 15], self-efficacy [16, 17], and self-determination [18, 19]. However, it is argued that many of these studies are exploratory and do not clearly define what motivation is, or even that they do not consistently follow any specific theoretical framework [20]. It is essential to point out that the coexistence of these theories with their different aspects demonstrates how complex and multifaceted motivation is. Table 1 presents a summary of the main aspects of some of the motivation to learn theories.

Much of the research on motivation to learn deals with the importance of the pedagogical context in which the students are inserted, as well as with their involvement and persistence for performing the learning activities [21]. Either oral and written communication, or teamwork skills are considered fundamental to undergraduate students in Computer Science, as future professionals in the field [22]. Thus, many authors propose project-oriented and teamwork activities to motivate and facilitate the development of both students' innovation and complex problem-solving skills that allow them to succeed in the labor market [21].

Concerning the achievement goal theory, students showing a strong commitment with learning present greater autonomy and cognitive strategies [23]. Additionally, they are more likely to seek help from colleagues and teachers when facing learning difficulties, both online and in classroom environments [24]. This is explained either by goal-oriented or by self-efficacy theories on motivation to learn [25].

Table 1. Main aspects of motivation to learn theories.

Theory	Aspects related to the practice of teaching programming
Achievement goal	• Students' academic and social goals influence their motivation; • Students have different goals and consequently different behaviors throughout their studies; • Students concerned with the development of their learning present greater autonomy, elaborate more meaningful strategies, and feel safer in seeking for help from their peers; • Students concerned about their reputation in terms of skills and expertise can also achieve good academic results; • Students enjoy recognition through rewards or feedback; • Tasks need to be challenging, but appropriate to the knowledge levels of students; • Tasks need to be fair, according to the level of the required effort to complete them; • Academic environments that promote more significant interaction among students tend to be better for learning
Interest	• Interest increases the chances of students developing their skills; • Interest can be generated from activities that promote self-study, active learning, collaborative work, and social interaction, for example, through Problem-Based Learning (PBL), serious games, social games, virtual worlds, gamification, etc.; • Constant support and encouragement help to develop students' interest
Expectancy-value	• The value attributed to a task and the expectation of its successful completion can contribute to greater student involvement; • Individual beliefs and perceptions, as well as the socio-cultural environment, influence students' motivation; • The social context, collaboration, and authentic activities closer to the workplace settings promote student motivation
Causal attributions	• Students develop hypotheses (attributions) about the causes that led them to success or failure in carrying out their activities; • Through optimistic attributions, students are confident to succeed in the accomplishment of a task; • Through pessimistic assignments, students have little confidence in completing a task successfully; • Through hostile assignments, students can develop anger and present aggressive behaviors
Self-efficacy	• Students with higher expectations of self-efficacy perform better; • Previous positive experiences, social models, persuasion, and physiological reactions originate and develop students' self-efficacy beliefs; • Reducing stress situations and enhancing positive emotional states help to motivate students; • task structuring and supervision aligned with task complexity enhance students' motivation to learn; • Self-reflection, collaborative work, and activities closer to the workplace environment enhance students' motivation to learn; • Problem-Based Learning (PBL) helps to achieve a more significant task involvement by developing students' positive feelings (e.g., task value recognition, social acceptance)
Self-determination	• Intrinsically motivated students usually take a greater interest in learning; • Extrinsically motivated students generally experience lower academic performance compared to intrinsically motivated students; • Social and environmental settings that meet students' needs in terms of autonomy, competence, and relational skills promote their motivation; • Regulatory processes influence students' motivational behaviors

Self-efficacy, in turn, is an indicator of success in solving mathematical problems [26]. This can be enhanced in Problem-Based Learning (PBL) environments; teachers who use PBL are more likely to assist their students in overcoming difficulties that may negatively impact their self-efficacy beliefs, such as team composition or task difficulty [27]. PBL and its derivatives are reported in the literature as methodological tools that can promote and maintain students' motivational aspects as [28], for example, their situational interest [29].

Pascual [30] describes a PBL approach to increase students' knowledge through a social construction process of learning. His approach aimed to maximize opportunities for knowledge sharing between students and professionals, uniting academia through the creation of communities of practice. These ideas were based on the theory of self-determination. The focus was on increasing students' intrinsic motivation by creating the conditions needed for their social relationships. Various activities and tools were developed during the intervention as, for example, the development of meetings between the communities of students, maintenance engineers and academics, the development of recreational activities inside and outside the university campus, and the development of a web-based decision support system. This author started from the hypothesis that this multimodal approach would enhance active learning and social interactions. As a result of the research carried out, an increase in students' motivation was identified, confirming that communities of practice and social relationships are relevant factors for effective student learning. Autonomy and other psychological needs of self-determination were also related to PBL, which favors social interaction and promoting active learning and self-study in engineering courses [31].

An innovative pedagogical project has been developed in a higher education course taught at the Faculty of Engineering of the University of Porto (FEUP) [32]. In this curricular unit, called Project Management Laboratory (PML), undergraduate and master students developed different learning projects within a simulated business-like environment. During one semester, the students were divided into different teams and created companies to respond to customers' problems. The learning activities were divided into four stages, with two oral and public presentations at crucial moments throughout the project. The project was initiated by the startup stage, where companies were created from kick-off meetings. The second stage was the conception, where weekly project planning, quality control and risk management were carried out, accompanied by written reports. At the end of this stage, intermediate presentations were made in public sessions. The third stage was the software development itself, planning and the development of weekly reports, quality control and risk management. After this stage, final oral presentations were made in public sessions. At the end of the project, during the last stage, self-evaluation and project delivery meetings were made with customers. Students developed knowledge about project management, entrepreneurship, marketing, communication, customer interaction, and teamwork in software projects.

In addition to studies on the motivational impact of PBL on engineering students' learning, research was conducted on the relation between students' motivation with online activities and tools. For example, multimedia resources and discussion forums increased student motivation in blended learning and e-learning environments [33]. Evidence indicates that such approaches increase students' interest and emotional involvement with learning [33]. These results were somehow expected since the main aspects of students' lives, such as leisure, friendships, social interactions, and civic activities, are mediated by these technologies [34]. This was also reflected in studies on the impact of games in students' motivation and learning. An increasing number of research have been conducted on how serious games [35], social games [36], virtual worlds [37], and gamification [38] are related to several personal factors, such as students' motivational, affective, cognitive, and behavioral factors. All these interactive technologies helped develop participatory cultures in which collaboration and networking define what is understood by social and cultural competences [39]. Such technological and social contexts allowed students interaction to search for information, share resources, and develop their curiosity, interest, and involvement with learning [40].

Due to the complexity of factors that influence student motivation and learning, planning, and executing projects in the classroom is a challenge for many teachers. To facilitate these activities, research has been carried out on how models based on the expectancy-value theory can help implement teaching approaches that promote the social aspects of learning, as collaboration and authentic activities closer to the workplace environment [41]. The results of these efforts highlighted the importance of pedagogical practices proposed by teachers, as well as the positive impact that social interactions and the use of technologies have on students' motivation and learning.

3 Research Problem and Question

The main research problem addressed in this paper is how to tackle the difficulty that students have in making the transition from a basic to a proficient computer programming level. Students do not seem to value the benefits that well-structured, organized code can bring in the long run during this transition. It is difficult for them to acknowledge the value of coding while thinking about its architectural features, mainly because they can make their programs work anyway, without this extra effort.

In this context, knowing that motivation has been identified as an important factor for students' learning success, we assume that the evidence generated by research on this topic can help to tackle the identified research problem. Thus, the research question addressed in our study was: How to bring the knowledge about learning motivation into the context of higher education intermediate computer programming classes in order to support students' transition from basic to proficient level?

4 Research Method

An action-research study was carried out within the curricular unit of "Programming Methodologies III" (PMIII), over three iterations/academic years, at the UTAD. The curricular unit has a duration of 4 months and is a mandatory subject of the second year of the undergraduate programmes in IE and ICT, with the main goal of introducing software architecture concepts to support the development of students' code organization skills.

An approach was designed and developed from a set of different learning problems related to the topics covered in the course. In Table 2, some instances of the problems are presented. For them, students, in groups, were asked to propose a solution. The activities were developed using PBL. Each group was assigned with a specific problem involving an architectural pattern related to MVC (Model-View-Controller) and pre-existing structures such as frameworks, libraries, or Application Programming Interface (API). At the end of each edition, the students' groups have to develop a written document explaining the approaches used to develop their code with the application of an architectural pattern with the pre-existing structure related to the assigned problem.

Throughout the research project, quantitative and qualitative data were collected from submitted files and logs in the information systems adopted in the curricular unit (e.g., Wiki PBWorks and Moodle), online questionnaires, semi-structured interviews, audiovisual recordings of some face-to-face activities and direct observation.

In the first iteration [42], students were challenged to solve the problem assigned with theoretical and practical components by researching technical-scientific literature, and by engaging with more experienced programmers in different social networks and/or online communities of practice. The goal was to motivate them to develop their computer programming skills by meeting and asking for help from other professionals, members

Table 2. Some of the specific problems assigned to student teams.

Problems
Write a detailed document that explains how to apply the MVC (Model-View-Controller) architectural standard to application development with libOpenMetaverse. This document should complement this explanation with concrete examples of the various forms of application that design
Write a detailed document that explains how to apply the MVP (Model-View-Presenter) architectural standard to the development of applications in the Windows Phone Application Platform, with the XNA framework. This document should complement this explanation with concrete examples of the various ways they conceive for applying the standard
Write a detailed document that explains how to apply the MVVM (Model-View-ViewModel) architectural pattern to the development of applications with Windows Forms. This document should complement this explanation with concrete examples of the various ways they conceive for applying the architectural pattern MVVM

of these online communities. The results of this first iteration showed that most groups were unable to solve their assignments successfully. Of the twenty groups (a total of 62 students) that were initially enrolled in the project, nineteen groups (a total of 59 students) performed some tasks. Seven groups performed the activities during all phases of the project, with four of them reaching an acceptable quality level regarding the learning outcomes achieved at the end. The overall quality of the reports from these groups that completed the project showed that the students acquired significant aspects on the themes of the proposed assignments and were able to provide useful examples of the approaches they developed; however, this effort was not reflected in the final grade of the curricular unit, which were much more dependent on the two written tests that students had to perform than the project itself- the latter only counted 20% for the final grade.

The second iteration occurred in the following year [43]. The activities were implemented with new teaching and learning strategies: they were more structured throughout the project (with weekly tasks and strict deadlines), and supervised by two tutors to provide support to the students through follow-up and feedback, which also facilitate three group dynamics conducted within the classroom. Compared to the previous cycle, it was found that more groups participated actively throughout the project. More specifically, nine of the twenty-one groups that started the project continually developed their activities and received feedback in the online communities of practice until the end. From the results of this second iteration, it was possible to identify and offer possible solutions to the students' main problems concerning their learning process, namely the lack of time to work, the lack of feedback on the development of the project, and the low motivation to complete the assigned activities. Based on these results, a motivational approach called SimProgramming was developed, which simulates a business-like environment and was then implemented in the third and last cycle of this research.

5 The SimProgramming Motivational Approach

Some significant changes were implemented in the third research iteration, reported already somewhere [44, 45]. One of them was creating a community of practice with students, alumni, and invited external programmers, instead of asking students to participate in the external online communities, and thus promoting a more significant interaction and strengthening the relationships among the different project participants. Better project management practices were also adopted to identify potential problems faced by students at an earlier stage, allowing the provision of supportive guidance by the teaching team according to their needs and, consequently, helping them to obtain better results. Therefore, it was also proposed a reformulation of the interaction and assessment strategies previously adopted, and a business-like environment was designed, and a popular project management method used in the workplace, known as Scrum, was implemented [46]. Other aspects, like continuous feedback, self-evaluation and hetero-evaluation strategies were also implemented. Below, the SimProgramming motivation approach is described according to its main conceptual foundations and application phases.

5.1 Conceptual Foundations

The SimProgramming approach is based on four conceptual foundations: (1) a business-simulated environment for learning, (2) self-regulated learning; (3) Co-regulated learning; and (4) formative assessment.

A Business-Simulated Environment for Learning (Situated learning). In this environment, each participant plays a role within a business roleplay context. The teacher plays the role of CEO - Chief Executive Officer (or General Manager), globally responsible for evaluating the progress of the projects, clarifying the specific doubts that students have and guiding them from the analyses made on the presentations in the face-to-face meetings and on the reports submitted. Tutors or Teaching Assistants take the role of project managers, responsible for closer monitoring, regular feedback, and mentoring. In all teams, one student plays the role of team coordinator, communicating with management (general manager and project managers). Among his duties are ensuring integration of other students/participants in the team, making sure that they maintain an overall view of the project and its status, as well as reporting issues, difficulties and doubts experienced by the teams to the managers (i.e., acting as a link). Team coordinators, like the project managers, are motivating agents for students. The proposal of simulating a business environment is based on the available literature about the influence that the pedagogical context has on the students' motivation.

Self-regulated Learning. SimProgramming promotes active learning, developing students' self-regulation, by enabling a study routine through weekly task deliveries, keeping students focused on course content. Weekly reports allow students to reflect on their work, planning what to do the following week, and identifying negative factors that prevent them from achieving individual and team objectives. This conceptual foundation also supports developing students' skills to avoid procrastination and improve time management. Thus, they are encouraged to adopt a study routine by promoting a motivational context for learning. In this way, students can gradually develop their accountability, doing their activities regularly and not delaying them to the last moment.

Co-regulated Learning. Students with little experience have only general ideas about the disciplinary field. When they acquire new responsibilities, performing more complex tasks, they gradually develop their identities against other participants in communities of practice. As they interact with others, they increase the opportunities to learn through their contributions and feedback. Thus, the teaching team must provide support to develop social and group interactions, guiding students' participation and gradual involvement in such communities. This development of co-regulation includes suggesting specific strategies for interaction. Such actions support the development of students' sense of being, informal interactions, and debating. This can also be promoted and monitored through social media groups created specifically for the curricular unit. Such an internal community can be maintained over the years, becoming a source of interaction between new students, former students still studying (e.g., MSc or PhD students), and graduates already in the labor market. Some of these alumni can play a role of business consultants, providing support and advice to the new teams.

Formative Assessment. This process includes motivational mentoring and constant feedback on the project development status, for example, on whether the work is progressing or deviating from initial expectations and goals. For this, weekly meetings are held based on Scrum - an agile method for planning and managing software development projects at the workplace. This support is provided face-to-face through weekly meetings that are scheduled with the team coordinators, in which three specific topics are addressed: 1) "What did the team do during the past week?"; 2) "What will be done during the current week?" and; 3) "What is preventing the conclusion of the activities? When specific problems (technical, personal, or others) are detected, meetings are scheduled with the teams that presented such difficulties, case by case. In addition to these meetings, all students need to answer the same three specific topics in an online form and submit it on a weekly basis. In addition to these forms, all students also need to submit reports on their interactions in the communities of practice on two specific occasions of the project (at the end of phases 1 and 2 - please see below in '5.2 Application stages'). These reports serve as formative assessment tools. At the end of the project, students make their self- and hetero-evaluation of their teammates. All these reports are excellent opportunities for students to reflect on their learning activities. There are still three presentations at the end of each phase of the project made by students. These presentations are evaluated by the teaching team and serve as a formative resource for guiding the students projects' progress. It is important to note that each meeting with the students is an opportunity to talk informally about the project and guide them on it.

5.2 Application Stages

The SimProgramming approach develops over 4 main stages, based on the conceptual foundations presented above. These phases represent the result of the reflections made by researchers on the entire action-research process. Table 3 presents a summary of the activities carried out during the four stages.

Table 3. Summary of SimProgramming stages and activities.

Stages	Activities
Stage 1 (design)	Organization of the teams; literature review; interaction in the communities of practice; initial presentation; weekly report
Stage 2 (development)	Interaction in the communities of practice; intermediate presentation; weekly report; report of interactions in the communities
Stage 3 (refinement)	Final presentation; final report
Stage 4 (closure)	Final report improved; self-evaluation and hetero-evaluation

Throughout all the project stages, weekly meetings are scheduled between project managers (tutors) and team coordinators, providing motivational support and clarification on more technical questions. When internal problems in any of the student's groups are identified, project managers can also schedule meetings with these teams or with any specific student to make more targeted interventions. Students also submit reports at the end of each stage, lasting one week, detailing what they have done, what they will do, and what eventually prevents them from performing the planned activities. On two occasions (end of Stage 1 and Stage 2), students still submit reports about their interactions in the communities of practice.

6 Results and Conclusion

According to the third cycle of this action-research study, in which SimProgramming was implemented, data was collected from a variety of sources, namely the students' forms filled in and submitted online, the notes from the direct observations of researchers, the audiovisual recordings of face-to-face meetings, the records of messages exchanged between the different actors, as well as the logs of the interactions in the information systems adopted for the curricular unit. During the application of the approach, it was possible to gather evidence on its adequacy to the proposed goals, and it was concluded that the SimProgramming proved to be an important motivational tool for students to develop their computer programming skills. In this cycle, more students participated actively in the project, and the results were reflected in the final grades of the curricular unit. Of the fifteen teams, eleven maintained a constant quality performance on all activities throughout the project. Of the four remaining teams, two worked regularly, but the quality of their reports was below the expected level, and the other two groups did not even start the project. In a total of 97 students, 66 completed the tasks, and 59 performed well in the learning activities. Table 4 summarizes the work developed by each team.

It is important to emphasize that the SimProgramming approach implied significant changes to the teaching practice, especially in terms of the relationship between teaching staff and students, both inside and outside the classroom. Maintaining a good relationship between all the actors guaranteed a safe and supportive environment that was of the utmost importance for the development of students' learning and academic success.

Table 4. Summary of students' teams in SimProgramming approach.

Team	Assignment development	
	No. members	Summary
T1	6	Regular individual and team task assignment completion. They created a Facebook group for internal interaction
T2	7	Regular individual assignment completion (except the last two weeks). Team tasks performed regularly
T3	7	Irregular individual assignment completion. The team delivered just two reports. One student quit the project and two others got negative grades. Tutor interventions were necessary via face-to-face meetings for feedback
T4	7	Irregular individual assignment completion. They carried out all team tasks but didn't perform the first presentation. Three students quit the project. Tutor interventions were necessary via face-to-face meetings for feedback
T5	7	Initially they weren't achieving the goals, but after replacing the coordinator (the original one quit the project), the team showed better results. Tutor interventions were necessary via face-to-face meetings for feedback
T6	4	Regular individual and team task assignment completion. Tutor interventions were necessary via face-to-face meetings for feedback
T7	7	The team quit the project. The students didn't respond to invitations for meetings with the tutors
T8	7	Regular individual and team tasks assignment completion
T9	6	Regular delivery (with some delays) of individual and team task assignments. One student quit the project. The coordinator was very committed and impactful for the success of the team. They created a Facebook group for internal interaction
T10	6	Regular individual and team tasks assignment completion. Two students quit the project
T11	6	The team quit the project. The students didn't answer invitations for meetings with tutors
T12	7	The team didn't work, and five students quit. Two students met with tutors and were instructed to perform compensatory activities. The other students didn't respond to tutors' invitations
T13	7	Regular for most assignments: individual (with the exception of one student) and team tasks
T14	8	Three students were regularly delivering individual and team task assignments. Tutor interventions were necessary via face-to-face meetings for motivation and feedback. Five students quit the project
T15	5	Regular individual and team tasks assignment completion. One student quit the project

Throughout the project, a relationship of trust between the teaching team and the students was built.

Thus, as the main contribution of this research, the SimProgramming approach is presented as a tool to support learning motivation in computer programming higher education courses, and specifically within the transition from basic to proficient level of programming skills. Another contribution is the whole research-action process developed in the context of this study, which educators can use as a guiding plan and method for the development of innovative pedagogical approaches in the computer education field.

Acknowledgments. This work is financed by National Funds through the Portuguese funding agency, FCT - Fundação para a Ciência e a Tecnologia within project UIDB/50014/2020.

References

1. Ibrahim, A., Aulls, M.W., Shore, B.M.: Teachers' roles, students' personalities, inquiry learning outcomes, and practices of science and engineering: the development and validation of the McGill attainment value for Inquiry engagement survey in STEM disciplines. Int. J. Sci. Math. Educ. **15**(7), 1195–1215 (2017)
2. Lucke, T., Dunn, P.K., Christie, M.: Activating learning in engineering education using ICT and the concept of 'Flipping the classroom.' Eur. J. Eng. Educ. **42**(1), 45–57 (2017)
3. López-Fernández, D., Ezquerro, J.M., Rodríguez, J., Porter, J., Lapuerta, V.: Motivational impact of active learning methods in aerospace engineering students. Acta Astronaut. **165**, 344–354 (2019)
4. Dicheva, D., Dichev, C., Agre, G., Angelova, G.: Gamification in education: a systematic mapping study. J. Educ. Technol. Soc. **18**(3), 75–88 (2015)
5. Hao, Q., Barnes, B., Wright, E., Branch, R.M.: The influence of achievement goals on online help seeking of computer science students. Br. J. Edu. Technol. **48**(6), 1273–1283 (2017)
6. Gorson, J., O'Rourke, E.: How do students talk about intelligence? An investigation of motivation, self-efficacy, and mindsets in computer science. In: Proceedings of the 2019 ACM Conference on International Computing Education Research, pp. 21–29. Association for Computing Machinery, New York (2019)
7. Slavich, G.M., Zimbardo, P.G.: Transformational teaching: theoretical underpinnings, basic principles, and core methods. Educ. Psychol. Rev. **24**(4), 569–608 (2012)
8. Hakulinen, L., Auvinen, T.: The effect of gamification on students with different achievement goal orientations. In: The Proceedings of the 2014 International Conference on Teaching and Learning in Computing and Engineering (LaTiCE), pp. 9–16. IEEE, Kuching (2014)
9. Banu, E.A., Hunsu, N.: Exploring the role of students' achievement goals and learning approaches in academic performance. In: the Proceedings of the 126th American Society for Engineering Education Annual Conference & Exposition, pp. 1–7. ASEE, Florida (2019)
10. Clapper, T.C.: Situational interest and instructional design: a guide for simulation facilitators. Simul. Gaming **45**(2), 167–182 (2014)
11. Rowe, J.P., Shores, L.R., Mott, B.W., Lester, J.C.: Integrating learning and engagement in narrative-centered learning environments. In: the Proceedings of the 10th International Conference on Intelligent Tutoring Systems - Volume Part II, pp. 166–177. Springer, Heidelberg (2010). https://doi.org/10.1007/978-3-642-13437-1_17
12. Chen, J.L.: The effects of education compatibility and technological expectancy on e-learning acceptance. Comput. Educ. **57**(2), 1501–1511 (2011)
13. Wu, F., Fan, W., Arbona, C., de la Rosa-Pohl, D.: Self-efficacy and subjective task values in relation to choice, effort, persistence, and continuation in engineering: an Expectancy-value theory perspective. Eur. J. Eng. Educ. **45**(1), 151–163 (2020)
14. Vivian, R., Falkner, K., Falkner, N.: Computer science students' causal attributions for successful and unsuccessful outcomes in programming assignments. In: the Proceedings of the 13th Koli Calling International Conference on Computing Education Research, pp. 125–134. Association for Computing Machinery, New York (2013)
15. Duron, T., Gallon, L., Aniorte, P.: Modelling learner's perseverance in education software. In: The Proceedings of the 35th Information Systems Education Conference (ISECON 2019), Galveston, Texas, United States, pp. 34–38 (2019)
16. Stolk, J., Harari, J.: Student motivations as predictors of high-level cognitions in project-based classrooms. Act. Learn. High. Educ. **15**(3), 231–247 (2014)
17. Starkey, E.M., Hunter, S.T., Miller, S.R.: Are creativity and self-efficacy at odds? An exploration in variations of product dissection in engineering education. J. Mech. Des. **141**(1), 012001 1–012001 11 (2019)

18. Hartmann, A., Gommer, L.: To play or not to play: on the motivational effects of games in engineering education. Eur. J. Eng. Educ. 1–25 (2019).
19. Zhao, L., Lu, Y., Wang, B., Huang, W.: What makes them happy and curious online? An empirical study on high school students' internet use from a self-determination theory perspective. Comput. Educ. **56**(2), 346–356 (2011)
20. Brown, P.R., McCord, R.E., Matusovich, H.M., Kajfez, R.L.: The use of motivation theory in engineering education research: a systematic review of literature. Eur. J. Eng. Educ. **40**(2), 186–205 (2015)
21. Johri, A., Olds, B.M.: Situated engineering learning: bridging engineering education research and the learning sciences. J. Eng. Educ. **100**(1), 151–185 (2011)
22. Adams, R., et al.: Multiple perspectives on engaging future engineers. J. Eng. Educ. **100**(1), 48–88 (2011)
23. Chen, C.H., Wu, I.C.: The interplay between cognitive and motivational variables in a supportive online learning system for secondary physical education. Comput. Educ. **58**(1), 542–550 (2012)
24. Vogt, C.M.: Faculty as a critical juncture in student retention and performance in engineering programs. J. Eng. Educ. **97**(1), 27–36 (2008)
25. Hutchison, M.A., Follman, D.K., Sumpter, M., Bodner, G.M.: Factors influencing the self-efficacy beliefs of first-year engineering students. J. Eng. Educ. **95**(1), 39–47 (2006)
26. Pajares, F., Miller, M.D.: Role of self-efficacy and self-concept beliefs in mathematical problem solving: a path analysis. J. Educ. Psychol. **86**(2), 193–203 (1994)
27. Schaffer, S.P., Chen, X., Zhu, X., Oakes, W.C.: Self-efficacy for cross-disciplinary learning in project-based teams. J. Eng. Educ. **101**(1), 82–94 (2012)
28. Bédard, D., Lison, C., Dalle, D., Côté, D., Boutin, N.: Problem-based and project-based learning in engineering and medicine: determinants of students' engagement and persistance. Interdisc. J. Probl. Learn. **6**(2), 7–30 (2012)
29. Rotgans, J.I., Schmidt, H.G.: Problem-based learning and student motivation: the role of interest in learning and achievement. In: One-Day, One-Problem, pp. 85–101. Springer, Singapore (2012). https://doi.org/10.1007/978-981-4021-75-3_5
30. Pascual, R.: Enhancing project-oriented learning by joining communities of practice and opening spaces for relatedness. Eur. J. Eng. Educ. **35**(1), 3–16 (2010)
31. Stolk, J., Martello, R., Somerville, M., Geddes, J.: Engineering students' definitions of and responses to self-directed learning. Int. J. Eng. Educ. **26**(4), 900–913 (2010)
32. Laboratório de Gestão de Projetos Homepage (Challenge). https://lgp.fe.up.pt. Accessed 20 Nov 2017
33. Sun, J.C.-Y., Rueda, R.: Situational interest, computer self-efficacy and self-regulation: their impact on student engagement in distance education. Br. J. Edu. Technol. **43**(2), 191–204 (2012)
34. Palfrey, J., Gasser, U.: Born Digital: Understanding the First Generation of Digital Natives. Basic Books, New York (2008)
35. Fonseca, B., et al.: PLAYER - a European project and a game to foster entrepreneurship education for young people. J. Univ. Comput. Sci. (J.UCS) **18**(1), 86–105 (2012)
36. Fonseca, B., et al.: BIZZY – a social game for entrepreneurship education learning and collaboration technologies. In: The Proceedings of the International Conference on Learning and Collaboration Technologies, pp. 33–41. Springer, Cham (2014). https://doi.org/10.1007/978-3-319-07485-6_4
37. Morgado, L., Varajão, J., Coelho, D., Rodrigues, C., Sancin, C., Castello, V.: The attributes and advantages of virtual worlds for real world training. J. Virtual Worlds Educ. **1**(1), 15–35 (2010)

38. Dicheva, D., Irwin, K., Dichev, C., Talasila, S.: A course gamification platform supporting student motivation and engagement. In: The Proceedings of the International Conference on Web and Open Access to Learning (ICWOAL), Dubai, United Arab Emirates, pp. 1–4. IEEE (2014)
39. Jenkins, H., Clinton, K., Purushotma, R., Robison, A.J., Weigel, M.: Confronting the challenges of participatory culture: media education for the 21st century. In: John, D., Catherine T.M. (eds.) Foundation Reports on Digital Media and Learning. The MIT Press, Cambridge (2006)
40. Arnone, M.P., Small, R.V., Chauncey, S.A., McKenna, H.P.: Curiosity, interest and engagement in technology-pervasive learning environments: a new research agenda. Educ. Technol. Res. Dev. **59**(2), 181–198 (2011)
41. Vekiri, I.: Information science instruction and changes in girls' and boy's expectancy and value beliefs: in search of gender-equitable pedagogical practices. Comput. Educ. **64**, 104–115 (2013)
42. Morgado, L., et al.: Social networks, microblogging, virtual worlds, and Web 2.0 in the teaching of programming techniques for software engineering: a trial combining collaboration and social interaction beyond college. In: The Proceedings of the Global Engineering Education Conference (EDUCON), pp. 1–7. IEEE, Marrakech (2012)
43. Nunes, R.R., et al.: Enhancing students' motivation to learn software engineering programming techniques: a collaborative and social interaction approach. In: the Proceedings of the International Conference on Universal Access in Human-Computer Interaction, pp. 189–201. Springer, Cham (2015). https://doi.org/10.1007/978-3-319-20684-4_19
44. Nunes, R.R., et al.: SimProgramming: uma abordagem motivacional para a aprendizagem de alunos intermediários de programação. In: Anais dos Workshops do Congresso Brasileiro de Informática na Educação, pp. 1099–1110. Sociedade Brasileira de Computação - SBC, Recife, Pernambuco (2017)
45. Pedrosa, D., Cravino, J., Morgado, L., Barreira, C., Nunes, R.R., Martins, P., Paredes, H.: Simprogramming: the development of an integrated teaching approach for computer programming in higher education. In: The Proceedings of the 10th International Technology, Education and Development Conference, pp. 7162–7172. IATED Academy, Valencia (2016)
46. Schwaber, K.: Agile Project Management with Scrum. Microsoft press, United States of America (2004)

A Proposal of a Classification Scheme to a Survey of Augmented Reality for Education and Training

Armando Cruz[1](✉), Hugo Paredes[2], and Paulo Martins[2]

[1] Instituto Politécnico de Viseu, Viseu, Portugal
cruz.armando1@sapo.pt
[2] Universidade de Trás-os-Montes e Alto Douro & INESC TEC, Vila Real, Portugal
{hparedes,pmartins}@utad.pt

Abstract. Augmented Reality (AR) is a field of knowledge that emerged in the middle of the last century, and its use has been spreading because of its usefulness, but also because of mobile platforms, accessible to most users. AR characteristics are valued in several fields of human activity, and also in the field of *Education and Training*, being AR pointed out as useful to the learning process. In this paper we search and analyse surveys and reviews of AR. We present a AR's definition, and we create a classification scheme of two dimensions for AR: the dimension of the fields of application of AR, and the dimension of the technologies of AR.

Keywords: Augmented reality · Virtual reality · Mixed reality · Education and training · Mobile platforms

1 Introduction

AR emerged in the middle of the XX century [1–3] with systems able to add artificial contents to the real world, from the user point of view. Since then, specific hardware and software was developed for AR, such as Head-Mounted Displays (HUD), haptic gloves, or visualization systems. More recently, with mobile platforms, AR has spread throughout the world, and its interest for research as grown accordingly [2, 3]. Along all these decades of AR development, many fields of human activity saw AR being used to support the field's activities. From industry, military, medical, to several other fields that have being using AR, and one in particular, *Education and Training*, is of major importance to us in this paper. As we are starting our research of the AR use for *Education and Training*, in this paper we intent to address the state of the art of AR, and how it has being used for *Education and Training*. Deeper research will follow this work.

In the next chapter we present the objectives of this work, and we describe the search process used, inclusions and exclusions, and the results of the search. In the third chapter we present the definition and a short history of AR. In the fourth chapter we explain and develop our classification scheme, presenting also the fields of application and technologies of AR. In the final chapter we present our conclusions and future work.

A. Reis et al. (Eds.): TECH-EDU 2020, CCIS 1384, pp. 519–531, 2021.
https://doi.org/10.1007/978-3-030-73988-1_42

2 The Search

The general objective of this work is to create a start point for future research in the area of AR applied to *Education and Training*. Our goal with this paper is to create a classification scheme for works in the field of AR that allow us to further analysis.

2.1 Methodology

AR is well known among researchers and public in general for several years now. Thus, any search for publications in this field will result in immense numbers of studies, hardly possible to analyse. Furthermore, there is debate about which databases to be included, depending on criteria such as field of study, citations, or publishing date, impact factor, etc. Usually several databases are included, which increases even more the difficulty of the search. To overcome these difficulties, our strategy is to use published reviews and surveys in the field of AR, usually based on those strict rules, and work over those studies. The search for those studies was conducted on Google Scholar [4].

We need to find enough studies that cover AR applications and technologies, and reuse them. And, to increase the likelihood of finding enough works with these characteristics, and provide a historical view of AR, we won't have any restrictions over the time window of the search, that is, we will search for studies of any date of publishing.

Two searches were conducted in Google Scholar [4]: one in search for surveys, and another searching for reviews. The keywords for searching surveys are "survey augmented reality", with the choices "all in title", and "since ever". With the same choices, for searching reviews, the keywords "review augmented reality" were used. The search includes articles from proceeding and journals, books, and technical reports. As exclusion criteria, are excluded those works which are out of theme, or are not surveys or reviews, are repeated, or are link errors.

2.2 Results

By application of the search filters described earlier, we obtained a total of 158 publications. Then, we applied our exclusion criteria. In the case of surveys, 96 studies were obtained, 29 of them rejected for being out of theme (3), repeated (6), link error (8), or not a survey (12), remaining 63 works. And in the case of reviews, 62 studies were obtained, with 22 rejected for being out of theme (2), repeated (2), link error (3), or not a review (15), remaining 40 works. The time span of the publications goes from 1997 to 2019, and the time span of their references goes from 1954 to 2019.

From the 103 works collected for this survey, only 15 refer explicitly the fields of application of AR, but several of them with examples. Along the time span of the sample, new fields are added, and somewhat different terms are used to name the fields. Many of the fields of application of AR are referred by several authors using the same designation or a similar one, and only a few of the fields where mentioned by only one author. They also are joined with other terms, or split, maybe reflecting the view of each author of the way to classify the fields of application of AR.

3 AR's Definition

The sample we achieved has several publications approaching general aspects of AR, such as the definition of AR, its characteristics, the relationship of AR and Virtual Reality (VR), and AR's history. In this chapter we approach these subjects in a brief way, but objectively with the purpose of creating a general picture of AR. For more details about any of these subjects, refer to the publications used.

Probably the most accepted definition of AR is Azuma's [5]. He sees AR as a variation of VR, distinguished from this last one by superimposing objects over reality, allowing the user to see both, rather than just a substitute of reality. From his point of view, AR systems have three characteristics: reality is combined with virtual objects, the combination is in 3D, and the systems are interactive in real time. Especially for the second characteristic, the idea to retain is that AR is the mixture of virtual information with real world information, but limited to visual information. Azuma's [5] definition of AR is also referred by [6–15]. Rabbi and Ullah [3] doesn't subscribes Azuma's [5] definition of AR, but they reaffirm the same characteristics of AR.

Other definitions were proposed, all of them similar in the idea that AR is some degree of mixture of virtual visual information and real world's. Some of those definitions set limits also to the contents used to only computer-generated information, namely: Thomas [16] who says that AR is graphical computer generated information registered over the view the user has of the real world; Kumar and Sahityapriyadharshini [17] saying that AR is the adding of virtual information in the real world using computer technology; Rabbi and Ullah [3] who says that AR are systems with which the real world is augmented by computer-generated objects; Hemamalini et al. [18] who says that AR is the combination of real world objects with digitally augmented data; Kim et al. [19] saying that AR is the enhancement of the real world with virtual information; and El-Khamisy et al. [20] defines AR as the projection of virtual objects and information on the real world.

In other hand, Sinha et al. [21], despite agreeing that AR combines the real world with computer-generated information, says that the information is not only visual, but also auditory, haptic, and somatosensory information. Sinha et al. [21] widens the scope of AR to other kinds of information besides visual, which is in agreement with the view of early dreamers, which was of mixture real information with artificially generated information, as it can be seen in the next chapter. Another interesting fact about these dreamers is that they weren't limited either to computer generated information.

4 Development of the Classification Scheme

Because the authors do not have a common classification scheme, we will need to create one, so we can organize the publications of our survey. In this chapter we present the results of our search, and our classification scheme. To develop our classification scheme, first we gather the terms referring to the same field of application of AR under one similar term. Then, we do the same with technologies of AR, after summarize them. We will adopt terms similar to those used by the authors, with preference to those more common in the publications. Based on the adopted fields of application of AR, of a total of 63 surveys and 40 reviews, we have been able to classify only 30 surveys and 34 reviews. That happens because there are works approaching several fields of application of AR at the same time, or approaching just technologies of AR and no fields, causing them to belong to several fields or to none at all.

Deeper analysis of our sample allowed us to distinguish three kinds of works: works approaching several fields at the same time, for which we created a new category called *General*; works approaching Education and Training and another field of application of AR, which were classified according the field more highlighted by the authors; and works approaching technologies only. For those about technologies only, we created a set of categories based on Kim et al. [22] by using the same concept of similarity used for the fields of application of AR. The classification scheme is based on the technologies of AR which are the subject approached on each work. Thus, we obtained a classification scheme with two dimensions: the fields of application of AR, and the technologies of AR. With these two dimensions we were able to classify all the works of our survey.

To develop this two dimensional classification scheme we will start by presenting the AR's fields of each author chronologically, and gather each field under one term that can encompass all the similar terms used by the authors. Then, we will do the same with the technologies.

4.1 Fields of Application of AR

In 1997, Azuma [5] referred the following fields of application of AR: *Medical, Manufacturing and Repair*, Annotation *and Visualization, Robot Path Planning, Entertainment*, and *Military Aircraft*. And in 2008, Papagiannakis et al. [7] referred *Cultural Heritage, Navigation and Path Finding, Endutainment and Games, Collaborative Assembly and Construction*, and *Maintenance and Inspection.*

In 2012, Adhani & Rambli [23] referred also the field *Medical*, and added the following fields: *Sports/Games and Edutainment, Cultural Heritage, Education and Training*, and *Marketing/Advertising*. Huang et al. [24] also mentioned *Entertainment and Advertisement*, and *Training and Education*, and added *Tourism and Navigation, Geometry Modelling and Scene Construction, Assembly and Maintenance*, and *Information Assistant Management*. Adabala & kaushik [25] in 2016, added the fields of *Construction, Emergency Management/Search and Rescue*, mentioned *Tourism and Sightseeing*, and *Gaming and Entertainment*, maintaining *Military, Education*, and *Medical.* In the same year, Manuri & Sanna [26] also mentioned *Sport, Tourism, and Architecture and Construction*, besides *Medicine, Assembly, Maintenanceand Repair, Entertainment, Education and Training, Marketing*, and *Military*. He also added *Collaborative Visualisation Space, Cultural Heritage and Museum Visits*, and *Teaching.*

In 2017 Chatzopoulos et al. [27] referred *Tourismand Navigation, Entertainment and Advertising, Training and Education, Geometry Modelling and Scene Construction, Assembly and Maintenance, Information Assistant Management, Representative and Big Data Driven Mobile AR*. In the same year, Alte and Patil [28] mentioned *Medical, Military, Historical Places, Entertainment*, and *Navigation.* Hemamalini et al. [18] mentioned *Education, Advertising and Marketing, Tourism*, and *Gaming*, and added *Language Interpretation.* And Sicaru et al. [29] referred the fields of *Navigation, Medical Environment, Education, Entertainment, Military, Assembly and Manufacturing, Robot Path Planning*, and *Pervasive AR*, this last one pointed out as a future progress.

Zhang [30] in 2018 mentioned the following fields: *Architecture and Construction, Entertainment, Medicine, Military*, and *Advertising and Marketing*. In 2019, Dubey et al. [31] added *Translation*, and referred the fields of *Education, Architecture, Engineering and Construction, Digital Marketing*, and *Entertainment*. And finally, Sinha et al. [21], besides referred the fields of *Education, Medical, Architecture, Entertainment*, and *Military*, he added the field of *E-Commerce*. As it can be seen, new fields of application of AR are introduced over time. It can also be seen that the majority of the terms used are the same or very similar. Next, we will use this similarity to gather them under the same terms.

4.2 Adopted Fields of Application of AR

The adopted term *Entertainment* [5, 21, 24–31] is the most used by the authors to refer entertainment, games, and sports. It includes the terms *Endutainment and Games* [7], *Sports/Games and Edutainment* [23], *Gaming and Entertainment* [25], *Gaming* [18], and *Sport* [26].

The adopted term *Military* [21, 25, 26, 28–30] is the most used to refer to military applications, and includes the term *Military Aircraft* [5, 32].

The field *Medical* [5, 21, 23, 25, 28, 29, 32, 33] is the most used by the authors, and is adopted to refer to applications in medicine and health care. It includes *Medicine* [26, 30].

Education and Training [23, 24, 26, 27] is the adopted term to refer the applications in education and/or training. It includes the term *Education* [18, 21, 25, 29, 31], and *Teaching* [26].

The term *Architecture and Construction* [26, 30] is used twice, and it includes *Collaborative Assembly and Construction* [7], *Construction* [25], *Architecture* [21], and *Architecture, Engineering and Construction* [31], to refer not only applications in architecture, but also construction, and engineering in general.

Marketing [26, 31] is used twice too, and includes *Marketing/Advertising* [23], and *Advertising and Marketing* [18, 30]. Is the adopted term to refer to applications in marketing and advertising, as the name suggests.

The term *Assembly and Maintenance* is adopted to refer to applications in manufacture in general, maintenance, and repair. It's used by [27], and includes the terms *Manufacturing and Repair* [5, 32], *Maintenance and Inspection* [7], *Assembly, Maintenance and Repair* [26], and *Assembly and Manufacturing* [29]. Again, all the authors used different terms.

Tourism [18, 26] is the term for applications in tourism, and navigation aids for tourists. It includes *Navigation and Path Finding* [7], *Tourism and Sightseeing* [25], *Navigation* [28, 29], and *Tourism and Navigation* [27].

To refer to applications for visualization of ancient monuments or environments, and for virtual visits to museums, we chose the term *Cultural Heritage*. Is a term used twice [7, 23], and includes *Cultural Heritage and Museum Visits* [26], and *Historical Places* [28].

We adopted the term *Robot Path Planning*, which is used three times [5, 29, 32], a term that is self explained. Also self explained is the adopted term of *Annotation and*

Visualization used twice [5, 32]. And also used twice is the adopted term of *Geometry Modelling and Scene Construction* [24, 27].

And finally, we adopted the term *Translation*, also a self explained term used one [31], and includes the term *Language Interpretation* [18]. We adopted also the term *Others* to refer to applications mentioned only by one author.

In the Table 1 are presented the several fields mentioned under the adopted term, what field is mentioned by the author, and the total of authors that mentioned each field. We can see in this that the field of *Entertainment* is the most referred by the authors (14 mentions), and the field of *Military* the second one (10 mentions), followed by *Medical* and *Education and Training* (nine mentions), *Assembly and Maintenance* and *Tourism and Navigation* (eight mentions), *Marketing* (seven mentions], *Architecture and Construction* (six mentions), *Cultural Heritage* and *Robot Path Planning* (four mentions), and finally, Annotation and Visualization, Geometry Modelling and Construction, and *Translation* (two mentions).

4.3 Technologies of AR

With the first dimension of our classification scheme solved, we'll now create the second dimension in a similar way. Kim et al. [22] compiled several authors that in fact were also found in our search, gathering them by technology used. This gathering was solved by Kim et al. [22] the same way we did for the application fields, by similarity of terms used, but they haven't defined categories.

We added to Table 2 Billinghurst et al. [39] and Sicaru et al. [29] according with the similarity rule, and defined the following categories for the second dimension of classification: *Tracking Techniques*, *Input and Interaction*, *Display Techniques*, and *Development Tools*.

By analysis of our sample we realized that there are many works that approach AR by the use of mobile platforms. These works, again, encompass several technologies at the same time that are supported by those platforms, which makes them belong to several categories of technology of our classification scheme at the same time. To solve this, we added another category to the technology dimension called *Mobile Platforms*.

Because there are cases of publications classified in more than one dimension, we created a priority rule of classification. As priority rule, we started by classify each work by the main field it approaches, which must be aimed explicitly by the authors. If that can't be achieved, we classify it by the technology aimed, again, explicitly. Finally, we created a category called *General* to encompass those works about several fields and/or technologies about AR, or approach AR in a "bird's eye" kind of view, and do not have any explicit field or technology aimed.

In Table 2 an adaptation of the compilation of Kim et al. [22] is presented. It can be seen in this table that there are too several terms equal or very similar. It can be seen also that two levels of classification are used, and in the second, more granular level, there are greater differences in the names used among the authors. We will use only the higher level of classification.

Table 1. Fields of application of AR mentioned by the authors.

Author	**Fields of Application of AR Mentioned**													
	Entertainment	**Military**	**Medical**	**Education and Training**	**Architecture and Construction**	**Marketing**	**Assembly and Maintenance**	**Tourism and Navigation**	**Cultural Heritage**	**Robot PathPlanning**	**Annotation and Visualization**	**Geometry Modelling and Scene Construction**	**Translation**	**Others**
Azuma, 1997 [5]	x	x	x				x			x	x			
Papagiannakis et Al., 2008 [7]	x				x		x	x	x					
Adhani& Rambli, 2012 [23]	x	x	x	x		x			x					
Huanget Al., 2013 [24]	x			x		x	x	x				x		Information Assistant Management
Adabala& kaushik, 2016 [25]	x	x	x	x	x			x						Emergency Management/ Search and Rescue
Frigoet Al., 2016 [32]	x	x	x				x			x	x			
Manuri& Sanna, 2016 [26]	x	x	x	x	x	x	x	x	x					
Alte et Patil, 2017 [28]	x	x	x					x	x					
Chatzopouloset Al., 2017 [27]	x	x		x		x	x	x				x		Representative and Big Data Driven Mobile AR
Hemamaliniet Al, 2017 [18]	x			x		x		x					x	
Sicaru et Al., 2017 [29]	x	x	x	x			x	x		x				Pervasive
Gallala et Al, 2019 [34]							x			x				Data visualization, simulation and design
Zhang S. , 2018 [30]	x	x	x		x	x								
Dubeyet Al., 2019 [31]	x			x	x	x							x	
Sinhaet Al., 2019 [21]	x	x	x	x	x									E-Commerce
Total	**14**	**10**	**9**	**9**	**6**	**7**	**8**	**8**	**4**	**4**	**2**	**2**	**2**	

Table 2. Compilation of technologies [adapted from [22]].

Authors	Technologies			
Zhou et al. 2008 [35]	**Tracking** • Sensor-based • Vision-based • Hybrid	**Interaction** • Tangible AR • Collaborative AR • Hybrid interface	**Display** • See-through • Projection-based • Handheld	
Krevelen & Poelman, 2010 [36]	**Tracking** • Modeling environment • User movement tracking	**User interface and interaction** • Tangible UI/3D pointing • Haptic UI/gesture recognition • Visual UI/gesture recognition • Gaze tracking • Aural UI/speech recognition • Text input • Hybrid UI • Context awareness • Biosensing	**Display** • Aural display • Visual display video see-through optical see-through projective • Display positioning head-worn hand-held spatial	
Carmigniani et al. 2011 [37]	**Trackings devices** – Optical-based – Sensor-based GPS/WiFi/Accelerometer/Magnetic/Ultrasound/Inertial/Hybrid/UWB/RFID	**AR Interfaces** • Tangible AR interfaces • Multimodal AR interfaces • Collaborative AR interfaces • Hybrid AR interfaces	**Displays** – HMD – Handheld – Spatial display	

(*continued*)

Table 2. (*continued*)

Authors	Technologies			
Rabbi & Ullah, 2013 [3]	**Tracking** • Vision-based marker-based/ markerless • Sensor-based magnetic/ acoustic/ inertical/ hybird • hybrid	**Interaction** • Acoustic • Haptic • Tangible • Gaze • Text-based		
Wang et al. 2016[38]	**Tracking** • Sensor-based • Vision-based marker-based/ markerless	**Interaction** • Glove-based • Desktop haptic • Hand-based Bare-hand UI/ Tangible UI	**Display** • HMD • Hand held display • Spatial display	
Manuri & Sanna, 2016[26]	**Tracking** • Optical marker-based/ markerless • Inertial • Mechnical • Magnetic	**UI and Interaction**	**Combiner** • See-through Monocular glasses/ Binocular glasses • Hand-held • Monitor-based	
Billinghurst et al. 2014[39]	**Tracking** • Magnetic tracking • Vision based tracking • Inertial tracking; • GPS tracking; • Hybrid tracking;	**Input and Interaction technologies** AR information browsers 3D user interfaces in AR Tangible user interface in Natural user interfaces in AR - Body Motion and Gesture; Multimodal Interaction Other interaction methods – speech recognition and sounds	**Display** • Combining of real with virtual images; • Eye-to-world spectrum: • Head-attached displays – HMD and goggles; • Handheld and body-attached displays • Spatial displays; • Oder sensory displays – haptic – audio	**Development Tools** Libraries and frameworks Rapid Prototyping/Development Plug-ins AR Authoring Tools

(*continued*)

Table 2. (*continued*)

Authors	Technologies			
Sicaru et al. 2017[29]	**Tracking devices** Mechanical, magnetic sensing, GPS, ultrasonic, inertia and/or optics	**Input and interaction** Tangible interfaces, collaborative interfaces, hybrid interfaces or emerging multimodal interfaces	**Display devices** Head-mounted display [HMD], hand held devices, monitors optical projection systems	**Software** Development tools

5 Conclusions

In this paper we have looked for surveys and reviews in the AR field of knowledge. We didn't make a systematic review, and the search was limited to Google Scholar [4]. Nevertheless, we managed to gather a large sample, covering all the fields of application and technologies of AR, allowing us to develop a classification scheme for AR.

AR has been used in many field of human activity. The fields of applications of AR seem to be a well separated set of categories, despite some degree of variation of terms used to name them. Nevertheless there's an exception of that separation with the field of *Education and Training*. It's notorious that this field invades some other fields of application of AR, such as in *Entertainment*, with *Endutainment* AR [23], for training in *Military* [26, 27, 29], and in *Medical* [5, 20, 23, 28, 29], *Architecture and Construction* [40, 41], *Translation* [30], and also in *Cultural Heritage* [42]. It would be interesting to research further to clarify how *Education and Training* relates to the other fields. It could clarify the importance of AR for *Education and Training* of the subjects of the several fields of knowledge that the other fields of application of AR represent.

In future work we intent to research deeper in the field of *Education and Training*. This field as revealed to be one with most interest by the research community, as it can be confirmed by the numbers of publications we've found. Other research interest would be mobile AR, not only in general, but also used in the field of *Education and Training*. Mobile AR is pointed as a very interesting platform for this field, because it's spread, not too expensive, and is accessible. Accessibility, now in the context of the impaired, could also be further researched. In our sample we found examples of AR being used to help in rehabilitation [43], autism [44], cognitively impaired [45], and disabled students [46].

Acknowledgments. This work is financed by National Funds through the Portuguese funding agency, FCT - Fundação para a Ciência e a Tecnologia within project UIDB/50014/2020.

References

1. Sutherland, E.I.: A head-mounted three dimensional display. In: Proceedings of the December 9–11, 1968, Fall Joint Computer Conference (pp. part I, pages 757–764). ACM (1968)
2. Jamali, S.S., Shiratuddin, M.F., Wong, K.W.: A review of augmented reality (AR) and mobile-augmented reality (mAR) technology: learning in tertiary education. Int. J. Learn. High. Educ. **20**, 37–54 (2013)
3. Rabbi, I., Ullah, S.: A survey on augmented reality challenges and tracking. Acta Graphica. **24**, 1–2, 29–46 (2013)
4. (n.d.). Google Scholar. https://scholar.google.pt/
5. Azuma, R.T.: A Survey of Augmented Reality, Presence: Teleoperators & Virtual Environments, vol. 6, no. 4, pp. 355–385. MIT Press (1997)
6. Cheshire, D., Omar, R, Ijab, M.T.P.: A survey of rendering techniques in computer augmented reality. In: Advanced Technology Congress, 20–21 May 2003
7. Papagiannakis, G., Singh, G., Magnenat-Thalmann, N.: A survey of mobile and wireless technologies for augmented reality systems. Comput. Anim. Virtual Worlds **19**, 3–22 (2008). https://doi.org/10.1002/cav.221
8. Danciu, M., Gordan, M., Vlaicu, A., Antone, A.: A survey of augmented reality in health care. Acta Technica Napocensis Electron. Telecommun. **52**(1), 13 (2011)
9. Thomas, B.H.: A survey of visual, mixed, and augmented reality gaming. Comput. Entertainment (CIE) **10**(1), 1–33 (2012)https://doi.org/10.1145/2381876.2381879.
10. Shoaib, H., Jaffry, S.W.: A survey of augmented reality. In: International Conference on Virtual and Augmented Reality (ICV AR 2015), pp. 34–43 (2015)
11. Aurelia, S., Raj, M.D., Saleh, O.: A survey on mobile augmented reality based interactive storytelling. Int. J. Emerg. Trends Sci. Technol. IJETST **1**(05), 567–578 (2014)
12. Marchand, E., Uchiyama, H., Spindle, F.: Pose estimation for augmented reality: a hands-on survey. IEEE Trans. Visual. Comput. Graph. **22**(12), 2633–2651 (2016)
13. Pelagia, K.:A survey of augmented reality technology in the field of cultural heritage. National Technical University of Athens & National Institute of Applied Sciences of Strasbourg (2018)
14. Şitompul, T.A., Wallmyr, M.: Augmented Reality For Encouraging Environmentally Sustainable Behaviors: a Survey. Rio de Janeiro, Brazil. Interaction Latin America (2018)
15. Sziebig, G.: Achieving total immersion: technology trends behind augmented reality - a survey. In: Proceedings of the 9th WSEAS International Conference on Simulation, Modelling and Optimization, pp. 458–463 (2009). ISSN 1790-2769, ISBN 978-960-474-113-7
16. Thomas, B.: A survey of visual, mixed, and augmented reality gaming. ACM Comput. Entertainment **10**(3), 458–463 (2012). Article 3
17. Ashok Kumar, M., Sahityapriyadharshini, K.: A survey of ARToolkitBased augmented reality applications. J. Comput. Appl. 5(EICA2012–3), 1–33 (2012). ISSN 0974-1925
18. Hemamalini, S., Priya, K.H., Raja, R.V., Poonkuzhali, S.M.: A survey of mobile applications using augmented reality. Inte. J. Pure Appl. Math. **117**(22), 209–213 (2017)
19. Kim, S., Jeong, Y., Park, S., Ryu, K., Gyuhwan, O.: A survey of drone use for entertainment and AVR (Augmented and Virtual Reality). In: Jung, T., Claudia tom Dieck, M. (eds.) Augmented Reality and Virtual Reality, pp. 339–352. Springer International Publishing, Cham (2018). https://doi.org/10.1007/978-3-319-64027-3_23
20. El-Khamisy, N., Amer, K., Riad, A., Mamdouh, R.: A survey on virtual reality, augmented reality and mixed reality techniques for liver surgical operations and training. Graph. Vis. Image Process. J. **18**(2), 13–22 (2018)
21. Sinha, G., Singh, P., Yadav, R.K., Rajdeep, V., Bhart, R.: A survey on augmented reality with its applications. Int. J. Sci. Res. Rev. **07**(03), 2710–2715 (2019)

22. Kim, S.K., Kang, S.J., Choi, Y.J., Choi, M.H., Hong, M.: Augmented-reality survey: from concept. KSII Trans. Internet Inf. Syst. **11**(2) 982–1004 (2017)
23. Adhani, N.I., Rambli, D.R.: A survey of mobile augmented reality. In: 1st International Conference on Future Trends in Computing and Communication Technologiesm, pp. 89–95 (2012)
24. Huang, Z., Hui, P., Peylo, C., Chatzopoulos, D.: Mobile Augmented Reality Survey: A Bottom-up Approach (2013). https://arxiv.org/abs/1309.4413
25. Adabala, D., kaushik, S.: Augmented reality: a review of applications. IJRAR- Int. J. Res. Anal. Rev. **3**(3), 22–27 (2016)
26. Manuri, F., Sanna, A.: A survey on applications of augmented reality. ACSIJ Adv. Comput. Sci. Int. J. **5**(1), 19 (2016)
27. Chatzopoulos, D., Bermejo, C., Huang, Z., Hui, P.: Mobile augmented reality survey: from where we are to where we go. IEEE Access **5**, 6917–6950 (2017)
28. Alte, B., Patil, B.: A review of augmented reality and an attempt of creating video book for kids. Int. J. Adv. Sci. Res. Eng. Trends **2**(10), 244–246 (2017)
29. Ciocianu, C.G., Boiangiu, C, Sicaru I.A.: A survey on augmented reality. J. Inf. Syst. Oper. Manage. **11**(2), 263–279 (2017)
30. Zhang, S.: Augmented reality in foreign language education: a review of empirical studies. J. Technol. Chin. Lang. Teach. **9**(2), 116–133 (2018)
31. Dubey, N., Thakore, M., Patel, D.: A survey on new paradigm of display using virtual and augmented reality. Asian J. Converg. Technol. (AJCT) **V**(I), 1–5 (2019)
32. Frigo, M.A., Silva, E.C.C., Barbosa, G.F.: Augmented reality in aerospace manufacturing: a review. J. Ind. Intell. Inf. **4**(2), 125–130 (2016)
33. Zhang, Z., Hui, P., Kulkarni, S.R., Peylo, C.: Enabling an augmented reality ecosystem: a content-oriented survey. In: Proceedings of the 2014 Workshop on Mobile Augmented Reality and Robotic Technology-Based Systems, Bretton Woods, New Hampshire, USA, pp. 41–46. ACM, New York (2014)
34. Gallala, A., Hichri, B., Plapper, P.: Survey: the evolution of the usage of augmented reality in industry 4.0. In: 3rd International Conference on Manufacturing Technologies (ICMT) (2019)
35. Feng, Z., Been-Lirn Duh, H., Billinghurs, M.: Trends in augmented reality tracking. In: Proceeding of ISMAR 2008: Proceedigs 7th, pp. 193–202 (2008)
36. van Krevelen, D.W.F., Poelman, R.: A survey of augmented reality technologies, applications. Int. J. Virtual Reality **9**(2), 1–20 (2010)
37. Carmigniani, J., Furht, B., Anisetti, M., Ceravolo, P., Damiani, E., Ivkovic, M.: Augmented reality technologies, systems and application. Multimed. Tools. Appl. **51**(1), 341–377 (2011)
38. Wang, X., Ong, S.K., Nee, A.Y.C.: A comprehensive survey of augmented reality assembly research. Adv. Manuf. **4**(1), 1–22 (2016). https://doi.org/10.1007/s40436-015-0131-4
39. Billinghurst, M., Clark, A., Lee, G.: A survey of augmented reality. Found. Trends Hum.-Comput. Interact. **8**(2–3), 73–272 (2014)
40. Khetani, T.: A review of augmented reality in field of electrical engineering. In: Engineering, International Conference on Emerging Technologies in Engineering, Biomedical, Medical and Science (ETEBMS) (2016). International Journal For Technological Research
41. Ali, D.F., Omar, M., Mokhtar, M., Suhairom, N., Abdullah, A.H., Halim, N.D.A.: Review on augmented reality application in engineering drawing classrooms. Man India **97**(19), 195–204 (2017)
42. Schiavottiello, N.: From survey to education: how augmented reality can contribute to the study and dissemination of archaeo-astronomy. Cosmol. Across Cult. ASP Conf. Ser. **409,** 464 (2009)
43. Al-issa, H., Regenbrecht, H., Hale, L.: Augmented reality applications in rehabilitation to improve physical outcomes (2012)

44. Adnan, N.H., Ahmad, I., Abdullasim, N.: Systematic review on augmented reality application for autism children. J. Adv. Res. Dyn. Control Syst. **10**(11), 26–32 (2018)
45. Blattgerste, J., Renner, P., Pfeiffer, T.: Augmented reality action assistance and learning for cognitively impaired people - a systematic literature review. In: PETRA 2019, Proceedings of the 12th ACM International Conference on Pervasive Technologies Related to Assistive Environments, pp. 270–279 (2019)
46. Sahri, M.S.B., Helmi, S.A.: Effect of augmented reality and virtual reality as teaching tools to increase spatial knowledge for students in stem education- literature review. In: Proceedings of The 2nd International Conference on Science, Technology, Engineering And Mathematics Education (ICSTEM2018), pp. 112–115 (2019)

Author Index

Akhmedjanova, Diana 193
Alves Diniz, J. 249
Amaral, Paula 380
Antunes, Filipa Oliveira 263
Araújo, Fátima 44
Avaca, Ivan Luciano 408, 421

Balula, Ana 398
Baptista, Mónica 124
Barbosa, Ana 32
Barroso, João 442, 451
Bastos, Nuno R. O. 156
Bellou, Ioanna 301
Bender, Benedict 225
Berk, Dawn 279
Bernardino Lopes, J. 111

Campaniço, Ana Teresa 432
Catarino, Paula 21
Cirillo, Michelle 279
Coelho, António 203
Cosma, Smaranda Adina 380
Costa e Silva, Anabela 203
Costa, Cecília 3, 61, 75, 111
Cravino, José 44, 210, 506
Cruz, Armando 519
Cruz, Gonçalo 506

da Silva Carvalho, Tiago 351
de Moura Oliveira, Paulo B. 442
Dias, Sofia B. 249
Dimitriadou, Catherine 181
Dominguez, Caroline 168

Fachantidis, Nikolaos 476
Ferreira, Paulo 263
Fesakis, George 313
Filipe, Vitor 432
Fleşeriu, Cristina 380

Gallo, Haroldo 263
Giannakoulas, Andreas 463
Gomes, J. A. 90
Gronau, Norbert 225

Hadjileontiadis, Leontios J. 249
Hadjileontiadou, Sofia J. 249

Jimoyiannis, Athanassios 320, 330

Karasavvidis, Ilias 287
Khanal, Salik 432
Koukis, Nikolaos 320, 330
Koutromanos, George 301

LaRochelle, Raymond 279
Liberato, Dália 380
Lithoxoidou, Angeliki 181
Lopes, B. 90
Lopes, J. Bernardino 3, 44
Lopes, José 168
Lui, Angela M. 193

Maia, Ana Margarida 506
Martins, Fernando 75
Martins, Iva 124
Martins, Paulo 21, 506, 519
Martins, Sónia 236
Mažeikienė, Viktorija 389
Melo, Carla 380
Mercier, Julien 408, 421
Mikropoulos, Tassos A. 301, 340
Mockienė, Liudmila 389
Monteiro, Carlos 61
Morais, Carla 124
Morais, Ceres 210
Morais, Eva 168
Moreira, António 370, 398
Moreira, Luciano 124
Morgado, Leonel 203, 210, 506

Negruşa, Adina Letiţia 380
Nunes, Paula Sofia 21
Nunes, Ricardo Rodrigues 506

Oliveira, Ana Patrícia 492

Papachristos, Nikiforos M. 340
Paradis, Ariane 408, 421
Paredes, Hugo 432, 506, 519
Pedrosa, Daniela 210, 506
Pereira, Heloisa Mendes 263
Pessoa, P. 90
Pires, E. J. Solteiro 442
Pisano, Carlotta 141
Pliasa, Sofia 476

Rapanta, Chrysi 141
Reis, Arsénio 442, 451
Reisinho, Pedro 492
Rocha, J. 90
Rocio, Vitor 210
Rudenko, Roman 451

Santos, Vanda 156
Sá-Pinto, X. 90
Satratzemi, Maya 463
Silva, Ana 111
Silva, Bruno 442
Silva, Cândida 380
Silva, Cátia 492
Silva, Helena 168
Silva, Ricardo 75
Soares, Armando A. 44
Sousa, José 451

Terzopoulos, George 463
Tognon, Marcos 263
Tsigaros, Theologos 313
Tsiotakis, Panagiotis 320, 330

Ullrich, André 225

Vairinhos, Mário 492
Vale, Isabel 32
Valūnaitė-Oleškevičienė, Giedrė 389
Vasconcelos, Sandra 380, 398
Velentza, Anna-Maria 476
Vladova, Gergana 225

Whissell-Turner, Kathleen 408, 421

Xinogalos, Stelios 463

Yu, Elie ChingYen 193

Zagalo, Nelson 492
Zhang, Yuxiong 370

The manufacturer's authorised representative in the EU is Springer Nature Customer Service Centre GmbH, Europaplatz 3, 69115 Heidelberg, Germany. If you have any concerns regarding our products, please contact ProductSafety@springernature.com

Printed and bound by CPI Group (UK) Ltd, Croydon, CR0 4YY
01/10/2026
02226550-0001